HAUSSMANN

HAUSSMANN

His Life and Times,
and the Making of Modern Paris

MICHEL CARMONA

TRANSLATED FROM THE FRENCH BY PATRICK CAMILLER

Ivan · R · Dee

Chicago 2002

First published in France, 2000, as *Haussmann*.

The publishers gratefully acknowledge the support of the French Ministry of Culture and Furthermore, a program of the J. M. Kaplan Fund, in the preparation of the English translation of *Haussmann*.

Library of Congress Cataloging-in-Publication Data:
Carmona, Michel.
    [Haussmann. English]
    Haussmann : his life and times, and the making of modern Paris / Michel Carmona ; translated from the French by Patrick Camiller.
        p. cm.
    Includes bibliographical references and index.
    ISBN 1-56663-427-X (alk. paper)
    1. Haussmann, Georges-Eugène, baron, 1809–1891.   2. City planning—France—Paris—History.   3. Urban renewal—France—Paris—History.   4. France—Officials and employees—Biography.   5. France—Politics and government—1789–1815.   I. Title.
DC280.5.H3 C3713 2002
307.1'216'092—dc21
[B]   2001052985

Contents

HAUSSMANN

· I ·

A DEDICATED ADMINISTRATOR

"How rich France would become if it were well governed—above all, well administered."
— Haussmann, *Mémoires*

I

➜➜➜➜➜➜➜➜➜➜➜➜➜➜➜➜

The Prince, Paris,

Haussmann

On September 24, 1848, a short, modest-looking man wearing middle-class dress stepped from a train onto the platform at the Paris "embarkation point" of the Northern railway. He was returning from exile, and his name was Louis-Napoléon Bonaparte. The embarkation point has since become the Gare du Nord, while the main courtyard running along its front side is today called the Place Napoléon III. Here began the incredible adventure through which Louis-Napoléon, the proscribed Napoléon III, was transformed into the "emperor of the French people." Seven months earlier, on February 24, 1848, Louis-Philippe had in turn been forced into exile by the popular uprising that instituted the Second Republic, and in his London refuge he had perhaps come across the pale figure of the young Louis-Napoléon, then scraping a dubious living as general factotum for a rich lady. But whereas the one had been pondering the collapse of his reign, the other had lived in constant hope that a few twists of fate would carry him to France on the lofty march to power.

Louis-Napoléon Bonaparte stood in the legislative elections of September 17, 1848, which the Second Republic expected to be free and democratic and to ground it upon a new legitimacy. The prince, as the election law allowed, presented himself in five *départements*: Seine, Yonne, Charente-Inférieure (today's Charente-Maritime), Corsica (where the imperial blood would tell), and Moselle. This multiple candidacy indicates how little chance he thought he had of being elected: the French people did not know him; he was still subject to the exile order that Louis-Philippe had imposed on all members of the Bonaparte family; and a long-distance campaign from London seemed hardly likely to yield a favorable outcome. In the end, however, a virtual landslide in each of the five departments made of him the people's chosen representative.

Exactly one week after the elections, the future Napoléon III was back in Paris. He had been there very little since childhood—just three or four times, and then only passing through. He still did not know whether he would be able to settle there for good, both because of the banishment order of 1832 and because he had no assurance that his fivefold election would be ratified. He stayed temporarily with one of his supporters, then moved to the Hôtel du Rhin, in the rue de la Paix, where he left his office on the mezzanine in the charge of the faithful Mocquard and took up residence on the first floor. Here he arranged his library of history books, military works, and treatises on political economy. One long roll of parchment seemed especially precious: it was a map of Paris, with zebra stripes of red, green, blue, and yellow that appeared to have been drawn at random.

In fact, there was nothing random about the composition of that document; for years Louis-Napoléon had had the aim of restoring Paris to its imperial splendor. Soon after the son of Napoléon I, the Duke of Reichstadt, l'Aiglon, had died in 1832, Louis-Napoléon himself—the son of Louis Bonaparte and Hortense de Beauharnais, born on the night of April 20–21, 1808, in Paris and the first of the emperor's nephews—began to put himself forward as the successor to the empire of the Bonaparte family. On October 30, 1836, to shouts of "Vive l'Empereur!" he and his friend Fialan de Persigny, who called himself the Count of Persigny, tried to raise the Strasbourg garrison with the complicity of one of the city's artillery commanders, General Vaudrey. The attempted coup came to an abrupt and inglorious end, and Louis-Napoléon was placed under arrest. To avoid the media impact of a major trial, Louis-Philippe shipped him off to New York on November 21, but it was not long before he was back on European soil. First he went to Switzerland, to be with his dying mother in Arenenberg, then settled in London to prepare a new rising which, he was sure, would be backed by elements of the French army nostalgic for the empire. One of his English friends said at the time: "Nothing can dissuade him that he will one day be Emperor of the French. . . . He constantly thinks of what he will do when he is on the throne."

The stage for Louis-Napoléon's second attempt was Boulogne-sur-Mer, on August 5, 1840. Once more the military coup was a failure, but this time Louis-Philippe reacted vigorously. The prince was brought before the Chamber of Peers, which on October 6, 1840, sentenced him to life imprisonment in a fortress of the realm. According to press reports, he stated to the court clerk who read the sentence: *"Monsieur, in France nothing is for life."* The prince was interned in the fort at Ham, in Picardy, where he was able to read, study, work, and publish. His time there—at the "University of Ham," as he later joked—was an intense period when his ideas acquired their final shape and the prisoner forged his image of a national savior. He had already published his *Idées napoléoniennes* in July 1839, and 1844 saw the appearance of *L'Extinction du paupérisme*, his most important work. Louis-Napoléon had a feel for the arresting formulation. Declaring himself a firm supporter of universal suffrage, he expressed his confidence in a top-down reformism driven by a real leader with extensive powers: "Today," he wrote, "caste rule is finished; it is possible to govern only with the masses." Or again: "The working class owns nothing; it must be given some property."

Early in 1846, the prince asked to be allowed to visit his ailing father, the one-time King Louis of Holland, so that they could spend his final days together in his Tuscan retirement. When the government of Louis-Philippe refused permission, Louis-Napoléon felt he had no option but to escape. On May 25, having shaved off his beard and mustache, he dressed himself in the clothes of a workman, Badinguet, shouldered a wooden plank, and calmly walked out of the fort to catch a train to Brussels, then the boat to England. By May 27 he was back in London, accompanied by the dog he called . . . Ham. Without a safe-conduct pass he could not make his way to Tuscany. His father's death there, on July 24, 1846, left Louis-Napoléon the first of the Bonapartes, the official claimant to the succession.

The escapee from Ham, not in the least discouraged by the successive failures at Strasbourg and Boulogne, continued to prepare determinedly for his accession to power in France. His father's legacy saved him from financial disaster, and his liaison with the wealthy Miss Howard in London gave him the means to pay spies, journalists, and associates. Imbued with the socialistic philosophies of the age, and especially with the optimism of the Saint-Simonians, he dreamed of initiating major projects to create jobs and riches, of spreading progress through the development of industrial civilization. In *L'Extinction du paupérisme* he had written: "My friends are in the workshops." The prince sincerely wished to improve the workers' lot by eliminating the plague of unemployment and by raising wage levels. He was close to the high-minded men of the left who took power in February 1848—those who established national workshops to give work for all in the construction of a progressive future, and who, on May 3, 1848, issued a decree for large-scale municipal works in Paris. Louis-Napoléon did not, however, approve of their methods. While still in exile, he saw France as "a powerful country, full of wealth and resources but wretchedly governed." It would be hard to say he was wrong, given the spectacle of the badly organized and unmanaged national workshops that were sinking into anarchy. Starvation riots broke out in Paris and were followed by the bloody repression of the June Days of 1848, when the bourgeois order shot the workers *en masse* in the popular districts of the capital.

June 1848 opened a fast route for the political ambitions of Louis-Napoléon. The prince had one element of superiority over the dreamers who were steering the country so badly: he believed in the virtues of organization. He was also convinced that the main problem facing France was the problem of Paris, of that effervescent, industrious city where misery existed side by side with luxury, and where the location of public buildings within a tangled web of narrow winding streets placed government at the constant mercy of the rifle. Three months later he was triumphantly elected.

Napoléon III has been a little-loved figure in histories of France. The coup d'état of December 2, 1851, the fall of the empire in 1870 amid military defeat and the Prussian amputation of Alsace-Lorraine, the lampooning and abuse directed at him by such talented figures as Henri Rochefort and Victor Hugo—all this left an image of "Napoléon le Petit" as a prototype of the unscrupulous and unintelligent adventurer, an idiot who did France nothing but harm. His ability to remain in power for so long (from 1848 to 1852 as president of the Republic, then until 1870 as emperor) did not prevent French historians—ever since the military disaster at Sedan—from presenting his regime as a mere (though utterly dire) historical parenthesis. Only since the early 1960s has the Second Empire been given fresh attention and, in some cases, fresh appraisal. Historians, politicians, and public opinion have acquired a taste for the people and things of that age. Haussmann's urban projects, treated for decades as mindless butchery of the charming old city of Paris for no other purpose than the crushing of the working class, are again becoming an object of study and reflection, sometimes even a model.

The plan that Louis-Napoléon Bonaparte brought in his luggage to Paris on September 24, 1848, was a set of notes for his refurbishment of the capital, the four colors—red, green, blue, and yellow—corresponding to the urgency of various points in the program. Its guiding principles were intended to meet the requirements of movement, public hygiene, and elegance. When one thinks of the determination and the precise thinking that must have gone into the plan, one cannot fail to be amazed by its excessive and slightly deranged quality, as if it belonged more to the dream world.

This feeling of disbelief, combined with the discrediting of the historical figure, explains why the role of Napoléon III himself in the transformation of Paris has been so often debated, challenged, or quite simply denied. We speak of "Haussmann's *grands travaux*," never of "Napoléon III's *grands travaux*." Victor Hugo ridiculed the emperor's supposed ignorance of the geography of Paris—and, of course, before his return in 1848 the prince's life had been almost entirely that of an exile. In *Choses bien vues*, published much later when he was himself an exile fighting the imperial regime, the famous writer even related: "Louis Bonaparte knows so little about Paris that, the first time I met him, at rue de la Tour d'Auvergne, he said to me: 'I've looked for you a lot. I've been to your old house.¹ So what is this Place des Vosges?' 'It's the Place Royale,' I replied. 'Ah! Is that an old square?' "

Historians have emphasized the decisive role of Eugène Deschamps, head of the Plan de Paris (the official survey department), in tracing the new thoroughfares, or of Fialin de Persigny (minister of the interior under Napoléon III) in financing the projects—and later of Adolphe Alphand in relation to parks and plantings, Eugène Belgrand in relation to water services, or indeed Haussmann himself, as organizer and person in overall charge of coordinating the *travaux*. It is also true that the transformation of Paris had been on the agenda for a number of decades, and that the men of the 1848 revolution had already energetically promoted large-scale public works. But although the prince president—later Napoléon III—benefited from the experience of a huge number of previous studies, plans, and actual operations, it was still he who gave shape to a veritable program, chose the people to implement his "plan for the embellishment of Paris," and overcame the opposition and obstacles in its path.

Haussmann, in his *Mémoires*, could not have been more explicit on this point. On June 29, 1853, the very day on which he was sworn in as prefect for the Seine department at the château de Saint-Cloud, Napoléon III hastened to take him into his study and to unveil his plans for the capital. These were summarized in "a map of Paris on which he had himself traced, in blue, red, yellow, and green according to their degree of urgency, the various new thoroughfares that he intended to have built."² A few pages further on, Haussmann adds a comment that clearly shows the degree of the emperor's involvement in the work of transformation: "Alone, I should never have been able to pursue, nor especially to fulfill, the mission he demanded of me, and in the accomplishment of which his growing trust gradually left me greater freedom of decision. I should never have been able to wage a successful fight against the difficulties inherent in each operation; against the ill will arising from sincere convictions or from base and unavowed, yet implacable, jealousies within the great bodies of state, the government, and His Majesty's own entourage; against the open attacks from parties hostile to the imperial regime which, while not daring to target the political direction impressed on the country by the sovereign, tried to combat it indirectly in the municipal undertakings dependent upon his initiative and inspiration; unless I had really been the expression, organ, or instrument of a great idea conceived by him and for which I should give him the principal merit—an idea whose implementation he promoted at every moment with a firmness that never failed. All the opponents of this idea, acting in good faith or not, personified it in myself—and so today I must recall that I was only the one who carried it out."[3]

This passage should not be ascribed to the pen of a prudent courtier, since Haussmann's *Mémoires* were first published in 1890, long after the death of Napoléon III, at a time when the only flesh and blood in the Bonapartist myth was a cousin of the late emperor for whom Haussmann felt both hatred and contempt. In that *fin de siècle*, when the Third Republic was paying open homage to the Paris prefect, Haussmann, no paragon of modesty, might quite easily have claimed the paternity that everyone awarded him. Why, then, should we not believe him when he says that it was Napoléon III alone who conceived and impelled the great enterprise? A similar view was expressed by another contemporary witness and participant in the venture, Charles Merruau, who was appointed general secretary of the Seine prefecture following the coup d'état of December 2, 1851, and remained in that post until his appointment to the municipal council in 1860. In his *Souvenirs*, first published in 1875, two years after the death of Napoléon III, Merruau writes: "The broad guidelines and the system [of the transformation of Paris] were already fixed in the prince's mind during the days of his presidency."

The speech that Napoléon III gave at Paris City Hall in December 1850, when he was still only Prince Louis-Napoléon Bonaparte, president of the Second Republic, resonates as a declaration of faith: "Paris is the heart of France. Let us put all our efforts into embellishing this great city, into improving the lot of those who live in it. Let us open new streets, let us clean up the populous districts that lack air and daylight. Let the beneficial light of the sun everywhere penetrate our walls." Should we be surprised at this expression of interest in the modernization of Paris? All the sovereigns who ruled France, as well as the successive presidents of the Fifth Republic, have considered that the state bears a special responsibility in the affairs of the capital. Almost uninterruptedly for more than 175 years, from 1800 through to the law of December 31, 1975 and the municipal elections of 1977, the Paris administration was placed under a special regime that made the prefect of the Seine department the true mayor of the city.

Haussmann tells us that Napoléon III never changed his view: "The Emperor obviously thought that in France, the country where centralization has been taken furthest, the head of state had a right to keep the administrative reins both of the capital, his official residence, and the seat of his government—and of the department formed by its suburbs; in other words, that he should rule at the Hôtel de Ville as he did at the Tuileries, just as the Pope, the head of the Catholic world who is sovereign pontiff of all nations, is at Saint Peter's the Bishop of Rome. . . . In Paris, where the interests of the state take precedence over municipal interests and should in many respects absorb them, a prefect has been created for the Seine who not only has the task, like his fellow prefects, of representing the government, of ensuring that laws, decrees, regulations, and measures of a general nature are enforced within his jurisdiction, and incidentally of managing the collective interests of his department, but also, over and above all these things, discharges the functions of the central mayor of Paris, since the existence of a mayor holding his mandate more or less from the population is held to be incompatible with the sovereign power in this city."[4]

In this conception, the link between central government and the Paris authority was a figure of crucial importance. If this link was to be the prefect of the Seine department, then the holder of supreme power in the country had to have a real delegate at the prefecture who administered the capital in keeping with the sovereign's views, and in whom the sovereign could have confidence. Haussmann was the ideal person for this role. From June 1853, Napoléon III kept him at his side for sixteen and a half years. Only at the beginning of 1870, when the Second Empire was mired in a thousand difficulties and the ailing emperor was torn between rival coteries, did he finally think it expedient to throw to the lions the prefect who embodied a particular conception of the centralization and solitary exercise of power.

This long collaboration between the two men is the best justification for what Haussmann says about his first steps as Napoléon III's prefect for the Seine: "Without a doubt, he was completely satisfied with the presence at

Paris City Hall of a prefect who had, as I had, long been absolutely devoted to his person, a depository of his thinking who understood it and used it as the inspiration for all his actions, ever ready to receive and obey his directives."[5]

2

Haussmann
Before Haussmann

GEORGES-EUGÈNE HAUSSMANN was born in Paris on March 27, 1809, in a small town house with a front yard and garden, situated in the Beaujon district then known as the faubourg du Roule, not far from l'Étoile. When he became prefect for the Seine and cut the Paris boulevard that bears his name, he had the house of his birth pulled down; its exact location was at the present junction between Boulevard Haussmann and the rue du Faubourg Saint-Honoré. In 1859, when the incorporation of some suburban communes increased from twelve to twenty the number of arrondissements into which Paris is divided, the faubourg du Roule left the former 1st arrondissement to become the heart of what we know today as the 8th arrondissement.

Less than a year separates the births of Haussmann and Louis-Napoléon Bonaparte. And yet the two men whom fate would yoke together for sixteen and a half years did not bear much resemblance to each other. Haussmann attached a lot of weight to the influence of his family. As he writes at the beginning of his *Mémoires*: "The milieu in which each of us is born, the education we have received, the feelings, ideas, and opinions we share as a result, have an influence on at least the early part of our life." He recalls with pride that his family originated in large measure from Rhineland Germany, but he adds: "We have been French for six generations before mine, and all have provided quite humble but devoted servants to the noble country that our forebears eventually chose as their adoptive fatherland." Haussmann's ancestors on his father's side, being attached to the Protestant faith, fled in the sixteenth century to Saxony and then to Alsace. The religious freedoms of

Alsace survived its union with France early in the reign of Louis XIV, and continued even after the revocation of the Edict of Nantes in 1685. The Haussmanns therefore remained French.

THE MARK OF THE GRANDPARENTS

≪ The Haussmanns were prolific—and enterprising. In 1775 one of them, Christian, created a printed fabrics factory in the Logelbach area of Colmar, whose workforce of four hundred placed it among the leading industrial businesses in Alsace. The rue de Logelbach, later opened in the Monceau district, would discreetly perpetuate its memory. Christian's brother Nicolas Haussmann, born in 1759, went into politics; he was to be our prefect's grandfather. Having settled in Versailles, he bought a private house in rue Montbauron and became the owner of a large country house at Chaville, on the road to Paris, where he spent the summer, and a smaller one opposite it, called Belle Source, where his grandson spent his early childhood years. Nicolas Haussmann was elected a deputy to the National Assembly in 1791, and to the Convention in 1792. He became administrator of the department of Seine-et-Oise, left to act as a commissar to the armies of the Rhine, then the armies of the North, and finally of Rhin-et-Moselle—a post he maintained until 1797. Wearying of the restlessness of public life, and of the ubiquitous informers who were the stuff of everyday life for a people's representative in the army, Nicolas then decided to retire to his house in Chaville. His functions had kept him outside Paris, so that he had not been present at the Convention at the time of the trial of Louis XVI. Grandfather Haussmann was the first who infected the family with the virus of a passion for public administration.

The prefect's father, Nicolas-Valentin Haussmann, was born at the grandparents' home in 1787. He showed up in the army during the Napoleonic wars, where he did his father proud by exercising the functions of war commissar and quartermaster. It was a heavy responsibility, as the armies needed food, ammunition, clothing, and billets. Napoleon I thought what one of his distant successors as head of state would also think: "The administration will provide support." Unfortunate quartermasters, guilty of all evils and all sins. But this did not much disturb the *joie de vivre* of Nicolas-Valentin. On June 6, 1806, at the age of nineteen, he took a wife, Marie-Caroline Dentzel, who was just seventeen, also from a Protestant family of German origin. In fact her father, General Dentzel, was born at Durckheim in the Palatinate in 1755. A comrade-in-arms of Rochambeau and Lafayette, he participated as an officer in the American War of Independence and, upon his return, received French citizenship from Louis XVI in 1784 and went on to serve the Revolution and the empire as a career soldier. By 1806 he was adjutant at Napoleon's general staff, and he was serving Prince Eugène (Eugène de Beauharnais), son of the Empress Josephine, at the moment when his daughter married Nicolas-Valentin Haussmann. In the following months, General Dentzel took part in the Prussian campaign and, when charged with the occupation of Weimar, protected the town of Goethe—especially his precious library—from pillage and disorder. The celebrated writer warmly thanked him for this, and after the return of peace Goethe's protector, the Grand Duke of Saxe-Weimar, presented a fine diamond ring to Madame Dentzel, the general's wife and grandmother of the future prefect.

General Dentzel had already been made a baron of the empire by Napoleon when Georges-Eugène Haussmann was born on March 27, 1809. He was the second child of Nicolas-Valentin and Marie-Caroline, who had had a daughter two years before and would have another son two years later. The new baby was given the forenames Georges (in honor of Grandfather Dentzel) and Eugène (in honor of Prince Eugène de Beauharnais), as we know from the birth declaration made the following day by the happy father. Georges-Eugène was then baptized a few days later at the reformed church of the Oratoire (the Haussmanns were Lutherans, and there was not yet a Lutheran church in Paris). General Dentzel, as godfather, also represented Prince Eugène, who had agreed to be the child's other godfather.

But war was calling the general back to arms—this time in Austria. In June 1809, Dentzel was appointed governor of Vienna, then occupied by Napoleon's forces, and as at Weimar he carried out his assignment with considerable tact. This earned him, from the thankful burghers of Vienna, a finely chased medal in a gilded box carrying the inscription: *To the comforter of the evils of war, from the community of merchant burghers of Vienna*. General Dentzel survived the retreat from Russia, retired from the army in 1816, and died at Versailles in 1828.

The young Georges-Eugène grew quickly, but his nervous constitution tired his mother. When he was two years old it was therefore decided to send him to the grandparents' country home at Chaville; his parents and the other children came to join him there during the summer months. How did Georges-Eugène experience this special treatment? He does not say a word about it in his *Mémoires*. But he clearly remained deeply grateful to his grandfather: "I can say that it was he who brought me up. Thanks to the great impressionability of all children, I was influenced by the methodical habits and principles that always reigned in the house of that truly wise man and in his clear, sensible, well-ordered mind. It is to his example—confirming his lessons and his advice, from which I never failed to seek inspiration—that I owe the sense of duty, the calm firmness, and the indefatigable perseverance that have given me the upper hand over so many obstacles; the moderation of character that prudence forbade me to exhibit too much but that my zealous friends could alone blame for the inspirations and the personal disinterest that made me prefer, over the satisfactions of wealth and honors, the less vain ones provided, even in misfortune, by a good conscience and the justifiable pride of a great task faithfully accomplished."[1]

Later, as a law student, he was influenced by a remark about France that slipped from his grandfather's mouth: "We don't know well enough how many resources France contains and how rich and powerful it would become if it were well governed—above all, well administered."[2] And in the evening of his life, without illusions about the quality of the rulers among whom he had always sought the embodiment of the ideal leader, Georges-Eugène Haussmann recognized how much his choice of career had owed to the comments of Nicolas Haussmann. Consider this one, for example, which does not lack weight coming from a former member of the Convention: "I sincerely believed in the Republic, as did so many people with a noble mind, a generous spirit. I admit it. An enlightened nation such as ours seemed to me capable of governing itself wisely, as the newly constituted United States had been doing, and I thought that, after it had reformed the abuses of the past, it could give to the world an example of honest, skillful, and fruitful administration. But I had to recognize that this philosophical form of government did not suit the spirit of France, the volatile character of a people still carrying the customs of our old society."

"I WANT TO BE A PAGE"

≪ In the ambience of the late empire, Child Haussmann had his mind filled with warlike and heroic dreams. He was old for his age. From time to time he would be taken to see General Baron Dentzel, then living at the Hermitage, the former domain of the marquise de Pompadour, near Trianon. The few summer months that he spent there plunged him into a completely military atmosphere. Georges-Eugène looked forward to the moment when his godfather, Prince Eugène, would keep his promise and make him one of the emperor's pages. One day he was accompanying his grandfather on a visit to Prince Eugène in Trianon, when the emperor himself appeared on one of the paths through the park. Dentzel stepped aside, but the little boy gave a military salute and shouted: "Vive l'Empereur!" Napoleon, feeling his thoughts suddenly interrupted, asked sharply: "Who is that child, general?" "Sire, he is my grandson, a future soldier of the King of Rome. He and I are waiting to be received by the viceroy of Italy [that is, Prince Eugène], his godfather." The emperor brightened and, having closely examined the young boy and noticed that he was dressed as a hussar (his uncle, Dentzel's son, was colonel in the Sixth Regiment of Hussars), retorted: "Do you want to join the army already, young man?" "First I want to become one of the emperor's pages," came the reply. Napoleon smiled and tweaked the boy's chin: "That's not the worst of choices. Well, all right, my lad, grow up quickly and learn to mount a horse, so that you can begin your duties."

Haussmann's future, however, was not to be in the army. The Russian campaign, the defeat, the invasion of France, the capitulation of Paris, and Napoleon's abdication would make a profound impression upon Georges-Eugène. In 1814 he was at Chaville with the women of the family while the men were off fighting. Wounded men kept pouring in, then the enemy troops. There was fighting close to the Hermitage at Glatigny, and at Versailles in the rue des Réservoirs. The woods of Chaville were occupied by the invading forces. Grandfather Haussmann, who was mayor of the commune, had to grant in silence the requests for billeting. Little Georges-Eugène came across the cossacks, stationed at Viroflay, Chaville, and Sèvres. "I could therefore contemplate these strange horsemen at close quarters, perched on mounts with flowing mane and tail. I could observe their seemingly endless lances and their uncultivated, not to say disgusting, carriage. I later found out that my poor little maid, Jeannette, who was no more than fifteen years old, saw them at even closer quarters, as did many other girls and women in the area who were victims of the odious brutality of those barbarians."[3]

In 1815 the Hundred Days again galvanized the Napoleonic faith of the Haussmanns and Dentzels. Even Grandfather Haussmann resumed duties supplying the army of the North. Waterloo (June 18, 1815) brought everyone back to Paris in more or less good shape. General Dentzel had one arm gashed by a bullet.

The second Restoration would be harsher than the first for Grandfather Haussmann. Under the terms of a law of January 12, 1816, the royalist reaction hit out at regicides in deed or "in intent." The police minister, the duc Decazes, issued an order for Nicolas Haussmann to leave the country, and the unfortunate grandfather took up exile in Basle. A letter from January 6,

1793, had been discovered in which the army commissar Merlin de Thionville (then serving on the Rhine with Nicolas Haussmann) and another member of the Convention, Reubell, claimed the right to cast a vote by letter at the trial of Louis XIV—a vote for sentence of death. A report to the Convention, attached to this letter and signed by the three commissars, gave an account of military operations and the needs of the army and ended as follows: "We are surrounded by dead and wounded. It is in the name of Louis Capet that the tyrants slit our brothers' throats, and yet Louis Capet is still alive!" The letter and report were read at the rostrum of the Convention on January 11, 1793. Louis XVI was beheaded ten days later. So did the vote count or not? Investigations carried out in 1816 exculpated Nicolas Haussmann; his reports to the Convention even showed him evading anything that might have a political connotation. In short, an administrator and nothing more.

The government of Louis XVIII authorized him to return to France. Marked by the ordeal, Grandfather Haussmann sold his properties in Versailles and Chaville and went to settle in the faubourg du Roule in Paris. To philosophize, to delight his grandson by reciting memories, to admire the masterpieces collected in the Louvre Museum: these were now the occupations of "that cruel bloodthirsty man." "Until I entered the departmental administration," writes Georges-Eugène, "I went regularly to visit him, to hear him and to listen to his advice, so full of life right up to his death in June 1846."[4]

THE AGE OF FRIENDS

❧ In February 1816, when he was just short of seven years of age, Georges-Eugène left forever the house at Chaville and moved to his parents' home in Paris, where the family had a month before acquired a fourth child, another girl. Together with his elder sister, he received lessons from a governess. But the proximity of his parents does not seem to have agreed with him, and if we are to believe what he writes, he himself asked to be sent to school. The one chosen for himself and his young brother was at Bagneux, again in the country, where a young former member of the Oratoire, Monsieur Legal, lodged and instructed some fifty pupils in a large and handsome property. Georges-Eugène made friends with a boy who, as he notes with emotion, would become "my oldest pal."[5] Théophile de Montour would, like him, be a prefect in the Second Empire.

Haussmann kept a lively memory of those years of board and education that he received from the former member of the Oratoire. Practical observations followed from theoretical courses; they collected plants and learned to recognize them, every child having responsibility for one part of the garden; they watched the stars in the evening; and some curious experiments impressed the laws of physics and chemistry upon the young minds. There was no lack of physical exercise: running, jumping, fencing, summer swimming, winter skating. Nor were Greek and Latin, design and music, neglected. Two most valuable years: "The ideas I received there about a whole host of things opened my naturally inquiring mind to the multiple studies that attracted it later on, furnishing it with varied knowledge that would be most useful in my career."[6]

He was eleven when his father took him away from Bagneux and sent him as a boarder to the Collège Henri-IV, the present-day Lycée Condorcet, "the most salubrious in Paris." Everything is relative, however, for Georges-Eugène had to interrupt his studies several times in mid-year, especially between the ages of thirteen and fifteen, in order to recover his health in the country. So, it was frail after all, this force of nature? Haussmann had chest problems, and those close to him constantly feared the possibility of "phthisis," that is, tuberculosis, "until the time when I decided to live in wool, both summer and winter, from my neck to the soles of my feet."[7]

No sooner did he enter the sixth grade at Henri-IV than he began finishing at the top of his class. On the benches he made friends with a new boy, none other than the duc de Chartres, the future duc d'Orléans, whose father (later to become King Louis-Philippe) had insisted that his sons should go to the lycée like everyone else—or almost like everyone else, because they were only semi-boarders and came to class accompanied by their personal tutor. The young Haussmann entered the circle of school friends of the young prince, who was familiarly called "Chartres," although no one dared to use the familiar *toi* in addressing him. One of these boys was Gabriel Bocher, "my neighbor in the study room, . . . the most excellent and most charming of my pals," even if life's fortunes would place them in opposite camps under the Second Empire. Another boy, Ferdinand Le Roy, would be general secretary of the Gironde prefecture after 1830, then prefect of Indre-et-Nièvre, before he was called by Georges-Eugène (then prefect of the Seine department) to the important post of director of the public works fund, the Caisse des Travaux de Paris. On the other hand, the little group liked to jeer at a good-looking boy, fair-haired and slightly effeminate, who was nicknamed "Mademoiselle de Musset."[8]

VORACIOUS LEARNING

≈ The young Haussmann had many gifts, especially an ability to learn things fast. He belonged to a school orchestra, where he played the violin, the cello, the organ, and occasionally other instruments. One of his music teachers, a Monsieur Choron who was director of the École de musique religieuse, gave him lessons in harmony.

But Haussmann's health was so worrying that his parents took him away from Henri-IV when he reached the age of sixteen and registered him as a day-boy at the Collège Bourbon. He took philosophy there in the class of Legouvé (a future member of the Académie Française) and passed the baccalaureate in grand fashion. He was seventeen when he enrolled at the École de Droit, where he proved a hardworking student. As the hill of Sainte-Geneviève was too far from the faubourg du Roule for him to have lunch with the family, he joined a reading room where he could leave his books and course notebooks and had a quick but comfortable meal either at Flicoteaux or at Vigneron in the rue Saint-Jacques, a little down from the Lycée Louis-le-Grand, whose owner had been a pastry cook before setting up on his own account. (Flicoteaux disappeared ages ago, but the Maison Vigneron still exists today.)

Haussmann used any time left over from his law studies to follow courses at the Sorbonne or the Collège de France. He was thus, as he said without boasting, an intermittent attender at the lectures of Victor Cousin in philosophy, Cauchy (the inventor of differential calculus and integrals) in mathematics, and Gay-Lussac in physics—as well as the geology classes of Élie de Beaumont at the École des Mines. Music still held an attraction for him, and he managed to put his name down to attend classes in counterpoint and fugue at the Conservatory. He saw a lot of Berlioz there—already the young romantic who was overturning classical harmony and shaking its defenders, such as the director of the Conservatory himself, the venerable Cherubini. Haussmann was witness to one scene between Cherubini and Berlioz that still delighted him many years later:

> I recollect that on an examination day Cherubini leafed through one of Berlioz's scores and, with that grumpy air that never left him, pointed to a general pause of two bars: "What is that?"
>
> "Sir, I wanted to produce an effect with that silence."
>
> "Ah! Do you think that this suppression of two bars will produce a good effect on those who hear it?"

"Yes, I do, sir."

"Well, get rid of the rest as well; the effect would be better still," the mischievous fellow said as he handed back the notebook.[9]

Haussmann did not share Berlioz's musical audacity, but he did excel in classical composition classes. What he liked more than anything else was "the development of a musical idea and, consequently, . . . the symmetrical construction of one of those opera fragments that are called cantatas."[10] Symmetry, already.

All these pursuits did not prevent the young Haussmann from fencing, pistol shooting, horse riding, swimming at the Deligny baths, or skating on the Ourcq Canal and at La Glacière.

As he had to think about the future, and as boys at that time were very early apprenticed in a profession, Georges-Eugène spent several hours each day, before or after dinner, in the office of the family's lawyer. For him it was a kind of work experience, which enabled him to understand "the practical implementation of the provisions in the Civil Code regarding property, inheritance, donations and testaments, marriage, sales and rental contracts, binding agreements, mortgages, etc., etc., whose theoretical principles were taught to me at law school."[11] Later in life, Haussmann the prefect felt that he owed to this training in the lawyer's office his undying taste for terminological precision.

SECRET WOUNDS

❧ Behind this apparently smooth and proper "childhood of a leader," secret wounds lay hidden.

First of all, Haussmann's German-sounding name must have made him the target of much sarcasm, as in the unhappy episode when his father declared the birth of his son to a registry official who stumbled over the double 's.' Thus when Haussmann came to write his memoirs so many years later— they were published in 1890, when he had already turned eighty—he preferred not to speak at all of the Haussmanns "before" France.

Similarly, he found himself excluded several times in his life because of the religion to which he was always fiercely attached, as we may glimpse from a few discreet lines he writes on the subject. "The reader will understand that, coming as I did from a family that had had to endure many trials to keep its faith, and having been brought up in a dissident community amid an often intolerant Catholic majority, I learned from childhood to detest persecution, whatever its source and whatever its object, and that, without having to make an effort, I respect in others any sincerely held religious or political belief."[12]

Then there is the father, the enigmatic Nicolas-Valentin Haussmann. All he is given in his son's memoirs is a short item of biographical information: "My father, who belonged to the army administration as a war commissar under the First Empire, was made a half-pay officer at the Restoration. This lasted until the July Revolution, when he was recalled to service in the Commissariat. But after an interruption of fifteen years that had been in every respect damaging to his interests—for it had allowed him to indulge his extravagant taste for new inventions—his career could not continue for much longer."[13] He was present at the siege of Antwerp, participated in the so-called Iron Gates expedition between Constantine and Algiers, and finally retired just before the 1848 revolution to occupy himself, "up to his death in 1876," only with "books and publications related to army supply and administration."[14] It is brief, factual, and lacking in warmth. There are obviously reasons for that.

Haussmann did not share his father's taste for "new inventions"—which we should understand to include republican ideas. Moreover, the childhood of Georges-Eugène, spent far from a father who had removed him alone from the family home, could not have encouraged him to regard that father with any great tenderness. Nor can we disregard certain remarks that Haussmann's later reputation, including among historians, has obscured beneath a shadow of contempt.

The remarks in question tarnish both the future prefect and his father. They are to be found in the *Journal* of Xavier Marmier, a well-known man of letters, originally from Besançon, who left valuable testimony about the Haussmanns. On Nicolas-Valentin: "Monsieur Haussmann's father, who was employed in the military administration, was at the center of several unpleasant scandals and was eventually pensioned off. Only the generosity of one of his bosses saved him from a major trial. He was in the habit of supplementing his income at the state's expense, in ways that the courts rigorously punish."[15] It is not much, but it is also a lot, for it allows the prefect Georges-Eugène to be simply lumped together with his father.

Marmier does not hesitate to do this. "Already in his youth, his son displayed a special taste for other people's goods, and was much inclined to enrich himself through means similar to those that his father had only slightly overused. As a solicitor's clerk, the young Haussmann started a fund among clerks at various offices to raise money for a memorial to one of their number. But once he had collected the money, he doubtless thought that it would do him some real good, whereas the dead man did not need a carved stone on his grave—and so he kept the contributions. At another office, where he was once asked to organize the recovery of 12,000 francs, the idea occurred to him as he was passing the Palais Royal that he could easily use his boss's money to make a bit for himself. He entered a gaming house, lost the 12,000 francs, and was in no position to reimburse it. It is the loyal and excellent M. De Ramb[uteau], his predecessor at the Hôtel de Ville, who told me of this."

True or false, the source of this youthful story in Rambuteau, the great prefect of the Seine in the time of Louis-Philippe, ensured that it was received with delight in the salons of Paris. This is a further reason why Georges-Eugène Haussmann preferred to take some distance from his father and—even if it meant facing severe criticism—to carry only the weight of his own errors without assuming those of Nicolas-Valentin as well.

POLITICS AND THE HAUSSMANNS

One thing that Georges-Eugène distrusted in 1828, 1829, and 1830 was politics, the fray into which some men in the family hurled themselves with abandon. The son of General Dentzel, Georges-Eugène's uncle Colonel Dentzel, joined all the conspiracies of the age. Arrested and released several times, he eventually had to leave France and went to place his sword in the service of Greek independence. There he earned his promotion to the rank of general, only to die at Epirus fighting the Turks. "I was distressed twice over: at this end to a life so brilliantly begun, and at the stain on it caused, in my view, by the involvement of this brave officer in sterile plots."[16] The colonel's death meant that Georges-Eugène inherited the title of baron from his grandfather—a title ("Baron Haussmann") that the prefect used after his appointment as senator under the Second Empire.

Haussmann's own father was also very active in the struggle against Charles X, both working at the offices of the paper *Le Temps* and writing articles for it. Georges-Eugène dissociates himself from this activity: "I remained a mere observer. . . . I had gained the conviction that there was no need . . . to engage in conspiracies or secret plotting, still less to sing the Marsellaise, Riego's anthem, or other musical productions of that kind. That is why I maintained a calm that was taken as indifference."[17] All the greater was Haussmann Senior's surprise, therefore, to see his son racing to the offices of *Le Temps* in rue de Richelieu when, in the summer of 1830, the police acted on Charles X's decrees on the press to seize and destroy the presses of *Le Temps* and its fellow oppositionist, *Le National*. Georges-Eugène went to stand beside his father, who was in danger of being arrested at any moment. But the insurrection that broke out on July 27 forestalled the police. The Hôtel de Ville was captured the next day, with the friends of Nicolas-Valentin Haussmann in the front line.

On July 29, fighting raged in the area between the Hôtel de Ville and the offices of *Le Temps*. Georges-Eugène offered to carry messages to the Hôtel de Ville, and he was naturally armed with a musket. On his way back he became caught up in battles around the Théâtre Français, where Swiss and Royal Guards protected the approaches to the Louvre. In the middle of the shooting, Haussmann found himself grappling with an officer of the Swiss Guard, who tried to run him through with a saber. The young man, being more robust and fighting for his life, managed to disarm the officer and ran off with the saber in his hand. Only then did he notice that he was bleeding profusely from a flesh wound above his right knee, and from a more serious one where a bullet had entered the fleshy part of his left thigh. Haussmann had these "scratches"[18] bandaged up, then went to deliver his report to the banker Laffitte, who was dining with members of the brand-new provisional government. "They were being served an iced melon that made me greatly envious." But duty called—and it would seem that Laffitte did not think it necessary to offer a melon to the unimportant young man. Haussmann went off to join Colonel Bro, an officer in the First Empire, who was reorganizing the National Guard of the 1st arrondissement in which the faubourg du Roule was located. Together with the colonel, Haussmann climbed the heights of Montmartre on horseback and helped to establish defensive positions against a return of the royal troops.

Haussmann finally went home to bed and stayed there for a few days. Once recovered, he went with Colonel Bro to receive the surrender of the fort at Vincennes. On August 7, 1830, the national deputies elected the duc d'Orléans, Louis-Philippe, king of the French. Two days later he took the oath in the hall of the Legislative Assembly. Haussmann, who was part of the royal escort in his capacity as Colonel Bro's orderly, met again his old fellow student, the duc de Chartres, on the steps of the platform.

A HERO DIFFICULT TO PLACE

The national compensation board, which was established after the July revolution, awarded Haussmann the title of hero and decorated him with the three-pointed cross commemorating the events. What advantage could the young man derive from it? He completed his law degree in the spring of 1830 and considered beginning work on a thesis in the autumn; the bar attracted him, but the administration of justice tempted him most. The duc de Chartres, now the duc d'Orléans following his father's elevation to the monarchy, suggested that Haussmann join the army with the rank of sublieutenant. But he did not wish to follow behind his younger brother, who had just entered Saumur College as a cavalry officer. He preferred to take his time finishing his studies. "After obtaining my final diploma, I went back to the duc d'Orléans and said I would definitely prefer the justice system to the bar. The prince talked me out of it. In his view, there was nothing important to be done in that branch of public service, whereas the administration of the country, previously entrusted to functionaries of whom nothing had been asked but blind devotion to 'Throne and Altar,' would open unexplored paths where, by working hard and using my education, I could distinguish myself and make rapid advances."[19]

Casimir Périer was prime minister as well as minister of the interior. He knew the Haussmann family—he had been one of the melon eaters at Laffitte's table on the evening of July 29. Moreover, Haussmann Senior had just resumed service in army supplies and had been seconded to the ministry of the interior to reorganize the administrative services of the National Guard.

Nevertheless, it was not a matter of course for Georges-Eugène to be selected. Would the story told by Xavier Marmier play some role? Marmier himself wrote in the same *Journal*: "The July Revolution, like all revolutions, did not closely scrutinize those who showed evidence of zeal. The young clerk, who had lost everything and was not highly thought of, was appointed subprefect in a department in southern France." In his *Mémoires*, Haussmann assures us that Casimir Périer told him in an obviously friendly spirit that, "in order to cover the royal prince vis-à-vis the Chamber (which was most jealous of influences on the Court), it would be good if my candidacy was supported by a few deputies."[20] Months passed, however, as Haussmann made approach after approach and requested the intervention of Colonel Bro and the national compensations board. Since it was necessary to mobilize some deputies, he applied himself to that task as well; a small delegation, led by his father's friend Monsieur Chevandier, deputy for the Meurthe, turned out in support of the young man.

All these efforts were finally rewarded on May 22, 1831, when Haussmann received an order appointing him general secretary of the Vienne prefecture. Was he disappointed? The letter of thanks that he sent to Casimir

Périer on May 26 displayed no great enthusiasm: "I understand the importance of the post that has been entrusted to me, and I shall attempt to justify His Majesty's choice and yours."

GENERAL SECRETARY IN THE VIENNE

❧ When the new general secretary of the Vienne arrived in Poitiers, the situation on the ground took him completely by surprise. Georges-Eugène would be working under a prefect, Monsieur Boullé, who was the son of a former prefect of Napoleon I and had himself once been a subprefect in the empire, a man of about fifty with a great capacity for work and undeniable competence. The problem was that Haussmann's predecessor as general secretary had limited himself to performing menial tasks, and Boullé had acquired the habit of conducting the affairs of the department with the help of his principal private secretary, leaving the general secretary simply to sign the finished documents. Clearly Haussmann would have to make his presence felt. And thanks to his legal expertise, he gradually succeeded in doing this. A good organizer, he introduced flow charts to monitor the progress of each dossier in the various sections, and to spot unjustified delays. In the end he regained control of the administrative side while policy remained in the hands of the prefect's private secretary.[21] "The obliteration of the general secretary," he wrote, had been carried so far that even the accommodation that came with the post had been claimed by the principal private secretary. Haussmann preferred to say nothing and soon chose to live with some good citizens of Poitiers, in a central street near the Place du Marché and the Palais de Justice.

All things considered, the prefect had a kindly attitude to the young man: he welcomed him at the table, and to some extent Georges-Eugène became one of the family. Yet the way of life in Poitiers society disconcerted the young man from Paris. The evenings were dreary. People killed time playing cards or billiards. Haussmann had the instinctive good sense to let himself be beaten in all the games at which the prefect excelled. He flirted in a pleasant way with the prefect's cousin, a slim young brunette who, since Haussmann's arrival, no longer spoke of going back home to Saint-Brieuc. She also ran the show at the mansion that housed the prefecture, and before the evening of a grand dinner or ball she would rope the Parisian into helping her organize the occasion.

Outside the prefecture, Haussmann got to meet the best families in

Poitiers. He made friends with Monsieur Garreau, a counselor at the royal court, who insisted that he should come and live in his house, in the more aristocratic upper part of town. Haussmann did not wait too often to be asked. He met interesting people there, some lawyers like himself, who were or would be making a career in the justice system. As keen on history as some of them also were, he traveled out to view the two battlefields of Poitiers: the one where Jean le Bon was defeated by the English at the beginning of the Hundred Years War and made prisoner by the Black Prince; and the one where Charles Martel was said to have broken the momentum of the Arabs bent on conquering Gaul. Nor was Haussmann indifferent to the realities of the present, as we can tell from the curiosity with which he looked around the blade factory at Châtellerault, or from the serious way in which he took his responsibilities as administrator by visiting all the districts and cantons of the department.

In the spring of 1832, Haussmann obtained leave to visit his family. Casimir Périer received him at five in the morning—a customary hour for that noted workaholic. He complimented him and gave him some advice: not to make fun of deputies' wives, for example. Haussmann was astounded to hear such things; he was beginning to discover the nature of a prefect's career, of the nobility, of the constraints that shaped the life of a young general secretary.

On May 16, Casimir Périer was carried off by the cholera epidemic sweeping the capital. No one knew where it had originated, how it was propagated, or what measures could be taken to defend against it; there was not yet the slightest notion that the disease might be spread through water. It has been estimated that this particular epidemic caused 18,500 fatalities. In Poitiers the opposition gloated over the death of Louis-Philippe's prime minister. Haussmann, feeling bitter, ended up having a row with a student during one lunch hour. A duel seemed inevitable. This was avoided when Haussmann's opponent preferred to retract what he had said, but the atmosphere remained heavy, and strolls around town were one long sequence of verbal skirmishes.

SUBPREFECT IN YSSINGEAUX DISTRICT[22]

✎ Providence manifested itself in the form of economies, as the 1833 budget prescribed the elimination of numerous posts of departmental general secretary. Haussmann left Poitiers for a new appointment as subprefect for Yssingeaux, in the Haute-Loire department, which he had accepted on June 15, 1833. The young man had grown attached to Poitiers and departed with some regret. But there was also the pull of the unknown, the seductiveness of seeing more of France.

When Haussmann published his memoirs in 1890, the generation in command of the country no longer had any idea of the difficulties that transport presented before the railroad revolution. In order to recall what it had really been like in the "good old days" now embellished with reflected colors, Haussmann gave a detailed account of his journey from Poitiers to Yssingeaux. First he dropped south on the Paris-Bordeaux stagecoach as far as Angoulême, where he picked up a mail carriage to Limoges via La Rochefoucauld, Chabanais, and Saint-Junien. The wait in Angoulême was long enough for him to visit a paper factory and the ship-cannon foundry of Ruelle. At Limoges he again had nearly a day to see the sights and to visit a porcelain factory, where he leisurely bought a few presents and had them sent to his friends in Poitiers. Another stagecoach made the connection to Clermont-Ferrand in thirty-six hours, with an overnight stop in the small town of Sauviat. When the climb was too steep, the passengers got off and walked alongside the comfortless old rattletrap. As he was struggling up one such hill at Bourganeuf, in the Creuse department, Haussmann thought he was really lucky not to have been appointed subprefect in that particular place. Aubusson, an active, lively town, was more to his liking. But the arrival at Clermont-Ferrand filled him with wonder. He treated himself to a fine hotel on the central Place de Jaude and reserved a seat on the next day's mail carriage bound for Le Puy. Having passed through Issoire and Brioude and spent a night on the road, he arrived at Le Puy in the early hours and alighted at an inn opposite the prefecture. He took a while to recover from the exhausting journey, but after a hearty lunch he went to the prefecture to pay his respects to the prefect of Haute-Loire—whose name was Du Puy, of all things.

After a friendly welcome, there followed the official swearing-in, formal visits to the general in charge of the army subdivision and to the local bishop, and a ritual distribution of cards to the various section heads, the tax officer, and the prefectural counselors. In the evening, back at the prefecture, Haussmann dined with the prefect and virtually all the leading administrative personnel in the department, gathered there for his benefit. The next day, off to Yssingeaux, after lunch at the prefect's house. It was only seventeen miles away, but the journey was so hard that it was already dark by the time they reached Yssingeaux. As they approached the town, they came across more and more drunkards. In front of the subprefect's office, a brawl had just left one man lying wounded on the ground. Haussmann had him taken to the hospital: it was his first act of administration.

The subprefecture was a bourgeois town house. His predecessor in the post was waiting for Haussmann there, impatient to bargain with him over the transfer of the furniture. (Only in 1853, at Haussmann's instigation, or so he claims, did the minister of the interior issue a decree making the departments responsible for the costs of furnishing the prefecture or subprefecture.) Haussmann was in no mood to argue: he kept everything and paid what the experts advised.

The deputy for Yssingeaux was the eloquent Legitimist Antoine Berryer, but the Orleanist bourgeoisie controlled the municipalities. The district of Yssingeaux, tucked away at the edge of the Cevennes, was quite densely populated at the time when Haussmann arrived: its forty-one communes had no fewer than ninety thousand inhabitants, eight thousand of them in the main town. There was a good deal of industrial activity in metalwork, silk-throwing, the ribbon trade, and lace making. Eager to discover new landscapes and to explore the local geology, Haussmann tirelessly rode on horseback around the region for which he was responsible—traveling from Mont Mézenc to the Viviers country and meeting an unfamiliar breed of people, different from those in the books: the Protestants of the Cevennes and the Ardèche. When he went to a sermon one Sunday morning, he found himself surrounded at the exit by members of the same faith, "who had never previously heard of a Protestant subprefect, and who in general struck me as a bit on the wild side." To his astonishment he saw that they lived with memories of the *dragonnades*[23] and went to church with a gun on their shoulder. More poetic was a trip to Mont Gerbier-de-Jonc, where he had lunch near the source of the Loire, and another one along the pretty Lignon Valley made famous by Honoré d'Urfé in his novel *L'Astrée*.

Haussmann, whose duties left him with a lot of time on his hands, also went to Saint-Étienne. His curiosity was aroused by its arms factories and collieries, and by "its horse-driven railway, still a novelty at the time"—in short, an industrial metropolis prefiguring future times. But the region could also be plunged into the most savage past, as on the road to Aubenas where Haussmann and his companion, a lawyer from Yssingeaux, stopped off at a sinister inn and decided to leave again that same night despite the innkeeper's rebukes. A few months later he heard that the innkeeper's specialty on pitch-black nights was to relieve travelers of their money and luggage and to dispose of their bodies in the oven.

Four months later, around mid-October 1833, Haussmann received notice that on the 9th of that month he had been appointed subprefect of Nérac, in the department of Lot-et-Garonne, the home town of Henri IV's mother Jeanne d'Albret and the scene of Henri's own youthful exploits, a land of milk and honey. He took leave of the prefect and arranged to move to his new residence. This time he passed through Lyons (another new discovery) and Paris on an exhausting journey of three nights and two days, then made for Poitiers (where he allowed himself a twenty-four-hour stopover to call on his friends) and on to Bordeaux. From there he took the Toulouse mail coach as far as Agen, where the new subprefect had to report to the prefect. For the third time in his short career, Haussmann took the oath of "loyalty to the King and obedience to the Constitutional Charter and the laws of the realm."

3

Subprefect in the
Age of the Bourgeois King

THE FRANCE of the "bourgeois king" Louis-Philippe was a France with an eagerness to modernize but also with major resistances and conservative characteristics. Paris lay at the center of the whirlwind; it was the crucible for innovations so intensely desired as well as the focus of numerous apprehensions. During these years, Georges-Eugène Haussmann pressed on with his career and became an ever more seasoned administrator. A lucid and enthusiastic observer of his times, he was at once liberal and resolutely conservative—and an equally enthusiastic player in the transformation of French society and the national territory. For the moment we find him, the Parisian, living in the provinces, waiting for destiny to recall him to Paris.

PEACE, MONEY, AND PROGRESS

The France of the bourgeois king had as its first aim to live in peace in Europe. His reign involved a few well-controlled military expeditions, to give the French back their pride, but nothing at all adventurist. The conquest of Algeria served as an outlet for the army and procured its share of glory. But the main necessity was to avoid any false steps: France was being closely observed by the conservative monarchies grouped in the Holy Alliance. Louis-Philippe adopted a reassuring profile, proposing a revolution to the French people that centered upon prosperity and economic development. "Enrichissez-vous!"—the watchword of Guizot, prime minister from 1840—was also the leitmotif of the epoch. When people are making money, they are too busy to engage in untimely reveries. The more they make, and the more they are attached to their property, the more conservative they become.

Modernization was a special concern in relation to agriculture. France was witnessing an acceleration of the agricultural revolution that had begun in England eighty years before: more modern farming practices, the use of fertilizers, crop rotation, introduction of leguminous and fodder plants that removed the need for fallow periods, expansion of livestock farming, and the rapid development of industrial plants such as dyestuffs. Sugar beets, potatoes, and corn were revolutionizing the countryside. But France had emerged from the Revolution with a sizable class of smallholders, and the creation of large farms was proving more difficult than it was across the Channel.

Large-scale industry—textiles, in particular, but also metalworking—was fast gathering momentum. These two industries in turn gave a major spur to coal mining. For this was the age of the steam engine: the transport of coal led to the pioneering use of rail vehicles at Saint-Étienne, pulled first by horses, then by steam engines capable of moving ever longer trains over ever longer distances, at speeds that were steadily increasing. The steam train, which had first appeared as a curiosity toward the end of the reign of Charles X, was now used to transport both passengers and freight. More than just another technical invention, it became the springboard for economic transformation and a social phenomenon that was changing the face of France.

The new businesses that sprang up had large financial needs. Short-term credit had been organized for centuries through the discounting of commercial bills; now the growth of small-scale and craft industry made it more necessary than ever to establish mechanisms that would permit discounting on a less parsimonious scale than that carried out by the traditional banks or the Bank of France. Industrial and mining firms, large textile factories, and railway companies all required new means of securing medium- to long-term investment in the modern sense of the term. The railway would be the vehicle for carrying new types of savers to the stock exchange.

Not all bankers saw things in the same way. Those at the top, including the Rothschilds, kept a cautious approach, whereas many others had a bolder and more innovative vision—Laffitte, for example, whose dual career as financier and political leader illustrated the close links between money and politics in this era of strong economic growth.

Faced with the rise of new industries and the surge of inventions both minor and major, the public was convinced that the Age of Progress was dawning. It was a sensational turnaround in the destiny of man. The dispute between Darwin and Lamarck was shattering any literal interpretation of the biblical tale of the creation. French people at the time of Louis-Philippe were thirsty for knowledge, thirsty for education. The main scientific and technical colleges, headed by the École Polytechnique, were the object of almost religious reverence. In fact, the institution of the Polytechnique—a temple where mathematics was regarded as a tool for mastering the world, rather than an immediately applicable body of knowledge—made France distinctive among European nations. A graduate of the Polytechnique was not a vulgar engineer; with his black uniform, sword, and kepi, he was a priest of the new scientific church, a guide leading humanity toward the light of Reason.

Access to knowledge had certain peculiarities in this world-conquering enterprise. Education in order to rise higher became everyone's obsession. Government, chambers of commerce, and employers saw it as the basis for technological development and a compulsory stage in gaining wealth. Another major aspect in the acquisition of knowledge was information. To know what was happening in the world and on one's own doorstep made it possible to anticipate events—for human activity was more and more turned toward, and shaped by, the future. Foresight was no longer the prerogative of government; it was considered one of the essential qualities of an entrepreneur, magnified as one of the prime human virtues. Information about new inventions, pioneering methods, the state of markets, and the state of fashion was a right and a necessity for each and all.

Cities were in the fore of this cultural effervescence, the places where ideas rubbed shoulders with people. Correspondence, too, underwent prodigious growth. Telegraphy, optical and later electrical, was still the preserve of the public authorities, but the day was near when it would be opened up to private messages. The press inspired both adulation and dread, yet continued its forward march despite the spoke that ruling politicians tried to put in its wheel. No one could escape its power, and the financial potentates of the age supported daily papers, often becoming shareholders, in order to control journalists and influence public opinion.

The cult of progress, however, accompanied a ferment in many people's minds. France, like the rest of Europe, had not fully recovered its bearings since the turbulence of the Revolution and the Napoleonic adventure. The seeds of the spirit of 1789 were still at work. The Romantic reaction to the numbing rationalism of the late Enlightenment was wreaking havoc in the shape of solitary reveries and feverish imaginings; people dreamed of dying Byron-like in the Greek struggle against the Turks, or joined one of the proliferation of secret societies, plots, and conspiracies. In France, Romanticism also drew sustenance from a nostalgia for the empire.

Utopian philosophers were springing up on all sides. Each head of a school felt vested with a mission to reform the world. Auguste Comte, Fourier, Blanqui, Proudhon, and countless others exercised high moral office and sometimes also political influence. But it was the Saint-Simonians who would have the most fertile posterity. Scientific progress, erected into a dogma in the name of civilization and world peace, was supposed to produce remarkable results in the wake of the transport and communications revolution: self-knowledge would lead people to stop desiring war; the shrinking of the planet through faster movement of goods and people, and through greater exchange of information, would become an ideological as well as an economic imperative. The Saint-Simonians made themselves the convinced and influential apostles of this trend.

One contemporary witness and champion of scientific progress, Maxime Du Camp, was rather less enthusiastic about the utopian systems of his time. He had a keen eye for what was going on around him. "It is a French disease to create a chimerical being and then shape institutions to suit it. . . . From 1830 to 1840 social, philosophical and religious innovation became a mania—I was about to say a vogue."[1] Judging by the political trends, one might think with Du Camp that the target of the multiple and persistent attacks of the opposition under Louis-Philippe was not the royalty but the social order of the Ancien Régime, which the Revolution had not brought crashing down in all its elements. It was "the constitution of the French tribe," in religion and relations between the sexes, which Du Camp thought to be under assault. People dreamed of renewing the old world and deifying humanity; they were in the grip of an insane pride. Among the apostles of a new era, the Saint-Simonians were "the only ones to whom our age owes any debt of gratitude. It was their impetus, both scientific and industrial, which set the ameliorative trend in motion. . . . Their theocracy was childish and their dress ridiculous, but their preaching and their efforts had a huge effect that has greatly improved the conditions of human life."[2]

AN EXEMPLARY ADMINISTRATOR

≈ When Haussmann arrived at Agen in the autumn of 1833, he was greeted by the prefect of the Lot-et-Garonne department, Monsieur

Croneau. A former general secretary of the Gironde, he was a hard worker and a mediocre public speaker. Haussmann judged him "an outstanding bureaucrat rather than a prefect."[3] All said, however, Croneau was an excellent man upon whom the young subprefect made a very good impression. Once Haussmann had been sworn in, he paid introductory calls on the presiding judge and the prosecutor general of the Royal Law Court, on the local bishop, the general in charge of the army subdivision, the tax officer, and the rector of the Academy. He also did the rounds of the section heads, including the chief engineer.

A Land of Milk and Honey? The chief engineer made the unpleasant disclosure that there was no main road from Agen to Nérac—or, to be more precise, that one was planned but was still only on the drawing board. This meant that Georges-Eugène would have to follow the Garonne twelve miles down as far as Port-Sainte-Marie, cross the river on a ferry, pick up the highway to Auch at Saint-Laurent on the left bank, then travel another twelve miles via Nérac and Condom before finally reaching the main town of his arrondissement.

Nor was that all. The chief engineer itemized all the highway routes in Haussmann's new territory that conformed to official standards: the portion of royal highway just mentioned, an eight-mile stretch of departmental highway between Nérac and Mézin, three miles between Barbaste and Lusseignan, a few more miles on the way from Saint-Côme to Boussès, and two miles between Damazan and Port-de-Pascau (on the land of the commune of Saint-Léger). And the rest? Some roads roughly drawn in the soil—that is, impassable for most of the year. "These revelations were like so many cold showers. I had just left a land that was reputedly wild yet crisscrossed by a good number of well-maintained roads and endowed with a reasonable vicinal highway, and was coming to administer an ostensible land of milk and honey that was almost entirely devoid of means of communication! It crossed my mind to return to Paris and say: 'I'd prefer something else.' But I reflected that the more I had to do in this backward land, the more merit there was in undertaking it and seeing it through. And seven years later— for I would remain no less than seven years in Nérac—the same arrondissement had been completely transformed under my care, people traveled everywhere by horse and carriage, and the value of all the land had considerably increased."[4] To build roads that afforded ease of travel and increased land values: the Haussmann of the Parisian *grands travaux* can be seen behind the mask of the subprefect of Nérac.

After a few social events in Agen—dinner at the prefect's house, visits to

individuals of note—Haussmann set off to take up his subprefecture. He
went over what he had already learned. The arrondissement of Nérac, one of
the four into which the department was divided, lived a life shut off from
the rest of the world. Moreover its partly Protestant population exhibited
some liberal tendencies whereas the other districts of the department had a
large Catholic majority. Being a Protestant himself, Haussmann did not encounter the difficulties he had feared, and in Nérac Catholics and Protestants
actually lived on good terms with each other. The deputy for Nérac was the
marquis de Lusignan, who owed his election to his Napoleonic past. The arrondissement of Agen had two deputies, one of whom, Sylvain Dumon, had
been a pupil at the Collège Henri-IV before Haussmann's time. A liberal
who had gone over to the Orleanist majority, he was considered a renegade
by his former friends in Nérac; he would later become a minister. Haussmann arrived after dark in Nérac, although it was most agreeably lighted by
streetlamps that distinguished it from Yssingeaux. A superb dinner was
awaiting him at the town's main hostelry.

Haussmann took possession of the subprefecture, which had been established in a former convent. He was immediately won over by the charm of
the town and by the valley of the Baïse that watered it. The châteaux of the
region included Bournac and Séguinot, and also Xaintrailles, where Poton
de Xaintrailles, maréchal de France under Charles VII, was said to have im-
mured alive his wife Mathilde de Sabran-Pontevès (whose bones were found
one day when Georges-Eugène, on a trip around the region, stopped off at
the château to pay his respects to the current owner, the marquis de Lusignan). Haussmann also liked to contemplate the little fortified town of
Lavardac, typical of the Southwest, and the famous windmill at Barbaste
that had been dear to the heart of Henri IV.

Haussmann's memoirs contain a veritable course in the natural and economic geography of the arrondissement of Nérac. In the northeastern moor-
land, the subsoil had an impenetrable crust similar to the rust-colored *alios*
of the Medoc and the Landes near Bordeaux, here called *terrebouc*, which, by
preventing the flow of water, transformed the whole area into one huge
marsh. But since 1832, Haussmann tells us, the sowing of maritime pine
(from which resin was extracted) had been transforming the landscape and
draining the water. Elsewhere, especially in the valleys of the Garonne,
Baïse, Avance, and Ciron, the land was rich, the wines plentiful, the agriculture and livestock farming prosperous.

Roads and Schools. Indeed, "it was means of communication that were
most lacking in this land favored by fortune." Sometimes a horse might sink

up to its chest in the clayey soil, or in the quicksand of the marshy part of the arrondissement. There was a real sense of urgency in the way that Haussmann tackled the problem of roads.

He went with budget proposals to the regional council, persuaded it to approve funding for the vicinal roads, and negotiated with residents bordering upon them a donation of land that would allow a road-widening program to go ahead. The 1836 law on vicinal roads, which provided for additional resources, was a blessing for our young subprefect. He made a start on the departmental highways, and by the time he left Nérac he had the satisfaction of knowing that all the projects had been carried out in accordance with the rules of the art. It was also under his administration that the Baïse was canalized between Nérac and Condom, and the swamps of Casteljaloux were cleared. Three suspension toll bridges replaced the three ferries that had been the only means of crossing the Garonne: one at Marmande (which did not affect those under his administration), one at Port-Sainte-Marie, and one at Port-de-Pascau. The three bridges were built through the awarding of concessions to private companies; Haussmann, as subprefect, was responsible for supervising the work on behalf of the state.

Haussmann attached at least the same degree of importance to primary education. A law of June 28, 1835, cleared the way for a primary school to be opened in each commune through a special system of funding: each commune would raise a special education levy of three centimes, or 3 percent, in addition to the four direct taxes that constituted its revenue base; and if this was not enough to cover expenditure—as was the case in most communes in the Nérac arrondissement—the commune could ask the department or, if necessary, the central government to make up the shortfall. This expression of public support made primary education accessible to all. Haussmann used all his energy to convince, one by one, the mayors of each of the sixty-seven communes comprising the seven cantons of the arrondissement. Nor did he forget the parish priests! Before the end of the summer holidays of 1835, the respective school premises had been converted, equipped, and furnished; the teachers had been appointed (he also helped the mayors with secretarial support, and the priests found in him a willing chorister); and the lists of pupils, including those entitled to free schooling, had been finalized.

The year 1836 saw the triumph of Haussmann's active approach as pastors and priests rivaled each other in zeal alongside him in the struggle against ignorance. On July 20, 1837, Haussmann received a letter from the minister of the interior, comte de Montalivet, informing him that as of the 17th he had been made a *chevalier* of the Légion d'Honneur. "Nothing had led me to expect such a reward at the age of twenty-eight," Haussmann claims in his memoirs. But the truth was different. The honor was the fruit of protracted trench warfare in which Haussmann had been his own worst enemy, although on the outside this role appeared to have been taken by the new prefect for Lot-et-Garonne, Monsieur Brun.

A *"Superior" Young Man?* In a note dated October 21, 1834, to the minister of the interior, Brun criticized Haussmann's tendency to swaggering: "People find him curt, thoughtless, superior [*avantageux*], to use the local expression; he indulges a little too much in the petty passions of small coteries and does not bring to his relations with others that scrupulous impartiality which one has a right to expect from an administrator." A few months later, at the beginning of 1835, Haussmann signed his application for the Légion d'Honneur. But Brun had another candidate, the subprefect for Villeneuve-sur-Lot, whom he put forward ahead of Haussmann. Georges-Eugène heard of this and requested the Nérac deputy, the marquis de Lusignan, to put in a word on his behalf. The reports required in support of his dossier were frankly bad, and eighteen months of pressure on the part of the marquis de Lusignan were necessary for Haussmann finally to obtain the red ribbon. When Brun was informed of the outcome, he made a point of recalling that it had never been his preference and requested that the restless subprefect be moved elsewhere.

Brun was a withdrawn and secretive Protestant from Bordeaux, with no taste for public displays, so that Haussmann's exuberance and need to have a hand in everything were naturally not to his liking. He also held it against Georges-Eugène that he used his connections a little too freely. The marquis de Lusignan had Brun transferred to the Vosges, but he could not prevent him from being brought back to Agen a few weeks later. For Brun enough was enough; he would now nurse a persistent grudge against his subprefect, considering him to be the main person responsible for his misfortune.

THE CHARM OF OCTAVIE—A PROTESTANT MARRIAGE

❧ Haussmann's unmarried status was also beginning to pose problems. Well-placed families sought him out, and Haussmann, carried away by his desire to shine, probably did not realize that he sometimes placed himself in embarrassing situations. Was it wise to pay such frequent visits to the young "Misses" of Nérac (there was a small English colony in the town), even if it was only for English lessons that seemed to bear fruit, since "in the end I spoke English quite fluently and—a more difficult achievement—could also

understand it"?[5] He flattered the deputies' wives, as Casimir Périer had recommended, and made a fuss over the children; indeed, ever since Poitiers he
had noticed that "by occupying oneself with them, one is assured of the
mothers' favor."[6] When he went to Paris, he took great care to run plenty of
errands for these ladies and went to see their little girls who had been sent to
boarding school there to learn "to speak in a shrill tone," as they say in Gas-
cony of Parisians.

When his father was sent to Algeria, his mother and sisters came to stay
with him for nearly a year. The arrival of these Parisians threw Nérac into
turmoil, but at least it protected Georges-Eugène from the maneuvering of
the local ladies. He greatly regretted it when his father's return from Algeria
and appointment to the more prosaic surroundings of Le Mans deprived him
of the sweet company of the women of the family. His elder sister married at
that moment a distinguished Hellenist, Monsieur Artaud, who progressed
under the Second Empire to become vice rector of the Académie de Paris and
a member of the municipal council in the capital.

Haussmann again became the center of all the matrimonial strategies in
Nérac. To put an end to it all, he made up his mind to ask for the hand of
Octavie de Laharpe, whose brother, a young pastor living in Bordeaux, was a
friend of the subprefect. The Laharpes were Calvinists, originally from Rolle,
near Lausanne in Switzerland. The family was rich. Haussmann, who found a
lot of charm in Octavie, heard that she would gladly consent to become his
wife. On the brother's advice—he had said to him that "marriage is one of
those things you need to do as soon as you decide on it, like blowing your
brains out"—Haussmann proposed on September 4, 1838, and was accepted. That month he spent many days in Bordeaux as well as at the large
estate of Octavie's parents outside Le Bouscat. But he divided his time with
Nérac, where he continued with his work as subprefect and set about rear-
ranging his bachelor's home to receive the young woman. As a good son who
respected the rules of family cohesion, he informed his parents and gained
their willing approval: the bride-to-be was a Protestant. The marriage took
place in early October, with the signing of the necessary contract; a civil ceremony followed at the *mairie* in Bordeaux on October 17, followed the same
day by a religious service at the church of the Chartrons, the part of Bordeaux where the merchant bourgeoisie lived.

Haussmann's parents were not able to come. This was one more reason to
present Octavie to all Georges-Eugène's close relatives; first to meet his
mother at Le Mans, then his Dentzel grandparents, the Artauds, and others
in Paris—which also gave Octavie her first taste of the frenetic activity of

life in the capital. But poor Octavie fell ill as a result, and the couple returned to Bordeaux in small stages, arriving only in January 1839. The young Madame Haussmann was left exhausted in her family's care, while Georges-Eugène made his way back to Nérac. Octavie finally joined him there in April and submitted with good grace to the ritual of introductions that started her on her new life. Not long afterward, a trip to the Southwest by the duc and duchesse d'Orléans took them to Nérac and put the social talents of the Haussmann couple to the test. A grand lunch brought together local authorities and notables. The duke and duchess left in the late afternoon, seeming pleased enough with the occasion. Haussmann noted: "Everything went well." Does a prefect's life not consist of dealing with the tricky situations that may always occur?

Well, a tricky situation was certainly looming. The raising of the marquis de Lusignan to the Chamber of Peers had made necessary the election of a new deputy. The minister of the interior, Duchâtel, had some ideas that the subprefect did not share. Then the prefect got involved, and in desperation Haussmann offered his resignation to the minister. It was rejected. The minister's candidate was elected only after three rounds of voting, by the kind of narrow margin that Haussmann had foreseen. That evening Georges-Eugène requested a transfer. It was the autumn of 1839.

THE SUBPREFECTURE OF SAINT-GIRONS

✽ By December, Octavie was pregnant and back in Bordeaux; Haussmann was still in Nérac when his daughter Marie-Henriette was born on January 17, 1840. A month later, Duchâtel was removed as minister of the interior, but not before he had obtained the king's signature for Haussmann's transfer from Nérac to Saint-Girons, in the department of Ariège.

It was a real fall from grace, and Georges-Eugène indignantly decided to request an explanation from the new minister. They were sympathetic at the offices in Paris, but they argued that Saint-Girons was a sensitive location on the frontier with Spain and itself prone to civil unrest, that Haussmann was the only person who could cope honorably with such a hornet's nest, and that it would later certainly earn him the subprefecture of Libourne, close to Bordeaux and the most beautiful on the Gironde, which he had his eyes on because of his marriage with a woman from Bordeaux. Haussmann saw the under secretary of state to the ministry of the interior, as well as the minister himself, and even the prime minister Adolphe Thiers. All vied with one another in the promises they offered. Feeling reassured, Haussmann left to take up his new post.

His journey took him first to Toulouse, then along the banks of the Garonne and the Ariège, through Auterive, Cintegabelle, and Pamiers, and finally to Foix, seat of the Ariège prefecture. Here, following a routine that he now knew by heart, he had a good scrub in a hotel room, dressed, had a meal, and at about 8:30 in the evening asked to be taken to the prefecture. The prefect, Monsieur Petit de Bantel, was a petulant Parisian who gave him a most hearty welcome. The next morning Haussmann was sworn in and then, on the prefect's advice, immediately set off for Saint-Girons. He needed half the day to cover the twenty-seven miles.

Haussmann did not reckon that he would be staying long in the Ariège. At the town's main hotel he came to an arrangement with the landlord, who was also a trader of bric-a-brac, that he should furnish the bare rooms of the subprefecture. Haussmann would go to the hotel for his meals, together with the prosecutor, the examining magistrate, and the forestry expert, all of whom were, so to speak, in the same boat as himself. He tirelessly familiarized himself with everything to do with the arrondissement, relying on the geological survey map and the annual statistical reports. He had the lieutenant of the gendarmerie explain the main roads as well as the tracks used by smugglers. He took an interest in the life of the local people, whose men had to migrate in the winter months to the towns of the plain in order to earn some money while the women kept jealous watch over the herds and fields. He was told about the numerous bears in the area, which the Ariégeois specialized in training for display at fairs and markets as far away as the capital, and he especially delighted to catch sight of some in semi-liberty.

One day he received Doctor Ferrus, the celebrated alienist with whom he would work in later years as prefect for the Seine. They discussed the causes of goiter, which troubled some sections of the population in the department. On his way out, Ferrus offered two pieces of advice that Haussmann would remember to his advantage: "Beware of fat men!" and "If someone has behaved badly with you, he will never forgive you for it!"[7] The arrondissement had a mental asylum, Saint-Lizier, where the inmates practiced all the trades—beginning with that of ward supervisor. Haussmann was fascinated by this: "In the end, this little population of the insane was not much worse off than many large modern nations, where the rights of reason, proclaimed and invoked on all sides, would lead one to think that reason was the common and generally respected rule. In both cases, I thought I could detect that order was the end result of a happy antagonism among mutually balancing and neutralizing elements of disorder. Can the various passions that grapple with one another in society not be likened to the corresponding cases of insanity: religious mania; frenzied ambition; obsession with grandeur, wealth, or power; persecution mania; liberty mania; rage at all constraints; the folly of love, and so many others? And if society can place effective curbs on all these conditions, and thereby maintain a state of equilibrium, is it not because, against each of them, it can enlist the support of those members of society who are not affected by it, and who are guided by reason insofar as their own mania is not involved?"[8]

Saint-Girons also saw the stirrings of the passionate interest in geology and hydrology that would later help Haussmann to deal successfully with the problem of the Paris water supply. At the same time he by no means neglected the defense of the frontier; one lucky ambush enabled local customs officers to seize a load of a thousand rifles. Feeling satisfied with his performance, the subprefect asked for leave in October of his first year, 1840. He went first to his old arrondissement of Nérac, where he was offered the chance to buy an estate near Houeillès on which he had had his eye for some time, then on to spend some days with his family in Bordeaux, and finally to see how the land lay at the ministry of the interior in Paris.

On October 29 the government changed once more, with Guizot as prime minister instead of Thiers. Rémusat was replaced as interior minister by Duchâtel, and it was now that Haussmann met him for the first time. Straightaway he noticed that Duchâtel was not only fat but bloated. Distrust, therefore. He was most surprised to find himself invited to dinner the next day. The atmosphere was pleasant, and Haussmann spoke a great deal without waiting to be asked. He returned to Saint-Girons very contented with himself—and with the radiant future he thought he could glimpse for his career. He even persuaded Octavie and his daughter to come and stay with him—which proved to be something of a holiday, despite the social round of introductions, lunches, and dinners. The end of civil war in Spain meant that the defeated troops were streaming across the frontier; Haussmann received them, disarmed them, and interned them. Then he asked for leave and for permission to reside in Bordeaux while awaiting a new appointment. In October 1841, his request approved, Haussmann left the Ariège for good.

SUBPREFECT AT BLAYE

❧ As the post at Libourne was not vacant, Duchâtel offered Haussmann another subprefecture in the Gironde, at Bazas or Blaye. He would have preferred Bazas, which was close to his new acquisitions at Houeillès, but he wisely turned for advice to the prefect for the Gironde, Baron Sers, and was told that this very proximity made it a bad choice. Haussmann therefore opted for Blaye and received the posting on November 23, 1841. It was a small arrondissement, very near to Bordeaux. Baron Sers advised Haussmann to think of Blaye as in every way the equal of Libourne and to move on only if it was to take up a full prefecture—and indeed, he did later turn down an offer of Libourne, being convinced that a prefect's job was in the offing. In the end, he remained in that holding post at Blaye for six years, until February 24, 1848, and the fall of the July Monarchy.

As soon as he was sworn in, Haussmann departed to take possession of the subprefecture. He found it to his taste: spacious, well ventilated, and with a pretty garden. Octavie, who liked Bordeaux or Le Bouscat better, did not set up house at Blaye. Each Saturday at midday, or sometimes at the same time on Friday, our subprefect took the riverboat from Blaye to be with her; he usually met a number of people on board and dealt with some administrative business there. On landing at Bordeaux, Haussmann went to have a chat with the prefect and often had dinner with him. Not only did this cement a useful relationship; he learned just as much about the wines of Bordeaux and began to lay down a cellar of his own, which would have quite a reputation during his years at the Seine prefecture.

Together with two great sons of Bordeaux, the duc Decazes and Mayor Duffour-Dubergier, he played a role in setting up the Bordeaux Horticultural Society. The ships that docked in the port brought with them a number of colonial plants, especially orchids. Haussmann would later use the evergreens in the parks and gardens of Paris. And here in Bordeaux he met a couple of other flower-loving inhabitants, Alphand and Barillet-Deschamps, whom he would later bring to work with him at the Seine prefecture. In the midst of this easy life, however, a stroke of fate drove it home that nothing in this world can ever be taken for granted: on July 13, 1842, the accidental death of the duc d'Orléans deprived him of a man who was in some ways his peer in politics and left him alone with himself.

Haussmann applied himself all the more zealously to cultivating the district potentates: the duc de Lamoignon, an imposing and distant figure who soon went the way of all flesh; the marquis; and especially the marquise de

La Grange (née Caumont-La Force). The marquis, the deputy for Blaye, was a pleasant enough character, while his haughty and caustic wife had a more difficult manner. But Georges-Eugène and Octavie had the good fortune to get on well with her: she thought they made "a nice couple" and broadcast this loud and clear. Haussmann was asked to organize parties and balls for the marquise—a skill he eventually mastered which would stand him in good stead.

According to Xavier Marmier, the support of the La Granges was decisive for Haussmann's career. "As subprefect at Blaye, he found the dull and scheming marquis de La Grange and his wife the marquise, even more scheming, bustling and mischievous than he. M. de la Grange was deputy for the arrondissement. M. Haussmann knew how to make a fuss of this vain couple and thereby to obtain friends in high places who could really do things for him. He was appointed prefect of Bordeaux and eventually called by the Emperor to the prefecture of Paris. It is from then that his terrible power dates."[9] Ah, connections! Can one ever get away from them? Without any feeling of shame, Haussmann calls this section of the chapter of his memoirs dealing with his time at Blaye: "Establishing important connections."

Haussmann displayed his talents in the art of decoration and lighting when two sons of Louis-Philippe, the duc de Nemours and the duc de Montpensier, paid successive dazzling visits to the region. Georges-Eugène illuminated all the heights along the Garonne and had powerful lamps hung from the wings of its numerous windmills. The magnificent effect won him compliments from the princes and the prefect.

The functions of subprefect at Blaye were not really engrossing. Haussmann opened some new roads. He improved the one from Blaye to Bourg-sur-Gironde, Saint-André-de-Cubzac, and Libourne, and another one from Blaye to Saint-Savin and Guitres. An old mayor paid him this compliment some years later: "You have written your name into roads all over our district."[10] Soon he had done the rounds of the arrondissement, which was less extensive than Nérac and already had good facilities.

Would he feel stifled in this narrow space? In any event, a murky record of illegal land transfer shows a tendency on his part both to ride roughshod over established procedures and to behave in a more and more cantankerous manner. His talents, real enough, seem to have led him to think that people owed him certain things, and his constant faultfinding earned him considerable hostility. This time it was a departmental councillor, Monsieur Pascault, who began in 1844 a campaign of press articles, petitions, and approaches to the ministry of the interior for Haussmann to be replaced. The prefect, Baron Sers, had to intervene to vouch for the integrity of the Blaye subprefect.

Haussmann's work included responsibilities for the communal schools. The buildings were impeccably equipped and maintained, and the schools themselves functioned well. He also took an interest in the system introduced in the seventeenth century by Dutch engineers to drain the marshes on the borders of Blaye. To prevent the drainage canals from silting up, boats of roughly the same width as the canals were fitted with sluice gates that could obstruct and lower the whole section of water; the downward flow carried the boats toward the Garonne, and the silt with them. The boats were then hauled upstream, with the sluice gates raised so that they did not touch the bottom. And the operation began over again, as many times as were necessary. The sluice boats that Haussmann developed to clear the sewers of the capital were directly descended from those of the Blaye marshes.

Baron Sers secured Georges-Eugène's promotion to the rank of officer of the Légion d'Honneur on February 20, 1847, and toward the end of the same year there was talk of his being appointed to a prefect's post. In January 1848 things became clearer: it would be the prefecture of Charente, based at Angoulême. The royal signature was expected any day, but then the revolution of February 24 erupted in Paris and swept away all his expectations.

4

The End of

Louis-Philippe's Reign

THE MONTHS BEFORE the fall of Louis-Philippe were filled with a variety of events heralding the collapse of the moral virtues of a bourgeois society that the king claimed to embody. The duchesse de Praslin was murdered by her husband the duke, a Peer of France, and the prefect of police "advised" him to commit suicide so as to avoid the scandal of a public trial. But the banker Pélaprat, the major general Despans-Cubière, and the former minister Teste did not manage to avoid the scandal of a trial for misappropriation of public funds. "French society," wrote Du Camp, "seemed to be falling apart, and those with a keen ear claimed to hear the cracking of the throne."[1] At the end of eighteen years, the regime was exhausted. The king himself was seventy-five, weary, and increasingly resembling the cartoons that depicted him as a rotten pear. His eldest son, the duc d'Orléans, had been killed in an accident in 1842. The heir to the throne was now the king's grandson, the comte de Paris, born in 1838 and still a child. If there was to be a regent, the argument centered on whether it should be his mother, a German Protestant who had the support of the left, or the eldest of his uncles, the duc de Nemours, a loyal dullard favored by conservatives.

The institutions were stable—too stable. The Soult-Guizot government had been in place since October 1840; it suited the king, and no one could see how a majority could be found to topple it. But for this very reason France had grown bored. And for want of a parliamentary tribune, opposition was expressed in other places. The Legitimists campaigned on behalf of Charles X's grandson, the comte de Chambord, in the salons of Paris and the châteaux of the provinces. The faubourg Saint-Germain was their citadel. They had brilliant polemicists, men such as Veuillot, who found Orleanism too Protestant and too petty-minded. The republicans, though few in number, had the young on their side; they were *patriotes*, who laid claim to the revolutionary heritage of 1789—indeed, most of their leaders were descended from the personnel of the Revolution. They believed in the emergent middle classes, the ordinary town dwellers enriched by the industrial changes amid which they had grown up—even if, in some cases, other kinds of suffering had made them rise up indignantly against the government of the rich. Lacking experience in a political system that had pushed them aside, the oppositional forces mobilized their energies in newspapers, novels, or essays. The surge of left-wing utopias and social romanticism was quite formidable, and the prospect of emancipation through force attracted all the Legitimist and republican enemies of the regime.

The electoral base of the July Monarchy appeared to be obsolete; the *pays légal* no longer reflected the *pays réel*. An election law of 1831 had increased the number of voters from 80,000 to 200,000, the qualification being annual payment of a certain tax quota, or *cens*, which has given the name *censitaire* in French to any such system. The educated classes put up with this mechanism, considering that universal suffrage would be premature as the popular classes would be easy prey for demagogues. Other Western countries did not disagree, although the electoral base was much larger in Britain and the United States. In France there was constant talk of a lowering of the tax quota and the granting of the vote to a larger number of "capable," if not necessarily affluent, citizens in high-profile social positions. But the reform did not see the light of day.

ELECTORAL REPRESENTATION AND MUNICIPAL LIFE IN PARIS

In 1842, Paris had 18,138 electors, one for each 52 inhabitants, nearly a tenth of the total number of electors in France. This proportion confirmed the wealth of the capital in comparison with the rest of the country, as the national average was just 1 elector for 170 inhabitants. In the capital, 60 percent of those entitled to vote were traders or manufacturers; and 47.4 percent—living especially in the central districts on the Right Bank—owned no property and reached their qualifying quota only by virtue of license-to-trade payments. Still, the fact that more than half of electors paid some tax on real estate is an indication that this form of property was becoming more widespread. More than 70 percent of Parisian electors were described as traders, food-sector professionals such as butchers, bakers, *charcutiers*, and café proprietors, or producers who sold some of their wares (especially clothing or furniture) direct to the public. The liberal professions were quite strongly represented: lawyers and business agents, public officials, doctors, pharmacists, architects, and so on. Magistrates, university staff, and senior civil servants, on the other hand, accounted for only 4.5 percent of the register. A tax reform in 1844 meant that a number of craftsmen and traders lost the right to vote, so that by 1847 the number of electors in Paris had fallen to 15,991. The king was turning his most loyal allies against him.

Paris was run by an appointed municipal committee, the true executive being the prefect for the Seine department. In each of the twelve arrondissements then in the capital, a mayor and two deputies were chosen by the king from among the local councillors. Reputation, celebrity, and competence were the chief criteria in the selection. The government tried to promote a Parisian elite that distinguished itself by social position as much as by money. Public opinion was not convinced of the need for an elected assembly in the capital, but the eviction of the "little people" made the atmosphere heavy. They were the most ardent in demanding the modernization of Paris. The lack of movement in the field of public works was the cause of great discontent. Notables who confronted one another across district boundaries were particularly held to blame, as in 1845 when a plan to move Les Halles to the Left Bank collapsed because the large dealers on the Right Bank were fiercely opposed to it. In short, the bourgeoisie wanted reforms. It was calling not for a revolution but for an evolution in the regime.

A BANQUET THAT WENT WRONG

The establishment of a railway network in France, which began amid doubts and heated debates, was regulated in 1842 through a law that provided for a stable partnership between the state and private operators organized into large financial companies. It was some time before the machinery was fully operational, but then it soon demonstrated its efficacy. In fact, it raced away. Everyone wanted to invest in the railways, to subscribe to the loans. The financial results were sensational at first, but then fell back to more reasonable levels. Some speculators who had taken too many risks amid the financial euphoria were suddenly ruined. The railway "bubble" burst in 1845, as other bubbles would burst in 1929 and later.

In 1846 the financial crisis was compounded by serious floods and a disastrous harvest. Food shortages, rising prices, and a slump in textiles, timber, craft metalworking, and the extensive cottage industries, piled up the difficulties and made calls for reform all the more insistent. The regime, whose legitimacy was based upon economic prosperity, found itself facing recession and rising unemployment.

Advocates of reform knew they had no interest in appearing to be seditious. They believed that a powerful mobilization of opinion, involving not street demonstrations but banquets, would make the government bend. The most hostile to reforms was Guizot's minister of the interior, Duchâtel, whose obduracy we have already seen on display in his relations with Haussmann. Rambuteau argued for a conciliatory approach, but he was isolated in the circle surrounding Louis-Philippe. Du Camp writes: "Only M. De Rambuteau, who, as prefect for the Seine, was in touch with the influential bourgeois figures on the municipal council, had made some timid remarks to the king and been answered with an indulgent smile: 'My dear prefect, you don't understand the first thing about all this.' "[2]

The royal government wagered that the banquet campaign would eventually lose momentum. In fact, was it wrong? Once the participants had eaten well, drunk a little, heard and acclaimed the leading lights of the opposition, and gone home to bed, the regime could continue its untroubled sleep. But what of the Parisian powder keg? In theory the city was in the solid hands of thirty thousand troops, who also had the support of the National Guard, a kind of bourgeois militia constituted under the law of March 22, 1831, and ever ready to take up arms against a popular movement, a political insurrection, or a hunger revolt. Until early 1848 the National Guard had perfectly discharged its task of putting down street rioting. But would it fire upon advocates of reform who expressed themselves in the form of banquets? And if the National Guard stayed put at home, would it be possible to count on the soldiers? In Rambuteau's view they would not shoot either—and he was right.

When the organizers of the banquet campaign, with Lamartine at their head, grew to feel that the movement had reached an impasse, they decided to hold an especially large banquet in Paris. They chose the Mouffetard area, in one of the poorest districts of the capital. For Lamartine, who no longer believed in success, this last meeting was supposed to go off like a final burst of fireworks, for the sake of honor. On January 14, 1848, the prefect of police issued an order prohibiting the banquet. The reformists were in a way relieved, as their chosen location presented too many risks. They set a new date, February 22. Every precaution was taken: the banquet would take place on a Tuesday, in the Chaillot part of town, with a high admission fee customized for the bourgeoisie. As an extra safeguard against excesses, the National Guard was asked to show up unarmed and to provide the steward-ing—a clever suggestion that would make it possible to gauge the popular-ity of reformist ideas among the Parisian middle classes. On February 21 the government forbade both the attendance of the National Guard and the ban-quet itself. The organizers backed down in the evening. But how were they to tell Parisians that the procession due to leave Place de la Madeleine for the banquet at 11:30 the next morning had been canceled? At 11:30 on Febru-ary 22, then, onlookers and many who had paid for their banquet tickets showed up at the appointed place. The organizers were not to be seen. Shouts rang out, various movements occurred in the crowd, the soldiers opened fire on the Place de la Concorde. An old woman and a worker were killed. Clashes broke out, and a few barricades were erected between Les Halles and the boulevards. Nothing really serious.

THE *JOURNÉES* OF FEBRUARY 1848:
THE PARIS BOURGEOISIE SWINGS ROUND

⇆ Only the dragoons (of whom there were at most three thousand in Paris) went into action on February 22. The next day the government brought in the line infantry. Onlookers shouted: "Long live the line!" The regime de-cided to heighten the impact by calling up the National Guard. The guards-men assembled at the council offices of the various arrondissements, as the regulations stipulated. But the turnout was not high, and the men appeared to lack motivation. When they were ordered to arms, they did not shoot alongside the soldiers but took up a position between the royal army and the insurgents.

Why did the National Guard abandon the regime? The petty bour-geoisie, which largely constituted the Guard, had been deprived of its right to vote through the taxation reforms of 1844, so why should it spill its blood? The crisis of 1847, which spared the big bankers and merchants, hit the artisans and shopkeepers of Paris very hard; their markets dried up at a time when many had gone heavily into debt to purchase or improve their premises. As the discounting system ceased to function, they encountered serious cash-flow problems and suddenly found themselves on the verge of bankruptcy.

It was not the first time that the Parisian bourgeoisie had had to face economic difficulties. In the past it had always rallied around the July Monarchy. But now it blamed the king's obstinacy for the outbreak of street agitation; Louis-Philippe had stopped being a defensive rampart and had become a sower of trouble. In the affair of the canceled banquet of February 22, the attitude of the National Guard did not pass unnoticed. By refusing to allow it to carry out stewarding functions, the government showed that it no longer had confidence in the support of the bourgeoisie, and the humiliated bourgeoisie responded by giving the government a sharp lesson.

Louis-Philippe, who was anything but stupid, understood the message and gave ground. On the evening of February 23 he dismissed Guizot and replaced him with the comte Molé. As the news spread, people exulted with victory cheers, lighted paper lanterns, and placed lamps or candles in their windows when the crowd shouted up from the street, "Light up! Light up!" The demonstrators walked about joyfully with torches attached to their wrists. Then the unpredictable happened. In front of the ministry of foreign affairs, on the Boulevard des Capucines, a standoff between soldiers guarding the building and the crowd trying to break into it took a dramatic turn. A sergeant, thinking his officer was in danger, opened fire. It was 9:30 in the evening. The soldiers panicked and began shooting at the crowd; twenty were killed and fifty wounded. The victims' corpses were piled into a cart, which proceeded to move by torchlight toward the Bastille. Some members of the National Guard were among the dead. Now the whole population of Paris was risen against Louis-Philippe. At one in the morning on February 24, the old king called on Bugeaud to crush the revolt. The first troops moved off at five or six o'clock and found the city center covered with barricades. Neither the men nor their officers had much drive in them. By nine, most of the city was in the hands of the insurgents. At eleven o'clock on February 24, 1848, at the Hôtel de Ville, the destitution of Louis-Philippe was announced and a new republic proclaimed.

The agitation spread from Paris like wildfire. In several towns an attack was launched on the weaving looms and the railway stations. At the gates of Paris, people set fire to the railway bridges at Asnières, Chatou, Croissy, and Maisons-Laffitte. Rails were torn up, and in some parts of Alsace houses belonging to Jews went up in flames. In the countryside, bands of peasants ordered a sharing out of the large estates. While the insurrection was carrying the day in Paris, the château of James de Rothschild in Suresnes was being set afire. The people demanded bread and work from the fledgling republic.

5

━━━━━━━━━━━━━━━━━━━━
⇻⇻⇻⇻⇻⇻⇻⇻⇻⇻⇻
━━━━━━━━━━━━━━━━━━━━

First Steps in the

Second Republic

THE BARRICADES of February 1848, which drove Louis-Philippe from the throne of France, established the Second Republic. A provisional government, formed on the afternoon of February 24, immediately faced three problems: the economic, financial, and social crisis; Paris; and Louis-Napoléon Bonaparte.

ECONOMIC, FINANCIAL, AND SOCIAL DIFFICULTIES

⇼ At once, a decree of February 25, 1848, proclaimed: "The Provisional Government of the French Republic undertakes to guarantee the worker's existence through labor. It undertakes to guarantee work for all citizens. It recognizes that workers must combine among themselves to enjoy the rightful fruits of their labor." There were two objectives: to provide work for the unemployed, and to establish trade union freedoms and thereby a greater distribution of the product of work. Of those who were masters of the hour, some wished to keep to the first objective while others, around Louis Blanc, wished to introduce a democratic social republic through "the organization of labor."

In the Luxembourg Palace left vacant by the hurriedly abolished Chamber of Peers, a so-called "Luxembourg Commission" set to work defining the principles and instruments for the new organization of society. A section of the working class passionately threw itself into the debates while those who owned property—whether the rich or simply members of the middle classes—took fright. A number of immediate reforms were adopted: the working day was limited to a maximum of ten hours in Paris, eleven in the provinces; contracts for the supply of labor through an intermediary (the ancestor of today's agencies for temporary employment?) were prohibited. The workers wanted their earnings to be maintained in full. This would have meant an increase in the hourly wage—a demand that the bosses viewed with terror in the difficult economic climate.

On February 26 the scale of unemployment led the government to provide for charity workshops, pompously called "National Workshops." Marie, the man responsible for public works in the Provisional Government, was appointed to get them up and running. It was thought that as many as fifteen thousand workers could be employed in this way. But the signing-on process in local town halls took place amid the greatest confusion. On March 3, Émile Thomas, a young engineer at the École Centrale, offered his services to Marie and was given carte blanche to organize operations. National Workshop recruits would receive two francs a day, as against one and a half francs on the dole. By March 5 a total of sixteen thousand had registered; by March 15 more than twenty thousand. The funding, for which the city of Paris had responsibility, was charged to the central government. It was unclear what should be done with all these people—especially as many had registered at the National Workshops who should not have been there: self-employed craftsmen, traveling salesmen, even individuals with small independent means or workers on strike over wage demands.

The February Revolution, far from solving the economic and financial crisis, gave it a hefty push. On February 26 the government ordered a ten-day moratorium on commercial bills. But since everyone in commerce and small-scale industry paid their suppliers with drafts instead of paper money, this measure had the unforeseen consequence that depositors rushed to the banks to demand their holdings in cash. The banks tottered on the brink of bankruptcy. And as confidence in the system evaporated, people began hoarding gold and the rich sacked their domestic staff or perhaps left Paris altogether. The family silver was put up for sale. Everyone wished to sell everything they had, but there were no longer any buyers. The president of the *tribunal de commerce*, a big banker, committed suicide. The finance minister, Goudchaux, another banker, practiced the Coué method of instilling confidence by autosuggestion. But he believed in it so little himself that he resigned on March 5, to be replaced by Garnier-Pagès, a broker originally from Marseilles. He had just been declared mayor of Paris and left that prestigious position with considerable regret.

The Bourse, which had been shut since the revolution, opened its doors on March 6. The 5 percent stock that had been quoted at 116.10 francs on February 23, shortly before closure, fell to 89 francs, and then on 8 March to 75 francs. But its descent was far from over: by the time it bottomed out on April 6 it was worth no more than 50 francs. Railway shares also collapsed, as did all other securities. No one had any more liquid assets at their disposal. Garnier-Pagès repeated a formula that had been successfully used in 1830: a series of decrees established discount bank branches in Paris and sixty provincial towns to get the circulation of commercial bills moving again, as well as a number of new warehouses that would enable loans to be made against the security of bonded goods. On March 19 the Paris discount bank began operations. On March 24, on the suggestion of Émile Pereire, a financier who became one of Garnier-Pagès's advisers, the government created a number of sub-banks covering particular branches of industry. All the bankers, beginning with the most famous, James de Rothschild, and the Pereires who were developing in his wake, closed ranks around the government and looked for ways out of the crisis.

In the housing market the situation was especially severe. For more than ten years, rents in the capital had been steadily rising as more and more people streamed in from the provinces. In March the political troubles and the economic morass suddenly threw the movement into reverse: rents fell by a third, many accommodations could find no takers at all, and the best building land remained unsold. When the rent-due date of April 1 arrived, many tenants refused to pay and demanded a new arrangement or even straightforward cancellation of the quarterly rent. Stubborn landlords soon gave in when a black flag was raised over their building or "Mister Moneybags" was burned in effigy.

The treasury needed money like everyone else: its money in hand had fallen from 192 million francs on February 25 to 107 million on March 6. Garnier-Pagès wanted to borrow, but there was no public confidence. The government therefore imposed a price for 5 percent stock and four- or six-month treasury bonds. It borrowed from the Bank of France, then convinced itself that only taxes could bring the necessary funds into the state coffers. A special surcharge of 45 centimes in the franc was added with immediate effect to all direct taxation—a levy that was financially salutary but also, one imagines, unpopular, especially in a time of recession. Farmers were hit hardest. The harvest was shaping up well, but the 45 centimes was a cause of lasting resentment against a Provisional Government seen as being under the thumb of Parisian workers.

As the bosses were given a hard time, spreading unemployment added fuel to social demands. In Lyons, the newly appointed prefect (or *commissaire de la République*) Emmanuel Arago drove the monks out into the streets, while Les Voraces—extremists from the Croix-Rousse part of the city, where nearly all the weavers were on strike—threatened to set up a revolutionary commune. In many towns, people took out their frustrations on foreign workers.

PARIS

Upon the fall of Louis-Philippe, the Seine prefect Rambuteau disappeared from the scene, as did the prefect of police, Delessert, and the chief functionaries in those two administrations. In the aftermath of the Revolution, Paris was high on the list of priorities for government action: a mayor was appointed by popular acclaim in the shape of Garnier-Pagès, with Guinard and Recurt as his two deputies. Moreover, the mayor regained all his autonomy vis-à-vis the Seine prefecture; and although the prefecture of police continued to exist, it came under his general authority.

For want of bread, the people were given culture. Ledru-Rollin, now minister of the interior, took over supervision of the Fine Arts and Museums department. On February 24, just after Louis-Philippe had taken the road of exile, Ledru-Rollin signed an order for the annual exhibition of painting, sculpture, and architecture—the famous Salon—to open on March 15. There was to be no selection: every submission would be put on display; five thousand canvases were squeezed in along the walls of the Louvre Museum. Ledru-Rollin even considered a plan to combine the Louvre and the Tuileries Palace into a single people's palace of recreation. Performances of the Théâtre Français were free for poorer sections of the population.

For the time being, people mainly headed for the National Workshops. When they eventually disappeared on June 20, 110,000 had registered with them—and another 50,000 were waiting to be admitted. Émile Thomas issued orders for the trees to be replanted on the boulevards, and for the level of the West Station (today's Gare Montparnasse) to be raised. And then? No one knew what next job to give the unemployed workers or clerks. Public opinion grew indignant: "Instead of being required to perform work that was honorable for themselves and profitable to the city, these men were left on the Champ de Mars with spades, picks, and wheelbarrows and told to destroy the embankments raised there on the Day of the Federation [July 14, 1790]. The workers themselves felt humiliated by such ridiculous labor;

they had no scruples about abandoning it and went off to fill the cabarets where people talked politics."[1]

On March 12, Garnier-Pagès moved to the finance ministry and was replaced as mayor of Paris by Gascon Armand Marrast. This former private tutor and journalist, for twenty years in the forefront of opposition to the monarchical regime, had come to know the damp straw of Louis-Philippe's dungeons before escaping and secretly returning to France. He was an energetic man, brimming with activity and enthusiasm. And although he stayed only four months at the Hôtel de Ville—from March 12 to July 19—he managed to get the administrative machine running again and to launch a major program of public works. In his view, as in that of his colleagues in the Provisional Government, the two priorities were to supply bread for the unemployed and to demonstrate the superiority of republican administration in seeing through the work on Paris for which everyone had long clamored but which the July Monarchy had never actually carried out. The decree of May 3, 1848, drafted by Marrast, had the following main clauses:

1) The Louvre Palace will be completed.

2) It will take the name People's Palace.

3) It will be reserved for the exhibition of paintings, for the exhibition of industrial products, and for the National Library.

4) All working people are called upon to assist in the work of completing the Louvre.

5) The rue de Rivoli will be continued in accordance with the same plan.

By a decree of March 24, the Provisional Government had already decided to resume work on the extension of the rue de Rivoli, which at that time came to an end at the rue de Richelieu. The new section of the rue de Rivoli, stretching from rue de Rohan to rue de la Bibliothèque, was to run alongside the wing of the Louvre that would eventually join the Tuileries Palace to the Cour Carrée, a project begun under Napoléon I, continued under Louis XVIII, but still far from completed. The decree of May 3 thus made the completion of work on the Louvre a matter of national interest and ordered the extension of the rue de Rivoli to rue Saint-Antoine and Bastille. This would mean no less than cutting through the Right Bank the east-west branch of the "great crossing" that had been demanded for so long. The city issued bonds to the value of nine million francs to fund the works.

The emergent Second Republic had neither the time nor the means to fulfill all these ambitions. One of its most valuable measures for the future, however, was a change in the law of 1841 on compulsory purchases, which had allowed the city to acquire only the precise area on which new roads were to be built, so that people living on either side had often retained tiny morsels of adjoining land. In the future the city would be able to purchase the entire portions of land affected by the new road-building program. Thus after the municipal works had been carried out, it would be possible to build comfortable and hygienic new apartment buildings—indeed, it was this option that first enabled Haussmann's projects to go ahead. In his *Souvenirs*, Charles Merruau later drew a perceptive balance sheet: "The makeshift draft was evidently wrong in form and went further than its authors had intended, but it did assert a new principle that was applied to the rue de Rivoli in the decree of 1848 and then more generally in 1852."

The decree that speeded up house-building along the new axis also provided for a seven-year exemption from property taxes and from the special tax on doors and windows. However, as Merruau points out, "at that time no capitalist would have ventured into the field of high-rental housing construction."

LOUIS-NAPOLÉON: "WATER THE POPLAR!"

News of the February Revolution took Louis-Napoléon by surprise, and he immediately reacted in accordance with the maxim that anyone not on the spot is always wrong. He left England on February 27, landing in France at the same time that Louis-Philippe was in Honfleur looking for a boat to take him to London. Louis-Napoléon arrived in Paris by train on the 28th. "I rushed to take my place beneath the flag of the Republic," he proudly recalled. Workers were demonstrating on the boulevards and chanting: "'Poléon, 'Poléon, we want 'Poléon!"

A song inspired by the prince's supporters was in the air:

Napoléon, rentre dans ton palais,
Napoléon, sois bon républicain.*

Lamartine received him on behalf of the Provisional Government and advised him to stay away; the law imposing his exile had not yet been repealed. On March 2, then, he was back in London.

Not for a moment were his followers inactive. Maxime Du Camp, in his *Souvenirs d'un demi-siècle*, categorically declares that the Bonapartes and their loyal supporters tried to use the revolutionary days of February 1848 to re-

---

*Napoleon, go back to your palace./Napoleon, be a good republican.

store the Empire.[2] Prince Napoléon-Jérôme, son of the former King Jérôme of Westphalia and brother of Princess Mathilde, was living as the comte de Montfort on a mezzanine floor on the Boulevard de la Madeleine, on the corner of rue de la Ferme des Mathurins (nowadays rue Vignon). On the morning of February 24, Persigny arrived there from Versailles, where he had been under house arrest. Louis-Napoléon's hired man said to Napoléon-Jérôme: "Your Highness, the circumstances are favorable—we must take advantage of them. The monarchy is collapsing and will be succeeded by the Empire; I will rush to Paris and start campaigning; but I need money for that, and I don't have any." "Nor do I," replied the prince, who had nothing to live on but the allowance of six thousand francs accorded him by his uncle, the King of Wurtemberg. "But I can't get the Empire proclaimed with trousers like these," Persigny continued, showing him all the places where they had holes. Napoléon-Jérôme burst out laughing and gave him forty francs: "Go and buy yourself some pants, and good luck."

Persigny went to buy some pants. Then, together with two conspirator friends, he called on Madame Gordon, a former mistress of Louis-Napoléon's. She had already been involved in the Strasbourg putsch in 1836, and as she was better off than Napoléon-Jérôme, she gave them three thousand francs. This allowed them to have some small posters printed with a few lines penned by Persigny: "Prince Louis-Napoléon, heir of the victor of Marengo and Austerlitz, is alone able to save France now that a shameful monarchy has launched it into the abyss. People of France, remember the glories of the Empire!" The conspirators also bought some knives, which Persigny, "on behalf of Prince Louis-Napoléon, nephew of the Great Emperor," handed out to those insurgents who came forward and presented themselves to him. At the same time he whispered to them: "The watchword is: 'Water the poplar!'" When Maxime Du Camp later asked Napoléon-Jérôme the meaning of these mysterious words, he was prosaically told: "Persigny said that just as he might have said something else."

Napoléon-Jérôme also decided that the time had come to do something. With a friend of his, Pierre-Marie Peitri, who the next day was appointed the Republic's special commissioner for Corsica, Napoléon-Jérôme took a rifle and went to shoot at some soldiers near the Palais Royal.

In following Lamartine's advice to return to London, Louis-Napoléon chose not to take the path recommended by Persigny. Instead he would try to gain power by legal means, having much greater faith in the effectiveness of a well-structured Bonapartist party than in another coup attempt that would have been dangerous and untimely. As Maxime Du Camp recognizes:

"Those who were thinking then of a restoration of the Empire were rather thin on the ground." And yet, given the verbal and other torrents that marked the first few months of the Second Republic, "people would not have been at all surprised at an ending in which verbiage and anxiety gave way to the peace and quiet that the nation needed."[3]

"Verbiage" did indeed have free rein, the planting of Trees of Liberty at each street corner being a good pretext for floods of eloquence. Clubs mushroomed as in the days of the Great Revolution, and it seems that the required pronunciation was the more popular-sounding *cloobs*. New labels appeared: "*démoc-soc.*," "*réac.*," "*aristo.*" The hit song:

> *C'est moi qu'on nomme avec orgueil*
> *Charlotte la républicaine;*
> *Je suis la rose plébéienne*
> *Du quartier Montorgueil.* *

Lyrical illusion, republican festivity. It was later called *l'esprit quarante-huitard*, the spirit of '48, to define the period of the nascent republic when everything seemed possible: universal suffrage, association between capital and labor, universal harmony, world peace by means of railways and other major public works, communism. Karl Marx carefully studied the 1848 revolution and drew many lessons for his future ideology, while its discourse increasingly scared the bourgeoisie and the peasantry.

In Paris on March 16 a demonstration by the conservative minority of the National Guard (and therefore by the Parisian bourgeoisie) was a pitiful failure. This "fur coat parade"—the derisive term that immediately caught on—was followed the next day by an impressive counterdemonstration in support of a social republic. Two hundred thousand people marched past in an atmosphere of cool determination. The conservatives began preparing for war: "It was only an alert," noted Maxime Du Camp, "but the good thing about it was that it put us on the alert. When the battle came, we were ready to welcome it."[4]

PREFECTURAL COUNSELOR IN BORDEAUX

The news of the proclamation of the republic, on February 24 in Paris, reached the Bordeaux prefecture by optical telegraph only the next day be-

---

*It is me they proudly call / Charlotte the republican; / I am the plebeian rose / Of Montorgueil district.

cause of an interruption in communications due to bad weather. Haussmann was informed in Blaye on the morning of the 26th. He took all the necessary security measures and asked the prefect for instructions. Sers expected that the new regime would replace him as prefect for the Gironde, but for the time being he remained at his post and ordered Haussmann to do likewise.

On March 14, Sers handed over his office to a Monsieur Chevallier, a moderate republican who had known Haussmann's father well and who expressed the wish that Georges-Eugène would stay on in Blaye. Haussmann invoked certain scruples and his oath of allegiance to Louis-Philippe. But in reply Chevallier read out a long list of illustrious figures who had rallied to the new regime. Faced with Haussmann's continuing reservations, he eventually suggested that he become prefectural counselor in Bordeaux. This position, more technical than political, involved the auditing of commune accounts and responsibility for official litigation—functions that make one think of the role of administrative courts and regional auditing bureaus in contemporary France. At worst he might have to carry out the tasks of secretary general of the prefecture, at the head of the administrative department, not to speak of the supervision of military conscription by lot or involvement in army medical boards. After thinking it over for a few hours, Haussmann gave in to Sers's persistence. The fact that his replacement as subprefect at Blaye would be a fine country doctor called Gornet gave Georges-Eugène further confidence about the moderate character of the new regime. On March 17, having been officially discharged from his functions as subprefect, Haussmann took over as prefectural counselor for the Gironde.

Haussmann thereby placed himself in a curious position. He had refused to remain in his post as subprefect in Blaye because of his seventeen years of service to the July Monarchy, yet here he was accepting a post as prefectural counselor under the new regime. Careful not to push himself forward in strictly political matters, he was content to play an active role in the administrative corridors of the prefecture: "I taught my younger colleagues how they should examine and adjust the accounts of the municipal tax collectors. I gave them lectures of sorts about the direct tax base, so that they could rule on applications for exemption or recalculation and judge what advice should be given concerning deferment or reduction. I directed their study of questions pertaining to administrative litigation—mainly businessmen's complaints against the payment of their costs by highway engineers and others. Outside working hours, I mixed with everyone as best I could."[5] In fact, Haussmann had moved to his father-in-law's apartment on rue Victoire-Américaine. He was a man of long-standing republican inclinations, and it was a good opportunity for Georges-Eugène to meet people who did not share his own views. He was curious about everything and eager to understand those he considered his adversaries. When he travelled around the department organizing the conscription by lot, he noticed that the republicans were active but not very numerous, and that the socialists were making no inroads in the countryside. Many villagers asked when a king would be appointed in place of the one who had been dismissed.

The Gironde was calm, but the prefecture was marked by instability. Chevallier, too moderate for some in the Provisional Government, was replaced on March 20 by a new special commissioner called Latrade, a former editor at the *National*, who encountered displays of hostility and soon returned to Paris. The man who replaced him, a Clément Thomas from Bonzac near Libourne, was mainly preoccupied with his campaign for the upcoming legislative elections; and it was not long before he too was back in Paris, appointed colonel of the 2nd Legion of the National Guard, with ambitions (fulfilled on May 15) to become its commander. Before he left for the capital, Clément Thomas suggested to Haussmann that he should replace him in the prefect's office. But Georges-Eugène was not interested. On his father-in-law's advice, he suggested that Clément Thomas appoint Henri Ducos, a moderate figure in favor with the republicans of Bordeaux. Clément Thomas took the advice, and it proved to be sound.

THE ELECTIONS OF APRIL 23, 1848

≈ The Provisional Government called upon the people of France to elect a constituent assembly. The more radical sections of the left managed to have the election postponed once, but the date of April 23 was eventually fixed. A demonstration was held on April 16 in the hope of forcing a further postponement, but the Provisional Government called out the National Guard and refused to budge. On April 20, on the occasion of the Festival of Fraternity at the Arc de Triomphe, the twelve legions of the National Guard in Paris (one for each arrondissement) marched past the members of the government from the morning until ten in the evening, joined by the four suburban legions as well as units of the regular army and the anti-riot Garde Mobile. It was clear that each side was counting its forces in preparation for a showdown that everyone could foresee.

The election was held on April 23 by direct universal suffrage; all male Frenchmen could vote at the age of twenty-one or be elected at twenty-five. A departmental list system operated, with the requirement of a simple ma-

jority. Printed voting slips were used for the first time in French history. Of
a total of nine hundred seats, the Seine had thirty-four while the least populous department, Hautes-Alpes, had three. It was possible to stand in several
departments at once. The right to vote included soldiers and (unlike in
1791) domestics. People voted enthusiastically, in closed ranks, with a participation rate of 84 percent. The results yielded seven hundred seats to the
bourgeois candidates who had rallied to the Republic and were grouped
around the *National* newspaper; one hundred seats to what were called "the
Reds"; and one hundred seats to the Legitimists. Three members of the
Bonapartist clan—Lucien Murat, Napoléon-Jérôme (son of Jérôme Bonaparte), and Pierre (son of Lucien)—were elected. They did not even bother to
ask Louis-Napoléon for his advice, and despite the banishment order still affecting him, they were allowed to take up their seats. Persigny, on the other
hand, was defeated.

Louis-Napoléon did not stand in the election. In a letter to his former
tutor, Vieillard, he set forth a position which, in rather different circumstances, nevertheless had many points in common with that of Haussmann.
"I did not want to stand in the elections because I am convinced that my position in the Assembly would have been utterly embarrassing. . . . Until
French society has recovered and the Constitution has been fixed, I feel that
my position in France would be very difficult for me, even very dangerous. I
have therefore resolved to stand aside and to resist all the seductive features
that the regime in my country might have for me."

In Bordeaux the election took place in an atmosphere of calm. A broad
list of conservatives and moderate republicans was put together. Those
elected, in order of their number of votes, included Lamartine, Billaudel
(former bridges and highways engineer), Lubbert (a naval captain), Aurélien
de Sèze (a lawyer and friend of George Sand), and Clément Thomas. Haussmann commented that, of the eleven elected candidates, two were long-
standing republicans, four "well-recognized reactionaries," and the other
nine "unquestionable conservatives" who "accepted the Republic without
the slightest enthusiasm as a necessity of the moment."[6] Lamartine, then at
the height of his popularity, was elected with a huge majority in no fewer
than ten departments. He chose to represent the Seine. The Gironde, where
his majority had been the greatest of all, therefore had to cast another ballot
for someone to replace him.

The Constituent Assembly held its first session on May 4, in a specially
constructed building in the court of the Palais Bourbon. A government was
duly formed. On May 10, the five-man executive committee of Arago,

Garnier-Pagès, Marie, Lamartine, and Ledru-Rollin was elected. (The last of these, the only stray "Red" among moderates, owed his presence on the committee entirely to Lamartine's eloquent advocacy.) Arago took the chair. The Committee of Five appointed a government whose members had had to be chosen outside its own ranks. The Five therefore gave up their ministerial portfolios. The committee established itself in the Palais du Luxembourg and at the Petit Luxembourg, the residence today of the president of the Senate.

The "Reds" attempted another show of strength on May 15, when they occupied the Assembly to present a petition in support of the Polish rising against the tsarist regime. The demonstrators booed the deputies; they shouted at "our clerks who have awarded themselves 25 francs a day and argue over our 30 sous" (the sum that the workers wanted as a guaranteed minimum wage). After some chaotic scenes, the National Guard moved in and cleared the Assembly. For the conservatives, it was clear that the supporters of social democracy had no interest in universal suffrage when it did not work in their favor. On May 17, General Cavaignac was appointed war minister. The following days were fraught with dangers. Work ceased in the national workshops. Trade virtually dried up as people bought only what was strictly necessary for their daily subsistence. Real estate values collapsed, and the 100-franc government bond was testing the 50-franc mark.

On May 21 the new Festival of Fraternity was only a limited success: the chariots of agriculture and chastity, or the patriotic choirs, were no longer the hits they had been just a month before. People were asking for a leader.

On May 23 the executive committee decided to close down the national workshops. A protest by Émile Thomas, a graduate of the prestigious École centrale des Arts et Manufactures, led to his unceremonious dispatch to the distant Landes region on a mission of supposedly great importance. The conservative deputy Louis Falloux asked the Assembly to put an end to "this permanently organized strike that is costing 170,000 francs a day." But the executive committee hesitated and eventually reneged on its decision of May 23; supplementary elections were due to be held on June 4.

In Bordeaux, Thiers was elected hands down to Lamartine's seat and passed up a number of other possibilities to serve as deputy (including in Paris). Paris had to choose eleven deputies, and this time Louis-Napoléon was in the running. Without waging a campaign, he won election in four departments: Yonne, Seine, Corsica, and Charente-Inférieure (today's Charente-Maritime). In Paris the only moderate to gain a seat was Goudchaux, who had once briefly been minister of finance. Four of the Parisian deputies were republicans: Caussidière and Lagrange from the Radical Clubs, and the utopians Proudhon and Leroux. The others were out-and-out supporters of order: Thiers, General Changarnier, and Victor Hugo (who at that time was in the ultra-conservative camp).

The results were declared on June 8. On June 11, still in London, Louis-Napoléon addressed a message of thanks to the voters who had expressed their trust in him, and said that he hoped one day soon to give "the world the great spectacle of a people regenerating itself without violence, without civil war, without anarchy." The Assembly had the task of ratifying the ballot. Some were concerned about the election of the prince. But Crémieux, minister in the Provisional Government, went to the rostrum to defend him: "Napoléon's glory belongs to France. We eagerly accept everything that is popular in that glory; it would be shameful to proscribe his family." Among the moderate republicans, Jules Favre—who represented Louis-Napoléon at his trial in 1840 before the Chamber of Peers following the Boulogne putsch attempt—also went to speak at the rostrum: "If Citizen Bonaparte was mad enough to dream up a kind of parody of what he did in 1840, he would be covered with the contempt of his fellow-citizens and of posterity."

At a demonstration that day, June 12, there were shouts of "Long live Napoléon! Down with the aristos!" The moderates grew worried. The Assembly ordered the arrest of Louis-Napoléon if he should dare to set foot on French soil, then changed its mind and ratified his election. The prince wrote to the Assembly: "If the people demanded certain duties of me, I would know how to carry them out." Tactlessness or a calculated challenge? Whichever it was, on June 18, Louis-Napoléon decided to resign as deputy. Once again events would prove him right—for in the next few days the government had much to deal with other than the ambitions of the Bonapartist pretender.

CLOSURE OF THE NATIONAL WORKSHOPS;
THE JUNE DAYS OF 1848

On June 19 and 20, the Assembly discussed Louis Falloux's proposal to close the National Workshops. A majority of deputies, including Victor Hugo, were up in arms about what they saw as waste and mismanagement, typified by the men in workers' overalls playing beneath the arcades of the Place des Vosges. (Hugo lived a few days longer at the corner of the square, in a house that is now the Victor Hugo Museum; the "June Days" and his wife's entreaties soon brought about his departure.) The men in question were playing to kill time. Another man in overalls was sleeping by the side of the wall. One of the players approached and pushed him with his foot: "What are you doing there, eh?" The sleeper woke up, raised his head, replied: "Well, I'm earning my twenty sous," and stretched out again. That, Hugo commented, was what the national workshops were about.

On June 21 the executive committee issued a decree that gave the 110,000 workers on the registered payroll of the workshops a choice between enlistment in the army and departure for the region of Sologne. Deputations from the workshops came to talk with the Executive Committee but found that it was not prepared to budge. On the evening of the 21st and throughout the next day, the workers formed up into groups, demonstrated in the streets, and sang the Marsellaise—at the Pantheon, at Place Saint-Sulpice, and at the Bastille. The slogans were somber: "Bread or lead! Lead or work!" On the same day, June 22, workers in Marseilles went further and rose up against the bosses who were trying to cut their wages in response to the new legal limits on the working day. But the state's representative in the city, the twenty-three-year-old Émile Ollivier, having failed to calm things, called in the army and put down the insurrection in a single day.

On the morning of June 23, however, the capital was covered with barricades. In the narrow streets of old Paris, the material came from overturned coaches and any scaffolding that was at hand; at the city gates it came from the walls of the historic tollhouses. When Arago bravely went to harangue the insurgents at the Pantheon, they answered him: "Monsieur Arago, you've never gone hungry; you don't know what it's like to be poor." The next day a state of emergency was decreed: the Assembly dissolved the executive committee and gave dictatorial powers to General Cavaignac. The first motley reinforcements arrived from the provinces. Fighting raged all day, and it was still continuing on the 25th when the archbishop of Paris, Monseigneur Affre, died as he attempted to intervene. The army, the anti-riot police, and the National Guard from the bourgeois districts gradually took back control of the city, suffering heavy losses in their own ranks and those of the insurgents. The army inched its way forward. Whenever it captured a barricade, it blasted away the houses at the nearest intersection so that they could not be used to form another barricade at the rear of the troops. By 11 A.M. on June 26, the sixty-five barricades erected between the faubourg Saint-Antoine and the Place du Trône had been swept away; the rebellion had been smashed. In the early afternoon, Cavaignac telegraphed all the prefectures: "Order has triumphed over anarchy! Vive la République!" Volunteers sent from the provinces to help the fight against the *partageux* (that is, those in favor of sharing out property) arrived after the battle was over but nonetheless did their fair share of the repression. On June 28 they paraded with shouts of "Down with the Montagnards! Long live the Republic of Decent People!" The same day Cavaignac handed his powers back to the Assembly, but it gave him executive power as president of the Council of Ministers until such time as a president of the Republic was elected.

According to Haussmann, the Gironde was fired up against the insurrection in Paris. "When the first news of the terrible June days reached Bordeaux, the exasperation with Paris knew no bounds. For the third time in barely four months, Paris was putting on a spectacle of insurrection for a quiet and peaceful France, and this time blood was truly flowing there. People talked of nothing less than forming a defensive confederation of the South-West departments, which would have been the start of a dismemberment of France."[7] If Paris was giving in to its old demons, the spirit of the Gironde was far from having deserted its native land. Haussmann, who hardly favored decentralization, would have approved even less of such overtly separatist feelings—and yet he helped in creating units of volunteers to be used against Paris. People enlisted en masse, equipped themselves, and began to report for duty carrying haversacks. They were about to be embarked on boats to Nantes for a final train journey to the capital when the official dispatch arrived that the insurrection had been crushed.

On the day after the drama, Renan toured the most severely affected areas of Paris. He wrote to his sister Henriette: "You have to have seen that, my dear, to imagine the great scenes of humanity. In rue Saint-Martin, rue Saint-Antoine, and the part of rue Saint-Jacques stretching from the Pantheon to the docks, there was not one house that had not been lacerated by cannon fire. Some you could literally see through. All the shop fronts, all the windows were riddled with bullets; abundant traces of blood and discarded or abandoned weapons still marked the spots where the fighting had been fiercest." The June Days strewed the streets of Paris with five thousand corpses. Still keeping a low profile in London, Louis-Philippe commented with bitter irony: "The Republic is lucky: it can shoot at the people." He could also see that the repression was discrediting the Assembly and creating more opportunities for his own cause.

On July 3 the national workshops were finally ended. Life at the Palais Bourbon resumed as before. Goudchaux returned as finance minister and ordered the collection of even such unpopular taxes as the special forty-five centimes levy and the duty on salt and drinks. In a surreal climate the Assembly proclaimed the traditional motto of the Republic: *Liberté, égalité, fraternité.*

THE RETURN OF THE PREFECTS

🙠 Cavaignac canceled the appointments of *commissaires de la République* and took the opportunity to revert to the more usual term of prefect. Order was returning. Haussmann was proposed as prefect for Bordeaux by a majority of the Gironde deputies, who appreciated his qualities, his good sense, and his determination. But Georges-Eugène did not wish to compromise himself by falling in with the shaky new regime at a time when Louis-Napoléon's star was rising in the political firmament: "Given the ever more pronounced trend in public opinion toward Prince Louis-Napoléon, I did not want to accept a position where my official duty might be to combat him when my personal feelings commanded me to support his cause."[8]

The mayor of Paris, Marrast, left the Hôtel de Ville on July 19 to assume the position of president of the Assembly. Taking advantage of his departure, the Assembly felt it had seen enough of Parisian autonomy and decided to restore the system established by Napoléon Bonaparte in Year VIII (1799) when he was First Consul, so that the Seine prefect again became the chief executive of the capital. Trouvé-Chauvel, a politician from Le Mans who had been chief of police since May 18, was appointed prefect for the Seine. He would remain boss of Paris for three months, during which time he continued Marrast's drive to put the city administration back on a sound footing.

On July 21, forty-eight hours after Paris, the Gironde also acquired a new prefect: not Haussmann but the former subprefect of four months, Monsieur Neveux, a man with a background as mayor's secretary in a Parisian arrondissement and subprefect at Rethel. It was a dazzling promotion—although the man himself was levelheaded and inclined to wait and see. The replacement for Doctor Gornet at Blaye was a remarkable scholar named Read, founder of the Society for French Protestant History, whom Haussmann would later bring to the Seine prefecture and appoint as keeper of the archives. As Thiers had resigned his seat at Bordeaux, a bye-election was held on September 16 that scarcely shook the political landscape. Count Molé, like Thiers a former prime minister under Louis-Philippe, received the highest vote.

THE ELECTIONS OF SEPTEMBER 16 AND 17, 1848:
LOUIS-NAPOLÉON A FIVEFOLD DEPUTY

After the most careful preparation, Louis-Napoléon also stood in the series of elections held on September 16 and 17. As we know, he swept the board in the five departments where he was a candidate—the Moselle joining the four that had already voted for him on June 4.

Louis-Napoléon chose to represent the Seine. When he arrived at the Assembly on September 25, the banishment order on him was suspended. The prince was able to find the kind of words that make people feel good: "The Republic has allowed me the good fortune of once more being in my home country among my fellow citizens. May the Republic accept my pledge of gratitude." Victor Hugo was filled with enthusiasm: "The man just named by the people as their representative is not the heir to the brawl in Boulogne; he is the victor of Jena. . . . His candidacy dates from the time of Austerlitz."

On October 13 a government reshuffle brought to the interior ministry Dufaure, a Bordeaux lawyer and friend of Haussmann's father-in-law. Dufaure proposed that Georges-Eugène should leave his post as prefectural counselor and take over the prefect's office in Charente-Inférieure (Charente-Maritime). But Haussmann refused, for the same reasons as before.

In late October the Assembly set December 10 as the date for the election of the president of the Republic. Louis-Napoléon immediately announced that he would stand. Without the least hesitation, Haussmann rallied to the prince's cause.

The triumph of Louis-Napoléon in the September ballot, and now his candidacy in the presidential elections, made the republicans doubt the wisdom of their institutional choices. Grévy was worried that the president would be elected by direct universal suffrage: "Until now, all republics have been swallowed up by despotism." Another republican deputy, Parieu (later a minister under Napoléon III), foresaw irresolvable conflicts between the Assembly and the president. Some would have preferred a president elected by the Assembly itself. But in the end Lamartine got the decision he wanted. Not only was the will of the sovereign people his one motto in politics; he also wanted to bar the way to Cavaignac, who would not be elected on a popular vote but would undoubtedly be the Assembly's own choice. "By what right," Lamartine asked, "could one prevent universal suffrage from expressing itself as it thought best? . . . Let God and the people pronounce! If the people wishes to surrender its liberty to something reminiscent of the Empire, so much the worse for the people!"

Louis-Napoléon was no great orator, and on the rare occasions that he spoke during his weeks on the Assembly benches he used a moderate voice that made him appear insignificant. Thiers saw him as a "cretin," Lamennais as "a kind of idiot," while Proudhon confided that he did not think "great fortune" lay in store for him. The majority felt reassured and regretted that they had not lifted the banishment order on all the Bonapartes.

The Constituent Assembly eventually adopted the texts of a constitution on November 4, 1848. Power would now be shared between two institutions elected by direct universal manhood suffrage: a National Assembly that held legislative power, and a presidency that held executive power. The Assembly, consisting of 750 deputies, would be elected for a term of three years. The president would hold office for one four-year term, would not be immediately reelectable, and would have no power to dissolve or suspend the Assembly. He would appoint ministers, who would be responsible to him alone.

In Bordeaux on November 19, 1848, the new constitution was presented with great pomp at the Place des Quinconces. Haussmann was not present on the VIP stand: he preferred to witness the ceremony from the less conspicuous position reserved for him as a captain in the Bordeaux National Guard.

THE PRESIDENTIAL ELECTION OF DECEMBER 10, 1848: 'POLÉON AS CANDIDATE

In Paris the constitution was officially proclaimed on November 22. Then the election campaign got under way. The *Moniteur de l'Armée* attacked Louis-Napoléon: "It is up to France to judge whether it can count on the patriotic feelings of a Bonaparte who has served Switzerland as a captain and England as a constable, and whose great achievement has been to fire a pistol shot at a French soldier in Boulogne from the foot of the column." Others sang a very different tune:

> *Voulez-vous du bon?*
> *Choisissez Poléon.**

In the Gironde, the influential Free Trade Society—whose sympathies tended more toward Orleanism—made a calculated decision to back Louis-Napoléon for president. Its leaders asked Haussmann to go and sound out

---

*Do you want something good? / Then choose 'Poléon.

the state of opinion in the arrondissement of Blaye. There a landowner friend of his, a departmental councillor, former Orleanist, and present supporter of Cavaignac, invited Georges-Eugène to lunch with him at his steward's farm in Prignac, near Saint-André-de-Cubzac. Haussmann reports the scene in French, but he notes that all the conversation took place in the local patois.

"So then," said the landowner after the meal was over, "we are going to have another election. What will people do around here?"

"Good Lord, sir," said the man, "a child at its mother's bosom knows just as much as I do about those things. We have voted this year for gentlemen who were completely unknown in these parts, although we were told they were good people. Some agree with us, others disagree. We don't know who to believe. This time we'd like to vote for a name we know."

"Well, my friend, go for General Cavaignac."

"Oh, monsieur, he doesn't have a good name in these parts."

Cavaignac's father, who had once been sent on a mission to the Gironde by the Convention, had left behind some very bad memories. Haussmann assures us that mothers used to tell naughty children: "*Qué m'en bao te bailla à Cabagnac!*"—which is patois for "I'll give you to Cavaignac." And old women used to shout at their stubborn mules: "*Hi! doun, Cabagnac!*"

"So what are you saying?" the landowner continued.

His steward replied: "This time round, monsieur, I want to vote for the emperor."

It was no good the landowner saying that the emperor was dead, his son too, and that his nephew had had some rather peculiar adventures. The steward listened with the greatest respect, but it meant nothing to him. "*Ta bé, Moussu, qué bouii bouta per el!*" he replied. "All the same, monsieur, I'm going to vote for him!"

Haussmann, uplifted, said to his host upon leaving: "Since you say you are his leader, believe me: this time you should follow your peasant, lest he get used to marching without you!"[9]

The Bonapartist party was well organized. Louis-Napoléon had an efficient aide in Persigny, who knew how to win over intelligent public figures. They printed posters, set up local committees, brought out newspapers with various shades of opinion to cast their net as widely as possible. On the evening of December 10, 1848, the prince won a landslide first-round victory with 5.4 million votes out of a total of 7.7 million—nearly 75 percent. A long way behind, with 1.4 million votes, came General Cavaignac, the man who had gunned down the workers. Then followed Ledru-Rollin (370,000), Raspail (36,000), and Lamartine (18,000). In the Gironde, Louis-Napoléon won 78 percent of the vote. Guizot commented in his *Mémoires*: "The experience revealed the strength of the Bonapartist party—or, more accurately, of the name of Napoléon. It is quite something to be at once a national celebrity, a guarantor of the revolution, and a principle of authority."

6

Prefect for the Var

ON DECEMBER 20, Louis-Napoléon was sworn in before the Constituent Assembly. He appointed the new cabinet under justice minister Odilon Barrot, and entrusted the interior ministry to Maleville. The government team had been selected by Thiers. That same evening the prince moved into the Élysée Palace and invited the loyal Persigny and other architects of his victory to a festive dinner. On December 24 he reviewed the troops of the first army division. To General Petit, who commanded the veterans of the Imperial Guard, he said: "The Emperor embraced you when he made his final review; I am happy to shake your hand as I conduct my first."

In the intoxication of his election triumph, did Louis-Napoléon perhaps think he had become master? The ministers around him immediately set about correcting any such idea. As Victor Hugo put it, he must have found it very unpleasant "to dream he was emperor and to wake up a puppet." Louis-Napoléon asked that the comte de Nieuwekerke, friend or lover of his cousin Princess Mathilde, should be put in charge of museums. Refused. He asked to be sent the sixteen boxes containing "his" files—the documents concerning the Strasbourg and Boulogne affairs. Refused. On December 27 he lost his temper and fired off a curt missive to Maleville, who had been complaining to Barrot of the prince's "arrogance." The government sided with Maleville and resigned en bloc. Louis-Napoléon apologized and the government remained in office, but Maleville stuck to his resignation. He was replaced by Léon Faucher.

Louis-Napoléon's conflict with the government emanating from the parliamentary majority showed that his hardest task still lay ahead: namely, to gain the upper hand over an Assembly that had not chosen him and distrusted his popularity. Universal suffrage is unpredictable. To consolidate his victory, Louis-Napoléon had to control Paris and to control the provinces; only then would his popularity have roots capable of long-term survival. The way to achieve this was through the appointment of good, efficient, and devoted prefects, without too many scruples. The situation of the prince president is well described in Persigny's *Mémoires*: "Returning after thirty years of exile to govern his country, he did not know where to get his instruments of government. Although carried to power by six million votes, he was reduced to such a state of isolation that he did not know any person with important interests, nor any friend whom he could properly make a minister."

FIRST MISSION OF TRUST:
HAUSSMANN'S APPOINTMENT AS PREFECT FOR THE VAR

No sooner had Faucher been installed as interior minister than he telegraphed for Haussmann to come to Paris. But when Georges-Eugène reported in, there was no real rapport between the two men. Faucher, much more Orleanist than Bonapartist, was taken aback by Haussmann's profession of dyed-in-the-wool imperialism. The latter, for his part, said of the minister: "I was struck by his puny, narrow, sickly mind, in contrast to his stiff and even pedantic air of importance. I felt that my new boss was totally lacking in prestige."[1] This first impression later gave way to admiration for Faucher's statesmanlike qualities. In any event, Georges-Eugène was featured on the list of nominations for prefect that Faucher submitted to Louis-Napoléon. The prince was waiting for him the next day.

The Élysée Palace, having been abandoned for twenty years, was cold and mournful when Haussmann presented himself the next morning to Louis-Napoléon's secretary, Mocquard, who had been subprefect at Bagnères-de-Bigorre during Haussmann's spell at Nérac. The prince president welcomed Haussmann. The two men were virtually the same in age, but not in size—Louis-Napoléon was short, almost stunted, whereas Haussmann was tall and sporty-looking—nor in character. Haussmann was impressed by the pretender to the Bonapartist family, to which he felt viscerally attached. The prince president made Haussmann talk about himself and his family, about his idolization of Prince Eugène and Napoleonic ideas. He thanked him for services rendered "in the cause of order" in the Gironde, and for his "active help in the success of his candidacy." Despite the cold surroundings, there was warmth in his voice as he confirmed to Haussmann that he would be appointed prefect.

A few days later, Haussmann was invited to dinner at the ministry of the interior. Louis-Napoléon was also present. When the meal was over, he took Haussmann aside and said: "I have appointed you prefect for the Var." Haussmann pulled a face: "It would be difficult to be appointed anywhere farther from Bordeaux." But Louis-Napoléon replied: "The Var is one of our worst departments. Demagogues are there in strength. They are defying the authorities in Toulon, our great military port, and in Draguignan where I need a prefect of whom I can be completely sure." The Var was one of the four departments that had returned a majority for Cavaignac in the presidential election. If Haussmann wished to win promotion on the prefectural ladder, he would have to become actively involved in politics—something he had always shunned. Louis-Napoléon added: "The police on our frontier with Italy need to be especially shrewd and vigilant at the present time." In fact, the Var then had a frontier with Italy, as Nice and the Comté de Nice belonged to the ruling dynasty of Piedmont-Sardinia. War was raging in Italy, and France was preparing to intervene in Rome. It was therefore a mission of considerable trust that the prince president was offering Haussmann. On January 24, 1849, Georges-Eugène received official notification of his appointment.

Disorders in Paris, which soon spread to Lyons, Marseilles, and Limoges, delayed Haussmann's departure. He finally left the capital on the evening of February 1, taking the mail coach from Paris to Lyons, then another one to Marseilles via Aix-en-Provence. The new prefect traveled on by delivery carriage to Draguignan and reached his destination only on the evening of February 4. Octavie joined him there—without haste, as he first had to organize the usual furnishing of the prefect's office. She came from Bordeaux in the course of April, accompanied, Haussmann tells us, by a veritable *smala* (originally, an Arab chief's retinue: the conquest of Algeria was imminent). There were the two daughters, their private governess, a chambermaid, and a valet-cum-maitre-d'hôtel.

DISCOVERING THE DEPARTMENT

❧ In keeping with his usual habit, Haussmann took possession of his new territory by meticulously combing through the statistical yearbooks and above all by traveling far and wide in every direction. The Var, with an area of 1.8 million acres, was larger in 1849 than it is today and was divided into four arrondissements: Brignoles, Grasse, Draguignan, and Toulon.[2] The prefecture was located in Draguignan, which had only 10,000 inhabitants, whereas Toulon—with 70,000 out of the departmental total of 360,000, as well as most of the headquarters of regional services—had a mere subprefecture. In fact, the only senior officials based in Draguignan were the prefect himself, the director of the Land Registry Office, the chief engineer, and the commander of the gendarmerie. The bishop was in Fréjus. The town of Hyères was the big winter coastal resort, Saint-Tropez, Saint-Raphaël, and Agay being three little ports of no significance. Cannes and Antibes were only just beginning to be developed. Between them lay the long shoreline of the Bay of Juan, where local people religiously showed off the large olive tree in whose shade Napoléon I was said to have dozed after landing from the island of Elba in 1815 to commence his triumphant "eagle's flight" to Paris.

Still passionately interested in geology and geography, Haussmann tried to understand how the landscape had influenced the character, opinions, and political affiliations of the local population. Waterfalls, caves, and places with historical associations also earned a visit from the cultured prefect, who was attracted by monuments that bore witness to ancient times. In his view, the key to the settlement and development of the region was the combination of fertile soil with sun and water, especially water: it was "the need to make common use of this veritable source of wealth, and not the fear of Saracen raids (the reason commonly given), which explains the original grouping of the agricultural communities of the Var . . . into large settlements averaging 1700 to 1800 souls, despite the wearying daily travel that the farmers had to undergo to get to their fields."[3] Haussmann also noted that little work had been done on the irrigation and watering that might allow greater profit to be derived from the abundance of natural wealth.

The coastal population lived from fishing, saltworks, and above all the navy. Haussmann clearly had little time for the sailors' tendency to dissipation and strong drink, which was such a joy to the heart of those who profited from it. Further inland, the olive was the crop that brought the highest income, followed by the grape. The annual harvest fluctuated around 2.3 million bushels, but the resulting wines were poorly converted and high in alcohol. Our prefect's long stay in Bordeaux had made him quite a connoisseur of wine. One day, invited to dinner by the Bishop of Fréjus and served two different Bordeaux, he impressed his host by identifying each one almost to the year.

Apart from the fruit trees and the perfumed plants around Grasse, the big business in the area was the production of silkworms. Mulberry trees were to be found almost everywhere. Haussmann's daughters, under the guidance of their governess, followed custom and began raising worms on the top floor of the prefecture, earning themselves a few extra francs in silk and the pride that comes from having made some money of one's own.

A considerable part of the department was covered with forest, mainly maritime and forest pine. Although Haussmann, with his experience as sub-prefect at Nérac, thought these forests were poorly exploited, they still aroused a good deal of covetous feelings. Many belonged to large landown-ers, often from aristocratic families, who had responded to the fall of the em-pire and the restoration of the monarchy by attempting to curb the traditional usage rights of the local population. The magistrates at Aix-en-Provence often ruled in their favor and imposed sentences for forestry of-fenses that Haussmann himself, though so attached to order and property, considered disproportionate to the damages. "In my view, the main reason for the fires that periodically devastate woodlands in the Var is not, as people think, the feelings of resentment among many communities and hatred among forestry offenders for large landholdings, but rather the extensive planting with resinous trees and the heat of a torrid sun. Nevertheless, such feelings make it understandable why socialist preaching has the reception that it does in these country parts."[4]

One problem on his mind was the common pasture covering much of the department, relatively unproductive tracts used chiefly by the large landowners who owned most of the livestock. From time to time an enter-prising notable would develop such land by planting fruit trees, but then the local population felt despoiled. On March 1, 1848, to the sound of a beating drum, the villagers of Montmeyant together pulled down the fences on a patch of common land that a notary had turned from forest into orchard. "This is the Republic," they shouted. "We have to live in the Re-public." Haussmann, for his part, responded to acts of surreptitious en-croachment by promoting, if not the straightforward division of common land, at least its allocation in small plots to a larger number of beneficiaries; the rents would help finance the budget of the local communes. Thus, barely forty days after his arrival in the Var, he sent a report along these lines to Léon Faucher. The minister congratulated the new prefect and encouraged him to continue his good work.

Alertness and clearheadedness seem to have been Georges-Eugène's two key qualities. Another aspect of his character, in which politics evidently had the upper hand over restless impatience, was his penchant for teaching through repetition. The hobbyhorse of common lands became a recurrent theme of his statements to municipal councils and gatherings of notables.

"Emperor Napoléon I," he later wrote, "considered repetition to be the most powerful rhetorical figure. I soon had reason to know the correctness of that maxim."[5]

REVIVING THE WORK OF ADMINISTRATION

As the prince president had warned, Haussmann found a departmental administration seriously adrift. In Toulon a worldly-wise subprefect who had been passed over in the promotion race made feverish use of the telegraphic link to Paris that Draguignan still lacked, breaking all the rules of hierarchy with a flood of hasty missives to the ministry of the interior that bypassed his own prefect. In Brignoles it was a down-at-heel journalist, a nice enough fellow, who carried out the functions of subprefect; he had left his wife and six children in Paris and sent them half of his meager remuneration. In Grasse the subprefect, a man from the area who had started as a mere tax inspector and risen through the ranks, had to be replaced because he was too embroiled in local politics.

In communes with a population of six thousand or more—which included Draguignan, Toulon, Hyères, La Seyne, Grasse, and Antibes—the central government appointed the mayor and deputy mayor but was obliged to choose them from members of the municipal council. It was a system that had not changed since the days of the July Monarchy. In the case of communes with fewer than six thousand inhabitants—of which there were 196 in the Var—a Republican decree of July 3, 1848, gave the municipal council the liberty to elect the mayor and his deputy. But the prefect could suspend them for a period of three months, and the government had the power to pass a decree of the Conseil d'État canceling their appointment. Having been removed in this way, the mayor or deputy could not be reelected for a period of a year.

In a report to the government, Haussmann argued that the mayor and deputy mayor should be replaced in 64 of the 196 communes, including the district centers of Brignoles and Cannes (which had a population under six thousand in 1849). "It was a dirty little town," he said, "with no more than three villas lying above it: those of Lord Brougham, Mr. Woodfield, and Sir Leader-Temple. None could be established on the beach, because the vast sand-flats [that is, the coastal domains] stretching from La Napoule to La Croisette—even those facing the town itself—belonged to the state. I opened negotiations with both the maritime authorities and the Public Property Department to procure the sale in portions of these arid and desolate-looking spaces. I managed to achieve this, not without difficulty. It was the starting point for a complete transfiguration of the vile settlement and for its future prosperity. In 1849 and 1850 I drew up plans for it to become a new French Nice, when the Var was still the outer limit of France and Nice was an Italian town."[6] "Dirty little town," "vile settlement": Haussmann does not mince his words. The fact is that the development of the Côte d'Azur, which owed its life to rich Englishmen like the ones he mentions, began only during this period.

In dealings with the departmental council, Haussmann was in his element as a trained manager. His priority was to bring the finances back into balance. The budget for 1850 showed the effects of excessive responsibilities (the Var had 373 miles of departmental highway and 476 miles of main roads) and of difficulties in raising loans. Haussmann therefore tried the new idea of turning the construction and public works firms that had invoiced the department for various works into bankers for the community. The prefect played the card seriously, as one can tell from the dozens of carefully drafted reports and his successful nonpolitical approach to the problem. Nearly all his proposals gained acceptance—even the one for loans relating to the prefecture, which was ideal ammunition for a revolt. Le Démocrate du Var, the paper of a resolute Republican opposition, felt a duty to explain to its readers why the left-wing departmental councillors had been so indulgent toward Haussmann: "It is remarkable that the prefect for the Var was secure from any personal opposition. It was well understood that he was a distinguished administrator, that his character was marked by loyalty, that he was less inclined than anyone in present times to serve the grudges of the jesuitism of 1815 to 1830 [an allusion to his Protestantism]: in short, that the man was worth more than the views, the administrator more than the civil servant. War was therefore not waged against M. Haussmann."[7]

CLUBS, CHAMBRÉES, AND THE PRESS

≈ Whether the administrator liked it or not, it was more often the politician who had to step to the fore. Politics was a ubiquitous presence in the Var, perhaps even more than at the national level. On March 15 the Constituent Assembly programmed its own death by scheduling legislative elections for May 13. A new electoral law reduced the number of deputies representing the Var from nine to seven. Among the nine outgoing deputies, seven had advanced ideas or else were very rich but anti-Bonpartist. It was Haussmann's task to find credible candidates for a balanced list to be drawn up—not necessarily Bonapartists, but likely to swing behind Louis-Napoléon. It was also his task to organize the propaganda for the forces of order and to combat that of the *"démoc-socs."* On March 24, in fact, the Assembly approved Faucher's proposal restricting the activity of the club movement, and as a result of this several clubs in the Var donned the mask of charitable or festive associations.

The club in Draguignan, with eight hundred people on its list, was the largest in the department. Its leader was the lawyer Pastoret, who in Haussmann's eyes was first and foremost a man of ambition. Club members infiltrated the system of *chambrées*, the traditional social evenings which, especially in Provence, had strongly religious origins. Some still bore the mark of this religious and charitable past while others were geared more to relaxation. Workers and farmers gathered there after work to play games, to smoke and drink together—and in this part of France, where words come easily, the talk often turned to politics. On occasion they were addressed by leading political lights who happened to be passing through.

Haussmann, not without reason, saw this network and the shrewd use made of it by the socialists as the explanation for the election success of Ledru-Rollin or Raspail, when most of those who voted for them by no means shared their advanced political ideas. The most recent *chambrées* were also those with the largest participation: 550 members in just one of Draguignan's, 350 in Vidauban, 250 in Cannes. Haussmann had little difficulty in tracking them down, but it was also necessary to prove that they were clubs in disguise. Pastoret was well versed in legal proceedings, so that months of wrangling (sometimes with one another) lay ahead for Haussmann, the court in Aix-en-Provence, the justice ministry, and the interior ministry, before the prefect for the Var was given final approval to apply the law on clubs to the *chambrées*. Closure orders were imposed on 23 of them.

Haussmann thus scored a point against Pastoret. He rejoiced even more in January 1850 when he saw the arrival in town of Émile Ollivier, a moderate, well-spoken republican who seemed to preach more than to call people to arms. Pastoret, by comparison, looked like a tribune from another age; he kept up the fight but his heart was no longer in it. After Louis-Napoléon's coup d'état in December 1851, he gave up politics and went to live in Nice, where he successfully resumed his career as a lawyer. Many years later, in 1866, Haussmann bought a villa on the heights of Mont Boron above Nice and took Pastoret as his consultant. They both smiled like old friends as they reminisced about their disputes with each other in the wild year of 1849 in the Var.

Chambrées were in general an ideal opportunity for those who knew how to take advantage of their convivial atmosphere. In this respect, the socialists were several steps ahead of Haussmann and the divided right; the two main socialist papers in the department, *La Voix du Peuple de Marseille* and *Le Démocrate du Var*, were distributed free of charge to all the *chambrées*. Haussmann recorded the existence of 900 *chambrées* and estimated at 28,000 the number of people who regularly took part in them—a veritable army if ever they were mobilized together. To compete with the socialist press, the only well-produced conservative paper in the Var was *Le Conciliateur*, a biweekly sheet founded in Draguignan a few days after Haussmann's arrival. But it was in no position to distribute 900 free copies, nor did Haussmann have the funds to cover the expense. He did a little to help by bringing the paper's owner-director onto his departmental staff. There was even a special Sunday supplement, partly in French, partly in Provençal, which Haussmann arranged to distribute in a thousand copies to carefully selected people.

Our prefect was all the more upset about the lack of money when he thought of the main paper in Toulon, the conservative-leaning *Sentinelle de la Marine et de l'Algérie*. The 1848 revolution had cut its owner-director off from the secret funding he had previously enjoyed, and he had turned the paper into a sheet which, according to Haussmann, intimidated civil servants with its criticisms as a way of extracting money from them. To help the Toulon conservatives, Haussmann could do no better than lend them for six months his own principal private secretary, a man gifted with the pen.

THE ITALIAN IMBROGLIO AND THE BATTLE AGAINST THE "REDS"

❧ Events in Italy were complicating the prefect's administration in the Var. The King of Piedmont, Charles-Albert, had taken up arms against the Austrians in the spring of 1848 that had brought all the states of Italy to a fever pitch, and the triumph of revolution in Vienna in March had weakened the fighting capacity of the Habsburgs' formidable army. But when the Austrian regime regained control of Vienna in the autumn, Charles-Albert was defeated and had to sue for an armistice. Meanwhile the revolution succeeded in the papal states, and Pius IX, driven from the Eternal City, took refuge at Gaeta in the Austrian-protected Kingdom of Naples. The Roman Republic was proclaimed on February 9, 1849. And when Tuscany rid itself of its grand duke, Charles-Albert thought he would be able to resume the struggle against the Austrians. He began the campaign on March 20, but three days later his army was crushed at Novara. He had no option but to abdicate in favor of his elder son, Victor Emmanuel, after the Austrians had granted another armistice but occupied parts of Piedmont, Tuscany, and the northern states belonging to the church. Refugees of all origins—political oppositionists, deserters, distraught patriots—now crossed the frontier with the Var. On March 26, Charles-Albert arrived in Antibes with an assumed identity. Haussmann turned a blind eye for forty-eight hours, allowing him time to say farewell to the young Victor Emmanuel and to embark for Barcelona. Six years later Georges-Eugène would meet Victor Emmanuel again in less tragic circumstances, when he laid on a magnificent banquet at the Hôtel de Ville in Paris in honor of the Italian sovereign.

Louis-Napoléon was nonplussed by the Italian situation and, in particular, by the thorny Roman question. Despite his youthful conspiracies against the papacy and his unconcealed sympathy for the cause of Italian unity and independence, the prince president felt compelled to intervene militarily in support of Pius IX—both to humor his own electorate and to strike before the Austrians did. Officially France did no more than offer to mediate between the pontiff and his subjects. On April 25, General Oudinot, the son of a Napoleonic marshal, landed at the papal port of Civitavecchia at the head of an expeditionary force of 12,000 men, but on April 30, Rome greeted him with cannon fire. In France, Louis-Napoléon found himself doing the splits between republicans favorable to the Roman Republic and Catholics demanding vigorous military intervention. Everyone accused everyone else of secret plotting. On May 11 the republicans demanded the impeachment of the prince president for violation of Article V of the Constitution: "France never uses its weapons against the liberty of any people." The motion was defeated. When Faucher then tactlessly forwarded to prefects a list of the deputies who had supported impeachment, virtually the whole of Parliament was up in arms about his action. On May 14 a vote of no confidence in Faucher won a majority of 519 votes to 5. The minister resigned at once, just as the legislative elections were taking place.

The elections of May 13 and 14, 1849, saw the triumph of the party of order. A powerful organization, the Electoral Union, had been established to defend the stability of society against anarchy. A public collection had brought in 200,000 francs, which had been used to flood the country with propaganda posters and brochures. In one of them, signed by Wallon, the future progenitor of the Third Republic, we can read the following: "A Red is not a man; he is a Red; he does not reason, he no longer thinks. He no longer

has any sense of truth or justice, any sense of what is beautiful and good. . . .
He sacrifices his own liberty, instincts, and ideas to the crudest animal passions: he is a fallen degenerate being." The campaign of the democrats and
socialists was equally active under Ledru-Rollin's leadership. It called for the
right to work and own capital, for a progressive income tax, and for state operation of the railways, mines, and insurance companies.

The turnout was a low 60 percent. The right emerged victorious with
500 seats, including 200 Legitimists and a few Bonapartists. But the social-
ist-democrats won 180—a result that had the Stock Exchange plummeting
in fear. The moderate republicans around Lamartine won only 75. In the Var,
the prefect's list ended up with 3 seats, against 4 for the advanced republicans. This halftone result was understandable enough in view of the local
quarrels, the challenge by conservative committees to outsiders parachuted
in by Paris (our prefect was particularly agitated about one Besuchet de
Saunois, describing him as an "unknown midget"[8]), the extreme diatribes
against the July Monarchy that angered Orleanists and made Haussmann
himself fly off the handle, and the constitution of a dissident list. The high
rate of abstention—nearly 50 percent—seemed to confirm the baneful effect
of division in the ranks of the right.

The new National Assembly held its first session on May 28, 1849. The
results of the elections did not satisfy the socialists, and in early June the agitation apparent in Paris, Lyons, Toulouse, and other big cities found a powerful echo among socialist circles in the Var and the *chambrées* close to them.
On June 3 a number of French soldiers were killed fighting in Rome against
local republicans. On June 11, at the Palais Bourbon in Paris, Ledru-Rollin
once again called for the impeachment of the president and his ministers;
once again the proposal was rejected. Ledru-Rollin warned: "We shall defend
the violated Constitution, even with guns in our hands." The streets of the
capital seemed more worried about the new outbreak of cholera that was
killing two hundred people a day; no less a figure than Marshal Bugeaud
died of it on the same June 11. Yet Ledru-Rollin decided to risk everything.
On June 13 National Guardsmen from the popular districts demonstrated
on the boulevards to shouts of "Long live the Roman Republic!" Étienne
Arago was among them. The crowd remained indifferent. General Changarnier dispersed the demonstrators at the rue de la Paix. The last square of insurgents held out for a while in the Arts et Métiers district and the
Conservatory of the same name, then disbanded in turn. Ledru-Rollin fled to
England. That evening, the prince president was acclaimed and a few shouts

of "Vive l'Empereur!" were raised. In Lyons, where barricades erected by the militant Voraces were destroyed by cannon fire, 80 soldiers and 150 workers were killed or wounded. Barricades also appeared on the streets of Grenoble, Perpignan, and Strasbourg.

ALERT IN DRAGUIGNAN

≈ A dispatch reached Draguignan on June 14 with news of the rioting and the state of siege in Paris. The Reds in the Var tried to occupy the prefecture. Public security, together with the underperforming administration, was the main weakness in the department. The commander of the Marseilles army division, which included the Draguignan area, had too few troops for his needs—and Marseilles and Toulon worried him more than Draguignan, especially as the task of frontier defense tied down major forces based in Antibes. Haussmann himself had long been preparing to meet a possible attack on Draguignan. In normal times he had available *in toto* some twenty soldiers of fortune—unemployed workers—whom he had to divide between defense of the prefecture and of the powder magazine adjoining the town. The National Guard in the department had been dissolved and disbanded, not without some difficulty, and Haussmann had taken the precaution of making its twelve hundred rifles unusable. Since the Var gendarmerie was the only solid force on which he could rely, he worked with its commander, Captain Duval,[9] to ensure that the twenty units closest to Draguignan could be concentrated there as rapidly as possible—which gave him a total of a hundred men upon whom he could draw if the need arose. It was not a large number, but Haussmann thought that the prestige of the gendarme's hat, based in turn upon saber, carbine, and powers of arrest, would give each one the strength of ten—so long as he used them with determination.

During the night of June 13 to 14, then, Haussmann brought in a hundred or so gendarmes in a number of small groups. The demonstrators called upon him to hand over the prefecture, sending a delegation to meet him that included the prefect's bootmaker. His reply was haughty: "Although there are ten thousand of you, I have on my side a hundred determined men who have just been given a hundred cartridges for each carbine. That makes a total of ten thousand, one for each of you." And he assured them that he was quite ready to vacate the building if the legal government, whatever it was, ordered him to do so, or if it appointed someone else to take over for him. News of the restoration of order in Paris dispelled the insurgency. Haussmann could breathe again, convinced that no prefect in France had been in such a critical position. Or anyway, he did not fail to point this out to his superiors in the hierarchy.

"IT IS TIME THAT THE GOOD TOOK HEART
AND THE BAD TREMBLED"

≈ After the collapse of the "Red" insurrection, Louis-Napoléon issued a proclamation that made a great impact on public opinion: "A few agitators are still daring to raise the standard of revolt against a legitimate government. . . . This system of agitation is maintaining the unrest and defiance that are the cause of so much hardship; it must stop. It is time that the good took heart and the bad trembled. The Republic has no more implacable enemies than those who, in perpetuating disorder, force us to turn France into a military camp, our projects for improvement and progress into preparations for combat and defense." The whole program of the Second Empire is contained in these few sentences: order in trust, grand projects to create wealth, to give everyone more, and to eliminate social tensions through prosperity. Seen from Paris or from Draguignan, the struggle is the same.

The maintenance of order is never easy, and again and again it cost Haussmann dear. Following incidents in Cogolin, he went in person to Grimaud to supervise the arrest of two rowdies. He did not have much support: just the lieutenant of the gendarmerie and three squads of gendarmes (together making a total of six men), soon reinforced by the later-celebrated force from Saint-Tropez. On the way back they ran into the whole population of the village of La Garde-Freinet and had a hard time getting through its hostile barracking. In the end someone shouted out, "Death to the prefect!" Haussmann stopped, looked around, and exclaimed: "Who is talking of death to the prefect? Let him step forward, this so-called republican: here I am, alone; let him lay a hand on the representative of the law." Haussmann's composure gave him the breathing space to leave the village and, by quickening his pace, to shake off his pursuers. But his anger reached new heights when the men he had arrested were released on bail and later acquitted—the familiar theme of a lawman's outrage at judicial laxity.

By July 3, 1849, the French expeditionary force was in control of Rome, and on the 17th it handed it back to the pope. He had the bad taste to ignore the counsel of moderation proffered by France and to embark upon pitiless repression. On August 18, Louis-Napoléon wrote to Colonel Ney, son of the Marshal of the Empire, who was then serving in Italy: "The French Republic did not send an army to Rome to stifle Italian liberty." The letter was published—as the prince president had intended—and caused intense emotion within the party of order and a break between Louis-Napoléon and his ministers; one of them, the staunchly Catholic Louis Falloux, resigned on September 7. Louis-Napoléon's liberal turn intensified just as the forces of reaction were winning on all fronts. In August, Austria retook Venice and, with Russian help, crushed the Hungarian revolution.

On October 31 the prince president demanded the resignation of the government. He did not appoint a new president of the Council of Ministers but instead brought in two legal experts from Auvergne, Rouher and Parieu, a banker, Achille Fould, and two generals. It was a fighting cabinet, and on the right there were cries of "A coup d'état is under way." Louis-Napoléon recalled his oath of loyalty to the Constitution while his half-brother Morny, who favored a forcible solution, regretted that he still had "scruples of integrity."

Yet Louis-Napoléon was still in the business of maintaining order, restricted as he was by a conservative National Assembly that he had the power neither to suspend nor to dissolve. The prefects, "frontline soldiers of order," had to go out into the arena. In Paris the police chief Carlier ordered the Trees of Liberty to be cut down, on the pretext that they interfered with the flow of traffic. In the Var, Haussmann began proceedings in March 1850 against those who had stirred up trouble at the Vidauban carnival on February 13. The mayor of the town had banned any procession, riding roughshod over an age-old tradition that on the first day of Lent a dummy was carried though the streets and solemnly decapitated on the main square. The anger of the townspeople was exploited by a very active republican *chambrée* which, with none other than Émile Ollivier at its head, defied the prohibition and organized an especially noisy and provocative carnival; the dummy beheaded with great pomp was a representation of the mayor himself. The anger of the conservatives found an echo in *Le Conciliateur* of February 17: "Base demagogic scenes disturbed the usually harmless celebrations at the end of the carnival. Our Reds gave themselves over to, we won't call them political demonstrations, but unspeakable orgies. . . . Are these the people who say they are in favor of reforms and progress?"

The main architects of the Arts et Métiers insurrection in Paris were convicted of sedition in October 1849, and the deputies among them were stripped of their mandate. The bye-elections to fill their seats were fixed for March 10 and 11, 1850. The Var was affected, since two of the deputies in question, Ledru-Rollin and Suchet, had to be replaced. The party of order presented Monsieur de Clappiers, although Haussmann considered him too Legitimist and clerical, and Siméon, a large landowner from Les Salins d'Hyères. Siméon was duly elected, whereas de Clappiers was defeated by the republican Clavier. The latter was disqualified by the National Assembly, however, and de Clappiers was declared the winner in his place. Now there were two Reds and five conservatives in the Var. Haussmann's political wager had largely paid off.

Reaction was on the march. But it was not all easy going. Despite official pressure, twenty-one left-wing deputies had nevertheless been elected instead of the thirty-one debarred "Reds" in the departments where voting had taken place in March. It was a good result for the socialists. The Bourse fell, rich foreigners abandoned Paris, and savings accounts emptied. The trials following the Vidauban carnival affair must also have left Haussmann with mixed feelings: in April the jury at the Assize Court found Émile Ollivier not guilty of incitement to public disorder, and in May ringing pleas from the attorney representing two female defendants (the attorney being Émile Ollivier!) led to their acquittal. Haussmann noted in *Le Conciliateur* that two other defendants had nonetheless been sentenced to terms of imprisonment.

Meanwhile, on March 15 the National Assembly passed the Falloux law establishing church control over education. As one of its supporters, the monarchist Montalembert, pointed out, "There is only one formula for making those who do not own property believe in property, and that is to make them believe in God—in the God who handed down the Ten Commandments and who punishes thieves for all eternity." But the results of the bye-elections showed that, while awaiting the fruits of the Falloux law, some action had to be taken at once. On May 31 the Assembly amended the election law so that three years of uninterrupted residence in the commune of registration became necessary to exercise the right to vote. This sleight of hand erased from the electoral rolls all workers who were compelled to go from town to town in search of work—a full 3 million out of an electorate of 9.6 million. Louis-Napoléon kept his peace, whereas Haussmann could hardly contain his joy. But by the time the law was passed, he was no longer prefect for the Var: he learned on May 15, 1850, that a decree signed on the 11th had named him prefect for the Yonne.

The next day, Georges-Eugène sent a farewell circular to the Var's departmental staff. Here we see the combative prefect, together with the man more than ever enamored of good management. First the manager: "The Var . . . offers the administrator magnificent country to fertilize with useful

measures, and it offers the political functionary intelligent local people devoted to their work if also, no doubt, left too much in the past." Then the
combative prefect: "It is necessary to win back [communities that have gone
astray] to the cause of order, through loyal and devoted administration as
much as through sustained vigilance and firmness." And finally a moral self-
portrait: "I hope to leave with you the memory of a public servant who was a
slave to his duties, anxious to impress on all his actions that stamp of meticulous regularity which is as distant from the violence of an excess of energy
as it is from the weakness of an excess of moderation."[10]

His farewells said, Haussmann hastened to Auxerre and entrusted his
wife with her usual task of solving the problems of the move. He took with
him his principal private secretary and personal secretary as well as his faithful domestic servant, Pierre Réau. There was just enough time to leave his
luggage in his new administrative center, and to complete his new residence
formalities, before he rushed to Joigny to catch the train for Paris. He arrived on the evening of May 19.

7

From Auxerre to Bordeaux

AUXERRE was not as large as the Metz prefecture for which Haussmann had been hoping. To be sure, the Yonne had the advantage of closeness and ease of communication with Paris, but Haussmann remained a little disappointed. He wanted some clarification of the meaning of the appointment as well as precise instructions about his new responsibilities. No sooner had he arrived in Paris than he received the key to the puzzle from the prince's secretary, Mocquard. The Yonne was the first department to have voted for Louis-Napoléon when he was still in exile, a citadel of imperial sentiment but one that the prince seemed to be losing as socialist propaganda scored heavily and the party of order came to be represented by monarchists opposed to him. Who was to blame for this? The two prefects who had been there previously. Louis-Napoléon, beginning to appreciate Haussmann's devotion, had therefore decided to entrust him with an important mission. He expected a lot from him.

Haussmann was already feeling greatly cheered by these explanations when he was received by the prince himself. Louis-Napoléon confirmed that, although the new post did not involve the promotion that Haussmann had every right to expect, a way would be found of compensating him for this. Haussmann could only repeat the assurances of his loyalty: "I place my career interests in Your Imperial Highness's hands, with a request that he always subordinate them, as now, to the weightier interests of his service."[1]

Next Georges-Eugène went to the ministry of the interior. He had never previously met the minister, Baroche, and it cannot be said that the two men hit it off. "He received me with the haughty arrogance that he adopted toward his subordinates and told me what I already knew: he had been intending me for a more important position than Auxerre—for which I thanked him with a respectful bow—but the prince president had thought that the qualities displayed by my administration in the Var—I shall omit the condescending details that I greeted in the same way—would be better employed for the time being in the Yonne than elsewhere."[2] Baroche drew him a picture of the political landscape in the department and analyzed each deputy's attitude to the government. But Haussmann noted that the minister did not take him into his political confidence as much as Louis-Napoléon had done. "Perhaps he did not yet read, and did not accept that he should already read in the future, everything that His Imperial Highness had allowed me to glimpse. He was not a born imperialist."

Haussmann was well aware that the prince's aim was to restore the empire, even if he officially denied it and even if his own government was sure it could prevent it from happening. In relation to Baroche and others—sometimes he openly told them so—Haussmann always experienced the pride that comes of being among the recipients of grace. Baron Haussmann's overweening humility made itself felt day after day. It was not the best way of winning friends. But what do trustworthy or not so trustworthy friends matter when you have the strength of a well-tempered soul who has won the support of your lord and master? On the train back to the Yonne, Haussmann received a visit from Louis Frémy, formerly Foucher's principal private secretary and now deputy for the Yonne, a man who, like Haussmann, was completely devoted to the prince. Frémy described the situation there to him. It would not be in the Yonne that Georges-Eugène would be able to satisfy his taste for administration. The circular sent on May 22 to the main public servants and elected representatives of the department reflected this realization: "Today, the practical work and studies involved in administration are all too often overshadowed by the numerous duties imposed on public office by the formidable task of ensuring public tranquility, preventing any attempt to sow disorder, containing all the evil instincts. . . . I do not wish to leave anyone in doubt about the energy with which I shall fulfil my mandate to make order prevail everywhere and in all things over disorder; the authority of the law over anarchic passions; respect for rules over the spirit of insubordination."[3]

METHOD BEFORE ALL ELSE

❧ Although the Yonne had a larger population than the Var, it posed incomparably fewer problems of organization. The department had a real capital in the active and prosperous town of Auxerre, and all its services had their headquarters there. On the other hand, the only person who might give the prefect a difficult time, the Archbishop of Sens, lived not in Auxerre but where one would expect, in Sens. Moreover, Auxerre was only forty leagues from Paris, so the prefect could catch a train and be at the Elysée in a couple of hours.

The Yonne had more communes than the Var (485 to 202), but the fact that it was divided into five arrondissements instead of four meant that the prefect had the assistance of four subprefects, based in Avallon, Joigny, Sens, and Tonnerre. Although the administrative staff was not all of equal value, all the public servants gave loyal service—another marked difference from what Haussmann had experienced in the Var. The eight deputies comprised two republicans, four Bonapartists, one royalist, and one independent conservative. Frémy, a Bonapartist deputy, was one of Haussmann's main pillars of support. The departmental council had a third republicans and a half supporters of Louis-Napoléon, and the large number of distinguished people who had links with the thirty-five councillors made it difficult to handle. Haussmann would have to use a lot of diplomacy rather than try to force things through. By and large, he managed this very well.

The soil was more fertile than in the Var. Vines covered most of the hillsides around Auxerre, Joigny, Tonnerre, and Chablis, producing wines justly reputed for their delicacy and body whose sale on the Parisian market brought a fine return. The tax revenue was in theory half as large again as that of the Var. There were plenty of navigable rivers and waterways; several sources of the Vanne were later tapped by Haussmann for the Paris water supply. Road haulage was a sizable business, but the railway gradually dealt a number of sharp blows to it. There was already a line from Paris to Tonnerre, and it had reached Montbard by the time Haussmann left the department. Public works were carried out on the state's behalf by two engineers: Haussmann had no great liking for one of them, Julien, but he saw eye to eye with Chaperon (it is true that he was from Libourne!). It was especially desirable that the prefect should get on well with those responsible for the railway infrastructure, because he was in charge of the funding and accounts for line construction.

In financial matters, Haussmann was faced with the problem of relations with the departmental council. One of his predecessors had obtained credits to build a small town house that could provide private accommodations for the prefect, just next to the splendid main building, an imposing but uncomfortable gothic bishop's palace that had been converted into the prefecture. Yet when he had asked for a loan of 3,000 francs to do up a billiard room, the departmental council had refused point blank. Haussmann's entourage advised him not to revive the dispute, so Georges-Eugène gave them a lesson in method. He went through the plans and estimates with a fine-tooth comb, added some extra work to the billiard room while avoiding any luxury expenditure, and changed some of the descriptions (the billiard room became salon No. X, for example, the grand staircase was demoted to the main staircase, and so on). The loan request was for much more than the 3,000 francs of the old billiard room: in fact, it came to 62,000 francs. Haussmann added an application for some repair work on departmental buildings. The total package, well wrapped and presented, obtained the necessary vote without encountering the slightest difficulty. This victory vindicated what Haussmann went on to make his guiding rule: "Within deliberative bodies, the opposition prefers to make a career for itself in small matters: first, because they are within the grasp of many more speakers than are larger matters; next, because certain malcontents or petty minds in the majority, who would not dare defect in votes on the latter, find in the former an opportunity to make up for it and demonstrate their independence."[4]

In return, Haussmann brought the departmental council a sizable subsidy from the ministry of the interior as well as introducing various economy measures. The Yonne was well endowed with roads, but the classifications were perhaps a little perfectionist in view of the sometimes modest amount of traffic recorded on them. Thus, apart from the 327 miles of national highway for which the central government was responsible, the department counted 511 miles of secondary roads and 834 miles of major and minor link roads, not to speak of the waterways (214 miles) and railway lines (91 miles). Truly a fine network—but a little excessive. Haussmann proposed to reduce the least used departmental highways to the rank of major link roads, whose upkeep would be less demanding. Selective counting would make it possible to know the exact volume of traffic on all the roads in the department.

During the 1850 session he also managed to persuade the councillors to vote for a loan of 400,000 francs: (a) to revamp the Auxerre mental asylum in accordance with the plans of Doctor Ferrus, which involved eliminating padded cells and making all inmates take part in communal life; and (b) to build a penitentiary where defendants awaiting trial could be kept separate from convicted prisoners—"an excellent measure, constantly demanded by criminologists."[5] Haussmann cooperated with the senior consultant at the mental hospital, Doctor Gurard de Cailleux, on the design of a new nursing home. He also asked him for medical advice about the spells of nervous dizziness that he had been suffering. The doctor urged him to take regular walks and to persist in them even when he was snowed under with work—a prescription that cost nothing and proved to have beneficial results. Later, when he had become prefect for the Seine, Haussmann appointed Girard de Cailleux departmental inspector of the treatment of mental patients and had every reason to be pleased with the serious way in which he performed his duties as well as with the medical advice that he himself received from time to time.

KEEPING ORDER AND APPEALING TO THE PEOPLE

To his great regret, however, Haussmann had to devote most of his energy to the maintenance of order in the department. A look at the forces available to him told the new prefect that he had no regular army units and that the police force was weak and poorly informed. Although he had the backing of the judiciary, the assize juries tended to be pusillanimous in their verdicts. Finally, as in the Var, he could more or less rely only upon the small force of gendarmes, whereas the secret societies in the Yonne were altogether more formidable than the clubs and *chambrées* of his former prefecture.

Georges-Eugène's period in the Yonne was punctuated by a number of grave incidents. On June 14, just three weeks after he had assumed his office, he encountered a railwaymen's revolt and an outbreak of rioting—although in this case rapid intervention by the gendarmes and the arrest of the leaders restored calm by the following day.

In the summer of 1850 the prince president adopted the two major strategic orientations that would remain unchanged until the coup d'état of December 1851. They may be summed up in two terms: order and social progress. Faced with a National Assembly in a frenzy over security issues, Louis-Napoléon came round to supporting various measures in the name of public order, such as the law of July 16 strengthening control over the press. At the same time, however, he pardoned many of those sentenced in the wake of the June Days of 1848—an act that so infuriated the Assembly that it began to talk of limiting his right of pardon. The prince president needed money and was asking for an increase in his civil list from 1.2 million francs to 3 million francs. But in fact the majority in Parliament was working to restore the monarchy. Louis-Philippe died in exile at a convenient moment on August 26, 1850, leaving the way open for the newly buoyant Legitimists to assert their claims. Unfortunately for the ambitions of the monarchist party, the grandson of Charles X, the comte de Chambord, stubbornly invoked divine right and would have no truck with a negotiated restoration. Nevertheless, Louis-Napoléon could not ignore the restorationist peril. In the race with the royalists, he knew he could beat them only by capturing long-term public opinion.

The prince president took advantage of the summer holidays for further visits to the provinces, including the regions where he was least popular. He denied that he was preparing to overthrow the Republic and declared with all the appearances of logic: "He who has been elected by six million votes carries out the will of the people and does not betray it." For the time being, he was not seeking to reestablish the empire; he considered that to be premature. But he did wish to see a revision of the Constitution that would allow him to be reelected.

On August 12, Louis-Napoléon left Paris on a visit to Burgundy, passing through Haussmann's Yonne prefecture on the way. He broke his train journey at Joigny for a military review, then continued to Tonnerre for a reception by the constituted authorities; he did not stop off at Sens, as Haussmann did not wish to take any risks in a town troubled by the opposition. Dreading fresh demonstrations by railway workers, our prefect put all the gendarmes on a war footing and had two hundred reinforcements sent to him from Troyes. In the end there were scarcely any hitches, despite a few shouts of "Vive la République!" among those of "Vive Napoléon! Vive l'Empereur!" The more daring did not hesitate to shout: "Vive la République démocratique et sociale!"—and as the word "social" was considered seditious, the gendarmes picked up the guilty parties. Louis-Napoléon affectionately shook his prefect's hand at the moment of farewell and expressed his satisfaction with how things had gone.

During the military reviews that took place at Saint-Maur and Satory in October 1850, the soldiers shouted "Vive Napoléon!" instead of "Vive la République!"—the latter having been abandoned to the opposition. On October 10 in Satory, some elements in the cavalry even raised enthusiastic cries of "Vive l'Empereur!" General Changarnier, who combined the command of the Paris army division and the National Guard, took umbrage at these seditious calls and talked of sanctions in the military hierarchy. The prince president played the appeaser, continuing to invoke his duty and the exacting religion of legality that ostensibly filled his mind.

While wrapping himself in the cloak of law and order, Louis-Napoléon tried to appear full of concern to effect social advances—the second component of his strategy—and did not hesitate to profit from the innovative social policy conducted in Parliament by one section of the party of order. Carried along by those of its members who believed, like the prince president, that there would be no lasting peace among the masses unless the axis of repression was complemented by progressive legislation, the National Assembly passed a number of acts for the conditional development of savings and pension funds as well as mutual aid societies. It introduced legal aid to provide access to justice for the poor. The Grammont law protected animals from human violence. The telegraph, hitherto reserved for the use of the government, was opened to the public. A single fixed charge for letters— twenty-five centimes whatever the distance—simplified the postal service and made private and business correspondence more democratic. The Catholic deputy Anatole de Melun, worried about urban destitution, put forward legislation to further the struggle against slum housing, and when a far from enthusiastic majority tried to bury the proposal in a commission, the prince president gave it the backing that eventually ensured its acceptance.

The republicans relaunched their agitation as this fratricidal struggle broke out between Louis-Napoléon Bonaparte and the monarchists within the party of order. In the Yonne, the difficulties facing Haussmann showed that calm often hung by a single thread. Serious incidents flared in early November 1850 at Ligny, a town considered Bonapartist, when the mayor ordered the cafés and bistrots to close at nine o'clock—a measure not exactly to the liking of local youth. After a number of clashes with the police, the mayor issued forty-three violators of the order with summonses. When the trial began on November 9, the defendants' families invaded the courtroom in angry protest. The two gendarmes on court duty arrested three particularly voluble protesters, but the crowd laid into the gendarmes, freed the prisoners, and took one of the gendarmes hostage while the other one managed to flee to Auxerre and solicit help. Haussmann immediately sent two squads of gendarmes from Auxerre, as well as the squads based in Saint-Florentin and Chablis. (A squad, we should recall, consisted of two men.) As an extra precaution, he added sixty soldiers from an infantry regiment. He himself picked up a couple of magistrates and the captain of the gendarmerie, then set off for Ligny and reached it in advance of the gendarmes and soldiers. The local people were nearly all celebrating in the various cafés, just to show that they could not care less about the municipal order. It was ten o'clock in the evening. Suddenly shouts rang out: "It's the prefect! It's the prefect!" The crowd recognized Haussmann in the man marching toward them and saying, "Make way! Make way!" Those who were there as simple onlookers were taken aback and began to shout: "Vive le préfet! Vive Napoléon!" Meanwhile, Georges-Eugène's unexpected arrival enabled the resolute force of gendarmes, who had been held at the entrance to the town by volleys of stones, to press on and regroup around the prefect. Haussmann called for silence and harangued the crowd, recalling Ligny's well-known attachment to Louis-Napoléon and expressing his sadness that he had immediately to open a judicial investigation. At that point—it was eleven at night—the soldiers and remaining gendarmes arrived, and the crowd eventually dispersed. The next morning, ten of the most heavily involved local people were arrested without incident and taken under escort to Auxerre.

Our prefect expected to be congratulated. Instead he received a dressing-down from his minister, Baroche, who accused him of inexcusable softness toward the rioters when he should have marched against them in force and issued military-style commands. Haussmann was not the kind of man to take that without reacting. "I pointed out to the braggart that upon my arrival I had no more than eight gendarmes for such an exploit; that I would have had to wait an hour at least for the drummer to arrive, if not for the infantry reinforcements, in order to effect the drum rolls that the law requires before any formal warning; and that the appearance of hesitation, by emboldening the crowd and encouraging the rebellion protected by darkness, would have led without fail to bloody fighting. 'I did not want,' I wrote in conclusion, 'to appear to doubt for one moment that my orders would be obeyed. The event proves that I was right to trust in the moral influence that an attitude of assurance on the part of one holding power always exerts over the masses.'"[6] In the Yonne department, at any event, Haussmann's calm courage made a strong impression.

A few days later there was a new alert. The Yonne bargemen, who floated regular convoys of wood in the direction of Paris, were in a state of effervescence. The subprefect in Avallon was beginning to lose control of the situation. On November 23, Haussmann decided to call upon the army for assistance; an infantry battalion was sent from Paris and arrived in Auxerre on the 27th. By then, however, Haussmann had been able to obtain a revocation of the order by the Ministry of Public Works that had provoked the bargemen's anger. Calm was restored.

CONTROLLING LOCALLY ELECTED COUNCILLORS

❦ The task of regaining control over the Yonne also involved controlling locally elected councillors. When Haussmann first arrived, the three main towns in the department—Auxerre, Sens, and Joigny—had neither a mayor nor a deputy mayor; for better or worse, their jobs were being done by municipal councillors. At Sens, just three days after formally taking over as prefect, Haussmann suspended the municipal councillors who were performing these functions and dissolved the town's battalion of the National Guard. As a sign of protest, the municipal councillors resigned *en bloc*. The new prefect took advantage of this to appoint a special delegation of three local notables to administer the town until fresh elections could be held. Meanwhile, on May 31, the National Assembly passed the electoral law requiring a minimum of three years' residence. Did this apply only to parliamentary elections or to local ones as well? Weeks passed before the Assembly specifically included local elections, and voting took place in Sens only on October 27 and November 3. The new council, twenty-seven strong, consisted of twenty-two conservatives and five supported by the "Reds." Haussmann was as satisfied as he could possibly have hoped. The law of May 31 was a mechanism for creating highly effective conservative majorities.

On December 3 it was the turn of the Auxerre town council to face Haussmann's wrath and be dissolved. Two days later he appointed another special delegation of three notables, headed by a leading civil servant now retired, Martineau des Chênets, former government accountant and under secretary of state for war under the July Monarchy, as well as a friend of Haussmann's father. The election took place on March 1, 1851, under the new provisions of the law of May 31, although as an extra twist Haussmann had divided the town into nine sections that each had to elect three councillors. The division was no random affair, of course. The opposition was so disgusted that it called for a boycott, and the twenty-seven candidates chosen by Haussmann were all elected. Martineau, who was one of them, was appointed mayor. Despite his age, he lost no time putting the town's finances in order and stepping up measures to improve the functioning of public services. As the distribution of water was inadequate, Haussmann sent him a civil engineer based in Avallon, by the name of Belgrand, who went on to produce miracles in Auxerre. Once Haussmann had become prefect for the Seine, he called Belgrand to Paris and gave him the task of designing and supervising an ambitious policy for the capital's water supply.

The favorable election results in Auxerre persuaded Haussmann to tackle the last main town: Joigny. On March 15 he asked the government to dissolve the town council, and this was done by decree on April 15. Four days later, another special delegation was appointed, and the municipal area was divided into three sections. Haussmann was resigned to cutting his losses: the opposition was certain to win one of the sections, but the newly drawn boundaries should ensure that the conservatives won the other two. On May 25 the ballot proved his analysis correct: of twenty-three municipal councillors, several were from the opposition and sixteen on the side of the government. Our prefect sent a victory bulletin to the ministry of the interior: "The three main towns of the Yonne, which were in the hands of the Reds less than a year ago and seemed forever pledged to socialism, have today been recaptured for the cause of order." He could not resist the pleasure of adding that the result in Joigny, together with those in Sens and Auxerre, furnished "three incontestable arguments for the effectiveness of the law of May 31."[7]

Haussmann continued to disagree with the prince president about the electoral law. Soon it would be at the heart of the final crisis between Louis-Napoléon and the National Assembly from which the coup d'état would issue.

REVISION OR DEATH

After the affair of the shouts of "Vive l'Empereur!" on October 10, to which he had reacted with considerable energy, General Changarnier thought he had won a decisive round against Louis-Napoléon. Much to its delight, the National Assembly seemed to have found in Changarnier the sword it lacked to counter the ambitions of the troublesome head of state. But that was to misjudge the prince, who was quite happy to keep his head down and jump back up when no one expected it. On January 2, 1851, the Élysée Palace opened the attack on Changarnier, and in his surprise he made a clumsy riposte at the rostrum of the Assembly on the morning of the 3rd. That evening the prince president dismissed him.

Each side had been preparing for an open crisis around May 1852, when elections were scheduled both for the National Assembly and for a new president of the Republic. Louis-Napoléon now formally requested the Assembly to revise the Constitution so that he could be elected for another term, a majority of three-fourths being necessary for this to be approved. Faucher had the idea of launching a petition in support of the constitutional amendment but forbade prefects and subprefects to become involved in the campaign. Haussmann was furious, believing that either you go to war or you don't. And although the Yonne supplied 32,000 signatures for the petition, he was convinced that the figure could have been higher if he and his colleagues had been allowed to do their part.

The prince president stepped up the pressure and began a new series of trips to the provinces, especially in Burgundy. He arrived in Sens on May 31, 1851; the reception at the station, the journey downtown, the hospitality at the archbishop's palace were occasions for a display of enthusiastic support punctuated with shouts of "Vive l'Empereur!" Louis-Napoléon left the next day, Sunday, June 1, after attending high mass in the cathedral. In the train taking him to Dijon, officials questioned the prefect about the feelings of the people in his department. Haussmann was categorical: everyone hoped that the president's mandate would be extended. Frémy was convinced; Dupin, president of the National Assembly, and Faucher, minister of the interior, much less so. They arrived at Tonnerre, where the welcome was just as warm. When the time came to part, at the limits of the department, Louis-Napoléon grasped Haussmann's hands in his own: "You fully justify the mission I gave you in the Yonne and the trust that your beginnings in the Var made me place in your great value as an administrator. I shall be counting on your devotion when the time comes." He could count on Haussmann. And Haussmann knew that, whatever happened, the prince president would not forget him.

Louis-Napoléon's speech that evening in Dijon marked an epoch: "For three years, I was always visibly assisted by the Assembly when it was a question of fighting disorder through measures of repression. But when I wanted to do good and improve the lot of local communities, it denied me its help. . . . From one end of France to the other, petitions were signed to demand an amendment to the Constitution. . . . Whatever the duties that my country imposes upon me, it will find me determined to carry out its will." Dupin expressed his approval. Faucher gave Le Moniteur, the official journal of the times, a somewhat toned-down version of Louis-Napoléon's remarks. When Haussmann learned of them, he lapped them up and wondered whether the things he had told him in confidence a few hours earlier had not helped to strengthen the prince's resolve.

Its bluff called, the Assembly rejected the constitutional amendment in July. If the prince president wished to remain in power, his only option now was to use force. He appointed as his war minister General de Saint-Arnaud, an Africa Army soldier from Algeria known for his lack of scruples. General

Magnan, a loyal Bonapartist, received the Paris command. Among those close to the prince, there were such regulars as Fleury, an army man very friendly with Princess Mathilde; Colonel Vaudrey, who had compromised himself for Louis-Napoléon in the Strasbourg affair; Mocquard, his personal secretary; Maupas, a prefect with a strong hand who later became chief of police; Persigny; and, above all, Morny.

As the Assembly was in recess from August 10 until November 4, the conspirators initially believed that they could use the summer break for their ends. But one of them, General de Saint-Arnaud, changed his mind on the grounds that deputies were more than capable of organizing resistance from their local constituencies. It was therefore decided to await the return of Parliament so that everyone could be picked up in the same dragnet. The tension mounted over the summer and autumn. Tradesmen stopped placing orders, looms no longer beat their rhythm in the countryside, the specter of unemployment returned. The fear worked to Louis-Napoléon's advantage, but secret societies were rearing their head again. The republicans did not intend to remain neutral; they were determined to play their hand. Then the prince president banged down his master trump: he proposed in early October the repeal of the election law of May 31, 1850. Parliamentarians were furious yet undecided when the new session opened on November 6. Some of the moderates thought it unwise to isolate themselves from the prince president, but the conservative majority saw his proposal as indicating a change of alliances and accused him of doing a deal with the Reds. In this climate, Louis-Napoléon gave proof of consummate tactical dexterity. While posing as the champion of universal suffrage against a reactionary Assembly, he was also able to cut the ground from under the feet of the republicans.

The prince's position caused a certain wavering among his supporters, or at least among some of them. After three weeks of equivocation, Faucher resigned as interior minister and precipitated the formation of a new government on October 27. Haussmann was too devoted to Louis-Napoléon to abandon the cause. And yet he remained a supporter of the law of May 31, 1850, and stuck to this view until the end of his days.[8] How was he able to reconcile this with the Napoleonic appeal to the people and the systematic recourse to plebiscitary universal suffrage that marked the prince's political system? Casuistry may have had a place in our prefect's Lutheran way of thinking. Here is how it may have gone. Universal suffrage, with its inherent solemnity, is suited to the manifestation of the national will in a presidential plebiscite; there it is like the water of baptism. But for other elections—parliamentary, cantonal, or municipal—the law of May 31, 1850, defines the necessary framework; the water of baptism is not for everyday use.

Certainly Haussmann distrusted universal suffrage. In October 1852 in Bordeaux, a few months before the restoration of the empire, he again made this clear to Louis-Napoléon: "Universal suffrage without limits strikes me as comparable to those wild cats which, fascinated by their tamer, grovel at his feet and act affectionately toward him, and him alone, but which tear him apart and devour him if, in a forgetful moment, his eyes cease to hold them under the spell of his magnetic power."[9]

Disagreement over the electoral law did not prevent Haussmann from devotedly serving Louis-Napoléon, nor the prince president from appreciating more than ever his fantastic prefect. After all, Haussmann believed that the opinions of French people could be summed up as follows: "For us, royalty has had its day," but "the Empire is a different matter." A pithy formula, but one that was music to Louis-Napoléon's ears and, if there was any need, further strengthened his determination.

One last test awaited Haussmann, the most serious of all those he encountered during his time in the Yonne. The departmental cantons belonging to La Puisaye, Saint-Fargeau, Saint-Sauveur, and Bléneau were racked by the propaganda of a mysterious "invisible army" that was recruiting among lumberjacks and bargemen and preparing a grand Twilight of the Rich. Police informers reported plans to pillage châteaux and divide up large estates. Early in November, Haussmann began to draw up a plan of arrests. But his subprefect in Joigny jumped the gun and nearly ruined everything by suddenly opening a judicial investigation that clearly had no legal foundation. On the evening of November 14, Haussmann called him in for a discussion. During that night they agreed to cancel the subprefect's actions but to begin at once a normal investigation through the prosecutor's office. Despite the dangers, Haussmann then left at dawn for La Puisaye, where he invited himself to stay at the château. Frémy joined him the next day and never left his side for a moment. "That day," Haussmann later wrote, "saw the beginning of the feelings of mutual trust and sincere friendship that have never ceased to exist between M. Frémy and myself."[10] In the end, everything went well. The judicial apparatus and the appearance of a few gendarmes impressed the seditious elements, as did the presence of the prefect himself. Fifteen arrests were carried out. On November 19 the prefect was back in Auxerre, conscious of having done his duty.

A MISUNDERSTANDING AT THE ÉLYSÉE

✍ On November 26, Georges-Eugène Haussmann was appointed prefect for the Gironde. The news overjoyed him, but it came as a complete surprise. Until then, two possible posts had been suggested for him: chief of police in Paris (an idea he flatly refused) and prefect for Lyons (which would have been greatly to his liking). Now he did not show any inordinate rush: he received and paid visits on November 29 and 30, prepared the departure of his *smala* household, then accompanied his mother to Paris on December 1 after her visit of a few days to Auxerre in the company of Georges-Eugène's unmarried sister. That evening he went to the Élysée Palace to pay his respects and to express his gratitude. The prince came to greet Haussmann with a broad smile and inquired: "Is Madame Haussmann very upset to be returning to Bordeaux?"—"Far from it, Your Highness," came the reply, "she is delighted. And for my part, I am all the happier in that it was the last thing in the world I expected."—"I cannot tell you now why I am sending you there," the prince continued, "but I want you to go immediately. Early tomorrow morning, as early as possible, go to collect your instructions from the minister of the interior and leave at once." As Haussmann looked at him without seeming to understand these rather unusual directions, the prince president dropped his voice and urged: "Go to see the minister before daybreak—that will be better still." He shook hands with Haussmann, who had the feeling that after such strange words this gesture contained a message.

As he was about to leave the Élysée, Haussmann ran into de Royer, the public prosecutor at the appeals court, and asked him if he knew whether the interior minister appointed on October 27, a certain Monsieur de Thorigny, happened to be there. Thorigny, whom Haussmann had never met before, had been de Royer's first advocate general. "There he is, next to the chimney," the prosecutor pointed him out. Thorigny, thinking that Haussmann wished to thank him, said: "It is to the prince himself that you owe your new post. My predecessor had planned for you to go to Lyons, but the prince took the view that you would give him better service in Bordeaux."—"His Highness deigned to explain that to me himself, and urged me to go and see you very early tomorrow morning to receive special instructions from you, so that I could leave without delay."—"But I do not have any!" Haussmann was dumbfounded, as Thorigny probably was too, and said on leaving: "The prince's order is so categorical that I cannot fail to obey it. His

Imperial Highness will, I presume, let you know shortly which urgent mission I have to carry out in Bordeaux."

The next morning, at five o'clock, Haussmann hailed a cab and went to the ministry of the interior, which in those days was at rue de Grenelle. At the Place de la Concorde he came across troops on the march. It was still pitch dark. At rue de Grenelle the main gate was open and the courtyard was brightly illuminated; an infantry battalion was standing at attention, its rifles on the ground. The hussars in the lobby recognized him and one of them asked: "Have you come to speak with the minister?"—"Exactly," Haussmann replied.—"With which one?"—"What do you mean, which one?" Haussmann exclaimed. "You can be sure it is not the navy minister."—"Is it Monsieur de Thorigny you wish to see, or Monsieur le comte de Morny?" At last Haussmann understood. "Announce me to Monsieur le comte de Morny." Then the doors of the minister's office opened and Morny (whom Haussmann had never met before) came toward him with outstretched hand: "Monsieur Haussmann, are you with us?"—Haussmann: "I do not know exactly what this is about, Monsieur le comte, but my life belongs to the prince; do not hesitate to make use of me." It was dawn on December 2, 1851.

DECEMBER 2, 1851: AT LAST THE COUP D'ÉTAT

☙ During the night of December 1–2, Maupas sent out police superintendents to arrest seventy-eight people: prominent parliamentarians and other ostensibly dangerous leaders. It was Morny who had persuaded a hesitant Louis-Napoléon to agree to this: "You don't have to clamp down against people in prison," he said, "and some intelligent arrests can prevent a civil war." And he added with complete cynicism: "To arrest someone in such circumstances is to do him the greatest of favors"—that is, by sparing him the risk of death on the barricades. Changarnier, Thiers, Cavaignac, and Lamorcière were picked up in this way. The Palais Bourbon was occupied and the whole of Paris taken over by Magnan's men. Morny installed himself at the ministry of the interior and made contact with all the prefects. During the night he had a proclamation printed and then pasted to the walls of the capital; the prince president was dissolving the National Assembly, repealing the electoral law of May 31, 1850, restoring universal suffrage, and calling citizens to the polls to endorse the constitutional amendment that allowed the president to be elected for a ten-year term. To the army Louis-

Napoléon forcefully declared: "I count upon you, not to violate the laws but to ensure respect for the country's principal law: national sovereignty."

Haussmann was given unlimited powers by decree and sent as a special prefect to ensure the compliance of the Gironde, a department where Legitimists and Orleanists were the dominant influence. To maintain secrecy, he would leave by the evening mail train and change at Poitiers (then still the end of the line) for the night mail coach to Bordeaux, arriving there late on the 3rd. Haussmann was annoyed at having to waste so much precious time, but the state of communications did not allow of a better solution. He also had a telegram sent to the trusted secretary general for the Gironde, Monsieur Dosquet, asking him to wait beside the bridge at La Bastide on the right bank of the Garonne with the carriage of Haussmann's father-in-law (who would be confidentially informed of his arrival). Meanwhile, Haussmann was champing at the bit and only reluctantly spent the day with his family and friends. He ascertained that Paris was calm and that people in the street, though a little surprised, were strolling around as if nothing had happened. He was told at the ministry that a few deputies who had tried to assemble at the *mairie* in the 10th arrondissement had been overcome without difficulty. Later he learned that in fact three hundred of them—mostly conservatives like Tocqueville and Berryer—had gathered in response to an appeal by Dupin, the president of the Assembly, and had soon been arrested.

Haussmann left as planned. At Angoulême he met the mail coach coming the other way from Bordeaux. The monarchists were in a rage, having been informed by telegraph of the coup d'état, but there were not yet signs of unrest. Haussmann arrived at La Bastide and found the secretary general waiting for him. They left for the prefecture. The city knew there was a state of siege in Paris, and the prefect for the Gironde, who was still Monsieur Neveux, had handed over his powers to General d'Arbouville, commander of the military forces in the area. Neither Neveux nor the general was a supporter of Louis-Napoléon. A state of siege had not yet been declared in the department, but the posters announcing it had been printed and were ready to be pasted up. When Haussmann reached the prefecture, he found in conference there Neveux, d'Arbouville, the mayor of Bordeaux, the public prosecutor, and a few departmental councillors, all of them Orleanists. A heated discussion ensued, and Haussmann could already see himself in a prison cell. He took out the order appointing him special prefect and canceled the powers that Neveux had handed over to d'Arbouville; he had the posters thrown on the fire, received the general's resignation, and issued his orders. At midnight, as he made his way on foot to the house of his parents-in-law, he was able to see that the city was sleeping peacefully.

Louis-Napoléon's appeal to the people was well received when it was pasted up in Bordeaux on December 3. Haussmann's decisiveness and his knowledge of people did the rest. Elsewhere, especially in Paris, things did not go so well. On the morning of the 3rd, a new government was formed with Saint-Arnaud, Rouher, Morny, Fould, and Magne. Parisians were at first indifferent to the dispute between the prince president and the reactionary Assembly. Sixty or so republican deputies, including Victor Hugo and Schoelcher, attempted unsuccessfully to rouse the population. A barricade was erected, however, in faubourg Saint-Antoine. A deputy proudly replied to a worker who had reproached him for his deputy's allowance of twenty-five francs: "You'll see how we die for twenty-five francs a day"—and did in fact get himself killed. That afternoon more barricades appeared in the Temple area; street warfare had started. Morny decreed a state of siege, with summary execution of insurgents, and withdrew his troops so that the rising would spread out and become easier to crush. On the boulevards people were shouting "Vive la République!" The impression in Paris was that the coup had failed.

The next day, December 4, there were barricades at rue Saint-Denis, rue Rambuteau, faubourg Saint-Martin, and faubourg Saint-Antoine. Common people were in the streets claiming victory: "Down with the pretorians!" But by early afternoon General Magnan had thirty thousand men on the move, converging from the four points of the compass on the centers of the insurrection in today's 1st, 2nd, 3rd, and 4th arrondissements. The column that had come from the west, under General Canrobert, advanced from the Madeleine down the boulevards to the Porte Saint-Denis. Blocked by a hostile crowd, it opened fire for ten minutes on anything that moved—demonstrators but also onlookers, passersby, shop assistants—and caused dozens of deaths. Resistance crumbled as the barricades were removed with great force; a total of four hundred people were killed, ten times fewer than in June 1848. Prisoners were shot on the Champ de Mars. The last barricades came down on December 5. Terrorized Paris would not stir again for nineteen years.

Morny kept his prefects informed and told them to act ruthlessly against anyone trying to follow Paris's example of rebellion. In the end, the provincial towns did not rise up. The bourgeoisie, terrified by the exaggerated and self-serving reports from Paris in the pro-government press, threw itself into the arms of the forces of order. The workers on the whole remained apathetic. The large market towns shook the most; the agitation, latent or overt, that had been the stuff of everyday life over the last two and a half years, for Haussmann in the Var and Yonne as well as for many another prefect elsewhere in the country, finally exploded under the pressure of resentment and malaise. The Southwest was one of the three main seats of revolt. Louis-Napoléon had not been wrong to send to Bordeaux a man with Haussmann's proven record of firmness.

BORDEAUX: PREFECT HAUSSMANN SHOWS HIS MUSCLE

The Gironde subprefect at La Réole had his own firmness to thank for the fact that he did not suffer the fate of his neighbor in Marmande (Lot-de-Garonne), who was driven from his office by insurgents and came with all the units of the gendarmerie in his department to seek refuge with his brave colleague. In Bazas, another subprefect panicked and called for reinforcements. Haussmann advised him to move around his area in force instead of remaining holed up in his subprefecture. And Georges-Eugène added the ironical barb: "You won't offer a larger surface for bullets; but you will run much less risk of being hit by one. The prudent as well as the dutiful course is to face up to danger when it appears."[11]

Show your muscles so that you won't have to use them: Georges-Eugène adopted this as his own personal motto in Bordeaux. On the morning of December 4 he had a tough proclamation pasted up: "When the whole people has made its will known, everyone will have to submit. . . . Whatever happens, the powers I hold from the government are extensive enough to keep the peace in the department and to ensure that the great test is a genuine test. From whichever side aggression may come, the energy with which I stamp it out will certainly prevent its return. Men of disorder should not expect leniency on my part." Fearing the contagious effect of the news from Paris, he thought it wise to back up the posters with a few forthright actions. On the evenings of the 4th and the 5th, he ordered cavalry charges to disperse crowds of demonstrators who had gathered in the area around the prefecture. And as his information gave him reason to fear something more serious for the evening of the 6th, he issued an order the day before that required people in the street to keep moving and threatened with summary shooting anyone in rebellion who was found to be carrying a weapon. "It was a little strong," Haussmann admitted, "but I knew the people I was dealing with."[12] On the 6th itself he ordered the arrest of a dozen well-known agitators, and the police carried out many more at random among people passing by. Even the chairman of the *tribunal de commerce*, who had been on his way to the prefecture to receive the daily telegram quoting values on the Paris Bourse, found himself clicking his heels in prison.

On December 7, General d'Arbouville, who had resigned but had not yet been replaced, asked and received permission from Haussmann to send a few army units to take back control of Marmande. Some of the troops went up the Garonne by steamboat while others took the road and met up with them at Sainte-Bazeille. In the cemetery there, the insurgents laid an ambush that cost the gendarmes several dead and wounded. But they had no more ammunition, and Marmande was subsequently retaken without resistance. Haussmann breathed again. His modest conclusion: "No doubt it was thanks more to the swift repression of the troubles in Paris than to the promptness of my own decisions that Bordeaux had just regained its habitual calm, and the order maintained in the rest of the department continued to reign there despite the attempts at sedition."[13]

It was in two departments south of the Gironde that the Southwest witnessed the most serious unrest: in Lot-et-Garonne at Marmande and Villeneuve-sur-Lot, which also fell into the hands of insurgent forces, and in the Gers. In the latter, columns of peasants—sometimes acting spontaneously, sometimes under the leadership of secret societies—attacked the towns and the public buildings that symbolized authority. Between eight and ten thousand, armed with hunting rifles, scythes, pitchforks, and sticks, converged on Auch, Mirande, Condom, and Fleurance; Mirande was actually occupied for ten days.

The agitation also affected the center of France—Clamecy, in the Nièvre, was the scene of a veritable uprising that was drowned in blood—and Languedoc and the eastern Rhône in the South. During the night of December 4–5, the peasants of the Ardèche marched on Privas, and the prefecture in Digne was occupied for five days. The resistance went on even longer in the Var. There the republican leaders were not always in the forefront of the movement, although the regime took advantage of the unrest to punish them severely. The secret societies played a role, but it was mainly the lumberjacks and the small peasants ruined by the division of common land who burst out in anger against social injustice.

The physical excesses committed against the gendarmes, as symbols of the order against which the armed bands were in revolt, did more than all the flights of rhetoric to rally a majority of the country behind Louis-Napoléon. For years to come, grim legends associated with the insurrection filled moderate and conservative opinion with horror. Morny had his chance to write to prefects: "You have just been through some trying days; you have just withstood in 1851 the social war that was due to break out in 1852." The regime's touch was far from light. Of the 27,000 people arrested, 6,000 were released but 5,000 were kept under house arrest in their home towns, 3,000 were interned in another town, 1,500 were banished, and 10,000 were transported to Algeria (half in a fort or camp, half in a residence of their choosing). In March 1852, Louis-Napoléon sent special commissioners to the provinces with instructions to review sentences and show greater leniency. Three to four thousand pardons were granted, but the repression following December 2 remained "the ball that one drags by the foot throughout one's life," as the Empress Eugénie said after the fall of Napoléon III.

A PRINCE PRESIDENT: THE PLEBISCITE OF DECEMBER 20–21, 1851

  ↪ On December 2, Louis-Napoléon called upon French citizens—all citizens, thanks to the repeal of the law of May 31, 1850—to vote by plebiscite on a constitutional amendment. The date was initially set for the 14th, but a second decree, on December 4, postponed it until the 20th. Some ten million electors were asked to cast their secret ballot between 8 A.M. and 4 P.M. on December 20 and 21, at the administrative center of each commune. The proclamation contained the principles to which the nation had to say yea or nay: a leader put in charge for ten years; ministers responsible to the executive power alone; a Council of State to draft laws and defend them before a legislature elected by universal suffrage, which then discussed and voted on those laws. The precise formulation requiring the voter's endorsement was: "The French people wishes to maintain the authority of Louis-Napoléon Bonaparte and delegates to him the necessary powers to establish a Constitution upon the basis proposed in the proclamation."

Montalembert recommended a "yes" vote: "It will arm the ruling power with the necessary force to quell the army of crime, to defend your churches, your homes, your women against those whose covetous desires treat nothing with respect." Louis-Napoléon, the savior of order, also offered various satisfactions to the church: he gave the Pantheon back for religious worship and made Sunday rest obligatory at public building sites. More than 8 million votes were cast, more than in April 1848: 7.5 million "yes," 650,000 "no." Some 1.5 million electors abstained. In Paris, of the 300,000 on the register, only 133,000 voted "yes," against 80,000 "no" and 80,000 abstentions.

In the Gironde, Georges-Eugène owed the excellent results to—among

other things—his patient work persuading the Bordeaux commercial aristocracy, his own family ties, and the network of connections he had built up
over the years. His brief spell in the National Guard in 1848 had put him in
touch with ordinary people—invaluable experience at a time when each citizen had a paper ballot to place in the box. Haussmann attached great value
to the support won from Duffour-Dubergier, the influential president of the
Bordeaux chamber of commerce. The two big cats could read each other's
minds, and Haussmann persuaded Duffour-Dubergier to head a committee
in favor of a "yes" vote in the plebiscite. But although the public appeals
made by this heavyweight of Orleanism certainly had an effect, they were
not sufficient to ensure a landslide for Louis-Napoléon. In the end, the figures for the city of Bordeaux were only 13,519 "yes" against 6,818 "no," although this was better than Haussmann and the prince president might
have feared and gave them every reason to feel content. The results for the
department as a whole were much better: 123,110 "yes," 15,232 "no." We
can certainly believe Haussmann when he said: "The result of 1851 . . . was
for me personally, and in the eyes of the prince, a considerable success. It justified my having been sent to the Gironde, and completely fulfilled the special mission I had received."[14]

On December 31 the official results were communicated to Louis-
Napoléon by Baroche, who implored him to defend order and authority:
"France has confidence in you. . . . Restore in France the principle of authority. . . . Tirelessly combat the anarchic passions that attack the very roots of
society. . . . May France be at last delivered from those men who are ever
ready for murder and pillage. . . . Give the country back . . . order, stability,
and confidence."

The prince president answered in a decidedly more measured tone. His
intention was to found "institutions that correspond both to the democratic
interests of the nation and to the generally expressed desire that the government should be strong and respected." Then he added a surprising sentence:
"France has understood that I departed from legality only to return to the
law. More than seven million votes have just absolved me of this!" On January 1 the prince president left the Élysée to take up residence in the Tuileries
Palace. The imperial eagle was placed on the flags.

THE CONSTITUTION OF JANUARY 14, 1852

≈ Louis-Napoléon had been given the presidency for a ten-year term. He
enjoyed the most extensive powers, commanded the armed forces, declared

war, concluded treaties, appointed officials to every position, received the oath of loyalty from civil servants, chose ministers and held them accountable to himself alone, had sole initiative in the drafting of laws, decreed all the rules for their observance.

Legislative power lay with a 261-member legislature elected for six years, unless it was dissolved earlier. The small size of this chamber was a guarantee of calm. Deputies were elected by universal suffrage, one for each constituency. This district-based system was preferred to proportional representation by department, which was thought to offer too many opportunities to strong oppositions. After the empire was proclaimed later in 1852, deputies were granted an allowance of 2,500 francs a month when Parliament was in session. The government reserved the complete power to change constituency boundaries as it saw fit. A circular to prefects did not disguise the advantages of such a system: "You should understand how much the intelligent or not so intelligent division of constituencies will influence the results of elections."

The mechanism for the drafting of legislation was a true masterpiece, resting as it did upon the principle of keeping the work of Parliament to a minimum and placing it under close supervision. Only the president of the Republic had the right to propose legislation; Parliament had no initiative in the matter. The plan for a law started with the relevant ministry and passed on to the Council of State, which had the responsibility for the preparation of a draft text. This was then sent to the legislature, where it was discussed within an ad hoc committee of seven members appointed by the legislature. The committee could submit amendments to the Council of State, which either accepted or rejected them; there was no appeal against its decision. The final text then came before a plenary session of the legislature, which either passed it or rejected it *en bloc*. The president and vice-presidents of the legislature were appointed by the government. It held one session a year, lasting three months; it sat in public, but only the official minutes written up by its president could be published.

Alongside the legislature was a Senate of 150 life members: some sitting there by right (cardinals, marshals, admirals), others chosen by the head of state "from among men known for their name or their wealth, their talent or their brilliance of service." A salary of 30,000 francs could be granted to them, and after the proclamation of the empire this became the rule. The Senate had the special role of examining behind closed doors any laws passed by the legislature, to ensure that it was not "contrary to the Constitution, religion, morality, freedom of worship, freedom of the individual, civil equality, the inviolability of property, the irremovability of the magistrature." It could also issue *sénatus-consultes* that interpreted or supplemented the Constitution, although these were subject to approval by the president of the Republic.

The people could be consulted by plebiscite, when they would be asked to answer "yes" or "no" to a question or questions posed by the president of the Republic.

A number of decrees subsequently completed the work of the Constitution. Two new ministers were created: a minister of state responsible for liaison between the government and the two chambers, since individual ministers never took part in their sessions; and a police minister responsible for the implementation of "laws concerning the national police, national security, and internal peace." Maupas was placed in charge of this new ministry, his inspectors being sent to the provinces "to ensure that the victory of order over anarchy bears fruit," to stimulate the zeal of prefects, and even to report those who seemed too halfhearted.

The National Guard was dissolved. The principle behind it was supposedly maintained, and the possibility remained of reviving it "where it is considered useful for the defense of public order." But in fact it would never reappear.

Bars were subject to licensing by the prefect, because they could always become "a hotbed of political propaganda." The last remaining Trees of Liberty were cut down. The 15th of August, the anniversary of the birth of Napoléon I, was declared a public holiday.

Here at last was the regime of Haussmann's dreams. As prefect for Bordeaux, in the mild Gironde region that had become his homeland by adoption, he could pass his life with his family, befriend the local notables and top wine merchants, sip the *grands crus* as a true connoisseur. What more could he ask of life? To increase his property, to embellish metropolitan Bordeaux with some well-designed public works, perhaps one day to crown his prefect's career by moving to Lyons: such were the limits of his ambition. It was not long before the return of the empire put quite a different complexion on things.

·II·

PARIS, THE CITY WITH ALL THE PROBLEMS

8

The Frenetic Growth

of a Capital

AT THE HEART of the French problem one always finds Paris. Perhaps the French are so used to it that they have stopped noticing. The period from the revolutionary days of 1789 to the crushing of the Commune in 1871 was deeply marked by the economic and political weight of the capital. Paris and France—but so often also Paris against France, or France against Paris. Born out of rioting in Paris, the July Monarchy foundered in another bout of Parisian rioting. The Second Republic that succeeded it lived according to the rhythm of the *journées* and the moods of Paris. When Louis-Napoléon took the reins of power and assumed control of Paris, he constantly examined, pampered, and ill-treated the huge city that had never really been calmed or brought into line. Certainly there was no lack of fine minds predicting catastrophe, calling for reforms and a reorganization of Paris as well as a better balance in the country as a whole. Each regime had tried to do something, the July Monarchy like the others. But it had not been enough.

Paris was a kind of myth, whose growth had accompanied the growth of France. Until the collapse of the Carolinigian Empire it had been only rarely the seat of power. Then it became identified with the drive of the Capetian monarchs to assemble an ideal France around themselves, its later contours following the accidents of dynastic succession and war until the Revolution and empire stretched them to their greatest extent. Capital city, concentrating ever denser, ever more complex administrative machinery, seat of political and therefore financial and military power, Paris inevitably became the country's main consumer market, main pool of labor, main industrial region.

It also saw itself as the center of French intellect and taste. "His glib tongue is all due to Paris": the Parisians' sense of superiority did not appear only yesterday. Growing faster than the rest of France, Paris has been the focal point of all ambitions. Like Balzac's Rastignac, people have come to Paris to make their fortune—or to lose body and soul in the vast ocean of the Paris streets, in the name of a freedom unknown in the provinces. For moralists, a corruption of standards, a modern Babylon. How could a better balance be struck between the provinces and the capital? How could Paris itself be saved from asphyxiation?

Maxime Du Camp—one of the best minds of the age, who bore active witness to the 1848 Revolution, the Second Republic, the Second Empire, and the beginnings of the Third Republic—set out to describe the city in a vast book *Paris: Its Structure, Functions, and Life to 1870*. This Parisian bourgeois covered a great deal of ground in his travels and observations. A friend of noted intellectuals, he also had an excellent grasp of economic, financial, and psychological realities. But though generally measured in style, he could not refrain from beginning his anatomy of the great city with a lyrical flight of fancy: "In my life as a traveler, I have seen many capitals: ones that are being born, ones that are growing, ones that are in full bloom, ones that are dying, ones that are dead. But I have not seen another city that gives such a vast impression as Paris does, nor one that gives such a clear sense of an indefatigable, nervous, living people, equally active beneath the light of the sun or the glow of gaslight, panting for its pleasures and its business, endowed with perpetual motion." The bluish smoke escaping from 500,000 chimneys hovered over rooftops, enveloping the city in a haze, distorting its buildings in a tangled confusion.

The capital was devouring France. Du Camp evokes March 1814, when the coalition of Russians, Prussians, and Austrians reached Paris. Two generals—the Austrian Schwartzenberg and the Russian Osten-Sacken—looked down from Montmartre upon the city lying at their feet. "The Russian, who carried the memory of Moscow in his breast, exclaimed: 'So there is Paris at last, and we'll be able to burn it!'—'Hey! Why burn it?'—'To take our revenge on France and to punish it.'—'That's the last thing you should do,' Schwartzenberg continued, pointing to the sleeping colossus, 'the very last thing. It will anyway be eaten up by chancre.' It was a dire prediction, but it did not seem irrational. With its insatiable growth, which demanded, sucked in, and absorbed everything, France really did look hydrocephalous. The head was no longer in proportion to the body."[1]

The very excess of Paris was sapping not only the vitality of France but its own vitality as well. In the fever of growth, its misfortune was not to have suffered such disasters as the Great Fire of London of 1666 or the Lisbon Earthquake of 1757, which allowed a more rational reconstruction on cleared space. Paris, by contrast, kept changing, raising its heights, filling empty spaces, patching up, trimming bits off the street, off gardens, yards, and marshes; the city expanded on top of itself. The task of controlling such a monster discouraged the strongest-willed people. For a regime eager to have peace and quiet, would not the best solution be to let the Parisians get on with it? No, replied Maxime Du Camp, for "Parisians in Paris are like the Hebrews in the desert; they would like manna to fall from heaven. Here, heaven is the public authority. They make fun of it, heap accusations on it— but at the slightest mishap they go running to it. If the bread is bad or the waters of the Seine are cloudy, if carriages have trouble moving, cabmen are impolite, the wine is adulterated or the dogs are unmuzzled, if the cafés sell bad-quality beer—then those in authority must take pity and protect us."[2]

WALLS AND BARRIERS

❧ To understand Paris, it is necessary to remember that it was a walled city. Even today nothing has really changed: the *boulevard péripherique*, which has taken the place of the last city wall, is a more effective barrier than the strongest of the old great walls. In the third century, following the barbarian invasions, a fortified enclosure was hastily thrown up around the Île de la Cité. Later, in the late twelfth and early thirteenth centuries, Philippe-Auguste built the first systematic wall and asserted Paris as the capital of the Capetian kingdom. On the right bank, the wall finished in 1190 absorbed the villages of Saint-German-l'Auxerrois, L'Abbé, and Thibourg, as well as Les Champeaux (the site of the future Halles) together with the adjacent vineyards and meadows. On the left bank, the works finished in 1210 left the abbey of Saint-Germain-des-Prés outside the walls but drew in Mount Sainte-Geneviève. At that time Paris had a population of fifty thousand and a surface area of 675 acres.

But from then on the city never ceased to grow more dense. Open spaces, gardens, and wasteland became increasingly rare; houses squeezed next to one another. By 1329 the population was close to 200,000. In a new surge of growth on the right bank, Charles V had a wall built from the gates of the Louvre (a mighty fortress) and what is now the Place du Théâtre-Français along to the Place des Victoires, rue du Mail, and rue d'Aboukir, then down the line of today's *grands boulevards* to the Bastille, Paris's defensive barrier on the east. Six fortified gates, or *bastides*, protected the entrances to rue Saint-Antoine, rue du Temple, rue Saint-Martin, rue Saint-Denis, rue Montmartre, and rue Saint-Honoré.[3] Constructed between 1356 and 1383, the wall of Charles V enclosed an area of 1,084 acres. It marked the boundaries of *le vieux Paris* of the nineteenth and twentieth centuries, the central areas of the capital that were the prime target for the urban transformation already outlined in the late eighteenth century and later accomplished by Haussmann and Napoléon III.

One hundred and fifty years after Charles V, the wall was outflanked. Henri II prohibited construction in the area outside the walls in order to promote the smooth administration of the capital, vitality in the provinces, and the defense of public morals. He was the first French sovereign to speak a coherent language about the problem of Paris. But nothing could stop the growth of the capital, and Henri II was forced to accept the futility of his prohibition and to allow the illegal extensions to be incorporated into the city. In 1551 he admitted his failure before the municipality of Paris: "We have realized that, for the embellishment and comfort of our said city that is the capital of our kingdom, it would be most right and proper to enclose the said areas within it by means of good walls, ditches, and ramparts."

Louis XIII and Louis XIV continued in the same vein. Louis XIII extended the wall of Charles V on the right bank, incorporating the Palais Royal district and the area around the faubourg Saint-Honoré, then had large boundary stones planted at the outer edge of the *faubourgs*: it was forbidden to build anything beyond. Louis XIV pushed them farther back in 1672, disguising his impotence with a display of grandiloquence: "In the manner of the ancient Romans, whose religion did not allow them to touch the sacred foundations of the city of Rome or to carry them farther except to those who had enlarged the empire through their conquests, the king, having expanded the limits of his states beyond the Rhine, the Alps, and the Pyrenees, has felt justly able to order the enlargement and embellishment of the capital of his realm." At the death of Louis XIV, Paris had half a million inhabitants.

Louis XV extended the capital twice more: in 1724 and 1765. And in 1785, Louis XVI authorized the construction of a new and larger wall, the so-called Barrier of the Farmers-General. This would be the last new demarcation until 1859–1860, when the city limits received their final extension (barring a few minor rectifications) under Napoléon III and the administration of Haussmann. The Paris enclosed by the Barrier of the Farmers-General was the Paris of the Revolution and the Empire, the bustling and industrious Paris of King Louis-Philippe, the Paris that Louis-Napoléon Bonaparte set himself the task of improving before he extended its area once more.

The Farmers-General wall, approximately twenty feet high, had no military value but made it easier to levy tolls at the entrance to Paris, as well as to keep an eye on comings and goings between town and country through its fifty-four gates. The construction of this barrier angered Parisians at the time, for the tolls that each year raised the handsome sum of 28 to 30 million livres meant an increase in the price of necessities. In the days preceding the revolution in 1789, just before the storming of the Bastille, Parisians attacked the barrier and set fire to it at many points. Victor Hugo alluded to this event in a famous acrostic:

Le mur murant Paris
Rend Paris murmurant.*

The extension of the Farmers-General wall testifies to the growth of Paris in the eighteenth century. *Vieux Paris* survived, more jumbled than ever, on the Île de la Cité and in the areas bordering the Seine. Louis XV undertook to complete the massive redevelopment of Île Saint-Louis begun under Louis XIII, but he could not successfully conclude the vast projects that had been haunting him. If the city changed, this was due not to the king but to the pressure of circumstances and a socioeconomic evolution.

The center of Paris remained the preserve of workmen, artisans, and the poorest layers of society. On the Place de Grève, now the Place de l'Hôtel-de-Ville, casual laborers gathered each morning with nothing to offer but the strength of their arms for construction work or the loading and unloading of boats. They lived nearby. The Marais, chief of the *beaux quartiers* under Louis XIII and Louis XIV, was now considered too close to the popular districts adjoining the Hôtel de Ville. After 1750 its well-off inhabitants began to move to the areas around the Luxembourg, the Palais Royal, and Concorde, leaving room for artisans gradually to take over the old town houses. The construction of the Odéon Theatre on the site of the Hôtel de Condé, between 1786 and 1790, gave birth to a new district; meanwhile, on the right bank, ten thousand houses sprang up between 1760 and 1783 in the Saint Honoré and Palais Royal areas.

The distinction between the *beaux quartiers* and the others became more pronounced, but one cannot yet speak of spatial segregation. In the Paris of

---

*The wall walling Paris / Causes Paris to murmur.

Louis XV and Louis XVI, different social groups were still more superimposed than juxtaposed to one another. Shops typically occupied the ground floor, nobles or rich bourgeois lived on the first floor, tradesmen or artisans on the second, manual workers, journeymen, or apprentices on the third. Domestics and newcomers from the provinces without a steady job were to be found on the fourth floor.

CLEARING AND EMBELLISHING

≈ Everyone suffered with irritation the problems posed by the constant growth of Paris. In 1749, Voltaire remarked: "We have in Paris the wherewithal to purchase kingdoms; every day we see what our city lacks and are content to grumble about it. Within less than ten years Paris could be made the wonder of the world. It would be the glory of the nation and an immortal honor to the city trades; it would encourage all the arts, attract foreigners from the far end of Europe, and instead of impoverishing the state would make it wealthier. It is time for those in charge of Europe's most opulent capital to make it more convenient and more magnificent."

Voltaire protested against the concepts of city planning held by sovereigns in the seventeenth and eighteenth centuries, which came down to little more than the laying out of large open squares. After Henri IV and the Place des Vosges, Louis XIV opened the Place des Victoires and the Place Vendôme, Louis XV the Place de la Concorde. The general public, like Voltaire, rebelled against an outmoded ideology that attached greater importance to royal swagger than to the everyday lives of citizens. Less and less did people understand why it should be impossible for Paris, in a whirl of renovation and development, to outstrip major provincial towns such as Bordeaux, Lyons, Nimes, Poitiers, or Nantes, which the eighteenth century transformed for the greater happiness of those living at the time—and of French people living today.

While those provincial cities were modernizing, the capital became mired in its problems. There were a number of reasons for this development gap. In the provinces, the sovereigns of the "administrative monarchy"— Louis XIV, Louis XV, and Louis XVI—put in place a series of great administrators, the royal *intendants*, ancestors of the prefects who had a power that the latter never possessed. With an extensive authority in financial, administrative, and judicial spheres as well as in police matters, they sometimes remained in office for decades and were thus able to carry out truly long-term projects. This was quite different from the situation in Paris, where the municipality came up against two representatives of the king: the *intendant* of the Île de France region, who had a chiefly decorative function, and the *lieutenant de police*, whose energy was focused on keeping the peace in a restive capital. Everyone talked of transforming Paris, but no one was officially responsible for it—and doubtless in the end no one really wanted to face the unpopularity it might arouse.

Furthermore, although the capital concentrated a large share of the national wealth, this benefited Parisians (or certain Parisians) more than it did the city. Since the Paris budget was not clearly separate from the central state budget, its credit could be and was used to help the latter offset its deplorable reputation. The practice of issuing "Hôtel de Ville bonds," for the profit of the Royal Treasury but presentable to the city of Paris, did not leave much latitude for the municipality to carry out large-scale public works, even if anyone had wished to do so.

THE ARTISTS' PLAN

❧ At the end of the eighteenth century, Paris had a population of approximately 650,000, a fortieth of the French total. It was by far the largest city in France, and second in Europe only to London (which already had more than a million).

Although the Revolution was scarcely propitious for the execution of major civic projects, it did give the necessary impetus to projects for the transformation of Paris. In the revolutionary assemblies there were people concerned about the state of the capital. The decrees of the Convention nationalizing the property of clergy and religious orders, and subsequently also of émigrés, made it easier to carry out such major works. For the fact that the public authorities now disposed of a large part of the land in Paris removed many obstacles to systematic development and the opening of new roads.

Before throwing itself into the great work of modernization for which enlightened opinion had been appealing, the Convention thought it necessary to appoint a special commission to draw up a program. This was the "Artists' Commission," so called because it consisted of artists, architects, engineers, and scholars.

The first priority for the Artists' Commission was the crossing of Paris by road. A first route from east to west would start from the Place de la Révolution (now the Place de la Concorde), run along the Jardin des Tuileries to the colonnade of the Louvre, then through the Saint-Germain-l'Auxerrois church (which would have to be demolished) and on to the Bastille. A second route from north to south was not agreed upon, however, as the commission could not decide among the various possibilities.

The artists who made up the commission had three concerns: to cut through the huge spaces occupied by convents; to enlarge the winding airless streets; and to plan embellishments that would be carried out "when circumstances became favorable." The commission planned a number of new roads leading off the east-west artery, within the walls of the Farmers-General. This first program for development of the capital, coming after the projects drawn up by the architect Patte between 1765 and 1789, envisaged the creation of roads in the area around Place Vendôme, in the Bastille district, and on the left bank between L'Observatoire, Val de Grâce, and Luxembourg; the destruction of the Grand Châtelet, the Temple, and the area around Place Saint-Sulpice, in order to show off Servandoni's façade to greater effect; and the construction of Les Halles in the area now known by that name and the opening of a road to serve them (the present rue Rambuteau).[4] It fell to Napoleon to put into operation the first building sites.

THE FIRST EMPIRE

❧ The first Napoleon was one of the great urbanists of Paris, and in many respects Napoléon III did no more than follow in his uncle's footsteps. The work accomplished under the First Empire is impressive, even though it lacked sufficient funds or a leading civil servant of Haussmann's stamp.

A number of streets were opened on the left bank—rue des Ursalines, rue Clovis, rue du Val-de-Grâce, rue d'Ulm—and the upper part of rue Soufflot was cleared. But it was mainly in the heart of Paris, along the Seine, that Napoléon I concentrated his efforts. Stone embankments were built all around the Île de la Cité and on the left bank between the rue du Bac and the Champ de Mars. On the right bank, the river was lined with a stone wall from the Pont Neuf to the heights of Chaillot.

Napoleon also set about increasing the number of bridges. To the eight already in place (Pont de la Tournelle / Pont Marie, the four bridges serving the Cité, the Pont Neuf built under Henri III and Henri IV, the Pont Royal commissioned by Louis XIV, and the Pont de la Concorde ordered by Louis XVI and completed under the Constituent Assembly with the help of stones from the demolished Bastille), the empire added another four: a footbridge linking the Île de la Cité and the Île Saint-Louis; two stone bridges, the Pont d'Austerlitz and the Pont d'Iéna; and the Pont des Arts, built in iron and reserved for pedestrians, between the Louvre and the Collège des Quatre Nations.

The transformation of the area around the Tuileries began in 1810, with work on the north wing of the Louvre that began at the Marsan pavillion. The Place du Carrousel was enlarged and adorned with a triumphal arch that served as a new gateway to the Château des Tuileries. Napoleon also ordered the rebuilding of the Grande Galérie that joins the Louvre to the Tuileries on the Seine side.

Without a doubt, the most important project was the new rue de Rivoli. The first stretch, from the Place de la Concorde, presented few difficulties as there were only gardens and convents between the Tuileries Palace and rue Saint-Honoré. By the time the empire was proclaimed in 1804, the sections running from the Passage du Manège to rue Saint-Florentin had already been completed, as had the rue de la Castiglione and rue de la Paix. A whole district sprang up. On the site of the old Convent of the Assumption and its adjoining gardens, fine buildings lined the new rues Mont-Thabor, Mondovi, and Cambon. The westward shift of the *beaux quartiers* was accelerating and taking shape. After 1804 the rue de Rivoli was driven on to the area around the Tuileries Palace. But then the lack of funds stopped further work. "Let's postpone it until another time," Napoleon is supposed to have said. "Architecture has often been the scourge of states. Architects ruined Louis XIV."

Over the years, however, the emperor repeated many of the traditional failings and concentrated more and more on monumental structures to perpetuate his own glory. One scheme, for instance, was to add a Greek façade to the Palais Bourbon that would be more in line with the tastes of the day and match the one on the Madeleine Church across the way. The palace interior had already been altered in 1796 to provide a hall for meetings of the Council of Five Hundred and later for the legislature under Napoleon. The Senate held its sessions at the Luxembourg Palace, where Chagrin meticulously created a chamber by dismantling the garden façade stone by stone and reconstructing it a few yards farther out.

Work was done to restore monuments that had suffered the effects of time or been left neglected in the revolutionary turmoil: for example, Porte Saint-Denis and Porte Saint-Martin, or Notre Dame cathedral. The imperial administration, in occupying the old town houses of the aristocracy, assured their later upkeep and maintenance. Thus the war minister established his office in the Hôtel de Brienne, where it can also be found today. The Navy

Ministry occupied the Furniture Storehouse at Place de la Concorde. The Interior Ministry took possession of the Hôtel de Brissac, while the Justice Ministry moved into the Hôtel de Choiseul at Place Vendôme and the Ministry of Religion into the Hôtel de Soyecourt at rue de l'Université. The Police Ministry took over the Hôtel de Juigné at the corner of Quai Malaquais and the rue des Saints-Pères.

Napoleon could not rest with such minor works. "Paris is short of buildings. It must be given more. There are occasions when twelve kings may find themselves together. They need palaces and everything that goes with them."[5] In addition to the work on the Madeleine and the construction of the triumphal Arc du Carrousel, a Stock Exchange was built on the model of a Greek temple. But the emperor did not personally see the completion of any of these projects. He had greater luck in the case of the redesigned public squares. He created the Place de la Bastille, decorated Place Vendôme with a column to replace the equestrian statue of Louis XIV that the Revolution had sent to the smelter's, and commissioned the Fontaine du Palmier on the Place du Châtelet, as well as the water tower on what is today the Place de la République. Napoleon dreamed of making Paris "something fabulous, colossal and unprecedented, whose institutions would be a match for its population";[6] and he planned to crown the heights of Chaillot with a huge edifice that would be the palace of the king of Rome, or his own residence in retirement. This extraordinary project, with a façade of 1,312 feet, never saw the light of day; it was swept away together with the empire.

Many of Napoleon's designs suffered from the failure to complete the projects of which they were part. The triumphal Arc du Carrousel, deprived of the setting of the Tuileries Palace (which burned down during the Commune of 1871) and isolated in the middle of a huge empty space, is no longer of the right scale. Similarly the rue de Rivoli, between Concorde and the Tuileries Palace, long remained a desert. As Chateaubriand notes, builders were not exactly lining up to start work: "In the winter of 1813 to 1814 I took an apartment in rue de Rivoli, opposite the first gate of the Tuileries Palace. Even by then, all you could see in that street were the arcades built by the government and a few houses rising here and there with their side teeth of waiting stone."[7]

If we are to believe what he later claimed in Saint Helena, the emperor personally had more taste for functional works than for illusory testimony to a misguided magnificence. "Everything in the character and tastes of the nation is provisional and wasteful. I often opposed festivities that the city of Paris wanted to put on for me. . . . In order to know how difficult it is to do good, you must have done as much as I have. Sometimes I needed all my strength to succeed. . . . When it was a question of extending the Tuileries garden, of improving the sanitation in certain areas, of clearing some sewers, of doing something in the public good that was not of direct interest to a few private individuals, I needed all my personality, to write six or ten letters a day and to fly into a temper. That is how I used as much as 30 million francs on sewers that no one will ever credit me with."[8]

These remarks made in exile show the extent to which the redevelopment of Paris was a matter for the prince. Everything rested on the emperor's shoulders. He was himself partly responsible for this, because he increased the state's control over the city by depriving it of a mayor and installing two high-ranking civil servants answerable to himself alone, the prefect for the Seine and the Paris chief of police. Since development work in the city had to be decided by the central government, and since its efforts tended to lapse into inertia for want of any broader enthusiasm among the public, it is hardly surprising that ten letters and the emperor's fury might be required to unblock a single sewer. The prince needed time and perseverance: "If heaven had given me just twenty years and a little free time, people would have looked in vain for Paris. No trace of it would have been left, and I would have changed the face of France."[9] Napoléon III pondered the lessons as he made plans to succeed where his uncle had failed.

THE RESTORATION

The works carried out under the Restoration were mainly due to the prefect Chabrol de Volvic, who, though sharply criticized by the former émigrés around Louis XVIII, enjoyed the king's unstinting support. On one occasion the king answered as follows the insistent calls for his dismissal: "Monsieur de Chabrol married the city of Paris, and I have abolished divorce." Charles X had the same confidence in him, and Chabrol went down in history as *the* prefect of the Restoration.

Chabrol took up where Napoleon had left off, completing the Bourse, the Saint Denis Canal, the Saint Martin Canal, the Halle aux Vins and Montparnasse Cemetery, and pursuing the work on the Madeleine Church. He also resumed construction of the Arc de Triomphe that Napoleon had scarcely begun; the project would perhaps never have been completed if skillful courtiers had not persuaded Louis XVIII to consecrate it to the glory of the duc d'Angoulême and the Spanish expedition.

Chabrol also commissioned several new bridges: the Pont de

l'Archevêché, the suspension bridge at the Allée d'Antin (which replaced the Pont des Invalides), and the pedestrian Passerelle de la Grève (on the site of the future Pont d'Arcole). These three bridges, all charging tolls, were built with a revolutionary technique involving suspension from steel cables instead of supporting pillars.

Finally, the Restoration gave new life to the plantations that had greatly suffered from the occupation of Paris by invading armies at the end of the empire. Chabrol also kept up the progress made under Napoleon with the systems of sewers and sidewalks.

THE JULY MONARCHY

≈ The July Monarchy gave Paris back its freedom. The departmental council of the Seine and the municipal councils of the arrondissements of Paris were elected by universal suffrage based on a tax qualification. Delegates from the twelve arrondissements constituted the city council. There was still no mayor of Paris, but the council elections restored a little of the importance that the empire had stripped from the Hôtel de Ville.

On June 22, 1833, the Seine prefecture was given to Charles de Rambuteau, a talented administrator who could also draw on his experience as a parliamentary deputy for his new career. According to the minister of the interior, d'Argout, the prefect was "called upon to put an important administration back on its feet, after a period in which it has been greatly neglected." "The Seine prefecture," he continued, "has almost the importance of a ministry, but patience and courage are required to set it right again." Rambuteau was successful and remained in his position until the fall of Louis-Philippe in 1848.

Rambuteau had trouble spelling his name. Prosper Mérimée claims that the prefect once called round to visit the comtesse de Montijo and, not finding her there, left his card with the additional words written on it: "I am Venus in person." Endowed with a practical and positive mind, he gave himself over to various useful accomplishments. He commissioned the prison of La Roquette, replaced the padded cells at Salpêtrière with dormitories, and began work on Lariboisière Hospital. The paving of streets made further progress, as did the building of public fountains, sidewalks, and drains. Rambuteau also supervised the leveling of the city's streets and boulevards, which were often bulging in a most unpleasant manner. On Boulevard Saint-Martin, one can still see today the opening he made in the "mound" of Bonne-Nouvelle—a disagreeable humpback right in the middle of the thoroughfare. The prefect had trees planted everywhere. Indeed, one of his grand ideas was to have a second line of trees placed along the boulevards where their width permitted it. But he had to face the complaints of shopkeepers, who accused him of causing lethal damage to their businesses.

Rambuteau completed the work on the Arc de Triomphe, the Madeleine, the Hôtel du Quai d'Orsay, Notre-Dame-de-Lorette, and the *mairies* on the Place du Panthéon and the rue de la Banque (today's *mairies* for the 5th and the 2nd arrondissements, respectively). Île Louviers, facing the tip of Île Saint-Louis, was half-destroyed to widen the fairway, while the other half was attached to the right bank where today's Boulevard Morland stretches out. The *quais* were extended from the Pont d'Austerlitz to the Grands Augustins on the left bank, and from the Arsenal to the Louvre colonnade on the right bank. The Seine was lined with stone retaining walls.

Elsewhere the first tarmac was tried on the road surfaces of the Palais Royal, and the gas supply spread through the granting of concessions to private companies. Economy, not to say parsimony, was the golden rule of Rambuteau's administration. Even hospital waste was carefully collected and used for the fattening of pigs.

The street that today bears the name of Louis-Philippe's prefect, rue Rambuteau, was the most noteworthy achievement of his long period in charge of the city administration. For the first time in the history of Paris, a decision was made not simply to straighten or widen an existing street but to cut straight into dense urban tissue. For this purpose, Rambuteau had to order a large number of compulsory purchases.

Rambuteau prepared and heralded the transformation of Paris that would be directed by Haussmann. But although the "bourgeois monarchy" laid the foundations for the larger, richer, better organized modern Paris of the Second Empire, it never really went beyond the preliminary stages. That is largely the reason why it died as it did. It proved incapable of carrying out the reforms demanded by Parisians—above all by the middle classes that constituted its political base.

9

The Splendor and
the Squalor

THE PARIS of the Restoration and the July Monarchy remained within the administrative limits laid down by the Revolution and the empire, limits at once fiscal and political. The city was surrounded by the old toll wall, an almost circular line corresponding to the outer boulevards, from Place de l'Étoile to Place de la Nation; it is the route of the metro lines from Étoile to Nation via Barbès-Rochechouart, and from Étoile to Nation via Denfert-Rochereau. More than a million people slept, worked, and lived in the tall narrow houses that lined the host of winding streets.

A few collections of historical buildings had been left behind, most of them along the banks of the Seine. The large royal squares—Place des Vosges, Place Vendôme, Place des Victoires, Place de la Concorde—ventilated the dense fabric of Paris. Along the central districts, especially toward the northwest, new housing areas were being occupied by a well-off clientele. The initial section of the rue de Rivoli opened up a magnificent perspective, still incomplete, along the Tuileries. The Champs Élysées referred only to the walkway between the Place de la Concorde (where the obelisk stood in majesty) and the Rond-Point des Champs-Élysées; the cobbled road beyond to the Arc de Triomphe was still called the chemin de Neuilly, flanked only by a few elegant houses in a country setting. The bridges of Paris, still too few in number, charged tolls that restricted their use.

The three divisions of medieval Paris could still be identified: the Town on the right bank, the Cité on the isle of the same name, and the University on the left bank. Beyond the toll barriers stretched mainly rural communes, administratively separate from the capital, which were beginning to play a role in its industrial development. Several of them housed the locomotive and freight wagon depots, the marshaling yards and railway workshops that Paris no longer had room to accommodate. These communes were themselves bordered, sometimes bisected, by the *enceinte* constructed by Thiers after 1842—a formidable wall that enabled Paris to escape a humiliating capitulation despite the hardships of the siege of 1870–1871.

THE ECONOMIC CAPITAL

≈ Paris was becoming the center of French economic life, the kind of phenomenon not seen before in the history of the country. By 1847, according to the *Statistique de l'industrie à Paris*, it was "the center where numerous communication routes came to an end, where large companies usually had their business headquarters, and where foreign firms opened their branches."[1]

One indisputable sign of the development of the Parisian economy was the sharp rise in the number of steam engines: 1,076 more authorized between 1830 (when the total stood at 131) and 1849, not including a little more than 500 steam boilers for the soaring needs of refineries, laundries, and industrial cleaning plants. On the eve of the 1848 revolution, the capital accounted for a fourth of all French exports. From the early 1820s to 1847, the last year of the July Monarchy, the value of exports from Paris increased threefold to 180 million francs—its share of the French total rising from 11 percent in 1821 to 23 percent in 1847.

Of course, the expansion did not take place without conflicts. The economic crisis of 1830, far from abating with the coronation of Louis-Philippe, was further intensified by political troubles and uncertainties. A large number of reputedly sound businesses went under, including one of the leading banks, Laffitte. In 1831, scarcely two thousand out of the ten to twelve thousand workers in the Paris bronze industry were employed, and even they were on a two-day or three-day week. The long-awaited upturn certainly took its time, becoming general only in 1834, but then it turned swift and healthy. The commercial dynamism of the capital rested upon the production of quality goods with an image of good taste, which flowed out to the provinces and abroad even in times of crisis—for the richest customers are always less affected than the poorest by difficulties in the economy.

Together with the large firms, small-scale craftsmen and shopkeepers made up the basic fabric of the Parisian economy. We should remember that, when the contemporaries of Louis-Philippe and Balzac talked of "the workshop and the store," many shopkeepers were also craftsmen, and many of the goods they sold were produced on the spot. It is not surprising, then, that many workers tried to cross the class barrier and set up their own business: "As soon as workers had some savings . . . , they hurried to open a shop that would make their fortune."[2] No prejudice stood in their way—on the contrary, public opinion was very pleased about the porousness of social boundaries.

The primacy of Paris was also based upon innovation. Together with the neighboring communes of the Seine department, it was the country's leading area for novelty and experiment. Paris was the birthplace of the artificial soda industry, gas lighting, commercial fertilizer, starch production, and the clothing industry. The latter revolutionized workers' living conditions by making it possible for them to buy new clothes—little more than a dream just a generation before. The Environmental Health Board (Conseil de salubrité), which authorized the introduction of new machinery, was particularly well placed to observe trends: "Do people not know that nearly all of today's large-scale industries started out or improved their position in this department? That often the initial experiments were carried out here, although the high price of raw materials, fuel, and labor could not offer the best chances of success and sometimes forced manufacturers to take their industry to parts of France with a better share of the material means of economic production?"[3]

To the surprise of many French people and even Parisians, this city of business, offices, and finance became the industrial capital of the country. By 1845 the president of the Paris court dealing with trade disputes could state as an obvious fact: "It is the center of all banking and financial operations, the registered location of all the large industrial associations, the most opulent city in the realm, and the one with the most manufacturing." And on the eve of the 1848 crisis, Émile Pereire could declare before the Northern Railways Board: "Paris is the principal manufacturing city in the kingdom."

This remarkable expansion was due to the sudden explosion of ingenuity, know-how, and enterpreneurship among the population of Paris. It did, of course, have the country's main reserves of labor as well as skills and capital with a long history behind them. But it was still a break with traditional caution that merchants, shopkeepers, even civil servants, should launch into new businesses and risk their inheritance on industrial ventures. The subjects of King Louis-Philippe were convinced that, in driving Charles X from power and thwarting his attempts to restore the noble elite, they had created the conditions for true equality that allowed everyone to chance their luck.

The *Journal des Débats* of April 15, 1839, declared: "Since 1830 there has been only one race, one nation in France. All French people are now truly equal before the law. The poor classes know that they are assured of this conquest."

SOCIAL CLIMBING

Everyone believed in social climbing, and thousands of individuals or families experienced it every day. In *Les Deux Parvenus*, serialized by the *Journal des Débats* in 1837–1838, the author, Frédéric Soulié, put the following words into the mouth of a wealthy man in the construction business: "It's been the story for all of us. . . . I started learning my trade by helping masons." In 1845 a letter from the Seine Employers' Federation reported that of 220 employers, two-thirds had been workers twelve years before. The upward mobility open to everyone was becoming an article of faith: "Anyone in the lower classes who has intelligence and honesty enters the ranks of the bourgeoisie along with his family, and he remains there with his family unless the spirit of idleness and dissipation later undoes the labor of activity and thrift. . . . The bourgeoisie constantly recruits among the people; new bourgeois families are constantly appearing."[4]

The *Journal des Débats* of November 29, 1837, saw this mobility as the strength of modern society: "Everyone is constantly moving up or moving down." For Tocqueville this was the essence of democracy: "Just as there are no longer poor breeds, there are no longer rich breeds; the rich daily emerge from the mass and ceaselessly return to it."[5]

The *notables* of the Parisian bourgeoisie had nearly all experienced a rapid ascent. Traditionally this happened by stages, from one generation to the next. But now the main factor in success was individual worth, exercised in the most diverse careers. Newcomers held the stage at every level. Shortly after the July Revolution, in a letter that he sent in November 1830 to the mayors of the Paris arrondissements, the prefect for the Seine announced that the king might be organizing festivities at the palace that winter, and added: "On this supposition you will doubtless find it appropriate . . . to draw up in advance a list of the persons in each arrondissement who might be allowed the honor of receiving the king's invitation. Some outstanding merit, honorably acquired, a justly celebrated name: such are . . . the conditions which, together with an honorable life, should direct you in the choices to be made. Would you kindly point out to me, among the magistrates, landowners, bankers, stockbrokers, notaries, lawyers, manufacturers, military officers, artists, and literary people resident in your arrondissement, the names of five or six of the worthiest in their profession."[6]

In his *Mémoires*, Rambuteau writes of a visit by the comte de Paris and the duchesse d'Orléans to the Cail and Derosne workshops. "I led the comte de Paris into a dark corner and said to him: 'Sire, it was from here, twenty-three years ago, that M. Cail started out a mere fitter and went on to head the great factory where he employs fifteen hundred workers.'"[7] The business, created in 1818 by Charles Derosne, the son of a Parisian pharmacist, had begun on a small scale with the production of distillation equipment for the sugar industry. Cail, having joined as a penniless ordinary worker in 1824, became foreman, then took a share in the business, and finally, in 1836, added his name to that of Derosne. From 1834 the company expanded under his influence and turned to the production of material for the railways; a first batch of locomotives was completed in 1844. Showing inventiveness and practical sense, Cail became one of the richest men of his generation.[8]

Another example of social ascent was Benoît Véro. He was the son of a miserly pork butcher who even charged him for his board. In 1807, Benoît married a Parisian caterer's daughter who inherited 40,000 francs from her parents. The couple succeeded brilliantly and by 1840 had increased their fortune to 800,000 francs. Véro was proud of his humble origins. Between 1823 and 1826, in association with a fellow butcher, he had an arcade cut between the rue du Bouloi and rue Saint-Honoré that bears their two names: the *passage Véro-Dodat*. People given to cheap punning said that it was *un beau morceau de l'art* between two parts of town—that is, a fine piece of art but also a piece of streaky bacon (*un morceau de lard*). The pork butchers let them chatter away. What counted was that "their" arcade had a marble floor, and that such a well-known celebrity as the actress Rachel once came to live there. By 1837 the arcade was worth 2 million francs, a million for each of the two partners.

The influx of provincial bourgeois seeking success in the capital also played a major role in its industrial development. The story of Charles Beslay is a good illustration of this. He was the son of a leather merchant in Dinan, who had branched out into banking and public works. In 1814, after studying in Paris, Charles became a partner in his father's business, was given a share of the profits, and then in 1820 full ownership of the commercial and banking company. At twenty-five he was thus at the head of one of the principal businesses in the Côtes-du-Nord (since renamed the Côtes-d'Armor). Beslay successfully tendered to build a section of the canal from

Nantes to Brest and completed work on it in 1832. Three years later, in partnership with a civil engineer, he put in a tender for the railway from Paris to Saint-Germain-en-Laye (or in reality to Le Pecq), but his rival Pereire won the contract. "It was easy to see from the first concessions that the government was under siege," writes Beslay in his *Mémoires*. "On the pretext of giving to these operations the most serious guarantees, ministers did not want to depart from the system that led them always to rely upon high finance. . . . Faced with the bias that made each concession an unequal contest between special people [the specialists, among whom Beslay counted himself] and bankers, I gave up trying to alter the balance in my favor and began making plans to create an industrial plant." It was in the faubourg Saint-Antoine in Paris that he accordingly founded a business to produce steam engines for the navy. He was already rich; he would soon be super rich.

The historian Adeline Daumard has calculated that, of a sample of Parisian bourgeois who were rich under the July Monarchy (more than 500,000 francs at their death) and who had married after Napoleon's coup on the 18th Brumaire, 21 percent had had less than 10,000 francs and 9.8 percent less than 1,000 francs at the time of their marriage. Among merchants these proportions are even higher: 32 percent and 15 percent respectively. But they are lower in the case of civil servants. To enter public service it was necessary to belong to a family that was already comfortably off. Haussmann was a good example.

<h3 style="text-align:center">DISAPPOINTMENTS, DOWNFALLS, BANKRUPTCIES</h3>

⇌ If there were brilliant and not so brilliant successes, there were also failures, social stagnation, and downfalls. Bankruptcies were not uncommon. Sometimes they spelled the end of a life, or at least a fall to the bottom of the ladder. The two eldest sons of the wealthy Benoît Véro both went bankrupt, and when one of them remarried in 1845 he was a mere butcher's assistant. A district collector of taxes in the Seine, whose fortune of 11.4 million francs in 1823 was one of the largest in Paris, later had to go into voluntary liquidation because he had lent too much to the big property developers of the time, and they claimed to be unable to pay him back. He died in 1831. In 1845 one of his sons was an ordinary clerk on the Rouen railway, another was a noncommissioned officer in the army, and his eldest daughter was married to a subprefect in a small town in the south. The family's decline had been spectacular.

Workers who tried to climb the ladder failed more often than the children of bourgeois. Moralists suggested only one reason for this: idleness and dissipation. But official receivers saw things differently. In their view, it was a lack of sufficient training that mainly accounted for the failure of company heads; it made them imprudent, leading them to borrow from other businessmen or small finance houses at exorbitant rates of interest. Official receivers also mentioned the risky nature of many ventures, the poor commercial sense of many small Parisian firms, especially those set up by workers. "More a worker than a tradesman" was one typical judgment. Or: "Good honest worker, but illiterate, incapable of keeping the accounts or understanding his commercial position." The self-made man was often assisted by his wife, who was generally better educated because of her higher social origin; upwardly mobile men married above their station.

Among rich people, bankruptcy was sometimes a testing episode that opened new paths on the road to success. The banker Jacques Laffitte went bankrupt, started a new business, again went bankrupt, then started up once more with greater success. Honorably to overcome such an ordeal could itself help the victim to bounce back. The founder of the Fould Bank in France, Berr Léon, went bankrupt in 1811. Stubborn and hardworking, he kept the trust of his friends and main partners because of the correctness he showed in winding up his business. He resumed his brokerage activities, won back his reputation in 1825, and was permitted to open a banking house again. The Maison Fould emerged from the desert stronger and better armed against difficulties. Berr Léon's younger son, Bénédict—later known as Benoît—became one of the leading bankers in the market; he successfully joined the adventure of the railways, shared the government loan market with the Rothschilds and other friendly (often Jewish) banks, and entered politics. His younger brother, Achille, joined the Jockey Club and became keeper of the nation's purse; he formed an alliance with the duc de Morny, gave financial assistance to Louis-Napoléon Bonaparte when he was no more than a penniless pretender, and in 1849 was rewarded with an appointment as finance minister when the latter became prince president of the Second Republic. He was involved in all the financial ventures of the early Second Empire, left the government, then returned as finance minister advocating the strictest financial orthodoxy.[9]

WHAT MAKES PARISIANS TICK?

According to Charton's *Guide pour le choix d'un état ou dictionnaire des professions*, the second edition of which appeared in 1851, the choice of a profession should fulfil three conditions: "First, it should procure what is necessary for the needs of life, provide the means to start a family . . . and to save for adequate comfort in retirement. Second, it should encourage the use of the faculties, . . . allow the requisite leisure to relax and cultivate the mind. . . . Third, it should be useful to society." The economist Jean-Baptiste Say, in his *Traité d'économie politique*, added a fourth criterion: "In the pleasure or displeasure of a profession should be included the respect or lack of respect that accompanies it. Honor is a kind of wage that counts among the profits of certain professions."[10]

The situation of the salaried employee did not earn much respect because it was seen as a form of dependence. French people, especially Parisians in the time of Louis-Philippe, wanted to be independent. The *Livre des cent et un*, a faithful mirror of the opinions of the age, asserts this as a self-evident fact: "In our century, independence is one of life's basic needs." It was a different matter for workers, of course, who had to rely upon their employer's goodwill to cover their daily necessities. But the civil servant or the engineer? People generally looked down upon employees in lower or even middle grades; only high-ranking civil servants were both respected and feared. As a subprefect, Haussmann was under the heel of *marquises* and other wives of prominent figures, who used him as they might a works supervisor or gardener. Public opinion did not distinguish very clearly between engineers (even those from the major technical colleges) and foremen coming from the ranks of the working class. You gained respect only if you had graduated from the École Polytechnique itself or if you performed the functions of a company director (administrators were often also directors and therefore salaried employees).

The liberal professions were the most prestigious. The lawyer's occupation commanded everyone's respect: it offered independence and embodied a typically French cultural ideal based upon the humanities and the art of speaking well. It also had the advantage of being "a kind of candidacy and general apprenticeship for all kinds of employment."[11] After the revolution of 1830, the young Georges-Eugène Haussmann hesitated between the legal profession and a job in prefectural administration. At a time when there was no college of administration, the career of prefect usually succeeded a preliminary apprenticeship at the bar. But Haussmann had a high idea of himself and thought that his courage in the battles of the July Revolution should earn him the favor of direct entry into the administration. Although he had the support of Louis-Philippe's own eldest son, it was several months before he was finally allowed to take this exceptional route.

The idea that work was necessary and eminently dignified was gaining considerable ground. "Everywhere emulation, everywhere competition!" we can read in the *Journal des Débats* of August 19, 1834. "People wrangle over fortunes in life, fight over reputations. This society, which does not have enough places for all those competing for them, does not permit idleness but brands it with contempt. Elegant idleness is no longer an acceptable position in the world." Tocqueville predicted the coming of a society divided into three classes: "The first class will consist of the rich. The second will comprise those who, without being rich, live comfortably in all things. The third will contain those who mainly live from the work given them by the first two."[12]

WEALTH AND APPEARANCES

≈ The overall wealth of Parisians had been increasing—from 100 million francs under the Restoration to 160 million francs on the eve of the 1848 Revolution. There was a high level of debt, and many took fright as they drew a parallel between private and public debt. Balzac, for example, wrote in *Le Diable à Paris*: "When one remarks the *floating debt* of the Treasury and becomes aware of each family's floating debt modeled on that of the state, one is terrified to see that half of France is *overdrawn* on the other half." Large fortunes were more sizable and more numerous than in the past, but the main difference was the rise of medium-sized fortunes. Real estate played a major role in the enrichment of Parisians. For a shopkeeper it was a sign of social advance to buy a house in Paris; and even if this meant running up the greatest possible debt, the constant rise in housing prices under the July Monarchy enabled him to go ahead without a great many risks. Someone from the upper bourgeoisie did not need to assert himself in this way; he could buy property later in his career as head of a company, and do so to make money rather than to gain other people's respect.

Those who owned real estate owned the whole building: joint ownership was unknown. The tradesman kept only the minimum space for himself, living on the mezzanine at the back of the shop and leasing out the rest as apartments. The furnishings were sparse: just the basic bed, wardrobe, and chest of drawers, without even a chair or armchair. As retirement drew near, two or three armchairs made their appearance, together with chairs, a writing desk, and a sofa; these made it possible to receive guests somewhere other than in the bedroom. Those with the best housing were generally the construction professionals, who readily took a luxury apartment for themselves in one of the buildings they had put up and kept as their own property. This did not mean that they remained particularly attached to it, however, and they did not hesitate to sell if an opportunity arose to do so at a profit.

Receptions were a common event among public servants or large private companies that were beginning to spread their wings. The bourgeoisie sacrificed a little but not too much for the sake of appearances, in ritual objects of display such as private libraries. Many of the early tradesmen had one, used more by their children than by themselves. Like musical instruments, they were institutional accessories of the social life of the epoch. Real readers of books tended to buy few and satisfied their passion in the many reading rooms.

The bourgeoisie always tried to avoid lavish expenditure. Thrift was a cardinal virtue. Here again is Jean-Baptiste Say: "Is it lacking in thrift to spend all one's income? I think it is. Foresight requires one to take events into account."[13] Everyone in Paris wanted to be rich: "Money is necessary over and above all other things . . . public opinion forces upon us as a law that we must make our fortune quickly, by whatever route."[14] One sold things off only if driven to do so by necessity, only if the debts for which one had mortgaged one's legacy made it compulsory.

Speculation was only a marginal activity; its professionals were large shareholders who risked only a fraction of their portfolio on the Bourse. The same was true of land. Investors speculated on land for construction but did not try to profit from rising values to sell rental blocks. Most of those who bought government bonds did so for the small but secure income they provided, not as a form of speculation. The urge to get rich justified all sacrifices, but one did not risk a fortune once it had begun to mount up. Enterprise then became more reflexive, more carefully weighed. The money in one's happy possession was primarily a means to independence.

RICH AND POOR: THE FIGURES

The population of Paris was administratively divided into two categories: those required and those not required to pay a property tax in accordance with the level of their rent. Since 1825 the exemption threshold had been an annual rent of 200 francs. This did not exactly correspond to the division between rich and poor, as there were sometimes quite marked differences in rent for similar accommodations in different areas of Paris. The tax inspector for the Seine department wrote in a report dated March 31, 1829:

"One may gain an idea . . . of the ratio of the well-off section of the population to the section made up of ordinary artisans and laborers (nearly all living in poverty) and to the poor strictly so called, if one bears in mind . . . that of 224,000 households in Paris, 136,000 are in poverty and 32,000 in a state approximating to it, . . . the section of the population that is really not poor accounts for only a quarter of the total number of rentals."[15]

In 1846, according to the census, the 945,000 inhabitants of Paris were divided among 357,000 households. Yet in 1847 only 100,000 heads of households were liable for the property tax. Of a population just below a million, therefore, there were nearly 650,000 poor,[16] a huge proportion. Moreover, far from having improved, the situation had grown steadily worse during the reign of Louis-Philippe. The proportion of tax-exempt rentals had been a little less than 68 percent in 1833, and by 1846 had climbed to 72.2 percent. The same conclusions may be drawn from the record of burials: between 1839 and 1847, an average of 78.6 percent of Parisians ended their days in a pauper's grave. Under the rule of the "bourgeois monarch," the numbers living a precarious existence remained constant between 65 and 75 percent of the total population of Paris.

Who were the others? According to an industrial survey conducted in 1847 by the Paris Chamber of Commerce, 35 percent of respondents belonged to the bourgeoisie. Of these, heads of businesses dominated with 54 percent, followed by the idle rich, the *rentiers* (22 percent); the liberal professionals, employees, and civil servants made up the rest. Most of the bourgeois had a servant, usually a maid. After workers and bourgeois, in fact, domestics were the third-largest social group in the Parisian population. Statistics of the time record that in 1846, 46,000 households had one in their employ. If we consider that there were an average of four persons in each bourgeois household—the parental couple and two children living with them—the total size of the Parisian bourgeoisie must have been around 185,000, or one Parisian in six.[17]

Although men and women from all walks of life daily rubbed shoulders in the bustling Paris of Louis-Philippe, and although it was relatively easy to move from one class to another, social barriers were very high. "One cannot imagine all the courage that a man of the people had to possess to call a bourgeois of some importance simply by his name, whereas the latter began by calling the worker simply by his name," wrote Corbon in *Le Secret du peuple de Paris*. Foreigners were generally struck by the courtesy that Parisian bourgeois showed toward members of the popular classes. But they still kept their distance. Petty-bourgeois of working-class origin were often the most rigid. Having raised themselves by sheer hard work, they regarded those who remained workers as fundamentally lazy.

People generally mixed with their kind. This was especially noticeable in the world of state administrators, for whom a lack of definite training meant that patronage (that is, connections) assumed considerable importance. It can sometimes be rather tedious to read Haussmann's *Mémoires*, especially when he talks of the meetings that punctuated his administrative life, or of the family connections between so-and-so and so-and-so. But he owed his career to such networks, and it was from his circle of friends and relatives that he preferred to select the people with whom he worked.

The bourgeoisie was driven by a keen desire for education. A bourgeois wanted a classically tinged education for his sons and suspected that a purely technical schooling would be a kind of "under-instruction" designed by the ruling classes to keep him in an inferior status. When Guizot pleaded for "modern education," bourgeois opinion unanimously rejected his project. Without Latin and the humanities, no salvation.

Education was also seen as a potent factor in the progress of the poor. True, the main purpose of those who drafted the law of 1833 on primary education was to combat immorality and to teach a spirit of submissiveness. True, workers who knew how to read and write were a trump card for industry, which needed an ever-better-educated labor force. Yet there was also a desire for general advancement through education. The duc de la Rochefoucauld-Dodeauville, president of the Société pour l'instruction élementaire, said to the general meeting of the society: "Let us consider the sad condition of the poor man. All he owns is himself; his human quality is his only possession. . . . Though poor as a church mouse, he was perhaps endowed by nature with certain gifts. . . . Let us therefore teach him to seek them out, to discover them. One day perhaps these still unknown treasures will produce the wealth and glory of our fatherland." The efforts in this direction were paying off, since a local committee for primary education (there was one in each arrondissement) estimated that less than 6 percent of children in Paris received no education. Another survey showed that, of 10,000 conscripts in the Seine department, 1,289 did not know how to read or write—that is, a little less than 13 percent, compared with more than 43 percent for France as a whole.

For the *Journal des Débats* of December 4, 1834, "the charity that endeavors to prevent laziness, destitution, and immorality is worth more than the charity that takes in and cares for the victims of these three scourges." This did not rule out compassion; public charity and private charity coexisted without difficulty. Although Parisians happily accepted that their taxes should buy bread or hospital care for the poor, the age was one of philanthropy. Women in the middle and upper bourgeoisie had "their" poor. Believing in the effectiveness of individual action in all walks of life, the bourgeoisie also applied this conviction to assistance for the least privileged layers.

The reason why the well-off were prepared to give such assistance was not fear of the working classes but a wish to see them integrated into society. This was expressed in a famous article on the "barbarians" of modern times that appeared in the *Journal des Débats* on April 18, 1832: "Unhappy, suffering workers who lack any security in their lives are a sorrow, a cause of suffering, a scourge for our society. . . . The workers are outside political society, outside the city: they are the barbarians of modern societies, barbarians brimming with courage and energy who, like their precursors, must reinvigorate our society with their resources of strength and life. They must enter our society, therefore, but after they have been through the apprenticeship of owning property." The Parisians of the July Monarchy had been brought up in the philosophy of the Enlightenment and believed in social progress and fraternity among all the classes; they were, in varying degrees, tinged with utopianism and the Saint-Simonian idea that, if people hate and butcher one another, this is only because they do not know one another well enough.

SPATIAL SEGREGATION

❧ Nevertheless, a city of rich people was growing up alongside an ever more congested city of the poor, and the most conscious elements among the population were becoming alarmed at the shape of things in the capital of the country. The "spatial segregation" between rich and poor areas, for which Haussmann is so often blamed, was developing long before he took over the Paris administration.

The tax statistics confirm that this trend was already far advanced on the eve of the fall of Louis-Philippe, although bourgeois pockets still existed in the middle of the poorer arrondissements. (The numbering of the Parisian arrondissements in the following description is the one used before the reform that brought the total to the present twenty.) The most affluent arrondissements were the 1st, the 2nd, and the 10th. In 1846 the proportion of tenancies liable for the property tax was 48.3 percent in the 2nd arrondissement and 40 percent in the 1st, but the figure rose to 61.1 percent in the Chaussée d'Antin area of the 1st and was above 50 percent in Palais

Royal (2nd), Vendôme (1st), and Tuileries (1st). The poorest arrondissements were the 9th, the 7th, and the 8th; the proportion of taxable tenancies
was 19 percent in the 9th (although this rose to 22.6 percent on the Île
Saint-Louis) and 16 percent in the 7th (although 24.7 percent and 22.9 percent respectively in the Mont de Piété and Sainte-Avoye areas of the arrondissement), while in the 8th the percentage was 27.5 percent in the
Marais and ranged between 9 and 12 percent in the three other areas of the
arrondissement, Popincourt, faubourg Saint-Antoine, and Quinze-Vingts.
The contrast was very marked between the poor arrondissements in the east
and the rich ones in the west.[18] With seeming inevitability, the percentage of
taxable tenancies was steadily declining in the poor areas and arrondissements and steadily rising in the rich arrondissements.

Under the bourgeois monarchy, attempts were made to understand the
reasons for this growing segregation. Occupational specialization by area was
clearly one factor. High finance and big business were concentrated in the
1st, 2nd, and 3rd arrondissements, the activity of workshops and stores in
the heart of the right bank. The 4th arrondissement, on the right bank, was
the most commercial. The fabric trade was concentrated between the Place
des Victoires and the rue des Bourdonnais. Firms specializing in public
works, engineering companies, factories, and the wallpaper trade were the
main presence in the faubourg Saint-Antoine; leather and pelts near the little Bièvre River toward the end of the Avenue des Gobelins and in the
faubourg Saint-Marcel; breweries and refineries in the 8th (Marais, Popincourt, Quinze-Vingts) and the 12th (Saint-Jacques and Saint-Marcel). The
utopian philosopher Victor Considérant and the municipal councillor Lanquetin attacked the location of the major facilities at Les Halles and the
Bourse on the grounds that Parisians preferred to live close to their place of
work. On the left bank, where the Hôtel des Invalides, the École Militaire,
and the Institut de France scarcely drew crowds, it was apparent that construction work was making little headway.

Charles Merruau, secretary general of the Seine prefecture after 1851,
added the commonsense argument that if "everyone with something to lose"
was drifting away from the center and *vieux Paris* in general, this was partly
because of the "revolutionary and insurrectionary traditions that persisted
thereabouts." "The area near the Hôtel de Ville," he noted, "has rarely been
free of tumult." The densely populated areas of the Cité, Les Arcis, and
Sainte-Avoye (the 4th and 5th arrondissements in the time of Louis-
Philippe) had each known episodes of rioting and bloodshed, such as the
sack of the archbishop's palace, the insurrection at the Saint-Merry Cloister,

or the massacre of rue Transnonain. It was hardly surprising, then, that more and more bourgeois residents had been moving out. One of the last diehards was Victor Hugo, determined to stay in his beloved house on the Place des Vosges. His wife Adèle, terrified by the street fighting of June 1848, finally convinced him to leave for the *beaux quartiers* in the west.

The center of Paris, which for so many centuries had symbolized its economic, human, and intellectual wealth, was growing so impoverished that owners of rental buildings were seriously worried. Griolet, mayor of what was then the 5th arrondissement (the area between Les Halles and the *grands boulevards*), was well aware of these concerns: "There is a readily visible trend among the population to go and live in a different area of Paris. Heading out from the Bourse area, it moves toward Chaussée d'Antin and follows the direction of Saint-Lazare, as far as the faubourg Saint-Honoré. This truly major phenomenon, which is tending to change the center of the city, to shift its tax base, and to create an entirely new town alongside the old, is arousing justifiable fears on all sides."

In 1842, Lanquetin asked the public authorities to step in and block this geographical "shift": "The movement of the population is by now too obvious to be denied, and it is easy to see the harm it is doing to real estate property in certain areas, where the rich are replaced only by the less comfortably off, and the latter in turn by the poor. It is easy to become convinced that unless the municipal and higher levels of the state, through their policy on public thoroughfares and the creation and funding of public services in relation to buildings and monuments, constantly seek to combat this tendency to relocation within Paris—or rather this drift that is already so active and deplorable and will one day leave the southeast areas of the city without life and resources—a general upheaval will occur in property values."[19]

DOWNTOWN OVERPOPULATION AND SLUM HOUSING

❧ The departure of the rich was more than offset, numerically, by the daily influx of newcomers into the stations and then the streets of Paris. The central arrondissements were overpopulated. By 1850 the 4th arrondissement (which contained the Saint-Honoré, Halles, Louvre, and Banque de France areas) had an average population density of 344 per acre, but in Saint-Honoré and Les Halles it was as high as 405 per acre. These were saturation levels. In the 7th arrondissement, another central area of the capital (corresponding to today's 3rd arrondissement) which contained the areas of Les Arcis and Sainte-Avoye, the population density had been steadily increasing

since the early part of the century: 324 per acre in 1817, 344 in 1831, 389
in 1851.

In these parts of the city, the quality of housing suffered as a result, and
slums were a common feature. The blame for this lay with the loose regulation of construction, which permitted the most outrageous abuses. Municipal regulations on public thoroughfares limited the height of street-side
façades to 57.5 feet for the widest streets, and 38.4 feet for streets with a
width of less than 25.6 feet; these were the most numerous categories in the
older arrondissements of Paris. As to buildings overlooking the inner courtyard, the regulations stipulated that none of their façades could exceed a
height of 57.4 feet, but said nothing about the dimensions of the yards
themselves. Frégier, a head clerk at police headquarters, described the consequences: "Landlords abuse the silence of the regulations in the most deplorable manner, making the constructions in their courtyards so high that
it is not uncommon to see very small spaces surrounded by buildings of six
or seven storys."[20] The Cité area had a bleak aspect, in stark contrast with the
nearby quays and historic buildings, furrowed by streets no more than 8.2
feet wide with lofty, time-blackened constructions on either side that made
them still more damp and gloomy.

The wildly increasing density in the city center left neither the time nor
the space for the necessary amenities to be introduced there. Sewers were too
few and their capacity insufficient; sanitation in the blocks was rudimentary,
with courtyards serving as garbage dumps and latrines; the water supply system was notoriously faulty, the dirtiness of the blocks revolting. Cholera
reaped its deadly harvest mainly in the overcrowded arrondissements: 5 percent of the population in the 11th, compared with less than 1 percent in the
2nd. Municipal councillor Horace Say, in his *Études sur l'Administration de la
Ville de Paris* (1846), commented on the 1832 cholera epidemic: "The fact
that the death rate was five times higher in the packed areas of the Hôtel de
Ville and the Cité than in the open aerated district of Chaussée d'Antin is
quite striking evidence."

For lack of space, most of the housing units in the city center consisted
of one all-purpose room. Frégier again: "These dwellings are dirty, badly lit,
badly shut. They are narrow, and as parents and children live and sleep in the
same room, the resulting overcrowding is a cause of insalubrity at the same
time that it is an offense to morals." Rents were low, and landlords used this
as an argument for their failure to carry out badly needed repairs.

SLEEP MERCHANTS AND "BOARDINGHOUSES"

☞ The owners of apartment buildings sometimes turned themselves into sleep merchants, converting the rooms into dormitories and renting out beds by the night. This activity was either conducted in secret or officially authorized as "the provision of boarding." The boardinghouse was today's furnished hotel. Parent-Duchatelet—a highly reputable Parisian doctor and member of the Environmental Health Board set up by the Paris police department—examined the drains and earth closets, investigated prostitution and the terrible conditions of hygiene accompanying it, and visited a number of slums and boardinghouses. His description of them is given in a coolly clinical style: "In Paris there are thousands of individuals who have no fixed address, who lie today on one bridge, tomorrow on another, and who shelter every evening in those houses where, for a sometimes very full and most often very modest reward, they are at least given somewhere indoors where they can lie. . . . A lot of workers mostly belonging to the group of bachelors, who have not been outside the capital for ten, fifteen, or twenty years, prefer this kind of life to residence in an isolated room."

Official records show a total of 3,000 hotels and boardinghouses in Paris at that time, accommodating 35,000 to 40,000 persons a night. Some of the hotels were comfortable places of residence. But in the view of Parent-Duchatelet, the majority were "disgusting lairs where people put up for six, four, or even two sous." To see "human creatures reduced to lodging in cubbyholes of this kind, in the capital of France at that," was an unbearable sight. He gave some idea of what he meant simply by quoting the hotel inspector's report to police headquarters during the cholera epidemic of 1832.

"Rue X, No. . . . This house draws attention to itself because of its excessive dirtiness; it is a veritable focus of infection; the only people staying there are thieves, smugglers, tramps, and streetwalkers. Rue Y, No. . . . This house stands out because of its contents and its dirty state. What one sees there are not beds but disgusting pallets; animal debris, intestines, all the leftovers from a cheap eating place lie rotting in the courtyard; all the rooms open onto a corridor completely without air or light; the sinks and latrines on each floor are disgustingly filled with garbage and fecal matter. Rue Z, No. . . . The greatest filth prevails everywhere; the windows have oiled paper instead of panes; the rooms are foul; on each floor the garbage thrown onto the toilets comes back onto the staircase."[21]

Another edifying testimony comes from Doctor Henry Bayard: "In a room on the fourth floor measuring barely five square meters, I found twenty-three persons, men and children, lying higgledy-piggledy on five beds. The air in this room was so foul that I was gripped with nausea. The candle giving me light nearly went out. The shoes and clothes of these persons gave off a sharp unbearable stench that covered the other exhalations."[22]

TRAFFIC PROBLEMS

These central areas where it was no longer pleasant to live were also impenetrable to traffic, forming a kind of barrier with the other arrondissements of Paris. Already in 1819 the prefect Chabrol was writing: "Considerable work has been undertaken to embellish the capital. . . . But this city, with its wealth of historic public buildings, lacks unrestricted and convenient communications over much of its surface." Hippolyte Meynadier observed that the public thoroughfares were completely unplanned; the streets were too narrow and winding, making it very difficult to get around in "a city where each minute is counted." In 1843, in his *Études sur la ville de Paris*, Perreymond expressed concern about the congestion that was choking the center to death.

During the first half of the nineteenth century, traffic in Paris meant horse-drawn carriages, horseback riders, and pedestrians. Prefects tended to take an interest only in the problem of carriages. Here again is Chabrol: "We know from experience the road width that is absolutely necessary in Paris for traffic to move in the main areas of the city; it is enough that, with a carriage parked on either side of the street, a third should be able to pass between them." The width of most streets was no more than 23 feet, that of the main arteries rarely more than 40 feet. And a vehicle took up between 9 and 10 feet.

From the point of view of urban strategy, this situation produced nightmares for every government. Haussmann was ritually accused of wanting only to create routes for the army by means of his *grands travaux*, and although he denied that this was his sole concern he had no wish to disclaim it—on the contrary. Among his contemporaries it was a veritable obsession; two overturned carriages, a table, a few chairs, and mattresses were enough for a barricade that could hold at bay the best troops in the regular army.

The number of horse-drawn carriages on the roads of the capital strikes us as very low. In 1853, thirty years after Chabrol and in the same year that Haussmann became prefect for the Seine, Texier gave precise figures for "harnessed horses" in his *Tableau de Paris*. The total passing in a period of 24 hours was: 10,750 on the Boulevard des Italiens, 9,609 on the Boulevard

Saint-Denis, 9,070 on the Boulevard des Capucines, 7,720 on the Boulevard Poissonnière, and 5,856 on the Boulevard des Filles-du-Calvaire. The number of vehicles was smaller than the number of harnessings, because sometimes two or three horses would be attached to a heavily loaded carriage. Thus no more than 6,000 carriages passed in 24 hours on the *grands boulevards*, and as the traffic was mainly concentrated during the day (let us say, over 12 hours), this represents 500 carriages an hour on the busiest arteries. Fewer than half that number passed on the Champs Élysées, and many fewer again in streets such as Saint-Denis, Saint-Martin, Saint-Jacques, or Saint-Antoine, where there were nevertheless a good many stores.

The carriage was the most common form of traffic, but there was the horse for the very rich and shank's mare for the great majority of people. Goods were carried on men's backs or in handcarts or wheelbarrows to and from workshops or stores—as one may see even today in rue du Sentier and thereabouts, or in the twisting alleyways of third world souks. People walked to go from A to B; there were constantly people walking in Paris. When the young Haussmann was studying at the École de Droit on Mount Sainte-Geneviève, he went on foot from his family home in the faubourg du Roule: it used to take him a good hour. In the evening he made the journey in reverse, again taking an hour or more. There was no way of doing it otherwise.

The line of the Paris streets did not help. Some more or less straight ones ran from north to south: the rues Saint-Denis and Saint-Martin on the right bank, Saint-Jacques on the left bank—but one could cross the Île de la Cité only through a warren of small streets. The east-west axis was more theoretical than actual: on one side the rue Saint-Antoine, on the other the rue Saint-Honoré, and in between impenetrable labyrinths; the rue de Rivoli stopped at the Tuileries in those days. In order to picture a major through road in mid-nineteenth-century Paris, one need only imagine today's rue Mouffetard as the only way of reaching the center from the route d'Italie, passing from the Place d'Italie through the Gobelins to the Pantheon.

There was a way round, of course, following the Farmers-General wall, the outer boulevards. But with the means of transport of the time, they were too far from the center. Closer in, the *grands boulevards* were congested, inconvenient, and ended in culs-de-sac; besides, they existed only on the right bank while people on the left bank had to be content with the incipient Boulevard des Invalides and Boulevard Montparnasse.

Traffic problems grew ever worse during the first half of the nineteenth century. The spectacular increase of the Parisian population would alone explain them, for there were more people who had to move around, more activity, and more goods to be brought into the city. The rising population also meant a greater need for administrative activities, therefore more offices at the Hôtel de Ville and police headquarters, more local police stations, more premises at the Palais de Justice.

The development of a centralized state administration for France also played a role, as the Paris-based ministries were greedy for space. Already there was the problem of having to concentrate ministries and administrative centers within a limited area in order to keep the time lost on transport to a minimum. And then there were the acres upon acres required by such booming services as the mail, the telegraph, gas (where should the gasworks be located?), water (the reservoirs), and, most demanding and congesting of all, the railway.

CHOKING UP

~ At the end of the reign of Louis-Philippe, all the main railway stations familiar to us in Paris were already there. Some were in a particularly poor location; all were very badly served with urban transport.

The first railway line opened on August 26, 1837, between Paris and Saint-Germain-en-Laye (or, in reality, Le Pecq). The terminus was at the Place de l'Europe. For a moment there was a plan to bring it down to the corner of the Madeleine and rue Tronchet, but in the end the second station was built above the tracks at rue de Stockholm, so that passengers gained access to the trains by means of ramps. The third station, the Gare Saint-Lazare, joined it in 1842. The façade, with its large hall built of metal by Eugène Flachat and Alfred Armand between 1851 and 1853, was much admired. But the location was not very practicable, at the intersection of rue de la Pépinière, the narrow rue Saint-Lazare, and the dead-end rue de Rome. Only the construction of the rue d'Amsterdam in 1843 conveniently linked the station to the Clichy gate farther north (Place de Clichy).

The Gare du Nord opened for business in 1843. Three years later the tracks were covered with a large hall that looked out onto a huge courtyard with wrought-iron railings. But this courtyard led to the rue La Fayette, an impasse dominated by the bulk of Saint-Lazare prison. There was no link worthy of the name with the center of Paris. The nearby Gare de l'Est was also built into the vicinity of the Saint-Lazare prison. In 1850 the Compagnie du Chemin de Fer de l'Est unveiled its monumental vaulted hall, with a façade topped by a rose window above the entrance gallery designed by François Duquesney. It was the first station that opened directly onto the city—although for the time being this meant onto the rue de Chabrol (the section between the corner of Boulevard Magenta/rue du faubourg Saint-Denis and the rue du faubourg Saint-Martin, which today bears the name "rue du Huit-Mai-1945"). Again there was no direct link with the city center.

Work on the Gare de Lyon began in February 1847, directly opposite the Nouvelle Force prison. The Boulevard Mazas (now Boulevard Diderot) ran alongside it, giving access to the Seine at the Pont d'Austerlitz after quite a sharp bend that caused traffic jams and accidents. The building of the rue de Lyon, decided the same year, would improve the connection in the future. On the other side of the river, the Gare du Paris-Orléans (today's Gare d'Austerlitz) was separated from the heart of Paris by the opaque screen of the Jardin des Plantes. Its façade looked onto the Boulevard de l'Hôpital, which led to the Pont d'Austerlitz in the north and the Place d'Italie in the south. It was a fine bypass, merely skating *vieux Paris* without actually going inside.

The Gare de Sceaux (now the regional RER station Denfert-Rochereau) had the best location, at the Barrière d'Enfer (today's Place Denfert-Rochereau, with the rue d'Enfer leading down to the Seine), but it also had fewer trains. Like the Gare d'Austerlitz, the station was also skirted by the outer boulevards. Finally there was the Gare de l'Ouest, later to become the Gare Montparnasse, which was situated at the Barrière du Maine, with good routes to the side but no access to the inner core of Paris.

In short, everything remained to be done. In the absence of a central station, links had to be devised between the various terminuses and access created to the city center. Moreover, as no one foresaw the future explosion of railway traffic, the areas available to the stations soon proved to be much too small.

The more traditional means of transport were no better off. The large six-horse coaches ended at rue Notre-Dame-des-Victoires, where the coach station was choking to death. The age-old navigation routes were suffocating too. Wooden rafts, newcomers to the scene in the mid-sixteenth century, could not be accommodated in Paris and had to stop at the Port à l'Anglais, near Charenton, where they were reduced to smaller pieces and taken on to the Port de la Rapée, below the tracks of the Gare d'Austerlitz, the Port du Vin, the Port des Invalides, and the ports of the Saint-Martin canal. Steamboat services carried passengers daily from Paris to Saint-Cloud, Melun, and

Montereau. Hay, wheat, and wine jostled for space, while the canal banks also accommodated nineteen cold baths, four hot baths and twenty-six wash houses, not to speak of the eight watering places where horses and dogs could be bathed.

The means of communication were also cruelly short of space. The letter post carried more than 145 million items around the country, a fourth of them in the capital. The main Paris Post Office, the hub of the whole postal system with collections and deliveries seven days a week, was cooped up in a set of buildings and temporary constructions between the narrow rues Jean-Jacques Rousseau and Coq-Héron. In the view of Maxime Du Camp, the layout of the offices was such a shambles that only the porter knew all its ins and outs.

Another means of sending messages was the telegraph, its central Paris office being in rue de Grenelle. Chappe's optical system was superseded in 1846 by an electrical system, but for some time the service was reserved for use by the state. Mounting demands for it to become available to the public, as in Britain, proved unsuccessful owing to lack of space and the attitude of officialdom.

Paris was suffocating. Parisians were by definition proud of their city. The capital was "the common center where all opinions check one another out, where all forces recognize one another, where all capable people display themselves."[23] "In a way Paris represents the whole of France; it is the dazzling image of the glory of the nation's greatness."[24] But Parisian pride was combined with a malaise due both to pauperization of the ever more numerous and restive popular classes and to the poor level of urban amenities.

TRANSFORMING THE CITY

≈ Proposed for the transformation of Paris were a number of projects, some fanciful, others surprisingly modern. The word "transformation" itself was just coming into vogue, and many an individual expressed the hope of seeing a new Paris emerge from the decrepit old city that seemed to be rotting before his eyes. Improvement and transformation were one of the most fashionable topics of discussion among Parisians in the 1830s and 1840s, not disdained by elected representatives or economists, newspaper columnists or writers, Eugène Sues or Balzacs.

Among the more authoritative ideas were those of Perreymond, who insisted on the need to win back the city center. He proposed to create a new administrative and commercial development on the Île de la Cité and the Île Saint-Louis, a new Lutetia (the Roman precursor of Paris) with a kind of giant shopping center to be called the "National Bazaar."

Meynadier's idea, by contrast, was to bring order into the existing Paris through a rational program to open it up. In 1843 he collected his proposals in *Paris sous le point de vue pittoresque et monumental*: "This study will focus on a system of major new communication routes for the city of Paris; on the examination and selection of the most favorable sites for its artistic monuments and public utilities that need to be built or rebuilt." Meynadier espoused a systematic driving of straight lines through the city. Some accused him of paying too much attention to historic buildings, on the grounds that the needs of urban movement should be the one and only priority.

Lanquetin, ever the cautious manager, preferred to make use of existing roads. He therefore advocated widening the rue Saint-Denis, rue de la Cité, and rue de la Harpe—three streets adding up to a north-south route that he considered highly advantageous. Meynadier thought this plan too limited and campaigned for a north-south breach on the right bank, which would start from the Châtelet, join the *grands boulevards*, and cut straight through to the *barrières* of Saint-Denis (today's Square de la Chapelle) and Saint-Martin (Rotonde de la Villette). This was more or less the line that would eventually be taken by the Boulevard de Strasbourg and the Boulevard de Sébastopol. In an east-west direction, Lanquetin argued in 1840 for a grand "rue Louis-Philippe" from the Louvre to the Bastille. Meynadier preferred a slightly different route, running in a straight line from Saint-Germain-l'Auxerrois to the Bastille. On the left bank, Meynadier, Perreymond, and others thought of creating roads that prefigured the later rue des Écoles and Boulevard Saint-Germain.

None of the problems of Paris really defied those living at the time. But the city lacked a conductor to turn the transformation from a dream to the reality that the great majority desired. Despising the idleness inherited from the past, Parisians respected success, exalted productive labor, and believed in the superiority of French civilization as it had emerged from the Revolution. Transforming Paris was therefore feasible, so long as it was done with perseverance and clarity of ideas.

10

The Transformation of Paris: The Curtain Rises, 1849–1853

PEOPLE OFTEN used to speak of "Haussmann's *grands travaux*" at the time when he sat as prefect for the Seine. But a mere glance at the chronology shows that the works actually began in 1849. The idea of transforming Paris, systematically developed by Louis-Napoléon Bonaparte, had been carried along by the thinking of a whole century—from Voltaire through Patte to the Commission des Artistes and Rambuteau.

Louis-Napoléon, with his somewhat fanciful spirit of adventure, loved great syntheses and sweeping plans. Convinced that creative vision on a grand scale was fruitful for humanity, he could well have adopted the motto of another great utopian, Auguste Comte: "Order and Progress" (which Brazil did make its own). The transformation of Paris was, in his view, one of those projects that are capable of mobilizing a whole nation; its image of organized society moving forward for the good of all offered a political response to the challenge of economic crisis that had been the downfall of Louis-Philippe. The prince president claimed to be achieving with "his" *grands travaux* what the National Workshops had failed to do. Were they also to fail, they would expose his unfitness to govern. The successful transformation of Paris, however, would be the best testimonial for the regime he aimed to create.

In accordance with Saint-Simonian thinking, the prince considered that

the development of amenities and infrastructure—in both town and country— encouraged initiative and the creation of wealth. Although it was not
possible to prove mathematically the multiplier effect that expenditure on
the building of a particular street would have upon the economy as a whole,
the fact that people would be able to move around more easily, communicate, and exchange goods and ideas could only encourage him to go ahead
with public works for the good of the whole community.

Another factor in the prince's mind was that well-organized urban life
had a positive effect on morals; the gutting of the unhealthy old districts
would help in spiritually uplifting the popular classes. In his *Mémoires*,
Haussmann mentions with pride the good marks he received from Cardinal
Morlot, the archbishop of Paris: "Your apostolate is helping my own. You are
combating moral squalor indirectly but with certain effect, by raising the
conditions and habits of life of the toiling classes. In wide and straight
streets flooded with light, people do not behave with the same slovenliness
as in dark, narrow, winding streets. To supply the housing of the poor with
air, daylight, and water is not only to make it physically healthy; it is also to
introduce new encouragement, a stimulus to good housekeeping and personal cleanliness that gradually has an effect upon the moral state of those
who live there."[1]

Was Haussmann, then, merely a kind of puppet for his master to wave in
the face of the opposition while himself calmly getting on with the job?
There is a little truth in that. The prefect for the Seine was indeed the whip-
ping boy whom enemies of the regime could happily take to task when direct criticism of the head of state threatened to cost them dear. One might
also say that he was like a piece of fuse wire—very strong, though, because
he remained in place for sixteen and a half years. So there must have been
something else there too. In fact, Haussmann was the loyal and devoted servant of a policy which, in order to move beyond its originating brain, needed
a great organizer to implement it. Otherwise the dream would have remained no more than that: a dream.

The most negative judgment of the prefect comes from Émile Ollivier:
"When he took over his post, the general plan of works had been ordered by
the Emperor and the funding had been worked out by Persigny. It is therefore not right to accord Haussmann alone the glory of an undertaking which,
once universally criticized, is today universally praised."[2] Persigny, minister
of the interior when Haussmann was appointed, is not much more qualified
in his appreciation: Louis-Napoléon, "with his constant passion for improvements and things on a grand scale, had for a long time been studying" vari-

ous projects for implementation in Paris, and the impetus for the *grands travaux* came from the prince himself. What of Haussmann, then? "Apart from the energy, order, and skill that he put into directing these vast operations, his real merit was to carry out these major works despite the vigorous, passionate, inexplicable opposition from influential members of the government. The history of his administration was one long struggle against the guardians of power, a series of hand-to-hand battles with a powerful coterie that was incapable of doing anything itself yet anxious that nothing should be done by anyone else."

With an eye on posterity, Haussmann took the greatest care to exalt the role of the prince, but he did not fail to underline his own merits at appropriate times. Should we regard his testimony as suspect? He wrote his *Mémoires* in 1890, when Napoléon III had already been dead for seventeen years. No one would have taken offense if he had claimed full responsibility for the *grands travaux*. In fact, the exact opposite had been happening. In 1882, Jules Simon, a onetime adversary of Haussmann's and a founding father of the Third Republic, took it into his head to praise Haussmann's work in an article in *Le Gaulois*: "It matters little to us today that M. Haussmann's accounts had the character of fantasy. He set out to make Paris a magnificent city, and in that he completely succeeded. . . . His work was at least as much fantasy as his accounts. Now we want only one thing: that what began under despotism should be completed in liberty." Haussmann was not altogether happy with this article, however, and in his *Mémoires* he strongly regretted that Jules Simon "did not give most of his admiration to the one who merited it: to the sovereign, my master. That 'dreamer' was not only the architect of the plans I carried out; he continued to give loyal support to the man he had chosen among all the prefects of France to interpret and execute his thinking—dare I say it, 'his number two' in Paris."[3]

THE MAIN PRINCIPLES

‽ Louis-Napoléon might have directed the effort at new towns on the outskirts of the existing city. This was what had been spontaneously happening since the Restoration, when Lanquetin and his colleagues had been so alarmed at the mushrooming development of building land to the west of the old districts of the city center. The conquest of Algeria had given birth to new, rationally organized cities, and some well-meaning people advocated similar solutions for Paris. Closer to our own times, General de Gaulle's prefect for the Paris region, Paul Delouvrier, did precisely create new towns on the periphery of the capital. But that was not the option chosen by the prince president.

Louis-Napoléon turned to the tradition of papal Rome, where new roads had been driven through existing built-up areas—with the difference that Paris had a much larger population of one million, living in an incomparably denser urban space. His plan was to regenerate the urban fabric, "to remake the city upon the city." Persigny realized that Rambuteau had shown the way: "The idea of improving the conditions of life in Paris . . . by directly opening a route through it . . . by means of compulsory purchases—an idea that was to transform Paris and our great cities with such happy effect—belongs to the reign of Louis-Philippe. M. de Rambuteau, prefect for the Seine, got it started with the building of the street that bears his name. The population of Paris was deeply impressed at the sight of this new road through a wretched, insalubrious district, which brought to it energy, air, light, and health. And the popularity of this development was such as to encourage its imitation."

Rambuteau, who witnessed Haussmann's *grands travaux* after his own retirement, had not waited for Persigny to put himself forward as the sensible innovator but had wittingly committed the resources of Paris. "I especially aimed for new roads that would create fine building land where the façades reached high prices; such as the rue de Rambuteau, which cost 9 million francs and whose roadside constructions must be worth 50." He certainly did show the way. But he could not decide among all the blossoming projects and never managed to gain the interest of Louis-Philippe, who was prey to a pathological fear of spending money. Unable to build the momentum he had wanted to achieve, Rambuteau did have the undeniable merit of launching the first timid operations.

For Louis-Napoléon, the redevelopment of Paris had to obey a number of principles. These were perfectly summarized by Charles Merruau, secretary general of the Seine prefecture, shortly after the coup d'état of December 2, 1851: "No railhead that needs to be served, no historic building to be given space, no center of the police force to be spread out, no stronghold of rioting to be opened, no grand promenade to be brought closer to the center, no part of town to be connected to the rest—not one of these is being neglected."

Undoubtedly the priority was to create good links among the various railway stations and between each of them and the city center. In his *Souvenirs*, Merruau stressed the prime importance that the opening up of the stations had for the prince: "Those admitted to his presence often saw him cover the map of Paris with pencil strokes and lines pointing in various directions. As the starting point for what he had in mind, he considered that the railheads or railway stations were henceforth the true gates of the city, instead of the old *barrières* at which the national highways ended. It was necessary to link these new gates, so that movement from one to the other—that is, from one region of France to the other—should take place quickly and conveniently through a common center; it was necessary to plan wide thoroughfares from these main points of arrival to the heart of the great city."

Louis-Napoléon's second major principle was to facilitate communication between the ministries and the headquarters of important administrative departments. It was a question of efficiency even more than of security, as Merruau made quite clear: "He [the prince president] knew that action by the authorities could be blocked at a crucial moment by obstacles separating them from the agents and instruments of execution."

One concern that Louis-Napoléon shared with the party of order—and indeed this third principle is often considered the main one behind the *grands travaux*—was to facilitate troop movements and to bore deep inside the traditional foci of insurrection. Merruau again: "It was also necessary, by means of avenues and major roads, to open breaches in the areas that had previously been closed as citadels of insurrection, such as the area around the Hôtel de Ville, the faubourg Saint-Antoine, or the two slopes of Mount Sainte-Geneviève."

The fourth principle was to unify the city. The thoroughfares beginning at the railway stations, ministries, and major public buildings were to come together at a number of central points, where other roads would radiate outward and link each district of Paris to all the others. It was a mesh system stemming from a highly modern concept of traffic organization.

Louis-Napoléon's fifth principle, based on the model of London, was to create planted areas and to plan public parks and gardens, so that each part of Paris would have its own green space.

The sixth and final principle expressed a much-debated aesthetic bias: namely, to create more space around historic buildings so that they could be better viewed and admired. The exaggerated clearing of the cathedral square in front of Notre Dame was one example of this, but the *grands travaux* did not lead to the destruction of any historic monument, and Haussmann prided himself on buying the ruined Hôtel Carnavalet and renovating it as a museum devoted to the history of Paris. The idea that whole districts should be treasured as parts of a historic legacy did not, with a few exceptions, enter into the aesthetic conceptions of the age. As to the newly built blocks, they followed the imperatives of the classical epoch: straight lines and regular façades. One may regret the tyranny of the rectilinear, but the Parisian cityscape owes its personality precisely to this monumentality, which we are used to calling "Haussmannian," though none of it actually comes from Haussmann.

All these ideas could be found on the map mentioned by Merruau, and Haussmann became their loyal interpreter after his early vision on June 29, 1853, the day he was sworn in as prefect at Saint-Cloud. The original map first hung in the prince's office in the Tuileries Palace and was then moved to Haussmann's office in the Hôtel de Ville. This document, like the copies that were made of it, was destroyed when the Hôtel de Ville was set on fire in 1871—the only exception being a copy given to the king of Prussia, Wilhelm I, when he visited Paris during the World's Fair of 1867. This was photographed in 1930 but disappeared in its turn in the destruction of Berlin in 1945. One can see from the photograph the state of the *travaux* already completed in 1859, as well as the further work that Napoléon III was planning to carry out in old Paris.

Shortly before his death in 1873, Napoléon III put together a most interesting document at the request of Merruau, who was then in the course of writing his memoirs. It was a color-coded map of Paris in 1871, incorporating the criteria defined by the former secretary general for the Seine prefecture. "The public highways opened or planned under his government are, so to speak, graded in accordance with his personal predilection and the degree of responsibility he assumed for their execution. One color indicates the boulevards or streets existing today that he thought he had especially wanted and commissioned; another color denotes the roads (all or part) that were not built but which he would very much have liked to be created; and a lack of shading on other new roads shows that he agreed to them but, though considering them urgent, did not order them to go ahead."

A comparison of these two plans clearly brings out the desire to embellish the capital with monumental roads and to create links between the various stations: the building of the Boulevard de Strasbourg and Boulevard Magenta made it possible to open up the Gare du Nord and the Gare de l'Est; the newly created Boulevard Mazas (now Diderot) served the Gare de Lyon and the Gare d'Austerlitz; Boulevard Saint-Marcel and Boulevard Arago made the Gare d'Austerlitz more accessible; and the Boulevard de Port Royal and Boulevard Raspail, as well as the rue de Rennes, served the Gare Montparnasse. On the other hand, two new roads reflected mainly strategic preoccupations: the Boulevard du Prince-Eugène (now Voltaire) and the rue Monge.

The initial plan, which Louis-Napoléon brought in his luggage when he got off the train at the Gare du Nord in September 1848, has since vanished, and we do not know what it might have looked like. But Charles Merruau assures us that "it existed only as a sketch before the empire" and that it was "finally adopted only after M. Haussmann's recommendation had been carefully considered." Although the eminent prefect suggested some alterations, "the general lines and system had already been decided in the prince's mind since the days of his presidency, and on many important points long before that."[4]

THE FUNDING

In a report dated December 25, 1843, Rambuteau congratulated himself on the progress of work on the rue de Constantine and the street that bears his name. Nevertheless, Louis-Philippe's prefect added that the last thing he wanted was to speed up the work, because he had "to provide for all the services out of ordinary funds, without staking the future, without venturing down the road of loans, an extreme measure which, for a city like Paris, should be employed only with the greatest circumspection and in grave circumstances." "What graver circumstances could there be than the need to provide clean air and space, those two necessary conditions of life?" retorted the architect Daly in the *Revue générale de l'architecture* (1844).

Berger, appointed prefect for the Seine in the first days of 1849, did not use different arguments from Rambuteau's. Merruau relates: "One day [in 1851] we saw the prefect returning worried and irritated from the Élysée. He had been summoned to a meeting of the Council of Ministers chaired by the prince; he had been given to understand that there was reason to commit the city at once to the considerable expenditure required for the rue de Rivoli to be extended through the populous shopping areas of the rue de la Monnaie, the rue des Bourdonnais, the area around Les Halles, the rues Saint-Denis and Saint-Martin, in order to join the Louvre with the Hôtel de Ville. There had been talk of starting the construction of Les Halles as soon as possible, of laying the foundation stone. The president of the Republic had been insistent; he wanted things done quickly."

Berger thought that, in the current state of the city's finances, it would be impossible to carry through all this work. Tax revenue was 4 million francs higher than in the previous year, but in his view it would not remain at that level. Besides, the city had only just taken out a loan of 25 million francs. "The city was his own home, the municipal finances his own finances, without any ulterior motive on his part. He administered the city as a good father would his family and did not want to run any risks," Merruau added. Those who worked with Berger, all sincerely devoted to Louis-Napoléon, knew that the prince president had little scope "to advance the public good at leisure," since the National Assembly was hostile toward him. Merruau viewed Berger's resistance as tantamount to resignation. He went with his principal colleagues to the prefect's office and found him already thinking it over; they finished off the process of persuading him. Berger climbed back into his carriage, returned to the Élysée, and finally gave his approval for a new municipal loan of 50 million francs to finance the rue de Rivoli extension from the corner of the Cour Carrée to the Hôtel de Ville and the rue Saint-Antoine.

The project and the loan were approved on August 4, 1851, and the demolition work began at once. A few months later, however, it appeared that 50 million francs would not be enough. Then Persigny came onto the scene. The former conspirator, Louis-Napoléon's oldest companion who became minister of the interior in January 1852, considered the *grands travaux* in Paris to be one of his most pressing matters. "The question of transforming Paris was virtually present before the public at the moment when I took over the ministry of the interior," he explains in his *Mémoires*. "The narrow streets of Paris were so congested, movement had become so difficult, that when everyone considered the rapid rise in the population along with the sight of the happily built rue de Rivoli, they called for new streets and new links to be opened—but without giving much thought to the means of funding them." When a new regime establishes itself, everyone goes to it with their suggestions. How are these to be implemented? That seems a secondary issue for others to address.

In this case, "others" meant Persigny. "It fell to me, as minister of the interior, to examine the matter. . . . Six weeks after I arrived at the ministry, in response to my report and proposal, the prince president of the Republic decided by a decree of March 10 [1852] to build the Boulevard de Strasbourg from the embarkation point on the street of the same name [the Gare de l'Est] to the Boulevard de Saint-Denis. But this project, whose execution could scarcely begin before the following year, and for which the state was supposed to bear the principal costs, was only a small detail in the *travaux* that everyone understood to be necessary." Necessary perhaps—but Berger and Louis-Napoléon remained totally at odds about the means of funding them. Moreover, the prince president did not intend to stop at that: he was already working on another program of public road-building. Persigny was evidently concerned about the budget. "It was the usual topic of my talks with the prefect for the Seine." Difficult talks: "M. Berger displayed a great reluctance to follow me on this issue."

In a sudden insight, Persigny saw the funding system that could meet the needs of the transformation of Paris. Early in 1853 he congratulated the Seine prefect on being told that the city's tax receipts again showed an unexpected surplus of 4 million francs over expenditure. Berger agreed to allocate the sum to new works, but then Persigny, pretending to think that this windfall would repeat itself every year, suggested that he should rather use it as security for a major loan that would make it possible to speed up operations quite considerably: "If, despite the charges on the last loan [the one of August 4, 1851, for the rue de Rivoli extension] and the provision for expenditure on the Boulevard de Strasbourg, you already have a rise in tax receipts of 4 million francs—a rise indicating such a marked upward trend in your receipts—why should you limit yourself to an insignificant 4 million for new works? Why not realize the capital of 4 million for both interest and repayment, so that you can continue with a large capital the system of works begun with the rue de Rivoli?" With Berger struck dumb, Persigny pressed the point within a broader economic vision. He argued that "the city of Paris, in becoming the center of a population growing in the same proportions, did not have to fear becoming stretched beyond its resources; that the immobilization of 4 million francs would actually be insignificant in such a state of prosperity; that once the capital had been constituted by the pledging of 4 million in annuities, the city could use it for a series of similar operations until it was used up; . . . that such works would certainly help the city's finances by producing a huge movement of business and wealth into the capital; and that, in accomplishing these major works, Paris would have increased and not reduced its own resources." In short, the *grands travaux* were a useful investment, "productive expenditure."

Persigny thus presented himself as the inventor of the theory of "productive expenditure." We shall see that Haussmann accorded himself the same merit. Each of the two men took all the credit for a system based on a number of self-evident facts: the added value of building land and the extra profit in comparison with real estate investment; the demographic growth of Paris; the fever of activity that had taken hold of the capital. Recuperation of the investment through major urban development was more complicated than through the building of a railway line, where payment could be charged for passengers and freight. Now it would be necessary to find additional or indirect tax revenue. The selling of land, made easier by the decree of 1848, would be one way of achieving this; increased property and patent taxes resulting from the rise in wealth and economic activity would be another way. And there was also a predictable growth in the toll revenue charged on all goods entering the city—a form of taxation that would boost municipal funds by falling upon construction materials, and on goods that ended up as food or clothing for construction workers or as equipment for construction companies.[5] The revenue would automatically increase with any rise in Parisian consumption.

Such ideas were familiar to contemporaries of Louis-Philippe, though not everyone worked them into a coherent theory as Persigny and Haussmann did. It seemed that only someone clinging to outdated conceptions, someone like Berger, could refuse to accept them. All that Haussmann's predecessor found to reply to Persigny was: "I am not one who will ever go along with ruining the city." According to Persigny, the prefect for the Seine did not shrink from a campaign of rumors against his minister of the interior and accused him of madness and adventurism. "But I did not have reason to regret this whole campaign against me," Persigny tells us in his *Mémoires*, "for it gave me the opportunity not only to have my ideas approved by the Emperor, but to present clearly to His Majesty the question of removing M. Berger from the Seine prefecture—which I had the satisfaction of obtaining."

THE LEGAL INSTRUMENTS

≈ Among the instruments available to the Paris administration for urban redevelopment, one of the oldest was *alignement*: that is, the power to set the line of public thoroughfares. A decision to review all the *alignements* in the capital was taken in 1765, and the municipality was instructed to carry this out. When it proved dilatory in performing the task, the royal authorities repeated in 1783 the order to "carry out a survey of all the streets in the city and faubourgs of Paris." It would be called the "Verniquet survey," after the name of the man who eventually completed the colossal work. A decree issued by the post-Revolutionary Directory made the ministry of the interior responsible for recording in this document any decisions on the widening or straightening of Parisian streets—a responsibility later transferred to the prefect for the Seine.

The conditions for the fixing or altering of the alignment plans were defined by an ordinance dated August 23, 1835. Such plans had to be opened
to a public inquiry that would guarantee the rights of landowners and the
local population as a whole before they were submitted to the municipal
council and approved by the Council of State. The aim of this procedure was
to ensure that the alignment respected certain standards and especially the
regularity of the street line (straight lines are part of France's heritage in aes-
thetics and regulatory practices); to enhance public safety by removing any
recesses where brigands might lurk or garbage and rubble might be illegally
dumped; and to promote the circulation of pedestrians and vehicles, and of
fresh air.

The regulations governing street alignment are still in force today, as
they have shown their usefulness down the ages. The system enables the
community to widen a street or to correct its line—generally by making it
straighter. In return for the piece of land that he surrenders to the city, the
owner of the relevant building is paid a reduction indemnity. Under the July
Monarchy, as we have seen, the municipal councillor Lanquetin was especially fond of this means of carrying out transformation work. But in practice the city must wait at the pleasure of the owner of a building affected by
alignement—and that can take decades, even centuries. In the present day
there are still quite a lot of streets in Paris untouched by Haussmann's operations that continue to wind in amiable disorder between residential blocks,
some of which (the older ones) jut out, while the more recent ones stand
back as the result of reconstruction following an alignment ruling. Lanquetin demanded the introduction of compulsory alignment. In reality, expropriation is the only legal means of altering the street plan with reasonable
speed.

Expropriation—that is, compulsory purchase—allows the community to
acquire new land at a time that suits it. The French Revolution, while establishing the rights of personal property, also set the principles of expropriation. The Declaration of Human and Civil Rights stipulated: "Property is an
inviolable and sacred right. No one can be deprived of it without fair compensation paid in advance." Two laws enacted under the First Empire on
September 16, 1807, and March 8, 1810, and ratified and complemented by
legislation of the July Monarchy on July 7, 1833, and May 3, 1841, authorized the community to expropriate land for the widening of an existing road
or the construction of a new one. On what remained of the plot of land, the
owner could build a new façade or a new building, but difficulties arose if
the plot was too narrow or irregular in shape. In 1848, Lahure, the architect

then in charge of public thoroughfares, complained that such spaces were "employed for the construction of houses without depth that are veritable broom cupboards, whose airless lodgings, both too small and too low, are as uncomfortable as they are unhealthy." Laws enacted in 1807, 1833, and especially on May 3, 1841, made provisions whereby owners could ask the administration to acquire the whole of the plot so that they would not be left with unusable land.

A decree of March 26, 1852, on the streets of Paris went much further than the law of 1841, since it authorized the community to carry out large-scale acquisitions on their own initiative. Article Two of the decree established that it was enough for the administration simply to declare which of the remaining parts "are not of the right size or shape to permit salubrious constructions to be erected upon them." It also stated that "plots of land acquired outside the alignments and not suitable for salubrious constructions shall be joined to contiguous landholdings, either by mutual agreement or by expropriation of such holdings." The way was thus opened for the city of Paris to expropriate on a large scale, to profit from the additional value that its road building and improvement gave to the land through which the roads passed, to reshape plots of land in a rational manner, and to encourage there the rapid and integrated construction of well-designed residential blocks. Berger, followed by Haussmann, made ample use of these possibilities, until a legal about-face took them away.

Expropriation involved a ponderous formal mechanism, the aim of which was to determine the public utility of the intended action and to establish, under a judge's supervision, fair compensation for the owner of the land and others entitled to receive it. The law of July 7, 1833, specified how this should work. The administration began by drawing up a plan for the area in question that mentioned any new road or roads as well as the land to be expropriated. The plan was displayed at the local town hall and thrown open to a public inquiry. The compensation board then set the level of payment under the supervision of a judge specializing in real estate, who could allow the transfer of ownership only on grounds of public benefit. Many further controls strengthened the guarantees offered to citizens: the plan submitted by the local authority had to refer to a certified copy of the original map of the city; each alignment reference on the map was officially recorded; the plan had to carry the seal of approval of the Seine prefect, who started the procedure of the public inquiry; after the inquiry, the plan and everything else in the file were sent to the Ministry of Education and Religious Worship, then to the Council of State, and finally to the minister of the interior for authentication that it was in the public benefit. Even then the expropriation could go ahead only after a meeting of the municipal council to consider the matter.

Expropriation, then, was allowable only for considerations of public benefit, which traditionally included the building, improvement, or widening of roads as well as the digging of canals, the improvement of watercourses, and since the 1820s the development of railways. Other possible grounds were the creation of fortifications and defenses, army camps, and barracks, and the construction of public buildings for civil use: the new Palace of Justice or the Louvre extension, or perhaps a new town hall, ministry, or covered market.

The Melun Law of 1850 on unhealthy dwellings added a further legal basis for expropriation: the creation of healthier conditions in residential blocks. Article One imposed an obligation on municipal councils to look into the measures that needed to be carried out in remedying insalubrious dwellings and outbuildings, rented out or occupied by anyone other than the owner. The following articles listed the courses of action open to the municipality. If the insalubriousness was the responsibility of a private owner, it was up to him to carry out the necessary improvements, on pain of a fine proportional to the delay. Otherwise it was up to the commune to take action by becoming the owner of the property in question: "It may acquire, within the limits of its capacities, all the property contained in the perimeter of the work to be carried out."

Until 1853 Paris had no "Service du Plan," no official survey department. The responsibility for alignment plans was given to Eugène Deschamps, who had the title of survey registrar. This architect, a former student at the École des Beaux-Arts before joining the city's team of architects in charge of public thoroughfares, had working for him only four surveyors plus one more to check their work. But he had no role in making proposals; the task of designing public thoroughfares lay with the Conseil des Bâtiments Civils, a consultative body under the Ministry of Public Works and the Ministry of the Interior that dealt with new road-building and architectural projects in the public domain. From 1854 on, Haussmann made of the reorganized survey department a remarkably efficient tool for the conception and preparation of public works programs; the Conseil des Bâtiments Civils was left to concern itself with the architecture of public buildings at the planning stage.

SUBCONTRACTING OR DIRECT EXECUTION

❧ The traditional state of the nineteenth century was quite jealous of its prerogatives, but once it had established them it was happy to delegate certain tasks to private operators under its own control. Its functioning was very different from that of the twentieth-century state, which intervenes in the economy and society on a much greater scale. Rather than do things itself, a nineteenth-century public authority preferred to get others to do them. Transport was private, as were the gas supply, the postal service, and the construction and operation of the railways.

In the realm of urban development, too, delegation to the private sector was the rule. The favorite technique was a division of labor whereby private developers built new streets such as the rue Rambuteau, the rue de Rivoli, and eventually the Berger and Haussmann throughroads while the public authorities maintained overall control and supervision. Just as a contract was awarded to a private transport company to operate stagecoaches or carriages, so a private company might be permitted to carry out public works on behalf of the authorities for an all-inclusive price. The scope for concessions varied quite considerably. The city might well authorize the company in question to settle compulsory purchases in advance of the actual work on the road, or else to sell any remnants of land after the work was completed. In such cases the contractor would advance the purchasing costs as well as expenditure on street equipment such as drains, water mains, and lighting, obviously in the hope that he would make a profit on the reselling of the land. But as this rarely enabled him to cover all his expenditures, the community made up the difference on the basis of what the contractor had actually spent on the street works and furnishings. This extra sum was usually paid only at the end, when the public works had been formally delivered, but the city also had the power to make interim payments.

Having become the banker of the city of Paris, the concessionary company thus bore the financial burdens and all the risks. For major operations the contenders did not exactly line up in the offices of the prefecture, and the misfortunes of Ardoin, Ricardo & Company during the work on the Boulevard de Strasbourg helped to cool the enthusiasm of others. On September 27, 1852, this company signed a contract with Berger and Merruau from the Seine prefecture for the purchase of land (both by mutual agreement and by expropriation), the road-building work, and the reselling of the surplus land, in accordance with a schedule attached to the contract—all in return for a subsidy of 7,750,000 francs, to be paid one-third by central government and

two-thirds by the city of Paris. The subsidy was to be paid in four annual instalments of 1,937,000 francs, the first falling due on December 31, 1852.
The contract was ratified by the Ministry of the Interior through a decree of
public benefit issued on November 8. Ardoin and Ricardo, counting on the
advantages offered in the decree of March 16, 1852, purchased more than
the amount of land for which the contract had provided. The expropriations
began in February 1853 and were completed by March 1854. Work on the
boulevard started on December 16, 1853, but the construction of new
blocks scarcely got off the ground. Financial charges were eating up a considerable part of the anticipated profit.

After this episode, no one was willing to sign a deal on the terms set by
the city. This was how things stood when Haussmann took over at the Seine
prefecture, and until 1860 nearly all the operations had to be carried out
under the *régie* system, whereby the city did everything itself: the expropriations, the works, the reselling of land. It was a cumbersome arrangement.
Instead of dealing with a concessionary company that took care of all the
bother, yielded to inspection, and advanced the necessary expenditure, the
public authorities had to create the relevant services and fund the whole operation either out of their own reserves or through a loan. The city saved
funds on the profit that would have gone to the contractor—but that was
cold comfort in view of the risks it had to shoulder. As the services of the
Seine prefecture did not have the right tools to face these unexpected responsibilities, the mistakes began to come thick and fast.

THE *GRANDS TRAVAUX* GET UNDER WAY

In the days of Louis-Philippe, Rambuteau had presented to Parliament
the idea of a city of Paris loan, to be used for improvements to Les Halles and
the rue de Rivoli extension up to the corner of the Cour Carrée and the
colonnade of the Louvre. A loan of 25 million francs was approved on July 3
and 30, 1847. But then the Revolution of 1848 and the fall of Louis-
Philippe intervened before Rambuteau had actually launched the work. A
decree of the Provisional Government on March 24, 1848, followed by Marrast's decree of May 3, endorsed the continuation of the Louvre and the extension of the rue de Rivoli. On August 24, the Constituent Assembly
passed a law confirming the vote of approval of July 1847 and thus gave the
city of Paris approval to borrow 25 million francs. This was the loan that
Berger had in mind when he said that municipal finances had gone beyond
the limits of the tolerable. In reality, Marrast's decree of May 3 went further

than Rambuteau's project because it stipulated that the rue de Rivoli would be extended as far as the rue Saint-Antoine. The works would be more expensive; the city of Paris therefore issued bonds to the value of 9 million francs, with the necessary expropriations as the first priority for their use.

Bidding for the loan of 25 million francs opened on March 26, 1849, but the operation was a failure: not one banker took it up. There were two main reasons for this: the general economic difficulties, which did not encourage risk-taking; and the skeptical attitude of the leading banks, whose sympathies were with Orleanism and which had little faith in the bold views of the prince president. The bad blood between Louis-Napoléon and the leading banks was a constant feature of his first period in power, lasting right up to 1860 or 1861. But as far as the loan was concerned, the situation was saved when the Bechet-Dethomas Company agreed on April 9, 1849, to come up with the 25 million francs for a fairly short term of ten years. By 1859, when the loan would have been repaid in full, the payments of capital and interest would have cost Paris 36 million francs. Hidden behind Bechet-Dethomas were the Pereire brothers and their front man Mirès, rising stars of a new generation of financiers willing to play the game of Louis-Napoléon and Persigny and to advance major loans for the country's modernization and the improvement of its public facilities.

The procedure for the rue de Rivoli extension now took shape. The city of Paris and the central government signed a contract on August 2, 1849, that was ratified by a law of October 4. This provided for the clearing and leveling of the space separating the Tuileries Palace from the Louvre, and the opening of the rue de Rivoli, with a width of seventy-two feet, between the Passage Delorme (now vanished, but then near the rue des Pyramides) and the rue de la Bibliothèque (near the corner of the Cour Carrée and the Place du Louvre), so that it would run beside the northern wing of the Louvre when the latter was completed (as it was in 1855). Next, a decree of December 23, 1852, declared that it was in the public interest to build the section of the rue de Rivoli that would give the Place du Louvre the shape it has today; work began on this in 1853 and was completed in the course of 1854. The same decree ordered the construction of houses with arcades on the sides of the two new sections. It also declared that the enlargement of the Place du Louvre and the Place Saint-Germain-l'Auxerrois was in the public interest, and ordered the construction of houses with architecturally uniform façades on the sides of the two *places*.

Central government met two-thirds of the net expenditure on the section between the Passage Delorme and the rue de la Bibliothèque. It also covered half of the costs of clearing the space between the Louvre Palace and the Carrousel as well as the area around the Théâtre Français and the Palais Royal.

The law of August 4, 1851, organized the extension of the rue de Rivoli from the Place du Louvre to the rue Saint-Antoine. A twenty-year tax exemption was granted in order to aid the construction of houses along this stretch of the street. But then the planners suddenly realized that they had cut things too fine and been insufficiently aware of the local geography, so that now they had to extend the area of the expropriations around the Tour Saint-Jacques. A decree of July 26, 1852, authorized this extension and promised the city two subsidies: 1 million francs to handle the new expropriations; and 500,000 francs for the reconstruction of the Pont Notre-Dame that had become unavoidable. Finally a decree of February 19, 1853, declared the enlargement of the Place de l'Hôtel de Ville (formerly known as the Place de Grève) to be a matter of public benefit. All this gave a strong impression of muddling through from day to day. For meanwhile the prince president had been forcing Berger in quick succession to launch the Boulevard de Strasbourg project to link the Gare de l'Est and the *grands boulevards* (decree of March 10, 1852), the Boulevard Mazas (now Boulevard Diderot) to open up the Gare de Lyon, the rue des Écoles, and the beginning of the rue de Rennes.

The rue des Écoles was the personal work of Louis-Napoléon, probably one of the projects to which he was the most attached. The prince was absolutely insistent that new thoroughfares should be opened in the particularly wretched and insalubrious districts of the left bank. Since the 1830s there had been a plan to open the rue des Écoles along the front of the Sorbonne and the Collège de France. But in 1849 the architect Portret published a more ambitious project to drive the rue des Écoles from the Jardin des Plantes to the École de Médecine. A paper setting out the case for this alternative was signed by prominent citizens living on the left bank, and a delegation handed it to the prince president on October 3, 1851. Louis-Napoléon had a weakness for fieldwork. A few days later, reported Louis Lazare in the *Revue municipale*, "the prince . . . visited the dark narrow streets of these districts; he studied all their troubles, understood all their sufferings, and resolved to put an end to them." Having heard the voice of the people, he issued a decree of public benefit on July 24, 1852, with regard to the section of the rue des Écoles stretching from the rue de la Harpe—

roughly at what is now the corner of the rue des Écoles and the Boulevard Saint-Michel—and the rue Jean de Beauvais, which marked the limits of the Collège de France to the east.

The street would have a width of 72 feet, as much as the rue de Rivoli. At the level of the Sorbonne and the Collège de France, it opened out to 131 feet and formed a huge space that would take the name Place de Cambrai. Its creation involved the expropriation of more than 215,000 square feet of land on which buildings already existed. The work lasted two years, 1853 and 1854, and cost the exorbitant sum of 13.6 million francs, shared equally between the city and central government. For this price, Berger laid out a fine esplanade in front of the Sorbonne and the Collège de France, but there was still a long way to go before the prince's dream of a great east-west route on the left bank saw the light of day.

Whether through makeshift methods or technical blunders, Louis-Napoléon risked slipping up at any moment because of Berger's ill will or lack of competence. He was too busy consolidating his regime to get on the wrong side of the Seine prefect and what he represented, a nervous Parisian bourgeoisie which had been ceaselessly demanding the transformation of Paris but without any inconvenience or expense—in short, the squaring of the circle. Clearly it would be necessary to get tough. As he waited for the right moment to acquire the means, the prince put in place the man who would share his grand designs and relieve him of the petty concerns of administration.

Haussmann with the imperial couple, visiting the site for Garnier's new opera house. *(Painting by E. Gilis, in Musée de Compiègne, RMN)*

Napoléon III in 1859, handing Haussmann the decree incorporating the suburban communes into the city of Paris. *(Painting by Adolf Yvon, in Musée Carnavalet)*

The cutting of the Boulevard du Palais (Boulevard de Sébastopol in
Haussmann's time); demolition of the rue de la Barillerie in 1859.
(Musée Carnavalet)

Demolition work in the Quartier Latin in 1860.
(Musée Carnavalet)

Official opening of the Boulevard du Prince-Eugène by Napoléon III, on December 7, 1862. *(Bibliothèque Nationale)*

Official opening of the Boulevard Malesherbes, August 13, 1861. *(Bibliothèque Nationale)*

The Place du Palais Royal before the work on the
rue de Rivoli.

The cutting of the rue de Rome in
1865. *(Bibliothèque Historique de la
Ville de Paris)*

The transformation of Mount
Sainte-Geneviève, seen from rue Saint-Victor.
(Bibliothèque Nationale)

The Barrière du Trône (Place de la Nation) in 1858.
(Bibliothèque Nationale)

Demolition of the Barrière de l'Étoile. *(Musée Carnavalet)*

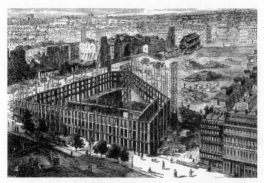

Construction of the Hôtel de la Paix.
(Musée Carnavalet)

Planting trees on the Place de la Bourse.

Bailly's new Tribunal de Commerce, completed in 1864.
(Bibliothèque Nationale)

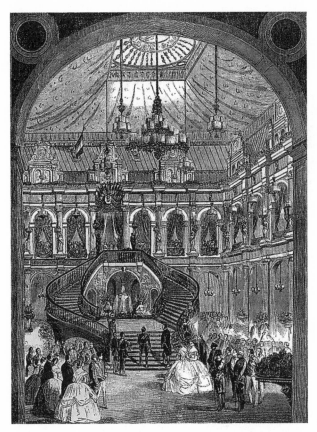

The Cour Louis XIV (at the Paris Hôtel de Ville),
which Haussmann covered with a metal shelter
on the occasion of the reception for Grandduke
Constantine in 1857. *(Bibliothèque Nationale)*

The "metal umbrellas" of the central Halles, during
the Second Empire. *(Photograph by Marville,
Bibliothèque Historique de la Ville de Paris)*

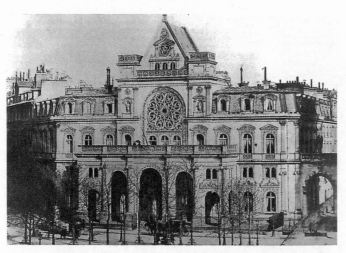

The *mairie* of the 1st arrondissement, designed by Hittorff.
(Photograph by Marville, Bibliothèque Historique de la Ville de Paris)

Baltard's Church of Saint-Augustin.
(Musée d'Orsay)

The Avenue de l'Opéra. *(Plate by J.-C. Doërr, Bibliothèque Historique de la Ville de Paris)*

General view of the World's Fair of 1867. *(Lithograph by Rivière, Musée Carnavalet)*

Demolition of the theatres on the Boulevard du Temple for the cutting of the Boulevard du Prince-Eugène.

New theatres on the Place du Châtelet. *(Print by J.-A. Peulot, Musée Carnavalet)*

A Morris column.

A rostral column.

A public convenience on the Place de la
Madeleine, in 1870. *(Photograph by
Marville, Bibliothèque Historique de la Ville
de Paris)*

HAUSSMANN
Recéleur de PARIS vendu
a la Destruction

Haussmann, depicted as a fence serving
time for receiving a Paris sold for
destruction.

Another lampoon of Haussmann.
*(Photographed by the Musées de la Ville
de Paris)*

·III·

PREFECT FOR THE SEINE

11

Paris Gets a
New Prefect

"IT IS THE first flight of the Eagle," exclaimed Dupin, one of the leaders of the Orleanist party, when a decree of January 23, 1852, ordered the sale of the property of the Orleans family.[1] Pro-Orleanist salons were up in arms about this measure, seeing it as an act of mindless resentment and, above all, an attack on the principle of private property. The government prevailed only with difficulty in the Council of State, and four ministers resigned: Rouher, Magne, Fould, and the minister of the interior Morny himself.

In fact, Morny's departure was probably due most of all to disagreements with Louis-Napoléon following his adoption of a coat of arms that featured a hydrangea and the motto *Tace sed memento* (Be silent but remember), both of which were too "outspoken." He had been the friend of the princes of Orleans, and he took this opportunity to leave the ministry vacant for Persigny. Not long afterward Morny recalled: "The prince bears no real friendship toward anyone, and he is disturbed by my special situation with regard to him. . . . He only reluctantly accepted my presence, and my services weighed heavily upon him. He is mistrustful and ungrateful, and he only likes those who obey and flatter him in a servile manner."

In Bordeaux the prefect Haussmann, though no longer an Orleanist, deplored Morny's retirement. Without going too far, he clamped down on those in the Gironde who were associated with the protest by the princes of the Orleans family. He also acted with restraint against republicans in the region. While a wave of repression swept France in the weeks following the coup d'état, Haussmann carried out no more than fifteen arrests. On the other hand, he had to lend out his prisons to accommodate the overflow from the neighboring Lot-et-Garonne: "Residents of the Gironde could judge from this contrast the moderate character of my harsh actions."[2] Basing himself on a circular of January 29, 1852, that authorized prefects to release "low-grade rioters," he soon set nine of his prisoners free. His philosophy: "Hit mainly at the leaders, and apart from a small number of really dangerous rogues, . . . spare the *vulgum pecus* [the common herd]."[3]

The institution of so-called joint commissions made it possible both to place under surveillance a number of significant opponents who had escaped the first dragnet, and to send the smaller fry on their way. Haussmann sat on the Gironde joint commission together with the public prosecutor for Bordeaux and General Le Pays de Bourjolly (who had succeeded General d'Arbouville as military commandant). It cleared more than four hundred accused persons and subjected another seventy-four to measures of internment or removal from the area. Clément Thomas, the ostensible head of the Gironde opposition, was first on the list of those sent away, followed by a number of journalists and lawyers, two judges, and several large landowners. In other departments the joint commission struck much harder.

In March 1852, Louis-Napoléon sent out special commissioners to review every sentence in a spirit of leniency; three thousand to four thousand pardons were granted, sometimes to the fury of those who favored a tougher course. At the same time, however, there was no slowdown in the regimentation of public opinion. A decree of February 17, 1852, tightened the regulation of the press. Higher education was forced into line: teachers were forbidden to wear beards, "considering that it is important for the last traces of anarchy to disappear"; and as some students or former students of the elite teacher training college, the École Normale Supérieure, had been led astray by leftist ideas, it was decided to do away with the *agrégation* exam in philosophy and history so that future teachers could return to their true vocation, the transmission of the values of literary culture. University teachers would have to submit to their rector advance written schedules of their courses.

Mayors and deputy mayors would be appointed by the government, even from outside the elected municipal council, and would have to appear at official ceremonies in uniform. Prefects, as the backbone of the new regime, were delegated important powers of decision, including the power to appoint lower-ranking civil servants, without having to refer to Paris. The prefect became the ruler of his department. Haussmann saw himself as the man behind some of these new provisions, especially those concerning levels of remuneration. Subprefectures were now divided into three categories, in the same way as prefectures, and the salaries attaching to both were substantially increased. More powerful and better paid, prefects were nevertheless kept under tight government control. Many were moved to a different department, some dismissed, all closely watched. Before Morny left the Ministry of the Interior, he started keeping files on them: one was "vulgar, course, curt, violent, tactless"; another had been involved in "unfortunate financial scandals"; yet another had been too parsimonious, or had shown excessive zeal.

The prince president stepped up his initiatives to restore order to the economy and to accelerate the transformation of the country. Political uncertainties had undermined confidence and wrecked the credit system. The railways and public works budgets had been savaged. The ultra-sensitivity of the National Assembly and the encumbering new Constitution had turned the crisis of 1847–1848 into a deep recession. Now the dictatorial powers of Louis-Napoléon would put an end to the disarray. The prince president imposed by decree the 1852 budget in which expenditure on new facilities showed a sharp rise. Business got moving again. A decision was made to build new railway lines to Lyons, to the north, and to Strasbourg and Basle. Telegraph lines were opened. The Crédit Foncier was created to make funds available to farmers for the coming surge of modernization, and later to serve as the main financial instrument of urban transformation. A number of friendly societies were established. The Pereire brothers founded Crédit Mobilier, the merchant bank that would accompany the equipment program so much desired by the new regime.

In the capital, where the number of large stores was on the rise, Marruau was already discovering a new Paris early in 1852: "The Hôtel de Ville saw its garrison return to barracks, while politics gave administration back its rightful place. The people roaming the city were no longer bands of insurgents but squads of masons, carpenters, and the like off to their place of work; if the paving stones were disturbed, it was not to pile them up in barricades but to make water and gas travel beneath the street; the threat to people's houses came not from cannon or fire but from the compulsory purchase order."

A decree law of March 17, 1852, halved the duty on drinks entering towns and abolished the 10 percent government levy on municipal dues. According to Haussmann, this greatly excited local people in the Gironde. A number of other projects also won support in the region: the railway link between Bordeaux and Sète, the completion of the canal by the side of the Garonne, the extension of the Bordeaux-La Teste railway line to Bayonne, the planned cross-country route linking Bordeaux, Clermont-Ferrand,

Lyons, and Geneva, and the start of a transatlantic liner service from Bordeaux.

ELECTIONS: THE BIRTH OF OFFICIAL CANDIDATES

~ The prince president and his men were concerned about the forthcoming elections to the legislature, and the prefects were in the front line when it came to proposing good candidates. Above professional politicians, they were supposed to prefer those who had "made their fortune through work in industry or agriculture, improved the lot of their workers, made noble use of their property." A legislative mandate was now incompatible with any public office and any position in the army or navy. The "organic decree" of February 2, 1852, allocated to each department one deputy for each constituency of 35,000 electors. Haussmann, whose task it was to draw the boundaries, managed to distribute the 177,847 registered electors more or less evenly among the Gironde's five constituencies: that is, Bordeaux with its suburbs of Bègles, Le Bouscat, Bruges, Caudéran, and Talence; the outer cantons of the district of Bordeaux, excluding Saint-André-de-Cubzac and Castelnau; the districts of Bazas and La Réole; the districts of Blaye and Lesparre plus the cantons of Saint-André-de-Cubzac and Castelnau; and the district of Libourne.

The regime instituted a list of "official candidates" for these elections, and prefects were instructed to draw them to the attention of the electorate. For those who might have qualms about this, Persigny wrote: "How could 8 million electors know how to distinguish . . . 261 deputies animated with the same spirit, devoted to the same interests, and equally disposed to round off the popular victory of December 20? It is therefore important that the government should enlighten the electorate about this." In the Gironde, Haussmann had no qualms, but he realized that paradoxically an official candidacy would not make it easier to recruit people to stand for the regime. Previous governments had always more or less secretly backed the men of their choice. "But strangely enough, people could never get used to the idea that a government, more honest and scornful of such hypocrisies, should openly show citizens eager to support it which candidates were worthy of all their confidence, while leaving them free to vote in accordance with their personal convictions."[4] After much negotiation, Haussmann eventually got his five quality candidates, who agreed to be named as loyal supporters of the regime.

The ballot took place over two days, February 29 and March 1, 1852; the mayors kept watch over the boxes during the night. A candidate could be elected in the first round only if he received half the votes cast and if that number represented at least a quarter of the registered electors—otherwise there had to be a second round, in which a simple majority sufficed. The official candidates were nearly all new men, either landowners or industrialists. The elections resulted in an overwhelming majority for Louis-Napoléon. Of 261 elected representatives, there were 3 Legitimists, 2 independents, and 3 republicans; the latter refused to swear an oath of loyalty to the president and resigned their seats. In the Gironde the five official candidates walked home. But the rate of participation was low—scarcely more than 50 percent—and varied widely from constituency to constituency. In four of the five there was only a single candidate, the only actual contest being in Libourne where it was easily won by the Bonapartist. On December 10 and 21, 1851, the plebiscite had given Louis-Napoléon the votes of 73 percent of registered electors. So the much lower turnout for the legislative elections was due in part to the certainty of the outcome, but it also showed that, once the great fear following the coup d'état had blown over, the population would return to more traditional political attitudes rooted in the local region. It was a warning to the government—and to the prefects. Haussmann took advantage of it to rail once more against universal suffrage.

The new institutions soon fell into place. When the list of 72 presidential appointees to the Senate was made public in January, it proved to consist of former ministers of Louis-Napoléon, former members of the Legislative Assembly, the Peers of France, generals, and judges. In addition there were 12 senators sitting by right: 4 cardinals and 8 marshals or admirals. The Council of State had Baroche as its chairman; the prince nominated his trusted men to the key positions; Rouher and Magne became heads of sections. On March 17 the state of siege that had been imposed in 32 departments was finally lifted. On March 29 deputies and senators were summoned to the Tuileries, the royal palace to which the president, in a symbolic touch, had decided to move his official residence from the Élysée. Saluted by 101 cannon shots, Louis-Napoléon made a solemn entrance and took up position on a raised platform—almost a throne—while the parliamentarians sat on rows of benches. The legislature went the next day to hold a session in the Palais Bourbon, in a hall that was now quite large enough to hold it. The temporary building erected in the courtyard in 1848 had disappeared, along with the rostrum from which representatives had previously addressed the Assembly; now they said what they had to say from their seats, facing the speaker of the house. Morny, who had been elected deputy for Clermont-Ferrand and Ambert, in the Puy-de-Dôme department, set his sights on his speaker's job, but Louis-Napoléon did not trust him and preferred Billau from the Ariège, a former Orleanist deputy who inaugurated his new functions by putting parliamentarism itself in the dock.

The legislature soon began debating the draft budget. Docile though it was, it loudly protested against the size of the deficit—40 million francs— and the floating debt of 750 million francs. Montalembert, who had taken his distance from Louis-Napoléon since the plundering of the Orléans family, announced that he would be voting against the budget. But the attempted revolt came to nothing. For the time being, the regime had managed to hold down the liberal and democratic aspirations in the country. Paris had a much livelier interest in railway speculation and the recently published *Uncle Tom's Cabin*. There were long queues to get into the Vaudeville Theatre for a performance of *La Dame aux camélias* by Alexandre Dumas, Jr. "The whole play is dripping with vice and debauchery," some thundered. Others forgot about everything in the excitement of balls offered by the head of state: a guest list of five thousand at the Tuileries, twelve thousand at the École Militaire. The festivities of August 15 offered the common people a magnificent fireworks display.

On May 5, the anniversary of the death of Napoléon I, a solemn funeral service was held at Notre Dame. But Louis-Napoléon still hesitated to take the decisive step of declaring the empire. Persigny fumed and fretted: "Nervous scruples suddenly gripped him."

The cantonal elections of September 1 also turned out favorably for the regime. In the Gironde, forty-five of Haussmann's protégés were elected to the forty-eight available seats, including General de Saint-Arnaud (who was appointed president of the departmental council), the inevitable marquis de la Grange, and Duffour-Dubergier. But the voter turnout was even lower than before. The session of the departmental council opened on August 23. Georges-Eugène, with all his experience of police and politics, was in his element here as the professional administrator. The finances were in bad shape, mainly because the length of the departmental highways had soared from 364 miles in 1847 to 480 in 1852—not excessive, perhaps, for the largest department in France, but requiring heavy expenditure, especially in the Gironde part of the Landes. The prefect argued that further development of the railway network should make it possible to downgrade some sections of highway. At the end of a busy fortnight, the forty councillors present at the closing session passed a motion congratulating Haussmann on his work.[5]

At its first session, all the councillors save one expressed a wish "that the Senate will take legal steps toward giving the government of Louis-Napoléon Bonaparte the form and stability required by the interests, the spirit, and the customs of France." Other departmental councils called more explicitly for a restoration of the empire. But what did the French people really want? In September the prince president decided to sound out public opinion by undertaking a major tour of the provinces. "I do not want the answer to be prepared," he ordered the government. Persigny naturally enjoined the prefects of the relevant departments to have crowds ready to shout "Vive l'Empereur!" And the agreed slogan was raised in Bourges, Nevers, and Moulins, as it was in Roanne, Saint-Étienne, and Lyons. The trip continued through Grenoble and Valence. At Avignon and Arles the prince was similarly acclaimed. At Marseilles, where Napoléon laid the foundation stone of the new cathedral, a plot was uncovered (or perhaps set up) by the police. At Montpellier the prefect had not done his work properly. The crowd shouted "Vive l'amnistie!"

In Bordeaux, Haussmann had arranged things remarkably well. On his own admission, his relations with the people of Bordeaux were not of the best. But Bordeaux was not like the rest of the Gironde. The landowners, whose harvest was bought up by the city's wine merchants, were in a position of economic dependence. But "the popular masses escaped this subjection, and both in the countryside and in Bordeaux itself they followed other currents of opinion than those of the upper or middle classes."[6] As much as memories of the imperial saga remained alive among the peasantry, the bourgeoisie of Bordeaux wished to base its choices on nothing other than the interests of the port and to modulate its political attitudes in accordance with what the government did for its prosperity. The First Empire meant the continental blockade and the loss of the colonies, a complete disaster for foreign trade: "In 1814 the people of Bordeaux acclaimed the return of the Bourbons and, with them, the return of European peace!"[7] The July Monarchy, which favored peace at any price, made Bordeaux richer; the city discovered itself to be Orleanist. If, in October 1852, Bordeaux suddenly began to feel differently and gave Louis-Napoléon an enthusiastic welcome, this was because the prince came with the solemn declaration: "The Empire means peace!"

The conversion was not effected by the wave of a magic wand. As the results of the legislative elections showed, Bordeaux remained aloof. Some in Paris blamed Haussmann for the poor showing. Colonel Espinasse, one of the architects of the December coup, put this view most strongly: "Like many others close to the prince," Haussmann later wrote, "the colonel doubtless attributed the relatively moderate character of my actions to the influence of old attachments."[8]

Haussmann had known for a long time that in every field things needed to be done gradually, and he took special care over preparations for Louis-Napoléon's visit. When putting the finishing touches to the route, he asked that Bordeaux be the last of the big cities to be visited, not the first as the original plan had envisaged. The reasons he gave Persigny for this were of a technical nature: work on the final Angoulême-Bordeaux section of the line to Paris was only just finished; the terminus would be at La Bastide Station on the right bank of the Garonne, where piles of rubble were still causing an obstruction; the prince's entry across the stone bridge over the river would not differ in any way from countless others, and its stereotyped ceremony would leave the population cold. In Haussmann's view, if Louis-Napoléon instead descended the Garonne and approached the city through the port, his entry would be guaranteed the necessary pomp. To this he added a psychological argument: "This beautiful city would like to justify . . . the high rank that it rightly occupies among the great towns of France, and the more the others have done, the more its just pride will command it to do when its own turn comes. The reception in Bordeaux should therefore be kept back as the finishing piece of the imperialist demonstration that the sight of the prince will everywhere occasion." Persigny agreed. It was up to Haussmann to show that he had not been mistaken and that he knew how to go about things.

The prince president was scheduled to stay in Bordeaux for four days: October 7, 8, 9, and 10, 1852. On the 6th, Haussmann went by boat to wait for Louis-Napoléon at La Réole, so that he could welcome him at the moment he entered the territory of the Gironde. Everything had been planned to the finest detail—everything except the demonstrations by Garonne sailors, whose enthusiastic shouts exceeded Haussmann's expectations. On the morning of the 7th, Haussmann greeted the prince at La Réole and presented the Gironde deputies and members of the departmental council. (Later he was told that he had addressed Louis-Napoléon as "Sire," a slip he had not noticed at the time.) The journey down the Garonne, from La Réole to Bordeaux, took place in splendid weather and was accompanied by crowds on both banks waving forests of flags and shouting "Vive l'Empereur!" Inhabitants of the ancient region of Aquitaine, which took in Bordeaux, were known to "make gunpowder speak"[9]—although the expression did not have the national notoriety that rugby and sports reporters would give it a century and a half later. This was October 7, 1852, and Haussmann cautiously placed it in inverted commas for the benefit of ignoramuses in the rest of France. Louis-Napoléon was struck dumb with wonder when he arrived at the "Port of the Moon": boats were decked out with flags, navy ships let their cannons be heard, and bells rang at each volley. The whole city seemed to have collected on the Place des Quinconces, where the prince came in to land. Louis-Napoléon eventually found a low voice to utter: "This is a capital city!"

On the evening of October 8 there was a dinner followed by a gala ball in the Grand Theatre. The monumental staircase caught Louis-Napoléon's eye. Charles Garnier, "the clever architect of the new Paris opera," would later have the good sense to take inspiration from it. The arrangement of the reception hall was the work of the civil engineer Adolphe Alphand, whose name would for many years be linked with that of Prefect Haussmann in the Seine department. Louis-Napoléon danced with Octavie, Haussmann with the sister-in-law of the mayor of Bordeaux.

Rain disturbed the program for the next day, leaving the prefect time to make preparations for the evening meal at the Chamber of Commerce. The president of the chamber, Duffour-Dubergier, was taken by Haussmann to see the prince president, who went over with him the finishing touches for the exchange of speeches. In the hall of the Bourse, a thousand prominent citizens took part in the final celebrations of the presidential trip: the famous "Bordeaux speech" in which Louis-Napoléon Bonaparte announced the coming restoration of the empire. "France seems to want to return to the Empire. Some say: the Empire means war. But I say: the Empire means peace." As if freeing himself of a great weight, the prince president outlined the main features of his program: national reconciliation, improvement of the lot of the still large section of the population who "are scarcely able to enjoy the bare necessities of life." He continued: "We have immense uncultivated lands to develop, roads to open, harbors to dig, rivers to make navigable, canals to finish, our railway network to complete. Facing Marseilles we have a vast country [Algeria] to integrate with France. We have all our great ports in the west to draw closer to the American continent through the swift communications we still lack. . . . Such are the conquests I have in mind, and all you around me, who want as I do the good of our nation, you are my soldiers."

The presidential tour was a plebiscite *avant la lettre*. Haussmann wired

Persigny: "This speech is a great event. It is a formal acceptance of the Empire." That evening another ball took place at the Grand Theatre. No women all dressed up, no glittering jewels: the city of Bordeaux invited its working-class population to dance. It was Alphand's idea. He chose the prince's partner, the daughter of a foreman. Haussmann also danced with a working woman. The next day the prince gave his prefect a gift to hand to his dancer; Haussmann was most happy to give one to his own partner of the night before.

At midday on October 10, the prince president caught the train at the Gare La Bastide and began the journey back to Paris via Angoulême, Rochefort, La Rochelle, Tours, and Amboise (where he told Abdel Kader that his captivity would soon be over). When he reached the capital on October 16, he was greeted by the president of the municipal council and then made his way along boulevards decorated with flags and little *arcs de triomphe*, to the sound of bells, cannon salvos, and shouts of "Vive l'Empereur!" The Austrian ambassador, Hübner, noted: "The public was fairly indifferent."

PROCLAMATION OF THE EMPIRE

❧ The Senate was convened—officially to offer a ruling on the wishes expressed by the departmental councils, but in reality to express its opinion on "changes in the form of government." Haussmann, who had no doubt about the result, did not wait before revising the electoral lists in the Gironde. On November 7 the Senate announced its decision: it proposed unanimously, barring one vote, to restore the dignity of empire in the person of Louis-Napoléon Bonaparte, with the right of inheritance through his descendants. The electorate was called upon to deliver its verdict in a plebiscite, on November 20 and 21. As one might have expected, Haussmann's appeal as prefect to the electors of the Gironde relied heavily upon the Bordeaux speech: "Never has a people displayed more directly, more unanimously, its will to free itself from worries about the future, by consolidating in the same hands a regime with which it is in sympathy. . . . It was under the impression of your warm and magnificent welcome; it was in Bordeaux itself that Prince Louis-Napoléon summed up . . . in a forever memorable speech his triumphant march through the departments of the South."[10]

Citizens were simply asked to say whether they agreed with the following statement: "The people wishes to restore the dignity of empire in the person of Louis-Napoléon Bonaparte." The number in favor was 7,824,189, or 96.9 percent, against 253,645 answering "no." In the Gironde the majority was even more overwhelming: 98 percent. The prefect estimated that, had torrential rain not kept a number of electors from going to the polling station, the result would have been still better.

On December 1 the Senate, the Legislature, and the Council of State went to the Château de Saint Cloud to give the prince the results of the ballot. Louis-Napoléon took the title Napoléon III, out of respect for the "Eaglet," Napoléon II, who had died in 1832. The next day, December 2, the empire was proclaimed and the new *empereur des Français* made his solemn entry into Paris. There he declared a wide-ranging amnesty. Saint-Arnaud and Magnan became marshals, Morny was awarded the grand cross of the Légion d'Honneur, and the civil list of the head of state was set at 25 million francs. In the various departments, official ceremonies marking the proclamation of the empire took place on Sunday, December 5. For Haussmann it was the high point of his career so far. He felt that he deserved some reward for the quality of his work, and he made this known to Persigny. On January 1, 1853, he was raised to the rank of commander of the Légion d'Honneur.

The proclamation of the empire caused much gnashing of teeth in other parts of Europe. The king of Piedmont-Sardinia was one of the first to recognize Napoléon III, followed by the king of the Belgians and the German princes. Prussia was not so sure. Great Britain was quite favorable to the prince, who had lived for a long time in London and whose Anglophilia was a known fact. London invited Austria, Prussia, and Russia to a secret conference, which took note of Napoléon III's support for peace and decided to recognize the new regime.

Napoléon III had more trouble finding a princess to marry him and ensure the future of the dynasty. After a series of refusals in the courts of Europe, he chose instead a marriage of love. On January 22, 1853, in the Throne Hall, he announced to the officers of the Senate, the Legislature, and the Council of State his forthcoming marriage to Eugénie de Montijo, comtesse de Teba, a very beautiful Spanish woman aged twenty-six. He himself was then forty-four. "When, faced with the old Europe, one is carried by the force of a new idea to the level of the old dynasties, the way to gain acceptance is not by making one's coat of arms appear older or by seeking at any price to enter the family of kings, but by always keeping in mind one's own origins, retaining one's own character, frankly assuming in relation to Europe the position of *parvenu*, a glorious title when one attains it through

PREFECT FOR THE SEINE

the free vote of a great people. . . . I have preferred a wife I respect to marriage with an unknown woman that would have had advantages mixed with sacrifices." The civil wedding took place on January 29 at the Tuileries Palace, followed on January 30 by a religious ceremony at Notre Dame.

The regime was shoring up its position. Festivities followed one another in quick succession, but the old nobility continued to sulk. "Etiquette is all the stricter if it is of recent date," the Austrian ambassador Hübner ironically observed. But what did it matter? If the poor grew richer, and the rich still richer, who would be so mad as to waste their energies in the sterile games of politics?

For the Gironde, where Mademoiselle de Montijo and her mother were well-known figures, the marriage of Napoléon III was an opportunity to send gifts and congratulatory messages to the imperial couple. On February 20, Haussmann was summoned to Paris by Persigny. In recognition of his services in various posts and especially at Bordeaux, Napoléon III had a flattering promotion in mind: namely, a place on the Council of State and an appointment as special state counselor, Rhône prefect/mayor of Lyons, and chief of police for the Rhône, with additional responsibility for the monitoring of political refugees in Switzerland. But Haussmann refused the offer. He preferred to serve out his career at the Gironde prefecture, where he was very busy with two projects close to his heart: attachment of the commune of La Bastide to the territory of Bordeaux, and construction of a ring boulevard around the city. In fact, Haussmann was proud to have been more or less accepted into the closed world of large wine merchants in the Chartrons area of Bordeaux. "Finally my wife and I had entered a milieu that nothing could replace for us, one that suited our family interests and degree of wealth, and in excellent relations with a world where our children's future seemed assured in advance by the great respect in which my wife's parents were held and the esteem that we ourselves enjoyed."[11] Having become a landowner in the Lot-et-Garonne, he could see only advantages in remaining at the head of a prefecture that promised him considerable leisure at such a short distance from his land. The emperor understood his reasons and acceded to his request; he appointed the former interior minister Vaïsse to the position in Lyons.

Georges-Eugène quietly returned to the Gironde. He no longer had in mind anything more than the extension of the limits of Bordeaux (his project eventually led to the fusion with La Bastide on January 1, 1865), the plans for a ring boulevard, and the construction of coastal defenses against the assaults of the ocean at the Pointe de Grave headland.

PREFECT FOR THE SEINE. WHO MADE YOU KING?

≈ On the evening of June 23, 1853, a day he had spent making a tour of inspection, Georges-Eugène was in the middle of dinner at the Bazas subprefecture when a dispatch rider from Bordeaux handed him an envelope containing a message sent by Persigny from Paris a few hours previously. It informed Haussmann of his appointment as prefect for the Seine and instructed him to proceed to the capital without delay. Haussmann continued with the dinner as if nothing had happened, merely asking the rider to take a dispatch back to Bordeaux after it was over. It was a forced display of calm—for, as he admitted in his *Mémoires*, "the dispatch I had just received caused me something more than astonishment: a great disturbance of mind. Nothing had suggested to me that I would receive this quite exceptional appointment. The thought had never even crossed my mind."[12]

The secret had been well kept. "A flash of lightning striking my dinner plate at the Bazas subprefecture would not have surprised me more than my appointment to the Seine prefecture arriving by dispatch in the middle of our dessert. But instead of the great satisfaction that it would probably have caused to others, I felt a sense of blank annoyance that grew as I thought more about it."[13] Haussmann retired to the subprefect's office and drafted a polite telegram to Persigny in which he thanked him but asked to be kept on at Bordeaux. As his secretary general had had the presence of mind to send to Bazas a prefectural counselor who could relieve him of the inspection operations, Haussmann was back in Bordeaux early on the 24th. That same afternoon, another telegram arrived from Persigny: the emperor himself had appointed Haussmann to the Seine prefecture; the appointment had already appeared in the official *Moniteur*, together with the name of his replacement in Bordeaux. He had no option but to send back his acceptance, which he did in a telegram dated June 24, 1853, 4 P.M.: "I have reason to believe that my experience of government administration will be of only little value in the exceptional post to which I have been called. Yet I belong unreservedly to the emperor, and however perilous for myself I judge the new position to which His Majesty has assigned me, I shall occupy it if that is his wish, and I shall bring to it the complete devotion of which I have already given more than one proof."

Haussmann just had time to say his farewells, to take leave of his colleagues, to pay his respects to the municipal and departmental notables. Then on the 27th he set off for Paris. He arrived the next morning and went straight to the Hôtel du Danube in rue Richepance, where a few relatives and friends had turned out to welcome him, and where Monsieur Buffet, the head of the supply department at the Hôtel de Ville, was waiting to take his order for furnishings and equipment. Haussmann already knew that bourgeois circles in Paris greatly regretted Berger's departure, and that they would be wondering about his successor. Those who knew him and had come to offer their congratulations found him looking pensive. Georges-Eugène wanted to understand the reasons for his appointment—the inside story, perhaps. To understand so that he could get his bearings in the new arena.

It was clear, first of all, that Persigny had played a role in the appointment. Haussmann takes his hat off to him in a passage of the *Mémoires* that also allows him to express the high opinion he has of himself: "M. de Persigny, my new minister of the interior, did not know me at all personally, but the exactitude, precision, and independence of my correspondence from Bordeaux had won me his sympathy. Struck by the results I had obtained there, he held me in very high esteem."

In fact Haussmann contradicts himself, because he writes elsewhere that he had already had at least one long meeting with Persigny, when the minister had offered and Haussmann refused the appointment in Lyons. We know from Persigny's *Souvenirs* that once it had been decided to replace Berger in the Seine prefecture, the problem arose of finding a successor with the necessary abilities and substance. For the first time in a long time, the regime rejected the idea of appointing a politician to the post—the established practice since the First Empire. They wanted a solid, experienced, battle-hardened administrator. Why not find one among the most seasoned prefects? "In my view," Persigny writes, "a departmental prefect alien to the coteries of Paris salons, but familiar with the ways of the bureaucracy, would sincerely accept the proposed system and everything it implied, and would have a thousand times better chance than a political figure of achieving success. But could I find the necessary independence of mind among prefects used to bowing before all-powerful ministers? That was the question." The only way to form an opinion was to meet the potential candidates. And so Persigny met for dinner and probed all the leading prefects: from Rouen, Lille, Lyons, Marseilles—and Bordeaux.

The minister already appreciated the efficiency of the prefect for the Gironde. As Haussmann says, he remembered the notes and reports that revealed a meticulous administrator, a man with a taste for detail and a real spirit of initiative. It all added up to quite an explosive mixture of cunning and inflexibility. Furthermore, the head of administration at the interior ministry—a man with whom Persigny was on excellent terms—was none other than the Frémy whom Haussmann had known for many years. Did Frémy perhaps remember the day when Georges-Eugène, revealing a bit of his true self, had rejected Faucher's offer of the job of Paris chief of police, on the grounds that the Seine prefecture could turn out to be much more important (which suggested that the position would not come personally amiss), so long as it was given not to Berger or "some other political war horse" but to "a man whose position in the state or record of service endowed him with sufficient authority to carry out works on a grand scale, and who had the vigor of mind and body to fight the routinism that is so strong in France and personally to direct many diverse and tiring projects, as well as fulfilling the considerable delegated duties in a manner worthy of his important role"?[14]

Persigny also alludes to Frémy's role: "As M. Frémy had predicted, . . . it was M. Haussmann who impressed me the most." But he adds that his dinner with Haussmann did much more than Frémy's recommendation to convince him that he had found the rare pearl he needed. "Strangely enough, what appealed to me was less the faculties of his remarkable intelligence than the faults of his character. . . . I had before me one of the most extraordinary figures of our times: big, strong, vigorous, and energetic, but also shrewd, cunning, resourceful—a bold man not afraid to show himself as he was. Visibly indulgent toward his own person, he set out the heroic deeds of his administrative career, not sparing me any detail. He could have spoken for six hours without stopping—provided it was about his favorite subject, himself. Anyway, I was far from complaining about this tendency of his. It revealed to me all the facets of his strange personality. There was nothing as curious as the way he told me of his hard work on the 2nd of December, his wrangling with the navy minister, the poor M. Ducos, whose hands were filled with two women, and especially his fights with the municipal council in Bordeaux. He spoke in the greatest detail of incidents during his campaign against formidable opponents in the municipality, of the traps they laid for him, the precautions he took not to fall into them, the crushing blows he delivered to them once they were on the ground. His forehead shone with the pride of victory.

"For my own part, I could not contain my pleasure as this absorbing personality laid himself before me with a kind of brutal cynicism. Here, I said to myself, is the perfect man to combat the ideas and prejudices of a whole school of economics, to take on cunning and skeptical people, mostly from the corridors of the Bourse or the legal profession, who are not choosy about the methods they use. Where a gentleman with the loftiest and cleverest mind, the deftest and noblest character, would inevitably come a cropper, this vigorous athlete with a strong backbone and thick neckline, this bold and skillful individual capable of countering tricks with tricks, ambushes with ambushes, would be certain to succeed. I toyed in advance with the idea of setting this big animal from the feline race among a pack of foxes and wolves banded together against the noble aspirations of the Empire."

All that remained was to have this choice confirmed by the emperor. And when Persigny proposed to Napoléon III that he should appoint Haussmann to the Seine prefecture, he agreed without hesitation: "When passing through Bordeaux, at the time of his famous 'the Empire means peace' speech, the emperor had been able to gauge M. Haussmann's abilities. He recognized in him that faculty peculiar to organizers which the prefect for the Gironde possessed to the highest degree: the capacity to take care of the details as well as the whole."

If we are to believe Persigny, then, it was he who "invented" Haussmann, just as he "invented" the financial system of productive expenditure, and sold the package to Napoléon III. But this may really be a bit much. Of course it was the responsibility of the interior minister, by definition, to propose the name of a prefect to the head of the executive. Of course the interior minister was by definition a key figure in the government, and Persigny had from the beginning been an especially close collaborator of Louis-Napoléon, joined to him through ties of friendship and shared turpitude. It is also true that Persigny was later marginalized as a result of the liberal evolution of the regime as well as a few personal mishaps, and that his manichaean vision of the prince's entourage drew a sharp line between the original clan of Bonapartists and the circles who jumped on the bandwagon of the state out of sheer opportunism. Haussmann would remain in place until the early days of 1870, a last survivor from among the figures symbolizing the authoritarian early period of the empire. And so it was quite natural that Persigny, a pillar of that authoritarianism, should in a way appropriate Haussmann for his own clan.

Persigny's only mistake was to forget that even in 1853, Georges-Eugène Haussmann was by no means unknown to Napoléon III. No doubt the account of his appointment that Georges-Eugène left for posterity in his *Mémoires* commits the opposite fault of implying that he owed nothing to anyone except the emperor and his own merits. Nevertheless, this also contains a share of the truth.

What does Haussmann actually say? "As I later discovered, M. Frémy—

then head of administration at the interior ministry—accompanied M. de
Persigny when a list of serving prefects was submitted to His Majesty at his
request so that he could choose one among them as the new prefect for the
Seine. Chance would have it that, as a result of several recent movements in
the administrative staff, I found myself, as prefect for the Gironde, at the
head of the highest-ranking prefects. The emperor immediately stopped at
my name, saying: 'There's no point going any further; this is the one I need!'
My appointment was thus made both by selection and by seniority."

The explanation seems too simple to provide a complete account of what
happened. But Haussmann adds at once a rather more plausible point: "The
head of state had doubtless recalled the exceptional circumstances that
brought to his attention my periods of administration in the Var and the
Yonne (where I received him twice before the Second of December); next, his
plan to send me to Lyons in 1851 at the time of the formation of the Lyons
agglomeration and again more recently in March 1853; and finally, and most
important, his entry into Bordeaux in October 1852, his three triumphant
days spent walking around that great and beautiful city, and the splendid
setting of the hall of the Bourse for that historic speech in which he summarized his magnificent program (so unfortunately belied by events): 'The Empire means peace.'" And in keeping with a book of memoirs in which, like
Persigny, he repeatedly claims his place among the "chosen few" or even the
"born imperialists," Haussmann goes on to say: "It is known that I was a
godson of Prince Eugène, to whose general staff my maternal grandfather
belonged as field officer. . . . Mocquard, the emperor's secretary, formerly
subprefect at Bagnères-de-Bigorre when I was subprefect at Nérac, was informed of this detail and thought it of some importance. Indeed, Napoléon
III always took great account of the assurances of loyalty that descendants of
those who served the First Empire seemed to give him."[15]

According to Haussmann, it was Napoléon III who decided to appoint
him on his own initiative. According to Persigny, he himself put Haussmann's name forward, but he gives the false impression that he had first met
him only a few weeks before. In view of the fact that the transformation of
Paris was one of Napoléon III's main policy objectives, it would not be at all
surprising if he decided on his own initiative to appoint Haussmann as prefect for the Seine, especially as Berger had given him daily proof of the disappointments that could result from a wrong choice for this post. In the end,
what does it matter? As Henri Malet put it: "Persigny's account seems to involve quite a large fictional element, added for the greater glory of its author. But it has left us a lively and spirited portrait of our prefect, at once

vicious and laudatory, which must on the whole bear him quite a fair resemblance."[16]

FIRST VISITS

≈ Haussmann hastened to pay a visit to Frémy, who gave him a first briefing on the causes and circumstances of Berger's disgrace. Then they went together to see Persigny. Haussmann's *Mémoires* give us a brief account of this meeting which acquires its full pungency only when it is compared with the words of Persigny quoted above. "M. de Persigny," he writes, "gave me a welcome even better than the one I had expected: with open arms. From the beginning of our personal relations, this excellent man had taken to me with unflagging affection and given me many proofs of his absolute trust. The results of my administration in the Gironde, particularly the incomparable welcome given in October 1852 to the future emperor by all classes of the population in the city of Bordeaux—a city considered an impregnable bastion of Orleanism—had filled him with enthusiasm. He therefore had no doubt that I would be able to tackle, apparently without extra effort, the difficulties awaiting me at the Hôtel de Ville in Paris, even though the new field of struggle would be much less familiar to me."[17] Persigny confirmed to him the reasons for Berger's departure and outlined the task that Napoléon III would entrust to him, leaving it to the emperor himself to explain the details. The minister of the interior concluded by advising Haussmann to be at the Palais de Saint-Cloud the next morning between ten and eleven o'clock, to take his oath of office after the session of the Council of Ministers.

Back at the Hôtel du Danube, Haussmann received a visit from Merruau. A graduate in history from the École Normale Supérieure, he had become chief editor of *Le Constitutionnel* and worked closely with Thiers before siding with the prince president against the Assembly; he had then joined Berger's team and remained secretary general at the Seine prefecture since the coup d'état of December 2. Merruau told Haussmann that he would consider it normal if he wished to replace him, and simply asked to be given time to find another position. In the meantime, the new prefect would be able to count upon his loyal cooperation. Haussmann immediately reassured him that, unless Merruau himself considered his fate to be tied to Berger's, he intended to keep him in the job. It might be natural that a prefect should take his private secretary with him at the end of his period in office, but there was no reason why a secretary general, who had a special remit from the head of state, should be at the mercy of a change in prefects. The same

applied to the two subprefects in the Seine (a department roughly corresponding to the area now divided between Paris, Hauts-de-Seine, Seine-
Saint-Denis, and Val-de-Marne): that is, the subprefects at Saint-Denis and
Sceaux. In principle, Haussmann no more intended to replace them than he
did Merruau. "In the absence of any other advantage, the arrival of a career
prefect in the Seine prefecture should assert the traditional principle of safe-
guarding the administrative personnel. Our hierarchy is open to all
merits. . . . Once inside it, no one should leave to suit a superior's whim or
convenience."

Merruau quickly pointed out that he had Napoléon III to thank, not
Berger, for his appointment as secretary general. "Well, then," Haussmann
replied, "that makes it perfect. I shall be very glad to keep by my side, as a
permanent witness to my actions, a functionary enjoying such patronage
who cannot be suspected of harboring any prejudice against me."[18] Merruau
returned to the Hôtel de Ville and was soon putting the other section heads
in the picture. Haussmann later heard that he had been presented as "a great
captain who would turn everything upside down."

That afternoon, Haussmann went to the Boulevard Saint-Germain to
meet the marquis and marquise de La Grange. The marquise's salon was one
of the most popular in Paris, while she herself had a biting wit whose barbs
always spared Haussmann's "gracious household." The couple said they were
delighted with Georges-Eugène's appointment, claiming it almost as a personal success, and predicted that he would have fewer problems than he
thought. It was not Berger's disgrace that surprised them but rather
Napoléon III's long forbearance in relation to a man who, though sincere in
supporting the empire, was "still imbued with the narrow ideas of another
age." Such judgments could not have failed to please Haussmann. The new
prefect hoped that the marquise would rally the faubourg Saint-Germain behind a Hôtel de Ville where everyone, from whichever party, could meet on
neutral ground.

Haussmann arrived at the Hôtel de Ville shortly before two o'clock.
Berger received him cordially in a small dark office, with just a single window looking onto the Place de Grève (today's Place de l'Hôtel de Ville).
"Well, come in, young man!" Berger called out. "You do keep people waiting! I've been longing to shake your hand." And he even added: "I am glad it
is you who are taking over from me, not one of those who slyly worked
against me in the hope of taking my place." Then Berger gave his account of
the "kind of conflict" he had had with Napoléon III over what in his view
were the emperor's extravagant plans for the embellishment of Paris.

Haussmann could do no more than listen in silence. He intuitively agreed with Berger's opposition to any increase in direct or indirect taxation that would weigh upon the population of the capital. Deep within himself, he felt caught between two contradictory arguments. On the one hand, the capital of a highly centralized country had a role to play in relation both to its own residents and to the country as a whole—and that meant a certain level of spending. On the other hand, the purse of its taxpayers was the city's true wealth and had to be preserved at all costs. Why not use that wealth to support a system resting upon trust—that is, upon a pledge that would not actually be mobilized but would allow sizable loans to be raised without tightening the fiscal screw? Haussmann knew that, whatever it might take, he had to find a way of serving the political interests of the imperial government that also safeguarded the city's finances.

The government's interest definitely seemed to lie in large-scale public works. "Despite my long time in the provinces (no less than twenty-two years!), my earlier memories and impressions had remained so strong that, when I was suddenly called in the space of a few days to direct the much-debated transformation of the capital of the Empire between the Tuileries and the Hôtel de Ville, I felt much better prepared than one probably imagined to carry out this complicated assignment, and in any event ready to go straight to the heart of the matters to be resolved."[19] Georges-Eugène understood that the transformation of Paris was a necessity. The capital was experiencing a major growth of population due to the feverishly woven network of railways that was making Paris one of the crossroads of Europe. Huge spaces remained unproductive on the outskirts of the capital while the city center was slowly choking to death. "I did not yet know what the emperor had planned. But I was born in Paris, in the former faubourg of Le Roule that is now part of the faubourg Saint-Honoré, at the point where the Boulevard Haussmann ends and the Avenue de Friedland begins; I went to school at the Collège Henri IV, the former Lycée Napoléon located on Mount Sainte-Geneviève, where I later followed courses at the École de Droit and— time wasted—at the Sorbonne and the Collège de France; I had gone for walks in every part of the city, and very often in my youth I had been absorbed in lengthy contemplation of a map of this motley city—which had shown me the imperfections of its network of public thoroughfares."[20]

Everything hinged on a solution to the problem of finances. Haussmann had a sense that Berger underestimated the revenue boost to be expected from the city's demographic growth and the inevitable rise in the number of floating French and foreign residents drawn there on business or pleasure by the greater ease of transport. The theory of productive expenditure, he admitted, had long been one of his articles of faith. And as he bid Berger farewell, Haussmann asked him to leave at his hotel some copies of the income and expenditure account for 1852 and the budget for 1853. The remaining visits he had to make were to the chief of police and the president of the municipal council.

Haussmann scarcely knew the chief of police, Pierre-Marie Pietri, but he sensed from the latter's loud rejoicing that he had not been uninvolved in Berger's removal. Pietri lived as an old bachelor at the run-down offices of the *préfecture de police* on rue de Jérusalem, a small street leading onto the Quai des Orfevres that has since made way for the Palais de Justice. Little attracted by the pomp of official events, he seemed to take real pleasure in his police work. The discovery of his pathological sensitivity was not an easy experience for Haussmann.

The presidency of the municipal council was in the hands of Delangle, an eminent legal expert, senator, and chief presiding officer of the Imperial Court. In the course of his career he had been a director of studies at a day school, an attorney, a public prosecutor, and a parliamentary deputy; he was proud to have raised himself by sheer hard work. Naturally cold in manner, he was positively glacial in his first encounter with Haussmann and did not conceal his feeling that he was sorry to see Berger go. The new prefect cut the meeting short.

Back at the Hôtel du Danube, Haussmann found the finance documents promised by Berger. He worked on them until very late, and the sleepless hours proved fruitful in revealing layer after layer of available reserves that had been carefully hidden beneath undervalued income and blatantly overvalued expenditure.

THE OATH OF OFFICE

❧ The next day, at 10 A.M. on June 29, 1853, Haussmann found himself in ceremonial dress in the billiard room of the Château de Saint-Cloud. The meeting of the Council of Ministers, chaired by Napoléon III, went on longer than expected, and Haussmann waited for more than an hour in the company of other prefects summoned to take their oath of office. When the meeting finally ended, Persigny showed them into the hall where Napoléon III was to receive them. The emperor told a proud Haussmann that he was glad to be awarding him a position to which he attached exceptional importance. Persigny read out the wording of the oath: "You pledge allegiance to the Constitution and loyalty to the emperor." Haussmann placed his hands between those of Napoléon III and said: "I swear." There he was: prefect for the Seine.

The other prefects in turn sweared the oath. The solemnity of the occasion was briefly interrupted when Persigny presented to Napoléon III the new prefect for Cantal, Monsieur Paillard, with a glowing report on his conduct. Thinking that he had heard "Bayard" instead of "Paillard," the emperor replied amiably enough, "I expect you to prove yourself worthy of the name."[21] Those present found it difficult to suppress the fit of laughter that came over them.

The oath-taking ceremony was followed by lunch. Haussmann, now topping the hierarchy as prefect for the Seine, was seated to the right of Empress Eugénie. A number of ministers were present, and Haussmann spoke freely—especially about himself and his family. With the empress he touched on the city of Bordeaux, his (and Eugénie's) godfather Prince Eugène, and the ancestry of Madame Haussmann. Taking stock of the meal, he was happy to have "positioned both my wife and myself at Court" on the very first day.[22]

The emperor took the new prefect into his office for a tête-à-tête and showed him the famous color-striped map. In his *Mémoires*, Haussmann assures us that it was only out of flattery that he expressed complete support for the emperor's projects. But he did stress that it would be necessary to proceed with caution, arguing that while the people of Paris were generally well disposed toward the development works, the aristocracy and upper bourgeoisie would be mostly hostile. In fact, the emperor seemed well aware of this danger and had decided to dissolve the municipal council; he suggested a few names for possible replacements. Haussmann asked for a few days to test the hearts and spines of the existing municipal councillors, in order to avoid waving a red rag in front of conservative opinion right from the start. If things went badly, there would still be time to dissolve the council. Napoléon III accepted these proposals, with their hallmark of common sense.

Haussmann also learned that the emperor had set up an unofficial commission outside the council proper to examine the various plans for new roads. This made a bad impression on the new prefect for the Seine, so bad that he regretted having accepted the job. With considerable skill, he suggested that the commission risked presenting municipal councillors with a good reason to turn against the emperor's projects. Either the head of state thought he could work with them—and then what was the point of a commission? Or he did not think he could work with the councillors—in which case, why had he not simply dismissed them? Napoléon III found the argument persuasive. The commission would meet in a few days' time, with Haussmann in attendance. Then it would be up to him to decide its fate.

Haussmann left Saint Cloud and returned to Paris. Once he had rid himself of the ceremonial dress, he made himself at home in the Hôtel de Ville and initiated the transfer of power. The Berger administration was over, the Haussmann era was just beginning. It would last sixteen and a half years.

12

Haussmann in Control

IN THE late afternoon of the same day, June 29, 1853, Berger and Hauss-mann met for a second time in the Hôtel de Ville for the traditional transfer of power. This simple formality had often been limited to the signing of a record of the newcomer's arrival. But as a courtesy to Haussmann, and per-haps also to put a brave face on adversity, Berger wished to give the proceed-ings an air of prestige. After the written record drawn up by Merruau had been duly signed, Berger presented to Haussmann the divisional heads and the city treasurer who together, under the direction of the secretary general, constituted the prefect's general staff. Then Berger withdrew from the stage, with the same dignity and the same perfect elegance he would always dis-play toward his successor. On Haussmann's side, one of the first acts of his administration was to propose that the street bordering the façade of the Halles should be named rue Berger. The Halles have since disappeared, but rue Berger still survives. It now runs along the south side of the Forum, par-allel to rue Rambuteau on the north side.

TAKING CHARGE

⁂ In taking leave of his section heads, Haussmann asked them to return at five o'clock to the so-called Throne Hall with all their colleagues from the internal administration—that is to say, members of staff actually working at the Hôtel de Ville. The various offices were spread among four divisions plus the Caisse Municipale, the city's treasury department. The first division was in charge of direct taxation, city dues, recruitment, and military affairs. The second division dealt with general, departmental, and communal adminis-tration, charitable institutions, religious worship, and public education. The third division was responsible for highways, local roads, major Parisian thoroughfares, waterways, public works, and architecture. The fourth division handled accounting, budgets, the administrative audit,[1] the uses of expenditure, and financial inspection. The distribution of responsibilities corresponded to areas of administrative activity and did not distinguish, in each case, what lay within the competence of the central government, the Seine department, or the city of Paris.

Haussmann, who had the feeling that Berger had reigned more than governed, was determined to get back on top of the prefectural administration. As he entered the Throne Hall, he took in his new subordinates arranged by division and office. The new prefect walked down their lines and had them introduced to him in turn, careful to say a few polite words to each. Then, positioning himself in front of one of the monumental chimneys at the end of the hall, he delivered the little speech he had been preparing for an hour or two. It did not seek stylistic effect—indeed, it seemed as if he was improvising. "*Messieurs*: Having just taken up my appointment, I did not want to delay making direct contact with all those who have become, more than my assistants, my fellow workers in the great task of administration entrusted to my dutiful charge." He followed this with a bow to the noble old lady that was the Paris administration: "Before all else, I intend to observe and study in motion the many different wheels of this administration. Resulting from the lessons of a now distant past, its organization has in its favor that authority of an established order which must always be seriously heeded. . . . If it is necessary for me to modify it, I shall do so in a gradual and measured manner, scrupulously respecting individual positions already acquired."

The experienced prefect, a public servant like those he addressed, went on to give some account of himself. "I am a functionary of already long service. . . . My entry into the administration dates from my first steps in life. I have moved through all the grades, sometimes quite laboriously, from the first to the highest—without jumping a single one. . . . I intend to form my own judgment of the merits and services of each one of you, so that I can be conscientious in distributing the favors—or rather, the rewards of all kinds—that I shall have the good fortune to dispense. Long accustomed to hard work, I shall set the example for you. Expect to see me demanding that it is followed. But the stricter I am for the good of the service, the more you will find me sympathetic toward good workers." And to end, a little ethics: "Avoid making recommendations. I take a dim view of them. On the part of the one being recommended, they express a lack of confidence in his own

merit or in the intelligence or fairness of his superiors." In answer to Haussmann's "I give you back your freedom!" came a ringing "Vive l'Empereur!"
Our prefect had certainly taken care to produce the right effects. But the
man himself, with his tall stature and air of resolution, gave off a kind of
magnetism to which everyone was susceptible. "Yes, *messieurs*," Haussmann
concluded. "Long live the emperor, who wants to make Paris the world's
leading city, a capital worthy of France."[2]

ORGANIZATIONAL MATTERS

The Hôtel de Ville was an enormous machine. The prefect was in charge
of departments that came under central government and of others that came
under the Seine department or the city of Paris. He had swarms of engineers,
architects, and clerks working under him. He was responsible for local taxes,
customs duties, river navigation, mines and quarries, railways, nursery
schooling, primary and secondary education, ministers of religion, hospitals
and old people's homes, insane persons and foundlings, the fire brigade, the
Paris Guard, and the Seine gendarmerie. It was physically impossible for the
head of such an oversized administration to check all its work in person—
hence the importance of the secretariat, the mail department, and the prefect's personal staff. The secretary general, in addition to supervising four
divisions plus the Treasury, ran the personnel department, organized the secretariat for the municipal council and the departmental council, and supervised the recording and sending of dispatches and the keeping of the city
archives and library.

The prefect's principal private secretary, the *chef de cabinet*, was in charge
of opening the mail and monitoring the newspapers, and also dealt with private matters, the fine arts, and the granting of audiences. For this position
Haussmann kept on Ferrier, who had been with him since Draguignan.
Every morning, by nine o'clock, he had to open the mail and sort it into two
piles; one was then handed to the prefect himself while the other was sent to
the secretary general to be recorded and forwarded to the relevant department. When it came to outgoing correspondence, Haussmann made the
secretary general and section heads responsible for handling (and, if appropriate, signing) routine official business, reminders, the sending of documents, notification of decisions, and so on. He kept personal responsibility
for documents and letters that gave expression to decisions, commitments,
or advice, as well as correspondence with the ministers and principal institutions of the state. Every evening, folders containing drafts for his signature

had to be left with his private office; he undertook to read them by the following morning, either signing them for dispatch or sending them back to be rewritten. Corrected drafts had to be back on his desk for signature at the latest by four o'clock that afternoon. This mechanism, which meant a heavy workload for Haussmann, functioned without a hitch throughout his time at the Seine prefecture. With rare exceptions, Georges-Eugène never retired at night before completing the task he had bound himself to perform.

For the authorization of the hundreds or sometimes thousands of expense claims that came up each day, he asked to be given the general payment orders drawn up by the chief accountant for each ministry (in the case of central government expenditure) or each section of the budget (in the case of the Seine department and the city of Paris). Having checked that they were in line with the relevant expenditure allocation, he then personally signed these general orders and delegated to the secretary general the task of signing each individual payment.

Haussmann asked Merruau, his right-hand man as secretary general of the prefecture, to draw up a set of rules incorporating these various dispositions and a list of delegated signatories. Merruau meticulously carried out these instructions; there would be no real clouds in his working relationship with the prefect. The most that Haussmann ever held against him was a certain glibness, due no doubt to Merruau's training as a teacher and his earlier work in education and journalism. An impressive capacity for work tended to make Merruau think that he understood everything, sometimes at the risk of not properly distinguishing between what was central and what was only secondary. Moreover, being unused to debate and argument, he did not always think ahead to objections that might be raised and to ways of combating them. He was certainly no jouster. Yet his solid education, good judgment, and total loyalty made him immensely valuable to Haussmann. In 1860, after the prefect had him appointed to the Council of State, he had to give up his position as secretary general. But the bonds of complicity that had developed between the two men did not disappear, especially when he joined the Paris municipal council and assumed the functions of secretary there.

After the transfer of office, the meeting in the Throne Hall, and the resolution of various organizational matters, Haussmann spent the rest of the evening and much of the night studying Berger's draft budget for 1854. He found in it confirmation of what he had noticed the night before in relation to the 1852 administrative audit and the 1853 budget: namely, a systematic underestimation of income and greatly inflated provisions for expenditure.

He was now quite persuaded. He would have the means to carry through the transformation of Paris to which he had already been completely won over.

SETTLING INTO THE HÔTEL DE VILLE

❧ At nine o'clock on the morning of June 30, an official cab picked up Haussmann at the door of his hotel and took him to his new residence, the Hôtel de Ville. He formally appointed Ferrier de Tourettes to his position as *chef de cabinet*.

Since the law of 28 Plûviose, Year VIII (that is, February 17, 1800, in the revolutionary calendar of the time), the capital had had the special status of a commune divided into twelve arrondissements, each with its own mayor. But there had been no mayor of Paris as such; the relevant duties had been performed by the Seine prefect. The limits of the Seine department extended beyond the capital, of course, and contained three communal districts: Paris itself, directly administered by the Seine prefect; and the districts of Saint-Denis and Sceaux, each under the authority of a subprefect. Matters involving the department as a whole were handled by its *conseil général*. A few months after the law of Pluviôse, a law of Messidor, Year VIII transferred responsibility for law and order from the Seine prefect to a Paris chief of police. Napoleon Bonaparte established the offices of the chief of police at rue de Jérusalem, while those of the Seine prefecture were fused with those of the municipality in 1802 and established at the Hôtel de Ville on November 19, 1803.[3]

The bringing together of the municipal and departmental services naturally increased the demand for office space. The First Empire accordingly drew up an ambitious extension plan, but the vagaries of politics kept it on the shelf until the coming of the July Monarchy. Its implementation was then entrusted to a couple of architects, Étienne Hippolyte Godde and Jean-Baptiste Lesueur. They retained the former mansion house, commissioned by François I in 1532 from the Italian architect Domenico of Cortona (known as Le Boccador), and extended its Place de Grève façade with two wings, each ending in a corner pavilion. Perpendicular buildings were built along the waterfront and, on the other side, along what would become the rue de Rivoli. Work began in 1836 and was completed by 1847. Haussmann therefore took possession of a group of virtually new buildings.

For the first time, the Hôtel de Ville was no longer attached to the houses next to it. The architects placed the trapezoidal courtyard of the old building within two new courtyards. The rear building that looked onto rue

Lobau was doubled in width, and offices were established in the constructions surrounding the northern courtyard. The committee and meeting
rooms of the municipal council looked onto the main courtyard, called the
Cour Louis-XIV because of Coysevox's statue of the Sun King in the middle
of it. The wing facing the Seine, separated from the river by a garden running the full length of the building, was allocated to the prefect; it included
several reception rooms on the first floor. The large Festive Hall, with other
rooms leading off it, was also on the first floor, in the building that looked
onto rue Lobau.

Buffet showed the new prefect round his rooms on the ground floor of
the riverside wing. The section looking back onto the Place de Grève had
been taken over by General Levasseur, commanding an infantry division, as
long ago as December 2, 1851, but with a little respectful consideration
Haussmann managed to ease him out. He lost no time in rigging up a private study there next to his bedroom; an internal staircase led directly to his
office on the first floor, the so-called King's Room, with its three fine windows looking over the Place de Grève, which led off from the great Throne
Hall in the central part of Le Boccador's building. The prefect thus had a
secretary on call round the clock for the dictation of messages. For although
Haussmann thought things through very carefully, he wrote them up with a
great sense of urgency. Sometimes a secretary or other member of staff, or
even the head of a section, worked by night to provide him with a figure or
clarification that he needed for a report due the next day.

REFURBISHING OF THE HÔTEL DE VILLE

❧ When Haussmann took office, the Festive Hall and the adjoining Room
of the Caryatids had just been redecorated. The year 1854 saw the installation of the paintings executed by Ingres and Delacroix for the emperor's
Salon (or War Salon) and the Peace Salon. Théophile Gautier has devoted
many pages in praise of Ingres's apotheosis of Napoléon I and Delacroix's *La
Paix ramenant l'Abondance* [Peace Restoring Prosperity], although the former
looks more like a general's triumph than an entry into the world of the gods,
and the latter has to contend with a high ceiling that blurs its shapes and
darkens its colors.

The new prefect much admired the Cour Louis-XIV. One of his first concerns, also in 1854, was to furnish it with a light metallic structure and glass
roof that would protect both people and façades against bad weather. The
next year, in preparation for Queen Victoria's visit to Paris, a temporary

monumental staircase was constructed to afford a prestigious way in from the courtyard to the Festive Hall on the first floor. Designed by Baltard, the municipal architect responsible for the building's upkeep, it drew upon the two-flight horseshoe-shaped staircase in the Cour du Cheval Blanc at Fontainebleau Castle. The two flights were supported by columns rising up from a large basin. So impressed was Haussmann that he decided to convert the temporary staircase into a permanent feature. The statue of Louis XIV was ruthlessly cleared from the courtyard—a move that would save it from the fire of 1871 that engulfed the buildings from top to bottom and devoured all the works of art inside.[4]

The prefecture suffered from a chronic lack of offices, for the staff continued to increase as a result of administrative reorganization. Once the rue de Rivoli extension had widened the Place de Grève to a majestic esplanade (which then took its present name of the Place de l'Hôtel de Ville), Haussmann made Baltard responsible for building an annex in the block between the Place de l'Hôtel de Ville, the Avenue Victoria, the rue de Rivoli, and (diagonally joining the other two) the rue de la Coutellerie; private houses were to remain on the part of the block that looked onto the rue de Rivoli. The city dues department, the Bakery Trade Fund, the Public Works Fund, and the municipal and departmental archives were all installed in the new annex. It also served as a model for the symmetrical building that housed the Public Assistance staff on the other side of Avenue Victoria. The prefect was only moderately satisfied with the result, as he would have preferred there to be more relief work with moldings and pilasters.

In 1859 the Salon du Zodiaque, which acted as a waiting room for people visiting the prefect, was furnished with Léon Cogniet's four painted panels of the seasons to complement the decoration that gave the room its name. In 1865, Haussmann commissioned Yvon to decorate the ceiling of the Council Hall with a set of allegories on the great moments of Parisian history: Clovis making Lutetia his capital, Philippe-Auguste before his departure for the Holy Land, François I laying the foundation stone of the Hôtel de Ville, Haussmann handing to Napoléon III the decree that incorporated the suburban communes on January 1, 1860, and thereby extended the limits of Paris from the line of the outer boulevards to that of the fortifications. Haussmann introduced many new statues and paintings, especially in the Gallery of Mirrors and the Gallery of the Secretariat: Alexander and Caesar, Charlemagne, Napoleon Bonaparte, the four divisions of the world, the views from such elevated points in the department as Saint-Denis, Sceaux, Châtillon, the hill of Montmartre, the Bois de Boulogne, Vincennes.

Finally, in 1868, the architect Vauthier was given the job of restoring the bell tower of 1608 that was showing signs of weakness. He raised the whole construction, originally a square mass topped with an octagonal level and a round lantern, by adding to it a new base that restored harmonious proportions with a façade that was now twice as long as Le Boccador's.

DOING THE ROUNDS

On that June 30, 1853, having just ordered the first work on equipping his office and private rooms, Haussmann embarked upon a veritable marathon of receptions and visits. In the order of protocol, Merruau first presented to him the team of five prefectural counselors. This was a small number for a department as large as the Seine, and Haussmann managed to have it increased to six in 1859, then to seven in 1861 and eight shortly afterward. But the burden of administrative litigation was so large that even the greater number of counselors were unable to carry out all its duties without support from a few auditors attached to the Council of State.

Haussmann next met the subprefects for Saint-Denis and Sceaux, followed by the mayors and deputy mayors for the twelve arrondissements of Paris. It was a constant source of friction that these mayors and their deputies, who were appointed by the prefect, took precedence over the municipal council. Their powers were quite limited: they acted as official registrars, prepared electoral registers, and chaired community school committees and charitable boards. Haussmann later added the prerogatives of settling the expenses of their respective *mairies*, paying the salaries of their employees as well as of schoolteachers, and covering the purchase of school equipment. In order to raise the image of these local *mairies*, Haussmann introduced the term "budgets" for the documents setting out these various items of expenditure. Anxious to develop what we would now call a neighborhood administration, he obtained for each of the new *mairies* built during his period of office (and, as far as possible, for the older ones too) adequate space, pleasant offices, and halls that could be used for special occasions. He also concentrated there the local court of first instance, a central police station, and offices for the public engineer, architect, and highway engineer of the arrondissement, as well as for the water, garbage, and streetlighting departments. The mayors thus had the maximum support staff at hand, and citizens could have most of their dealings with the administration under one roof.

Among the twelve mayors who came to greet Haussmann in 1853 were two notaries, a former solicitor, a banker, three trial lawyers, a retired archivist at the Hôtel de Ville, and a member of the Council of State. Representatives of the liberal professions and senior civil servants were thus in a majority; the remaining three were a manufacturer (from the Japy family), a cloth wholesaler, and a merchant. Haussmann was aware of this imbalance and tried to widen the social spectrum. In 1858 he chose a timber merchant called Frédéric Lévy as mayor for the faubourg Saint-Antoine. And after the number of arrondissements was increased to twenty in 1860, he took advantage of the opportunity to appoint several more merchants, a bronze foundry owner, a businessman involved in transport, an army doctor, a curator at the Louvre, a head librarian at the Bibliothèque Sainte-Geneviève (Rataud, who was appropriately named mayor for the fifth arrondissement), a navy hydrographer, a former tax inspector (who might come in handy), and two or three landowners.

At the last round of presentations, with officials outside the departmental administration proper, Haussmann met the director and assistant directors of the Public Assistance Board, the director of the Mont de Piété pawnshop and his secretary, the director of the city dues department and his two managing agents. Three lower-ranking directors brought up the rear: those in charge of administering stallholders' fees, parking charges, and so on, the Butchers Fund, and the various tontine schemes.

Now it was Haussmann's turn to go visiting. First to the presidents of the Court of Cassation and the National Audit Office. Next to Marshal Magnan, army commander in Paris. Then to Monseigneur Sibour, the archbishop of Paris.

CONTACT WITH THE MUNICIPAL COUNCIL

≈ It was just four in the afternoon on June 30 when Haussmann, back in the Hôtel de Ville, received the Paris municipal council and the Seine *conseil général*. In fact, they did not yet have these names. The former was still called the "Paris municipal commission" until May 5, 1855, while the latter was still the "Seine departmental commission."

The municipal commission was appointed by the emperor, and this remained the case throughout the years of the Second Empire. In 1853 it consisted of thirty-six members, including bankers such as André, d'Eichtal, and the comte d'Argout (governor of the Bank of France); leading judges such as Delangle, first president of the imperial appeal court in Paris, and Chaix d'Est Ange, then a trial lawyer but soon to become public prosecutor;

members of the Institut de France such as the painter Delacroix, the chemist Pelouze, and the printer Firmin Didot; the stockbrokers' representative; and several members of the Council of State. In 1860 the size of the commission rose to sixty after the expansion of the city limits. The departmental commission comprised the members of the municipal commission plus eight representatives of the districts of Sceaux and Saint-Denis (one for each canton). Its chairman was the chairman of the municipal commission. All these figures were local dignitaries and, though appointees, could sometimes prove troublesome for the Seine prefect.

Haussmann was met with complete silence when he walked into the room to receive the councillors. He greeted those present, and then Delangle, the chairman of the municipal commission, returned the greeting and delivered a speech marked throughout "by the dry, peremptory tone that seemed to come naturally to him." It was perhaps not a declaration of war, but it was certainly a cold shower: "Whatever we may know of the value of your past services and of the outstanding talents to which it testifies, we cannot remain silent about the intense sympathy we feel for M. Berger in his early retirement. But we are devoted to the emperor and full of respect for his decisions. We owe our loyal cooperation to the man who represents his authority. You can therefore be assured of such cooperation for any measures not exceeding the powers of the city that might contribute to its splendor and to the well-being of its inhabitants."[5]

Haussmann was careful to display no ill-feeling on his part. His cheerful reply expressed confidence in the future, and Delangle became aware of the sharp contrast with his own curt remarks. More gracefully he introduced the councillors one by one to Haussmann, who tried his hardest to find a personal compliment in each case. The ice was beginning to break. As the councillors gradually went their way, the prefect had the impression that they were behaving rather more warmly toward him. He even wondered whether Delangle had not been mainly expressing his own feelings of resentment, and he said to himself that it should not be too difficult to gain the trust of most of the councillors.

On the evening of that long 30th of June, Haussmann went to the large property that Persigny had rented for the fine summer days at Ville d'Avray and told him of how the meeting with the municipal councillors had gone. Persigny's young wife made a bad impression on Haussmann: a spoiled child, frivolous and whimsical, more likely to cause problems than to give effective support to her husband (whom she called "Totor"). As for the minister, he advised Haussmann to report as soon as possible to Napoléon III.

When he gave his report two days later, Napoléon was unhappy with Delangle's attitude and could not make up his mind whether to take away his presidency or (the solution he found more attractive) to dissolve the municipal commission altogether. Haussmann pointed out that the threat of dissolution was often more valuable than dissolution itself, as the effects of the latter were unpredictable and could prove worse than the disease it was supposed to cure. Talkative as ever when the opportunity arose, he related that in the Var in 1849, and later in the Gironde after the coup d'état of December 2, 1851, he had faced similar situations and dealt with them by adopting a prudent but determined attitude. Napoléon agreed to let events take their course—and in the end dissolution did not prove necessary.

THE BUDGET BATTLE

∾ Haussmann had to submit the city's budget for approval by a regular session of the council. He had just eleven days to revise Berger's draft and to justify the changes he intended to slip into the text so that sufficient funding would be available for the policies of Napoléon III. On July 14, Haussmann was facing the council. Scarcely had the session begun when he read out his report on the state of the city's finances. This caused great alarm in the assembly: "It was extremely measured in form, but I turned inside out the skillful structure that had been consciously deployed to conceal from inexperienced eyes the size of the resources that the city could annually contribute to these major works. I seemed to have stirred up a hornet's nest."[6]

Haussmann systematically said the opposite of what Berger had argued, but in a veiled manner and without fully spelling out the implications that the councillors feared and expected to hear. In Berger's budget forecast, as we have seen, all the income had been deliberately undervalued and the expenditures cautiously overestimated. In reality, income would be as high as 69 million francs because of carryover from previous years, while expenditure would be as low as 51 million—which left a surplus of 18 million francs to play with. Income for 1852 had been more than 54 million francs. So by what right had Berger actually reduced the figure for 1853, when revenue had been continually rising throughout the first six months of the year? Haussmann's charge of income underestimation surprised many of the councillors. As he took apart the "Berger system" piece by piece, he suggested a real total income of 55 million francs, whereas ordinary expenditure seemed unlikely to exceed 32 million. The city therefore had at its disposal a surplus of more than 22 million francs to deal with extraordinary expenditure. "In normal circumstances, such a situation evidently allows the city to achieve great things!"[7]

To be sure, Paris had to service the debt run up in previous years. But according to Haussmann's calculations, the repayments would not rise above 12 million francs for each of the years 1854, 1855, and 1856, then fall to 10 million for 1857 and 1858, to 8 million for 1859 and 1860, and finally to 7 million and below for the years up to 1870. With the extra 22 million francs, that would still leave a margin of 10 million or more a year. Consequently, "however sizable the projects already started, the state of the city's finances appears to permit the administration to plan without apprehension, as capable of achievement in the near future, some more beneficial works of public concern that would continue the transformation of old Paris that you so courageously initiated."[8]

Haussmann did not yet mention the idea of allocating the extra 10 million francs to cover a large loan, in keeping with the theory of productive expenditure. No doubt he thought he had enough trouble for one day. Besides, such a loan was not necessary to complete the building projects already under way: the central Halles, the rue de Rivoli extension, the opening up of the area around the Louvre, the lowering of the Pont Notre Dame. The sum required for these operations was estimated at 100 million francs. Of this total, 18 million would come from the selling of materials and plots of land remaining in municipal ownership under the terms of the law on compulsory purchases; and another 14 million had been promised by central government. For the rest, a loan of 25 million had been contracted in 1849 for the building of the central Halles, although a considerable part of this had been reallocated to cover the extraordinary expenses of the 1848 Revolution and the June Days of the same year; and another loan had been floated in 1851 for 50 million francs. Thus, of the 75 million raised through loans, the city had precisely 61,691,000 francs available to add to the 32 million from other sources to finance the current program of major works. That left a little more than 6 million to make up—a sum that Haussmann proposed to find from the balance of 6.75 million remaining from the 1852 budget.

Delangle, sensing he had a tough opponent, sent these proposals to be examined by the finance committee, whose chairman, the chocolate producer Devinck, was one of the council's most influential members. Devinck disputed it every inch of the way while Haussmann tried to steamroller every objection as it came up. On July 29 he submitted a more detailed report that set precise figures on all the points in the original and highlighted a number of irregularities in the older budgetary material. The fault certainly lay with the Berger administration, but the municipal council—and, in particular, its finance committee—carried its share of the blame. This revelation took a lot of the wind out of the sails of Devinck and Delangle.

The municipal council eventually let itself be persuaded and approved the budget almost unanimously. Only five members held out in opposition and announced their resignation from the council: they were Ernest André and d'Eichtal (two of the three bankers then on the council), Dupérier, Fleury, and Riant. Devinck dramatically came out in support of Haussmann. Open opposition to the emperor's ideas was much weaker than Haussmann had thought. There was clearly no need to dissolve the council.

Yet all was not yet won, as many councillors continued to display a muted unease. On January 16, 1854, Haussmann was able to reassure them by announcing that the city's income had exceeded 55 million francs on December 31, 1853. The fact that 41 million of this total had come from the city's dues (levied on local consumption) was irrefutable evidence that the capital's economy was picking up again. The budget surplus had overshot the expected 10 million by a full 8 million (final accounts put it as high as 24 million francs). Resignations and good financial results gave Haussmann a free hand to finish the projects already under way and to launch the new road-building program of which the emperor had dreamed.

13

Friends and Enemies

ALTHOUGH Haussmann had been chosen and appointed by the emperor, it cannot be said that all was now plain sailing. His victory in the summer of 1853 over a restive council was but one episode in a long campaign in which not every engagement went in his favor. The prefect counted up his friends and enemies, his allies and opponents. Did he have any idea at first of the hostility and dissension that he would encounter within his own political "family"? The least we can say is that he was working in an institutional context full of sharp contrasts.

THE PARISIAN INSTITUTIONS

❧ Haussmann's first aim was to get rid of the consultative committee that the emperor had himself established to study the Parisian *grands travaux*. Napoléon III called Haussmann before a meeting of the committee in order to acquaint him with two of its reports. But in our prefect's view they were a collection of banalities. The first to present a report was the duc de Valmy, a dignitary from the days of the First Empire who lacked the slightest knowledge of administration—indeed, Haussmann soon concluded that he was on the committee only because he had skillfully put together Berger's criticisms for the emperor's ears. The second rapporteur was Count Siméon, whom Haussmann had already met during his days in the Var, a man with some weight in the administrative, political, and social landscape. In fact he was the grandson of a member of the Council of State who had become a senator under the First Empire and a Peer of France under the Restoration; the son of a prefect under Louis XVIII and Charles X; and himself prefect for the Vosges under Louis-Philippe, then deputy for the Var in 1849, and a senator since the coup d'état of December 2. Married to the daughter of the banker Seillière, he possessed a huge fortune. In March 1853, Haussmann had had the opportunity to chat with him, and he had made no secret of his ambition to take Berger's place in the Seine prefecture. Count Siméon drew in his claws when dealing with Haussmann, but who could say that he would not take the first opportunity to trip up the man installed in the position he coveted?

At the end of the session, Napoléon III asked Haussmann to remain behind and asked him how he thought it had gone. "Sire," our prefect replied, "the committee strikes me as much too large to do a good job of work. When there are a number of us here together, the slightest remarks take the form of a speech, and reports, instead of being brief, degenerate into learned dissertations. The work would progress better and faster if the committee consisted of the emperor as chairman; the Seine prefect as secretary, responsible for examining business submitted to His Majesty and implementing his decisions; and finally, between the sovereign and his most humble servant, the smallest possible number of other members."[1] Napoléon III concluded: "So, it would be even better if there were no committee?" And Haussmann agreed that that was indeed his basic view. Whims aside, Napoléon III recognized that his new prefect was right. There would be no more talk of the committee on the Parisian *grands travaux*.

The disappearance of the committee left Haussmann to tackle the municipal council face to face. Until 1858 it continued to be chaired by Delangle, who was still also a senator and the first president of the imperial appeal court in Paris. He was extremely touchy, and no one could do anything about this. In fact, Haussmann readily admitted that he should not be blamed for the ill humor Delangle had displayed since Haussmann's own arrival on the scene; the least propriety would have required him to be, if not consulted, then included among the first to know of Berger's replacement.

Four years later, in 1857, Delangle again gave vent to his ill humor—and this had the side effect of giving Haussmann a most unexpected promotion. One evening, at an after-show supper given in his honor, Grand Duke Constantine of Russia and his personal guests had the privilege of being served in the Throne Hall while the rest of the company was spread among other rooms where buffet tables had been laid. As the Paris council had issued the invitation, its members were permitted to move around all the rooms, and a piece of jewelry bearing the city's coat of arms was issued as a kind of pass for their wives and unmarried daughters. Delangle decided to show the preparations in the Throne Hall to a very pretty young woman who was neither his wife nor his daughter, nor wearing the required jewelry. When the usher on duty barred their way, Delangle took great umbrage and exclaimed: "Do you not know me? I am the president of the municipal council." To which the usher politely replied: "I do indeed have the honor of knowing you, sir, but my orders do not apply to you. They are only for the lady."[2] The loyal Merruau was not far away and hurried over at the sound of the altercation; he offered his apologies and opened the way for Delangle and his companion to enter the hall.

The next day, at a session of the municipal council, the councillors exchanged impressions of the previous evening. Delangle, still in the grip of anger, rubbed everyone up the wrong way with a fierce tirade against the absurd instructions that had not allowed for his credentials as president of the council, *and* first president of the imperial court, *and* senator of the empire. He concluded by turning his fire on Haussmann: "For I am a senator and therefore a dignitary of the Empire!"[3] Haussmann apologized and promised that in the future all the staff on duty would be formally instructed to obey the president of the municipal council as they would himself. He knew that the quick-tempered president of the council was essentially in the right, and that afternoon he called round to repeat his apologies in person. A few days later, when Haussmann had ended a working session with Napoléon III and was walking toward the door, the emperor called him back: "By the way, Monsieur Haussmann, I have decided to make you a senator!"—"Sire!"—"Yes, I don't want anyone from the municipal council or elsewhere to be able to say to my Seine prefect: I am a senator and you are not."[4]

Shortly afterward, Delangle left the municipal council to become minister of the interior, and from that time he behaved as one of Haussmann's most reliable allies. Once there were no longer any problems of precedence between them, he placed his perfect knowledge of Parisian realities at Georges-Eugène's service. In particular, he was a driving force behind the redistribution of powers in 1859 that benefited the Seine prefecture at the expense of the Paris *prefecture de police*.

Delangle's place was taken by the chemist Jean-Baptiste Dumas, who would remain president of the municipal council until 1870. Haussmann had known Dumas as minister of agriculture and trade when he himself had served at the Yonne prefecture. He had brought him onto the Paris council as one of several strong personalities meant to erode Delangle's position of dominance—and Dumas had played the game well. With Delangle out of the way, the great chemist was happy to work more in cooperation with Haussmann than as a counterweight. Calm and composed by temperament, he liked to get to the bottom of things and became enthusiastic over matters within his area of scientific competence: for example, the Paris water supply, the disinfection of the drains, the production and distribution of gas for artificial lighting.

The municipal council included a number of other intellectuals respected in their fields: the dramatist Scribe, the painters Delacroix and Paul Delaroche, the physiologist Flourens, the architects Caristie and Duban, the vice rector of the Paris Academy (and brother-in-law of Haussmann) Artaud. Although they all had absorbing interests outside the council, they took their political responsibilities very seriously. But they had no time to waste, and the form of cooperation that Haussmann introduced in the name of efficiency was one that suited them. After the initial clashes, relations between the prefect and the council soon settled down. The councillors met once a week, in the morning, for committee sessions that lasted less than two hours; then they had lunch and met in a plenary session at which reports were delivered in succession. The councillors were divided among four committees, the most sensitive, of course, being the two that dealt with public thoroughfares and finances. A report was immediately given on any plans that the prefect had submitted in the morning. After 1853 the council generally approved the budget without further discussion. No stenographic record was kept of debates, and any that did take place were not open to the public. Confidence in the system began to crumble only in 1866 when a dispute broke out with the national audit office over alleged financial irregularities of the Haussmann administration.

THE NATIONAL POLITICAL ASSEMBLIES

❧ Haussmann regularly had dealings with the Legislature—that is, with national deputies. Matters concerning Paris could not be of indifference to anyone at the Palais Bourbon. State funding of the *grands travaux*, introduced by Napoléon III with the first operations entrusted to the Berger administration, necessitated a number of conventions between the central state and the city of Paris, and when these came up for debate in the Legislature it had to be explained why the whole nation had a stake in the building work planned for Paris and should therefore make a special financial contribution to it. Haussmann tirelessly repeated the argument that Paris did not belong to Parisians alone; that it was quite normal for the city to be placed under the tutelage of the state and for some of the Parisian expenditure to come out of the national budget. But this meant that the Legislature, where provincial deputies were obviously in a large majority, closely scrutinized the affairs of the capital. It was not too difficult to explain that the completion of the Louvre, together with the adjacent road-building and the opening up of areas around it, would have financial implications for the municipality that it would be only fair to offset through a state subsidy. A more difficult case was the road programs that had no connection with the Louvre or other buildings owned by the state—although in the early days of the empire an overwhelming majority of deputies were prepared to bow to government wishes. The argument from authority enabled Haussmann to force decisions through, but it also set him up as a perfect target for anyone wishing to attack the emperor in all but name.

This is what happened after 1860, the year that marked a decisive turning point both in the evolution of the Second Empire toward liberalism and parliamentarism, and in the philosophy of public works applied to the newly expanded territory of Paris. The republican opposition was on ideal ground in mounting its attacks on Haussmann, for these fell on attentive ears among a small and medium bourgeoisie alarmed at the ever larger loans required to carry the development program beyond the old districts of Paris.

The Legislature had to approve these loans, and the prefect's relations with this assembly followed the trend set by the political evolution of the regime. The first loan was voted through in 1855 in a climate of consensus. Three years later, a second loan was authorized by a large majority, but it was actually launched only in 1860 after it had been picked about with a fine-tooth comb. The third loan was passed with difficulty in 1865. And in 1869 the debates on a fourth loan precipitated the demise of Haussmann's system and were soon followed by the prefect's own removal from office.

Some oppositionists found themselves propelled into the public limelight as a result of disputes with Haussmann. Jules Ferry, for instance, was no more than a highly respected lawyer when he published his *Comptes fantastiques d'Haussmann*[5] in 1868—a series of articles that launched him on a major political career.

Under the imperial system, the Senate was packed with Napoléon III's loyal supporters plus a few members who were there by right; it was no more than a rubber stamp. As we have seen, Haussmann himself joined it in 1857 and never had a major problem with the institution.

THE SENIOR BRANCHES OF THE CIVIL SERVICE

⇜ The same was not true of the Council of State, one of the main wheels in the regime. Many of its members were senior civil servants with a background in Orleanism who shared the cautious attitudes of that milieu. Opposed in principle to the massive loans envisaged by Napoléon III, they proved hostile to any policy of major public works in Paris or elsewhere, and some in their ranks—beginning with the council chairman, Baroche—had little personal liking for the Seine prefect. Haussmann had some rather unkind things to say on his side too: "From the rostrum M. Baroche struck me more as a dazzling lawyer than a powerful orator. But as regards administration, this bourgeois from the Parisian middle classes was imbued with narrowly routinist ideas and totally hostile in his innermost core to our *grands travaux*."[6] The Council of State was frequently used by those in the emperor's entourage who were out of sympathy with Haussmann. Unable to come too much into the open, since Napoléon III was himself involved in the transformation of Paris, they applied themselves to legal quibbling in the hope it would wear down Haussmann's resolve and influence the emperor's will. On two occasions, this petty skirmishing ended in open conflict.

The first time, in 1858, Baroche persuaded the Council of State to modify the decree of 1852 on compulsory purchases by making it more favorable to landowners and therefore more onerous for the city's finances. Under the new provisions, landowners could keep for themselves any extra value produced by the municipal works. In Haussmann's view this would be both materially and morally ruinous; he protested to the emperor that "this whole decree was inspired by reaction against the great work that would be one of the glories of the reign," and that in any event a government decree with the force of law could not be changed by mere fiat.[7] Napoléon III, however, was not willing to disown Baroche. The new decree of December 27, 1858, weighed heavily upon future operations, facing the city with an added expenditure of 400 million francs (Haussmann even spoke of 465 million).

The second conflict erupted in 1859, when the plan to extend the city limits of Paris by incorporating suburban communes was under debate. Baroche was hostile to the idea, but this time Haussmann generally had the upper hand. Nevertheless, for reasons that remain obscure (Haussmann suggested that landowners friendly to Baroche had a hand in it), Baroche managed to alter the plan so that the city limits ran along the line of the fortifications instead of 273 yards farther out, as Haussmann wished, in the zone *non aedificandi* where building operations had not been officially permitted—although in reality this strip of land had for decades been outside all municipal control and would soon become an extralegal area inhabited by the marginal and dispossessed.

Six months later, Haussmann took stunning revenge. A decree of January 11, 1860, gave him the right to attend general meetings of the Council of State whenever it considered matters pertaining to the work of his administration.

The Court of Cassation also entered the fray with a judgment in case law that was extremely unfavorable to the municipal finances—on this occasion, with regard to the position of tenants in cases involving compulsory purchases. The previous view had been that such persons were entitled to compensation if their tenancy agreement was terminated, but that they had no claim if the city allowed it to run its normal course. But on June 12, 1860, the Court of Cassation ruled that the holder of a tenancy agreement in a block marked down for compulsory purchase was entitled to compensation in every instance. Haussmann embarked upon a lengthy legal battle and obtained in his favor five rulings by the Seine court of first instance, as well as one by the imperial court of appeal in August 1862, that gave him partial satisfaction. But it was to no avail, as on January 20, 1864, the Court of Cassation reiterated its new ruling. This too would cost the city of Paris hundreds of millions of francs in additional expenditures.

Haussmann's difficulties with the National Audit Office were equally serious. In theory the Seine prefect was accountable only to the central government, but the National Audit Office was able to get at him indirectly by publishing observations on the management of the city's treasury department (which was under the office's control). As Haussmann saw it, the National Audit Office was filled with retrograde elements: "Family traditions perpetuated among most of them the mentality of that body which has forever been closed to progressive ideas."[8] He accused them of retreating into a narrow conception of their functions. If the only purpose of the National Audit Office was "to tick off figures, to check additions down to the last centime," if it was there only "for nitpicking," then the best course would be to abolish it. But Haussmann's indignation was useless against the power of the institution. The Audit Office would take the prefect to task for the liberties he had taken with financial orthodoxy, and would play a not insignificant role in his eventual undoing.

THE IMPERIAL STAFF

❦ The prefect remained in office for nearly seventeen years by the grace, and with the constant backing, of Napoléon III. In spite of this, or perhaps because of it, several members of the emperor's entourage—and even of the imperial family—campaigned more or less openly against Haussmann.

During the early years of the empire, the prefect was assured of unanimous government support. On the day when he took his oath of office at Saint Cloud following a meeting of the Council of Ministers, he met the ministers who came to attend the ceremony. He already knew most of them. There was Persigny, of course, but he was also on the best of terms with the war minister General de Saint-Arnaud, with the minister for agriculture, trade, and public works Magne, and with the foreign minister Drouyn de Lhuys. He had good relations with Ducos, the navy minister, and with Abbatucci, the minister of justice. He met for the first time the minister without portfolio Fould, the finance minister Bineau, and the minister of public education and religious worship Fortoul.

On the other hand, Haussmann did not get on well with the chief of police, Pietri, largely because of the lack of clarity about their respective spheres of competence. Things changed when Boittelle replaced Pietri in 1858. "M. Boittelle differed in every respect from M. Pietri. He was a man from the best society, with perfect manners, who weighed his actions and words and was very correct in all things."[9] The following year, a redefinition of the responsibilities of the prefect and the chief of police gave Haussmann the freer hand he wanted in managing the city's affairs.

The close bond that developed between Haussmann and Napoléon III aroused the growing jealousy of a number of leading figures in the empire. Both Haussmann and the chief of police had the privilege of working with the sovereign on a daily basis and of taking their orders directly from him: "A few ministers, following the example of M. Persigny, understood the necessity of this situation and had no hesitation in going along with it. These were at the interior ministry M. Boudet, the marquis de La Valette, and especially M. Ernest Pinard. Others resigned themselves but not always with good grace. A certain number, which included some of the most eminent personalities, tried another way and did not feel any better for it. In any event, their secret, persistent, systematic antagonism was not the least of the nuisances that made my work more difficult."[10]

The wrangles were muted but sorely trying. Rouher, the strong man in the late empire, felt especially resentful at Haussmann's influence over

Napoléon III and methodically sought to counter it. Thiers took malicious pleasure in adding fuel to the fire: "M. Rouher was flattered and called vice emperor; but the vice emperor was the prefect for the Seine." If Haussmann requested a special ministry for Paris, Rouher blocked it. If the Legislature took the prefect to task over his financial management, Rouher defended him in such a way as to make things a little worse. He acted as a barely disguised adversary at the time when Haussmann, still as authoritarian as in the early days of the empire, was beginning to worry those who supported the more parliamentarist evolution of the regime. In their view, the persistently poor electoral results in Paris were proof that his policies had failed to quiet the capital and were giving daily ammunition to republican propaganda and the enemies of the empire. When the official candidates in Paris were all defeated in the legislative elections of 1869, Haussmann exclaimed: "That's good. It will teach the emperor that Paris can't continue to be treated with kid gloves." This outburst delighted his opponents within the regime, who spread it around wherever they could. Rouher would make his peace with Haussmann only after the fall of the empire.

One of the prefect's chief enemies was the emperor's own cousin, Prince Napoléon-Jérôme, a major inspiration behind the move toward a "liberal" empire. The target in his sights was not the prefect as a person but the system of administration in Paris and the heavy-handed control to which it was subjected. His favorite theme was: let us give Paris back its freedom; let Parisians elect their own representatives, choose a mayor by universal suffrage, and decide for themselves the city's future (and, implicitly, the public works they want to have).

As a clear sign of his lack of respect for the existing organization of the city, Napoléon-Jérôme made it a point of honor—as did the republican leaders—to continue speaking of the "municipal commission" even after it had officially become the "municipal council." At a special session of the Council of State that Haussmann dates to 1863, there was a debate in Napoléon III's presence about problems concerning the Paris administration. When the emperor attended meetings of the Council of State, Napoléon-Jérôme had the right as a royal prince to be present too, seated on a stool close to the imperial throne. On this occasion, then, the prince was there when the Seine prefect referred in the middle of a sentence to the municipal council of Paris. Defying every convention, Napoléon-Jérôme unceremoniously interrupted him: "Say the municipal commission." Haussmann calmly parried: "Your Highness, I give to the municipal council of Paris the title it holds by virtue of our organic laws [from 1855], which no one, however highly placed he may be, has the right to dispute." The prince retorted: "No law can make an unelected body be anything other than a commission." Haussmann: "I cannot regret too much that Your Imperial Highness continues to describe a body as devoted as the municipal council of Paris is to the emperor by a name that His Majesty's enemies constantly fling in its face as an insult to paralyze its legitimate authority." Napoléon-Jérôme: "An unelected assembly could not have authority because it lacks independence!" The prince had trapped himself. It was easy enough for Haussmann to answer: "Your Imperial Highness forgets that the great body within which we now sit is itself not the product of an election; that all its members have been appointed by the emperor, as have the members of the municipal council of Paris; and that nevertheless the Council of State gives daily proof of its independence—and, I would add, its loyalty—through the complete liberty of its decisions and its opinions."[11] The blow struck home, but Napoléon-Jérôme did not cease to lend his authority and influence to attacks on the Seine prefect.

NAPOLÉON III

❧ The emperor's confidence in Haussmann was the cornerstone of the prefect's system; it never failed until the final months of their relationship, in late 1869 and early 1870. Haussmann is quite frank about it: "Alone I could never have completed the mission he gave me, for the accomplishment of which his growing confidence left me a progressively larger freedom of decision. I could not have wrestled with the difficulties . . . if I had not really been the expression, the organ, the instrument of a great idea that he had conceived and for which I should give him the principal merit. At all times he watched over its progress, with a firmness that never flagged."[12]

Haussmann had to face the hostility of senior branches of the civil service, the jealousy of some of the emperor's loyal supporters, the pressure of the republican opposition, and the imprudence that sometimes resulted from his ever more authoritarian impulses. If he managed to hold up, it was thanks to the favor he found with the sovereign. He therefore suffered the consequences of Napoléon III's physical decline, as countless tasks and demands pressed down upon a character not cut out for too long a haul. Haussmann perceptively observed the emperor's psychological evolution: "Concerns of a higher order both inside and outside the country—food shortages, the Crimean War, and so much else besides—took up more and more of the sovereign's time. The numerous grave questions that were his foremost duty to address meant that the infinite details involved in a serious project for a new thoroughfare were scarcely worthy of his attention: details such as the exact line of the road, the alignments, the achievement of a standard level (a crucial point too often neglected, as the emperor could see from recent examples) between the old roads that had to be cut up and the ones that were supposed to create broad openings for them, and finally the sewage system, water supply, and gas pipes that needed to be organized and coordinated with the bold new strokes of urban development! All this soon tired and even disgusted a mind that was alien to such minutiae and haunted by political combinations quite different from them in importance."[13] Things were not easy for Haussmann as he became aware of the emperor's growing lack of application to the problems raised by the transformation of Paris.

14

The First New System

WHEN Haussmann took office, two projects had already come to fruition under the previous administration. One was the Boulevard de Strasbourg, opened in 1853 between the Gare de l'Est and the Boulevard Saint-Denis. The other, on the left bank, was the first section of the rue des Écoles—which included the new space around the Sorbonne and the Collège de France, and the eastward thrust toward the rue du Cardinal Lemoine. The redevelopment of this part of the Latin Quarter did away with a number of old streets, such as the rue du Clos-Bruneau, rue Saint-Nicolas, rue du Mûrier, and rue du Bon-Puits, and initiated work on the north-south axes linking Mount Sainte-Geneviève to the banks of the Seine. The part of rue Saint-Jacques that runs from the Boulevard Saint-Germain to the rue des Écoles was widened; the seventeenth-century and eighteenth-century façades on the left side as one goes up the street stand in sharp contrast to the Second Empire blocks facing them on the right side. The Thermes were cleared of obstructions. The Hôpital des Mathurins stretching between the Palais des Abbés de Cluny and rue Saint-Jacques was pulled down, so that the palace itself became visible again and looked onto a pretty little square decorated with plants, the present-day Square Paul Painlevé. The entire project, carried out under direct public control, cost more than 13.6 million francs, a large sum that was shared in the same proportions as the Boulevard de Strasbourg: a third by central government, two-thirds by the city of Paris.

In these two projects, Haussmann's only role had been to close the accounts. His responsibility, competence, and personal touch would all be expressed, however, in the three major projects featured on the emperor's color-coded map: the great east-west axis on the right bank extending the rue de Rivoli along to the Bastille; the east-west axis on the left bank involving the continuation of the rue des Écoles; and the opening of the north-south axis right across Paris, beginning with the Boulevard de Strasbourg and crossing the *grands boulevards* down to the Châtelet and on through the Île de la Cité and the left bank. The emperor launched two other major projects: the construction of the central Halles and the development of the Bois de Boulogne. Haussmann would have to take a definite position on the Place de la Concorde/Champs Élysées promenade and on the triumphal route to the Étoile roundabout. And there were also the improvements to the water supply, the sewage system, the omnibus network, the price of bread, and the "imperial festivities"—all matters in which Haussmann and the Hôtel de Ville would have to play an important role.

After the fortunate discoveries he had made about the city's finances, Haussmann thought he had the resources to tackle all these challenges head-on. But he still had to gear up the various municipal departments for the task. Most urgently, he had to solve a problem whose misassessment had precipitated Berger's downfall: Paris did not have an official survey map, as the disastrous affair of the Tour Saint-Jacques had revealed.

THE TOWER OF SAINT-JACQUES DE LA BOUCHERIE

≈ One of the reasons why the emperor decided to part company so dramatically with Berger was his huge disappointment with the work on the rue de Rivoli extension from the Passage Delorme (between rue du Louvre and Place Saint-Germain-l'Auxerrois) to the Place de l'Hôtel de Ville. The project had not been properly thought through. When the works reached the vicinity of the Church of Saint-Jacques de la Boucherie, it was suddenly realized that the variations in land height were much greater than the planners had thought, and that the continuation of the road would require a drop of several yards. But how could it then be joined to adjacent streets? Would it be necessary to bring to the same level the whole Arcis *quartier* that it was supposed to serve and would then cut in two? How would it be possible to gain access to the Pont Notre Dame, which was already being criticized as too steep? Changes would also have to be made to the height of the right bank *quais* and to the Petit Pont—not to speak of the stability of the tower of Saint-Jacques de la Boucherie, which was planted at the top of a hillock and would be threatened by digging almost directly below it. It would have to be either pulled down or underpinned with a costly new base that would still not put it out of risk.

The initial plans for this section of the rue de Rivoli, from the Place du

Louvre to the Place de l'Hôtel de Ville, envisaged the compulsory purchase and demolition of 236 houses; the total cost of the project, including the construction of a large sewer, had been estimated by the prefect's technical department at nearly 19 million francs. To alter the level of the area around the Tour Saint-Jacques, a decree of July 26, 1852, had permitted a further round of compulsory purchases that led to the demolition of another 187 houses, at an additional cost of more than 9.5 million francs (after allowances for the reselling of land and materials). The bill for reconstruction of the Pont Notre Dame came to 1.34 million francs, while the isolation, under-pinning, and restoration of the Tour Saint-Jacques cost 580,000 francs. The decree of July 26, 1852, did promise two government subsidies to the city of Paris: one of 1 million francs for additional compulsory purchases, and one of 500,000 francs for work on the Pont Notre Dame. But these were tiny sums in comparison with the overall expenditure, which would involve a drain on the city's finances of 11,611,000 francs above the original estimate. The final cost to the city, which Haussmann had to take on board, was in excess of 30 million francs.

Technical problems were not about to set back Napoléon's III's schedule of operations. He had ordered the work on the Place de l'Hôtel de Ville in February 1853, when Berger was still in office. The government could not expose itself to further setbacks, and Berger's successor was required to be first and foremost a good administrator. Of course he had to have a strong character and the will to ride roughshod over the traps lying within the Parisian microcosm. Georges-Eugène Haussmann was not lacking in these qualities. But he was mainly called upon to demonstrate his capacities as an organizer. He had shown that he knew how to muzzle the municipal council and to unearth hidden resources. Would be he able to produce a magic for-mula for the *grands travaux*?

THE *PLAN DE PARIS*

❧ Haussmann must have been astonished to discover not only that there was no comprehensive survey of Paris—all that existed were partial surveys aligning the public thoroughfares—but that there was not even a land sur-vey indicating spot heights. In other words, pot luck had more or less been the rule for road-building work in the capital. This was all the more surpris-ing in that the railway construction program had posed many problems con-cerning slopes, variations in land height, or bends in the track that made precise topographical plans an absolute necessity.

Haussmann found at the prefecture the kind of rare pearl who could create the necessary technical support; he was none other than the Paris land surveyor, Eugène Deschamps, whose title corresponded to no reality but who had what it took to satisfy the new prefect's demands. Haussmann liked to think that his old habit of working directly with subordinates had given him a good knowledge of people, and beneath Deschamps's rather unsophisticated exterior he detected his latent abilities. To be more precise, Haussmann had on occasions summoned section heads and lower-level civil servants to explain to him hidden aspects of complicated cases, and Deschamps, though not very talkative, had soon impressed him with his clear, exact, and logical answers to questions.

The homage that Haussmann pays to Deschamps in his *Mémoires* has a moving quality, coming as it does from a man not much given to sentimentality. His insistent presentation of the humble architect and former student at the École des Beaux-Arts as a key wheel in the Parisian *grands travaux* is especially unusual. Deschamps was allowed various superlatives: "a man of unequaled merit," he showed "unquestionable superiority" over a period of seventeen years.[1] "He had kept that special disdain for form which too many of our young artists seem to have in relation to their own dress, manners, and way of living, even as they devote themselves to its solemn worship."[2]

It was to this overgrown student that Haussmann gave sufficient responsibility to propel him to the level of the city hall potentates. "I intended to make M. Deschamps my immediate assistant for the principal and certainly the most arduous part of the great project for which I had become responsible: first, to draw up the whole system of major roads that needed to be opened in Paris to implement the emperor's program (the Boulevard de Strasbourg and the barely finished sections of the rue de Rivoli extension between the Louvre and the Hôtel de Ville being only two initial specimens); then, as this vast program was gradually implemented, to study the route of each section in minute detail; to decide on the spot which properties had to be taken over; and finally to estimate their value."[3]

In 1853, Deschamps's office was an insignificant part of the *voirie de Paris*, which could be found in the same division as the government department of civil engineering, the Paris regional highways department, the water board, and the pavements, architecture, and quarries departments. Haussmann began by doubling the size of the *voirie de Paris* and promoted the survey office to its second bureau, headed by Deschamps. In 1859, Haussmann took advantage of the extension of the city limits to create the *Plan de Paris*, a major department responsible for official surveys and maps, again with Deschamps at its head. These two men, so dissimilar to each other, would spend the next seventeen years working in close collaboration. What would Haussmann's project have been without a proper survey map, without Deschamps' ability to make it solid and effective? "Always ready and willing, that invaluable civil servant deserved every ounce of confidence both for the integrity of his character and for the soundness of his work— two essential qualities in the position he occupied. And if his name is not as well known as others have deservedly become, outside the administrative circles where his fruitful activity was highly appreciated; if people do not generally know that it was he who drew all the major maps that are today admired for their fine order and scale, this doubtless has to do with the modest habits of his reserved existence, with his complete lack of interest in externals, with his neglect of the important personal connections that his official position enabled him to treat as assured. In any event, it is my duty to do for M. Deschamps what he did not know how to do himself: to save from oblivion a name that has remained too much in the dark, to recognize his right to feature among my most useful collaborators."[4]

In order to have a technically up-to-date plan of Paris, Haussmann asked Deschamps to prepare a triangulation project for the area of Paris contained within the *mur d'octroi* and to cost it for submission to the municipal council. (After the incorporation of the suburban communes, the triangulation was extended to the line of the Paris fortifications.)

The council accepted the need for such an operation and authorized Haussmann to take up the large credit it would require. The triangulation took more than a year to complete. The first task of those involved in the project was to divide the area to be surveyed into a series of adjacent triangles and to measure their lengths and angles. After ensuring that all the triangles "fitted" with one another, they could go on to make a detailed survey of each division, whether it was built upon or not. All these micro-surveys were then put together to form the general map of Paris, the document used by Deschamps's department to draw the alignments of the old roads and, as the program advanced, the lines of the new roads. Not a single mistake occurred to blemish the quality of the work.

Haussmann had the survey map of Paris made to a scale of 1:5,000 on large sheets containing all the information necessary to his various departments. He then had these sheets mounted in a frame on casters and placed behind a screen in the middle of his study, so that he could consult it at any moment to check a detail or hunch and to ponder the routes that would best link each part of Paris with the other parts. To make the city a single whole became a kind of obsession for him—"to recognize the topographical correlations between the different arrondissements and neighborhoods of Paris," as he would later put it.[5] Haussmann guaranteed the fame of "his" map by publishing a 1:10,000-scale reproduction (which was still rather cumbersome at 5 x 8 feet), and then a 1:20,000 version for the general public.

The other task was to measure the contours of the land so that spot heights would be visible. Because of the building work under way and the new projects ordered by Napoléon III, it was not possible to wait until the general survey map of Paris had been completed. Although it was not a very logical way to proceed, Haussmann was forced to begin the contouring of Paris at the same time as the triangulation operations.[6]

Much was at stake economically in the Paris survey, as new roads affected real estate values and could enrich or impoverish owners of the land. Surveyors from the special topographical department, whose job it was to plot new roads and to identify the buildings that might have to be compulsorily purchased, found themselves in the firing line. They were obliged to maintain complete confidentiality. "Until the moment when the plan for a new public road was submitted to an inquiry, it was important to keep safe from any indiscretion both the precise route of the road and the area of the compulsory purchases it would require. This denied speculators the means of profiting without risk from the fact that interested parties were not yet in the know, or of hatching one of those frauds through which so many landowners, and dishonest tenants even more, have been awarded exorbitant compensation by overindulgent panels."[7]

But there was also a second, later responsibility that placed Deschamps in the sights of anyone eager to benefit from inside information. Once the compulsory purchase orders had been issued, highway engineers prepared the reports on the basis of which the municipal council fixed the amount of compensation to landlords and tenants and calculated the price it should ask for leftover demolition material and pieces of land for which the city had no use. The actual selling was not part of their remit; that fell to the city department in charge of state-owned property. But their expert functions gave considerable power to the highway engineers. In 1859, Haussmann therefore placed them under Deschamps's *Plan de Paris* department. This says a lot about the ethical standards expected of Deschamps and all those with whom he worked.

THE RUE DE RIVOLI

↜ When Haussmann took over from Berger, the rue de Rivoli (which started at the Place de la Concorde) had progressed no farther than the Passage Delorme, just beyond the Pavillon de Marsan near the present-day rue des Pyramides. Between the Louvre and rue Saint-Honoré, on the major part of today's Place du Carrousel and the space that has become the Place du Palais Royal, "a foul area made up of squalid houses and criss-crossed by narrow alleyways"[8] stretched as far as rue de Richelieu. Between rue de Richelieu and rue Saint-Roch, things did not look much better. Dilapidated houses from the early seventeenth century flanked the Butte des Moulins, a huge garbage dump nearly a hundred feet high that blocked the flow of water and turned the ground into a noxious quagmire; its name came from the few windmills perched on top. A number of wretched shacks lay on the lower slopes of the hillock, together with piles of building rubble. After the fall of Napoléon III, the artificial hill was eventually razed to make way for the Avenue de l'Opéra, and today the only record of its existence is the rue des Moulins, which runs between rue Thérèse and the rue des Petits Champs in the first arrondissement.

Balzac expressed his outrage: "The Louvre blares out through every mouth of its pierced walls and yawning windows: 'Get these warts off my face!'" The light of day did not manage to create a passage for itself among the crumbling houses. Let us follow Balzac on the tracks of the pretty Madame Marneffe, who has been installed in the rue du Doyenné by Baron Hulot: "The block of houses still existing alongside the old Louvre is one of those gestures of protest that the French like to make against common sense, so that Europe is reassured about their fund of wit and no longer goes in fear of them." His description dates from 1836: "The rue du Doyenné and the impasse of the same name are the only streets inside this gloomy and deserted block of houses whose occupants are probably ghosts, since you never see anyone there. The sidewalk is much lower than in the rue du Musée and at the same level as in rue Froidmanteau. Now sunken beneath the rise in the ground, these houses are wrapped in the eternal shadow of the upper galleries of the Louvre, themselves darkened on this side by the wind from the north." Balzac's conclusion: "The usefulness of this rough area has doubtless been recognized, as a necessary symbol in the heart of Paris of that deeply rooted combination of squalor and splendor which characterizes the queen of capitals."

Émile de Labédollière showed in 1860, in his *Le Nouveau Paris* illustrated by Gustave Doré, that on the eve of Haussmann's *travaux* this wretched neighborhood was scarcely any better than in Balzac's picture. "In 1848 the Carrousel area was a desert. . . . From the Place du Carrousel to the Louvre, most of the houses lining the public road were inhabited by bric-a-brac merchants, who were selling old prints, coins and medals, arrows once used by savages, rusty armor, heads of Zealanders, stuffed crocodiles, traveling boxes, and mummies. . . . When night came, the darkness that enveloped the surrounding area was intensified by the dark mass of the palaces, and any late passerby trembled as he ventured into these solitary places, not far from which a sinister population was hidden from view inside seedy taverns and houses of ill repute."[9]

Haussmann destroyed this area during his early days in Paris—"with great satisfaction," as he put it. This part of the rue de Rivoli extension, begun under Berger, was completed by the end of 1854. But on November 15, 1853, a further decree authorized him to raze the rectangular area lying between rue Saint-Honoré and the Louvre, from the Passage Delorme to the rue des Poulies. The demolition operations made it possible to modify the cross streets: rue de l'Échelle, rue de Richelieu, rue de Rohan, rue Marengo, and rue de l'Oratoire, whose widening had been ordered by the same decree. The Place du Palais Royal came into being; a new *quartier* took shape. Finally, between the Louvre and Saint-Germain-l'Auxerrois, a huge new esplanade highlighted the colonnade of the Louvre for the first time since its construction under Louis XIV. After deducting the land acquired for public roads, nineteen thousand square yards remained on the city's hands.

It proved difficult to resell the surplus land. Haussmann was unable to find a purchaser because the transformation of Paris was in too early a stage for financial operators to be sure that it was worth deeply involving themselves in building projects along the roads in question. But the Pereire brothers, when asked for help, found Haussmann the means to post a positive result while themselves doing a good stroke of business. At the head of a syndicate of bankers, they paid the city 7.3 million francs for all the land it had put up for sale. Haussmann made the condition that all the building work on this land be completed by May 1, 1855, the date on which the World's Fair was due to open.

The Seine prefecture was in a hurry. On July 25, 1852, the first stone was laid for the new wing of the Louvre designed by the architects Lefuel and Visconti, which would eventually close up along the rue de Rivoli the set of monumental structures formed by the palaces of the Louvre and the Tuileries. The rue de Rivoli façade was completed in 1855. The new Louvre-

Tuileries complex, including the Place du Carrousel now laid out as gardens, was officially inaugurated on August 14, 1857.

Central government assumed responsibility for a large part of the expenditure.[10] The land acquisition cost more than 36 million francs, the works only 360,000 francs. Direct government subsidies came to 12 million francs, in addition to which it accepted financial responsibility for 15.5 million francs corresponding to the value of the land included in the joining of the Louvre and the Tuileries Palace. That meant a total reduction of 27 million francs for the city, which had to find only the extra 9 million. "It was fair," Haussmann commented. "The state's interest in the operations . . . was evidently greater than the city's."[11]

After the Louvre colonnade, the rue de Rivoli extension up to the Hôtel de Ville had already been decided under the law of August 4, 1851, and the decree of December 23, 1852, declared the enlargement of the Place du Louvre and the Place Saint-Germain-l'Auxerrois to be matters of public benefit. When Haussmann took office, Napoléon III settled the exact path of this section of the rue de Rivoli. A sketch going back to the time of the Artists' Plan envisaged an outward projection at the Place du Louvre; the street would then continue in a line from the colonnade to the Hôtel de Ville. The prince president and Berger also wanted to open a perspective on the colonnade of the Louvre by pulling down the Church of Saint-Germain-l'Auxerrois. No one at the time attached much importance to the edifice, but on March 1, 1852, Victor Hugo published in the *Revue des Deux Mondes* an article entitled "Guerre aux Démolisseurs!" [War on the Wreckers]. "A street a league long![12] Just think how nice that will be: a straight line drawn from the Louvre to the Throne Barrier. From the *barrière* one will gaze along to the Louvre. It is true that the whole merit of Perrault's construction is in its proportions and that this merit will vanish in the distance.[13] But what does that matter? We'll have a street a league long." The scale of the opposition led Louis-Napoléon to alter the plans for the rue de Rivoli so that it would continue the line flanking the side of the colonnade as far as rue Saint-Antoine. The prince took advantage of this to increase its width to seventy-two feet, the same as for the section between the Place de la Concorde and the Place du Louvre.

But the prince's decision did not eliminate the threats to Saint-Germain-l'Auxerrois, for the clearing of the area around it would leave the church alone facing the colonnade. The minister without portfolio Fould, who had the fine arts as one of his areas of activity, called in Haussmann soon after his appointment and confided that he was thinking of having the church pulled down. The prefect shared Fould's view that it had little artistic value apart from a porch that seemed to merit preservation, but he objected to its destruction on the grounds that the bells of Saint-Germain-l'Auxerrois had sounded the signal for the Bartholomew Night's Massacre on August 24, 1572. "Like yourself," he said to Fould, "I am not inclined to worship old stones when they lack that artistic vital spark; but Saint-Germain-l'Auxerrois brings to mind a date that I abhor as a Protestant, and that I therefore do not feel at liberty as prefect to erase from the soil of Paris."— "But I am a Protestant too," the minister broke in.—"Really?" Haussmann just stopped himself from adding that he had thought Fould was a religious Jew; he did not know that he had converted to Protestantism. Keeping his composure, he continued: "Then it's much worse! Two Protestants plotting together to pull down Saint-Germain-l'Auxerrois? No one in the world would see it as anything other than revenge for Saint Bartholomew's Night!"[14] Fould agreed that Haussmann was right.

The prefect wanted the square to be laid out in such a way that Saint-Germain-l'Auxerrois would be shown off to better advantage. Its façade was not parallel to the colonnade. Haussmann therefore thought of building a new town hall for the arrondissement that would also slant away from the Place Saint-Germain-l'Auxerrois, but in the opposite direction from that of the church; a tower serving the church would link the two structures to each other. The blocks of houses that would frame the far end of the square would give the otherwise rather airy-looking colonnade its proper proportions. "In fact," Haussmann noted, "although a historic building must have enough air around it to allow a visitor to grasp it as a whole, it must not have too much. The truth of this could be seen in the case of the École Militaire, which seemed to be slithering on the ground ever since the emperor had made me remove the little mounds of plants on the Champ de Mars that served to frame it."[15] Haussmann was clear and precise when it was a question of pointing out the faults of Napoléon III, but less forthright when the fault was his own. He said nothing at all about his mistake in excessively clearing the square in front of Notre Dame.

The church tower of Saint-Germain-l'Auxerrois was built between 1858 and 1861, to a design by the architect Ballu. According to Haussmann, its neo-Gothic style gave it considerable charm. But the emperor discovered that it could be seen from the Tuileries emerging above the roofs of the Louvre, to the left of the central pavilion, thereby emphasizing the lack of alignment between the Louvre and the Tuileries. The top part had to be shortened, and the prefect tried to redeem himself by placing a clock on the tower. The town hall of the 1st arrondissement (at that time the town hall of the 4th arrondissement) replaced the buildings on rue du Chevalier-du-Guet, which had been pulled down during the opening of the rue de Rivoli. The architect, Jacques-Ignace Hittorff, thought he had been given to understand that the prefect wanted a pastiche of the church, and that is what he produced. Work on it began in 1857 and was completed by 1859. It aroused universal sarcasm, some comparing the church, town hall, and intervening tower to an oil and vinegar cruet. Haussmann blamed Hittorff for it all: his only fault was to have allowed him to go ahead.

Haussmann soon had work under way on the rue de Rivoli extension from Place Saint-Germain-l'Auxerrois to the Place de l'Hôtel de Ville. A general razing of the Arcis neighborhood solved the problem of the differences in ground level in the area surrounding the tower of Saint-Jacques de la Boucherie. Haussmann perched a statue of Pascal on top of the tower, in memory of the famous gravity experiments that the philosopher had conducted there. His preparations then turned to the next stages: the extension of the rue de Rivoli in the direction of the Bastille; the redevelopment of the central Halles; and the boulevard perpendicular to the rue de Rivoli that would cross Paris from north to south.

A few months before Berger was removed, a decree of February 19, 1853, declared the enlargement of the Place de l'Hôtel de Ville to be a matter of public benefit. Haussmann worked up a development plan for the space between the Hôtel de Ville and the Place du Châtelet, and on June 29, 1854, this too was declared to be in the public benefit. A central avenue linked the two squares, known after 1855 as the Avenue Victoria. Opposite the Hôtel de Ville, Haussmann built two structures of uniform architecture to accommodate the *octroi* department, the municipal archives, and the public assistance board. In the direction of the Châtelet, Avenue Victoria passed Square Saint-Jacques on the right, now improved thanks to the demolition of the church of Saint Jacques de la Boucherie and the leveling of the mound of the Tour Saint-Jacques; it was Paris's first *square*, in the English sense of a small public garden. The Place du Châtelet opposite sported two new theatres: the Théâtre du Châtelet and the Théâtre Lyrique (today's Théâtre de la Ville). Between rue Saint-Denis and Boulevard Sébastopol, facing the Seine, a new building housed the Chamber of Notaries.

THE CENTRAL HALLES

❧ After years in which the project had been studied and debated, Napoléon III decided that the central Halles would be built on land around the church of Saint-Eustache, where markets had been held since the Middle Ages. The area in question was huge, with a dense population. When Haussmann took over, 147 houses had already been pulled down. But the new prefect realized that that would not be enough and decided to ask for a larger area to be set aside for the Halles, involving the destruction of another 180 houses.

Much more serious perhaps, Haussmann entered the scene in the middle of a storm over the architecture of the new structure. The design for the Halles had been entrusted to a municipal architect, Baltard, who had once won the Grand Prix de Rome. His project, approved by the civil construction committee and all other relevant bodies, consisted of eight pavilions. The first of these, facing the front of Saint Eustache, was completed just days before Haussmann took office as Seine prefect on June 22, 1853. It was so heavy that the public immediately nicknamed it "the Halle fortress." When Napoléon III visited the site on June 3, he was so shocked at the aspect of the pavilion that he decided to stop further work on the Halles and to open a new round of consultations. With his great admiration for the glass-covered metal frame of the main hall at the Gare Saint-Lazare,[16] which had just been finished by the railway engineer-architect Armand, the emperor looked to this as a model for the Halles. He instructed Haussmann to examine and classify the first preliminary designs for the replacement of Baltard's project, including one by Armand. "What I must have are huge umbrellas—nothing else," he confided. And he penciled the shape he had in mind on a piece of paper that Georges-Eugène carefully preserved.

Haussmann got down to work. On a map he drew the broad road he thought indispensable to carry traffic between Saint-Eustache and the Place du Châtelet, with the eight pavilions distributed on either side in two groups of four. Then he simply transcribed Napoléon III's sketch eight times onto a sheet of paper and added the ingenious idea of covering the cross street itself with metal roofing. Haussmann was quite fond of Baltard, a fellow Protestant who had finished his secondary education at the Collège Henri IV just as Haussmann had been starting his. He called in the unlucky architect and handed over the file he had prepared for him. "Now's the chance to get your revenge," he said. "Do a preliminary plan for me as soon as possible, using these directions. Iron, iron—nothing but iron."[17]

Baltard protested volubly. Steeped as he was in classicism, the use of iron in architecture was nothing short of heresy. Twice, three times he presented Haussmann with an outline that the prefect turned down as insufficiently stripped of pillars and brickwork. Finally one satisfied him, and he submitted it to Napoléon III without revealing the designer's identity. The emperor was excited at the anonymous sketch and would have been willing to approve it then and there. But Haussmann, not wanting to expose himself to another setback, asked for a model to be made up first. The prefect's staff took four months to complete this, but the result was an original conception that showed to scale not only the eight metal pavilions (whose exact proportions could thus be appreciated) but everything in their vicinity such as residential blocks, streets, sidewalks, streetlights, carriages, even pedestrians. Napoléon III was more convinced than ever and confirmed his decision. As he left the Hôtel de Ville, he finally got round to asking the name of the talented architect who had so well sensed what he had in mind. "Baltard," Haussmann revealed. The emperor's face darkened. "It's the same architect but not the same prefect," Haussmann added by way of explanation. As for Baltard, although he always showed perfect correctness in his dealings with the prefect, he never forgave him this hurtful claim to paternity over the Halles pavilions; he even went so far as to vote against Haussmann's application to join the Academy of Fine Arts.

The initial area of the Halles, including the demolition of 147 houses, had cost 14,688,000 francs. The acquisition of another 180 houses would mean spending almost the same again (14,680,000 francs). The provision of mains services would cost 1,339,000 million francs, or less than 5 percent of the 29,368,000 spent on the land. The price of acquiring and developing the land thus came to more than 30 million francs, not including the actual construction of the pavilions.

Haussmann was not very happy with the organization of the roads around the Halles. The major cross street, which took the name rue Baltard, connected with the Palais Royal area via rue Saint-Honoré, but the way in which it opened out toward the Châtelet had to be rethought. The prefect obtained Napoléon III's agreement for a decree of June 21, 1854, that declared a public interest in extending rue Baltard down a 66-foot-wide rue du Pont-Neuf to the bridge of the same name. Just before the river, it would be joined from the right by the rue de la Monnaie, which was linked via the rue du Roule and the rue des Prouvaires to the Bourse du Commerce on the western edge of the Halles. The decree also ordered the opening of the 66-

foot-wide rue des Halles, which would run diagonally down to the Pont au
Change, picking up rue Saint-Denis in its final stretch. To the north, the rue
des Halles and rue Baltard would issue into rue Montmartre, another diagonal street leading to the *grands boulevards*. To the west, Haussmann would
have liked to complete the system by extending rue Rambuteau on the
northern edge of the Halles toward the rue des Valois, at the corner of rue
Saint-Honoré and the Place du Palais Royal. But as the emperor thought
this less urgent, it did not go ahead. The Seine prefect secured central government support worth 3 million francs toward the 13,651,000 francs required for the road-building program decided by the decree of June 21,
1854. Total spending on the Halles and the surrounding area would thus
come to 44 million francs.

THE RUE DE RIVOLI EXTENSION TO RUE SAINT-ANTOINE

The last extension of the rue de Rivoli, between the Place de l'Hôtel de
Ville and Place Birague (where it was to join rue Saint-Antoine), was declared to be of public benefit under a decree of September 29, 1854. On the
other side of the Hôtel de Ville, however, the project ran into a layout problem similar to the one at Saint-Germain-l'Auxerrois. Behind the municipal
buildings, the rue de Rivoli opened onto the Place du Marché Saint-Jean in
front of the church of Saint-Gervais-Saint-Protais, from where rue Saint-
Antoine wound down to the Place de la Bastille. Shopkeepers wanted the existing route to be kept, even if it meant widening rue Saint-Antoine. But
Haussmann brushed this aside and drove the rue de Rivoli straight on to the
Lycée Charlemagne and the Church of Saint Paul at Place Birague, opposite
the present-day rue de Sévigné.

Haussmann was thus able to clear the area at the back of the Hôtel de
Ville and to open up the Napoléon Barracks that had been built on the other
side of rue Lobau just before his appointment. Behind the barracks, he enlarged the little Place Baudoyer and had the town hall of the 4th arrondissement built there. It would be the largest of all the local town halls
constructed through his efforts, the reason being that it was eventually supposed to serve as an annex (or "branch office," as he put it[18]) for the Hôtel de
Ville. The cost was 2,147,000 francs, not an insignificant amount, but the
architectural elements, due to Bailly, worked out rather well. The section of
rue Saint-Antoine between the church and Place Birague was renamed rue
François-Miron, so that Saint-Antoine now applied only to the stretch be-

tween Place Birague and the Place de la Bastille. The east-west road across Paris on the right bank was now complete; a wide, direct, and often monumental route linked Concorde to the Bastille.

THE BOULEVARD DE SÉBASTOPOL

✎ Haussmann next turned to the north-south branch. To improve access to the Gare du Nord and the Gare de l'Est, the Berger administration had opened the Boulevard de Strasbourg as far as Boulevard Saint-Denis. Napoléon III and Haussmann decided that it should continue to the Châtelet, then cut across the Île de la Cité to the Carrefour de l'Observatoire. The decree of September 29, 1854, declared this great artery to be of public benefit; it was meant to be called the "Boulevard du Centre," but after the victory in the Crimea it became the 98-foot-wide Boulevard de Sébastopol. Under the terms of a decree of October 18, 1854, the government agreed to contribute a third of total net expenditure on the new boulevard, with a ceiling of 23.5 million francs.

The same decree launched several other projects in the vicinity. The first was the creation between rue Saint-Denis and rue Saint-Martin of three cross roads, each sixty-six feet in width: the rue Réaumur extension past the church of Saint-Nicolas-des-Champs, the rue de Turbigo, and rue Étienne-Marcel, as well as a road fifty-two feet wide opposite the entrance to the Conservatoire des Arts et Métiers. The second operation was the extension of the rue des Cygnes, rue de la Grande-Truanderie, and rue de la Cossonerie, between rue Saint-Denis and the new boulevard. The third was the widening to fifty-two feet of rue Grenéta and rue La Reynie. The fourth and last was the complete or partial elimination of a number of streets: the rue du Ponceau, the passages de la Longue-Allée, Basfour, de la Trinité, Guérin-Boisseau, du Grand-Hurleur, du Bourg-l'Abbé, du Petit-Hurleur, Salle-au-Comte, des Trois Maures, de la Vieille-Monnaie, and the impasse de Venise.

These various undertakings were to be spread over five years, from 1855 to 1859. Haussmann congratulated himself on having built new roads that would make it easier to move around the city but also be an obstacle in the way of troublemakers. "It meant the gutting of *vieux Paris* [in fact, only the Arts et Métiers neighborhood], the area of riots and barricades. Cutting right through this nearly impassable labyrinth was now a large central road, as well as side streets whose continuation would round off the work. The later completion of the rue de Turbigo removed rue Transnonain from the map of Paris."[19]

Was this an admission that strategic considerations had been para-mount? Haussmann was anxious to qualify this point in his *Mémoires* while recognizing his concern to maintain law and order: "To be sure, in planning the Boulevard de Strasbourg and its extension to the Seine and beyond, the emperor did not have its strategic usefulness more in mind than he had in the case of many other roads, such as the rue de Rivioli, for example, whose straight line made it unfavorable for the usual tactic of local insurrections. But if he did not seek this result above all else, as the opposition claimed, it cannot be denied that it was the very fortunate consequence of all His Majesty's great road-building programs to improve and clean up the old town. This result, in conjunction with a number of other good reasons, served to justify in the eyes of France (which had a primary interest in the peace of Paris) the government's share in these costly undertakings. As to myself, who promoted the additions to the initial project, I can say that when I combined them in this way I never gave the slightest thought to their greater or lesser strategic importance."[20]

The line of the Boulevard de Sébastopol, which continues that of the Boulevard de Strasbourg, strikes us today as logical enough. But it was fiercely criticized at the time, and the prefect was urged instead to change the alignment by widening one side of either of the two north-south streets inherited from earlier times, rue Saint-Denis or rue Saint-Martin. Hauss-mann had a fine time showing in his *Mémoires* that, at the rate of progress common before he took over the prefecture, such a project could easily have taken a century or two, and that it was anyway easier to carve a route through gardens, small courtyards, and low-rise buildings than to tackle res-idential blocks that were sometimes highly priced and endowed with a handsome façade. "It is easier to pass through the inside of a pie than to cut into the pastry," he quipped. This route allowed him to spare the buildings with architectural or historical value that were scattered around the area. Only the chevet of the Church of Saint Leu was given a hard time, when it was forced to lose thirteen feet in height. Haussmann put Baltard in charge of redesigning its apse in the form of an ellipsoid instead of a semi-circle, and to make up for the lost space, the church acquired a new catechismal chapel and a presbytery. Baltard showed great skill in carrying out these tasks; only a trained eye was able to spot the suture.

There remained the problem of Haussmann's cherished perspective across the Seine. As the dome of the Sorbonne was not straight in line with the Boulevard de Sébastopol, he thought of a new *tribunal de commerce* built on the Île de la Cité, at the corner of the Quai de Corse and the future Boulevard du Palais, as a pendant to the great glass wall of the Gare de l'Est that closed the view in the north. The old commercial court was located at the Bourse, where it occupied much of the first floor of the Palais Brongniart, but the space available there was proving inadequate. The din from the stock dealing tended to disturb the tranquillity of the judges, especially as women were not allowed on the floor of the Bourse and often invaded the court-rooms in the hope of catching some rumor or piece of information. At the new site proposed by Haussmann, the court would have a building to itself in the heart of Paris, opposite the Palais de Justice. Haussmann put Bailly in charge of the architectural side of the project and urged him to consider a monumental structure directly in the line of the Boulevard de Sébastopol. Bailly came up with the idea of a dome-topped staircase, around which all the parts of the building would gravitate. The construction was completed in 1864. On the embankment side, the dome rose above a richly decorated façade for which the architect (at Napoléon III's request) had drawn inspira-tion from the Lodge of the merchants of Brescia in northern Italy. The work cost 5,437,000 francs.

THE LEFT BANK ROUTE: RUE DES ÉCOLES, BOULEVARDS SAINT-MICHEL AND SAINT-GERMAIN

⮜ Haussmann did not have much difficulty in persuading the emperor to accept the idea of a southward extension of the Boulevard de Sébastopol through the Île de la Cité, the Pont au Change, and the Pont Saint-Michel, then on to the rue des Écoles and finally the Barrière de l'Enfer (today's Place Denfert-Rochereau). The opening of the rue des Écoles, which the emperor had marked on his color-coded map as forming the east-west route on the left bank, got under way in 1853. But Haussmann was highly critical of the fact that, being on the slopes of Mount Sainte-Geneviève, the street could not be given sufficient width to carry large volumes of traffic. He therefore proposed to Napoléon III that a second, much wider road be built on level ground closer to the Seine: the future Boulevard Saint-Germain.

Napoléon III insisted on the rue des Écoles, but Haussmann eventually extracted from him the solution that we know: the rue des Écoles would stop at the junction with the rue du Cardinal-Lemoine, rue Saint-Victor, and the rue des Fossés-Saint-Bernard that ran alongside the Halle aux Vins (today's Campus Jussieu); a new street (the first section of rue Monge) would go up toward the École Polytechnique; and in the other direction, to the west, the rue des Écoles would end in the vicinity of the École de Médecine. Boulevard

Saint-Germain would become a pendant to the rue de Rivoli on the right bank.

Haussmann now devoted all his attention to the early work on the Boulevards Saint-Michel and Saint-Germain. He ordered the creation of Place Saint-Michel, on the south side of the Pont Saint-Michel, where there had only been an irregular crossroads formed by the lower ends of the rue de la Harpe, rue d'Enfer, and rue Hautefeuille. The opening of Boulevard Saint-Michel, from Place Saint-Michel to the rue de Médicis/rue Soufflot crossing, was declared to be of public benefit on August 11, 1855, and in 1856 the boulevard pressed on to rue Cujas. Another decree of August 11, 1855, allowed Boulevard Saint-Germain to be driven between rue Hautefeuille and the Quai des Tournelles. In 1857, once the land had been acquired, this stretch of the boulevard was built in three sections: the first, from rue Hautefeuille to rue Saint-Jacques, crossed Boulevard Saint-Michel and at last fully opened up the Thermes to view; the second went from the Seine to Place Maubert; the middle section, between Place Maubert and rue Saint-Jacques, was more complicated because it involved connecting the rue des Écoles with Boulevard Saint-Germain while continuing the construction of new roads through the Latin Quarter. The Saint-Michel/Saint-Germain crossing was finished some time in 1857, but it was only in 1861 that it became possible to travel Boulevard Saint-Germain all the way from rue Hautefeuille to the Quai des Tournelles.

LEFT BANK: THE FAUBOURG SAINT-MARCEL

The development of the faubourg Saint-Marcel and the Gare area on the left bank south from Mount Sainte-Geneviève to the Place d'Italie began in 1854. The decree for the creation of rue Jeanne d'Arc was published only a month after the one declaring the Boulevard du Centre (Boulevard de Sébastopol) to be of public benefit. Haussmann opened up rue Jeanne d'Arc from what is now Boulevard Vincent Auriol to the rue de Domrémy, halfway between rue Dunois and rue Nationale. Shortly before the Jeanne d'Arc/Domrémy crossing, it proved necessary to clear a rectangular esplanade, Place Jeanne-d'Arc, in the middle of which the church of Notre Dame de la Gare was constructed. In 1855, Haussmann decided to extend rue Jeanne d'Arc south along the rue de Patay. (Its northward extension, between Boulevard Vincent Auriol and the Boulevard de l'Hôpital, would have to wait until 1913.) The road system was completed with the creation of Boulevard Saint-Michel, under the terms of a decree of 1857.

LEFT BANK: THE RUE DE RENNES

During the same period, Haussmann pressed on with Berger's project for the rue de Rennes. The first sixty-six-foot-wide section, starting at the Gare Montparnasse (then called "the Western Railway Embarkation Point"), was planned to meet the rue du Vaugirard/rue de Regard intersection. Napoléon III and Haussmann wanted to extend it to the embankment and take it straight across the Seine on a new bridge, but the creation of such a bridge would have meant demolishing the Institut des Arts and the Pont des Arts—an evident impossibility. They therefore considered a number of other projects, particularly an X-shaped bridge whose two branches would have encompassed the Institute. But this idea found no greater favor among a public deeply attached to this exceptional cityscape, and the problem was declared insoluble. After 1866 the rue de Rennes was finally extended as far as Boulevard Saint-Germain and Place Saint-Germain-des-Prés.*

THE PLACE DE LA CONCORDE

The Place de la Concorde had scarcely changed since it was designed by the architect Gabriel in the age of Louis XV as the western edge of urbanized Paris. Work on Gabriel's project began in 1754 and was finished by 1764. It retained its shape during the turmoil of the Great Revolution, when it became the main site for the numerous executions of the time, including that of Louis XVI. On August 20, 1828, on the initiative of the prefect Chabrol, a law gave the city of Paris ownership of the Place de la Concorde and the Champs Élysées, including state property as far as the foot of the Tuileries terrace, on condition that it provided for the upkeep and maintenance of the places in question, carried out improvements to the value of at least 2.23 million francs within a period of five years, and retained the existing purpose of the land (which was declared inalienable). It was then that the transformation of the Champs Élysées began: elegant cafés opened their doors, the François I neighborhood was urbanized, and new streets opened onto the Marbeuf gardens. Chabrol decided to redesign the Place de la Concorde and launched an architectural competition that was won by Jacques-Ignace Hittorff. But the revolution of July 1830 brought Louis-Philippe to the throne,

*The dispute of the 1860s recurred in an unexpected form in the late 1990s. For the land originally acquired for the abandoned stretch between Saint-Germain-des-Prés and the Seine had left the city of Paris with a major "private domain" of residential blocks in the rue de Seine and rue Jacob, whose apartments were often rented out to friends at a rather friendly price. The resulting scandal shook the majority that had emerged from the local elections of 1995.

and the architect had to wait until 1831 for the new Seine prefect, Rambuteau, to put him in charge of the project. Building work began in 1834 and lasted until 1840.

Hittorff kept to the spirit of Gabriel's design. The sentry boxes built by his illustrious predecessor to mark the square as a place of closure were now topped with statues symbolizing the main towns of France, and the creation of central islands stressed the order of the main roads. Just then Egypt offered an obelisk to France; Hittorff managed to have it erected on the main island in the square, in a line with the Avenue des Champs Élysées and the Arc de Triomphe at l'Étoile, which was nearing completion. The base used for the obelisk was Hittorff's own work, as were the two fountains framing it, the street lamps, and the twenty commemorative naval columns. These columns and the statues symbolizing the major towns of France were unveiled with great pomp in July 1838.

The fall of Louis-Philippe did not damage Hittorff, who was linked to the Bonapartes, Prince Napoléon-Jérôme, and, through him, the prince president. Not only did he keep his architectural functions in the city of Paris, he was chosen by Louis-Napoléon as the right-hand man of Varé, the chief landscape architect for the Bois de Boulogne. As well as doing various jobs for Napoléon-Jérôme, he was given responsibility in 1853 for the construction of the Maison d'Éducation Eugénie-Napoléon, a reformatory founded by Empress Eugénie in the faubourg Saint-Antoine; he had it finished by 1856. Also in 1853 Hittorff completed the Church of Saint Vincent de Paul that had been started ten years earlier. His problems began when Haussmann appeared on the administrative scene in Paris. Was this because the architect, like Haussmann, originated from the Rhine region, or because a certain jealousy made it hard to endure the favor that the prefect enjoyed with Napoléon III? In any event, Haussmann seemed to be forever thwarting Hittorff's initiatives, or even humiliating him.

A great lover of polychromic architecture in imitation of ancient Greece, Hittorff proposed to apply this decorative schema to Saint Vincent de Paul. But Haussmann wanted to show who was boss: "He had a dispute with me. . . . In my view, the widespread daubing of color over churches in Italy and elsewhere to imitate unaffordable wall hangings or tapestries was unworthy of the majesty of these historic buildings." Haussmann had very fixed ideas on this score: "Whether Greek, Italian, or French, the use of colorwash . . . to replace the coldness and monotony of stone with a variety of flat colors has the great disadvantage of also hiding the simple and noble beauty of the uniform material used in the construction. And when this coat of paint is further brightened with detail that reminds me of the tattoos used in place of clothes by barbarous peoples to conceal their nakedness, I cannot find this pretentious form of decoration anything but grotesque." That certainly has the merit of clarity. "I therefore asked M. Hittorff," Haussmann continues, "to be more moderate in his use of color for Saint Vincent de Paul. I allowed him the porch paintings on enameled lava, although the clergy was shocked at the nudity displayed in them and later asked for them to be removed. I got off lightly inside, with gold stars smeared on blue for the vaults, and a big order for works of art to make up for the crude paintings I did not wish to see there."[21]

Whether the prefect was right or wrong, the emperor was not involved in such disputes and found it quite natural in 1854 to gave Hittorff the task of redesigning the Place de la Concorde. Having himself a strong penchant for festivals, parades, and mass demonstrations, both as spectacle and as tool of government, Napoléon III suddenly realized that the flow of a crowd down the Champs Élysées toward the city center on festive evenings created the risk of serious accidents. The authorities were obsessed with the tragic disaster of 1770, which had caused dozens of fatalities during a major festival on the Place de la Concorde. More recently, on July 29, 1844, a number of people had been killed or injured when a firework in front of the Palais Bourbon led to a collision between one group of spectators moving toward the Champs Élysées and another group trying to move away from it. The immediate issue facing the emperor now was the traffic and crowd flow problems bound up with festivities at the World's Fair he had decided to hold in 1855 on the Carré Marigny, between the Rond-Point des Champs Élysées and what is now Place Clemenceau. The erection of the obelisk and the Hittorff fountains meant that the open space in the Place de la Concorde had considerably shrunk. Moreover, as the flower borders had been dug below the level of the actual *place*, there was a danger that, even if these were fenced off inside railings, some pedestrians might fall and come to grief in a sudden surge of the crowd. The flower beds were part of Gabriel's original design, but they no longer corresponded to patterns of urban movement in the middle of the nineteenth century. To give Parisians more space, it was therefore necessary either to move the obelisk or to fill in the flower beds.

Haussmann was quite willing to move the obelisk, as there was no shortage of alternative sites. But Hittorff, who had designed the whole group in the middle of the square, did not wish to touch either the obelisk or the two fountains framing it. The affair eventually came before the emperor. Hittorff had experience and professional competence on his side, being both an artist and a scholar (as Haussmann himself recognized). Napoléon III therefore decided in his favor and agreed that Gabriel's flower beds should be removed. The Seine prefect, who had tried without success to win over influential members of the emperor's entourage, could do nothing other than reluctantly comply with his wishes. He would never admit that the disappearance of Gabriel's ornaments did not necessarily harm the general appearance of the square, although he did remark that from then on the crowd could move without obstruction on festive occasions or other days of dense traffic. The wound to his pride had stung him, and Haussmann was bent on revenge.

He went about this in a rather mean-spirited way, toppling the lamps from their tall stands in the Place de la Concorde. In fact, Hittorff had designed the proportions of the lamps with just such a base in mind, but Haussmann claimed that they were too high to provide sufficient lighting and overruled the architect by bringing them closer to the level of the street. Nor did this petty act suffice to quench the prefect's thirst for revenge. Each new opportunity to contradict Hittorff was welcomed: the layout of the Place de l'Étoile and the Bois de Boulogne, the opening of the Avenue de l'Impératrice (today's Avenue Foch), and the later landscaping of the Champs Élysées. Was it any surprise that Hittorff bequeathed his precious library to his home town of Cologne instead of to Paris?

THE ROND-POINT DE L'ÉTOILE

≈ Haussmann began considering plans for L'Étoile within weeks of taking over at the Hôtel de Ville. He wanted it to be a very special operation. The Arc de Triomphe was then outside the actual city limits, just behind the *barrière* marked by Ledoux's two tollhouses. The Avenue des Champs Élysées that led down to Paris was wide and planted with trees, but it still contained only a modest highway at its core.

The view from the Arc de Triomphe encompassed the capital in one direction and the plain of Neuilly in the other. The superb monument to the glory of the Grande Armée, begun under Napoléon I, continued by the Restoration and completed by the July Monarchy, had a very lonely air. When he was still in London, Louis-Napoléon Bonaparte had conceived the idea of opening a number of new avenues at L'Étoile—most importantly, Avenue Foch (or the Avenue de l'Impératrice, as it was first known), Avenue Kléber, and Avenue Friedland. But soon after his appointment as prefect,

Haussmann concluded that the emperor's plan lacked the necessary scale and inspiration; he set about correcting this.

It must be recognized that the merit is Haussmann's alone for this twelve-armed star radiating from a huge square 262 yards in diameter. He wanted the whole complex to be symmetrical, with similar houses all around it, but he ended up with a few irregularities because of some of the previous streets. He intended to eliminate the covered way, the *barrière*, and Ledoux's tollhouses, but to ease the flow of traffic he provided for a circular road (rue de Tilsitt/rue de Presbourg) that would run around the Arc de Triomphe and link up the avenues. As the suburban communes had not yet been absorbed, Haussmann made the Seine highways department responsible for road-building outside the city limits—most notably in the case of the Avenue de l'Impératrice, which was begun very soon after he took over as prefect.

The provisions for the Place de l'Étoile came under a decree of August 13, 1854, signed by Biarritz. The strip of land bordering the square was to be enclosed in railings, with no building allowed within fifty-two feet, and to open only onto the avenues and the circular roadway. The iron railings in the square and on its sides and street façades were to be identical in both height and external decoration: they would rest upon a low freestone base and have cast iron embellishments. The façades were to be in freestone, with pilasters, balusters, molding, cornices, and other stone ornaments. No trade signs were permitted. The roofs around the square were to be in zinc, with two slopes linked by a cast iron channel, and holes in their bottom part would open into attic rooms. The Seine prefect would issue instructions regarding levels and alignments. In fact, he gave instructions about much else besides: the railings and façades had to be kept clean in accordance with his specifications; the ground between the buildings and the railings had to be laid with approved flower beds and could not be used as a public meeting place; no trade could be practiced in the area between the square and the circular roadway unless it was approved by the Seine prefect, who would decide each case on its merits and could revoke a permit at any moment.

Hittorff, indispensable as ever, carried out his task of devising a model for the "marshals' homes" to be built around the square. When Haussmann denigrated his plan as petty and restrictive, and asked for another story to be added to the constructions, Hittorff replied that that would ruin the fine proportions of the Arc de Triomphe. Again Napoléon III followed the architect's opinion. To flesh out the buildings, Haussmann planted trees between them and the central part of the square. But his conception of the radiating star comforted him for these few disappointments, and our prefect declared himself very happy with the overall result, "this beautiful layout, which I am very proud to have thought up and which I consider one of the greatest successes of my administration."[22]

EARLY PROJECTS ON THE RIGHT BANK

❧ Various projects on the right bank paved the way for the future road-building programs. In 1854 a public benefit decree authorized the construction of the future Boulevard Malesherbes northeast from the Place de la Madeleine to the rue de Monceau. In 1855 the municipal council approved in principle a *"boulevard du Nord"* (later to be called Boulevard Magenta), which would provide a link between the Gare de l'Est and the Gare du Nord. A number of streets were added along this main route to improve access to the Hôpital Lariboisière and the Gare du Nord. The boulevard was conceived as having a uniform width of 98 feet. Work was scheduled to begin with the central stretch from the Boulevard de Strasbourg to rue Saint-Quentin, where the opening up of the railway stations had become a matter of urgency. The rue de Maubeuge, which cut diagonally across the boulevard a little farther north, would link the Notre Dame de Lorette neighborhood to the Boulevard de la Chapelle. In 1857, Avenue Parmentier was built between Place Voltaire (today's Place Léon Blum) and the rue du Chemin-Vert, the first road system in the eastern *quartiers* situated between the present Place de la République and the faubourg Saint-Antoine.

Other programs on the right bank aimed to improve the layout of certain *places*. At the Place du Châtelet, for example, Haussmann decided to have the Palmier Fountain moved so that it was in a line with the new Pont au Change—a task he entrusted to Ballu. On April 21, 1858 (some sources say April 22), the twenty-four-ton monumental structure effected its journey by means of capstans and props and slid down the rails onto its new site before an audience of thousands lost in admiration of the technical feat: thirty-nine feet in just twenty-four minutes. Fully serviced and sporting a brand new base, the fountain returned to operation on January 1, 1859, much to the joy of curious onlookers.

The *grands travaux* were also an opportunity to lay out the green spaces for which the Anglo-obsessed Napoléon III would use the English word *squares*. The first was the Square de la Tour Saint-Jacques de la Boucherie, decreed on June 29, 1854, and completed in August 1855, with railings by the same Ballu. The Square du Temple opened in 1857 on land given by the state to the city of Paris. Work on the final stage of the Square des Arts et Métiers began in late 1857 and was completed in 1858.

THE BOIS DE BOULOGNE

❧ The Bois de Boulogne was one of the jewels of Louis-Napoléon's urban policy. Steeped in hygienist ideas as much as in Saint-Simonian concepts, the prince president wanted the road-building program that would raise the city's productivity to proceed in tandem with the planting of huge green spaces that would offer people the relaxation of body and mind essential to a better quality of life. As soon as he took over as president of the Republic, at the beginning of 1849, he ordered work on the Bois de Boulogne to begin. The state-owned land lying outside the historic fortifications, and therefore outside the city limits of the time, was given free of charge to the city of Paris, on condition that it carried out the minimum work necessary for the area to be given over to walking and relaxation.

The initial plan involved the digging of a sinuous watercourse along the lines of the Serpentine in London's Hyde Park. But in 1853 the project seemed about to collapse in ridicule when it turned out that Berger's men had lost the thread of things and underestimated the gradient, so that the river was dry in its upper stretch and a quagmire down below. As in the Tour Saint-Jacques affair, improvisation was necessary to save the situation. Haussmann divided the river into two sections, turning them into two lakes separated by a waterfall. By April 14, 1854, Berger's blunder had been rectified, and the emperor and empress could inaugurate the first stage of the works in the Bois. Water from the Seine was conveyed along an artificial canal to the Rond-Point Mortemart, where the watercourse flowed on to supply the upper lake and the lower lake, then the forest streams, the Great Waterfall, the Lake of Armenonville, and the Lake of Longchamp. For the occasion, workmen had decorated with flags and banners the rock where the water would burst forth at a given signal. A bust of the empress sat enthroned at the top of the rock. On the insignia placed on the side of the rock, it was possible to read: "From the workers to the Emperor and Empress." Haussmann gave the signal. The water rose, covered the rock, and fell powerfully down into the river. Napoléon III applauded, but deep down he would never get over the failure of his Serpentine to materialize.

Strengthened by success, Haussmann rid himself of the landscapist appointed by Napoléon III, Master Varé. He also brought in Davioud to replace the architect who had had the job of designing all manner of chalets and other structures—none other than Hittorff. But the problem was not one that could be solved by changing architects. Haussmann needed proper technical backup for the rest of the operations, not some acrobatic feat to repair past neglect or inconsistency; the Serpentine affair was a kind of carbon copy of the one involving the Tour Saint-Jacques de la Boucherie. He therefore decided to call to his side one of the men with whom he had worked at the Bordeaux prefecture, the tried and tested civil engineer Adolphe Alphand. A few months later, Alphand was installed at the Seine prefecture in charge of a specially created Walks and Horticulture Department, a veritable military machine directly answerable to the prefect in person. In addition to his work on the Bois de Bouologne and the urban green spaces, Alphand would later play a considerable role in the program of *grands travaux*.

For the moment, Haussmann began a new battle over the Bois de Boulogne in which he was opposed to Napoléon III. On aesthetic grounds he wished to extend the area of the Bois to take in the plain of Longchamp, the plain of Bagatelle, and the Parc de Madrid, whereas the emperor did not see what was to be gained by this, especially as it would mean buying out a large number of market gardeners. Haussmann could not find a way round the obstacle, but then Morny suggested a clever maneuver. Morny, apart from being Napoléon III's half-brother, was a prominent member of the Jockey Club (officially called the *Société d'encouragement pour l'amélioration des races de chevaux en France*, the "Society to Promote Better Horse-breeding in France"); he also organized the popular races at the prestigious but inconvenient location of the Champ de Mars—a source of trouble for the military authorities, who could use the area only on days when races were not being held. Morny's idea was that Haussmann should create a new racetrack on the plain of Longchamp, where the Jockey Club would have more spacious and suitable facilities and be better able to compete with the racetracks in England. At the same time, the army would be delighted to regain full use of the Champ de Mars, while the fact that the new racetrack would extend the Bois de Boulogne right to the banks of the Seine could only be of benefit to Haussmann's ambitious project. The case was put to the emperor with great astuteness, and on August 29, 1854, he signed a decree authorizing the government to meet half the costs of creating the new racetrack.

Next it was necessary to acquire the land in question. Discussions at the Council of State and the Legislature proved long and difficult. On April 13, 1855, a public benefit law was finally passed enabling the city of Paris to purchase not only the future racetrack area but all the land in the plain of

Longchamp and the Parc de Madrid, as well as to resell parts of the domain lying outside in Neuilly, Auteuil, and Boulogne. The total cost was estimated at 4 million francs, of which half would be met by the city and half by government subsidy.

Haussmann moved quickly to open avenues that would both serve and clearly demarcate the areas of land for reselling. These areas were separated from the Bois only by ditches that did not obstruct the view across, while at the rear they ended at fortifications that Haussmann concealed by planting new vegetation. The reselling of land that the city decided not to keep brought in a total of 8 million francs. Plans for the racetrack proceeded without delay. Haussmann acquired the land and paid out the compensation in record time, so that development work was able to begin in the final months of 1855. With Alphand's talent and hard work, no more than eighteen months were needed to complete operations. On June 24, 1856, Haussmann signed the order whereby the city of Paris ceded Longchamp racetrack for fifty years to the *Société d'encouragement*.

The official opening took place on April 26, 1857. Haussmann thus killed two birds with one stone: the racetrack itself was an instant success; and it drew Parisians to the transformed Bois de Boulogne, which now covered an area of 3.3 square miles bordering the Seine. In the final balance, it had not cost the city anything.

THE AVENUE DE L'IMPÉRATRICE

    More suitable roads were needed to serve the Bois de Boulogne. The traditional access via the Avenue de Saint-Cloud (now Avenue Victor Hugo) was narrow and in poor repair. On his color-coded map, the emperor had drawn a major artery starting from the Place de l'Étoile. Hittorff (he again) was placed in charge of the planning and came up with an avenue 131 feet (40 meters) wide, the largest ever in Paris. But Haussmann had bigger things in mind and once more took the architect to task: "Forty meters? But *monsieur*, we need something twice, three times wider; yes, three times: 120 meters!" To Hittorff's original plan, Haussmann added two grass verges 105 feet each in width, that is, four times wider than the two 26-foot roads serving the properties along the side—which did indeed add up to 120 meters (393 feet). Haussmann could not disguise his gut reaction to the architect: "The avenue . . . corresponded almost exactly to the plan I had just improvised in keen response to M. Hittorff's banal and petty-minded scheme. He could not persuade himself that my plan was serious. But I proved that it

was when I said to him: 'Please do not forget to attach to your plans, corrected in line with my figures, a sketch for the railings that should close off
the bordering pieces of limited-ownership land both from the avenue and
from one another. With your perfect taste, you will surely find a model that
is simple yet also suits the scale of the new road.' Then he withdrew in a
daze."[23]

Going even further, the prefect would have liked to impose a ban on construction within 33 feet of the avenue—which would have meant a total of
460 feet between the houses on one side and the houses on the other side.
Thanks to the harmonious layout of the actual highway and of the green
spaces lining it, there would have been nothing disproportionate in such a
great width. But the Legislature, which had a say in the matter because the
whole Bois de Boulogne project was linked to the opening of the Avenue de
l'Impératrice, began whispering about "megalomania" and forced Haussmann to abandon the idea of prohibiting construction along a 33-foot roadside strip. On the other hand, the prefect laid out the grass verges with
uncommon luxury. As a good courtier, he suggested the name of Avenue de
l'Impératrice—which was later changed to Avenue Foch. Situated entirely
within the city limits of the time, the avenue would cost Paris 1.7 million
francs, and the Seine department a further 300,000 francs.

THE LOAN OF 1855

≈ Money was certainly becoming an important issue. Some projects benefited from central government participation, but many were undertaken
with the city's resources alone. The new roads and development schemes,
new equipment for police quarters and town halls, the many churches of
which no mention has been made, the drains and water pipes on which
Haussmann first reported to the municipal council on August 4, 1854—all
these things happening before the eyes of the public, or due to happen when
the suburban communes were incorporated into the city, meant that money
had to be found somewhere. The city's budget had to face an additional burden at once, and an even greater one in the years ahead.

To meet the cost of the operations under way, the city was authorized by
a law of April 16 and 24, 1855, to secure a loan of 75 million francs. In the
event, it raised 60 million francs by means of an issue below par, which involved the following mechanism. The city issued 150,000 bonds with a face
value of 500 francs, repayable in fifty years at an interest rate of 3 percent,
each of which was entered in a twice-yearly lottery that gave out total prizes

of 300,000 francs a year. The capital that the city had to reimburse came to 75 million francs. But purchasers paid only 400 francs for each bond, since the city issued below par by awarding a "bonus" of 100 francs per bond. The sum coming into the city's coffers was thus 150,000 x 400 francs, or 60 million francs in extra cash, and the total real cost of the loan for the municipal finances was 4.87 percent. This was still quite an acceptable figure, but it was a little high in terms of market rates in 1855—since potential bond owners would not be pleased that the city of Paris had been increasing its rate of borrowing and had already raised two loans in recent years, in 1849 and 1852.

Other formulas would have to be devised for the next stages in the transformation of Paris. Napoléon III and Haussmann worked in great secrecy upon a vast program of public works to expand and integrate the measures already begun, with large-scale government involvement and the raising of a major loan. The year 1855—the year of the World's Fair but also of the Crimean War, which got off to a bad start and dragged on longer than anticipated—did not lend itself to a debate on such schemes. The return of peace in 1856 did not make the climate more propitious, and in 1857 a financial crisis meant that any talk of a loan was strictly taboo. And so it was only in 1858 that discussion began of the terms and conditions of the "180 million agreement" between central government and the city of Paris, which would provide the framework for the new phase of the *grands travaux*.

The 180-million-franc agreement led to a retrospective classification of "systems" [*reseaux*] involved in the transformation of Paris. The habit soon arose of grouping all projects prior to the agreement in a "first system," which had begun with the law of October 4, 1849, and was more or less completed by 1858.

The term "system" suggests that the *grands travaux* followed from the outset a rigorous and perfectly planned schedule. It was an impression that some of the main players—Napoléon III, Merruau, Persigny, and Alphand, as well as all the leading politicians and senior administrators of the age—certainly wished to convey. Alphand's speech at Haussmann's funeral was no exception: "The first system was a coordinated project that brought air, light, and cleanliness to the dark, winding, unhealthy streets that used to make up the old *quartiers* of the Tuileries, the Louvre, the Palais Royal, the Théâtre Français, the central Halles, the Hôtel de Ville, and the Cité." The account in Haussmann's *Mémoires* is more accurate, however, and shows that the transformation of Paris was worked out "along the way." It was certainly coordinated, but there was also a lot of room for improvised solutions, second thoughts, and priority shifts.

The "systems" of 1849–1858—which included new roads opened under the Haussmann administration as well as projects inherited from Berger—had not really been graded by importance, utility, or urgency, although each of these criteria had had some role to play. The "first system" was a tributary of the road-building programs launched under the Revolution, the First Empire, the Restoration, and the July Monarchy. It was the reflection of a particular epoch, with its own contradictions, economic fluctuations, political vagaries, personal appetites and ambitions. Nowhere was this more visible than in the mad period of festivals, military expeditions, and feverish speculation that marked the time of the World's Fair of 1855.

15

Imperial Festivities

ON JANUARY 4, 1852, Berger had offered a grand ball in honor of the prince president, then still surrounded by the aura of the coup d'état. Haussmann had other things in mind: he wanted to make the Hôtel de Ville the center of Parisian life—after the royal palace, of course—and to show that he knew how to receive people. On August 14, 1853, the eve of Napoleon's Feast Day, 140 guests gathered in the Throne Hall around Napoléon III and Eugénie, the archbishop of Paris, various ministers, and the presidents of the constituent bodies. Haussmann proposed a toast to the emperor and thanked him for "the unprecedented prosperity that the city of Paris owes him."

In September, Haussmann spent two days in Dieppe with the imperial couple, and a bond of friendship began to develop between sovereign and prefect. They breathed the sea air but mainly worked on plans for the next operations in the capital. The emperor's inauguration of the Boulevard de Strasbourg on December 16 would mark the acceleration of the general program for the transformation of Paris.

On January 26, 1854, Haussmann opened a series of balls at the Hôtel de Ville, in the sumptuous setting of the Festive Hall and its adjacent galleries. No detail of the city hall's new magnificence escaped Émile de Labédollière. In his *Nouveau Paris* (1860), a kind of bulky guide to the Parisian metamorphosis for cultured readers, he meticulously described the Festive Hall—164 feet long by 41 feet wide, with a height also of 41 feet—and the veritable history of civilization contained in Henri Lehmann's paintings of more than 180 subjects that decorated the walls and ceilings. Lehmann depicted in turn a man defending his home (by driving an uprooted tree into a tiger's face); a frightened woman clutching her child to her breast; the taming of animals and then of fire and metal; song, poetry, astronomy, tragedy, comedy, philosophy, and religion. The prefect showed that the splendors of the Second Empire were not a whit inferior to those of the old monarchy. The thousand guests at the Hôtel de Ville received with their invitation a one-word instruction that applied to gentlemen and especially to ladies: *elegance*. Flared skirts were the fashion that year; crinoline had just made its appearance; the wicker hoops keeping precious fabrics afloat were still reasonably proportioned; the waltzes were merry enough. The prefect brought whole trainloads of fresh flowers and greenery from the south, and he seemed to have installed lighting everywhere. Haussmann's party was a great social success. The Legitimist salons of Boulevard Saint-Germain could steer clear as much as they liked.

The ring of marching boots in the east did not overly disturb the peace of Parisians: the Black Sea, where Russian and Turkish ships were exchanging cannon fire, seemed so far away. The French and British governments were heading for a war they would have preferred to avoid and for which they were not in the least prepared. On March 27, 1854, France took the plunge and declared war on Russia. On April 10, Britain and France signed a treaty of alliance whereby each undertook not to seek any particular advantage for itself. What was the purpose of the war? Napoléon III found himself dreaming of Poland, Italy, the East.

There was to be a rude awakening. To make war on the Russians meant seeking them out where they were. But where was that? The allies chose the Dardanelles. First they had to occupy Piraeus to protect themselves against a Greek government which, in the name of Orthodox-Christian solidarity, had taken up the cause of Russia. The Anglo-French fleet entered the Black Sea and bombarded Odessa. But it had still not been decided where the main thrust should be made. Some thought of attacking the mouth of the Danube, but the enemy slipped away. The head of the French expeditionary corps, Saint-Arnaud, was desolate: "The Russians are robbing me by running away." The British government had the final say: the showdown would be in the Crimea. In August, cholera struck the allied troops, but they landed nevertheless close to Sebastopol.

By the time Napoleon's Feast Day came round again, on August 25, 1854, the Seine prefect had fully settled in and offered a profusion of festivities to Parisians who wanted nothing more. The emperor was away in the south of the country, where he was given a rapturous reception. But this time Haussmann wished to excel himself in his honor. At six in the morning the cannon at the Invalides roared out its announcement of the occasion. The escort vessel *Le Galilée*, anchored in the middle of the Seine, mingled its salvos with those from the Invalides. Public carriages were festooned with little tricolors and golden eagles in a frame of miniature bouquets. In the afternoon, Parisians flocked to the embankment and the terrace of the Tuileries gardens to watch the water tournaments between the Pont Royal and the Pont d'Iéna. For two hours all the theatres opened their doors to the public without charge. Mademoiselle Rachel, the most famous actress of the time, came specially from Brussels for a performance of Racine's *Andromaque* at the Théâtre Français. On the Champ de Mars, a military mime show in front of 200,000 spectators celebrated the exploits of France's Turkish allies. At five o'clock a huge balloon bearing the gilded names *Turquie, Angleterre,* and *France* rose into the air opposite the École Militaire. At the *barrière* in the Trône district, young people practiced their skills on greasy poles as acrobatic acts were interspersed with mime shows. At seven o'clock a band of 200 musicians began to play in the Tuileries gardens. In front of the Hôtel de Ville, which had been hung with velvet drapery, banners, and garlands, two military bands on either side of the main gate played without a break. There was also dancing in the drawing rooms—a lot of dancing. From the Tuileries Palace to the Place de la Concorde, then right up the Champs Élysées to L'Étoile, 124 archways of greenery marked a triumphal route shimmering in light. At nightfall the cannon roared out again from the Invalides to herald a spectacular fireworks display, in which there were pictures representing Napoleon I, War, and Peace. The people of Paris went to sleep very late. The art of stage direction no longer held any secrets for Haussmann.

A month later, on September 19, 1854, the Russians tried to block the allied advance at the little Alma River. The allied forces broke through the next day, but they were too few in number and too badly equipped to capture Sebastopol. The ensuing siege became ever more grueling as autumn set in. The Russians took advantage of the changing weather to launch a counterattack. On October 25 they were stopped by the heroic charge of the English light brigade—but not for long. On the night of November 4–5 the Russians attacked at Inkermann; the allies held their position but incurred terrible losses. The soldiers passed New Year's Eve in the trenches, where various medals were handed out. Paris was disappointed: the masses expected a blitzkrieg, not siege warfare. Prince Napoléon-Jérôme, who had conducted himself bravely in the fighting at the Alma River, was brought back to Paris and held up as a hero. But it was better not to expose him to too much danger: he was second in line to the throne in case anything should happen to the emperor.

The government did not wish to make the public uneasy by canceling celebrations for the new year. Haussmann organized a grand ball that over-shadowed the one of the previous year; there was no end of praise for the magnificence of the Hôtel de Ville ball of January 22, 1855. From nine in the evening, several lines of carriages advanced along the embankment and the rue de Rivoli to drop off the crowd of guests. The porticoes and court-yards of the palace had been decorated with exquisite taste. People stopped to look admiringly at an improvised fountain in the Louis XIV courtyard, whose water cascaded down the steps of a stone staircase and disappeared into a pool surrounded by beds of greenery. Lighting effects and skillful per-spectives added to the magic of the arrangements. The municipal council and the Seine prefect had invited six thousand lucky people to attend, but the Hôtel de Ville was large enough for them to move around with ease. There was dancing in three of the *salons*; polkas and mazurkas set couples on fire. Refreshments and solid food were laid out on buffet tables in all the rooms. There were so many that "it was exceptionally easy to get at them"—to quote one eyewitness who was certainly speaking from experience. "The program promised a brilliant evening; it was positively enchanting."

THE SUICIDE OF GÉRARD DE NERVAL

The paper lanterns at the ball had scarcely been extinguished when sad news shook literary Paris. In the early morning of January 25, 1855, the life-less body of Gérard Labrunie—better known as Gérard de Nerval—was found hanging from a bar of a cellar window on the rue de la Vieille-Lanterne. He was known to be depressive, but no one had expected him to take his own life. One of his closest friends, Alexandre Dumas, poured out his grief that same day. His testimony was also a passionate protest against the alleyways and squalid houses that still covered much of the central areas of Paris.

"If you who read these lines were perchance to plan a funeral pilgrimage to the place where the body of our poor friend Gérard de Nerval was found, you would only have to follow, as a mourning pilgrim, the strange route we shall now describe. First stop at the Place du Châtelet. Opposite one side of the column raised to Desaix, on the left of the statue of Victory that sits on top,[1] you will see a street that is called the rue *de la Tuerie*.[2] This street is it-self intersected diagonally by two other streets: the rue de la Vieille-Tannerie on the left, rue Saint-Jérôme on the right. Then the street becomes narrower. You can read in large letters on a wall opposite: 'Bains de Gèvres.' And beneath that: 'Boudet, locksmith's business.' At the foot of the wall bearing these two inscriptions, a staircase begins with an iron handrail. A narrow, sticky, sinister staircase. On one side, to the right, the steps touch the wall. On the other side, a meter-wide extension of the street leads to a locksmith's shop that has a large key painted in yellow as its sign. In front of the door a crow hops around and now and then gives out a high-pitched whistle. The staircase and the blacksmith's shop are already part of a different street: the rue de *la Vieille-Lanterne*.[3] Do you remark the strange coincidence of these two names: rue de *La Tuerie*, rue de *la Vieille-Lanterne*?

"You go down this street, in fact just a deep alleyway that seems to sink beneath the Place du Châtelet by the staircase we have described. You are afraid to put a foot on the slippery steps, or a hand on the rusted rail. Opposite you at head's height, the extension that leads to the blacksmith's arches over. In the darkness at the end of this arch you discover a window of the same shape, with iron bars similar to those on prison windows. Go down five steps, stop on the last one, lift your arm to the iron bar. You are there: this is the bar to which the string was tied. A piece of white string, like that which is used to make the cord on a bonnet. Opposite is an open drain with some iron grating over it.

"It is a sinister place, as I said. Facing you, the rue de la Vieille-Lanterne runs up toward rue Saint-Martin. On the right a boardinghouse—which you have to see to form any idea of it—has a lantern with these words: *We offer overnight lodging. Coffee with water*. Opposite this boardinghouse are some stables, which remained open during the long icy nights through which we have just passed, as shelter for individuals too poor even to seek accommodation across the way. You have stopped on the last step, haven't you? Well, it was there that his still warm body was found at 7:03 A.M. on Friday morning, his feet barely two inches from the step, his hat still on his head. The death agony had been gentle, for the hat had not fallen to the ground."[4]

A public benefit decree of June 29, 1854, had ordered the demolition of the area separating the Place de Grève (Place de l'Hôtel de Ville) from the Place du Châtelet—an area that contained the rue de la Tannerie, rue des Teinturiers, rue de la Vieille-Tannerie, rue de la Vieille-Place-aux-Veaux, rue Saint-Jérôme, rue de la Vieille-Lanterne, rue de la Tuerie, and rue de la Joaillerie. At the rue de la Tannerie, on December 5, 1854, a five-story house had collapsed and killed a number of people. At the rue des Teinturiers, the street was so narrow that "the worm-eaten façade of one of the houses in panels of roughly plastered wood tried in vain to fall down; all it could manage was to rest against the façade of the house opposite."[5] The demolition began

on the first days of fine weather in 1855. By August the straight strip of avenue that would take the name of Victoria was unrolling amid a field of
ruins. The rue de la Vieille-Lanterne made way for the Théâtre de la Ville;
the bar from which Gérard de Nerval hanged himself had been directly
above the prompter's box.

THE WORLD'S FAIR OF 1855

≈ On March 2, 1855, barely two months after Nerval, Nicholas I of Russia died. For a while it was hoped that some accommodation could be
reached with his successor, Alexander II, but the new tsar continued his father's policy, and it would be the end of the year before the hostilities in the
Crimea came to an end.

In April, Napoléon III and the empress paid an official visit to London.
The couple stayed at Windsor and visited the Crystal Palace, and Napoléon
III was awarded the Order of the Garter at a reception at the Guildhall. He
made his reply in English. Victoria fell under his charm. He also spoke of the
Crimea with the British government. Napoléon III dreamed of going himself to Sebastopol and taking command of the allied army. The British, not
trusting his military genius, tried to dissuade him.

For France, in any event, 1855 was mainly the year of the first Exposition Universelle in Paris. The Seine prefect did not have direct responsibility
for the organization of the world's fair, but his various departments—especially the highways department—helped make a success of it, and much to
his satisfaction the Hôtel de Ville was one of the places that everyone had to
see.

Napoleon I had staged two exhibitions of French industry in the capital,
in 1801 and 1802, and others had followed in 1819, 1823, and 1827. These
fairs took place on the Champ de Mars, in the galleries of the Louvre, and at
the Invalides. Their growing success led Louis-Philippe to decide that there
should be one every five years, and that special provision should be made to
accommodate them. Temporary structures were therefore raised: in 1834 on
the Place de la Concorde, and thereafter, in 1839, 1844, and 1849, at the
Carré Marigny.

These fairs were limited to French production. But in 1833 the natural-
ist Boucher de Perthes had already floated the idea of one that would be open
to the whole world. "Why are these fairs restricted to our country? Why not
open them up on a truly grand and liberal scale? How beautiful and magnificent a world's fair would be!" This idea was taken up in many quarters and

also found an echo in Britain. In fact, the first world's fair of all time was held in London in 1851. It revealed the hidden potential of metal as a construction material, in Paxton's spectacular design for the ethereal Crystal Palace. Louis-Napoléon was fascinated by the sight of it, and a decree of March 27, 1852, authorized the planning of a huge structure to accommodate future industrial exhibitions in France, of which the next under the schedule fixed by Louis-Philippe was due to take place in 1854. Taking its inspiration from the Crystal Palace, this building would become the Palais de l'Industrie on the Carré Marigny, on the Champs Élysées. But meanwhile the prince president became emperor and began to revise the plans; a decree of March 8, 1853, canceled the national exhibition due in 1854 and ordered the opening in May 1855 of a "world's fair of agricultural and industrial products" in Paris. On June 22, 1853, another decree commissioned a world exhibition of fine arts to take place alongside it, and on December 24 the final piece fell into place when Prince Napoléon-Jérôme was appointed to head a committee for the organization and supervision of the exhibitions.

In the end the Palais de l'Industrie, designed by the architect Viel, had only distant affinities with the London palace: it was a two-story rectangular building, monumental without being heavy in appearance. While it was under construction, so many requests to exhibit came in that it was decided to add a long, four-thousand-foot gallery on the Cours la Reine, parallel to the Seine, for the display of industrial machinery. Bulky objects and models would be shown in another area, and carriages and agricultural machinery in an open shed. Yet another annex, at the end of Avenue Montaigne, was reserved for the fine arts exhibition. Gardens and fountains were dotted around the somewhat disorderly site on which thousands of workers were kept busy.

On April 16, Haussmann left on a trip to London. He had a dual mission: to make contact with the London local authority, and to prepare Queen Victoria's visit to Paris. During his time there he saw as much as he could of sewers, parks, and municipal services, and asked for information about the city's organization and its use of concessions. He was delighted by the lord mayor's toast at the end of a banquet: "Recent visitors to the capital of France have admired the improvements made there under the direction of the emperor and through the good offices of the Seine prefect."

From April 25 the Crimea was linked to the West through a cable under the Black Sea. The general public, awaiting the opening of the Exposition Universelle, showed no real concern that the siege of Sebastopol was taking such a long time. But the emperor was quite worried, especially since the failed offensive of April 8, 9, and 10 against the Russians' advanced position at the fort of Malakov. He used and misused the telegraph, flooding army commanders with sometimes contradictory messages that they had to struggle to interpret. The emperor would so much have liked to notch a victory while thousands of workers were busy putting the finishing touches to the World's Fair. But the victories did not come. And, worse for the regime, an Italian called Pianori originating from the Papal States fired two pistol shots at Napoléon III on the Champs Élysées. The emperor stayed extremely calm and continued his walk as if nothing had happened. The would-be assassin was arrested, tried on May 1, found guilty, and sentenced to death. The incident reminded people of the fragility of the imperial regime. Napoléon III no longer talked of going to the Crimea. Pianori was executed at dawn on May 15, 1855.

On the same day the great "Expo" opened amid bare plaster surfaces— for the internal decoration work had not yet been completed. The Palais de l'Industrie played host to the wonders of mining and metalworking, agriculture and fisheries, chemicals, paper and rubber, electricity and photography. Heavy machinery embodying the genius of nineteenth-century man was lined up in the gallery of the Cours la Reine.

The highest branches of the state apparatus and of the Paris justice and administration were represented at the opening ceremony in the Palais de l'Industrie. The wives, all dressed up, took their place on benches in the nave, to the left and right of the throne that had been installed there a few hours before. Everything was in place at one o'clock, when the imperial couple left the Tuileries Palace to the sound of cannon fire from the Invalides. Prince Napoléon-Jérôme greeted the emperor on the threshold. The sovereigns walked toward the throne. The prince read a long speech that outlined the work done by his organizing committee. The procession then moved off to visit the stands, many of which were still empty or in the course of installation. The orchestra played the march from Rossini's *William Tell* as the officials made their way to the exit. The exhibition would really be up and running only in late June.

The capital had been filled with visitors since the early days of 1855, and hotels were putting up "Full" notices long before the date of the official opening. Many visitors were forced to sleep in the open air. For six months the price of furnished rooms and à la carte meals skyrocketed. The sound of fun and festivities was deafening.

On June 6 and 7 another surprise attack on Malakov ended in failure, and on June 17–18 yet another. Questions were starting to be asked. The actor Grassot exclaimed on the terrace of a Parisian café where the waiter was keeping people waiting: "It's like Sebastopol here; they don't manage to get anything!" He was reported to the police, arrested, and imprisoned. Napoléon III criticized his generals: "The war they have been waging in Algeria does not make them fit for large-scale military operations." Alexander II ordered his troops to counterattack, as the siege was costing him a thousand men a day. On August 16 the Russians were repulsed at Traktir Bridge. The Sardinians who took part in the action alongside the French and British had 28 dead and 160 wounded. Cavour would know how to remind Napoléon III of this when the time came.

Queen Victoria and Prince Albert arrived in Paris two days later, returning the visit that Napoléon III had made to London. Paris put on a festive show to welcome the queen. As the newly renovated Gare du Nord looked onto a maze of blocks undergoing demolition, the Northern railway line had been hastily joined to the Eastern line. The Gare de l'Est, with the new Boulevard de Strasbourg stretching up to the Boulevard Saint Denis, offered a worthier setting for the royal entourage. Many buildings close to it were still under construction, but false façades of wood and painted cardboard had been put up to fill the gaps. Thousands of curious onlookers (800,000, it was said) lined the entire route to the Palais de Saint Cloud, and banners displaying the word "Welcome" were spread over each house and over hundreds of modest or majestic *arcs de triomphe*. The sovereigns went to look around the World's Fair, where the products of British industry had taken the lion's share. Victoria also insisted on bowing at the Invalides before the tomb of Napoleon I while chapel organs played "God Save the Queen." She was enchanted by the beauty and gaiety of Paris and greatly appreciated the emperor's company; she spent twelve to fourteen hours with him each day, very often in private.

On August 23, Haussmann organized a reception of unparalleled splendor at the Hôtel de Ville in honor of the British sovereigns. The rue de Rivoli and part of the embankment were illuminated and decorated with flags. The Place de l'Hôtel de Ville was surrounded with flags flying on Venetian poles and large pyramids made of colored glass. An elegant marquee had been installed in front of the main entrance, and the grand staircase in the Cour Louis XIV was being used for the first time. From each of the courtyard windows hung gold-lined crimson-velvet drapery bearing the intertwined monograms of Victoria and Albert, Napoléon and Eugénie. A platform covered in red velvet and topped with a crown awaited them in the Festive Hall. At 10 P.M. the emperor opened the ball with Queen Victoria,

Prince Albert with Princess Mathilde, and Madame Haussmann with Prince Adalbert of Bavaria. Eight thousand invitations had been issued. On every floor, buffet tables stood in the rooms not set aside for dancing. Haussmann had taken care of the slightest detail: even the ventilation was beyond reproach, despite the large number of people. The sovereigns retired at 11:30, but the festivities continued until morning.

At Haussmann's request, the queen agreed that her name should be given to the fine avenue that had just been opened from the Place de l'Hôtel de Ville to the Place du Châtelet. Victoria and Albert left for London on August 27, but not before the queen, as a token of her appreciation, had recommended the Seine prefect to the good offices of Napoléon III. The next year, this would earn Georges-Eugène elevation to the dignity of Grand Officer of the Légion d'Honneur.

On September 5 a new allied offensive opened against Malakov, and on September 8, MacMahon's Zouaves succeeded in capturing the fort. The Russians evacuated Sebastopol, which was occupied by allied troops during the day of the 10th. The siege had lasted 322 days. Alexander felt disposed to begin negotiations: the magnificent resistance had saved the honor of the Russian forces. Through the intermediary of Austria, he accepted that a peace congress should be held in Paris in late February 1856.

The Exposition Universelle thus ended on a happy note, although the day when French troops entered Sebastopol also saw another attempt on Napoléon III's life, this time by a lunatic named Delmarre who fired two shots wide. On September 13 a fervent Te Deum in thanksgiving for the capture of Sebastopol brought the usual ceremonial crowd to Notre Dame; the Boulevard du Centre, still under construction, became the Boulevard de Sébastopol, and a street took the name rue de Crimée. On October 18 exhibitors at the fair offered a superb party for Prince Napoléon-Jérôme and the imperial organizing committee. At the closing ceremony on November 15, speeches by Prince Napoléon-Jérôme and the emperor were followed by thousands of medal presentations and special mentions.

The 5 million recorded visitors were able to see for themselves the *grands travaux* in the capital—whether they left with feelings of amazement or of outrage. Foreign newspapers induced them to return there soon to witness the incredible earthquakes being unleashed by the authorities, and each visit was an occasion for more and more fun. Haussmann was already winning one part of his wager: the *grands travaux* were getting themselves talked about, and some of the large sum spent by tourists was flowing into the city's coffers and enabling it to repay the debt. At the Seine prefecture, there was considerable excitement at this first striking confirmation of the theory of productive expenditure.

On November 22 the king of Sardinia, Victor Emmanuel II, arrived with his chief minister Cavour in Paris, mainly to discuss with Napoléon III the future of the Italian peninsula and their goal of unity against Austria and the temporal sovereignty of the pope. Haussmann had first come across Victor Emmanuel in Antibes, when he had been prefect for the Var and the kingdom of Piedmont-Sardinia had been passing through tragic moments. This made all the more sumptuous the reception that the Seine prefect offered on November 24 at the Hôtel de Ville.

The year 1855 ended on a note of triumph. On December 29 a section of the troops returning from the Crimea entered Paris. Napoléon III welcomed them at the Bastille, then went to Place Vendôme (specially decorated by Baltard) to receive the standards before thousands of guests. The *fête* that set Paris ablaze that evening and well into the night seemed to seal the unity between the emperor and his people.

The Peace Congress opened in Paris on February 25, 1856. It endowed Napoléon III with his greatest prestige as the arbiter of Europe. The emperor did his utmost to spare the Russians, so much so that he aroused the suspicions of the British. On March 30 the Treaty of Paris was signed with a feather plucked from an eagle in the Jardin des Plantes: Turkey's territorial integrity was maintained, but the sultan's regime was forced to recognize the de facto independence of the provinces that would later become Serbia and Romania; the Black Sea was neutralized and the Danube declared an international waterway. France confirmed its position as the main protector of Christians in the East. Napoléon III asked Prussia (which had not taken part in the conflict) to sign the treaty along with the parties directly involved. In the days that followed, he also secured the adoption of several measures concerning international trade. On April 8, protests from Austria notwithstanding, mention was made of the position of Italy.

One happy event that occurred during the work of the Congress was the birth of a son to Empress Eugénie on March 16. In order that everyone might share in the widespread rejoicing, Napoléon III purchased 21,500 square yards of land on Boulevard Mazas (today's Boulevard Diderot) for the construction of inexpensive working-class housing. The baptism of the imperial prince on June 14 was the occasion for the municipal council and the Seine prefect to offer a banquet in honor of the emperor and empress in the Festive Hall at the Hôtel de Ville. Several charitable foundations bearing the name of the young prince were established. The country seemed content.

But the festivities of some could not efface the hardships of the many. Wages were increasing, but so was the cost of living in Paris. On October 7, Napoléon III received in Saint Cloud a delegation of Parisian workers who had come to complain about high rents; he asked the Seine prefect to look into possible solutions. On November 7 he sent 100,000 francs to the chief of police, Pietri, so that he could organize a number of soup kitchens. Over a period of 29 days, these kitchens distributed 1,244,756 meals at a very low price. On December 28, at the end of the faubourg Saint-Antoine near the Place du Trône, the Fondation Eugénie-Napoléon was set up with the 600,000 francs that the city of Paris had voted through to buy a necklace as a wedding-gift for the empress, but that she had preferred to spend on the occupational training of girls from poor backgrounds.

THE APOGEE OF THE SECOND EMPIRE

❧ The *arcs de triomphe* and fireworks displays organized by the Seine prefect marked the apogee of the Second Empire. Napoléon III was intoxicated with his popularity. Indeed, Pietri complained that he was obsessed with shaking people's hands—although the chief of police, true to his profession, added that he made sure the emperor never shook the hands of anyone other than a plainclothes policeman. Napoléon III remained at bottom a "forty-eighter," anxious to do good and to change the world. He knew Italian, English, and German—quite a lot for a time when there was little familiarity with foreign languages. He took little interest in either the arts or literature, and his empress, though lively and devoted, was not exactly intelligent. His respected uncle Jérôme, the onetime king of Westphalia, occupied a prominent place beside the emperor. So did Jérôme's two children: Prince Napoléon-Jérôme, an anti-clerical republican at heart, and the highly cultured Princess Mathilde, whose *salon* was one of the centers of literary and artistic life in the capital.

Napoléon III and Eugénie imposed strict etiquette on the imperial court. On January 1, 1854, four hundred ladies in dress and train paraded before the sovereigns to offer their respects and best wishes for the new year. The Austrian ambassador Hübner, a man usually given to sarcasm, was rather taken aback: "Very few of them had aristocratic names, yet they came out of it quite well."

On an ordinary day the empress received people between four and six in the afternoon. In the evening there was generally a ball, concert, or show. At first there was dancing to music from a barrel organ turned by an army general, but Napoléon III was afraid that professional musicians would hawk around venomous comments on what they had seen. Once the regime felt surer of itself, it grew bolder and held a ball every Thursday for eight hundred guests. For those who might be worried about the cost, it was said in advance that "the expense of a grand ball later falls as golden rain on every industry."[6] Masked balls, in particular, were all the rage. There were also enthusiastic sessions of table-turning and hypnosis. At one open-air reception in 1857, guests even played at the capture of Malakov: the empress and her ladies defended the tower while the emperor and his courtiers attacked. In monarchist circles it was said that the emperor advanced on all fours and that he even grabbed the ladies by the feet. Napoléon III was also fond of charades and blindman's buff. This was all grist to the Legitimist mill, which was soon producing denunciations of court "orgies." In 1856 receptions began to be held at Compiègne, where guests were invited in groups for eight days at a time.

The emperor's amusements were in keeping with those of the Parisian bourgeoisie. That whole world adored classical opera, particularly works by Rossini, Meyerbeer, Donizetti, and Verdi; the corps de ballet interested the gentlemen as much as bel canto and the divas. Who did not have his little darling or star dancer to protect? Haussmann himself did, as we shall see. The Comédie Française shone brightest in the firmament, but many preferred the vaudeville or social satire of boulevard theatre. A new genre of *opéra bouffe*, tending toward and not always clearly distinguishable from operetta, enjoyed a meteoric success and would come to symbolize for future generations the Second Empire and its "imperial festivities." The name of Jacques Offenbach attracted considerable attention in the world.

Jacques was the seventh of ten children of Isaac Offenbach, a cantor at the Cologne synagogue, and grew up surrounded by music. By the age of thirteen he was a virtuoso cellist and had begun to compose music of his own. Drawn to Paris, he did not find it easy to make a living and more than once returned to Cologne under the pressure of hunger. On July 30, 1850, fate smiled on him when Arsène Houssaye, the new director of the Comédie Française, took him on as its conductor. But it soon became clear that Offenbach's place was not there. Houssaye held him in high regard and said he was performing wonders; the pope of French music, Adolphe Adam, described one of his entr'actes as "a little masterpiece of color, originality, grace, and delicacy."[7] The members of the Comédie Française, however, did not appreciate him. In 1854, Offenbach bitterly considered emigrating to America, then changed his mind and decided to become his own boss. The

World's Fair of 1855 gave him the opportunity. Opposite the Palais de l'In-dustrie, on the Carré Marigny, was an unoccupied wooden theatre that had once served the conjurer Lacaze before he fell on hard times. Offenbach asked to take it over.

On June 4 he received the necessary permission from the chief of po-lice—on condition that the hall not be used to perform opera or *opéra bouffe* (on which the Opéra and the Opéra Comique had a monopoly). In fact, the license authorized only mime shows, five-character harlequinades, musical stagings with parts for two or three characters, mystery shows, Chinese shadow puppets, conjuring tricks, step-dancing with a maximum of five dancers, and comic songs with one or two costumed or noncostumed performers. Offenbach replaced the name Salle Lacaze with the Bouffes Parisiens. The opening night was July 5, 1855. Offenbach went to some trouble to prepare the Parisian public for the event, with unstinting help as always from Villemessant's newly founded *Le Figaro*. He recruited a highly talented young writer, Ludovic Halévy, a bored ministry employee who was trying his hand at writing for the theatre. The high point of the evening was a farce in song, *Les Deux Aveugles*, the first operetta ever performed in Paris. There was a great crush to get into the hall. A quarrel between two blind impostors to find the best spot for begging was at once funny and cruelly philosophical. The play was still running in 1856 at the time of the Con-gress of Paris, when Napoléon III asked for a special performance to be held at the Tuileries Palace for international delegates.

The success enabled Offenbach to resign from the Comédie Française. Once the World's Fair was over, he moved the Bouffes Parisiens to a hall in the Passage Choiseul that was both larger and easier to heat. For the inaugu-ration on December 29, 1855, Offenbach wrote *Ba-ta-clan*, a disguised po-litical satire helped along by the wildest fantasy. Halévy signed the libretto. Then in 1856, after various ruses to ease the crushing burden of debt and to keep the bailiffs at bay, Offenbach demonstrated his flair for publicity by launching an operetta competition. He the Rhinelander, who spoke French with a strong German accent (so that he was eventually suspected of deliber-ately overdoing his Teutonic manners), gave himself the mission of defend-ing the inexhaustible sparkle of the old *gaîté parisienne*! In 1857, Georges Bizet and Charles Lecocq were declared joint winners of the competition, having composed works on the same subject. The Bouffes Parisiens pre-sented Lecocq's *Docteur Miracle* on April 8 and Bizet's on April 9.

Offenbach himself went on composing without a break. He mocked Vic-tor Hugo and the Romantics, poked fun at the Bourse, at dupes and

swindlers alike, at the whole society of appearances. Paris was wildly enthusiastic about his *Tromb Al-Ca-Zar*, with its aria about Bayonne ham, its
pseudo-lyrical quartet, its Gigolette bolero; the emperor wanted it performed immediately at the Tuileries Palace. The range of shows permitted to
the Bouffes grew steadily larger. In 1858, Offenbach gained the right to use
a chorus and to have as many characters as he wished. At once he delivered
Mesdames de la Halle, a great musical work on the basis on a libretto that par-
odied the melodrama so much in vogue at the time. Then came another operetta, *La Chatte métamorphosée en femme* [The Cat Transformed into a
Woman]. And on October 21, 1858, *Orpheus in the Underworld* won instant
recognition at its first performance, with music by Offenbach and a libretto
by Ludovic Halévy (who did not sign it because of a flattering promotion at
his ministry) and Hector Crémieux. Everyone recognized Napoléon III in
the womanizing Jupiter, Empress Eugénie in the jealous wife, and the republican opposition in the revolt of the other gods who, with the *Marseillaise*
playing in the background, preferred the liberty of the Underworld to the
dictatorial azure of Olympus. The allusions were veiled, never aggressive,
and there was laughter at the imperial court. But Offenbach would remain
just a comic actor, to be invited to the Tuileries to entertain the prince's
guests; he never attended one of the "group parties" at Compiègne, where so
many intellectual and artistic worthies, or semi-worthies, of the time put in
an appearance. It is yet another paradox of his destiny that he has come to
embody a Second Empire that never recognized him as one of its own, just as
the galop in *Orpheus in the Underworld* remains the most famous "French cancan" of all time, although he composed it twenty years before the invention
of the cancan and no one who listens to it today has any idea that he was its
author.

ECONOMIC CHANGE

❧ In the realm of economics, Napoléon III at first continued Guizot's policies and made little attempt to innovate. Many of his political staff had done
their studies in the time of Louis-Philippe, and several ministers of the empire—men such as Fould, Magne, or Billaut—had formerly served in the
Guizot government: Morny was the great wheeler-dealer of the regime: it
was enough to say with a knowing look, "Morny has a hand in it" for capital
to come pouring in. The telegraph made it possible to speculate in the
provinces as well as in Paris. The theatre too was caught up in the speculative fever: Ponsard in *L'Honneur et l'Argent* (1853) and *La Bourse* (1856),

Émile Augier with *Le Gendre de Monsieur Poirier* (1854). In Augier's *La Cein-ture dorée* [The Golden Belt] of 1855, the play's hero Roussel has made a fast 3 million and is upset that no one wants to marry his daughter. In 1857, Alexandre Dumas, Jr., set his *La Question de l'Argent* against a background of stock-market shocks. So long as the emperor's own person was not touched, Napoléon III did not take umbrage and generally laughed in a good-natured manner at these vitriolic satires.

The emperor was supported by the Saint-Simonians, the leading force in economic thought and the spearhead of bold entrepreneurship. The "father" of the sect, Prosper Enfantin, dedicated his works to Napoléon III and felt no twinge of conscience in justifying the loss of political freedoms. "The plat-form and the press must remain quiet for a while, so that the hammer alone can echo where powder used to speak, so that man can write his iron hiero-glyphs on the land and not political rebuses on sheets of paper." A number of prominent Saint-Simonians were on close terms with the emperor: the Pereire brothers, both financiers of great talent; Michel Chevalier, the econo-mist and apostle of free trade; Guéroult, the journalist who had already been a personal friend of Prince Napoléon. The Second Empire did not limit itself to a repetition of Guizot; it also witnessed a profound change in the eco-nomic and financial structures of France.

The rapid spread of the railways played a major role in the moderniza-tion of the country. At the beginning of the Second Republic, the Valenci-ennes, Boulogne, Nevers, Chalon-sur-Saône, and Nancy lines had been completed; France had a total of 2,237 miles of railroad. Some 20 companies shared the network, each with its separate fares, and travelers were forced to make numerous transfers in the course of a journey. Many of the companies groaned under the weight of excessive charges for the use of track, and after the initial craze the value of their stock plummeted on the Bourse. An at-tempt was made to improve their financial health by extending their conces-sions to 99 years, and the state promised to underwrite a minimum of 4 percent in interest for half that period. In return, the railway companies were unofficially but firmly requested to consolidate into a smaller number of groups—a process that led to the formation of the Compagnie du Midi (for southern France) in 1853, the Compagnie de l'Est in 1854 and de l'Ouest in 1855, and the PLM (Paris-Lyons-Mediterranean) in 1858, through the merger of the Paris-Lyons and the Paris-Mediterranean. By the end of 1858 there were almost 10,000 miles of railroad. Between 1854 and 1857, Paris had been linked to Marseilles, Nantes, Bordeaux, Limoges, Clermont-Ferrand, Grenoble, Basle, Mulhouse, and Metz. Eight days after Louis-

Napoléon's coup d'état, a decree called for the creation of a right-bank circle line inside the city fortifications to link all the rail networks whose routes ended in Paris; a left-bank circle line would follow a bit later.

The banking system also underwent modernization. Until the Second Empire, it consisted mainly of small banking houses that advanced loans to businesses in return for binding guarantees, such as the deposit of merchandise or the assignment of letters of credit or government bonds. A few major companies, often headed by Jews or Protestants, made up the whole of a (very cautious) sector of "top business banking" that dealt in public loans and in finance for industry and the railways. Credit played a crucial role in the phase of development that marked the France of Napoléon III. Prosper Enfantin, in his *Économie politique et politique*, made this point very clear: "In a society where some possess instruments of industry without having the capacity or the will to put them to work, and where others who are industrious do not possess instruments of labor, the purpose of credit [must be] to ensure that these instruments pass as smoothly as possible from the hands of those who possess them to the hands of those who know how to activate them." The banker was an intermediary between the supply and demand of capital. The purpose of credit was to increase production and thereby to further the progress of society. Enfantin advocated the specialization of banking by trades in order to make this process as efficient as possible. Louis-Napoléon shared his analyses.

When the prince president was first elected, on December 10, 1848, the chief banking sector was still deeply Orleanist in both economics and politics and refused to accompany him down the road charted by the Saint-Simonians. This explains why Louis-Napoléon III and Persigny jumped so expectantly at the Pereire Brothers' idea of launching Crédit Mobilier.

Founded in 1852, Crédit Mobilier was an ambitious institution designed to provide loans for industry, trade, and major works of public benefit. Persigny later confided: "I wanted an instrument that would free the new regime of the domination that financiers usually exercise over governments, especially as I could already sense the hostility that major financial interests would have toward the regime. Had it not been for the support of Crédit Mobilier, which dragged the financiers along and forced them to keep moving forward, the emperor would have had to make allowances for the top banking sector and his policies would not have been as bold and free from restrictions as they were." The political risks involved in the attitude of the banking world were demonstrated on November 8, 1852, less than a fortnight before the referendum on the restoration of the empire, when the

stockbrokers' federation decided to require forward buyers and sellers to provide cover of 150 francs a share as of December 1—a measure that encouraged a fall in stock values. To pursue the policy of productive expenditure,
however, Persigny, Napoléon III, and Haussmann needed to speed the circulation of money, not slow it.

The idea for the Crédit Mobilier came from the inventive Mirès, a man
whose mind was as much that of a journalist as of a businessman. In 1851 he
announced that he intended to set up a joint stock fund, the *Caisse des actions
réunies*, with a capital of 5 million francs—of which he himself did not have a
cent. Benoît Fould, head of the Banque Fould, agreed to discuss the project
and thought he could give it a major impetus, so long as he was able to rely
upon a team of capable people. Then he thought of Isaac and Émile Pereire,
and the legal instruments were drawn up on September 9, 1852. The new
institution, initially called the *Banque des grands travaux*, would have a capital of 60 million francs; its activity would be discounting and loans for new
or developing businesses in industry, trade, and public works, both through
the purchase of their shares (provision of equity capital) and through the extension of overdraft facilities or other forms of credit. The new bank would
issue bonds to equip itself with the necessary funds. When the finance minister, Bineau, objected to the use of the word "bank" in its title, the founders
changed its name to *Société générale de Crédit mobilier*.

Some ministers wished to strengthen the supervisory functions of the finance ministry, but without calling into question the tutelage exercised by
the ministry of the interior. But the interior minister himself, Persigny, took
a more liberal position. He wrote in a note dated October 30, 1852: "The
planned company may perform real services if, as there is every reason to
hope, the management is in the hands of cautious, skillful, and quick-witted
people; it may help to bring closer the moment when our railway network is
complete, when the metallurgical wealth of our land is under exploitation,
when we reap the rewards of the *grands travaux*, some conducted with public
funding and assistance, others through individual efforts alone, which
should rejuvenate our cities." Magne, the minister of public works, nevertheless asked for further guarantees, and on November 7, Benoît Fould and
the Pereire Brothers accepted reality and agreed to his demands. The redemption date of Crédit Mobilier bonds had to be at least forty-five days
from the date of issue (to avoid creating excess liquidity); the total sums received from overdrafts and bonds issued for less than a year had to be not
more than double the amount of actual capital; and the total sum of bonds of
every length had to depend on the size of the capital and in any event could

not exceed 1.2 billion francs. The decree of authorization was signed on November 15, 1852, by Louis-Napoléon, then in his last few days as prince president (before the restoration of the empire was approved by referendum on November 20–21 and officially proclaimed on December 2). He did not even bother to consult the Bank of France.

Rothschild versus Pereire. On the same November 15, the spokesman of the *haute banque* sector, James de Rothschild, sent the prince president a long critique of modern financial capitalism and argued that it was dangerous to give Crédit Mobilier the possibility of issuing bonds in such large volume. Despite the various precautions, he wrote, those behind the project "will have thrown into circulation, with the government's support and permission, a considerable quantity of credit values that are based only upon variable and uncertain guarantees." Moreover, "the government would be organizing a frightful domination of trade and industry for the profit of a nameless entity devoid of personal responsibility. . . . As their whims and interests dictate, the unaccountable directors of this bank will be masters of every enterprise. They will be able to favor one business over another and exaggerate its value, raise this one up and hurl that one down, impose their own conditions on one and all. By the total value of their bonds, they will lay down the law in the market—a law without supervision and without competition. . . . With the new means at its disposal, the bank will penetrate all the managements of railways, mines, and canals, change the composition of those managements to suit its own whim, and run the companies through its own agents or persons of its choosing. It will thus gather in its hands or under its control the largest share of the public wealth. That would be more than a danger; it would be a calamity. It would be the end of all competition, the annihilation of all individual strength. The result would be disastrous for trade and industry. It would make the country's prosperity depend upon the will, adroitness, inexperience, or interests of a small number of men who would be only indirectly bound by their actions and would not bear personal responsibility for their faults and mistakes."[8] This long memorandum left the prince president unmoved. Relations between Napoléon III and James de Rothschild would remain icy for years to come.

While the Pereire Brothers redoubled their efforts, Rothschild went into a sulk that kept him out of the funding for new railway lines and major urban operations. Already in March 1849 the chief banking sector had caused the breakdown of the first tender for a 25-million-franc loan to the city of Paris. The second tender had succeeded thanks to the Maison Bechet-Dethomas (with Mirès behind it)—Crédit Mobilier did not yet exist. But when Haussmann, in the autumn of 1853, tried to find a purchaser for the land on the rue de Rivoli, the big banks were not interested. The prefect got himself out of difficulties with the help of the Pereires.

While the *haute banque* continued to predict their imminent collapse, the men at Crédit Mobilier were busy bringing in the capital. The first annual shareholders' meeting on April 29, 1854, heard Isaac Pereire set out his proposed strategy to gain hegemony: "The idea for Crédit Mobilier came out of the lack of credit instruments for the country's leading areas of business, the state of isolation to which the forces of finance had been reduced, and the lack of a center powerful enough to link them to another. . . . Crédit Mobilier might establish among the debts of all the major railway companies a bond uniformity that gives rise to close attachments, a centralization whose beneficial effects cannot be underestimated." The Pereire Brothers realized that it was necessary to divide up the risks, but they also saw that monopoly had something to be said for it. In his report to shareholders for 1855, Isaac Pereire returned to the charge: "In general, when we intervene in a branch of industry, our main wish is to secure its development not through competition but through association and fusion, not through opposition and mutual destruction of the forces in play but through their most economical use. . . . The principle of association and fusion mainly applies to industries in which the usefulness of individual efforts fades in comparison with the employment of means of action that can be obtained only with the help of large amounts of capital." This was true of heavy industry, the transport industry (not only the railways but also sea transport, which was being revolutionized by the construction of metal ships and the development of steam propulsion), and of course the real estate business and the road-building programs in Paris, Marseilles, or even the southwest fishing port of Arcachon. The Pereires snapped up land in the plain of Monceau as well as in the Opéra district of Paris, providing a model for Zola's character Saccart in the novel *La Curée* [The Scramble for Spoils]. The bond that developed between them and the leading figures of the Second Empire was more than one of mutual sympathy; it was a kind of complicity, and Haussmann was too attached to the success of the *grands travaux* not to feel its force.

Between 1854 and 1857, huge programs of public works were launched in France as in many other parts of Europe. The Pereires thought that, with the railway-driven unification of the national market, the size of firms would become a major problem and that only large ones would be able to meet the conditions for growth. To begin with, Crédit Mobilier tried to bring about the merger of all the railway companies; indeed, the Pereires themselves had important positions in the rail networks of the east, west, and south. The government pushed all the harder for these mergers and regroupments because new concessions were generating a need for major sums of capital. The *grands travaux* in Paris led Haussmann to make an appeal to the capital market in 1855. The Pereires ensured its success, but the cost of money was rising. Just then, in February 1856, Crédit Mobilier announced that it would have to raise a billion francs on the Bourse—a sum equal to everything hitherto invested—in order to follow through on the concessionary awards. This time, however, the government took fright.

The Rothschilds chose this moment to mount a counterattack by organizing a syndicate under the name of Réunion Financière and waging all-out war on Crédit Mobilier. Apart from the Maison Rothschild itself, the other members of the syndicate were the Protestant banks of Blount, Paccard-Dufour (later to become Mirabaud), F. Durand, F. Vernes, A. Marcuard (later Neuflize), as well as the Maison A. Dassier, the Swiss Hentsch-Lütscher, and the Belgian Cahen d'Anvers, and two directors of railway companies, Talabot from the Paris-Lyons-Mediterranean, and Bartholony from the Paris-Orléans, a great friend of Morny and a former opponent of the Rothschilds who was now lined up behind the holy union against the Pereires. The efforts of Réunion Financière soon bore fruit. An official government note of March 1856 forbade Crédit Mobilier to issue any more bonds. The Pereires no longer found favor among circles close to the emperor. In a memorandum of March 13, 1856, the emperor's secretary Mocquard wrote: "In the end, although this institution has been helpful in some ways, I think it has excessively developed in France the mentality of speculating on option bargains and the passion for gambling beyond all measure." Morny delivered the fatal blow. Having had railway interests of his own in the Massif Central, he had helped the Pereires in 1854 and 1855 to create (with British capital) the Grand Central company. Now, in a striking about-face, he refused to associate Grand Central with Crédit Mobilier and signed an agreement with Réunion Financière instead; a Crédit Mobilier director, the duc de Galliera, followed suit and went over to the enemy. In response, the Pereires wrote to the emperor on July 21, 1856, protesting against the spokes that had been placed in their wheels and the slanders that were being spread about them (for example, that two ministers close to Napoléon III were in their pockets).

Birth of the CIC. The Rothschilds and the *haute banque* had finally understood that they were missing the boat, that their excessive reserve was leaving the Pereires huge scope to take the initiative. Now that some balance had been restored, they got down to the job of assembling a rival project. On

December 4, 1856, a plan for the banking sector was presented to the government, but a recommendation issued by the Council of State on December 20 was not favorable to it. Some of its proponents then went straight to Napoléon III. Among them were the Englishman Gladstone and the French bankers Donon, Bartholony, and Delahante (the last of these being very close to Morny). On February 27, 1857, Donon created, subject to government permission, the *Société internationale de crédit commercial*, with a capital of 120 million francs; its lead bank was Arlès-Dufour of Lyons, linked to the Saint-Simonians, Enfantin, Talabot, and Rothschild. On April 3, 1857, various certifications were filed with the notary Dufour; the capital of 120 million francs was divided in parts of a third each among the French, the British, and a group of German financiers.

For more than a year there was open war between Rouher (linked to the Pereires) and Morny (who had an interest in the new project). At a conference of ministers held at Compiègne on November 24, 1858, Napoléon III repeated that he wished to see the rapid creation of a large discount bank. Rouher attacked Morny without naming him: "I am convinced that the public will regard this new institution as mainly due to the pressing demands of a private interest, established as it was through the influence and with the entourage of a man subject to attacks which, though doubtless sometimes slanderous, have been most vigorously made in connection with his unwarrantable interference in too many businesses." Napoléon III paid no heed, and on January 13, 1859, the Council of State finally passed a decree authorizing the creation of the *Société générale de crédit industriel et commercial*; the CIC of later fame was born. Meanwhile the antagonism between Rothschild and Pereire had subsided. Since 1856 the atmosphere at Crédit Mobilier had been less triumphalist; and besides, the large industrial groups were customers of both institutions, and all the fund-raising networks were required to meet growing needs.

Crédit Foncier. In February 1852 a decree of the prince president's government created the framework for *banques foncières*, that is, "land banks," whose function was to advance long-term loans against a mortgage, repayable in annual instalments at an interest rate of 5 percent plus 1 or 2 percent loan repayment. These banks were intended mainly for farmers wanting to develop their land; the new element of annual redemption payments was inspired by examples in Germany. The first banks opened in Paris, Marseilles, and Nevers. The Banque Foncière de Paris was created by the decree of February 17, 1852.

In the course of 1852, Napoléon III decided to merge the various banks into one large institution, and Crédit Foncier duly came into being early in 1853. Its operations covered the whole of France. But when farmers stayed away, it turned its attention to urban landowners and fueled the construction fever that took hold of Paris and, to a lesser extent, other cities. Thanks to a government subsidy of 10 million francs raised from the property of the Orléans family, Crédit Foncier now advanced loans at an annual rate of 5 percent, including repayment. The size of the loans could not exceed half the value of the land or property put up as guarantee.

Haussmann developed very friendly relations with Crédit Foncier, which had large sums of money to offer at attractive rates. It played a truly major role in the transformation of Paris: first, by standing surety for public works firms and allowing them to rediscover the joys of prefectural contracts; second, by lending money at a low price to the Pereires and later to their real estate rivals; and third, by giving the city of Paris hundreds of millions in barely legal disguised loans, which enabled Haussmann to carry out his projects but eventually cost him his job.

ASPECTS OF EVERYDAY LIFE

≈ Numerous changes were making an impact on everyday life. The telegraph had been open since 1850 for private communications, and the new electrical system meant that it worked round the clock almost instantaneously in any weather. In 1855 it reached Mende, the last prefecture to be linked telegraphically to Paris. Gustave Claudin wrote in 1862 that it was on a par with the railway as an agency of economic and social modernization: "The completion of the railways and the use of the electrical telegraph have been the two main causes of the happy disturbance that has come to change our customs and habits, to revolutionize our various systems, and to furnish our will, our needs, and our whims with a strength that might previously have been considered fanciful. . . . At present, one hour is enough for the prices in every stock exchange in Europe to become known in Paris and London."[9]

Paris was also transformed by the rapid growth of street lamps and technical improvements in the gas supply, and then in 1855 by Haussmann's compulsory amalgamation of the concessionary companies into a single Compagnie du Gaz under the leadership of the Pereire Brothers (who doubtless found cause to justify their taste for monopoly). Café terraces and windows, theatre façades, shop fronts—all were glistening with light. There were thousands of cafés in the capital. The Bignon was said to be the one

with the most men in evening dress, the Véron the one with the most vaudeville artists, the Café des Variétés the most actors, the Café du Helder the
most army officers, the Café Anglais the most Spaniards, the Café de Paris
the most engineers. As to Peters restaurant, it had a clientele of stockbrokers
in the evening, while those who frequented it in the morning were so bois-
terous that one corner came to be known as "the slapped faces market."[10]

The Café de Suède on Boulevard Montmartre had a diamond market on
its upper floor. On the ground floor, the journalists Émile de Girardin for *La
Liberté* and Villemessant for *Le Figaro* pooled their information to make up
miscellaneous news items together. Malicious gossipers claimed that some
theatre critics had set up a "mutual admiration society" there: each wrote for
a major newspaper, and all they had to do was reproduce their friends' reviews together with some glowing comments for every member of the group
to gain an impeccable reputation in record time.

This was all rather different from the Café Beuglant, where people drank
their beer or absinthe amid curls of pipe smoke. In winter its premises were
in rue Mazarine, while in summer it set up shop in a little street near the rue
Saint-André-des-Arts. The customers listened to songs, but they were forbidden to clap or whistle or to join in the chorus; they could express their
appreciation for the performers by offering them a small bunch of flowers.[11]
Paris ate too—from the simplest to the most elegant meals. The 1855 exhibition saw a plethora of guides to the tables of the capital, with discussions
of menus, prices, and atmosphere, just as in today's guides.

"Parisians are a peripatetic people," wrote the chronicler Alfred Delvau,
"and if movement had not existed, they would have invented it. Paris has
shady gardens filled with flowers and birds, minders of children and war veterans; a peaceful and majestic river packed with laundry boats and swimming schools; picturesque embankments lined with booksellers and cabmen;
tarmac roads and asphalt sidewalks enlivened with countless shops and wine
merchants: a whole world of strange objects to devour, a whole America of
little pleasures to discover! It is for this that the population abandons its
houses. Its houses are dirty inside, while its streets are swept every morning.
Its hundred thousand dwellings are damp, unhealthy, and dark, while its
public squares, its intersections, its embankments, and its boulevards are
flooded with sun and light! . . . How could one remain confined between
four walls, and between three or four worries—those of yesterday, today, and
tomorrow!"[12]

Behind the fine façades that lined the new road systems, the city's apartments were as unlike one another as they could possibly have been. Yet they

were united by the same curse of overcrowding: "Everyone is everyone's slave in these dreadful Parisian cages, where you are condemned to every sound, every smell, every illness of those with whom you share your chains."[13] The lack of soundproofing was the most trying problem. The squeaking of a door or a chair could banish all sleep; it was necessary to wear slippers out of consideration for the lady upstairs suffering from migraine; the piano of the girl from a good family was a torture for everyone else living in the block. Some landlords eventually found it easier simply to ban pianos, children, and dogs. The small courtyard gave off pestilential exhalations, and if the concierge decided to make cabbage soup in her broom-cupboard quarters, the whole staircase was soon filled with the odor.

Hygiene often left much to be desired. People waited for prefect Haussmann to make a start on his other grand project: the provision of running water for the population and the creation of a modern drainage system. Out of necessity, but often also out of sloppiness, people tended to be not all that clean. Haussmann was exceptional in having a bath every day.

"All the luxury is outside: all the riches are on view, all the enticements on display, all the pleasures walking the streets."[14] Window-shopping and real purchases were another reason to go outdoors. Alongside the traditional shops were large stores offering what had once been luxury goods at more affordable prices made possible by mass production and low-margin bulk marketing. What temptations were to be found in the Ville de Paris, Saint-Joseph, Le Grand Condé, Le Petit Saint-Thomas, La Belle Jardinière, Le Bon Marché, Le Printemps!

On February 22, 1855, Haussmann gained his imperial decree ordering the merger of 11 omnibus companies into a single Compagnie Générale des Omnibus; it owned 347 carriages, which in the course of 1855 would carry a total of 36 million passengers. Since 1853, double-decker omnibuses had become the norm, with 14 passengers downstairs and 12 more upstairs in the open. The price of a journey was 30 centimes down and 15 centimes up, so that, as Maxime Du Camp said, "workmen, smokers, and young people [had] a means of traveling at insignificant expense."[15] It was the unified operation that made it possible to offer journeys all over Paris at this modest price; for it gave full effect to the system of transfers which, since 1834, had offered journeys on two routes for the price of one. The creation of the Compagnie Générale, which had been the object of lengthy negotiations with the chief of police, was a personal success for the Seine prefect. "From now on," Jean des Cars points out, "there were swift and well-thought-out ways of traveling from one place to another, so that manual and white-collar workers could work and find entertainment in areas other than the one in which they lived. The to-and-fro movement characteristic of Paris came into being. Leaving one's own neighborhood involved a revolution in lifestyles."[16] Maxime Du Camp was ecstatic that one could go direct from Bercy to the Porte Maillot for a few centimes. The Compagnie Générale des Omnibus opened up new horizons for Parisians.

A LEADEN BLANKET

∼ People left their houses, laughed, and bustled about. But political life was placed beneath a leaden blanket. The regime relied upon the church to guarantee moral order and satisfied many of its needs in return. In Paris the government restored or rebuilt a number of churches. As the 1850s drew to a close, it was completing Saint Clotilde and finishing the restoration of Notre Dame, and Flandrin was painting frescoes at the Church of Saint-Germain-des-Prés. Prefects had orders to show honest religious zeal. For Haussmann the Protestant, the question was not posed. And some of his colleagues at the prefecture, officially Catholic but with an agnostic background that had erased any memory of religious practice, found themselves a figure of amusement as they kept trooping off to mass, wildly crossing themselves and standing or kneeling at the wrong moments.

The police kept close watch on all the people did. "Terrible corruption in Paris, terrible repression in the country, painful silence and darkness on all sides," recorded Louis-Philippe's former minister Duchatel. And Victor Cousin: "No one dares to speak in the provinces or to write in Paris. The bourgeoisie . . . thinks only of making money." The government was so sure of itself that in April 1857 it dissolved the Legislature. Prefects drew to the voters' attention the candidates who had the support of the authorities. Declarations by other candidates, when there were any, were neither published nor put up on posters. Nevertheless, at the elections of June 21 and 22 the opposition won 15 percent of the votes: 665,000 against 5,471,000 for the official candidates. It still had some coherent structure, especially in Paris where it won 5 of the 10 seats, in Lyons, and in a few provincial towns that had kept their attachment to the Republic. In the capital the republican victors were Carnot, Goudchaux, Cavaignac, Ollivier, and Darimon. On July 9 the interior minister, Billaut, darkly commented on the results: "The whole point now is to find ways of reducing the number of malcontents from Paris to Lyons." But it was clear that the malaise came from workers in large-scale industry. "A long time ago," he added, "I should have liked to pass a decree or propose a law preventing the construction of any new factories in Paris; but you also know all the objections that this proposal aroused." Haussmann too could clearly see that, in spite of the *grands travaux* and the benefits they brought to less well-off sections of the population, the capital remained hostile to the regime and each year was splitting more and more into a republican working-class Paris and a bourgeois Paris wedded to order. He wrote: "A two-tone map representing how the majority of electors voted in each *quartier* would show Paris divided into two almost equal parts, as in the time of the barricades."

THE BAKERY TRADE FUND

 The financial plan for the Parisian *grands travaux* depended upon the size of the city's annual budget surplus, and not long after Haussmann took over at the Hôtel de Ville a food shortage threatened the whole edifice. The wheat harvest was poor in 1853 and even worse in 1854. By September 1, 1853, the price of bread in Paris had shot up to forty centimes a kilo, so that the popular two-kilo round loaf was costing more than eighty centimes. The population expected the government to act, as it always had done in the past, by setting a ceiling of forty centimes on the price of a loaf. The popular reaction was all the more natural in that the bakery trade was subject to government controls: the number of bakers was limited, each one was obliged to keep a three-month stock of flour, the oven had to be adjacent to the retail outlet, and even the number of daily batches was regulated by the administration. Haussmann could not bear the thought, however, that lines of beggars would again form before the local arrondissement offices to collect (sometimes fraudulently issued) bread tokens, and that the city's finances would be damaged by its having to make up the difference between the high market price of flour and the low price charged to bakers.

The prefect had not forgotten the example of Mauvezin, the former miller become mayor of Nérac, who had combated the extreme price variations for bread by making an agreement with local bakers who had once been customers at his mill. Under this system, they paid a little more than the market price for flour in years with a good harvest and thus helped the town to form a "cushion" that would allow it to subsidize bread in years of shortage. Haussmann remembered that the same system had existed at Blaye in 1846, and he decided to apply it in Paris—or rather, in the whole of the Seine department. But whereas the mayors of Nérac and Blaye, with the sound wisdom of the peasantry, had begun by setting money aside during a number of good years, Haussmann in 1853 did not know where to turn to find the initial outlay.

Unable to count on the central government and unwilling to burden the city or department with debt, he had the idea of using credit. In fact, one of the institutions under his authority had recourse exclusively to lending to finance its activities: namely, the Mont de Piété, whose pawnbroking service was built upon interest-bearing bonds that Parisians—from traders at Les Halles to members of the Comédie Française—lost no time in snapping up. "Ma Tante," as it was popularly known, operated on the difference between the interest it paid on these bonds and the interest it charged its borrowers, any surplus going by statute to the Public Assistance. Why should the same privilege not accrue to bonds issued by the Bakery Trade Fund and underwritten by the city of Paris and the Seine department? Haussmann submitted his project to Napoléon III, who immediately referred it to the Council of State. There Haussmann ran into opposition both from conservatives, who wanted him to make do with the old system of bread tokens, and from liberals headed by Michel Chevalier, who were outraged by the infringement of the principle of free trade. The prefect said that some of his fiercest opponents even accused him of socialism. In fact, in the right circumstances he was no enemy of state intervention.

The organic decree establishing the Bakery Trade Fund was signed by the emperor, and the new system got off the ground on September 1, 1853. It rested upon the issuing of bonds for various terms, payable either to the bearer or to named persons, with an interest rate that varied with the date of maturity. The high-price period, which eventually lasted from September 1, 1853, to June 15, 1856, cost the fund more than 53 million francs. When prices fell again, the fund levied 1 to 3 centimes a kilo from bakers, so that over a period of six years it collected 62 million francs that enabled it to cover the bond issue, interest payments, and its own running costs. The system of compensation proved a success.

In 1863 the supporters of free trade secured the opening up of the bakery trade, on the recently introduced model of the butchery trade. As Haussmann could no longer levy anything directly from bakers, he settled for a duty of one centime on wheat, flour, and ready-made bread. It was a good thing he did, for a new period of shortage (from November 10, 1867, to May 31, 1868) would cost the fund 3.3 million francs. Nevertheless, on the eve of Haussmann's departure in late 1869, the fund still had 18 million francs in its coffers. He later noted in passing that the opening up of the bakery trade did not cause the price of bread to fall; while household bread consumption remained constant, the increased number of bakers turned to novelty loaves and Viennese pastries that could be sold without weight conditions, so that their return was much higher and in any event outside the control of officialdom.

THE WATER SUPPLY

⮞ The 1.2 million inhabitants that Haussmann estimated Paris to contain in 1853 had at their disposal an average of 29 gallons of water a day. This was a fifth of present-day consumption in Paris, and a sixteenth of the 475 gallons a day that the population of Rome is generally thought to have had under the Caesars. A team that Haussmann sent to London reported that the metropolis seen by everyone as their model provided 20 gallons of water a day per capita. The situation in Paris was therefore not critical, but distribution was a disaster.

Most of the available water (131,000 cubic yards) came from the Canal de l'Ourcq. The point of arrival, in the Villette basin, was too low to serve the high-lying *quartiers* of the capital—for simple reasons of gravity—and the supply pipes were neither large enough nor sufficiently well coordinated to allow the city to tap more than half this source of water. Pumps located at the Pont d'Austerlitz and at the foot of Chaillot drew 40,285 cubic yards of often cloudy water from the Seine. Finally, the water sources to the north (Belleville, Les Prés-Saint-Gervais) and to the south (via the Arcueil Gervais aqueduct) brought in 3,139 cubic yards; the artesian well at Grenelle another 1,046 cubic yards. The 194 miles of supply pipes in Paris were only laid in the earth; the 18 reservoirs were uneven and poorly coordinated; and the 33 monumental fountains had no more than a decorative function. For their personal consumption, Parisians could draw water from 69 wells and, between certain hours, from 1,779 street fountains. In addition, 113 commercial fountains were run by water merchants. Private supply pipes served a small number of registered customers: 7,771, to be precise, of which 157 were part of government, 3 of the departmental administration, and 223 of city and hospital services; the remaining 7,388 were private households.

There had long been talk of making greater demands on water from the Seine; it had a good reputation, unlike the springs in a large area around Paris that were gypseous and unsuitable either for washing or for the cooking of vegetables. When Haussmann took office in 1853, he found no fewer than five proposals of this kind on his desk. None of them captured his imagination, however, and he decided first to investigate whether good-quality spring water could be brought to the city in sufficient quantity and at the necessary height for large-scale private consumption. Early in 1854, Napoléon III mentioned to him a proposal from a powerful financial syndicate headed by Laffitte to obtain the contract for all water services in the capital, along the lines of the London model that the emperor regarded as a perfect solution. This project, like all the others so far proposed, would rely on pumping lightly filtered water from the Seine into reservoirs situated at the highest possible altitude.

Napoléon III wanted this plan presented as soon as possible to the municipal council. Haussmann had two objections to it. The first was of a legal and ethical nature: "I hastened to tell him [the emperor] that the direct concession of such an undertaking to private industry, without the guarantee of free competition and rival bidding, would from every point of view be extremely serious. It was at least necessary to examine very closely, with the most detailed attention, all the terms and conditions of the contract proposed by the person whom the emperor seemed to want to favor in the matter."[17] The second objection was of a technical nature. Haussmann explained his doubts about the water from the Seine and his belief that it was possible to supply the capital with plentiful spring water of perfect quality. As the emperor showed interest in what he said, Haussmann went on to insist that it was also necessary to attend to the problem of adequate drains for waste water. He did not hide his concern about the limited capacity of the gently sloping Seine to purify itself, and about the whole problem of sewage. In short, he wanted a comprehensive investigation of all these matters. The emperor agreed to his request, and the Laffitte group's dossier disappeared for good into a drawer in the prefect's desk.

Haussmann now went straight to the ministry of public works, to see Franqueville in the bridges and highways department. There he asked about the functions of Belgrand, his former colleague in the Yonne who knew so much about the waters of the Paris basin. Having discovered that he was in charge of river navigation in the Lower Seine and various hydrological researches, the prefect wrote and asked Belgrand to come and join him. Belgrand was duly seconded by the Public Works Ministry to the Seine prefecture, and in the course of April 1854 he began the investigation commissioned by Haussmann. Its purpose was to compute the springs in the Seine basin from which water could reach Paris at a minimum height of 230 feet above sea level, and to estimate the cost of channeling it to Paris, storing it there, and carrying out the necessary filtering. A report was on Haussmann's desk on July 8, and on August 4, 1854, the prefect produced his first of four memoranda on the Paris water supply. The municipal council gave it-self time to reflect, and it was only on January 22, 1855, that it approved the water and sewage system that would remain as one of Haussmann's greatest claims to fame.

BARON HAUSSMANN, IMPERIAL SENATOR

&ezh; We have seen the circumstances in which Napoléon III made Hauss-mann a senator. The appointment took place on June 9, 1857, but when it was reported in *Le Moniteur* on the 12th the number of his enemies multi-plied tenfold. The new rank came with a salary of thirty thousand francs a year, which helped to alleviate Haussmann's financial difficulties. It also flat-tered his pride, of course, especially as Napoléon III—his eye fixed as ever on the model of the first Napoleon—wanted every senator to be given a title of nobility. He spoke openly to Haussmann and asked why he should not be-come a duke. But Haussmann ruled himself out and suggested that the em-peror simply allow him to take the title of baron that his grandfather Dentzel used to have, as his son had died in 1830 without a male heir. No sooner said than done. Georges-Eugène became Baron Haussmann, senator of the empire.

A few days later, when he was lunching with the emperor at Fontaine-bleau, the conversation turned to the question of nobiliary titles. One of the guests, who had some grounds for bitterness on that score, involved Hauss-mann in his reflections and expressed surprise that he was not a duke—the duc de Dhuys, for example, after the name of the river whose waters Hauss-mann was thinking of channeling to the capital. That would not be enough, Haussmann objected. So, a prince? No, he replied with Offenbachian humor, "I should be made an aqueduke,[18] and that isn't in the list of nobiliary ti-tles."

THE SAINT-MICHEL FOUNTAIN

&ezh; In 1858, Haussmann assigned Davioud to build a fountain on the cor-ner of Place Saint-Michel that had been cut off to reduce the angle of inter-section formed by Boulevard Saint-Michel and Boulevard Saint-André. (The latter boulevard was to have been the first part of a major road leading to the Odéon theatre, but which was completed only over the section correspon-ding to the present-day rue Danton.)

The Saint-Michel fountain was Haussmann's own idea; he wanted a theatrical setting that would strike anyone coming straight over Pont Saint-Michel from the Île de la Cité and the right bank. In his *Mémoires*, Georges-Eugène mentions some youthful memories that explain his choice: "Only my contemporaries can testify to the wretched aspect of the old Place du Pont-Saint-Michel seen from the old bridge that used to tower up like a desk more than sixty years ago when, as a young law student, I had to pass it every day in order to answer my teachers' roll call. . . . [On passing] Pont Saint-Michel, I had to go through the poor little square where the water poured as into a sewer from the rues de la Harpe, de la Huchette, Saint-André-des-Arts and de l'Hirondelle. . . . Eventually I entered the meandering rue de la Harpe, climbed Mount Sainte-Geneviève, and reached . . . the corner of the École de Droit. The fine view of the Saint-Michel fountain that one has from the new bridge, as one arrives on the raised, enlarged, and cleared *place* surrounded by magnificent houses, is my revenge for the gloomy sight that I had to face for four years in a row to gain my college grades."[19]

The Seine prefect greatly appreciated Davioud's work, even though he thought it should have given a little more prominence to the grand composition that features the Archangel felling the Devil. Not everyone shared his admiration. The fountain was officially unveiled on August 15, 1860. Haussmann was radiant, but some vicious couplets were circulating in the streets of Paris, where "The devil is worth nothing at all" and "Saint-Michel is not worth the devil"!

ORSINI'S ASSASSINATION ATTEMPT

On the evening of January 14, 1858, Napoléon III and the empress were due to attend a benefit performance at the Opera for the baritone Massol.[20] At approximately 8:30, Haussmann was beneath the portico waiting for the couple to arrive. Then, just as the imperial carriage was drawing under the overhanging shelter, three bombs exploded, one after another. The emperor's face was slightly grazed by fragments of glass from the carriage. But he kept his composure, offered his arm to the empress, and walked to their box as if nothing had happened. "Take care of the wounded," he had time to tell Haussmann in a low voice. Help was organized. Haussmann made sure that those who could stand the journey were taken to Lariboisière hospital and that those who could not were treated on the spot. Altogether there were 106 wounded, two of whom died in the following minutes; the imperial bodyguards had paid a heavy tribute. The chief of police began investigations and sent his men to pick up the culprits, who had been trailed for several days. When Haussmann reported to the emperor during the first intermission, he played down the number of casualties.

The final toll of the assassination attempt was 8 dead and 150 wounded. Orsini, the ringleader, wanted to punish Napoléon III for forgetting the Italian cause and betraying his youthful fervor once he had come to power in France. Napoléon III, for his part, took a fatalistic attitude to the event: it was one of the risks of the trade. But imperial dignitaries and political personalities showed greater concern, as it reminded them of the fragility of the regime to which they had tied their fates. Morny laid into the British for their indulgence in granting asylum to political refugees of whatever origin. Military leaders offered the services of themselves and their men as a reliable pillar of the regime, and on February 7, General Espinasse was appointed minister of the interior in place of Billault. Hard-liners saw the assassination attempt as a good opportunity to strengthen the repressive apparatus. On January 18, in his speech opening the new session of Parliament, the emperor announced a number of emergency measures. The law on public safety that came before the Legislature a few days later created the new offenses of incitement to assassination, manufacturing of explosives, and arousal of others to hatred or contempt for the emperor's government; the minister of the interior received new powers to order internment in France or Algeria and to expel any suspect or any opponent of the imperial regime, whether young or old. The law was passed in February 1858 by a majority of 227 votes to 24, with only the republicans and a few Legitimists against.

Haussmann, using his senatorial title for the first time, raised some objections to the text of the law when it came up for debate in the Senate. His intervention did not bear the marks of liberalism; it was rather the pragmatic defender of law and order who spoke out: "In calm times such a weapon is pointless; in cases of extreme danger it is up to everyone to look to the prevailing risks and perils, and then laws do not count for much." But he did not go as far as MacMahon, the victor of Malakov, who cast the only senatorial vote against the law.

The political effect of the new legislation was soon put to the test. In April 1858, Parisians were again called to the polling stations, as two of the republicans elected in June 1857, Carnot and Goudchaux, had refused to swear an oath of loyalty to the emperor. Repression had its limits, however. The Paris electorate returned two more republicans to the Legislature: Ernest Picard and the lawyer Jules Favre, who had just acted as defense attorney at Orsini's trial. Favre and Picard, together with Émile Ollivier, Darimon, and the Lyons representative Hénon, would form the hard-core "Five" that led the republican opposition to the regime. Determined to fight Napoléon III with all the means allowed under the Constitution, they took the oath of "obedience to the Constitution and loyalty to the Emperor."

LONG LIVE THE *GRANDS TRAVAUX*!

≈ Orsini's action had an impact on the emperor's thinking that the authoritarian clan did not suspect at the time. For by accelerating his involvement in Italian affairs, it caused him to fall out with part of the Catholic electorate and encouraged him to look for support on the left through a liberal evolution of the regime.

The emperor thought that one of the best ways to draw the sting of the opposition was to speed up the economic modernization of the country and thereby bring about growth and social progress. On January 18, 1858, in the same speech before the Legislature in which he announced tough new measures of repression, Napoléon III gave a detailed account of the state of the nation and announced new programs for the transformation of public space and new victories of man over his environment. The emperor enumerated the *grands travaux* that had just been completed: the railway network covering France, the Saint-Nazaire wet dock, the canal from Caën to the sea, the enlargement and modernization of the ports of Le Havre, Marseilles, Toulon, and Bayonne, the draining and subsequent afforestation of the marshlands of Sologne and the Landes that was bringing health and prosperity to the local population. The public wealth was measured by the constantly rising tax revenues—43 percent over those of 1851, with no change in taxation rates. In the great cities of Lyons and Paris, new streets were boring through old unhealthy districts and opening them up for the free circulation of air, people, and the products of trade and industry. The housing stock was growing larger and better as comfortable modern blocks replaced the squalid and wretched old lodgings.

At 2:30 P.M. on April 4, 1858, starting from the corner of the Chambre des Notaires, Napoléon III rode on horseback down the Boulevard de Sébastopol, twenty paces ahead of his general staff. Splendid weather and a large enthusiastic crowd marked this official inauguration, just three months after Orsini's assassination attempt. Feelings were still running high, and many Parisians turned out on this public holiday to express their attachment to the emperor. Workers in overalls were no less eager than others to acclaim the head of state as he rode along this 98-foot-wide road, which stretched for more than a mile between the Place du Châtelet and Boulevard Saint-Denis.

The crowd kept moving up and down the new boulevard until late in the evening, and when it grew dark they could see that the improved model of gas lamps gave a brighter light than before.

At the Gare de l'Est, Napoléon III received his ministers and the municipal council and spoke in praise of Haussmann. Turning to the municipal councillors, he congratulated them on the fine achievement and immediately added: "Your task, gentlemen, is far from accomplished. You have approved a general plan that shall continue what you have begun so well. The Chamber will, I hope, soon vote it through, and each year we shall see the opening of new major roads and the clearing of crowded districts; rents will tend to fall as ever more buildings go up, the working class will grow richer through labor, poverty will dwindle as charity is better organized, and Paris will more and more answer its lofty calling." A new phase in the transformation of Paris was beginning. Make way for the 180-million-franc agreement.

16

The 180-Million-Franc Agreement

SHORTLY AFTER the speech opening the Boulevard de Sébastopol, deputies were apprised of a draft law authorizing the so-called "180 million agreement" between the government and the city of Paris. Under the terms of this convention, which was signed on March 18, 1858, the city of Paris undertook to build 18 miles of new road within a period of ten years, at an estimated cost of 180 million francs, to be paid one-third by the central government and two-thirds by the city. Haussmann submitted a coherent plan involving nine separate schemes, but discussions with the government proved arduous, and he did not get everything he wanted. In fact, Rouher and his Ministry of Agriculture, Trade, and Public Works feared that the scale of the program might cause Parliament to freeze up and therefore took the initiative of deleting a number of projects that they considered too ambitious.

Conservative circles and various provincial deputies were annoyed at the special treatment given by the government to the program of public works in Paris, but the Legislature approved the plan on May 28. The provincial rebels did succeed in removing several planned operations and in lowering the government share of funding to 50 million francs. This took the city's share up to 130 million francs, not counting the many risks for which it had to allow. At the same time the Legislature authorized the city of Paris to raise a major loan to cover its share of the costs. The deputy Leclerc d'Osmonville took advantage of the debates to question Haussmann's morals, as he had been seen rather often with a dancer called Céline or Francine Cellier:

"It is distressing that the Prefect for the Seine should bring the Opera into areas where it has no right to be." According to Émile Ollivier, such statements caused great mirth in the assembly. Georges-Eugène also had an interest in the dancer Marie-Roze from the Opéra Comique—which led humorists to poke fun at his alternation between "the paths to the storeroom [*cellier*] and the fragrance of the rose." Octavie decided to return to Bordeaux for good, and all the empress's diplomatic skills were required to bring the couple back together.

THE SECOND SYSTEM

In the public mind, the inauguration of the Boulevard de Sébastopol marked the completion of the "first system" of redevelopment projects. The financial overrun on these operations amounted to the sizable sum of 60 to 70 million francs, which Haussmann blamed mainly on the fact that most of the work had been directly executed by the public authorities and on the need for additional compulsory purchases. It was true that firms had not exactly lined up for the contracts, so that municipal departments often had to take on projects for which they were not properly equipped. Only as the projects advanced did bolder entrepreneurs test the contract market and see that it was not as risky as they had feared.

As to the soaring cost of land purchase, Haussmann attributed this in the early days of the *grands travaux* to the mechanism put in place by his predecessor. In order to guard against the canvasing and sponsoring of claims, Berger decided that all displaced landowners and tenants—even those open to amicable negotiations with the city—should be referred to land-pricing tribunals. But as this evidently increased the length of the procedure as well as the eventual level of compensation awards, Haussmann set up a special compensation board with a brief to seek amicable agreements and only in the event of failure to refer the matter to land-purchase tribunals—the precise course set out in the legislation on compulsory purchases. The board was chaired by a prefectural counselor and selected from among the most experienced members of the municipal council, plus the head of the highways department and the municipal attorney.

Later Haussmann gave the board responsibility for setting the sale price of expropriated land surplus to the city's requirements and, when subcontracting again became common practice, for sifting through the applications. In other words, the board carried out a kind of limited adjudication of the various proposals and prepared draft contracts for submission to the municipal council; the final nominees were then sent to the government for approval. "I always remained completely outside the work of this board," Haussmann later insisted, "and I never gave it any recommendation one way or another."[1]

Nevertheless, projects that fell under the 180-million-franc agreement—those comprising the so-called second system— witnessed a considerably higher degree of budget overrun. In Haussmann's view, this was largely due to the fact that the city and the central government had agreed to spread the works over ten years, to avoid "too large a concentration of workers in Paris." Another reason for the lengthy time scale was "to reduce expenditure by making it easier for the interests under threat, especially industries scheduled for displacement, to carry out their move, and for the city to grasp every opportunity to buy up the residential blocks they needed on favorable terms and to await the expiry or lessening of the term of the leases in which the blocks were entangled."[2] Neither the prefect nor Napoléon III nor the planning strategists, however, thought that the city of Paris would have to face upward pressure on all construction costs caused by the construction works themselves. The price of materials and labor increased; the growing technical complexity of the projects pushed up expenditures; and the value added to real estate by the *grands travaux* made both compulsory and amicable purchases more expensive as well as increasing the amount of compensation payable to evicted tenants.

The lengthy schedule also made it easier to engage in fraud at the city's expense. Unscrupulous industrialists were able to cook their books at leisure over several financial years and to submit these in support of exorbitant claims for compensation. And the acquisition of blocks several years before they were scheduled for demolition—which was supposed to be a way of saving money—turned out to be a complete disaster when, as we have seen, the Court of Cassation reversed a previous ruling and forced an immediate settlement of eviction compensation claims even where the city intended to allow the leases to run their course.

The upward pressure on costs was compounded by a fall in revenues due to a decision by the Council of State to restrict the conditions under which expropriated land could be resold. Most of the added value on which the city had been counting thus ended up instead in the landowners' pockets.

In the end, though, the loan authorized by the vote of May 28, 1858—which gave the municipality the 130 million francs it needed for its share of the funding—proved to be a good business deal. It was floated in 1860 in the form of bonds identical to those of 1855: that is, with a face value of 500 francs, repayable after the same period and offering the same advantages. This is how it worked. Of the 150,000 bonds covering the loan of 1855, 143,809 were to be repaid in 1860. When they fell due, Haussmann issued 287,618 new bonds—exactly double the original amount. This made the lottery element more attractive than before, since the new bonds were in two batches of 143,809, each bearing the same numbers as the 143,809 not yet repaid from 1855. Subscribers would thus treble their chance in each draw. Haussmann maintained that the investment was highly valued by customers, but things were not quite so simple. Although the bond was initially offered at 475 francs (that is, with a bonus of 25 francs to make up the face value), subscribers played hard to get. Only when the price was further reduced to 450 francs (doubling the bonus to 50 francs) was the loan fully covered, with a total of 133,548,925 francs in the city coffers. But this was more favorable to the city than in 1855, when the bond issue had involved a bonus of 100 francs. All things considered—bonus, lottery stake, 3 percent interest on the face value of 500 francs—the real cost of the 1860 loan was still barely 4 percent.

IN EACH *QUARTIER* OF THE CAPITAL

The first new road system had concentrated on historical Paris: the Place du Carrousel, Place Saint-Germain-l'Auxerrois before the Louvre colonnade, the area between the Place de Grève and the Place du Châtelet, the rear yards through which Boulevard Strasbourg/Sébastopol had been driven without too much difficulty. But the second system, while changing the face of the capital, created the apocalyptic impression noted in so many accounts of the time. On the right bank it transformed the Place du Château-d'Eau neighborhood and the Monceau and Batignolles areas, and went straight through the center of the Chaillot *quartier*; on the left bank, Gros-Caillou and the Pantheon became the scene of feverish building: "If one thinks of the huge number of heavy carts harnessed to draft horses that brought in the construction material and removed the debris, or the disorder caused by trenches for the installation of water and gas pipes, drains, and so on, one will not be too surprised that the peaceful burghers had such an impression of cataclysm as they watched the swift and total transformation."[3]

The nine projects comprising the second system came under sharper attack than the previous ones. Both in the workshops and the retail stores, people had for decades been clamoring for the transformation of *vieux Paris*—and yet the new round of public works did not correspond to their actual concerns. Many saw it all merely as spending for the fun of spending, an expression of the megalomania of the Napoléon III/Haussmann pair, an opportunity for profitable collusion with speculative circles. Every suspicion crystallized around the projects of the second system and its chief promoter, especially as the expenditure forecast was eventually exceeded by the dizzying amount of 230 million francs.

1. *The Place du Château-d'Eau and the Redevelopment of the Eastern Quartiers.* The first projects of the second system were the facelift carried out on the Place du Château-d'Eau and the opening of three dazzling new thoroughfares: the Boulevard du Prince Eugène (today's Boulevard Voltaire), Boulevard Magenta, and the rue du Turbigo.

The Boulevard du Prince Eugène, which crossed the faubourg Saint-Antoine from one end to the other, gave it new air and light—as well as making it easier for troops to move in and restore order. Opponents of the empire concentrated their attack on the *grands travaux* by arguing from this example that Napoléon III and his Seine prefect were guided only by strategic concerns. In his *Mémoires*, Haussmann does not disguise the importance of military considerations in the choices that were made concerning the Canal Saint-Martin and the Boulevard Richard-Lenoir. Yet these projects also undoubtedly helped improve the flow of traffic. The rue du Turbigo brought air to the old Arts et Métiers neighborhood and created a new strategic route through one of the traditional bastions of barricade-makers. And Haussmann was openly content to see the back of rue Transnonain and all its gloomy memories. In 1834, after emergency laws provoked rioting in Lyons and the Saint-Merry area of Paris, Interior Minister Adolphe Thiers had given Marshal Bugeaud forty thousand men to crush the uprising. When a shot fired from a house in the narrow rue Transnonain killed an already wounded officer, the soldiers burst in and, being unable to arrest the person responsible, murdered everyone there in their sleep. This massacre perpetrated under the July Monarchy was the inspiration for one of Daumier's masterpieces.

The extension of Boulevard Magenta to the Place du Château-d'Eau, authorized by the decree of March 12, 1859, did not correspond to any special strategic consideration but chiefly served to link the main railway stations: the Gare du Nord, the Gare de l'Est near the Boulevard de Strasbourg intersection, and then down to the Gare de Lyon via the Boulevard du Temple, Boulevard des Filles du Calvaire, and Boulevard Beumarchais, and the rue de Lyon.

The opening of the Boulevard du Prince Eugène posed several problems.[4] The project required demolition of the theatres on the Boulevard du Temple—a move that aroused great opposition among the audience for vaudeville and murder plays on "Crime Boulevard," as it came to be popularly known. The list of victims was long: the Théâtre Lyrique, Théâtre du Cirque, Théâtre des Folies Dramatiques, Théâtre de la Gaîté, Théâtre des Funambules, Théâtre des Délassements Comiques,Théâtre du Petit Lazare. The construction of the Winter Circus, at the corner between the Boulevard du Prince Eugène and the Boulevard du Temple, was little compensation. Some of the destroyed theatres would later be rebuilt, but in different areas of Paris.

The other problem was the technical challenge posed by the intersection of the new boulevard with the Canal Saint-Martin, for at that time the canal was several yards above the level of the road. Various ideas were considered, such as a swing bridge or a raised bridge with access ramps, before Haussmann and his men resigned themselves to the most costly but only really satisfactory solution: namely, to lower a large tract of canal by twenty feet between the Récollets lock and the Arsenal basin. It was a gigantic task, but in addition to achieving the best possible route for the Boulevard du Prince Eugène, it did away with the need for three locks. This reduced the clogging of the canal with barges and made it possible to turn the embankments into huge streets; the canal itself could thus be covered for a length of a mile and a quarter between the rue du Faubourg-du-Temple and the Place de la Bastille, and the land (the central part of Boulevard Richard-Lenoir) arranged as a ninety-eight-foot-wide promenade, with four rows of trees and a number of lawns and fountains. "It was after many anxious nights without sleep," Haussmann wrote, "that the idea occurred to me of that heroic cure to the disorder threatening nearly a league of the great artery that had already been almost entirely opened between the Place du Château-d'Eau and the Place du Trône [today's Place de la Nation]. I quickly got M. Belgrand to make a study of my plan, and as soon as he had accepted its practicability I hurried with the news to the emperor, who immediately mounted a horse to go and see for himself."[5]

Napoléon III was excited that the covering of the canal would remove an obstacle favorable to the erection of barricades. In a more peaceful vein, Boulevard Richard-Lenoir received its name from two patriotic and popular industrialists of the First Empire; it was a little blandishment for the working-class inhabitants of the neighboring *quartiers*.

The Boulevard du Prince Eugène was one of the longest roads in Paris

and the main new thoroughfare in the eastern section of the city. Its inauguration by the emperor on December 7, 1862, was an occasion of exceptional
pomp: Baltard had an *arc de triomphe* built on the Place du Trône, together
with a colonnade modeled on St. Peter's in Rome and a monument to the
victorious armies of the empire.

The construction of Boulevard Magenta did not raise the same difficulties, but the scale of the project made potential contractors think twice, and
it was only on August 15, 1864, that a deal was finally struck. Work on it
was completed in 1866. A northward extension along Boulevard Ornano
(whose first section, starting from the outer boulevards, was later renamed
Boulevard Barbès under the Third Republic) was decreed on May 23, 1863,
and completed in 1869.

The cramped little square with a modest water tower (opposite the
present-day rue Léon-Jouhaux) was expanded into the fine quadrilateral we
know today. The Prince Eugène Barracks, an important element in the military surveillance of the eastern *quartiers*, had been in place since 1857; today
it houses firemen's quarters (the Caserne de la République). A pendant on
the other side of the rue du Faubourg-du-Temple contained the buildings of
the Magasins Réunis department store in the same style. As to the water
tower, it was rebuilt in 1869 in the middle of what had become a kind of un-
fenced garden square. Shortly afterward the Third Republic had it pulled
down, and in 1889 the present monument to the glory of the Republic was
installed in its place. The lions that used to ornament the water tower were
then sent to the center of Place Daumesnil, where they still stand today.

Boulevard Magenta and Boulevard Saint-Martin (the first on the string
of the *grands boulevards*) issued into the Place du Château-d'Eau, and this was
also where the rue de Turbigo met the rue du Temple, and the Boulevard du
Temple met the Boulevard du Prince Eugène. The initial version of the
agreement with the central government provided for a direct-access road to
Père Lachaise, with the same width as Boulevard Magenta, but that idea was
withdrawn so as not to scare off the Legislature. The Avenue des Amandiers,
today's Avenue de la République, was begun only in 1857 and later completed as part of the "third system."

The Boulevard du Prince Eugène issued into the Place du Trône (now
Place de la Nation), which had been made more regular in shape. Haussmann's love of symmetry ensured that it was at the same distance as Boulevard Mazas (Diderot) from the rue du faubourg Saint-Antoine, which faced
the Avenue de Vincennes. He would have liked new roads to cut through the

arcs of the circle formed by the existing roads, but these plans had no place in the 180-million-franc agreement and got off the ground only at a later date.

2. *Avenue Daumesnil.* Another major new development in the east of Paris was the opening of the 108-foot-wide Avenue Daumesnil, twice the length of the Champs Élysées, as far as the Bois de Vincennes. The forest was then undergoing transformation, on orders from Napoléon III, so that it would become a popular brother of the aristocratic Bois de Boulogne and maintain the balance between the east and west slopes of the capital. "The faubourg Saint-Antoine should also have its Hyde Park." A Senate ordinance of 1852 had allocated the Bois de Vincennes to the crown, and on July 24, 1860, the emperor ceded it to the city in return for a promise that it would be suitably arranged.

Avenue Daumesnil gave residents of the faubourg Saint-Antoine and neighboring popular *quartiers* easy and majestic access to "their" forest. It began at the Place de la Bastille and initially stopped at the Reuilly *barrière* on the rue de Reuilly, at the site of the future Place Daumesnil created after the extension of the city limits. In a later stage, the avenue was then driven right into the heart of the forest, between the lake at Charenton and the School of Arboriculture.

3. *The Development of the Place de l'Europe and the Clearing of the Space Around Gare Saint-Lazare.* The moving of the west "embarkation point" from the Batignolles *barrière* to what is now the Gare Saint-Lazare required the gutting of the old Place de l'Europe with a deep trench. To avoid cutting it in two, Haussmann decided to build a crossroads bridge at the point where the rue de Londres intersected the rue de Vienne.

To clear the space around the Gare Saint-Lazare, he opened the sixty-six-foot-wide rue de Rome between the so-called Barrière de la Réforme (at the corner of today's Lycée Chaptal) and rue Saint-Lazare, and extended the rue de Madrid to the rue du Général-Foy that linked it to the rue de la Bienfaisance. He also opened the rue de Rouen (now rue Auber) and rue Halévy, two streets that paved the way for the future Opera *quartier*. Haussmann and Napoléon III did not breathe a word about the construction of the Opera, or about the roads intended to give this *quartier* its new shape. But the gossip network was still thriving, and an allusion to the future Opera could be read into Leclerc d'Osmonville's remarks concerning Haussmann's liaison with the dancer Céline Cellier.

4. *Boulevard Malesherbes and the Organization of the Monceau Quartier.* Boulevard Malesherbes was started under the July Monarchy, when the name

of the man who defended Louis XVI before the Convention had been given to the short section between rue Royale and rue Boissy-d'Anglas.

On the prince president's color-coded map, the new road was to join the outer boulevards at the Monceau *barrière*. As the hilltop location of the *barrière* meant that access to it could be rather difficult from the lower-lying rue de Laborde and rue de la Pépinière, Haussmann had the idea of carrying the boulevard to the lowest point behind Monceau Park by means of a detour starting at the rue de la Pépinière, and of compensating for the angle created by the change of direction with a new Church of Saint Augustin—just as a fountain had been installed on Place Saint-Michel. Napoléon III accepted Haussmann's argument.

The first part of the boulevard, starting at rue d'Anjou, did away with one of the city's most squalid neighborhoods, La Petite Pologne, which owed its name to a fashionable open-air café of the 1830s. Eugène Sue has left a graphic description of these streets running through wasteland, where a shady local population lived in makeshift huts and the rag-traders' stocks mingled with caches of stolen objects. "There were no streets, only alleyways; no houses, only shanties; no sidewalks, only a little carpet of mud and trash that would have stopped the noise of carriages from disturbing you if any had passed—though none actually did. From morning till evening, and especially from evening till morning, there was no end to the shouts of: Help! Guards! Murder! But the guards could not be bothered. The more people were knocked senseless in Petite Pologne, the fewer there were to arrest! It was swarming with people in there—you had to see them. Not many jewelers, goldsmiths, or bankers, but there were hordes of organ-grinders, clowns, punchinellos, people displaying strange animals."[6]

The land in Monceau was also abandoned, but it did not look at all like La Petite Pologne. Endless legal wrangling complicated matters for the city of Paris, as the 50 acres of Monceau Park (formerly part of the Orléans family estate) belonged half to the state and half still to the Orléans. The decision to open Boulevard Malesherbes through one of its outlying parts thus forced Haussmann to purchase the estate on behalf of the city. In order to avoid any appearance of a political settling of accounts with the former ruling family, Haussmann turned to the good offices of Émile Pereire, who secured an amicable agreement whereby the city paid a total of 9,387,000 francs in compensation to the Orléans family and to the state. In gratitude to Pereire, the city sold him 8,100 square meters (2 acres) of land (at a price of 1,000 francs per square meter) that was not needed for road-building or for the perimeter of the future public park; in 1853 the Pereires had paid 460 francs a square meter for the land along the rue de Rivoli—prices had been rising since then. On this land sold to them in Monceau, the Pereires built the residential blocks of the Monceau plain. The new *quartier* compelled recognition as one of the most elegant in Paris and became a jewel in the crown of the Crédit Mobilier group. Private houses sprang up around the park, their owners enjoying direct access to the gardens. It was here that Zola's hero, the financier Saccart, had an insolently luxurious house built for himself.

During the same years, the rue de Londres and the rue de Constantinople were extended (under the name of the Avenue de Villiers) as far as Porte Champerret. Place Malesherbes, like the Place du Château-d'Eau, was laid out in the manner of a fenceless garden square. We shall meet the Pereires again in connection with the Boulevard Malesherbes extension beyond the Boulevard de Courcelles—a project that was not part of the 180-million-franc agreement and would be carried out only after the incorporation of the suburban communes into Paris in 1860.

The land at Les Batignolles in the northwest area of Paris was still sparsely inhabited. The building of Boulevard Malesherbes and its annexes, the rue de Madrid and rue du Général-Foy, and then of the Avenue du Villiers, opened them up to real estate investors. Businesses had set up there under the July Monarchy, at the rue des Dames and rue de Lévis, outside the wall of the Farmers-General. The development of the Boulevard des Batignolles between the rue de Rome, rue des Batignolles, and the Barrière de Clichy (today's Place Clichy) gave a spectacular impetus to the neighborhood around the church and *mairie* of Les Batignolles, and accelerated the urbanization of the area tapped by the parallel rue des Dames, rue de La Condamine, rue Legendre, and rue Cardinet.

Boulevard Malesherbes was inaugurated on August 13, 1861, by Napoléon III in an atmosphere of heated debate, for seventeen town houses had been pulled down in the parts of rue de la Madeleine and rue Lavoisier affected by work on the boulevard. Some denounced what they saw as Haussmann's destruction mania while others hinted at murky speculative deals. It was the first time that upper-middle-class residences had been touched by the demolition contractor's pickax, and the event served as a signal for a press campaign of unprecedented violence. The emperor rode over on horseback from the Tuileries Palace to the Madeleine and spoke in words that no one could ignore: "Gentlemen, nowadays there is nothing extraordinary about the inauguration of a new communication route, and I would not have made a public ceremony out of it if I had not wanted to demonstrate my sympathy for the municipal council in its constant zeal on behalf of the city's interests, my satisfaction with the Seine prefect for his tireless perseverance in pursuing a great objective, and my approval of all those who are so well supporting my efforts."

Haussmann took the opportunity to settle acounts with the Orleanist bourgeoisie, which he held responsible for the outbreak of polemic. "When groups of people involved in industry or commerce have had their interests profoundly shaken through the opening of the rue de Rivoli and the Boulevard de Sébastopol, they have endured the most irksome displacement while showing respect for the duly declared public benefit and without vainly protesting against the executive authority. And this year, when the task facing us has no longer been to throw into turmoil workshops and retail stores whose customers and own prosperity are often bound up with a given situation, but only to disturb the habits of people blessed by fortune for whom a move of house is no more than a passing nuisance, we have had to endure language of unparalleled violence. As such persons are unfamiliar with the harsh necessities that the duties of life reserve for others, it is understandable that, in respect of compulsory purchases, they should have felt unpleasantly surprised when they were hit by the democratic rule of equality before the law. But their complaints have found a passionate echo among those who claim to be liberal *par excellence*—a fact that can hardly be explained by a systematic intent to contradict every act of the administration."

5. *The Place de l'Étoile.* The 180-million-franc agreement provided for an extension of Boulevard Beaujon (part of today's Boulevard Haussmann/Avenue de Friedland) between Boulevard Malesherbes and the Place de l'Étoile and a rectification of the outer Passy boulevard (since incorporated into Avenue Kléber), which both fell under the category of redevelopment of the area around the Arc de Triomphe.

We have already seen that the guiding principles for the layout of the Place de l'Étoile were fixed by the decree of August 13, 1854. By 1860, when Labédollière published *Le Nouveau Paris*, "this decree has started to be implemented. Leroux's tollhouse constructions of 1787 have been pulled down along with the wall, and sizable earthworks have been made to link the circus with the new boulevards. Symmetrical town houses rise above the *place*. It is illuminated by gas lampposts with branched lamps, each resting upon an octagonal base with cut corners and ornamental molding. The shaft consists of a bundle of spears, its lower part decorated with corbels ending in griffin heads. Fifty-four of these branched lampposts are spaced around the circus; the others illuminate the heads of the twelve boulevards."[7]

The arrangement of the *place* entailed a certain design for the surrounding area. The emperor's color-coded plan envisaged only three avenues: the Avenue de l'Impératrice, which was realized as part of the first new road system; Boulevard Beaujon (Avenue de Freidland); and a new avenue intended to prolong the transverse axis of the Arc de Triomphe toward the Trocadero (the Avenue du Roi de Rome, later changed to Avenue Kléber). But Haussmann had to take account of the existence of other roads, most in very poor shape, that prefigured the radiating plan: the Boulevard de Bezons (Avenue de Wagram), which was extended to Place Wagram and would later be joined there by Boulevard Malesherbes after the growth of the city limits; and the Avenue de Wagram and Avenue Kléber, intersected at the right angle formed by the Avenue des Champs Élysées and the Boulevard de Neuilly (which became after redevelopment the Avenue de la Grande Armée). Haussmann also had to give some thought to the Avenue de Saint-Cloud (today's Avenue Victor Hugo), which was too narrow adequately to serve the Bois de Boulogne.

With all these constraints, it was far from easy to work out a symmetrical arrangement for the Étoile. Haussmann began by opening the Avenue de l'Impératrice halfway between the Avenue de la Grande Armée and Avenue Victor Hugo, so that the land for building would be equal on either side; the rest of the arc of the circle, between the Avenue de la Grande Armée and Avenue Kléber, was nearly twice as large. Haussmann decided to do the same again between Avenue Kléber and the Champs Élysées by opening the Avenue d'Iéna and Avenue Joséphine (today's Avenue Marceau), which together formed two equal little arcs and another one almost double them in size. He reproduced this arrangement between the Avenue des Champs Élysées and the Avenue de Wagram, so that the Avenue de Friedland and the Avenue de la Reine Hortense (Avenue Hoche) coming up from Monceau Park formed the same angles as Avenue Marceau and the Avenue d'Iéna on the other side of the Champs Élysées. Then he repeated the operation one last time with the Avenue du Prince Jérôme (now Mac-Mahon and Niel) and the Avenue d'Essling (Carnot), corresponding to Avenue Victor Hugo and Avenue Foch; the line of Mac-Mahon/Niel stretched down to Place Pereire (now Place du Maréchal Juin) while Avenue Carnot would join the Avenue des Ternes.

The 180-million-franc agreement, as we have seen, allowed for only two road-building projects: the Avenue de Friedland with its Boulevard Haussmann extension to the Place Saint-Augustin, where it crosses Boulevard Malesherbes; and the straightening of the part of the wall-walk situated between Passy cemetery and Étoile (Avenue Kléber). The other projects would have to be carried out purely with municipal funding, outside the framework of the second system.

6. *The Chaillot and Trocadéro Quartier.* The 180-million-franc agreement provided for two 131-foot-wide boulevards from the Pont de l'Alma toward the right bank: the Avenue de l'Alma (George V) was to be a direct continuation of the bridge, between Quai Debilly and the Avenue des Champs Élysées; the Avenue de l'Empereur (Avenue du Président Wilson) was to be the pendant west of the bridge to Avenue Montaigne, establishing a direct link between the Place de l'Alma, Place d'Iéna, and the Trocadéro. The Avenue de l'Alma was completed by rues François Ier, Pierre-Charron, Marbeuf and de Marignan, which constituted the skeletal structure of the Chaillot *quartier.* After 1860 the Avenue du Président Wilson was extended beyond the Trocadéro by Avenue Georges Mandel and Avenue Henri Martin as far as the Muette (Place Tattegrain)—where it was joined by Avenue Victor Hugo—and from there to the Porte de la Muette. This created a pleasant route to the Bois de Boulogne.

7. *The Boulevards and Avenues of the École Militaire and the Invalides.* The road-building program on the left bank was equally ambitious. Starting from the Pont d'Alma, two ninety-eight-foot-wide avenues were envisaged: Avenue Bosquet and Avenue Rapp. The Avenue de la Tour Maubourg, which ran alongside the Invalides, was extended to the Pont des Invalides in a line with the Avenue d'Antin (Avenue Franklin Roosevelt).

8. *Mount Sainte-Geneviève and the Faubourgs Saint-Jacques and Saint-Marcel.* At the eastern end of the left bank, new roads broke open the area between the *vieux Paris* of the University, the Porte d'Italie, and the Barrière Denfert. Boulevard Saint-Marcel and the Boulevard de Port Royal, which were created between the Boulevard de l'Hôpital and the Boulevard de Montparnasse, completed the line of the inner boulevards on the left bank that the emperor had drawn on the color-coded map. Another road was planned to run from the Gobelins circus across to the Barrière d'Enfer (Place Denfert-Rochereau): this was the Boulevard Arago, which partly covered the route of the old rue Saint-Hippolyte. The Paris survey department proposed it in order to open up Place Denfert-Rochereau to the east; Deschamps had already planned to do the same to the west by means of the Boulevard d'Enfer (today's Boulevard Raspail). Napoléon III agreed to proceed with the latter project as far as the Boulevard du Montparnasse, but the continuation of Boulevard Raspail up to the Sèvres-Babylone circus and the rue de Bac/Boulevard Saint-Germain intersection would have to wait until the Third Republic.

On the other hand, the "circling" of Mount Sainte-Geneviève was successfully carried through. The first stage was the creation of the Avenue des Gobelins by widening to 131 feet the section of rue Mouffetard between the

Barrière d'Italie (Place d'Italie) and the rue Censier/rue de Lourcine cross-roads.[8] This crossroads was linked to Place Maubert by the sixty-six-foot-wide rue Monge, which skirted Mount Sainte-Geneviève to the east. And rue Claude-Bernard, starting from the same crossroads and also sixty-six feet in width, skirted Sainte-Geneviève to the south; its continuation through rue Gay-Lussac eventually joined the bottom of rue Soufflot, where it comes out onto Boulevard Saint-Michel. Haussmann considered the line of rue Monge and rue Claude-Bernard/Gay-Lussac to have been his personal contribution to the opening up of the Quartier Latin, due to his excellent knowledge of the terrain. "The emperor substituted them on his map for less simple and less effective schemes."[9]

9. *The Île de la Cité and the Left Bank*. The last article of the 180-million-franc agreement concerned the Île de la Cité and *vieux Paris*. It provided for a widening of the Boulevard de Sébastopol in the Cité, an extension of the same boulevard on the left bank, between Place Saint-Michel and the Observatoire circus, and the opening of a sixty-six-foot-wide street (rue Médicis) that insulated the Luxembourg Gardens opposite rue Soufflot.

The Île de la Cité. In the Cité, a widening of the old rue de la Barillerie created the Boulevard du Palais. In fact, half of the island was turned into one huge building site. Before Haussmann's *travaux*, twenty thousand people had lived on the Île de la Cité, packed into often decaying houses in small dark streets. Eugène Sue had made its *tapis-francs* famous: "The *quartier*, which stretches from the Palais de Justice to Notre Dame, . . . very limited in space, closely watched, is nevertheless a refuge or meeting place for a large number of Parisian criminals, who gather together in its *tapis-francs*. . . . A *tapis-franc*, in the slang of theft and murder, means the lowest kind of tavern or cabaret. A habitual criminal (who in this vile language is called an ogre) or a similarly degraded woman (who is called an ogress) is the typical custom at these taverns frequented by the rejects of the Parisian population. Ex-convicts, swindlers, thieves, and murderers are found there aplenty."[10]

The opening of the Boulevard du Palais was complemented by a new street running perpendicular to it, the rue de Lutèce, which marked the northern boundary of the land on which the Seine prefect meant the new commercial court to be built. Suddenly the flower market there became larger and more orderly. To the south, another operation cleared the rectangle formed by the Boulevard du Palais, the rue de Lutèce, rue de la Cité, and the Quai du Marché Neuf. A single building would occupy the space, intended as a headquarters barracks for the Paris Guard and the Fire Brigade. When work on it was finally completed, after Haussmann's departure from the scene, it was allocated to the *préfecture de police*—which is still its function today. Thus, between the Quai de la Corse, the rue de la Cité, the Quai du Marché Neuf, and the Boulevard du Palais, everything was pulled down to make way for two huge public buildings.

Should any tears be shed for these old *quartiers?* Haussmann expressed no regrets at having decided on "the compulsory purchase of all the houses and the disappearance of that ignoble *quartier.*"[11] Eugène Sue, though usually more compassionate toward old stones and, as a republican, often at odds with Haussmann, seemed no more affected by the loss: "The mud-colored houses, very occasionally perforated by worm-eaten window frames, almost touched each other at the top, so narrow were the streets. Dark foul alleys led to even darker and fouler staircases, which rose so steeply that you could barely climb them with the help of a rope attached by iron hook-nails to the damp walls. Displays had been laid out by coal merchants, fruiterers, and sellers of bad meat on the ground floor of some of these dwellings. Although the items were not worth much, the merchants feared the daring local thieves so much that they had put iron bars on nearly all the shop windows."[12]

Work on the Boulevard du Palais involved the reconstruction of two bridges: the Pont Saint-Michel in 1857 and the Pont au Change three years later. Arched and narrow, the early seventeenth-century Pont Saint-Michel crossed the Seine at an angle; it had been lined with houses until 1807. The Pont au Change was more solid, but it was also too narrow and no longer fitted in with the major roads already opened or under construction. Its new location was chosen to preserve the alignment with Boulevard Saint-Michel bordering the Thermes on the left bank, but this meant it was not lined up with the Boulevard de Sébastopol. On the right bank it joined the Place du Châtelet on its western edge, almost in a line with rue Saint-Denis, so that one could gain access to it either from the Boulevard de Sébastopol or from rue Saint-Denis and Les Halles (via the street of the same name). The bridge slightly deviated as it became the Boulevard du Palais on the Île de la Cité, in order to spare the clock tower at the corner of the Palais de Justice and the Quai de l'Horloge. The final plans were fixed in September 1858. The work of demolishing the old bridge had already been completed by late December, thanks to an efficient technique that involved placing winches on two metal footbridges with a capacity to shift the bulkiest stones in just a few hours. A pedestrian footbridge then replaced the main bridge for the duration of the works. Within barely eighteen months, on August 15, 1860, the new bridge was officially opened.

The reconstruction of the Pont au Change involved redesigning three of the adjacent *quais*. It also opened the way for new structural work on the Palais de Justice: restoration of the Sainte-Chapelle, and restoration and enlargement of the areas allocated to the justice department, the Conciergerie, and the *préfecture de police*, which at that time was in a jumble of buildings that looked onto the rue de Jérusalem and the Quai des Orfèvres.

Work on the Sainte-Chapelle restoration had already begun in 1848 on the initiative of the provisional government. The committee in charge of supervising operations included Mérimée, the architects Caristie and Duban, various members of the municipal council, representatives of the Seine departmental council, the attorney general, and one member of the Council of State. In 1854 the stained-glass windows were restored and the spire put back in place (on vaulting only seven inches thick). As the Sainte-Chapelle was enclosed within the buildings of the Palais de Justice, the idea had been briefly floated of separating it off altogether—but this was soon abandoned because the work in the Palais de Justice would have been too difficult. The enlargement and isolation of the palace was entrusted to the Paris city architect Duc, who had raised the July column on the Place de la Bastille during the reign of Louis-Philippe. Work began just as Haussmann was arriving in Paris to take over his new prefecture. It was a complicated business, involving the central government in matters relating to the Court of Cassation and the imperial (appeals) court, where Duc was responsible for the building work together with his assistant Coquard. But it also concerned the Seine department in relation to the assize courts, the Conciergerie, the Seine court of first instance (which alone required more space than the imperial court and the Court of Cassation together), the holding cells, and the rebuilding of the *préfecture de police*. For all of these projects, the chief architect was Daumet—except that Gilbert and Diet had responsibility for the *préfecture de police*. The city of Paris was involved only in connection with the police court.

All these projects required compulsory purchases along the rue de Harlay separating Place Dauphine from the Palais de Justice and the *préfecture de police*. In 1853 it was decided to demolish the old police headquarters to make way for the justice department, so that it became necessary to find replacement space. The houses on either side of the rue de Harlay were one possibility, and after a decree of March 2, 1854, authorizing their compulsory purchase, the offices of the *préfecture de police* were installed there. Walkways were put up to make it easier to pass between the two rows of houses above the rue de Harlay. But the structures were in worse shape than had been thought: cracks began to appear in 1857, and in August 1863 a huge piece of plaster fell from the fifth floor and crushed a little girl playing on Place Dauphine. In 1868 it was finally decided to pull down the whole row of houses on the east side of the rue de Harlay; the police offices were moved to the new buildings of the Palais de Justice overlooking the Quai des Orfèvres. In the middle of the rue de Harlay and backing on to the Quai de l'Horloge, Duc had built between 1856 and 1867 the buildings that housed the assize courts and the Court of Cassation; they lined the street with a monumental façade preceded by an imposing flight of steps. Naturally Duc supported the decision to pull down the houses on the west side of the street, as this highlighted his façade even more.

The need to avoid any interruption to the services in question meant that the building work had not been completed by the end of 1869. But the Court of Cassation was installed in its new location, as were the court of first instance and the two new rooms of the assizes. Work had been finished on the Salle des Pas Perdus along the Boulevard du Palais as well as on the holding cells and some of the offices allocated to the *préfecture de police*. Haussmann had planned to continue the demolition right up to the Pont Neuf, sweeping Place Dauphine away in the process. Indeed, already in 1855 the *place* had decayed so much that the *Grand Larousse Universel* announced, without a word of regret, that its demolition was imminent. Ten years later, Amédée Gabourg predicted in his *Histoire de Paris* that the "aged structures" of Place Dauphine would soon disappear: "These vast public works, only just begun, are connected with the transformation of the Cité, the cradle of Paris, whose face has already changed so much that the present generation will soon be ignorant of this strange and picturesque *quartier* that lasted through fourteen centuries." The historian A. Poirson, writing in his *Histoire du règne d'Henri IV* also in 1865, was one of the few to swim against the tide of public opinion that seemed to have doomed the old houses of Place Dauphine to destruction: "Place Dauphine—at least, so everyone says—will be leveled forthwith and turned into a square in front of the new façade of the Palais de Justice. . . . Place Dauphine wiped out! What destruction—and destruction that seems to concentrate on historical buildings from the reign of Henri IV! . . . Too often in France . . . the mania for leveling and starting anew has ruled supreme."[13] The plan for the square certainly did exist. At Haussmann's request, Duc had designed a green space for the center of the area de-

limited by the Quai de l'Horloge and the Quai des Orfèvres—an area surrounded by galleries and (along the Quai des Orfèvres) lined with offices
that would house the *préfecture de police*.

Notre Dame Cathedral. The restoration of Notre Dame and the clearing of
the space around it were another of the great enterprises undertaken during
the reign of Napoléon III. The restoration was entrusted to Viollet-le-Duc.
Thanks to the demolition of the former archbishop's palace, the southern
façade regained a majestic aspect, although Labédollière, for one, expressed
reservations about the construction of a "niggardly sacristy."[14] The central
spire was put back in place. Until 1864, Viollet-le-Duc kept himself busy
reinventing the statues that had disappeared from the façade, restoring the
mutilated sculptures, and bringing fragments of fresco back to life. Behind
the apse, the pretty walk in the Notre Dame gardens was given a fountain in
a Gothic style reminiscent of the cathedral itself. Invisible at the southern
tip of the island was the Morgue, whose construction Haussmann had assigned to Gilbert.

The cathedral gradually emerged from its matrix. "For a true appreciation of the majestic lines of Notre Dame de Paris," Labédollière opined, "all
that remains is to destroy the Hôtel-Dieu, whose patients do not have
enough air or space, and whose removal to another location has long been in
question." The clearing of the cathedral square, long desired by majority
opinion, was the great operation carried out by the regime. The whole area
between the rue de la Cité and the façade of Notre Dame was leveled. The
street clearing and resurfacing affected the Hôtel-Dieu, the old Paris hospital that then stood not on its present site but at the southern end of the Île
de la Cité, in a way spanning the smaller branch of the Seine since it also had
buildings on the Quai de Montebello on the left bank.

Haussmann had no hesitation in deciding to get rid of the old Hôtel-
Dieu: "I could never forget the sinister air of that bit of river wedged between two hospital complexes with a covered walkway between them,
polluted with evacuations of every kind from a mass of patients eight hundred strong or more."[15] Haussmann would have liked to build the new hospital outside the Île de la Cité, in an area with greater space. But Napoléon
III, with public support, wanted to keep a hospital in the city center—even
if it meant moving it to a different site. The hospital was therefore given the
rectangular space bounded by the Quai de la Corse, the rue d'Arcole, the
Notre Dame cathedral square, and the rue de la Cité: a total area of roughly
five acres. The plan attached to the decree of May 22, 1865, concerning "the
siting of the Hôtel-Dieu and the clearing of the area around it" entailed fur-

ther demolition in the Ursins *quartier*; all that would remain of it in the end would be the small part still visible today between the rue d'Arcole, the Quai aux Fleurs, and the cathedral, around rue Chanoinesse. Bent as he was on destruction, Haussmann would gladly have flattened that too in order to build in its place the new residence of the archbishop of Paris. As in the case of Place Dauphine, the prefect did not have the spare time to see his plans through to the end—plans that would have meant turning the whole island into an administrative city.

By the end of redevelopment, the resident population had shrunk to five thousand. Among the establishments that had to make way for the Hôtel-Dieu was La Belle Jardinière, one of the oldest department stores in Paris. Its founder, Pierre Parissot, had set up there in 1824 on the Quai aux Fleurs, and by 1856 the business was doing so well that it had expanded into the twenty-five adjacent houses. After Parissot's death in 1861, his nephews reached a private settlement with Haussmann relating to the sale of the rectangle allocated for the new hospital. La Belle Jardinière then moved to the corner of the Quai de la Mégisserie and the rue du Pont-Neuf.

Haussmann was worried about hygiene conditions at the new facility, but his mind was eventually put at rest: "All around this area of land [were] masses of air cleansed by the currents of the two branches of the river that nothing separated any longer, and whatever was said about the area, in every possible tone, it would have been difficult to find anything as good elsewhere from the point of view of health. I would add that, at the time in the morning when the cathedral might temporarily block the hospital, the sun was already high enough on the horizon for the southwest corner of the hospital not to be completely in its shadow."[16] Gilbert's project, in its first version, was imitation Gothic, but Napoléon III was concerned more about air and light than about any artistic flourishes—and anyway he did not like the Gothic style. Gilbert's second version was resolutely modern, involving a number of semi-detached four-story buildings separated by planted courtyards; together they would be able to accommodate the planned total of eight hundred beds. But even after various refinements and the addition of flower beds and fountains, the project came in for sharp criticism. The medical profession, which generally favored smaller hospitals and wards with fewer beds, thought the design much too dense. Enemies of the prefect also attacked the system of wings and the fact that patients were not sufficiently separate from one another.

Georges-Eugène grew indignant. At a time when the Public Assistance Board had to face escalating costs due to the expansion of the Parisian population, was it right to be advocating such radical and expensive solutions for the problem of hospital treatment? "One had only to think of how most of its clients lived at home, packed together in low-ceilinged hovels that were barely furnished, with neither air nor light, freezing in winter, stifling in summer; in six-story houses whose courtyard, if there was one, was more like a well; in narrow, dirty, stinking streets. Should one not recognize that their admission into a hospital located like the one we were planning, with airy and well-lighted buildings (even if they did have four storys) that were heated in winter and ventilated in summer; in raised wards gleaming with cleanliness; in real beds with real mattresses and really white sheets and curtains—that this would amount to such a change in their fate that their illnesses would be relieved before they had received any treatment."[17]

Aesthetic arguments came in support of the medical ones, four storys appearing too high at such a short distance from Notre Dame cathedral. Finally the emperor agreed to forgo the top level: the new Hôtel-Dieu, begun in 1866, would be built over three storys. Scarcely had it been completed, however, when the dispute flared up again under the Third Republic and another story was lopped off to leave just two! As to those who advocated the clearing of the area in front of Notre Dame, they had every reason to feel satisfied with the size of the square: no less than 492 by 656 feet. It was an empty space exceeding what its designers had intended.

The Luxembourg Gardens Dispute. The widening and (for part of the route) straightening of the rue d'Enfer constituted the final section of Boulevard Saint-Michel. (The present rue Henri-Barbusse corresponds to one of the parts of the rue d'Enfer that were not used for the building program.) In order to bring down the ground level by six and a half feet at the bottom of rue Soufflot and along the École des Mines, it was necessary to acquire all the houses in the lower section of rue Soufflot. The ensuing demolitions did not trouble Haussmann, for he could then make the narrow section of rue Soufflot between rue Saint-Jacques and Boulevard Saint-Michel as wide as the upper section between rue Saint-Jacques and the Place du Panthéon.

The driving of Boulevard Saint-Michel up to the Observatoire circus absorbed the through traffic that had previously been taken by the Avenue de l'Observatoire. The avenue, now reserved for local traffic, could thus sustain a fine tree-lined promenade over its entire length.

The last project envisaged under the 180-million-franc agreement was the link road between the rue Soufflot crossroads and the rue Corneille/rue de Vaugirard crossroads: that is, the rue de Médicis. Sixty-six feet wide, it was intended as a convenient way of traveling from the Odéon *quartier* to

Mount Sainte-Geneviève—a scheme similar to one that had already figured in the Artists' Plan. But since the planned route would chip a corner off the Luxembourg estate as it passed through the Senate outbuildings, stables, and service dwellings, the dignitaries who would be directly affected—the marquis d'Hautpoul (the Senate's grand auditor) and the marquis de Gisors (its chief architect)—demanded postponement and a reexamination of the project. The affair dragged on until May 1861, when a compromise was finally reached. The rue de Médicis received in sacrifice the marquis d'Hautpoul's stables and the architect's house, but the latter was rebuilt in the nearby rue Guynemer. The Médicis fountain was moved a few yards from the residential blocks to which it had been attached, and, more important, was turned around so as to become the basic decoration of one of the paths in the gardens.

THE LOAN OF 1865

✑ The second system therefore touched the whole city, bringing it the respiration and irrigation it would need as a modern metropolis. Contrary to a stipulation of the 180-million-franc agreement, the nine sets of projects were not all completed by the deadline of 1870—but the worst surprise was that they had cost 410 million francs instead of the 180 million for which allowance had been made. The reasons for this overrun of 230 million francs— more than twice the initial estimate—were the ones we have just seen Haussmann identify. As the central government share of the costs was limited to a total of 50 million francs, the city of Paris had to fund the *travaux* to the tune of 360 million. Haussmann had borrowed 130 million, and although this became 133 million in 1860, it was still a long way short. Another loan was therefore floated in 1865—officially to cover the costs of incorporating the suburban communes, but in effect mainly to fill the gaps created by the second system.

The loan of 1865 was similar in kind to the others we have encountered. The city issued 600,000 bonds of 500 francs repayable in 50 years, at an interest rate of 4 percent and with a free entry in a quarterly lottery for which the prize money was set at 1,140,000 francs a year. The bonds were issued below par at 450 francs (with a bonus of 50 francs), and thus brought in 275 million francs for a nominal capital of 300 million. With the benefit of hindsight, Haussmann thought the interest rate too favorable to bondholders, who received a dividend of 20 francs per bond whereas the loans of 1855 and 1860 had netted them 15 francs. In his view the dividend should have been set at 18 francs and the lottery prize money at 600,000 francs a year. As someone had to take the blame for everything, he singled out the municipal council for its failure to keep steady.[18] The real rate of interest weighing upon the city for the 1865 loan was 5 percent.

Some read the lessons rather differently. When the Paris city loan of 1860 had been floated, Rothschild—by then on better terms with Napoléon III—had been given the job of negotiating the unsubscribed issue for a sizable commission of 1.8 percent. By 1862 he had still not fully delivered, and Haussmann had slighted him by awarding the negotiation of the remaining bonds to a banking syndicate in which Crédit Mobilier played a not insignificant role (22,785 bonds, or 9 million francs). In 1865, however, Haussmann did not go to the same trouble of consulting rival bidders: when Crédit Mobilier and the Pereire Brothers offered to guarantee negotiation of the 270 million francs of the new loan for a commission of just 1 percent, the prefect signed with them. In a letter to Baroche dated July 20, 1865, Finance Minister Achille Fould—an enemy of the Pereires—bitterly complained that he had not been consulted: "Is it admissible . . . that an operation of this size should be publicly launched without any approach to the minister in charge of credit matters for his opinion on its wisdom. At this time of year, with this heat, it will be difficult to attract subscribers."[19] Fould's prediction proved wrong: the issue was a brilliant success. It was even said in Paris that the loan was at the origin of the stock market upturn that began around that time. On September 6, Fould wrote again to Baroche: "Attempts are being made, with *Le Constitutionnel* in the van, to claim that the recovery is due to the city loan and Crédit Mobilier. On the contrary, they have been the obstacle in the way of the recovery."[20]

Be this as it may, the uptake of the 1865 loan made it possible to cover more than the 230 million francs owing on the second program of *travaux*. Haussmann even had enough to launch new operations, and he did not fail to grasp the opportunity. The extension of the city limits, which was decided in 1859, meant that certain projects left out of the 180 million agreement could be taken up again, at the same time that new roads would help redevelop the suburban communes newly incorporated into Paris. Thus, in parallel to work on the second system scheduled to last from 1858 to 1868, Haussmann launched a number of projects that would be grouped under what came to be known as the third system. They too would involve financial overruns and supplementary loans, which the prefect continued to handle without tax increases by mobilizing the large extra sums that flowed into the municipal coffers in confirmation of the theory of productive expenditure.

A SECOND REPORT ON THE PARIS WATER SUPPLY

❧ The municipal council vote of January 22, 1855, on Haussmann's first submission concerning the Paris water supply, authorized the continuation of Belgrand's investigations into a possible routing of good-quality water into the city at a sufficient height. The results were presented to the council in a second submission, which Haussmann delivered on July 16, 1858. According to Belgrand's report, the most plentiful and best-quality source of water was the Somme-Soude, which flowed into the Marne between Châlons and Épernay; the cost of an aqueduct to convey 113,000 cubic yards of water a day to Paris, at a minimum slope of 262 feet, was roughly estimated at 25 million francs and then more precisely at 26 million. Belgrand's project called for the construction of a 26-mile aqueduct and 107 miles of mains. A public benefit decree of June 21, 1856, authorized the construction of a reservoir in Passy to hold this water after it reached the capital, and a further decree of January 24, 1858, approved the building of another one at Buttes Chaumont; a third reservoir was later planned for Montsouris. The cost of these new reservoirs was estimated at 12 million francs.

At the same time the municipal council resolution of 1855 authorized the prefect to take steps to improve the distribution of water in Paris. Haussmann's men drew up two projects. The first, which related to water for private consumption, provided for the laying of 62 miles of primary and secondary pipes (with diameters between 12 and 43 inches), and 267 miles of piping with a diameter of less than 12 inches. The second project, which covered water for public use (sprinkling and cleaning of streets, sprinkling of parks and gardens, supply of fountains), scheduled 47 miles of primary and secondary pipes plus 95 miles of small-diameter pipes. The cost of the two pipe systems was put at 8 million francs.

Finally, drawing on engineer Mille's research trip to England, Haussmann proposed main sewers to carry rainwater and wastewater from Paris to the Asnières loop in the Seine 3 miles downstream from the Pont de la Concorde, and a system of primary and secondary sewers linked up with them. In 1853 there were a little more than 66 miles of sewers. Five years later, thanks to Haussmann's efforts, the figure had climbed to 106 miles. Preliminary studies made by municipal engineers in 1858 suggested the construction of a further 35 miles of large-diameter sewers and nearly 145 miles of smaller ones. By the time the program was completed, the total length of sewers was supposed to reach 336 miles, at an estimated expenditure of 50 million francs.

Haussmann outlined all these points on July 18, 1858, in his second submission to the municipal council on the Paris water supply. As on the first occasion, the council took its time to consider the matter, and it was only on March 18, 1859, that it formally approved the diversion of water from sources of the Somme-Soude, and secondarily from sources close to the Dhuys, Sourdon, and the Vertus system. The council gave the prefect a good mark for his work on water distribution and sewage in Paris.

THE CAISSE DES TRAVAUX DE PARIS

To make budgeting easier for the *grands travaux*, Haussmann had long dreamed of creating a special fund. In 1858 he got what he wanted, thanks to the 180-million-franc agreement (which made the establishment of such a fund indispensable) and to the success of the Bakery Trade Fund, which had shown the huge potential of issuing bonds on para-municipal institutions.

The creation of a public works fund, the Caisse des Travaux de Paris, was initially a response to certain constraints within the local finance system. As a general rule, except in the case of consumer or real estate credit, it was unusual for a borrower to spend the whole of the sum advanced in the hours or days following its release; the unused portion was invested, and the income it yielded was especially welcome as the interest on the loan started to build from day one. But when a local community was the borrower, in Haussmann's day as in our own, it was not allowed to invest unused portions of the loan in a bank; it had no choice but to place them with the Treasury, where they earned an insignificant return and slept away the time until they were put to use. Any other procedure would require a para-municipal body that could borrow in accordance with current needs, instead of one which, as in the case of the city of Paris, floated a huge loan every four or five years and left most of it tied up at first in the Treasury.

The second reason for a special fund lay in the very nature of development projects. For Haussmann's *travaux* were spread over long periods of time: it was necessary to acquire land, either by private sale or by compulsory purchase, then to carry out the demolition work, to seek assistance from outside companies, and to launch the actual building works. All this involved successive expenditure. But money always came into the coffers in stages: demolition material could, by definition, be resold only after the demolition was complete; and building land on the new streets could be sold only once the work on them was over. Hence there was always a need to advance expenditure that would be offset by income only at a later date (with little chance, moreover, that the two would exactly balance). This was a crucial budgetary problem, especially if the city of Paris was pursuing projects under its own control.

The Caisse des Travaux was therefore called upon to play the role of a "second" municipal fund, specialized in the funding of exceptional public works. Where was the money to come from? It might be thought that the city itself would give it a major subsidy, and Haussmann did indeed allocate it an initial 20 million francs. But this sum, though large, fell a long way short of what was required. At this point in the sequence of ideas, the Seine prefect had only to take the further step of invoking the example of the Bakery Trade Fund, which had shown how easy it was for a municipal body to borrow money through a medium-term bond issue that carried weight with savers and basked in the longstanding reputation of good municipal management.

Haussmann went to explain all this to the emperor. He showed that a 130-million-franc loan, together with a ten-year phasing of the second system of works, would render the city incapable of budgeting for these operations unless it could rely on the existence of a special fund. The 180-million-franc agreement had given Haussmann the opportunity for which he had anyway been waiting, and it was also a point in his favor that the fund was in principle intended for projects connected with the second system. On November 19, 1858, after consultation with the Council of State, an imperial decree duly established the Caisse des Travaux de Paris to serve the requirements of the second system. On December 27 a further decree gave it financial autonomy from the Caisse Municipale de Paris by making it directly accountable to the National Audit Office. On January 6, 1859, a third decree specified the details of how the new service should be organized.

The precise functions of the Caisse des Travaux were to settle all the landowners' and tenants' compensation payments, either agreed privately or ordered through the courts, as a result of compulsory purchases or evictions connected with *grands travaux* in the city of Paris pursuant to laws, decrees, or ministerial authorizations; and to pay expenses of any kind related to such works. It also collected payments in respect to the sale of demolition material, and resold land surplus to requirements after the completion of public works. Any excess of expenditure over income was supposed to be paid out of credit balances in the budget of the city of Paris, on whose behalf the Caisse received and paid out all moneys. The Caisse issued bonds, similar to Treasury bonds, for a maximum term specified in each instance by a vote of the municipal council, within overall limits set for each financial year; final approval was required in the form of a vote in the Legislature on the general budget. The Caisse submitted to the Legislature all the necessary documents tracing its movement of funds and precisely identifying the public works operations in question. After the vote in the Legislature on the budget, it was up to the finance minister to approve each issue of bonds on the merits of the case. Interest payments and negotiation fees were payable by the city of Paris, as were the running costs of the Caisse itself.

The Caisse had a director. He was placed under the supervision of a committee similar in composition to the one for the Bakery Trade Fund, except that the three members of the departmental council were in this case replaced by three members of the Paris municipal council.

From January 3, 1859 (the day when it started operating) until December 31, 1869 (the eve of its abolition), the Caisse paid out on the city's behalf an average of 108 million francs a year—that is, a total of nearly 1.2 billion francs over a ten-year period, or 1,188,812,145 francs, to be completely precise. Expenditure on the second system accounted for a little over 411 million francs of this total. The funding was effected through the issue of duly authorized bonds.[21]

The Caisse, then, played quite a major role. Total road-building works carried out in old Paris under the Haussmann administration came to a sum of nearly 1.3 billion francs (or 1,297,445,134 francs, to be precise). Out of this, operations performed under contract accounted for a little under 500 million francs; all the rest, accounting for almost 800 million francs, was carried out under municipal control, with all the well-known risks that this involved for the city. The Caisse made it possible to spread the impact of these risks over a period of time. Moreover, total income from the reselling of materials and of surplus land came (very precisely) to 364,828,444 francs and 19 centimes. It was a fine result, but it had been necessary to support the works with additional financing, since the sums were received with sometimes quite a long interval after expenditure.

Though extremely useful for the *grands travaux*, the Caisse clearly exceeded its original brief of funding the operations of the second system. Haussmann took it upon himself to step outside the regulatory framework that he had himself called into being. Necessity knows no law, he would later argue; it was either that or a halt to the transformation of Paris. Such words still persuaded the man for whom they were mainly intended: Napoléon III. But how much longer would they continue to do so? And was Haussmann not risking too much by systematically flouting parliamentary and public opinion?

17

Incorporation of the Suburban Communes and the Third System

As THE *grands travaux* developed over the years, Haussmann seemed more and more puffed up with success, more and more domineering, his sights set on becoming "minister" for Paris. His methods were those of an autocrat, whereas the imperial regime itself was evolving toward a greater degree of liberalism. The Seine prefect's position grew daily more precarious. Napoléon III's support was not lacking, but he was a man weakened by illness and rebuffs whose ambitions were seeking fulfilment in the international arena. The victorious Italian campaign of 1859, which seemed to mark the apogée of imperial policy and coincided with Haussmann's greatest successes, turned out to be the prelude to later disappointments and failures.

ITALIAN MANEUVERS: MAGENTA AND SOLFERINO

☙ The beautiful Countess of Castiglione, who had Napoléon III under her spell, was enlisted by Cavour as early as 1856 in the cause of Italian unification. But it was Orsini's bombs that persuaded the emperor to act. Queen Victoria understood that his motive lay in a desire for revenge against the victors of 1815 combined with a fear of assassination.

On July 21, 1858, returning to his conspiratorial habits, Napoléon III had a four-hour meeting with Cavour at Plombières, in the Vosges Mountains. The emperor, who had not informed his government beforehand, promised France's military support in the event of an Austrian attack—and they agreed that one would be provoked. The future Italy would take the form of a confederation of three states: the North unified under Victor Emmanuel, whose kingdom of Piedmont-Sardinia would absorb the Austrian possessions of Lombardy and Venetia as well as the northern part of the papal states; Central Italy, including Tuscany and Umbria, which would be taken away from the sovereign pontiff; and the kingdom of Naples. The pope would reign over a rump state but in addition would exercise the presidency of the confederation. In return for its support, France would receive Nice and Savoy. Prince Napoléon-Jérôme would marry Clotilde, the daughter of Victor Emmanuel; Napoléon III defended the prince, whose morals were not his strong point, and argued that he had been faithful to his mistresses and would make a good husband.

Over the next few weeks, in a sign of a change of policy toward the Holy See, newspapers close to the regime suddenly let loose against pontifical obscurantism in connection with the Mortara affair, so called after the Jewish child in Bologna who had been secretly baptized by his Catholic servant, taken away from his family, and hidden in a convent.

French diplomats busied themselves securing the tsar's benevolent neutrality, even though this meant postponing the dream of Polish emancipation. Napoléon III had less success with Prussia, whose king was distrustful of his adventurous spirit, and with the British, who were furious at the prospect of the upheavals he was preparing. But Queen Victoria's pleas failed to move him, and on December 10, 1858, he signed a treaty of alliance with Piedmont confirming the Plombières accords and promising the dispatch of 200,000 men to Italy. At a reception for the diplomatic corps on January 1, 1859, Napoléon III said in response to the greetings of the Austrian ambassador Hübner: "I regret that our relations with your government are not as good as in the past, but I would ask you to tell the emperor that my personal sentiments have not changed." A threat or a blunder? Whichever it was, the Bourse and business circles panicked. A few days later, in a speech from the throne whose wording had been seen and corrected by Napoléon III, he declared that he could not remain insensitive to the "cry of pain" reaching him from so many parts of Italy. Napoléon-Jérôme left to get married in Turin—accompanied by General Niel, who took the opportunity to evaluate the Piedmontese forces.

Napoléon III, who knew all about campaigns to influence public opinion, prompted a brochure *L'Empereur Napoléon III et l'Italie*, which explained that Napoleon I had thought it necessary to conquer other nations to free them, whereas his nephew aimed to free them without conquest. At the same time, however, Morny reminded his half-brother the emperor that peace was the primary good in modern societies and that "rapid international communications and publicity have created a new European power with which all governments are forced to reckon: the power of public opinion." Opinion, he continued, "may waver or stray for a moment, but it will eventually side with justice, legality, and humanity." Neither Morny's warnings nor the threats issued by the States of Southern Germany (which spoke of attacking Alsace if France moved against Austria) altered the emperor's resolve.

Britain then offered to mediate. Indeed, an international congress seemed to be in prospect when Austria rejected the proposal from London and, on April 23, suddenly issued an ultimatum requiring Piedmont to disarm. The next day, troops were already embarking at the Gare de Lyon, cheered on by the faubourg Saint-Antoine where the war of liberation was very popular. On May 3, Napoléon III declared in a message to the nation: "I do not wish for conquest . . . ; the aim of this war is to give Italy back to itself." And with his eye on Catholics, he added: "We are going to Italy not in order to sow disorder or to weaken the power of the Holy Father, but to shield it from any foreign pressure." On May 10 he rode through a capital decked with flags and himself set off from the Gare de Lyon for Marseilles and Genoa.

There had been a complete lack of preparation for the war. France twice defeated the Austrian armies—on June 4, 1859, at Magenta, and on June 24 at Solferino—and between the two battles, on June 8, Napoléon III made a triumphant entry into Milan alongside Victor Emmanuel. But the attitude of the Germans gave him cause for concern. In the days following Solferino he proposed an armistice to the Austrians, who accepted it on July 7. Britain and the tsar pressed him to negotiate, while his Piedmontese ally displayed appetites pointing well beyond the Plombières accords. Besides, the French victories had been costly; the emperor was deeply shaken by the sight of battlefields strewn with dead and wounded.

Franz-Joseph said he was willing to talk with Napoléon III, and a meeting between the two men on July 11, at Villafranca, resulted in an agreement. Austria ceded Lombardy to France, which would hand it over to Piedmont. Franz-Joseph held on to Venetia, with a promise of major reforms. Otherwise the Italian confederation planned by Napoléon III came into being under the presidency of the pope, who also undertook to introduce liberal reforms. The Italians felt swindled. Cavour, whom Napoléon III would not even receive, promptly resigned. On July 15 the emperor rode through Turin, where the shop windows had been decorated with pictures of Orsini. Victor Emmanuel tried to put on a good show by instructing policemen and hired extras to applaud Napoléon III.

On July 17, back in Paris, the emperor was not exactly happy with himself, and he naturally refrained from demanding the cession of Nice and Savoy. But public opinion was proud of the army's exploits and satisfied with the swift end to hostilities; the Bourse began to rise again. On August 14, 100,000 soldiers who had been in Italy paraded through the streets of Paris. At the Bastille the prefect's technical staff had erected triumphal arches symbolizing Milan Cathedral. At Place Vendôme, where Haussmann had deployed his stage arts to full effect, Napoléon III received the army banners in homage and was congratulated by his generals. Windows overlooking the square were rented out for 600 francs, balconies for between 1,500 and 2,000 francs. In the evening a banquet at the Louvre brought together the emperor and 300 leading military officers. The next day, August 15, Pont Solferino and the Square Louvois were officially inaugurated, and a decree was published whereby anyone sentenced for a political offense was given a full amnesty.

REDEVELOPMENT OF THE CHAMPS ÉLYSÉES

⪻ While the emperor was off in Italy and Eugénie was exercising his powers in France, Haussmann managed to make some progress with a number of projects—even if he thought that the empress's inexperience and lack of firm resolve occasionally clipped his wings. The prefect also took the opportunity to settle accounts with Hittorff once again.

In 1828 the city of Paris acquired ownership of the Champs Élysées, except for the so-called "Chaillot promenade" running up the left side of the avenue from the Rond-Point to the Place de l'Étoile. Cession of this space was in turn authorized on certain conditions, and with certain charges, under a law of the prince president on July 8, 1852, and an imperial law of June 22, 1854. In return the French state regained provisional ownership of the Carré Marigny for the construction of the Palace of Industry.

The Promenade des Champs Élysées, the great rectangular space between the Place de la Concorde and the Rond-Point des Champs Élysées, had been laid out long before Napoléon III appeared on the scene. The planting of trees in alternate rows corresponded to a design already worked out under Louis XIV. The elms charged with history had witnessed the parades of Napoleon I's victorious armies, then suffered the humiliation of sheltering Cossack tents in 1814, and British and Prussian tents in 1815, which had certainly not left them in better shape than before. In 1817, Louis XVIII ordered some of the most visible damage to be repaired, and a row of chestnut trees was planted on either side of the great square. The Cours-la-Reine was also laid out around that time.

During the reign of Louis-Philippe, Hittorff was appointed architect for the Champs Élysées following his work on the Place de la Concorde. In June 1838 he handed Rambuteau a design for fountains on the promenade as well as a plan for new buildings. In May 1839, Hittorff's Théâtre du Panorama des Champs-Élysées was opened near the Rond-Point, on the corner of the Avenue d'Antin (now Avenue Franklin Roosevelt, south side), and two years later the Winter Circus was in place opposite it. Cafés and restaurants licensed by the city of Paris sprang up on both sides of the promenade. But lawns and trees came under growing pressure from strollers and the merry-making clients of the places of entertainment. There came a time when the planted areas had to be given a serious facelift.

Taking advantage of the Italian campaign that had drawn Napoléon III outside France, Haussmann decided to bring the *promenade* more into line with how he thought it should look, at the same time inflicting a fresh humiliation on the detested Hittorff. "I took it upon myself to authorize the removal of the withering trees that had remained in those damp rows. I had the large areas of newly cleared ground placed under the cover of undulating turf, clumps of choice trees and shrubs, and round beds of greenery and flowers. I also distributed a number of fountains to freshen the air with their tiered sheets of spouting water."[1] Just in case the point was not understood, he added: "M. Hittorff had nothing to do with the transformation of the Champs Élysées, which came four years after that of the Place de la Concorde."[2] Revenge is one of those dishes that can be eaten cold again and again.

"It was a surprise for the victorious sovereign to discover this unexpected change in the scenery fully complete by the time of his return."[3] As for surprises, the emperor was greatly annoyed at the sidelining of Hittorff, who had been due to supervise the work in question. More generally, he found to his displeasure that the prefect had become a little too sure of himself and tended to do as he pleased as soon as the master was away. Napoléon III did not make the slightest reference to the incident. But "it was a meaningful silence on his part, concerning as it did a major operation accomplished entirely during his absence."[4] As ever, Haussmann was a good judge of the little signs that weave the fabric of everyday life for a senior civil servant.

The prefect's revenge for the imperial ill humor was the satisfaction of being able to contemplate in later years a renovated area of forty-six acres, decorated with fine chestnut trees and interspersed with theatres, cafés, and restaurants constantly buzzing with activity. The cost of the operation—1 million francs—was largely offset by the value of these businesses operating under municipal license. The Champs Élysées had become a nonstop show that Parisians of all social classes put on for themselves. But it may be that Haussmann's tactless behavior was one of the reasons why the emperor refused to grant his ambition by appointing him "minister for Paris" in 1860.

THE ENLARGEMENT OF PARIS

🙠 Under the July Monarchy, Thiers had decided as president of the Council of Ministers to surround the capital with a line of fortifications (1841–1844), and since then the question had been posed of incorporating into Paris those communes or part-communes contained between the fortified line and the wall of the Farmers-General that communicated with the region beyond only by means of gates under military guard. Many wanted to move the tollhouses out to the new line and to incorporate all the space within it into the municipality of Paris. But not everyone agreed. Rambuteau, for one, was proud to have blocked the extension of Paris during his term as Seine prefect. "The municipal council demanded many times the incorporation of the communes located between the two lines," he wrote in his *Mémoires.* "I never gave my consent to this."

Napoléon III also dreamed of annexing the suburban communes. It seemed a rational course of action, but it also had some drawbacks. For the inhabitants of the communes, the cost of living was lower because they received all their supplies from the countryside at significantly less than the Paris rate of taxation; and industries could draw upon cheaper labor and raw materials. For the city of Paris, on the other hand, the incorporation process would obviously come with a high price tag, as it would be necessary to pay compensation for a potentially lengthy period of transition and to bear the costs of providing these areas with urban facilities such as streets similar to those in central Paris, complete with planted and illuminated sidewalks, gas and water pipes, drains and sewers. New buildings would have to be found for administrative, educational, and ecclesiastical purposes, as well as extra staff for the servicing and administration of the new parts of the capital.

A commission was appointed by Napoléon III in 1856 to survey the problems posed by extension, to define the new city limits, and to prepare a list of the measures that needed to be taken. Chaired by Haussmann, this commission included Delangle (the public attorney at Royer's Court of Cassation), various members of the Council of State, one senator, and Devinck, chairman of the municipal council's finance committee. The sessions of the commission lasted from April to June, but its final recommendations did not choose between incorporation of the whole area between the fortified line and the wall of the Farmers-General, and incorporation only of the communes of Les Ternes, Passy, and Auteuil, with or without the Bois de Boulogne. Haussmann passed on the commission's reports to the emperor. They are documents "of unique interest . . . because of the psychological testimony they give us, especially about the mentality of these leading civil servants—which reflected the opinion of many of their contemporaries, the opinion of suburbs that needed Paris and were above all needed by it, and for that very reason were destined to remain different from Paris."[5]

At the beginning of 1859, the emperor asked Delangle—by now minister of the interior—to draft a new memorandum on whether incorporation should go ahead. Delangle's text, which amounted to an enthusiastic plea in favor, was published in Le Moniteur on February 12. Napoléon III was won over. A decree on February 9 had already ordered the opening of a public inquiry in all the town halls of the Seine department. On March 7 the municipal councils of the communes in question gathered at a special meeting, and on March 11, Haussmann presented the results of the inquiry to the Paris municipal council. He underlined the problem that the presence of 350,000 people at the gates of Paris posed for public order—a mass barely integrated at an administrative level, and including as many poor people as were to be found in the whole of Paris but with a population three times smaller. "An industrial city comprising eighteen distinct communes has established itself as a dangerous belt around the capital; it profits from the schools, hospitals, and theatres and all the other advantages of its neighbor, without paying local duties or bearing the costs." On March 14 the district councils of Saint-Denis and Sceaux began debating the issue in their turn.

The Seine departmental council held a special meeting at the end of March. Haussmann commented on the votes that had come in from the municipal councils, two of which—in Bercy and La Villette—were against the incorporation project. He made the following analysis of the widespread unease about the level of duties. "It should first be pointed out, with regard to the workers, that many have their dwelling place on one side of the *barrière* and their work and eating place on the other side. A large number lodge outside, enter Paris every morning, and leave only in the evening; others reside in the city's inner *faubourgs* and go off to spend the day in the outer railway stations, on the suburban building sites that have been springing up everywhere in recent years, or in the numerous factories or various workshops that are contained in the suburbs. It would appear that, in choosing to live in Paris or outside the *barrières*, the worker's main concern is the size of his rent, and that he remains convinced that this choice has little impact on the price of items that he consumes alone or as part of a family."

The draft law on incorporation was adopted by the Council of State on April 30, 1859, and passed to the Legislature on May 3. The parliamentary opposition criticized only the cost of extending the city limits, not the basis of the law itself, and it was duly enacted on May 26 by 228 votes to 13. It was the spring when Napoléon III was off campaigning in Italy, but the machinery did not slow. On June 6 the Senate cast all its 91 votes in favor. The law was signed by the empress on June 16 and promulgated on November 3, 1859. The administrative incorporation was immediate; the extension of the city taxes took effect on January 1, 1860.

NEW DIMENSIONS

❧ The incorporation of the suburban communes had important consequences for the development of the capital. The population of Paris increased by a third over the previous total of 1.2 million, in an area that more than doubled. Many empty spaces could thus either go to waste through incompetent management or, on the contrary, be intelligently organized by means of extensive road-building, the provision of new facilities, and the harmonious allocation of areas for housing, trade, leisure, and other activities.

A glance at today's inner Paris shows that major projects are reshaping, and will continue to reshape for some years to come, vast areas of the 13th, 15th, 18th, and 19th arrondissements. The whole northern fringe of the city remains to be conquered. A century and a half after they fused administratively with the central part of Paris, the so-called peripheral arrondissements have not ceased to form a distinct spatial and sociological entity within the capital. With hindsight it is easier to understand the huge challenge that faced Haussmann's administration and those that succeeded it. How much time and money were necessary for Paris to integrate those outlying communes dotted with farms, dairies, and market gardens, that disparate collection of urban islands within vast rural territories?

When Louis-Napoléon had been in his London exile, he had not thought of extending the city limits of Paris. His famous color-coded map remained inside the wall of the Farmers-General, except for the future Avenue de l'Impératrice linking the Étoile *barrière* to the Bois de Boulogne in the "foreign" territory beyond the fortifications. In his time at the Gironde prefecture, however, Haussmann had been able to gauge the advantages of aggrandizement for the city of Bordeaux; he was therefore already convinced of the need to do the same in Paris.

In the eyes of the law, the Paris municipal boundaries were fixed at the foot of the glacis on the outer side of the fortifications. One must imagine what the 459-foot-wide enclosure was like. It began almost in the middle of today's outer boulevards, with the military road that ran along inside for nearly its entire length. Next came the terreplein of the rampart, strengthened at regular intervals by bastions, and then a 131-foot-wide ditch (just 66 feet forward of the bastions). In front of the ditch rose a lawned embankment, the counterscarp, with a path on its inner side that allowed people to move under cover. On the outer side, the counterscarp sloped gently back down to the ground by means of a glacis.

In 1861, Haussmann doubled the width of the military road and thereby turned it into a ring of boulevards surrounding the city—the *boulevards des maréchaux*, as they were known, because they bore the names of the marshals of the First Empire. (Many years later, the law of 1919 authorizing demolition of the fortifications made it possible to widen the boulevards at the expense of the old enclosure.)

Haussmann would have liked to extend the Paris city limits by another 820 feet by encompassing the zone *non aedificandi*. Napoléon III planned to build a wide ring road on this land that would allow goods to be transported around Paris when there was no good reason for them to pass through it. The emperor also thought of adding to it a tree-lined promenade for the benefit of the neighboring communes. But as we have seen, Baroche took advantage of Napoléon III's absence (and Eugénie's lack of experience and authority) to defeat the project in the Council of Ministers.

Haussmann moved quickly to demolish the wall of the Farmers-General and to widen the outer boulevards. In 1860 there were still fifty-six toll barriers in place, most of them lodges built by the architect Ledoux between 1784 and 1789.[6] All that escaped destruction were the two lodges on Place Denfert-Rochereau, the so-called Chartres roundhouse located at the entrance to Monceau Park, the roundhouse of La Villette, and the two lodges on the Place du Trône (Place de la Nation). A square "toll lodge" also survived at the beginning of the Quai de la Rapée, virtually in the foundations of the finance ministry; it had been built to replace a circular building that went back a century to the time of Ledoux.

The incorporation process involved eleven whole communes: Auteuil, Passy, Batignolles-Monceau, Montmartre, La Chapelle, La Villette, Belleville, Charonne, and Bercy on the right bank, Grenelle and Vaugirard on the left bank. It also took in thirteen part-communes and severed them from their former administrative center: Les Ternes (which belonged to the town of Neuilly), Saint-Mandé (dependent on Vincennes), the Gare *quartier* (formerly part of Ivry), La Maison Blanche and La Glacière (dependent on Gentilly), Le Petit-Montrouge (part of the commune of Montrouge), Le Pré-Saint-Gervais, and pieces from the communes of Clichy, Saint-Ouen, Aubervilliers, Pantin, Vanves, Bagnolet, and Issy.

To appease industrialists in the areas newly incorporated into Paris, Haussmann agreed to keep business taxes at the old rate for five years and to allow a a kind of bonded goods option for ten years whereby products could be brought in duty-free for assembly, packaging, and subsequent dispatch outside the area.

TOWARD A GREATER PARIS?

✍ The ambition of Napoléon III and Haussmann was to achieve a much greater extension of the city limits. In their view, it would be natural for the capital to expand throughout the territory of the Seine department and at some points even beyond it.

They enlisted figures in support of their analysis. At the time of the incorporation of the suburban communes, the Paris within the wall of the Farmers-General covered an area of 12.7 square miles and had an official population of 1,174,246 (although the real total was certainly above 1.2 million). The territory destined for incorporation measured 14.7 square miles and had a population of 331,593 according to the 1856 census (although Haussmann put it closer to 400,000). On January 1, 1860, the enlarged city therefore formed a concentration of 1.6 million inhabitants over an area of 27.4 square miles. Haussmann thought it could hold 3.5 million people without difficulty, in "well built, well aired [*quartiers*] in which it was easy to move around."[7]

The population in the areas of the department outside Paris, which comprised 80 communes before the incorporation and 69 after, was obviously smaller but was nevertheless growing at a rapid rate. In fact it had just doubled in five years, from 135,011 in 1851 to 201,480 in 1856—a gain of 66,469, or 49 percent. One year after the extension of the city limits, census figures showed that the total population in the area in question was 257,519, representing a further growth of 26 percent since 1856. By 1866 it had climbed to 325,642—up another 68,123 (or 21 percent) in the space of five years. In 1870 there was no census, but the population of these 69 communes had increased by a further 55,000 and was by then in the area of 380,000. During the intervening four years, the population of Paris also increased, though much more slowly. The 1861 census counted 1,696,141 inhabitants within the new city limits; the figure for 1866 was 1,825,271 (a rise of 129,130, or 8 percent, over five years); and the estimate for 1870 was 2 million (which would have meant a sharp increase on the order of 175,000 over the previous four years).[8]

Despite the growth of the other communes, the weight of Paris within the Seine population as a whole was quite overwhelming. In 1856 the capital (within its 1860 limits) had roughly 68 percent of the total population of the department; by 1861 the figure had risen to 86.82 percent. The same picture emerges from a comparison of tax figures: Parisians accounted for 90 percent of total tax revenues in the Seine department.

This did not prevent (nor was Haussmann surprised by) very rapid population growth in the 69 communes outside Paris. For the outer arrondissements of Paris itself accommodated over time new settlers drawn by the relatively cheap land and rents, and now that these districts were being administratively absorbed into the capital, at a time when prosperity and the effects of the *grands travaux* were driving up the cost of living there, the outer communes answered the same need for cheaper rents and consumption prices.

Haussmann's conclusion was that these communes should have been included in an expansion of Paris that took in the whole area of the Seine department, involving the creation of eight additional arrondissements. But this project, which the emperor had thought of forcing through since 1858, encountered firm opposition from a large part of his own entourage. Haussmann's enemies could see that such an enlargement of Paris would inevitably make its prefect-mayor a figure with ministerial rank.

Napoléon III even contemplated casting the net wider and incorporating a number of communes from Seine-et-Oise, such as Saint-Cloud, Sèvres, and Meudon, in compensation for which he would have transferred to Seine-et-Oise a few communes in the north of the Seine region far from Paris. How did Haussmann think these schemes of aggrandizement could be reconciled with the fact that the attraction of the outer communes was precisely their *non*-integration into Paris and its tax regime? Was he so dead set against the poor and so determined to drive them farther out? He claimed that this was not at all the case. Communes outside the existing Paris enclosure, he argued, would still have a lower flat-rate duty that retained the benefits gained by their inhabitants and businesses; they would not suffer financially, and indeed could only profit, from a suppression of the sixty-nine internal duty regimes.

RURAL LANDSCAPES AND INDUSTRIALISM

Some of the newly incorporated communes were villages with a rural landscape that had already been vitiated by industrial activity. Labédollière was full of praise for the banks of the Bièvre in what became the 13th arrondissement: "A stroller coming from rue Mouffetard who turns right onto the rue du Petit-Gentilly is suddenly faced with one of the most beautiful landscapes in Paris. He has before him a valley watered by the Bièvre but is not yet close enough to breathe its harmful and nauseating emanations; washerwomen hang out laundry on pegs in the meadows bordering the river; cows graze as in the heart of the countryside; here and there, in gardens planted in the eighteenth century by wealthy gentlemen seeking pleasure and repose in these distant *quartiers*, the verdant tops of fruit trees rise up or the remnants of their many arbors continue to form arches of greenery. The tanneries dotted around the area, with their skylight attics, resemble Italian villas; the valley rises again a kilometer or so from the spot where we imagine the observer to be placed. The imposing lines of the Manufacture des Gobelins look down upon a mass of roofs, most of them degraded by time. Standing out against the sky above the houses are the Observatory, the domes of the Val de Grâce hospital and the church of Sainte-Geneviève [the Pantheon], the bells of Saint-Jacques du Haut Pas and Saint-Étienne du Mont, and the tower of the Lycée Napoléon [Henri IV]. We could not recommend this view too highly to travelers; it deserves to be better known."[9]

In the little village of Auteuil, Boileau's house was still the rustic villa of the seventeenth century: "Who has not halted with emotion before the house in which Boileau used to live, still so evocative of the past? As you look around it, you think you can still hear echoing in your ear . . . the arduously flowing verses that Despréaux composed beneath a large chestnut tree opposite the door."[10] Auteuil had a population of 4,982 on the eve of its attachment to Paris.

As to Passy, it was still a spa at that time. "The location of Passy would have alone sufficed to heighten its importance, but its main attraction for many Parisians and strangers to the area was the discovery in 1658 of two hot springs. Within a very short time the south slope and summit of the hill were covered with pretty houses. . . . The waters of Passy, which drew good society to the area, were on land owned by Baron Delessert. The garden where they flowed amid lawn and flowers was huge, wooded, punctuated with shady paths—a little Eden for those who came to drink. There were many English people among them: an enchanting view, healthy air, and the proximity of the Bois de Boulogne even led quite a few of those island folk to stay in Passy for the winter. In this well-built neighborhood, with its population of scarcely more than 2,400, the main street chiefly consisted of houses that were not a whit less elegant than those of the *beaux quartiers* of Paris."[11] Yes, that is right: there were just 2,400 people living there when these lines were written in 1836. But growth was then rapid. By 1841 the population had reached 4,545, rising to 7,000 during the summer months. In 1851 it was 11,431, and by the time of its incorporation into Paris it stood at 17,594.

Belleville still had only 7,728 residents in 1841; it was a village. Visitors were shown the tavern from which Cartouche, the famous local leader of a gang of thieves, was taken away and broken upon the wheel in 1721 on the Place de Grève; the establishment was later taken over by the restaurateur Ramponneau, who came to settle there in 1760. The past of Belleville also included the descent at daybreak with the eccentric Milord l'Arsouille from the Courtille, an enchanting retreat described by the poet Grandval in 1721:

Dans le nombre infini de ces réduits charmants,
Lieux où finit la ville et commencent les champs,
Il est une guinguette au bord d'une onde pure,
Où l'art a joint ses soins à ceux de la nature.
Là tous les environs, embellis d'arbres verts,
Offrent contre le chaud mille berceaux couverts. . . .
C'est le charmant réduit qu'on nomme la Courtille,
Lieu fatal à l'honneur de mainte et mainte fille!*

---

*In the infinite number of these charming nooks, / Places where the city ends and the fields begin, / There is a dance café beside waters pure, / Where art has joined its attentions to those of nature. / There all the surroundings, embellished by green trees, / Offer a thousand arbors against the heat of the day. . . . / It is the charming retreat called the Little Court, / So deadly to the honor of maiden upon maiden!

In 1826 the authors of *Vie publique et privée des Français* painted a more seemly picture: "La Courtille is the venue for nearly all the wedding feasts of the petty bourgeoisie, small-scale merchants, and workmen from areas of the capital adjoining this *barrière* and even as far as the right bank of the Seine." The 1856 census gave Belleville a population of 57,699, making it the most populous of the newly incorporated communes. Its residents would have liked it to form an arrondissement of its own within the new Parisian area, but Haussmann divided it in two so that the boundary between the 19th and 20th arrondissements ran down the middle of the rue de Belleville.

Some suburban communes were highly industrialized. Les Batignolles, for example, which still had a residential character near the outer boulevards, contained major factories in the Épinettes area: the Ateliers des Batignolles employed two thousand workers in 1856. At Vaugirard the Javel factories were well-known for their chemical products, especially the eponymous water. At La Chapelle and La Villette the railways had brought the development of numerous workshops. La Villette, with its river port, had ten thousand workers out of a population of thirty thousand. The commune protested against its incorporation into Paris on the grounds that no fewer than seventeen industrial groups would have to fear for their survival. Labédollière mentions in no particular order the production of candles, soap and perfume factories, glassworks and crystal factories, timber yards, ironworks, rolling mills and foundries, coach factories (producing three to four thousand a year), the Érard piano manufacturer, bone black makers, breweries, distilleries (sixty to eighty, employing more than a thousand workers), salt refineries, factories producing matches, metal pens, and so on.

LONG LIVE THE ARRONDISSEMENT!

🙠 The newly incorporated communes would have to bow to the discipline characteristic of the capital's administration, and in particular to fit into the framework of its arrondissements (whose number would obviously have to increase). Haussmann was not hostile to the maintenance of certain communal structures within the new Paris. The *mairie* of Montrouge thus became the *mairie* of the 14th arrondissement; that of Vaugirard was allocated to the 15th, that of Les Batignolles to the 17th, and that of Belleville to the 20th.

The extension of the city limits made it necessary to redivide the arrondissements and to increase their number from twelve to twenty. The time had come to do away with the illogical older pattern. Haussmann drew up a checkered plan—with smaller, less populous squares in the center and larger ones on the periphery—which aroused hardly any opposition. But residents of Passy were up in arms about his proposal to place them in the new 13th arrondissement, largely because "getting married at the registry office in the [nonexistent] 13th" had previously been a jocular way of referring to non-marital cohabitation. Possoz, the mayor of Passy, protested to Haussmann, who agreed to revise the numbering if a coherent justification could be given for the whole system. After several sleepless nights, Possoz came up with a numbering system that started from the 1st arrondissement where all the imperial palaces were located—honor to whom honor was due—and spiraled round clockwise so that the 13th fell in the east while Passy and Auteuil together formed the 16th.

The Paris municipal council was also reorganized to take account of the newly incorporated communes. It increased in size from thirty-six to sixty members, all still appointed, of course. At the same time Haussmann sought to enhance the role of the arrondissements. He had noticed on a trip to England that the London boroughs each had their own largely independent administration and indeed were so distinct from one another that Queen Victoria was starting to take control of services such as the police and sanitation that needed to be organized citywide. Paris, by contrast, had gone toward extreme centralization, and it was this which Haussmann tried to moderate by establishing in the law of incorporation that each arrondissement must have two councillors sitting on the municipal council. Forty seats were thus allocated in advance; the remaining twenty came under the discretion of the central government, which would have to balance things out so that each arrondissement was represented in accordance with the size of its population. This rule was not so easy to enforce, however, "partly because some arrondissements did not have enough candidates with real housing of their own, while others concentrated most of the prominent figures in each category; partly because the changes of residence that were so common in Paris constantly disturbed the sought-after equilibrium."[12]

On the occasion of the renewal process in 1869, Haussmann prided himself on having composed a municipal council in which the representation of the various arrondissements was perfectly balanced. It "limited to a maximum of four members the representation of the more populous arrondissements, the ones with the most interests to defend and the most candidates to present, while availing itself of the right to reduce to a minimum of two the representation of those least well endowed in the latter respect." Nor did Haussmann neglect (indeed, he tried "to apply more fully") the "excellent rule" that "positions in the municipal Senate of the great city should be allocated to the largest possible number of constituted bodies and of different social situations."[13] Haussmann's eventual aim was to organize arrondissement councils, separate from the municipal council, which would have their own powers and train people to operate efficently as members of the broader municipal council.[14]

"PARIS BELONGS TO FRANCE"

Although Haussmann was anxious to develop forms of local democracy, he remained fiercely opposed to a regime for Paris with a basis in common law—that is, with an elected municipal council and a central mayor, such as existed in other parts of France. He explained his view on a number of occasions. Paris was not a commune like the rest, since the capital was the collective property of the whole country. Paris belonged to France, not to Parisians either by birth or by adoption, and still less to "the changeable population living there in lodgings, which distorts the meaning of ballots by casting unintelligent votes, that crowd of nomads—to use an expression held against me but in my view correct—whose best members go to the big city in search of more or less regular work but remain attached to their place of origin and intend to return when the right moment comes."[15]

On November 14, 1859, Haussmann spelled out his vision of the capital at the ceremonial opening of the sixty-member municipal council that had just been expanded under the law of incorporation. "Although Paris is a great city, a center of commercial and industrial activity in its own right, as well as of special lines of production, prodigious consumption, and ceaseless trade, it is above all the capital of a mighty empire, the residence of a glorious sovereign, the seat of all the bodies through which power is exercised in France, the universal home for literature, the sciences, and the arts."[16] It was therefore normal that the state should directly intervene in the affairs of Paris. The central government did a great deal for the capital: it created and maintained historic buildings and museums, participated in the policing of the city, and subsidized municipal activities that were beyond the resources of the city alone.

In 1864 the municipal council underwent important changes. Haussmann repeated the principles underlying Paris's special status for the benefit of council members—and for a public opinion worked upon by the republicans and supporters of a liberal empire grouped around Prince Napoléon-Jérôme. As everyone knew, the special status had been established by law: the emperor appointed the members of the Paris municipal council, as also of municipal councils in all the communes of the Seine department, thereby affirming the specificity of the region around the capital. The special status existed because the 2 million inhabitants of Paris were not united by one civic link or common origin. "Most of them belong to other departments, many to foreign lands in which they still have their kith and kin, their most cherished interests, and often the greater part of their wealth. For them Paris is like a great consumption market, an immense workplace, an arena for personal ambitions, or simply a meeting place for pleasure. It is not their country."[17]

Not without a certain eloquence, the prefect describes young people flocking from far and wide to follow courses in finance, trade, and industry at the Grandes Écoles and various faculties, then setting off again with what they have learned to build their lives elsewhere. For most of them Paris was a place through which they merely passed. Hundreds of thousands of workers also streamed into Paris in search of high wages, hoping to save up a nest egg for retirement in their own or another region. Some managed to climb the social ladder, perhaps even to the highest echelons of society, while all too many others were tossed from workshop to workshop, lodging house to lodging house, veritable nomads often forced to knock on the door of relief committees. Civil servants moved from the provinces to the heart of the political administration; men of intelligence came to conquer fame or fortune, a precious acquisition for the life of the capital. Shining less brightly were the new arrivals who had come down in the world—inventors of fanciful schemes, unscrupulous adventurers driven to the great city by the need to be forgotten and a desire to find new dupes.

Genuine Parisians existed, but they were a minority in the city. How were they to be identified? How could they be attached to a particular arrondissement, to the bells of a parish, when each of them moved house and neighborhood with the greatest of ease and when families often scattered to the four corners of Paris? How could one think of applying a system of universal suffrage to these unlocatable Parisians, or of trusting them with the defense of communal interests impossible to identify?

Paris was the fruit of centralization, the child of governments that over the centuries had made it the soul of France. Paris was also centralization itself, the place where "opinion, with its understanding and sudden insights and often also its errors and aberrations, sprang up from one hour to the next and exerted an irresistible influence into the distant future."[18] To imagine that it could form a state within the state was therefore unacceptable. The history of France provided many disastrous examples of the consequences of autonomy; the United States of America, on the other hand, furnished an opposite example in Washington, D.C., which was considered the common property of all the states and not a state in itself.

Haussmann did not shrink from any of the consequences of this irresistible logic, and in particular insisted that the examination and approval of the Paris budget should be "a matter for the whole nation" through its Legislature. "If Paris belongs to the whole of France," he wrote, "it is up to the Legislature representing France to ratify all the taxes of every kind that the inhabitants of this city of all French people should have to pay every year."[19] If Haussmann failed to gain acceptance for this idea—or for the extension of Paris to the limits of the Seine department—this was because the political class (especially within the central government) saw it as a clever maneuver cooked up by a prefect well known for his guile and obstinacy in order to strengthen the case for a special minister in charge of Paris. Most historians have also questioned Haussmann's good faith. It is true that Georges-Eugène, with typical self-assurance, never failed to argue that a national parliamentary vote on plans and budgets pertaining to Paris would inevitably strengthen his hand "against the bunch of pygmies at the ministry of the interior, whose authority over the Hôtel de Ville had been growing purely nominal."[20] He could hardly have made himself clearer.

Despite the lack of support for his proposal, Haussmann returned indefatigably to the charge. On May 20, 1868, in a report to the emperor, he again pointed out that he had been fighting in vain for many years to ensure that there was some legal sanction for the Paris budget. Yet such a reform would have many advantages. This time he did not mention any pygmies, but he did produce another argument from his box of tricks. Such a reform, he said, "mainly had the great merit of putting an end to the traditional antagonism of the provinces toward Paris, and of replacing it with better and juster impressions of solidarity."[21]

Paradoxically, the difficulties that Haussmann would encounter on all sides in 1869 in connection with his financial acrobatics eventually led in part to the reform for which he had so long battled. But what a different context it was then! The imperial government threw some ballast overboard amid the storm and undertook to have future extraordinary budgets for Paris (its investment budget) voted on by the Legislature. Haussmann was living his final months at the Hôtel de Ville, and the Second Empire itself was not to last much longer. The tempestuous events of 1870–1871 would then sweep away a project that might once have been a considerable advance but was suddenly without a future.

THE DIVISION OF RESPONSIBILITIES WITH
THE *PRÉFECTURE DE POLICE*

❧ In parallel with the extension of Paris, a solution was at last found for the thorny problem of a division of tasks between the Seine prefecture and the *préfecture de police*. For too many years, sordid neighbors' quarrels had pitted the two against each other. Inquiries and working groups had been set up to devise a more logical distribution, and the Seine prefect seemed indisputably better in the daily running of the city. Yet it was all continuing to drag on, despite the urgency of the issue. In many areas the existing situation produced quite surreal results. For example, the new roads in Paris were "macadamized" in accordance with the emperor's liking for this originally English process. But this meant they had to be cleaned and sprinkled with the utmost care, as heavy-handed treatment might make the surface fall apart in a downpour, and excessive watering during dry weather might transform it into mud. Responsibility for these tasks was therefore given to the *préfecture de police*. But day after day, Haussmann's engineers complained that the men working for the police department took malicious pleasure in degrading the road surfaces with inappropriate methods and deliberately wasted precious water during periods of shortage.

Maintenance of the drains and sewers also fell to the *préfecture de police*. Haussmann made many vain efforts to introduce sluice-boats so that the sewers would be cleared by the simple flow of water, as in the system he had observed in the Blaye marshes. But the *préfecture de police* preferred to continue the age-old system of sludge clearance with buckets, which hired hands brought to the surface along pulleys delicately supported on three poles as dangerous to the workers as they were to public health.

Street lighting was another example of incoherence. Haussmann's engineers directed the laying of gas pipes and the installation and maintenance of lampposts, but the lighting and cleaning of the actual lamps was the responsibility of the *préfecture de police*. Haussmann went to enormous trouble to win acceptance for the cheaper and more efficient gas lamp developed by Dumas. Again, in the case of street markets and covered halls, the Seine prefect's departments had nothing to do with stall allocation and charging; it was the *préfecture de police* that collected the various fees. All this was completely illogical and a source of endless conflict between the two prefectures, so that the head of state invariably had to act as umpire and settle the matter himself.

Napoléon III had introduced some much-needed reforms in 1856. But ill will on Pietri's part, as well as veiled opposition from Interior Minister Billault, kept progress at a snail's pace. In the fall of 1857, Billault warned Haussmann in a letter not to keep calling on the emperor at every turn. Then Napoléon III decided to put an end to the situation. Orsini's attempt on his life, which led to Pietri's replacement by Boittelle at the *préfecture de police*, made things easier. And the appointment of Delangle as the new interior minister speeded up the drafting of a decree, which the emperor wished to be examined with some urgency after his return from Italy. Napoléon III put pressure on the Council of State, where Baroche as ever was merrily dragging out the debates, and on October 10, 1859 he was able to sign a decree that restored to the Seine prefecture the administrative functions transferred to the *préfecture de police* some sixty years earlier, on 12 Messidor, Year VIII. These functions concerned street lighting, road cleaning, sewer clearance, the emptying of cesspools, fares on public carriages, the calculation and collection of municipal taxes, the bakery and butchery trades, supplies, the allocation of contracts, and so on.

ADMINISTRATIVE REORGANIZATION OF THE SEINE PREFECTURE

❦ The government service responsible for Paris had already made quite a leap between 1853 and 1859, with a doubling of the amount of business it handled. The extension of the city limits now meant that the Seine prefecture faced an even greater increase in its workload. Haussmann first divided the offices at the Hôtel de Ville in two. The Seine prefecture proper exercised the general functions delegated to all prefects as representatives of central government: public administration, the handling of community interests in the department, the supervision of local communes, the supervision of hospitals and the relief committees of the districts of Saint-Denis and Sceaux. Paris city hall and its various services were a separate entity.

Haussmann was especially keen to reorganize the city departments, which had the main role in the transformation of the capital. In calling Alphand and Belgrand to come and work with him, he had started the process of breaking up the powerful department in charge of public works. Its director, chief engineer Dupuit—a man highly valued by Haussmann who had designed the Tuileries sewers, among other projects—was opposed to the prefect on the question of the water supply. A firm supporter of using the Seine, he conducted a fierce campaign against Haussmann's and Belgrand's plan to channel spring water into the capital. Alphand's and Belgrand's departments were therefore directly attached to the prefect's office until Dupuit left in

1856 and was replaced by another chief engineer, Michal. Haussmann then introduced a more rational organization by appointing Michal to head a directorate in control of three services: public highways, including road building and maintenance, under the engineer Homberg; water supply, under Belgrand; and promenades and planted areas, under Alphand, assisted after 1858 by Davioud (who was an architect by profession, not an engineer like the other three just mentioned).

As to the Paris survey department, from 1857 it constituted an office within the main administration on the same footing as the directorate. In 1859 it acquired a separate technical branch, which comprised an alignment and demarcation section and a section in charge of actual surveying. In 1862 Dechamps was appointed director of the Paris highway department, which then absorbed the survey department.

That same year, Haussmann created an architectural planning department under Baltard, who directly ran its first section responsible for the upkeep of the Hôtel de Ville and religious buildings. A second section under Toussaint Uchard was in charge of school buildings, while a third under Antoine Bailly had responsibility for university buildings, *mairies*, and courts of first instance.

Apart from a few minor details, the variously termed municipal departments had their equivalents in the prefecture responsible for the affairs of the Seine. The directors were the same men, for the sake of unity: Alphand in charge of public thoroughfares and planted areas, Belgrand of water, Deschamps of road maintenance, land surveyors, and highway designers. But the offices were kept separate. This coherent and efficient new structure underwent a series of further improvements until 1869.

The incorporation of the suburban communes, which was the justification for all this reorganization, was also the reason given by Napoléon III for a decision that overjoyed Haussmann. By a decree of January 11, 1860, the emperor gave him the right to take part in any deliberations of the Council of State that concerned the affairs of the city of Paris.

THE MARRIAGE OF MARIE-HENRIETTE

≈ The marriage of Haussmann's elder daughter, Marie-Henriette, took place soon after these events, and once again Napoléon III gave a striking demonstration of his close ties to the Seine prefect.

Marie-Henriette, just turned twenty, had fallen passionately in love with an impecunious employee at the prefecture. Haussmann took a very dim view of this and moved to organize a more fitting match. While her lover was sent off to work in a subprefecture, Mademoiselle was quickly joined in matrimony to Camille Dollfus, secretary at the French embassy in Berlin, whose father was a Protestant Alsatian industrialist (as was only proper) and a director of the Eastern Railway alongside Émile Pereire. In fact, it is not impossible that Pereire arranged the marriage at the prefect's request.

The affair did, however, raise the sizable problem of a dowry, as Haussmann's personal wealth was by no means comparable to that of the Dollfuses. Dumas, the president of the municipal council, spoke about the matter with other councillors (not, one suspects, on his own initiative), and they told him to seek the emperor's permission for a special municipal grant that would allow Haussmann to bring the bride's dowry more into line with that of her future husband. As soon as Georges-Eugène got wind of this, he thanked Dumas but rejected the idea. Misunderstanding his reasons, Dumas gave him an assurance that when the time came the council would find a way to make the same gesture for his younger daughter.

Haussmann felt that he had no option but to refer the matter to Napoléon III, pointing out that it was morally impossible for him to accept a gift from the municipal council because it would place him under an obligation to the council. The emperor agreed, but then added: "What the city won't do, I'll do myself." Haussmann begged him to desist and explained that the Dollfuses were well aware their son would not be marrying a wealthy heiress; and that they had even expressed their satisfaction with the size of Marie-Henriette's dowry, which was unambiguous proof that the prefect had kept his hands clean. Napoléon III was finally persuaded and, together with the empress, duly signed the marriage contract.

On March 27, 1860, the civil wedding took place in the Throne Hall at the Hôtel de Ville, and the religious ceremony at the Temple de l'Oratoire. The bride's witnesses were the president of the municipal council, Dumas, and the minister of the interior; the bridegroom's were Émile Pereire and the foreign minister. Afterward, Haussmann laid on a wedding dinner for ninety, a gala ball, and a supper for twelve hundred guests. Staff at the prefecture were given half a day off work. Camille Dollfus was soon transferred to Paris, and the arranged marriage between Marie-Henriette and himself did not turn out to be any worse than others. A few years later, when Haussmann married off his younger daughter Valentine with even greater haste, splendor and decorum would once again unite in the same ways.

WATER FROM THE LOIRE OR THE SEINE?

❧ The incorporation of the suburban communes was not yet planned on July 16, 1858, when Haussmann presented his second memorandum on the Paris water supply. The doubling of the city's size would subsequently add another 400,000 to the total number of consumers and absorb the heights of Montmartre and Belleville that were 197 feet above the highest points within the old city limits. It fell to the Seine prefecture to integrate the new areas as rapidly as possible with the old ones. The changed scale of the problems was certainly a stimulus for the planners. Thus the civil engineering directorate called upon Haussmann to submit an ambitious plan to the municipal council for the pumping of water from the Seine, together with another proposal by a member of the directorate to divert 654,000 cubic yards of water from the Loire to Paris. Water from the Loire or from the Seine? The two solutions were studied by prefectural engineers and presented to the municipal council in a memorandum dated April 20, 1860. The council eventually rejected them both.

To meet the needs of outer arrondissements as quickly as possible, Haussmann wanted to start work on the capture of water from the Surmelin Valley, especially from the sources of the River Dhuys, whose initial height of 426 feet meant that water could reach Paris at a height of 354 feet above the datum line. But since the maximum flow was not expected to exceed 52,000 cubic yards, Haussmann also asked the municipal council to put Belgrand in charge of feasibility studies concerning the capture of water from the Vanne and the channeling of water from the Somme-Soude, even though he was personally convinced that the Somme-Soude would provide much less than Belgrand's optimistic calculations led one to suppose. On May 18, the municipal council voted in favor of the conclusions of Haussmann's reports and authorized him to implement the Dhuys program, at an estimated cost of 14 million francs.

Over the next few months, Parisians spoke of nothing other than the Paris water supply and Haussmann's projects. The newspapers published the data supplied by the prefect. Each resident of the capital consumed 45 gallons of water a day: 20 gallons for private and industrial use, 20 gallons for the sprinkling of streets, firefighting and unforeseen occurrences, and 5.3 gallons for fountains and lakes. As the population had by then reached 1.7 million, the daily water requirement was 379,000 cubic yards. But only some 200,000 cubic yards were currently available to the city, from the Ourcq canal (131,000 cubic yards), the springs of Belleville and Prés-Saint-

Gervais (654 cubic yards), Rungis (2,093 cubic yards, via the Arcueil aqueduct), the artesian wells of Grenelle and Passy (9,810 cubic yards) and pumping from the Seine (56,765). A further 179,000 cubic yards were therefore needed. The Dhuys would provide 52,000, the Somme-Soude 78,500, and the Vanne 91,500.

By the time Belgrand's men had completed a detailed study of the operation, a decree of March 4, 1862, had declared the tapping of the Dhuys to be a matter of public benefit. Water channeled to the new reservoir at Ménilmontant, at a height of 354 feet, was pumped up to the highest points in Montmartre and Belleville (420 and 423 feet, respectively) and then allowed to flow down to the rest of the city by simple force of gravity. The distribution of water from the Dhuys officially commenced in Paris on October 15, 1864.

TOWARD THE LIBERAL EMPIRE

☙ Several months earlier the regime had executed the turn that would lead from the authoritarian empire to the liberal empire. The principal cause impelling this was the situation in Italy. Since returning from the war, Napoléon III had thought only of implementing the Villafranca accords. But what was to be done with the four states of Florence, Modena, Parma, and Bologna, whose populations had risen up against their lawful sovereigns and voted for union with Piedmont? The emperor had ordered Victor Emmanuel to give them up and published a note to that effect on September 9, 1859. But the four states had given themselves a military commander, Garibaldi the republican, whom the emperor did not trust.

Napoléon III, together with the British, eventually chose union with Piedmont as the lesser evil. It was true that Bologna belonged to the pope, but on December 22 the emperor brought out a pamphlet, *Le Pape et le Congrès*, which explained that "the smaller the territory, the greater the sovereign." On January 1, 1860, when he received the general commanding the French troops who guaranteed his safety in Rome, the pope expressed his anger at this "monument of hypocrisy and base tissue of contradictions." Catholic circles in Paris grew restless, and the Académie Française made its protest by electing the religious writer Lacordaire to its ranks. The liberal press laid into the pope tooth and nail. But in March 1860 the union of the four states with Piedmont went ahead.

Napoléon III then demanded his due: Nice and Savoy. The British were furious. The emperor said that his only thought was for the right of nations to decide their own future. Plebiscites held on April 22 and 23 gave a majority in Savoy of 130,000 to 235 in favor of union with France (despite the Swiss claims on Thonon and Bonneville), and an equally overwhelming majority in Nice of 15,000 to 160.

But then the Italian question flared up again. Naples revolted in April, and in May Garibaldi landed in Sicily at the head of his famous Thousand and captured Palermo. The young king of Naples, Francesco II, called on Napoléon III for help, but the emperor fell in line with the British position of nonintervention. Garibaldi was able to make a landing in Calabria. On September 6, Francesco II lost control of Naples and took refuge in the citadel of Gaeta. Garibaldi then decided to march without a break to attack the Papal States from the south. Soon he was close to Ancona, whose defense had been entrusted to a small international force under the command of the Frenchman Lamorcière. The Piedmontese intervened to block Garibaldi's path—and routed the pontifical forces at Castelfidaro on September 18; Lamorcière, shut up inside Ancona, capitulated a few days later. The kingdom of Italy absorbed Naples and Sicily, so that now the only outstanding business to complete the unification of the peninsula was in Venetia (still in Austrian hands) and Rome (where the French were protecting the pope). Catholics understood they had been tricked by Napoléon III when it became clear that he had allowed Piedmont to forestall Garibaldi outside Ancona. *Fate, ma fate presto*—"Do it, but be quick!" he was reported to have said. Catholics then broke once and for all with the regime.

At the same time the imperial regime was sailing into stormy waters on the economic front. Since the summer of 1859, Michel Chevalier, the Saint-Simonian economist very close to Napoléon III, had been secretly negotiating a free trade agreement between France and Britain, based on the elimination of trade restrictions and a lowering of customs duties. The discussions took place in a conspiratorial atmosphere; ministerial staff and diplomats were kept in the dark, as was the finance minister Morny, who was known to favor protectionism. The secret was finally revealed a few days before the signing of the treaty, on January 22, 1860. A wind of panic seized industrial circles, especially in the textiles sector. Factory closures and mass layoffs became more and more frequent.

Sir Charles Grenville astutely observed in his *Journal*: "To brave both the clerical party and the protectionist party at the same time, the emperor must have extraordinary confidence in his personal prestige." On Morny's advice, in fact, the emperor had mainly decided on a shift of alliances by opening up the institutions of the empire in a liberal direction. A decree of November

24, 1860, restored the "right of address": that is, the right of the Legislature to reply to the sovereign's speech formally declaring it open. It was the start of a genuine dialogue between Parliament and the head of the executive branch.

MINISTER FOR PARIS?

❧ Was this the best moment for Haussmann to try to force through his appointment as minister for Paris? He may have thought that the Rouhers, Magnes, and other dinosaurs of the authoritarian empire—who daily sought to impose on him the niggling supervision of the ministries of the interior, public works, and finance—had been sufficiently shaken by recent developments. The Seine prefect did not need the title of minister to continue dealing directly with the emperor on matters concerning Paris, and he also assured everyone that it was not at all a question of satisfying his personal vanity. On two occasions in the past he had refused an invitation to join the government: in 1858, when General Espinasse left the Ministry of the Interior; and a few months later, when he was asked to take over from Magne at the Ministry of Public Works and Agriculture. For the truth was that he wished to continue his work in the capital and to join the government only if he could do so as minister for Paris.

Faced with the prevarications of Napoléon III, Haussmann sent him a long memorandum on December 16, 1860, in which he argued that a special ministry for Paris would strengthen his position on the Council of State and gain him time and energy for the greater glory of the emperor. He attached to this a draft decree containing two crucial sentences: "Baron Haussmann, senator and Seine prefect, has the rank of minister and the right to sit in this capacity on our councils. He shall take the title of minister for Paris." But however much he wished to humor Haussmann, the emperor feared the violent reaction of Rouher and other members of his government and felt unable to agree to such a promotion. Haussmann could insist as much as he liked that the true mayor of Paris was the emperor himself and that a prefect-minister would only be a delegate of the head of state. The proposal advanced no further.

The emperor was looking for a compromise, however, and he came up with one a few days later. A decree of December 22, 1860, gave Haussmann access to the Council of Ministers to argue for texts concerning Paris—but without any special title. In practice this meant that he reported to the Council of Ministers on any decrees or laws concerning the city of Paris or the Seine department that he had drafted in accordance with instructions given him by Napoléon III as if he had been a "real" minister. The emperor patiently listened to the objections that were frequently raised against Haussmann's projects—the fiercest opponent invariably being Baroche. Then Haussmann replied and Napoléon III pronounced final judgment, usually in the prefect's favor. If the decree was straightforward, it was signed by the competent minister. If it involved the Council of State, Haussmann went to defend it before that body, with or without the competent minister. The procedure was the same for draft legislation, because the Constitution stipulated that the Council of State must forward the proposed text to the legislature and make a case for it before that body.

Napoléon III kept piling on the honors. Haussmann was awarded the Grand Cross of the Legion of Honor in 1862, on the occasion of the official opening of the Boulevard du Prince Eugène (today's Boulevard Voltaire). The emperor also ordered that another new road henceforth be called Boulevard Haussmann, as it still is today.

The Seine prefect would have to be content with these satisfactions and to give up any ambition to become a full minister. Georges-Eugène found this hard, and in his *Mémoires* he bitterly remarks that his opponents in the government, led by Rouher, never let slip an opportunity to make him feel the difference. "Those gentlemen no longer heeded anything more than the obligation that it [Napoléon III's decision] imposed upon them to treat me as a sort of equal, sitting on a par with them on His Majesty's councils. There were no petty means they did not use to make me feel, and to highlight in every quarter, that our positions in the hierarchy remained the same as before; that a distance still existed between us; that I was a mere prefect (hence their underling), invested by the emperor for passing reasons with certain exceptional powers, but whose official rank had not changed. This is what was later said against me when it came to settling my pension."[22]

Georges-Eugène's character, however, did change. We have come to know a Haussmann at the Seine prefecture who was sure of himself but also pedagogic and diplomatic in manner, a man who could argue a point with infinite patience. But as the lion grew older, he became authoritarian, impatient, cantankerous. Nor was his behavior free of pettiness. A little story told by Xavier Marmier is one of many examples: "He put people down whenever the fancy took him, often in the interests of one of his speculative schemes or one of his own protégés, sometimes with an idea of taking revenge. We know, for example, that he made the rue de X impassable out of hatred for M. Maigre, one of the main owners of land in the street. But on that occasion he received quite a sharp lesson, when M. Maigre demanded compensation for the damages he had suffered. M. Haussmann ironically offered him 2.50 francs—to pay for his cab fare. The jury to which M. Maigre presented his appeal awarded him 750,000 francs."[23] Marmier adds a perfidious insinuation to which we shall return later: "During the huge program of public works in Paris, M. Haussmann bought houses that he knew to be destined for compulsory purchase, or land whose value he would increase by making a boulevard pass across it. In this way he amassed a colossal fortune, and the Pereires were his accomplices in more than one venture."[24]

THE THIRD SYSTEM

The incorporation of the suburban communes was the signal for the third system of redevelopment projects. This program involved two categories: operations within the old city limits of Paris to complete public works begun under previous programs; and new roads to organize the space in the outer arrondissements.

Place du Château d'Eau and Place du Trône. The development of the Place du Château d'Eau continued with the Avenue des Amandiers (costing 1.5 million francs) and the Avenue Parmentier extension (nearly 2.5 million). Haussmann completed the Place du Trône project by creating around it Avenue Philippe Auguste (2 million alone), Avenue Taillebourg, and the Avenue de Bouvines.

Pont Caulaincourt. The incorporation of the suburban communes gave a new dimension to the Gare du Nord development. It was necessary to extend link roads such as Boulevard Ornano that had been driven out to the limits of the old city enclosure. One of the projects was the work on rue Caulaincourt. As it needed to span Montmartre Cemetery on a bridge, several hundred tombs had to be moved—and one of them was the tomb of Admiral Baudin, nephew of the deputy Baudin killed on the barricades in December 1851. The opposition accused Haussmann and the imperial regime of hounding even in the grave the family of that emblematic defender of republican legality. On May 1 and 2 a senatorial commission debated a petition from the sons of Admiral Baudin. Haussmann scraped through with a majority of 50 to 38, but that was not the end of the wrangling, and the Caulaincourt bridge would not see the light of day until the Third Republic.

Rue de Châteaudun. Haussmann completed the network of roads serving Gare Saint-Lazare by widening to 66 feet rue Saint-Lazare and the rue de la Pépinière, between the Place de la Trinité and Place Saint-Augustin. The driving of rue de Châteaudun between the Place de la Trinité and rue Lafayette opened up the Church of Notre Dame de Lorette and, above all, created a first-rate link between Gare Saint-Lazare and the Gare du Nord and Gare de l'Est. These operations cost 25.5 million francs.

Gare du Nord. It would cost even more to finish the Gare du Nord development: 32.5 million francs. The scheme adopted by the Seine prefecture rested upon two streets: the rue de Mauberge went from the rue du faubourg Montmartre to the Boulevard de la Chapelle, crossing Boulevard Magenta on its way. Rue Lafayette, extended beyond the Gare du Nord to the Porte de Pantin, became the longest street in Paris, at 3 miles, forming a major road from the northern outskirts of the capital to the new city center taking shape around the Opera; but although it was 66 feet wide, it unfortunately proved too narrow for the volume of traffic.

These operations gave their full meaning to the twin principles that had constantly guided Napoléon III's approach to the transformation of Paris: linking the center to the periphery, and linking the railway stations to one another.

The Opera Quartier. The most spectacular achievement of the third system, however, was the birth of the new *quartier* of the Opera. Plans for it were drawn up in the first year after Haussmann's appointment; the outlines became apparent during work on the second system, as rue Auber opened up Gare Saint-Lazare and led to the point chosen for the new Opera building, while rue Halévy added further touches of its own. The Place de l'Opéra having gradually taken shape, the final step was to build the crowning glory of the new *quartier*: the Opera itself. On December 29, 1860, Walewski, the minister responsible for the arts, opened a competition for architects. Rohault was initially chosen, but then the emperor changed his mind and launched a new round of consultations. As hurdle followed hurdle, the number of candidates was whittled down from 171 to 5 and then to 3. The final shortlist consisted of Ginain, Giraud, and Garnier. The selection committee chaired by Hittorff unanimously chose Charles Garnier's plan, and on June 6, 1861, Walewski officially appointed him architect for the new Opera.

At that time Garnier was still unknown. He had won the Prix de Rome in 1848, then followed the classical stages of a sojourn at the Villa Médicis and a trip further east (to Greece and Constantinople) in 1852. His plan did not please Empress Eugénie, however, who preferred the architecture of Viollet-le-Duc (who had also been in the running for the Opera). When she asked Garnier to name the style informing his plan, he proudly replied: "The Napoléon III style, *madame.*" Garnier's plans were accepted, and the first stone was laid on July 21, 1862. But the construction work ran into numerous technical difficulties, and work was still continuing on the building when the war of 1870 and then the Commune forced it to be broken off. Garnier's Opera finally opened on January 6, 1875. At the time of the original competition, the estimated cost had been 8 million francs. The final bill came in at 35.5 million, in addition to the 27 to 28 million for the clearing of the site and the surrounding area.

Work on the Opera was supervised by the architectural department of the Seine prefecture. At the same time a new rue du Quatre Septembre (in fact, an extension of rue Réaumur) was added as a kind of pendant to the rue de la Paix, linking the Place de l'Opéra to the Place de la Bourse at the very high cost of 66 million francs. Avenue Napoléon (today's Avenue de l'Opéra) had been completed only at its two ends when Haussmann left the scene, and would be completed under the Third Republic after the leveling of the Butte des Moulins.

The development of this *quartier* included the section of Boulevard Haussmann between Place Saint-Augustin and rue Taitbout; its continuation to the Carrefour Richelieu-Drouot would also have to wait until the Third Republic. The crossing with rue Meyerbeer and rue Scribe opened up the Opéra on its north side, while to the west the extension of the boulevard as the Avenue de Freidland linked the Opera *quartier* to Étoile.

The Chaillot Quartier and *Place Victor Hugo*. The urbanization of west Paris gathered pace. All the new roads opened in the Chaillot *quartier*—with the exception of the Avenue de l'Alma (today's Avenue Marceau), which was funded out of the 180-million-franc agreement—entered into the costs of the third system and drew 24 million francs out of the municipal coffers. New structures rapidly sprang up on the Champs Élysées. The Chaillot hill, still half countryside, acquired a central focus with the Place du Trocadéro, which was the starting point for the Avenue du Président Wilson, Avenue Georges Mandel, and Avenue Henri Martin. The developers also carried out an enlargement of rue Benjamin Franklin, while awaiting the completion of Avenue Paul Doumer that depended upon the relocation of part of Passy Cemetery. Haussmann also took an interest in Place Victor Hugo, giving it a regular star shape through the harmonization of Avenue Victor Hugo with the new Avenue Malakoff, Avenue Bugeaud, rue Boissière, and rue Copernic.

The Rond-point des Champs Élysées. Haussmann finished the development of the roundabout by driving the Avenue d'Antin (today's Avenue Franklin Roosevelt) through to the church of Saint-Philippe du Roule on the rue du faubourg Saint-Honoré, where another street, rue La Boétie, had appeared as a continuation of the rue de la Pépinière at one end and rue Pierre Charron at the other. The prefect, still a stickler for symmetry, was pleased to see that the angle at which rue La Boétie intersected the Avenue des Champs Élysées was exactly the same as the one formed by the avenue and the rue de Marignan. The Avenue d'Antin extension cost 5 million francs, and the regularization of the Rond-point another 3.5 million.

Left Bank. Major works on the left bank included the opening of Boulevard Saint-Germain from the Pont de la Concorde to the rue du Bac, the completion of the rue des Saints-Pères and the rue de Rennes (up to Place Saint-Germain-des-Prés), the development of the area around Place Monge, and the extension to the rue de la Glacière.

THE MONCEAU PLAIN, A BUDGET SQUEEZE, AND THE FIRST TROUBLE FOR THE PEREIRE BROTHERS

≈ On the eve of the incorporation of the suburban communes, Haussmann was negotiating with the five main owners of the huge areas of land on the Monceau plain beyond the wall of the Farmers-General: namely, Pereire, Chazelles, Deguingand, Jadin, and d'Offémont. They agreed to cede free of charge the land needed for Haussmann's road schemes: Boulevard Malesherbes as far as the Porte d'Asnières, Place Malesherbes, the Avenue de Villiers, Place Wagram, and Place Pereire, in all 20.4 acres. The landowners' profit would come from the value added by urbanization to the land that remained in their hands. But it was still necessary to "expropriate" a few isolated landowners who were not part of the Group of Five. Pereire, who conducted the laborious negotiations with Haussmann, signed a contract with the prefecture to build the new roads (classed as departmental roads) with a subsidy of 1 million francs. For the department the total cost of the Pereire contract plus the compulsory purchases of land came to the relatively modest sum of 3.2 million francs.

After the failure of his plans for a Paris ministry, Haussmann too began to look as if he had had his day. The public works were costing too much, criticized *La Revue des Deux Mondes*. And economics slipped over into politics: "There can be no good financial government without rigorous supervision by representative assemblies and vigilant polemic in a free press." In other words, it was becoming permissible to shoot on sight wherever the Seine prefect threatened to invade. The *Revue* received an official warning for its pains. But while this was going on, Fould was appointed finance minister. His program: to forgo any further loans, to strengthen supervision by the

Legislature, and to guard against unforeseen events by transferring credits between ministries without increasing overall expenditure. The emperor liked the idea. A senatorial order of December 31, 1861, accordingly banned the government from opening additional credit lines between budgets in the absence of special legislation.

Haussmann's links with the Pereires kept tongues wagging. Things were no longer looking so good for these buccaneers of high finance: they had never been very particular about their methods; now they were suffering their first setbacks. Their man Mirès, director of the General Railways Fund, was arrested in Mazas on February 17, 1861, and sentenced to five years' imprisonment on July 11. The next year, on October 25, 1862, a vote was carried in suspicious circumstances in favor of a merger between the Société Immobilière (which the Pereires controlled) and the Société des Ports de Marseille (in which they had a minority shareholding). Other holders of shares in the Société des Ports tried to block the merger in the courts. Nine sessions between late 1864 and early January 1865 dealt with the case, and on February 18, Émile Pereire and two of his cronies, Chaumont-Quitry and Crochard, were ordered to pay heavy fines. The sentence was less severe than some judges would have wished, but the emperor himself had intervened. In any event, the Pereires had suffered a breach in their financial citadel and went in fear of further court cases. Humorists joked that they had been sentenced to six years of forced honesty and that they would not serve out their time. This was one quatrain that did the rounds:

> *Sur la place Vendôme, un jour dans sa malice,*
> *Le destin a placé Pereire et ses bureaux,*
> *Afin qu'il travaillât sous l'oeil de la justice,*
> *Entre l'auteur du code et le garde des Sceaux.*[*]

For Haussmann it came as a grave warning. Financial difficulties were looming that would soon bring about his downfall.

---

[*]One day, spiteful fate placed Pereire and his offices on Place Vendôme, so that he would work beneath the gaze of justice, between the author of the code [a reference to the statue of Napoleon I in the square] and the keeper of the seals.

18

Financial Difficulties

IN PARALLEL with the liberal evolution of its institutions and political practices, the imperial regime adopted a social orientation that bore the personal imprint of the author of *L'Extinction du paupérisme*. Napoléon III did not forget that the popular districts of Paris had acclaimed the troops as they set off to wage a war of liberation in Italy against conservative Austria. And Prince Napoléon-Jérôme, for his part, had a number of meetings with printworkers, the elite of the working class, which led to the publication of an anonymous series called "Pamphlets of the Palais Royal." That was where he had his residence.

In October 1861 a couple of Saint-Simonians—the Lyons industrial banker Arlès-Dufour, and Guéroult—launched a campaign to assist French workers wishing to travel to the World's Fair in London scheduled for the following year, so that they could study British industry at close quarters and take the opportunity to meet some British fellow workers. Private donations brought in thirteen thousand francs, to which the government and the city of Paris each added a further twenty thousand francs; history tells us nothing about how Haussmann felt when he had to pay the bill for the emperor's invitation. The workers' delegation returned from London filled with admiration for the efficiency of the British trade unions, which had managed to win a fifty-five-hour week and wage guarantees. There was talk of forming an international labor union, but some thought that the way ahead for the struggle was an alliance with the republicans, while others wished to remain independent even if it meant negotiating improvements in the workers' lot with the imperial regime. In the elections of 1863 the typographer Blanc was the only workers' candidate in Paris, but the republicans picked up all its seats in Parliament.

Workers' candidates were no more successful in the 1864 round of by-elections. In their disappointment they asked the regime to give a spur to pro-labor reforms: the first was the right to strike. (In 1862 an illegal print-workers' strike had given rise to prosecutions and convictions, but the emperor had amnestied the strikers with public support.) Morny submitted a bill to the Legislature and named the republican Émile Ollivier, Haussmann's old enemy from their days in the Var, as the deputy who would formally speak to introduce it. Despite resistance from conservative circles, the bill permitting strike action so long as it was not marred by violence won a large majority in the spring of 1864. Ollivier replied to those who taxed him with opportunism: "I'll take something good from whichever hand it comes."

The appointment of Victor Duruy as minister of education in 1863 helped to modernize particularly the secondary school system. This history teacher at the Lycée Saint-Louis, whose chief merit was to have helped Napoléon III write his *Life of Caesar*, restored classes in philosophy and contemporary history as well as the teaching of foreign languages; he also introduced vocational education without Latin for pupils geared to a career in industry, agriculture, and trade. Declaring himself in private to be "a free-thinker in the marrow of his bones," Duruy became the *bête noire* of Catholics at a time when the Holy See—through its encyclical *Quanta cura* of December 8, 1864, complemented by a *Syllabus* of "the errors of our time"—was hardening its stance against "false opinions and doctrines" of the modern world. Napoléon III let Duruy publish a report in *Le Moniteur* arguing for free and compulsory education. Catholic and conservative circles were aghast. The crisis reached the upper levels of the civil service and even the government itself; the vice-president of the Council of State, Parieu, attacked Duruy at a plenary session of the assembly.

On September 28, 1864, three representatives of the French workers' movement attended the inaugural meeting of the first Labor International. Napoléon III let them go, as he had no reason to feel worried: the workers' struggle was directed against capitalism, not against the political regime. The French Section of the International had five hundred paid-up members; the Paris branch met in a little room on the ground floor at 44 rue des Gravilliers. The first congress of the International was held in Geneva in September 1866.

But the liberal evolution of the imperial regime was halted when Morny, the man most capable of leading the change, died suddenly on March 10, 1865. His disappearance left the emperor at a loss, torn between the sometimes clumsy entreaties of Prince Napoléon-Jérôme (who was leaning ever more to the left) and the diehard authoritarianism of the austere Rouher.

SETBACKS ABROAD: MEXICO AND PRUSSIA

❧ The regime had to face setbacks in foreign policy. The combination of Morny's financial appetites and Napoléon III's ambitious reveries took France into the Mexican expedition that began in December 1861–January 1862 alongside British and Spanish forces. It then continued with the French alone, who suffered a humiliating defeat before Puebla on May 5, 1862. A second battle of Puebla, in May 1863, gave them revenge and opened the road to Mexico City. French troops entered the capital on June 10, 1863.

But what was to be done with the victory? After some procrastination, Paris decided to support the Archduke Maximilian of Austria, who had been invited by some Mexican political forces to accept the crown of the Empire of Mexico. In April 1864, Maximilian set sail for Mexico, where a thousand frictions with Bazine's French expeditionary corps awaited him. Massacres were making the war a daily bloodier ordeal, and the United States, just emerging from its civil war, was determined not to tolerate an aggressive return of old Europe to the new continent. Early in 1866 the French press unanimously called for withdrawal; the *Revue des Deux Mondes* spoke of "gigantic deafness" that had to be ended with the utmost rapidity. On July 8, Empress Charlotte, the wife of Maximilian, set sail for Europe to persuade Napoléon III to continue his support.

A few days earlier, on July 3, the Prussian army had defeated the Austrians at Sadowa after a blitzkrieg, for supremacy in Central Europe. The Italians, whom Napoléon III had allied with Prussia, were defeated by Austria on June 24 at Custozza. But there was a reward for their participation in the war: in return for his neutrality, the emperor received Venetia from the government in Vienna, and he handed this over to the kingdom of Italy. Napoléon III, who had not negotiated any agreement with Prussia, now held out his hand to them in order to obtain territorial concessions on the left bank of the Rhine. This "policy of gratuities," as Bismarck contemptuously described it when he published his account of the indiscreet French demands, aroused the indignation of the peoples of Germany. The government in Paris lost everything—beginning with the sympathy of the whole of Europe. Even the Italians felt humiliated at their inability to capture Venetia without relying upon Napoléon III. But the emperor did not lose heart, and in January 1867 he asked Prussia to hand over Luxembourg—with as little success as before. When the World's Fair opened its doors on April 1, 1867, French and Prussians were beginning to say to each other that war was inevitable.

PARKS AND GARDENS

❧ The populist orientation of the imperial regime was expressed even in the *grands travaux* commissioned for the capital. Lower-income groups were cajoled by Napoléon III—and therefore by Haussmann, though he did more than his share of grumbling.

Special effort was put into the green spaces in the east of Paris. A law of July 24, 1860, in the year following the incorporation of the suburban communes, ceded the Bois de Vincennes to Paris on condition that the city convert it within four years into a public area for walks but also retain its military installations (the castle and fort of Vincennes, the hospital, the redoubts of Gravelle and La Faisanderie, the camp and ground used for army maneuvers). As in the case of the Bois de Boulogne, the city received authorization to sell 296 acres of land to private purchasers, with architectural restrictions as rigorous as in the west. In 1864 the 2,224 acres of the Bois de Vincennes were laid out and equipped with an elaborate system of artificial lakes: the lac de Gravelle drew water from the Marne to serve as a general reservoir and in turn supplied the lac de Saint-Mandé, lac de Bercy, and lac des Minimes. The excavations made it possible to increase the height of the Butte de Gravelle, from which there was a magnificent view east over the Marne Valley and the Seine Valley. Barillet-Deschamps organized the planting of trees and lawns, Davioud built the cafés, restaurants, and refreshment kiosks as well as a racecourse that acted as a more popular pendant to the one at Longchamp in the west.

In 1890, when Haussmann was writing his *Mémoires*, his temper still had not cooled. The Bois de Vincennes, "exceeding all forecasts, made quite a large hole in the city's finances; some who were not favorably disposed to sumptuous [sic] works wondered whether the final result was worth what it had cost: 12 million francs net. This might be reduced to 10 million to take account of the capital represented by fees and rents payable annually to the city, but it still amounts to five times more than the comparable sum spent on the Bois de Boulogne."[1] The prefect blamed the surprising discovery of dry sandy soil—which made the park much harder to lay out than the Bois de Boulogne—and the fact that the revenue from resold land fell far short of the results obtained in the west. "On this side of Paris, close to the *quartiers* of Reuilly, faubourg Saint-Antoine, Charonne, and La Roquette, we should not have expected price increases comparable to the value added . . . over in Boulogne and Neuilly, close to the new *quartiers* of Passy and Auteuil, and the most sought-after of the city's older neighborhoods."[2]

As we see, Haussmann was never an enthusiastic supporter of the Vincennes operation. On the other hand, he was the person behind the new park of Buttes-Chaumont, at the northern end of the Belleville heights. Before the project started, a fringe population lived there in unhealthy shanties amidst a vast garbage dump spread over ancient paths. Haussmann's idea was to replace this with a public park of sixty-two acres; this could hardly have been more to the liking of Napoléon III, who immediately accepted the proposal. On July 22, 1862, a decree of the Council of State duly declared the purchase of the area to be a matter of public benefit. The park opened to the public in spring 1867, at once becoming a symbol of the empire's achievements and an obligatory stopping place for official visits.

The work on Buttes-Chaumont proved to be difficult and expensive. It was necessary to fill in the holes left by the old gypsum tracks, to tackle the large drop from the upper to the lower part of the site, to dig a lake all around the island formed by the central promontory, to open avenues with sufficiently gentle slopes for vehicle traffic, and to bring in plant mold for the cultivated areas. Special machinery drew water from the Ourcq canal to supply a 105-foot-high waterfall. Two bridges permitted access to the panoramic viewpoint in the center of the park; a third was to be built in the northern section over the circle railway that cut through it. Davioud designed a rotunda, summer houses, chalet restaurants, warden's lodges, and duty quarters for the Parisian force of park rangers who supervised areas used for walks. Finally, the park was completely enclosed with railings.

The whole development cost nearly 6 million francs (2.5 million for the land purchase, 3 million for the actual works, and 500,000 for the various constructions). This was obviously more than Haussmann had been expecting, and he issued recriminations in the name of "spatial fairness." By what right had one part of Paris been favored to this extent when so many others had needs at least as glaring? The only response was to start building more parks. "The size of these figures . . . placed my administration under an even more pressing obligation to create another park in south Paris (as it had already planned), so that the outer 13th and 14th arrondissements would acquire benefits equivalent to those that the Parc des Buttes-Chaumont had given the new *quartiers* in the north of the city."[3]

The creation of the Parc de Montsouris was declared a matter of public benefit on June 22, 1865, when work was still under way on the Parc des Buttes-Chaumont. As the land in the area was split among many small owners, the aspects involving municipal acquisition were particularly complicated and dragged on from 1865 to 1867. The park covered nearly 40 acres. It was cut at two places, by the circle railway and by the Sceaux line (today's southern branch of the RER B line), and so it proved necessary to build three bridges. A large stretch of water was dug in the lower part, where it benefited from the proximity of the Montsouris reservoir. At the top of the hill, near the Observatoire de Paris, rose the Bardo, a faithful copy of the Bey's palace in Tunis, which the city purchased at a price of 150,000 francs for the World's Fair of 1867; it would later be converted for use as a weather station. Access to the central *quartiers* of Paris was facilitated by a new road (the future Avenue René Coty) leading from the lower section of the park to the Barrière d'Enfer (now Place Denfert-Rochereau). The cost of the work was 1.75 million francs, or half that of the Parc des Buttes-Chaumont, but the land purchase pushed the total expenditure up to 4,125,000 francs.

In the end, the popular *quartiers* did not have much reason for complaint, especially as several of Haussmann's garden squares were created in parts of the capital inhabited by lower-income groups. As far as the new arrondissements were concerned, the squares in the west (Batignolles, Boulevard Victor, Square de Grenelle, Place de Commerce) had their counterparts in the north and the east: the two squares at La Chapelle in the 18th arrondissement, Belleville in the 19th, and La Réunion in the 20th.

FOURTH REPORT ON THE PARIS WATER SUPPLY: PUBLIC AND PRIVATE

❧ During this period Haussmann perfected his plans for the capital's water and sanitation system. In 1865, in his fourth and final report to the municipal council on the Paris water supply, he gave up the idea of tapping the Somme-Soude, as the springs there were too irregular and the landowners highly resistant to municipal acquisition. To make up for the 78,500 cubic yards of water that could no longer be expected from that source, Haussmann proposed the diversion of 131,000 cubic yards from the Vanne—a project originally planned for a later date. Two resolutions of the municipal council gave him the necessary authorization, and a public benefit decree was signed on December 19, 1866; he had had the council's agreement since 1860 for the acquisition of springs in the Vanne Valley. The construction of the Montsouris reservoir drew upon cement techniques that Haussmann had already discovered during his days in the Yonne, when he had visited one of the main cement works in the department. The building of the aqueduct would be completed only after his departure from the scene.

While waiting for Vanne water to come on tap, it was necessary to extract a greater contribution from the Parisian watercourses. In 1864, on the occasion of the work on the Bois de Vincennes, Haussmann had purchased the concession on the canal and plant at Saint-Maur. The turbines were able to raise 17,000 cubic yards of water for the needs of the woods, but their later strengthening made it possible to add 60,000 cubic yards to the Ménilmontant reservoir for household consumption. In 1866, at Belgrand's request, he purchased the windmills at Trilbardou and Isles-les-Meldeuses on the Marne, downstream from Meaux. The project was declared a matter of public benefit on April 11, 1866. Then Haussmann had two hydraulic machines set up to pump 52,000 cubic yards each from the Marne into the Canal de l'Ourcq that passed nearby.

Another purchase at the time of the incorporation of the suburban communes was that of the concessions and plant of the Compagnie Générale des Eaux; Haussmann wanted everything under his control. But as a good administrator, he was eager to separate what he considered to be the areas of public responsibility from the commercial aspect of distributing water to consumers. He laid down his guiding principles as early as 1860. "Municipal execution of all work on the channeling of spring water, the two distribution networks [that is, for public use and for sale to private consumers], and the sewer tunnels; the administration and free disposal of water from all sources to be kept in the hands of the municipal authority; water for private use to be handled by a purely commercial company, which will purchase from the city at a moderate fixed price the amount of spring water that it is assured of selling and that it has been authorized to allocate to individuals within the limits of an agreed scale of charges; the city to set a minimum daily volume of water for which it is paid by the company, even if the latter uses only part of that volume."[4] The purpose of this minimum was to spur the company to make landlords bring water up to the higher floors of residential blocks. Naturally enough, the Compagnie Générale des Eaux became this partner for the city of Paris, in the framework of a shared-interest contract that would be amended twice during the Haussmann years, on December 26, 1867, and December 20, 1869. Haussmann favored the concentration and centralization of powers in single hands, preferably his own. But when it came to the tasks of running the service, he happily delegated these to a private company on the grounds that it would have a stronger commercial motivation than any municipal department and would prevent an excessive burden upon the city budget.

THE HONOR OF VALENTINE HAUSSMANN . . .

  Being an ardent champion of green spaces and spring water, Haussmann was less than happy with his second daughter, Valentine. Some felt that she looked like a hussy; others, while sharing this view, thought that the blame was Haussmann's for having slipped her into the emperor's bed. When she once inadvertently took Madame Oscar de la Vallée's place at a ball at the Tuileries Palace, the latter said to her rather sourly: "I will give up my place for you, *mademoiselle*, seeing that you are obviously the mistress here."[5]

The incidents between father and daughter were public—and sometimes stormy. Xavier Marmier describes one in his *Journal*: "Recently Mlle. Haussmann was dancing at a gala ball. Her father came up and said to her in a jovial way: 'You dance like a good-for-nothing.'—'Well, what's this then!' she exclaimed to her cavalier. 'My father running down his own commodity?'" It was intended that the beautiful young woman would marry Monsieur Grammont-Caderousse, who shortly after he came of age had started eating up his fortune with such gusto that a guardian had been compelled to intervene. He was now living on income from the estate of his brother, who had sailed off on *Le Président* fifteen years earlier and was no longer mentioned. Many a paterfamilias would not have cared to entrust his daughter to a man with such an odd background. By marrying him, however, Mademoiselle Haussmann would become a duchess; and if he ended up broke, she was rich enough for the two of them."[6]

Valentine did not marry Grammont-Caderousse, however, because the great pleasure-seeker died of consumption in 1865, at the age of just thirty-two. The journalist Henri Rochefort was very fond of him: "He was one of those predestined men who have wit and almost genius, senses and a tender soul, vices and never absurd habits." In any event, Grammont-Caderousse did not accept responsibility for the child to which Valentine gave birth on February 26, 1865, a boy, Jules-Adrien, who in all likelihood was the emperor's work. When he reached the age of eighteen, in 1883, he applied to take the name Hadot and went on to become paymaster general at Melun and to marry a former mistress of Morny's.

Valentine eventually married on February 23, 1865, the husband being Maurice-Joseph, vicomte de Pernetty. In Paris, as always, there were songs to round it all off:

Haussmann à Pernetty* vient d'accorder sa fille.
Si beau que soit l'hymen, je plains le marié,
Car on risque en entrant dans pareille famille,
D'être, comme mari, bientôt exproprié.

Haussmann, ne voulant point imiter les apôtres,
Au bien d'autrui s'arrange à plaisir, sans façon,
Et pour faire à sa fille une bonne maison,
Il nous prend toutes les nôtres.[†]

. . . AND THE HONESTY OF THE BARON

❧ At first the accusations of favoritism and corruption had been veiled, but now they were circulating freely. The memorialist Viel-Castel attacked the Seine prefect by name in connection with three affairs: Montulé, a section leader at the prefecture, refused to sign the report he had prepared on the Bakery Trade Fund on the grounds that Haussmann had altered some of the figures in it; next, the directors of the Société des Petites Voitures—a cab hire company—claimed to have paid a lot for a license issued by Haussmann; and finally, a bidder for the Boulevard du Prince Eugène development project said he had heard that acceptance of his offer would depend on payment of a commission to Haussmann (the "going rate for patronage," as Viel-Castel called it).[7] Young republicans began spreading a riddle: "What is the difference between a panther and Baron Haussmann?" Answer: *"C'est que la panthère est tachetée par nature, tandis que le baron est acheté par les entrepreneurs"* [A panther is spotted by nature, whereas the baron is bought by contractors—where the French for "is spotted" and "is bought" are homonymous].

During the debates on the financial arrangements for the *grands travaux*, which occupied no fewer than eleven sessions of the assembly in 1869, the deputy Calley de Saint-Paul expressed doubts about the openness of the municipal contracts and deals. Haussmann, who did not have the right to at-

---

*Pernety or Pernetty—one finds both spellings.
†Haussmann has just given Pernety his daughter's hand. / However beautiful the marriage, I pity the groom, / For when you enter such a family, / You risk, as a husband, swift dispossession. / Not wanting to imitate the apostles, / Haussmann just does what he likes with the property of others, / And to make a good home for his daughter, / He takes away all of ours.

tend the Legislature, replied shortly afterward at a session of the Senate. He explained that Calley de Saint-Paul was scarcely in a position to make such accusations, because in Berger's days the Calley bank had reached a deal for the floating of a 50-million-franc loan by the Seine department. When Haussmann had taken over, he had noticed that the Calley bank was incapable of meeting its commitments; he had given it several extensions and thereby caused himself considerable trouble with the competition. Would Calley de Saint-Paul dare claim that he had bribed the prefect? "This banker knows perfectly well how business is handled at the Hôtel de Ville, and I would like to think that, if necessary, he would defend it instead of incriminating it."[8] According to Haussmann, Calley apologized after the debates for having said things that might be misinterpreted. "He would have done better to disavow them spontaneously from the rostrum. But he would have had to say who was the target of his insinuations."[9]

These few words allow us to reconstitute what happened. Calley discussed several times with Haussmann a renegotiation of the terms of the loan contract. Haussmann, as usual, cannot have been an easy person to deal with. Calley looked for someone to intervene on his behalf with Georges-Eugène and to make him a little less inflexible. An obliging figure appeared and said he could sort something out if there was a sizable gift for the prefect. Calley accepted, continued the discussions—and reached an agreement with Haussmann. Calley obviously concluded that it was thanks to the commission in prospect that he had been able to reach the agreement. Did the middleman actually arrange anything with Haussmann? Or was it one of those typical maneuvers by someone in the corridors of power whereby money was demanded in the name of a leading politician or official who knew nothing about it? Was the bribe meant all the time to remain in the middleman's pocket? In any event, Haussmann never managed to obtain the name of the person touched by Calley's insinuations in connection with the 50-million-franc loan.

During the same debate in 1869, the virulence and precision of Calley's attacks—which added to those of several other parliamentarians—forced Rouher to reply in his capacity as minister without portfolio representing the government. In addressing Calley, however, his falsely reassuring manner could only add to the suspicions: "I too," he said, "have heard the rumors to which you allude; I have followed them up with concern; I have tried to pin them down and find proof for them; I have never been able to do this."[10] Haussmann acquitted for lack of proof—hardly a glorious outcome!

Inevitably Haussmann's relations with contractors also laid him open to

criticism in the assembly because of the huge cost of operations. He was accused of making too little use of concessions before the start of the third system; we have already seen how things stood and how difficult it was to find
contractors capable of taking on a major concession at their own risk. He was
also accused of embezzlement, in that the awarding of concessions supposedly lacked a thorough transparency, and he himself was suspected of having
derived considerable pecuniary advantage from the process. But the deputy
Du Miral wrote in his report on the draft legislation: "Be this as it may, we
can now state that everything to do with these concessions took place without the least irregularity, that a number of precautions were taken to avoid
any possibility of error, and that the honesty or morality of these operations
is evident to any impartial judge and defies the most passionate suspicion."[11]

   In his *Mémoires*, Haussmann himself describes two attempts at corruption to which he was exposed. The first came from a company offering to
sign a fixed-price contract for the Boulevard de Strasbourg: "One of my relatives by marriage confided to me that he had an interest in the deal, in the
form of a sum of 500,000 francs placed at his disposal to ensure its success.
He was prepared to give me 400,000 in return for the helping hand that his
approach was tending to receive from me."[12] Haussmann refused the money,
broke off talks with the company in question, and decided that the Boulevard de Strasbourg would be built under local government control. On the
second occasion, in 1867, a company applied to be awarded the Avenue de
l'Opéra contract at a fixed price of 30 million francs, and sent a messenger
round to offer Haussmann a commission of 2.5 million francs if he agreed to
the deal. Haussmann: "I did not move a muscle, and after a moment's silence
I gave the following answer. 'Excuse me, *monsieur*, you will find me very in-
quisitive, but I don't grasp the connection between the two sums. Why 2.5
million and not 2 or 3?'—'The deduction can be 3 million if you think it
necessary. All our calculations have been correctly made: 27 million can be
enough for everything.'—'Well, *monsieur*, please thank your friends on my
behalf. I take it from what you have said that a municipal grant of 30 million francs would be excessive, and I am noting in the file that they are prepared to reduce it by a tenth."[13]

   The other charge weighing upon the prefect was that he had used inside
information for his own profit and perhaps that of several accomplices. Who
could know for sure where a new road would pass? Prefect Haussmann. And
when someone had this information, all he had to do was visit the owners of
buildings scheduled for compulsory purchase and offer to buy their property
at the current market price. A few months then went by, the decision to

build the road was made public, the buildings were acquired, and a tidy profit was made on the difference between the compensation payment and the purchase price. Apparently Octavie let slip at dinner parties that she had no luck with her real estate purchases because whenever her husband advised her to invest in a particular block, it was always pulled down a few months later. It is the mechanism described in Zola's *La Curée*: Saccart, the main character, owes nothing to Octavie, but his story does remind one a lot of the Pereires.

Who would not be struck, for example, by the farsighted way in which the Pereires massively bought into the Opera neighborhood well before it began to take shape, and by the extraordinary coincidence between their investment decisions and the plans that the prefecture would publish only at a later date? In 1853, acting through the *Compagnie des immeubles et de l'hôtel de la rue de Rivoli* (of which they were the owners), they purchased the Hôtel Osmond in rue Basse-des-Remparts, corresponding to what are today Nos. 6 to 10 of the Boulevard des Capucines. In 1859 the company expanded—changing its name to *Compagnie immobilière de Paris*—and borrowed the sizable sum of 11 million francs from Crédit Foncier. This sum enabled it to buy up most of the land in the southern part of the future *quartier* of the Opera. Within a few months the demolition was over and construction work had begun on four residential blocks on the corner of the future Place de l'Opéra (the ones at 8 and 10, Boulevard des Capucines, and at 2–4, rue Halévy), even though the final layout of the square would be opened to a public inquiry only considerably later, on April 15, 1860, and approved by decree on September 29.

By early 1861 the Compagnie Immobilière de Paris owned nearly all the land between rue Scribe and rue Caumartin. This real estate enabled the Pereires to execute a series of constructions that were impressive in both size and architectural coherence. The crowning piece was the Grand Hôtel de la Paix, whose architect, Armand, had already been responsible for the main hall at Gare Saint-Lazare. Work on the hotel began in April 1861 and continued round the clock for fourteen months, reaching completion on June 30, 1862. The vast uniform building occupied a whole block between the Place de l'Opéra, the Boulevard des Capucines, rue Auber (then rue de Rouen), and rue Scribe. It was organized around a huge main courtyard, in which six hundred people could be seated at a table beneath a canopy. The hotel contained eight hundred rooms, some of them with private bathrooms and toilets. It also had a smoking room, a ladies' room, a bureau de change, a mail service complete with translators, a post and telegraph office, a theatre booking office, and a reading room where one could find nearly all the news-papers of Europe and the Americas. One of the first hydraulic elevators was in use there and much admired, and electric lighting competed with older gas lighting.

Very soon the first banks appeared on Pereire land close to the hotel. The Café de la Paix, designed by Armand, opened in 1863. Nearby buildings, somewhat smaller than the grand hotel, followed the same architectural stereotype: colossal pilasters on the façade, a central courtyard covered with glass. Office space was snapped up, but the apartments (opulent as they were) did not enjoy the same success. Apart from bank directors with living accommodations above their place of work, well-off Parisians preferred to live in the western *quartiers*, even if they worked in the Opera area that was becoming the main business center in the capital. Large stores also estab-lished themselves here. Le Printemps opened its doors in 1865 but without owing anything to the Pereires; its owner, Jaluzot, had bought the land him-self.[14]

After Haussmann's death in December 1891 Adolphe Alphand, who had been one of his closest collaborators (perhaps the closest of all) throughout the prefect's tenure in the Seine department, paid homage to him in a speech at the Academy of Fine Arts. Noting the existence of rumors, he gave a number of reasons connected with Haussmann's character to dismiss any idea that he had been corrupt. "His lack of selfish interest did not prevent slanderers from attacking the honor of this public servant. It was possible to rebut these attacks, and no one today is unaware that Baron Haussmann left the Hôtel de Ville knowing he had always done his duty and strictly ob-served the rules of the most scrupulous conduct. Such a man, haughty and proud as he was, could never have agreed to the humiliation of a dishonest deal that would have made him bow his head before an accomplice, whoever he might be."

THE WORLD'S FAIR OF 1867

❧ The operations of the second and third systems were not yet complete when the World's Fair opened in 1867. This new exhibition made further demands on the prefecture as well as helping to speed the building work al-ready under way and to justify the launching of new projects.

The Champ de Mars was chosen to accommodate the fair in preference to the Carré Marigny, which was considered too small and cluttered. A massive oblong structure made of metal covered an area of some thirty-six acres.[15]

Seven concentric galleries almost fifty feet wide enclosed a huge central garden under canvas. Other gardens were spread around the gallery for the repose and pleasure of visitors, and all the resources of the city hall's conservatories had been mobilized to create a delightful environment of greenery and flowers. As one looked at the main entrance in front of the Pont d'Iéna, one could see at the other end of the Champ de Mars the majestic façade of the École Militaire. But when one turned back to face the Seine, all that was visible were the vast wasteland and escarpments of the Chaillot hill, then several yards higher than it is today, whose crest was occupied by part of the Passy Cemetery. Haussmann had had to level the top of the hill—an operation that had taken no more than three months. The earth dug up by thousands of workers had been removed on two hundred little trucks along a railway of less than a mile operating round the clock. The Place du Roi de Rome (today's Place du Trocadéro) then remained clear for ten years or more, until a new world's fair furnished it with a Moorish-style building that became the ancestor of the present Palais de Chaillot (itself the fruit of another world's fair, held in 1937). The Eiffel Tower was raised on the occasion of the World's Fair of 1889, almost on the spot where the main entrance to the "Expo" of 1867 had stood.

The style of the massive iron-and-glass structure was universally criticized by people with taste as heavy and vulgar. Yet 10 million visitors, including an impressive number of crowned heads, flocked to this temple of industrial production—and of all the world's cuisines. To speak of gastronomy would not be quite right. Beneath the awning were restaurants and refreshment stands where people could eat and drink in the French, English, German, or Russian style. They laughed at the supposedly Dutch or Italian waitresses who acknowledged their orders with a local accent. The exhibition revealed caviar, salmon, or Italian dishes to curious diners who knew of them only by reputation. Beer—from Strasbourg, Bohemia, Bavaria, and Belgium—also made its appearance on the lists of Parisian brasseries and restaurants, never to leave them again.

The seven galleries juxtaposed in the form of an ellipse were linked at right angles by walkways, like the spokes of a wheel, which joined the center to the extremities of the huge building. Each gallery illustrated a particular theme: the machine gallery, which gave its name to the whole, included the galleries of raw materials, clothing, furniture, equipment, liberal arts, and fine arts; the final one, the gallery of the history of work, circled the central garden. A clever layout meant that the cross paths linked stands from the same country in each of the seven galleries.

There were many novelties at the exhibition, ranging from compressed gas machinery to railway safety signals. Aluminium also made its appearance, along with phenol for the effective combating of cholera; oil was beginning to display its varied potential. The consumer society was also beginning. Rocking chairs from America were a great success, and poorer visitors could admire such gleaming new objects as silver-coated zinc chandeliers, whitewood bed frames, colored wallpaper, wicker cradles, and cardboard dolls. Workers' homes were on display in the machine gallery, alongside a huge section of bric-a-brac in which an enormous Krupps cannon jostled ambulances and country ovens. The park around the gallery was an international bazaar where various *tableaux vivants* offered the public a distillation of the clichés associated with each culture: Russians with horses in front of their *izba* home, Arabs in a tent, Mexicans on Aztec tombs, Chinese women beneath a pagoda, Tunisian cafés, and lots of Turks. Bibles were handed out, and there was preaching in all languages. The photographic studios were a big hit.

Princes who visited the exhibition were struck by the wide range of French products and by the impression of wealth and abundance provided by the Expo and the capital itself. Haussmann took part in the festivities. He returned to the Hôtel de Ville to organize the receptions and gala evenings which, from April 3 through to October 26, honored the emperors of Russia and Austria, Wilhelm I of Prussia together with Bismarck and Moltke (future general commanding the German armies during the war of 1870–1871), and the kings of Belgium, Sweden, Portugal, Greece, Bavaria, and Württemberg. Queen Victoria had been inconsolable since the death of Prince Albert, and her place was taken by the much-acclaimed Prince of Wales. People also cheered the sultan of Turkey and the viceroy of Egypt; the Suez Canal, then being built under the auspices of the Saint-Simonian Ferdinand de Lesseps and largely funded by French savers, would open two years later and was widely seen in Paris as a French achievement. The tsar arrived on June 1 and drove along a route that tactfully avoided the Boulevard de Sébastopol. The next day, as he was visiting the Palais de Justice, shouts of "Long live Poland!" echoed in the air. And on the afternoon of June 6, as he was returning from a parade at Longchamp, a bullet fired by the Pole Berezowski missed its target thanks to the presence of mind of one of Napoléon III's horsemen. "We have seen fire together, so now we are brothers-in-arms," Napoléon III said, with more reasons than one. Nor did the tsar's reply depart from his usual calm: "Our lives are in the hands of Providence."

Still more than in 1855, the whole of Paris benefited from the curiosity and the money of the visitors who streamed into the city. Guidebooks led them through the maze of cafés and restaurants; there was something for every taste and every pocket, starting with the à la carte restaurants on the right bank: the Boeuf à la Mode, the Véfour, the Café de Chartres or de Margeuery or de Brabant, the Maison Dorée, the Café Riche, Café du Helder, and Café de la Paix, the Lucas on Place de la Madeleine, or Ledoyen on the Champs Élysées. On the left bank, well-off customers had the choice between the Tour d'Argent, Lapérouse, Magny, the Fleurus café, or the Café d'Orsay. Other restaurants offered fixed-price menus—for example, the Dîner de Paris, the Dîner du Rocher, the Dîner du Commerce, or the Dîner Européen, where it was possible to lunch on 2 or 2.50 francs and have an evening meal for 3 or 4 francs. There were many even cheaper places—from the Odéon and Colbert restaurants to Tavernier's, Demory's, and Catelain's—where a meal could be had for 1.25 francs. For several years a fashion for foreign cuisines had been spreading. In 1840 there had been only two Italian restaurants where the better sections of society could show themselves: Biffi on the rue de Richelieu, and Broggi on rue Le Peletier. Now there were ten or more. English restaurants were also in the running: the Taverne Britannique on the rue de Richelieu, Byron's Tavern on rue Favart, Hill's Café on the Boulevard des Capucines, or London's Tavern on the rue du faubourg Saint-Honoré. The less affluent tourist could find wine merchants on every street corner, some of which had a specialty like the *Tripes à la mode de Caën* at Joanne's, or eating places such as the Duval chain, whose twelve establishments had fanned out from the parent house in a former dance hall on rue Montesquieu.

Guidebooks also listed the musical cafés that were much in vogue at the time. The most chic was the Café des Îles, which had been operating in the Bois de Boulogne since 1865. The Beuglant still held the favor of intellectuals. But visitors were spoiled for a choice between the Vert-Galant, the Pavillon de l'Horloge run by the Pole Markowski, the El Dorado, the Folies-Marigny, the Café du Géant, the Bataclan on the Boulevard du Prince Eugène (Boulevard Voltaire), and the Café de France on Boulevard Bonne Nouvelle, where there was a crush every evening. Visitors could also relax at dozens of dance halls—from the Jardin Mabille through the Ranelagh and Château des Fleurs to many a Tivoli, Vauxhall, Élysées-Montmartre, or Château-Rouge; from the Constant, Dourlans, Commerce, Reine-Blanche, or Pré-aux-Clercs to the Auvergne-style hall of La Musette on the rue du Four.

More ribald guides explained how to find one's bearings among the ladies of the night, the demimonde of *cocottes*, *lionnes*, and *biches*. The top of the range could not be had for under a million francs a night—celebrities with such names as Anna Deslions, Juliette Beau la Marseillaise, Cora Pearl, Blanche d'Antigny, and La Païva (whose private house, still visible on the Champs Élysées, bears witness to the fortunes that some of these women managed to accumulate). The most famous of all was not a professional but an actress called Hortense Schneider. Offenbach guessed her talent when he gave her the role of Hélène in *La Belle Hélène*, which maintained its popularity from opening night on December 17, 1864. Men who had done well out of life went to pay homage at the feet of Hortense Schneider, so much so that she acquired the nickname "Passageway of Princes."

The Parisian theatre proved up to the level of the World's Fair. A few months earlier, on October 31, 1866, Offenbach's *La Vie parisienne* had had its premiere at the Théâtre du Palais Royal, and it was used in the main publicity for the Expo. His *Grande-Duchesse de Gérolstein*, which opened on April 12, 1867, had people flocking to see it. In a different genre, Gounod's *Romeo and Juliet* attracted aficionados of lyrical art when it opened on April 7 at the old opera house on rue Le Peletier. The days of that building were numbered, since work was already far advanced on Charles Garnier's monumental Opera House.

The imperial court tasted the pleasures of *tableaux vivants*, a rather unusual genre constructed around mythological themes in which beauties showed off their charms in diaphanous and (this being Antiquity) somewhat skimpy attire. After one such performance, the electrified crown prince of Prussia turned to his ambassador in Paris, Baron Goltz, and said: "I am glad you are not married, my dear Goltz. If you were, I would feel compelled to ask my father to recall you—because there is too much fun and games here." His father, Wilhelm, had other interests. He went with Haussmann to visit the Buttes-Chaumont park, whose view over the capital inspired him to say: "It was through that gate that we entered in 1815." Haussmann thought he had a duty to reply: "Yes, but we have built some forts since then." More courteously, Alexander of Russia congratulated the prefect with words that were soon doing the rounds of the city: "Before the queen that is Paris, we are no longer more than bourgeois." The reception held on June 8 at the Hôtel de Ville in honor of the two visiting sovereigns gathered together eight thousand guests and remained in memory as one of the most dazzling of the World's Fair.

A few days later, Paris learned that Maximilian of Mexico had been abandoned by Bazaine's French troops, captured by enemy forces at Querétaro, put on trial, and shot on June 19. As a sign of mourning, galas and official receptions were canceled. And when the festivities resumed, people's hearts were no longer really in it. Meanwhile Berezowski was tried and, much to the tsar's chagrin, was not sentenced to death but only to forced labor for life.

Napoléon III and Empress Eugénie felt the need for a change of air and arrived in Salzburg on August 18 to stay with Franz-Joseph. It was a visit that Bismarck took very badly. Back in France, Napoléon III said in a public speech at Lille: "Black spots have darkened our horizon." On October 23, Franz-Joseph paid a visit of his own to Napoléon III. At a banquet held at the Hôtel de Ville on October 28, the emperor of Austria spoke of peace in Europe before a number of crowned heads. It was the last display of fireworks at a lavish feast already darkened by threatening clouds.

Soon the guns were talking. In December 1866, French troops left Rome after the Italian government had promised not to try anything against the pope. In the autumn of 1867, Garibaldi—probably paid by the king of Italy—threatened what was left of the Papal States. Napoléon III massed his troops at Toulon, and after much hesitation decided to send them to Rome. By October 30, the French were back in the Eternal City. On November 3, papal forces attacked Garibaldi's men at Mentana, a few hours' march from Rome, and when they found themselves in difficulty some two hundred French soldiers intervened in their support and inflicted heavy losses on the Garibaldians with their new chassepot rifles. In Paris, the head of the expeditionary force praised the new weapon in his report: "The chassepots worked wonders." It was the end of the Franco-Italian friendship. For good measure, Rouher was applauded by conservatives as he declared to the Legislature: "Never shall Italy lay hold of Rome. Never shall France support such violence to its honor, to the Catholic Church." It is said that Napoléon III congratulated Rouher on his speech and reminded him of his own remark to the court clerk who read out his life sentence after the trial at Boulogne-sur-Mer: "In politics, you must not say *never*." As if in direct response, Victor Emmanuel muttered: "We shall make him see his Never."

THE PREFECT ATTACKS THE RESTING PLACE OF THE DEAD

☙ The Seine prefect was also in difficulty. First he was the object of fierce attack in connection with his plans for cemeteries. The affair of Montmartre Cemetery and the moving of Admiral Baudin's tomb was but one aspect of a wider problem posed by the bringing into Paris of three cemeteries that had previously been outside the city limits: Père-Lachaise, Montparnasse, and Montmartre. Their combined area was 151 acres, and they could not expand further. Until 1859—that is, until the incorporation of the suburban communes—the average number of burials had been around 32,000 to 33,000 a year, with high points in 1853 and 1854 (years of food shortages) and 1855 (the year of the World's Fair). But improvements in living standards and public health had been lengthening the human life span, which averaged 42 years by the end of 1869.

Haussmann needed extra space corresponding to a total of 44,000 to 47,000 burials a year. Furthermore, higher incomes and greater sensitivity toward the dead meant that contracting out was on the rise and that ever fewer Parisians were being buried in a pauper's grave. As cemeteries in the newly incorporated communes were rather small (a total of 35 acres) and close to saturation, Haussmann concluded that the only solution was the development of cemeteries outside the new city limits. But he needed to find 57 acres a year—that is, over a fifty-year period, between 2,595 and 2,965 acres. It then occurred to him that it might be best to look for a single large space well outside Paris, in one of the rural communes where land was cheap. He set his sights on Méry-sur-Oise, but this did not stop him from setting up a commission to look into sites closer to the capital, at Blanc-Mesnil and Massy, which could offer 4,942 acres and 741 acres of land respectively, at a price significantly higher than in Méry and with hydrological conditions rather unsatisfactory from the point of view of environmental health. Strengthened in his original conviction, Haussmann examined the feasibility of a special rail link that relatives could use to accompany or visit their dear departed. The final plan was on his desk on July 5, 1867. A week later he launched the public inquiry, and at his request the prefect for the Seine-et-Oise department did the same. Haussmann was concerned to forestall speculation in the area, and so he had started buying up the land in early 1866 without waiting for authorization from the municipal council. Thus when the public inquiry opened, the city of Paris already owned 1,268 acres at Méry without being aware of it.

The inquiry reports were favorable. As soon as they were delivered to

Haussmann, in November 1867, he set in motion the procedures required for municipal approval and for a declaration of public benefit. Then a dispute broke out over the special rail link as hostile petitions flooded into the offices of the Senate, Legislature, and emperor. Haussmann had to modify his plan: funeral processions would still take place to the existing cemeteries, where relatives could proceed to a specially furnished room and, without tiring themselves, travel by train for the twenty minutes to Méry. He also made the big mistake of publicly referring to costs and profitability. Everything he said by way of explanation seemed to trigger a fresh dispute. Napoléon III postponed his decision.

On April 21, 1868, *Le Figaro* published a long article from a reader, Olympe Audouard, whose son lay at rest in Montmartre Cemetery. Drawing a connection between the Méry project and the Pont Caulaincourt affair, she waxed indignant about a prefect who had forced "millions of families" to leave their homes and was now attacking the resting place of the dead: "All nations, even those we call barbarian, have kept their respect for the dead. The field of rest is inviolable among them." Baron Haussmann was turning everything into a question of money, whereas tears and pain knew no price.

Haussmann waited out the year before trying to revive the project, but then Rouher suddenly decided that a law was required to settle the issue. As there was a lot of business on the legislative agenda, the bill did not come up for discussion before Haussmann found himself out of office. It was raised on several occasions under the Third Republic, but the reactions were the same and the option of "Parisian cemeteries" in communes closer to the capital was finally adopted.

MORE TAXES OR MORE LOANS?

❧ Haussmann had wanted to retire upon the close of the World's Fair, but the emperor had persuaded him to stay on. Now he was ever more bitterly regretting it. Close on the heels of the Méry affair came a much graver challenge to his record of financial management.

After the cost overruns on the second system, the third system had run into financial difficulties right from the start. Should the tax burden on Parisians be increased? Haussmann had made it dogma that there should be no increases. Napoléon III wanted to lower the duty on articles of consumption, which affected everyone, and to increase personal and property taxes that touched only those with high incomes. Haussmann had to impress upon him that there was no comparison between the revenues from the two categories: 6 million francs from direct taxes in 1853, scheduled to rise to 12.5 million by 1870; but 41 million rising to 107.5 million from indirect duties. How could this manna be forgone without endangering the *grands travaux*?

Haussmann's argument did not stop Napoléon III from telling municipal councillors on August 13, 1861, at the inauguration of Boulevard Malesherbes: "I urge you above all, in examining your budget, to reduce the duty on basic necessities by as large an amount as finances permit. You will thereby acquire new rights to my gratitude."[16] While Napoléon III was growing impatient, Haussmann explained in his "Report to the Emperor on the City's Financial Situation" (dated May 20, 1868) that the rising cost of living had been accompanied with an increase in the average income of Parisians, and therefore a decline in the relative weight of duties expressed in constant francs. But he also provided the good news that there would be no difficulty in halving the duty on wine from 44 million francs to 22 million a year. Napoléon III was satisfied—although the reduction still had to be endorsed by the government, as a tax payable to the Treasury was involved in addition to the municipal duty. As one might have expected, the finance minister was opposed. Haussmann's departure and the war of 1870 then buried the whole idea.

Haussmann's success in defending his tax pledge still left the question of how additional funds were to be raised. Borrowing was out of the question, given that the Legislature, as well as the Council of State and all political forces in both the majority and the opposition, were against it. Since Fould's return as finance minister and the reconciliation between Napoléon III and Rothschild in the early 1860s, use of the Bourse had become wiser and less frenzied. The leading banks wanted to impose mechanisms whereby they would regain a preponderant position in the raising and allocation of investment credit. They were also behind the creation in 1864 of the Société Générale, which became not only the country's foremost deposit bank, with a huge network of branches siphoning off the money of small savers, but also a major commercial bank supporting industrial investment and business connected with public works and construction. The Société Générale thus became a player in the Parisian *grands travaux*, where it challenged the near-total dominance of the Pereires. This surge of activity on the part of the banks was one of the factors enabling Haussmann to find without much difficulty the contractors who would carry out work on the third system at a fixed price. The Société Générale financed, for example, the firms that handled the Avenue Kléber project (where the bank's involvement was as high

as 4 million francs), the rue de Turbigo extension, the opening of rue Réaumur, and the development of the Rochechouart *quartier*.

IRREGULARITIES OF MANAGEMENT?

<≈ The relaunching of public works under the contract system gave Haussmann the idea of credit certificates, which allowed him to "hold out" for another ten years before engulfing him in disaster.

Let us recall the mechanism of a contract operation. When a firm agreed
to open a street for a fixed price, it undertook to make delivery within a period set by the city under the terms of the contract. It negotiated with the
relevant landlords and paid compulsory purchase or eviction compensation
on behalf of the city; it carried out the road works and supplied all the requisite amenities, under the supervision of the municipal authorities; and it
resold demolition material and land in excess of the city's requirements.
Nothing prevented it from buying the surplus land itself—indeed, the city
favored the practice, because it speeded up construction along the elegant
new boulevards and helped to ensure that they were not blighted by waste
land for years to come. As the contractors' income from these sources was less
than their outlay, the city made up the difference by means of a subsidy
payable on acceptance of the completed works. The firm was thus in a way
the city's banker. In return, it had to deposit a sum equal to the value of its
undertakings. The resulting play of sureties and credits opened up interesting possibilities for the banks, which on occasion took the plunge themselves and invested in the construction of new blocks.

For the contractors, the fact that the subsidy was payable only at the very
end of their work created formidable cash-flow problems. Haussmann therefore authorized them to issue "credit certificates" [*bons de délégation*] for a
sum equal to the agreed subsidy—veritable bills drawn on the city and recognized by it which could, of course, be discounted by credit institutions.
The certificates were a permanent loan that did not call itself such, completely illegal since the city was entitled to borrow money only by a vote in
the Legislature. This first illegality was compounded by a second. For the
certificates were payable by the Caisse des Travaux de Paris, which, as we
have seen, had the right to issue in any one year bonds to a value not exceeding 100 million francs; the credit certificates represented an annual equivalent of nearly 70 million francs on top of those 100 million, so that the total
obligations of the Caisse des Travaux amounted to some 170 million francs a
year and were in breach of its operational rules.

All the banks in the Paris marketplace discounted the credit certificates since they bore the signature of the Seine prefect representing the city. Most of the certificates, however, gradually ended up in the hands of Crédit Foncier, which offered the most advantageous terms to entrepreneurs. At the end of 1867 the city issued credit certificates to the value of 465 million francs, of which 398 million were held by Crédit Foncier; the annual payments were spread out between 1868 and 1877. The director of Crédit Foncier at that time was none other than Haussmann's old friend Frémy. Berryer, who took a close interest in the credit certificates, used them as the basis for a stand-up fight with the imperial regime and denounced from the rostrum of the assembly what he considered to be the illegal procedure they involved. Rouher defended Haussmann on behalf of the government, arguing that the city had not entered into any unauthorized loan agreement, but at the same time he warned the Seine prefect to put things in order as soon as possible. On December 2, 1867, Haussmann and Frémy signed a contract whereby Crédit Foncier accorded a loan of 465 million francs so that the city could pay off all the certificates; the rate of interest was set at 5.41 percent and the repayment period at sixty years. This was a loan true and proper, which required the consent of the Legislature. The Seine prefect drafted a report for this purpose and had it published in *Le Moniteur* of December 11. Numerous articles and statements took this report to pieces, and it became clear that Haussmann now had very few friends and allies.

In conservative circles it was Léon Say who fired the first shot. His two articles in the *Journal des Débats*, published on May 2 and 3, condemned the system of credit certificates but mostly laid into Crédit Foncier for the excessive amount of money it had made on the operation. As Léon Say was a company director on the railways, and also a financier himself when he felt in the mood for it, people suspected that he was settling old scores with Frémy in his criticisms of the city of Paris. A few months later he was joined by Augustin Cochin, whose arguments were quite similar to his own.

The criticism that caused the greatest stir, however, was that contained in Jules Ferry's series of articles, "Comptes fantastiques d'Haussmann," which appeared in *Le Temps* between December 1867 and May 1868.[17] The end of 1868, he pointed out, would be a crucial date, for it was then that the 180-million-franc agreement was due to expire, and then too that the city was supposed to have finished the *travaux* it had undertaken on its own account. Ferry then reviewed the record of the three road systems. The first system, which had given Paris more than 5 miles of new roads (31,060 feet, to be precise) had cost 272 million francs, 121 million of which had been funded by credit. "This first part of the city works—the most serious part, in our view, and the least subject to criticism—was completed and paid for a long time ago, and it gave rise to no difficulty."[18] Ferry also expressed satisfaction with the second system, comprising nearly 17 miles of new roads (88,563 feet), which had cost 410 million francs and been subsidized by central government in the amount of 50 million francs. "Its purpose had been to link the center of Paris, already opened up by the *travaux* of the first system, to the outer parts; the *quartiers* of the perimeter to the buildings housing the public authorities; and the whole city to the railway termini."[19] It was the third system, "purely and simply M. Haussmann's personal system," which drew Ferry's fire. He saw in it nothing more than "massive demolition" combined with 17 miles of development, striking every neighborhood in Paris, at a scheduled cost of 300 million francs that seemed without any justification. All in all, work on the three systems, on the incorporation of the suburban communes and the various municipal undertakings, would end up costing the city of Paris more than 2 billion francs.

Ferry next tried to show that the Seine prefect had no right to complain of the rulings by the Court of Cassation and the Council of State concerning compulsory purchase and eviction compensation. In his view, the agreement with Crédit Foncier was a fool's deal for the city of Paris—more or less what Léon Say had said. More serious, he denounced the credit certificates as completely illegal and covered the Caisse des Travaux de Paris with the same opprobrium, even casting doubt on the reality of the surpluses evoked by Haussmann. The only conclusion was that the system should be urgently wound up, and that the political career of Baron Haussmann should be terminated at the same time.

The social criticism underlying Ferry's attack was that while the *travaux* had been an ego trip for Haussmann, probably facilitated by shady maneuvers of one kind or another, their main function for the Second Empire born of the bloody coup d'état of December 2 had been to deport the working-class population. In 1869 a pamphlet entitled *Les Finances de l'Hôtel de Ville*, by J. E. Horn, a liberal economist and journalist of Hungarian origin who had taken refuge in Paris, contained a similar analysis of the social and economic context of the transformation of Paris. Horn, like Ferry, took issue with the theory of productive expenditure. Haussmann's great good fortune was that the theory had worked out on this particular occasion; the ever growing revenue generated by the *grands travaux* had enabled the city of Paris to assume without difficulty the huge financial burden they had imposed upon it. But the wager could just as well have turned out badly.

The ordeal was certainly turning out badly for Haussmann, as the National Audit Office took charge of the affair. It declared that the credit certificates were disguised loans and also challenged the propriety of all the contract agreements and the Caisse des Travaux itself—virtually everything to do with the operations, in fact.

These judgments made an enormous impact. The settlement agreed with Crédit Foncier was deposited in the offices of the Assembly in February 1869. The committee that examined it held no fewer than thirty sessions, but it eventually backed the draft on condition that the repayment period was reduced from sixty to forty years; there can be no doubt that several members of the committee, because of their own professional activity, were envious of what they saw as Crédit Foncier's good fortune. The reporter, Du Miral, exonerated Haussmann of the other charges against him and recommended that the Legislature accept the agreement as amended. The debate on the floor of the assembly lasted for eleven sessions, from February 22 to March 8. It was a bitter affair. The big names—Jules Ferry and Léon Say, supported by Thiers and Ernest Picard—threw themselves into it with gusto. Thiers put the Second Empire and its financial methods in the dock: "There are as many sorcerers in France as there are spendthrift prefects." Members of the majority saw it as an opportunity to let off steam at little cost: "We believe it is important," one of them said, "for the Chamber to show by a deliberate action that it does not approve of any of the irregularities that have been committed, and that it demands respect for the law from one and all."

Sensing which way the wind was blowing, Rouher bestowed a few words of praise on the baron before moving on to a withering assault. First, he rejected any notion that the emperor himself was implicated: "No doubt the emperor was able to perceive the necessity of the transformation of Paris. But it is an unacceptable error to make him responsible for matters concerning the city's accounts and management." To condemn Haussmann was not to attack Napoléon III. "I do not hesitate to admit that the local administration went beyond its rights. . . . But the Chamber can feel assured. In future there will be no more contracting out, no more discounting of bills, no more disguised loans. The Caisse des Travaux Publics will soon be wound up. There will be no more credit certificates." Haussmann's faults could not stain the glory of the imperial *grands travaux*. "We have founded the great city, the queen of cities. We have accomplished a great endeavor. If there was also some irregularity of management, this will be forgotten and the grandeur of the enterprise will remain in the memory."

Haussmann defended himself before the Senate: "I admit that, as far as I am concerned, repentance is weak because there is not a complete conviction that a sin has been committed." If there had been faults of management, the urgent necessity of the transformation of Paris excused and justified them. "The municipal administration understood that boldness of resolution was needed to match the size of the danger, and that it should not recoil from any effort to avoid a patent failure of duty toward the state."

The Legislature finally approved the agreement with Crédit Foncier by a large majority: 185 in favor, 41 against, 27 abstentions. Without asking for it, the city was granted the right to borrow money to repay Crédit Foncier ahead of schedule; Frémy's enemies hoped that this would deny him at least a part of the cake. Under considerable pressure, Haussmann immediately borrowed 250 million francs, in the form of 400-franc bonds sold for 345 francs, with an interest rate of 3 percent, or 12 francs per bond. The finance minister also compelled him to set up a syndicate to guarantee the loan—a syndicate which, in a sign of the times, would be led by Rothschild, Hottinguer, and the Société Générale. On April 19, 1869, Haussmann had a decree passed to ensure that the Caisse des Travaux de Paris was liquidated by January 1, 1870. He knew that his own days were numbered.

THE DEPARTURE OF BARON HAUSSMANN

⪻ The legislative elections of 1869 went badly for Napoléon III. The opposition, speaking through Thiers, demanded the "necessary freedoms." The emperor issued a message on July 12 that went farther down the road of parliamentarianism, giving the Assembly the right to appoint its own presiding committee and enlarging its right to amend legislation and to demand answers to questions. Rouher was thanked for his services on July 13, and a transitional cabinet was formed under the moderate Forcade de la Roquette. Rouher had himself suggested to the emperor that he appoint Haussmann minister of the interior. "In the end, his superiority is undeniable and he will be most capable of defending himself from the rostrum." But the plan came to nothing. Long discussions were held with Émile Ollivier, who eventually agreed to serve as minister of justice and religion instead of heading the government; he did not dispute the emperor's choice for war minister and navy minister, but he wanted to have the final say over all the rest. He also wanted Haussmann's head. The new government was formed on January 2, 1870. As Ollivier testifies, Napoléon III did all he could for his prefect to remain in place: "The emperor wanted to keep Haussmann. I myself shrank from thrusting aside a man of such superior administrative abilities. But it was quite impossible to keep him on. His administration, to which justice was not yet done, had caused too much of an outcry."

The emperor eventually yielded, and proposed as his replacement Senator Chevreau, the Rhone prefect and the man with the longest service in the highest rank after Haussmann. Napoléon III sent Georges-Eugène a signed letter asking for his resignation. Haussmann refused: he wanted to be dismissed. On January 6 the decree was published: "M. Haussmann is relieved of his functions and replaced by M. Henri Chevreau." The news was received with jubilation. Émile Ollivier was right: it was one of the symbolic gestures that people needed. Girardin wrote: "History will not believe that the author of the transformation of Paris could have been dismissed."

Haussmann packed his bags. Loyal colleagues danced attendance upon him, messages of sympathy arrived in such number that special registers were opened to record them. Madame Baroche could not get over it: "More people kept flocking to the Hôtel de Ville than for a gala evening with a multitude of guests." On the afternoon of January 6, Haussmann was received by Napoléon III in private audience. For two hours the sovereign explained and apologized; the empress appeared and bemoaned the fact that state interests could require a sacrificial victim high enough to satisfy public opinion but not so close as to touch the emperor's own person.

On January 7, as Haussmann was preparing to take leave of the municipal council, its president Dumas took the initiative of organizing a visit by its collected members to say farewell to the fallen prefect. A written record was made of the meeting. "Having been informed that Baron Haussmann had been relieved of his functions as Seine prefect and that he intended to come and say his farewells in the ordinary meeting hall, the members of the council unanimously and spontaneously took themselves off to him at once to communicate their deep sympathy for the eminent administrator they had had the honor of assisting for so many years in the work of transforming Paris, and whose high intelligence and tireless activity they had so often had occasion to appreciate. Upon returning to the council hall, the President interpreted the feelings of the assembly and decided that mention should be made of this action in the minute-book, and that the words spoken on this occasion by Baron Haussmann should be recorded there." Haussmann was moved and became a little entangled, not avoiding a certain grandiloquence. He spoke of the general who falls dying in the last moment of battle, as well as of England, the French administration, patriotism, and the sense of duty.[20]

On January 10, Haussmann was still there, waiting for Chevreau to leave

Lyons and to come and replace him. The interior minister, Chevandier, did not wish the situation to drag on forever and asked the departing prefect to present his main colleagues to himself. With a provocative hauteur, Georges-Eugène led the gleaming procession of uniformed heads of department with impeccable order into the minister's reception room. Chevandier paid homage to the prefect, who stood with his sword at his side and briefly replied: "I feel especially flattered by this appreciation for my career, and in particular for my work in Paris, because I must confess that I did not expect it on your part. I joined the state administration under the government of the illustrious Casimir Périer, in 1831. Your revered father was one of those who vouched for me at the time. I could not feel happier that, after thirty-eight years, his son has become minister in his turn and wishes to recognize in public that I have not compromised that honorable recommendation." Haussmann bowed and walked toward the door.

19

The Lion Grown Old

HAUSSMANN was in no hurry to leave Paris; he had a thousand things to do. Scarcely eight days after his departure from the Hôtel de Ville, he learned that some left-wing deputies intended to demand that charges be laid against him. In the press, Henri Rochefort supported these calls with his pen: "M. Haussmann does not own a single property in Paris; his known fortune is a few hundred thousand francs. . . . He has nothing, but his son-in-law, M. de Pernetty, is a millionaire a hundred times over; his daughter owns twenty houses and his wife has hundreds of thousands of meters of land." Haussmann took up his pen to hit back at such detractors, and also overwhelmed the emperor with recriminations and advice on the conduct of political affairs.

Quarrels surrounding the baron were soon eclipsed by more serious concerns. On January 10 the Victor Noir affair broke into the open, so called after the republican journalist who challenged to a duel Prince Pierre Bonaparte (son of Lucien and therefore cousin of Napoléon III) and, in circumstances not fully explained, was killed by a pistol shot from the prince. The opposition drew a comparison with the Republic murdered on December 2, 1851. *La Marseillaise* appeared the following day with black borders and an editorial by Rochefort: "I was weak enough to believe that a Bonaparte could be anything other than a murderer. . . . For eighteen years France has been in the bloodstained hands of these ruffians who, not content with gunning down republicans in the street, draw them into vile traps in order to slit their throats at home. People of France, do you really not think there has been enough of it?" The government reacted promptly: Prince Pierre was arrested, *La Marseillaise* impounded, Rochefort prosecuted. On January 12 the funeral was the occasion for a huge demonstration, said to have been a hundred thousand strong, but as darkness fell everyone returned home. Scattered disturbances continued, and on February 7, Rochefort was placed under arrest.

The government was certainly scared, but the regime held fast. On April 20 the Senate adopted a text codifying the liberal reforms, and electors were called upon to say "yes" or "no" to the following formulation: "The people approves the liberal reforms that the emperor, with the help of the great institutions of the state, has operated under the Constitution since 1860, and endorses the senatorial judgment of April 20, 1870." The plebiscite held on May 8 gave a majority of 7.5 million "yes" against 1.5 million "no," with 1.9 million abstentions. The big cities, headed by Paris, had a majority against. But thanks to the rural vote, the empire gained the same results as in 1852; it seemed to everyone to be more solid than ever.

At the Hôtel de Ville, Henri Chevreau pressed on with Haussmann's work. Devinck, who still chaired the finance committee, presented his report on the special budget for 1870 to the municipal council: "The prefect asked us to examine the financial situation, to call the directors before us, and to conduct the most exhaustive inquiry." These were not the methods of Chevreau's predecessor, and one imagines that the speaker, like the majority of the council, thought that while courtesy toward councillors might be in the air, it should not result in abdication of the prefecture as an institution. In any event, Chevreau limited himself to continuing the current operations, with the same staff and the same mechanisms as before.

Meanwhile, Haussmann decided to rest for a while in Nice with his family. A few years earlier, he had purchased a former oil mill among the olive trees of Mont Boron, and he had had it converted into an elegant villa with gardens laid out by Alphand and a wonderful view of the sea. The previous year Haussmann had enlarged the property by acquiring six or seven acres of rocky ground. Almost next door, Frémy owned a splendid villa of his own, and he had also come to spend a few days in Nice. The two friends went walking, Haussmann in his overcoat and Nice-style hat. But he saw no one apart from his family and Frémy, and never went down into the town. He still had not absorbed the shock of his eviction. Although he had brought it upon himself, he had perhaps even then only half-believed that it would happen.

Haussmann made a few return trips to Paris. On May 21 he went to the Louvre for the official declaration of the results of the plebiscite. It may be that he heard the emperor declare: "More than ever we should look fearlessly ahead to the future." On June 12 he was at Longchamp racecourse for the

Grand Prix. Napoléon III noticed Georges-Eugène from his stand and sent Pietri to call him over.[1] He then invited him to dinner the next day at Saint-Cloud, where the two men spoke freely together for quite a long time. The emperor confided that he would like to bring Haussmann into the government, and his "cohabitation" arrangement with Émile Ollivier gave him control over a number of sensitive ministerial appointments. But Haussmann was clear-sighted enough to realize that, with his unyielding convictions, excessive self-confidence, and abrupt manner, he would make a poor minister.

The month of June appeared calm. No one spoke any longer of laying charges against Haussmann; it was as if his very existence had been forgotten. At the rostrum of the Assembly, Émile Ollivier declared: "Wherever we look, we can see no irritant in operation." Some politicians who looked more closely, however, knew that war had become inevitable. In Berlin, Bismarck wanted it in order to complete German unification around Prussia; Paris did not want war, yet accepted its coming as a fact and set about reorganizing the army.

At the beginning of July, a Hohenzollern bid for the Spanish throne ignited the fuse. Prince Leopold von Hohenzollern, a relative of Wilhelm I of Prussia, had in fact been offered the crown of Spain. France protested to Wilhelm, and on July 11 the prince withdrew his candidacy. This victory for the French government enraged Bismarck, who felt humiliated and thought of resigning. But then Paris asked the king of Prussia to make his decision valid for all time, and to put it in writing. Wilhelm, who still believed in a word of honor, thought he had made enough concessions and refused to go further. Bismarck falsified the record of his sovereign's last interview with the French ambassador, and this became the famous Ems telegram, a red rag to the bull of Gallic pride. The result is well known: on July 15 the Assembly declared war on Prussia.

For diametrically opposite reasons, war was also welcome both to Émile Ollivier—who went so far as to tell his fellow deputies: "Today begins a great responsibility, which we accept with a light heart"—and to Empress Eugénie, who thought that victory in battle, together with the emperor's standing down, would be the surest way of ensuring her son's future with herself as regent. Napoléon III, his will totally sapped by illness, let her persuade him to set off at the head of the armies. On July 28 he left by coach for the camp at Châlons. But he was in no state to command any action and merely paralyzed the generals with his presence. Eugénie, driven on by her reactionary entourage, sought to profit from her husband's absence and the patriotic fever to reverse the liberal tendency of the regime. Émile Ollivier demanded that the emperor return to Paris; the empress fiercely opposed it. When the Assembly adopted an agenda hostile to the government, Ollivier resigned. The empress regent formed a new cabinet under General Cousin-Montauban, comte de Palikao, all too celebrated for his sacking of the Winter Palace in Beijing in September 1860.

There was talk of bringing Haussmann into the government. Ollivier had already considered the idea in judging that "the only practical, farsighted and effective combination" to succeed him would be "a vigorous government including, apart from Rouher, staunch first-rate people from whom one need fear neither desertion nor pusillanimity: Granier de Cassagnac, Persigny, Haussmann, Pinard, Forcade." The empress urged the baron to take the Ministry of the Interior. Haussmann accepted—but only on condition that the emperor returned to Paris. The empress would not hear of it, and so the ministry was given to Chevreau. Magne took over as finance minister.

Haussmann remained in Paris and took his place in the Senate, where he presented several legislative measures concerning national defense that had been proposed by the Palikao cabinet. When Prussian troops captured Châlons-sur-Marne without meeting any resistance, he lambasted the mayor's conduct before the upper house. The mayor wrote to the Senate in defense of his attitude. His letter arrived on September 3; Haussmann read it with emotion to his fellow senators and made honorable amends for the harsh things he had said a few days before. Public opinion was calling for the return of the emperor and the appointment of General Trochu to defend the capital from impending danger. The empress rejected the second demand as well as the first, since Trochu had the reputation of being a liberal. But time had already run out. On September 2 the ailing Napoléon III surrendered with MacMahon's army at Sedan. Parisians heard the news when they rose on the morning of September 4.

With Napoléon III a prisoner, the empress fled distraught from Paris without trying to cling to power. The deputies representing Paris, all republicans, went to the Hôtel de Ville and declared the end of the empire. The *journées* of September 4 and 5 passed without bloodshed, but soon the crowd wanted the heads of Rouher, Baroche, and Ollivier. Former dignitaries of the empire prudently left Paris, most of them soon to go abroad, while Haussmann decided to head for Bordeaux. When the Gironde prefect learned of his presence there, he asked Paris for instructions. But as these were a long time coming, and as Haussmann thought they would not necessarily be favorable to him, he took to the road again and crossed over to Italy with a false passport, under an assumed name.

For Baron Haussmann, the fall of the empire was a moral and also a material disaster. It was the end of his days at the Senate, with its annual income of 30,000 francs; he could no longer hope for more than a prefect's basic pension of 6,000 francs a year. Gone was the briefly cherished dream of a reward for services rendered to the city of Paris. He never ceased to complain of the thoughtless attitude that had left him burdened more with debts than with wealth at the end of his tenure at the Hôtel de Ville—or anyway, less well off than he had been in 1853 when Napoléon III had called him to the Seine prefect's job. Now, at the age of 63, he would have to find work to supplement his pension in order to lead a decent existence. But for the time being he was in Italy, in exile.

A study of the baron's correspondence at this time seems to suggest, however, that his situation was not as desperate as he wished people to believe.[2] On his way to Italy, he stopped off for a few days in Nice in the company of a certain "Fr.," who must have been—as Jean des Cars suspects—Francine Cellier. Octavie, fully in the picture, poured out words of advice!

The Haussmanns, who did little to conceal themselves, made do with a single domestic servant. Georges-Eugène traveled incognito to Florence, Pisa, and Rome, where he arrived in December and chanced to meet some Italian friends. No more incognito. The former Seine prefect spent a few days in Naples, discovered Pompeii, then returned to Rome and was asked by the authorities of the new capital of unified Italy to take charge of its redevelopment. Haussmann was flattered and gave a few recommendations, but he could not conceive of living anywhere other than in France.

Just then, on January 28, 1871, the Franco-Prussian War came to a halt. An armistice negotiated by Jules Favre allowed the people of France to elect representative institutions, whose first task would be to reach an agreement with Germany. The conservative-dominated Assembly turned to Thiers, who formed a government on February 19 and presented a draft peace agreement on March 1. The Assembly ratified this and promptly moved its own location to Versailles. A few days later the Commune took power in Paris. Thiers launched the assault in May. Coming on top of the damage caused by German bombardment, the streetfighting and arson attacks resulted in enormous destruction in the city.

The restoration of order permitted such former servants of the empire as Haussmann to return to France. Toward the end of his stay in Italy, some Alsatian friends of his had made the extraordinary offer of a seat in the upper house of the new German state of Alsace-Lorraine, assuring him that it had Bismarck's personal approval. But Haussmann did not think twice before turning it down.

Back in France, Georges-Eugène had to focus on material problems. Five years earlier he had sold his estate at Houeillès, a few miles from Nérac in the Lot-et-Garonne department, and now he wished to do the same with the villa in Nice, which cost a great deal to maintain. He put it on the market but managed to achieve the sale only much later, in 1881, to Princess Kotschoubey, when he would note with a touch of bitterness that it had brought him in much less than it had cost him. The main property left was the Cestas estate, a little south of Bordeaux, which his wife had inherited from her parents in 1862, and which had expanded in stages until it covered almost 2,500 acres.

Haussmann had carried out near-princely construction work at Cestas, as he had done before at Houeillès—reception rooms, a huge library, a study for the lord of the house, visitors' rooms, and outbuildings for a large domestic staff. But that had been in the days of the Seine prefecture, when nothing had seemed too grand. At Houeillès and Cestas, Baltard had assisted Haussmann in the work of planning and supervision: "I had not been so fortunate in readily accepting M. Baltard's obliging offer to direct the work with architects or agents of his choice. In both cases, it seemed natural that he treated me as a client—but not so natural that he treated me as one for whom no expense should be spared, even though I had told him that my resources were much more limited than my high position might lead him to believe. When it came to settling the final bill for the work, . . . despite all possible reductions for various items, I had to pay much more than double the estimate both for the work carried out and for the percentage fees from which M. Baltard himself took a large share."[3]

Cestas was the kingdom of flowers and decorative flowerbeds. The baron's gardener, proud to serve such a great figure and perhaps eager to show that people knew how to lay out gardens in Cestas as well as in Paris, surprised him each year with a new arrangement of flowers. Once he produced a display in the form of a Legion of Honor decoration complete in the smallest detail, against a background of red sage in bloom. Another time he showed that he could also handle simplicity by planting round-shaped canna beds in huge baskets.[4]

Such a property was hard to maintain and difficult to sell because of its sheer size, especially as the phylloxera then starting to ravage the region did not encourage investment in wine. Haussmann ruled out any idea of settling down in Cestas, for he would have had to lead the life of a rich gentleman-farmer without the means to support it. Besides, it was only in Paris that he could hope to find some professional activity again—although there could be no question of his buying an apartment there, as he had once planned. In the end, he was happy to rent a pied-à-terre, a three-room apartment on rue Boissy-d'Anglas.

HAUSSMANN THE BUSINESSMAN

✾ Haussmann thought his experience and his financial abilities might be of interest to a banking or industrial group, especially as his career had always given the impression of an accomplished negotiator. When the six companies holding gas concessions in Paris had merged to form a single one in 1855, they had signed a new contract with the city of Paris. At the time this had been the responsibility of the chief of police, Pietri, only minor matters coming within the province of the Seine prefecture. But Haussmann had felt obliged to enter the fray to help Pietri (of whom he later wrote with pity) cope with all the complexities of the deal. "My colleague, M. Pietri, Sr., could not handle alone this discussion with the ablest businessmen in Paris, headed by MM. Émile and Isaac Pereire. My intervention helped greatly to bring it to a successful conclusion."[5] Nevertheless it was to the Pereire brothers that he now offered his services. They immediately suggested that he take over as chairman of Crédit Mobilier.

Crédit Mobilier had been suffering major setbacks. On January 29, 1866, Napoléon III arranged for authorization for the bank to double its capital—this decision not being unconnected with the success of the Paris city loan in summer 1865. But then the Austro-Prussian War (from May to July 1866) delivered a crushing blow. In 1867 the Bank of France demanded the resignation of the Pereires if it was to continue supervising the operations of Crédit Mobilier. After the Franco-Prussian War and the Commune, the Pereires' bank was virtually bankrupt. But Haussmann, with a fine show of optimism, felt capable of turning things around and took over as managing director of Crédit Mobilier on September 3, 1871. Installed in its handsome offices on Place Vendôme, where the Hotel Ritz is located today, he began looking for the fabulous contracts that would bring money flowing in again.

The Pereires had long had close relations with Turkey. In June 1870 they were asked to back the reconstruction of a part of Constantinople that had recently burned down with four thousand dwellings. Haussmann was the man for the situation. In March 1873 he went to the capital of the Turkish empire, where the viceroy of Egypt entertained him in his palace on the Bosphorus—and showed him the gardens designed there by Barillet-Deschamps. Haussmann stayed four months in Constantinople and founded the Société de Finances et de Travaux Publics de l'Empire Ottoman, a subsidiary of Crédit Mobilier. But the methods of the local administration put him off: he did not feel comfortable in a country where there did not seem to be the assurance of a stable legal framework; and in the end—this may have been the main reason—the city of Constantinople had no money. Haussmann returned to France and shortly afterward resigned from Crédit Mobilier.

Again in search of a lucrative occupation, he considered developing a riverboat service from Le Havre via the Rhone to Marseilles. But it was a tricky route to navigate, and Les Forges et Chantiers de la Méditerranée soon gave up work on a specially designed boat to tackle its furies. Haussmann too gave up the project.

He examined a number of other possibilities, either alone or with his son-in-law Dollfus. He was still interested in Crédit Mobilier, which had sizable assets, and tried to assemble a stable group of shareholders to relaunch the bank. Another "raider," the Belgian Philippart, had the same idea; he managed to put together an independent empire in Belgium, northern France, and Normandy out of various railway companies and industrial enterprises, and he needed banks to support his system of financing acquisitions with the stock of his own companies. A stockholders' battle ensued between Haussmann and Philippart, which the latter won at a general meeting of Crédit Mobilier held on March 2, 1875—a success that allowed him to dream on for another eighteen months before going under. As to Haussmann, he remained in good spirits and turned to new pastures in Paris real estate.

In September 1879, thanks to the support of the Banque Parisienne group, Haussmann and Dollfus founded Rente Foncière. The real estate subsidiary of Crédit Immobilier, known by the name of Compagnie Immobilière, went into liquidation on July 30, 1872, still with large assets valued at 259 million francs on December 31, 1869. In addition to its huge holdings in Marseilles, the company owned in Paris property on the rue de Rivoli, rue Scribe, and Boulevard Malesherbes, the Hôtel du Louvre block, the Grand Hotel block and many other buildings near the Opéra, and dozens of buildings on the Monceau plain. The war of 1870–1871, followed by the Commune and the postwar recession, did not favor major real estate initiatives. But prices were rising again when Haussmann decided that the moment had come to buy. On August 20, 1879, the liquidators of the Compagnie Immobilière put up for auction (with a reserve price of 33 million francs) the Grand Hotel block, the Hôtel Scribe, the building at No. 1, rue Scribe, the Grand Café, and the Courcelles Laundry. Rente Foncière beat the competition with an offer of more than 36.5 million francs—which, together with additional charges, represented an outlay of more than 40 million.

Baron Haussmann's company, with a capital of 12.5 million francs, would never have been able to achieve its ambitions if, two days before the auction, it had not reached an agreement whereby Crédit Foncier opened it a credit line of 200 million francs for future acquisitions, at the extremely favorable interest rate of 4.05 percent. At the time Rente Foncière did not even have a juridical existence. Its deal with Crédit Foncier became known as "the 200-million-franc agreement," a wording that certainly brought back memories. It was signed on September 20, a few days after the official birth of Rente Foncière, having been approved by finance minister Léon Say, an enemy of Haussmann's in 1869 who had since been reconciled with him. Three representatives of Crédit Foncier joined the board of directors of the company chaired by the baron.

The activities of Rente Foncière seemed destined for a rosy future. After the spectacular purchase of blocks in the Opéra *quartier* and investments in the 1st, 2nd, and 9th arrondissements, Haussmann concentrated on real estate in the popular neighborhoods of the 10th and 11th arrondissements, and later in the 18th, where he negotiated the purchase of a whole new *quartier* in Clignancourt comprising 88 blocks with 3,000 dwellings and 189 shops.[6] But the market judged that Rente Foncière had paid too much for the buildings in the Opéra area, and the investment in petty bourgeois or popular neighborhoods created further reservations. Rente Foncière securities plunged so dramatically that Crédit Foncier eventually stepped in to take control of the company. Its one condition was that Haussmann, personally identified with the company's adventurous image, had to go.

Haussmann and Dollfus next tried to start a bank, the Comptoir Foncier, but it proved no more of a success. Clearly the job of creating new companies was harder than the baron had realized.

In 1873, Haussmann became a director of the Compagnie des Entrepôts et Magasins Généraux, and the following year he took over as chairman. The business was in a very bad way: its warehouses had caught fire during the *se-*

maine sanglante that ended the Commune, and many of its debtors (small traders and Parisian industrialists) had been ruined by the Franco-Prussian War and civil war. Haussmann turned things around through force of energy, continuing to chair the company until his death and leaving it in a prosperous condition.

HAUSSMANN IN POLITICS

In the wake of defeat, empire loyalists continued to work for the restoration of Napoléon III. In March 1871, Rouher had already returned with instructions from his master's new home in Chislehurst, near London, and worked alongside Chevreau founding newspapers (*L'Ordre* and *L'Appel au Peuple*), organizing demonstrations, and demanding a plebiscite. On July 2 three Bonapartists were among forty-six new deputies to emerge from a series of by-elections. Haussmann had been sounded out for the Seine list, and the right-wing Union Parisienne de la Presse had mentioned his name. But the republican papers reacted violently and denounced the ghosts from the past; Haussmann did not persevere. When Rouher entered the Assembly in 1872, things seemed to be going well for an imperial comeback. It was not possible to win popular enthusiasm for a bedridden figure, however, and in fact Napoléon III died on January 2, 1873, following an operation to remove a stone. Now the hopes of the Bonapartist camp would focus on the imperial prince, then aged twenty.

On May 23, 1873, the Assembly rid itself of Thiers and appointed Marshal MacMahon to succeed him as head of state. MacMahon charged de Broglie with the formation of a government, and the Bonapartist Fortoul took over at the education ministry. Methods typical of the empire began to appear again, as 1,300 civil servants were dismissed and municipal councils dissolved. On May 20, 1874, Baron de Bourgoing, a former imperial equerry, trounced his radical opponent in a by-election in the Lièvre. As the 1876 elections approached, *Le Figaro* suggested to conservatives in the 1st arrondissement that they should run the former Seine prefect as their candidate. "His name stands for an enlarged, embellished Paris with improved sanitation; M. Haussmann is not a party man." His candidacy was indeed proposed but also sharply contested within the ranks of the right. In the first round, the republican Tirard finished on top with more than 6,000 votes; Haussmann won only 2,958. Deeply disappointed, he preferred to withdraw before the second round took place.

On May 16, 1877, de Broglie dissolved the Assembly, and elections were called for October. This time Haussmann wished to stand at Lesparre, in the Gironde, where the outgoing deputy had made it clear that he would be happy to support him. The local papers vigorously opposed him while the Bonapartist committees made use of his name. The plan ended in failure. Rouher, for his part, was elected in Bastia, Ajaccio (where he beat Prince Napoléon-Jérôme), and Riom, and he eventually settled for his home town of Riom. This meant that a by-election had to be held in Ajaccio, and since the prince was the empress's bête noire, she asked Haussmann to stand in order to bar his way. Georges-Eugène landed at Ajaccio in the second week of September to stand as the candidate of the empress and the de Broglie government, against Napoléon III's cousin backed by Gambetta and the republicans. The prefect had received orders to support Haussmann. And the bishop, duly lectured by the papal nuncio and the archbishop of Paris, also supported the candidate, "not only [because he is] presented by a government that maintains public safety and respect for religion, but also because in Paris he is unanimously held to be a truly conservative figure as favorable as anyone can be to Catholic interests." The Protestant become the candidate of the clergy! He was also supported by the police and by their cousins, the bandits. He was elected in the first round, having collected more than 8,000 votes to little more than 4,400 for Prince Napoléon-Jérôme.

So now Haussmann represented Corsica in the Assembly, finding himself in good company among forty Bonapartist deputies. During the four years he held a seat, he showed a predilection for committee work; his reports were sensible, well balanced, and farsighted. He filed into the voting lobby with the *Appel au Peuple* group, but he was certainly not cut out for the role of deputy and spoke only twice on the floor of the house. On the first occasion it was to answer Nadeau's aspersions on his past record of management. On the second, in 1878, he appealed for the conservation of Philibert Delorme's central wing of the old Tuileries Palace, which had been reduced to a ruin by the fire of 1871. But his speech had no effect; the government chose to destroy whatever was left of the palace. Haussmann also fought for local Corsican issues and won acceptance that the Ajaccio-Bastia railway should be built in one effort rather than in successive stages.

On June 1, 1879, the imperial prince died in an ambush fighting the Zulus and left the Bonapartist party in complete disarray. The natural successor was Prince Napoléon-Jérôme, but the deceased prince had held him in abhorrence and, in his will, had named Napoléon-Jérôme's son Victor to succeed him at the head of the Bonapartist cause. Napoléon-Jérôme, for all his republican sympathies, declared himself to be the pretender to the imperial throne, in opposition to the testament left by the imperial prince and in opposition to his own son. Haussmann was disgusted by the spectacle that the imperial family was making of itself—a spectacle repeated when the body of the imperial prince was brought back to England. Wild rumors spread in France, some even saying that the corpse was not that of the prince. So Haussmann and the last group of loyalists asked that his coffin be opened. When the empress adamantly refused to allow this, Haussmann insisted: "France has a right to know what the English are giving back to us." Eugénie finally yielded: the corpse was identified and buried close to that of the prince's father.

In July 1879 the Paris municipal council wished to change the names of certain streets on the grounds that they were too evocative of the empire, one such name being that of Boulevard Haussmann. Georges-Eugène, still at that time a deputy for Corsica, tried to calm his indignant friends: "An inscription can be erased. As long as Paris lives, my name will be engraved in all its stones." The council's proposal was rejected by Haussmann's successor at the Seine prefecture, on instructions from the government. Boulevard Haussmann kept its name, even though Victor Hugo got a little caught up in the affair. For the poet thought that his name was going to be given to the boulevard, whereas in reality it was the Avenue d'Eylau (formerly the Avenue de Saint-Cloud) that would eventually become Avenue Victor Hugo.

By the time Haussmann was in his seventies, the internecine disputes of the Bonapartist clan no longer belonged to his era. He supported Prince Victor, out of obedience to the will of the imperial prince and hostility to Prince Napoléon-Jérôme. But how could he fight against Napoléon-Jérôme again at the forthcoming legislative elections? The answer was that he could not. Haussmann did not stand in the elections of 1881.

Besides, the conservative republic suited him well. He was above all a man of action, and as such easily forgot the quarrels of yesteryear. As we have seen, he made up with Léon Say after he had become finance minister. And when Jules Grévy was elected president of the Republic, Haussmann paid him a visit during which the two men saw eye to eye and found that they actually liked each other. In May 1882, *Le Gaulois* published the article by Jules Simon (quoted at the beginning of this book) which paid striking homage to the baron's past activity. Alphand, his former colleague and now himself the city's big man, continued Haussmann's work, lavished upon him the marks of sincere deference, and assisted him in his affairs.

In 1885, Haussmann was asked to head the Gironde list of the Conservative Alliance at the legislative elections. He was defeated. At seventy-six years of age, the time for political struggle was over for him.

Georges-Eugène was now happy enough to court the Muse. In his first published work, *Une campagne administrative dans les Pyrénées*, he evoked playful memories of the subprefecture of Saint-Girons:

> *Le pays est fécond en très aimables filles,*
> *Belles souvent, gracieuses, gentilles,*
> *Presque toujours aux coeurs hospitaliers,*
> *Faisant l'amour gratis et surtout volontiers.* *

In *Fleurette*, published in 1882, he drew on the loves of Henri IV in the Nérac region:

> *Un bellâtre peut bien fasciner mainte femme;*
> *Mais c'est pour le courage ou bien pour le talent,*
> *Pour la gloire surtout que la beauté s'enflamme.* †

Next was *Dans les bois, À propos d'Alfred de Musset*:

> *Musset, mon camarade, était moins fort que moi*
> *—Et notamment en vers—sur les bancs du collège.* ††

Then came *Le Joli Sentier, Sur l'Amour* in October, and finally *La Confession d'un lion devenu vieux*. Despite his fine presence, Haussmann suddenly felt himself to be an old man. On March 5, 1890, his daughter Marie-Henriette died. The baron feverishly speeded up the writing of his *Mémoires*. When the first volume appeared, his publisher noted that the name of the "great baron" had come to stand for "any great program of municipal works." The book aroused widespread interest among the public—as well as a few recollections of forgotten points or even corrections of inaccuracies. The baron attended with even greater regularity meetings of the Academy of Fine Arts to which he was proud to have belonged for nearly a quarter of a century; he had been elected to it on December 7, 1867.

On December 24, 1890, Octavie died. Haussmann acknowledged the

---

*The land abounds in most lovable girls, / Often beautiful, gracious, and pretty, / Nearly always with hospitable hearts, / Making love for free and above all gladly.

†A fop may well entrance many a beauty; / But it is for courage or for talent, / And above all for glory that beauty ignites.

††Musset, my classmate, was not as strong as I / —Especially in poetry—on the school benches.

blow. On January 9, 1891, he chaired a meeting of the board of directors of the Compagnie des Entrepôts et Magasins Généraux with the same application that he had always given to everything he had done. The next day he stayed home to correct the proofs of volume three of his *Mémoires*. The weather had been cold for several days, and Haussmann sometimes had difficulty with his breathing. After dinner he felt he was choking. His relatives called a doctor, who diagnosed an untreatable congestion of the lungs. Haussmann died in the early hours of January 11, 1891, at the age of eighty-two. A few months earlier he had concluded the preface to his memoirs: "I wait in peace for the end of my earthly existence. My only hope now is that death will strike me standing up, as it has struck so many people in the strong generation to which I belong. I shall anyway leave this world, if not with my head held high as in my public life of former years, then at least with a steadfast heart and—as far as heaven is concerned—full of hope in the merciful justice of the Almighty."

The funeral procession crossed Paris from the Place de la Concorde to Père-Lachaise. A military detachment accompanied Haussmann's remains and paid him the homage due to the Grand Cross of the Legion of Honor. The government was not represented, nor was the Seine prefecture or the municipal council. Wreaths were sent by finance companies and Bonapartist committees. Among the two or three hundred people who followed the hearse were personal friends, a few members of the Institut de France, Alphand, municipal councillors in a personal capacity, and representatives of the empress and Prince Victor. The speeches at the cemetery were short and cold. Haussmann lies today in Père-Lachaise, not far from Fould, Baroche, and Musset.

A few months later the Academy of Fine Arts elected his replacement: Adolphe Alphand. In the mouth of the man who had been his closest colleague, and with whom he had established relations of esteem or even affection, the eulogy went beyond the limits of an obligatory ritual: "In his various positions, and later in Paris, Haussmann displayed an outstanding administrative talent, a resourceful ability, an unshakable firmness of character, tireless activity, and an extraordinary capacity for work. He liked to say that the head of a prefect—whose administration encompassed all the public services—should be a kind of encyclopedic dictionary. His investigative mind was always stimulated; it constantly led him on to new questions, which he did not abandon until he had rendered them more profound. His amazing power to absorb new material enabled him to understand everything and to retain everything, so that often, in complete good faith, he took to be his own ideas that he had once adopted from elsewhere. He found the means to do everything and was able to tackle head-on, without tiring, the numerous and varied duties for which he was responsible—without ever avoiding the social obligations that came with his high position."

·IV·

HAUSSMANNIZATION

20

The Ends and the Means

OVER THE PAST 150 years, French people have grown so used to Haussmann that they forget the existence of Berger before him and do not take the trouble to remember the name of his ephemeral successor. For them, as for international public opinion, the *grands travaux* of the Second Empire are the baron's great work. In the climate of polemic and accusation that we have described, new words have emerged to revile excessive use of compulsory purchase powers, blind demolition, and large-scale deportation of the poor: these words are "to Haussmannize" and "Haussmannization."

Time has not calmed the passions, and some continue to regard "Haussmannization" as the criminal work of a modern Nero bent on vandalizing *vieux Paris*, a lackey of property speculators, and a ruthless enemy of the common people. In this view, the apocalypse of the Paris Commune was the supreme protest of workers against a city corseted with pilasters, domes, and barracks that had been superimposed for at least two decades upon the Paris of popular liberties and surging fraternity. Others just as passionately see in Haussmann the model farsighted organizer of a hygienic and bustling city productive of wealth and festivities, the initiator of a style that has remained the *ne plus ultra* of urban redevelopment. He laid everything to waste or he invented everything: those are the two rival views. He was contemptuous of the democratic foundations of city life, some maintain. City planning can flourish only under the iron rule of a prince, others retort. The debate is less academic than one is tempted to think, for Haussmann is here the focus of implacable struggle between two ideologies. This makes it all the more necessary to draw up a balance sheet of his endeavor; we shall now try to sketch its main features—even though the fire at the Hôtel de Ville in 1871 has deprived us of essential archival materials.

For seventeen years Napoléon III and Haussmann exercised joint rule over Paris through a single will, a single constancy, a single team. The driving *will* was essentially that of Napoléon III—yet we know virtually nothing of the thinking behind his redevelopment plans. In the opening pages of this book we saw him alight at the Gare du Nord in 1848 with a color-coded map of the future road systems under his arm. He had certainly read the *Mémorial de Sainte-Hélène*. Indeed, his first steps in the transformation of Paris were a spectacular continuation of his uncle's policy: the closing-up of the Louvres and the Tuileries, the rue de Rivoli extension, the linking together of straight roads, some of which served as major thoroughfares across Paris while others established a grid pattern that made it easier to open up parts of the city for redevelopment. In his *Mémoires*, Haussmann spoke of the "Artists' Plan" as a document that he had once been able to consult. Perhaps Napoléon III also studied it after his return to Paris in 1848. Unfortunately his published works—*Les Idées napoléoniennes* and *L'Extinction du paupérisme*—tell us everything about what he believed with regard to political organization, economic development, and social progress, but remain silent about his conception of the city.

From the moment when Haussmann was called to the Seine prefecture, the two men shared one and the same vision. Maxime Du Camp has given us precise information about the books consulted by Haussmann, as well as precious testimony that when he moved out of the Hôtel de Ville, he left behind a plan he had devised (together with the emperor?) for the future Paris. "M. Haussmann's dream map of the future Paris exists, and it will be to the eternal honor of the man who thought it up. Any administration that wishes to recast Paris will be obliged to consult it and to follow its directions, just as M. Haussmann himself fruitfully consulted Poncet la Grave's *Projet des embellissements de la ville et des faubourgs de Paris* (1756), Dussaussoy's *Citoyen désintéressé* (1767), and especially the *Mémoires sur les objets les plus importants de l'architécture* (1769) by Patte, architect of the Prince de Deux-Ponts [Zweibrücken], a strange book, ahead of its time, which contains a complete system of hydraulic sewers, sidewalks, street lighting, drains, and roads. Although this major work was dedicated to M. De Marigny, no one took any account of it, and the ideas it put forward waited nearly a century before they were realized."[1]

The second characteristic of the *grands travaux* was their *constancy*. In the years before Haussmann arrived on the scene, construction sites were opened without any apparent plan, owing to Berger's negative attitude and the poor organization of his departments. More than once Haussmann had to over-

turn his predecessor's plan, to take measures on the spur of the moment such
as the saving of the tower of Saint-Jacques de la Boucherie, or the digging of
two lakes in the Bois de Boulogne to replace the unviable Serpentine. Other
projects could be completed only with substantial modifications: for example, Napoléon III questioned the architectural design for the Halles when
one wing of it had already been built. The second system of *grands travaux*
set out for the first time a coordinated series of projects to be performed over
a ten-year period. There would be considerable cost overruns, as well as mistakes such as the start of work on the Boulevard du Prince Eugène before it
had been decided which technical means would be used to take it across the
Canal Saint-Martin. Some projects were simply abandoned: Haussmann regretted that it had not been possible to extend the rue de Rennes as far as the
Seine, or that he had been unable to persuade the emperor of his views concerning the Pont Sully design or the building of Pont Caulaincourt. The fact
remains, however, that definite programs existed and were carried out as
planned, usually within the agreed schedule. This gave the impression of a
grand design that was being inexorably realized year after year.

Haussmann's long tenure at the Seine prefecture does not explain everything, since Chabrol and Rambuteau also held the prefect's office for many
years. During his seventeen years, Haussmann had every opportunity to
equivocate, to maneuver, to change doctrine, with few risks to his career, especially as Napoléon III had the volatile character so typical of a dreamer. In
the battle of the *grands travaux*, however, the emperor justified his reputation of being "gently stubborn" while Haussmann proved himself to be ob-
stinate and mulish. Stories about their disagreements over the line of a road
or some minor feature illustrate their extraordinary tenacity—a phenomenon sufficiently rare in political life and public administration to be worthy
of underlining.

The third characteristic was the formation of a *solid team*. If Napoléon III
deserves all the merit for planning the transformation, Haussmann played an
irreplaceable role as the sovereign's loyal executant; he insists on this point
throughout his *Mémoires*, as well as on the help given by people whose qualities he recognized and whom he could motivate to give of their best. We
have seen the fulsome tribute, not always unmixed with criticism, that he
paid to his team in the *Mémoires*: to Deschamps, Merruau, Alphand, Belgrand, and Barillet-Deschamps. Deschamps and Merruau (the latter changing his job in midcourse) remained with Haussmann from the beginning to
the end of his time as prefect. Belgrand spent fifteen and a half years by his
side, Alphand and Barillet-Deschamps almost as long. Several of them con-

tinued to do "Hausmmann's work" after his dismissal. Engineers or architects such as Dupuit and Mille, Hittorff, Baltard, Davioud, Duc, and Bailly
marked the city with the stamp desired by Napoléon III and Haussmann.

GREATER PARIS

 ↜ Napoléon III's color-coded map referred only to the city within the wall
of the Farmers-General, plus the Bois de Boulogne. Although Haussmann
zealously executed his master's instructions, he was not only the representative of the French state with the functions of a mayor of Paris; he was also
prefect for the Seine department and, as such, responsible for the administration of an area covering more than eighty communes, all operating, as in
Paris, under a system of specially appointed municipal councils. It is hardly
surprising, therefore, that both emperor and prefect thought of using this
common framework to enlarge the limits of Paris so that they coincided
with those of the department; Haussmann unreservedly supported this plan,
which in the end came to nothing.

During his time as prefect in the Gironde, Haussmann had already
shown his ability to think in terms of urban space on a grand scale. The incorporation of La Bastide commune on the right bank of the Garonne had
been only one part of a vast project to expand the territory of Bordeaux.
What were the reasons for expanding the city limits of Paris to coincide with
those of the Seine department? Haussmann explained that a uniform local
duty would be to the benefit of industries, since their location decisions took
account of the labor market and the supply of raw materials throughout the
area in question. Haussmann was well aware that the Paris of the Farmers-
General did not form a homogenous area with the outer arrondissements and
the zone beyond the fortifications, and in his view a program for new housing units would have to base itself upon both the similarities and the peculiarities of these three zones. This analysis of a zonally differentiated market
was one of Haussmann's major ideas. Since rents tended to exceed the workers' means within the modernized parts of the capital, it would be necessary
to gear their housing supply to what they could afford to pay—and that
would preferably be in the outlying areas.

What we see here is a modern vision of Greater Paris. It was obviously
linked to an older administrative conception that inserted Paris within the
Seine department as a region with a variable geometry. A unified command
was provided by the prefect and the municipal and departmental councils,
while local life regained all its rights within the arrondissements that Hauss-

mann strove to consolidate into *le Paris des vingt arrondissements*. If his project had been carried through, the capital would have had a total of twenty-eight arrondissements—twenty inside the walls, and another eight outside.

Haussmann's guiding principle was *the unity of urban space*. Whereas, in 1848, transport difficulties had kept Paris divided into an archipelago of largely autonomous islands, he waged a campaign to organize fast omnibus routes between the various parts of Paris. Without using the term, he was concerned with the unity of the labor pool: that is, the possibility for everyone to work and go about their business in any part of the city. The introduction of a unified public transport system in 1855 allowed anyone to cross Paris from one end to the other for just a few centimes. At the city limits, moreover, the fortifications did not prevent relations between the space inside and the space outside: many Parisians worked in the outer area, and many who were resident there daily traveled to work in the city center; a number of bus routes were extended to take in the inner suburbs. Yet the unity still existed, as did the highly centralized structure of the whole system.

THE MEANS

To tackle a program of this scale, it was first of all necessary to have the *administrative means*. Haussmann was at one and the same time head of central state functions in the Seine department (excluding those that came under the chief of police), chief executive for the local Seine community in relation to the departmental council, and mayor of Paris. His powers were considerable, then, but they were not unlimited. We have already described his demarcation disputes with the chief of police and his not always smooth relations with the municipal and departmental councils, both appointed bodies but no less difficult to handle on occasion. Haussmann's administration was subject to supervision by, and sometimes forced to compromise or maneuver with, the Legislature, the Senate, the Council of State, the Court of Cassation, and the National Audit Office. All of this was part of the institutional framework of a country highly structured from both a legal and an administrative point of view, where civil procedure might either supplant or supplement political decisions.

If the *grands travaux* were able to make daily progress against procedural blocking in the various bureaucratic departments, it was because Haussmann had all the legal tricks at his fingertips. As an experienced prefect, he was used to negotiations but also knew how to force things through when the need arose. Persigny was not wrong in thinking of Haussmann as an animal specially bred to launch into the Parisian arena, for the position required great staying power and a capacity to take a lot of buffeting, especially as the emperor abhorred legal quibbling and soon wearied of obstacles accumulating in his path. It was Haussmann's job to ensure that the imperial will did not lose its cutting edge amidst the legal ambushes prepared by his enemies.

Berger the politician was succeeded by Haussmann the administrator. The future baron established a clockwork mechanism whose various pieces had to function without any defect. Even details that looked minor from the outside, such as the distinction between municipal and departmental functions, or the organization of the mail, were crucially important conditions for the efficient running of the whole—hence the twenty-four-hour rotation for his secretariat, and hence too the refusal to accept the slightest error in the survey department.

We have seen that Haussmann always paid close attention to *technical* aspects: he prioritized triangulation and accurate surveying in order to have effective maps at his disposal; he concerned himself with geology and hydrology in working out a water distribution policy for Paris. He also took an interest in Dumas's development of high-performance gas lamps, in the work of the cemeteries commission on the oxidization qualities of different areas of land, in the early use of electricity for street lighting, in the relative merits of certain road surfaces, and sometimes even in tree varieties or the development of a meter for cab fares.

Haussmann was eager to have well-organized teams of engineers chosen from the most capable people in the profession and clearly had great respect for the civil engineers of the Ponts et Chaussées, even if he occasionally railed against some of the peculiarities of that body. He generally showed much consideration for diplomas and grades: he nearly always wrote of a chief engineer as a mathematician combined with a scientist, weighing more in his scales than an ordinary engineer but less than a chief inspector. He surrounded architects with marks of appreciation and established hierarchies to favor those with the highest titles, particularly the Grand Prix de Rome. But he also knew how to size people up as individuals. He guessed Deschamps's qualities beneath the manners of an eternal student, and although Davioud had not gained the Grand Prix de Rome but only a secondary title in architecture, Haussmann still considered him a great artist and entrusted him with a number of projects.

Lastly, Haussmann knew how to obtain the *financial means* for the *grands travaux* desired by the emperor. Here the first test concerned his ability to locate and release the necessary room for maneuver. The problems of financial administration came next; they involved an element of acrobatics, as we have seen, but that too was part of Haussmann's talent.

THE PRINCIPLES OF AN URBAN POLICY

☙ Enjoying the highest organizational and technical support, as well as an adequate supply of funds, the transformation of Paris proceeded in accordance with a number of *principles*.

First, there was a consistent policy of urban engineering: any new thoroughfare should involve a road to facilitate movement by pedestrians and vehicles, but also help air to circulate more freely within the dense urban space. In an age preoccupied with epidemics of still uncertain cause, the quality of air was the major factor in the drive to create healthier living conditions. Trees—and the wider streets to accommodate them—were intended to freshen the air, and Haussmann defended them against civil engineers who argued that they increased humidity.

Healthier conditions also required the efficient draining of rainwater and domestic or industrial wastewater. A preference for roadway with a central camber and a gutter on either side, in place of the older model with a central drainage pipe, dated back to the time of Rambuteau. The Haussmann administration made this the new technical standard, so that now a water main and a sewer had to be installed beneath each street. His engineers developed a system of tunnels (some wide streets even had two) where the various pipes generated by modern progress could be installed. This clever idea avoided the necessity of digging new trenches and made it easier to connect each block to the municipal network.

On the sidewalks, streetlamps cast a light whose profusion was part of the image of Paris; they created the conditions for night life and changed the way in which people living in the great city perceived the hours of darkness. Fountains, benches, and public conveniences were dotted around to complete the range of street services, making life easier and more pleasant for the population.

Second, the roads were the major factor of articulation in city planning. Haussmann was interested only in public space; the inside of buildings (unless they were in official use), the private space of Parisians, was not his concern. Permission to build involved the fixing of a boundary line between public and private, the specification of certain dimensions in keeping with area planning requirements, and perhaps a number of restrictions on façades in special cases such as the Place de l'Étoile, the Avenue de l'Impératrice, or the streets bordering the Bois de Boulogne or the Bois de Vincennes.

None of this was new. The building line was an ancient legal principle; the first building regulations went back to the days of the Ancien Régime; and the coordination of façades did not differ in principle from that which had once governed the appearance of Place Dauphine, Place Vendôme, or the Place des Vosges. If Haussmann's contemporaries as well as later generations have spoken of "Haussmann-style urban planning," this is because it concerned the whole of the public space in question, and because the building of residential blocks along the new roads rested upon certain economic conditions.

As the Seine prefecture did not concern itself with what these blocks were like on the inner side of the street façade, the Haussmannian projects often led to the creation of mere screens behind which the old structures remained intact. In fact, the structure of the blocks was rarely changed by the road-building programs of the Second Empire; it is possible to speak of complete reconstruction, or "urban renewal," only in the case of the Opéra *quartier*. Yet Haussmann himself had nothing to do with this fact, since it was private players—especially the Pereire brothers—who actually took the initiative.[2]

Similarly, Haussmann-style city planning never concerned itself with the functions of buildings but only with the provision of "salubrious" streets as the precondition for "healthy" blocks (or rather "houses," as they were significantly called in this context) to be built along the way. The actual manner in which lodging, productive labor, or trade was organized inside these structures did not concern the city of Paris. In no sense did the city originate the first business quarter around the Opéra; it was because the rental apartments as well as the offices and stores could not be easily let that they eventually became part of the businesses active in the area.[3]

The third principle was that the road-building had to accord with superstructural development. This idea was not invented by Napoléon III and Haussmann; the First Empire, in particular, then the Restoration and the July Monarchy, attached great importance to the supply of new amenities. The Second Empire was acting within an established tradition when it built the central Halles, slaughterhouses, local town halls, courts, hospitals, schools, and barracks as well as the religious buildings that the concordat had placed within the charge of the public authorities. The main difference with earlier epochs was the scale of the projects carried out over seventeen years in the Paris area.

The creation of all these new facilities, which made a strong impact upon the Parisian cityscape, corresponded to a certain way of thinking about their functions. The local "town halls" that emerged arrondissement by arrondissement were conceived in accordance with Haussmann's politically inspired notion of the services that each one should provide. Hospitals, prisons, and mental asylums also conformed to coherent and progressive ideas in medical and penal policy.

One real innovation in superstructure was the emphasis placed by Napoléon III, and perhaps even more by Haussmann, upon a hierarchically ordered network of green spaces. In addition to the Bois de Boulogne and the Bois de Vincennes, which were laid out for Parisians to use on days of rest, Haussmann also opened the great public gardens of Buttes-Chaumont, Monceau, and Montsouris, and sowed the garden squares which (according to Alphand) he wanted each arrondissement to have.

The final principle was that of *mobility* within the city. Haussmann's aim was to make this easier both through new road systems and through the organization of public transport. Since the time of Louis XIV, when Pascal had set up a company to offer carriage rides for a cheap fare of five sols, transport in the capital had been operated privately under a system of municipal contracts. Haussmann imposed the amalgamation of the various operators into a single company, the Compagnie Générale des Omnibus. This unified public service was universally agreed to be efficient and successful. Its combination with new road systems provided a mobility that was another innovative feature of Haussmannian planning.

THE LOGIC BEHIND THE PLAN

≈ In Haussmann's operations, the system of major roads structuring the Parisian cityscape can be seen to fit together with the great cross routes (one from east to west on either side of the Seine, and one from north to south) and with the concentric circles ringing the city. The basic idea still governs the layout of Paris and its immediate surroundings a century and a half later.

The backbone of the *grands travaux* was the route across Paris devised by the Artists' Commission in the time of the post-Revolutionary Convention. We have seen the difficulties that Napoléon III and Haussmann encountered in achieving their purpose. Nor had it been fully achieved by the time of the fall of the Second Empire, since Boulevard Saint-Germain had taken shape over only two-thirds of its final length, at its eastern and western ends.

Napoléon III and Haussmann also wanted to organize a system of roads that would make it possible to bypass the city center. On the right bank, the *grands boulevards* were already there and were now corrected, adjusted, and complemented with adjacent streets. On the left bank, Haussmann's line of boulevards coming down from the Pont de l'Alma and the Invalides, which joined the Boulevard du Montparnasse and enveloped the 5th and 6th arrondissements, expressed a desire to close the loop on either side of the Seine. After the expansion of Paris, a second concentric ring was organized. Profiting from the destruction of the wall of the Farmers-General, Haussmann had the outer boulevards built with exceptional speed. But he would not have time to complete a third ring connecting up the new arrondissements with the Tolbiac-Alésia-Vouillé-Convention axis on the left bank, rue Michel-Ange and Avenue Mozart in the 16th arrondissement, and the line adumbrated by rues Marcadet, Ordener, Riquet, and Crimée in the 18th and 19th. The fourth ring, which Haussmann made very large in scale, was formed by the so-called *boulevards des maréchaux* on the inner side of the fortifications. As we have seen, however, he was unable to achieve the ring that Napoléon III wanted outside the fortifications, which would have been the fifth in the Parisian system.

Once this skeleton had been established, the organization of space within it still had to be decided. Haussmann might have continued with a linear scheme along the lines of the great cross route and ended up with a checkerboard arrangement. But that it not what he chose—and perhaps his role was greater here than Napoléon III's. We know from Du Camp that Haussmann read a number of fundamental works on Paris city planning, and it is also clear that he was influenced by star-shaped patterns and crossroads. Yet these were not the most convenient in terms of traffic flow. Their spread indicates that the Seine prefect was here applying an ideal model that owed more to a certain image of the city than to a functional analysis of transport needs. Without a doubt, the star model with roads radiating over 360 degrees (the model of ideal cities in the Italian Renaissance), or the partial star with roads radiating over only part of the circumference, as in Versailles or Washington, corresponded to the ideology of the Prince, who, according to Machiavelli, was supposed to watch over the city from the castle or monument symbolizing his power.

In the history of the Parisian *grands travaux*, it was not so much Napoléon III as Haussmann who seemed obsessed with such radiating or semi-radiating patterns. We owe to the Seine prefect a long list of such *places*: the Place de l'Étoile, the Rond-Point des Champs-Élysées, Place Wagram, Place Pereire (today's Place du Maréchal Juin), Place Raymond Souplex, Place Malesherbes, Place de l'Opéra, Place de la République, Place Voltaire (Place Léon Blum), Place Gambetta, Place de la Nation, Place Daumesnil, Place d'Italie, Carrefour des Gobelins, Place Denfert-Rochereau, Place Saint-Germain-des-Prés, Place Fontenoy, Place Vauban, Place de Breteuil, Place du Trocadéro, and Place Victor Hugo. Some were completed under the Haussmann administration, others only designed. Sometimes the baron based himself upon existing elements to guide (or to complicate) the implementation of his plan. In any event, his preferred treatment of façades and cut-off corners (with circular tops, for example) underlined the symbolic significance of the *places* as a basic decorative element of the cityscape.

The way from one *place* to another passed along great diagonals. These were part of a vision of perspective in which Haussmann remained faithful to the classical principles fixed in the sixteenth century in papal Rome. He thus argued against Napoléon III for the diagonal line of the Pont Sully, so that there would be a perfect perspective from the column of the Bastille to the dome of the Pantheon, whereas the emperor preferred a bridge at right angles to the river. Irritated by Haussmann's stubborn defense of his position, Napoléon III accused him "of sacrificing too much to correctness of line, and of looking too hard for viewpoints that could justify the direction of public roads."[4] As Haussmann refused to budge, the project remained pending, and the empire fell before the issue was settled. It was left to the Third Republic to choose, like Haussmann, perspective and straight lines.

21

Modern Infrastructures

THE BARON'S *grands travaux* gave a formidable impetus to a modern style of planning in which the city is built around empty public spaces. The key role of linked streets and open spaces within the Haussmannian scheme earned them every favor, beginning with considerably increased width. In the end, the surface occupied by roadway, sidewalks, service roads, and tree-lined promenades was not far short of 20 percent of the total municipal area— more than 30 percent if one adds the Bois de Boulogne and the Bois de Vincennes.

In order to make the operations pay for themselves, both in overall profitability and in their immediate impact on the price of land resold by the city of Paris, the residential blocks had to be densely occupied. This was one of the purposes of the building regulations adopted in 1859, which increased the permitted height. The public provision of amenities became more justified the more people benefited from them. Thus, long before the modern debates on urban density, Haussmann showed a strong preference for a "compact" over a "dispersed" city. In his view, Paris up to the fortifications could easily accommodate a population of 3.5 million.

As we have already pointed out, since Haussmann's time Paris has never had more than 3 million inhabitants, and for a number of years the figure has stabilized at just over 2 million. Demands on the city's space are no longer the same as they used to be. In fact, the wide tree-lined streets and nearly uniform façades mask the fact that Haussmann's Paris was much more compact than the high-rise blocks that provide our own image of overcrowding. It is reckoned that the land occupation coefficient (that is, the number of square meters of floor space per square meter of land), which is today fixed at a high upper limit of 3 in Paris, was somewhere between 5 and 6 in the Haussmannian residential blocks.[1]

THE STREETS OF PARIS

❧ A few statistics will give us a clearer picture of the scale of Haussmann's road-building drive. In 1852 there were 239 miles of avenues, boulevards, and streets in Paris; programs before the incorporation of the suburban communes eliminated 30 miles but added another 56. By 1860 the network within the old city limits was finer and more extensive, with a total of 261 miles having risen from 303 yards per acre in 1852 to 332 yards in 1860. In the suburban communes, which were then still undergoing urbanization, the total length of road was only 221 miles in 1860, or barely 216 yards per acre. Here, Haussmann's activity did away with 3 miles but added a little more than 46; the network increased to 264 miles, and road density to 243 yards per acre.

At the moment of Haussmann's departure, the total Parisian road network therefore covered a length of 525 miles; 33 miles had been eliminated while 102 had been added as a result of the *grands travaux*. In other words, in Paris in the year 1870, 1 street in 5 had been created in the course of the previous 17 years.

Even more significant was the width of the new thoroughfares—a veritable obsession for Napoléon III and Haussmann. Within the old city limits, the *grands travaux* had doubled the average width of streets from thirty-nine feet to seventy-nine feet; while in the suburban communes it had risen from forty-three feet to fifty-nine feet over the ten years from 1860 to 1870. The eliminated roadway did not exceed an average of twenty-three feet in width.[2]

As to the road specifications, Haussmann introduced no novelties. As we have seen, he simply applied Rambuteau's options in a more systematic manner, abandoning the old model of streets with a central channel in favor of a gutter on either side.

The road surface caused the baron greater concern. The traditional paving used in Paris consisted of sandstone cubes with sides measuring 9 inches—a formula that resulted in roads that were jolty and noisy but also solid and durable and therefore economic. Haussmann wanted to switch to smaller porphyry stones measuring 1.5 to 3 square inches, which were capable of lasting 20 years (against 15 for sandstone) and provided a much smoother surface. Napoléon III, however, was an ardent supporter of macadam, which he had seen in widespread use in England. Haussmann argued that this would lead to a frightening burden of extra costs because it would not stand up well to heavy carriage wheels and would need to be constantly sprinkled, dried, and resurfaced. But it was the emperor who had the final word.

The prefect did the best he could, using flint and crushed granite instead of the original limestone, and covering at least the gutters with small porphyry stones. He had also examined the possibility of timber paving blocks and asphalt, but they both had the drawback of making the road slippery in rainy weather. Napoléon III was closed to any discussion: "Being an accomplished horseman, the Emperor would not hear of wooden blocks or asphalt, and especially not of granite or porphyry, for our major roads."[3] In desperation, Haussmann began to dream that the best solution would be to replace iron horseshoes with leather or an adhesive coating, which, though more expensive, would prove less costly in the long run.

Road maintenance techniques made great advances under Haussmann. From 1860, steamrollers made it possible to strengthen the cohesiveness of materials. New mechanical sweepers could be drawn by a horse and a single operator, and there were also new automatic sprinklers that could be supplemented, where necessary, by workers using water hoses. The cost of street cleaning was 4 million francs in 1869, although a special tax paid by people living along the route reduced this sum by a million. The prefect also had to provide for special teams in time of snow or frost, and after successful trials he introduced the general use of sea salt as a thawing device.

Another improvement was the spread of sidewalks. In 1859 many streets still did not have one: there were only 263 miles in all (178 miles within the old city limits, 85 miles in the suburban zone), with a total surface area of nearly 495 acres. Ten years later their total length was 676 miles, and their area represented nearly a quarter of the total public roadway. They were covered either with asphalt or with large slabs that were costly but very hard-wearing.

Haussmann also increased the number of service roads. By 1869 their total length was 697 miles, and the number of trees lining the roads had nearly doubled since 1852, from 50,000 to more than 95,000. As we have seen, these were criticized by the civil engineering department on the grounds that they kept the road damp, and by the emperor on the grounds that they obscured the view of street façades. In reality, Napoléon III was as little inclined to see trees planted in open areas as he was to have them cut down once they had become a nuisance. To enlarge the planted areas that could be used for public walking was another of the baron's priorities. When he left office, such areas—including the Champs Élysées, the Avenue de l'Observatoire, the Avenue de l'Impératrice, Boulevard Richard-Lenoir, and the Trocadéro—covered more than 200 acres. Parks and squares represented some 148 acres in Paris, with the Bois de Boulogne and the Bois de Vincennes adding 2,093 and 1,977 acres respectively *extra muros*.

Haussmann considerably improved street lighting. In 1853, Paris within its old city limits had only 12,400 gas lamps (2,484 in the incorporated suburbs). By 1869 there were more than 30,000 of a new and more powerful type, as well as 1,500 oil reflectors. Haussmann participated in experiments with electric lighting, but he was not won over by "the pale lunar glow" of the Edison model, "which hurt or tired the eyes."[4] Less inspired than on other occasions, he risked predicting "that, apart from its inventor, popularizers, and apparatus manufacturers, the only ones to support it after a while will be opticians and eye specialists."[5]

All these new amenities came at a price. Between 1852 and 1870 the total cost of road programs was 1.43 billion francs; that of sidewalks and service roads, street lighting, and green spaces was 178 million. "Installation maintenance" was the largest item in the city's running costs: the upkeep, cleaning, and lighting of public highways absorbed 18.75 million francs in 1869, plus another 2.45 million for planted areas and public places intended for walking. These figures illustrate the size of the legacy that Haussmann's administration bequeathed to the capital.

The construction of bridges and embankments was a central government responsibility, but the city of Paris contributed 17 million francs of its own during Haussmann's time as prefect. Preliminary studies and the actual work of construction were carried out by the "national" technical departments of the Seine prefecture, which rebuilt no fewer than ten bridges between 1853 and 1869. These were, in order from east to west, the Pont de Bercy, Pont d'Austerlitz, Pont Louis Philippe, Pont d'Arcole, Pont Notre Dame, Pont au Double, Petit Pont, Pont au Change, Pont Saint-Michel, and Pont des Invalides. Some had been showing signs of weakness: the Pont d'Austerlitz (an iron bridge built under the First Empire) and the Pont d'Arcole and Pont des Arts (both suspension bridges that left much to be desired in terms of solidity). The others, no longer suited to traffic requirements or street trajectories, had been widened or replaced to conform to the line of the new streets.

WATER AND SEWERS: "A CITY UNIQUE IN THE WORLD"

≈ One of Haussmann's most remarkable contributions to the modernization of Paris was undoubtedly the improvement of the water supply: "I especially like to dwell upon this major achievement . . . because it is mine. I did
not find it in the Emperor's program for the transformation of Paris, and no
one in the world suggested it to me. It was the fruit of my observations, my
assiduous research as a young civil servant, and my reflections in later life. It
was my own conception."[6]

Unlike other schemes of the time that focused on water from the Seine,
Haussmann tried to increase the supply of *spring water* for private consumption, keeping the river for public uses such as sprinkling, cleaning, and decorative functions. During his time at the Seine prefecture, the daily quantity
of water available in Paris per head of the population doubled: from 29 gallons (in 1852) to 46 gallons (in 1869) and, when the Vanne aqueduct came
into service, to 59 gallons.

In the Paris contained within the wall of the Farmers-General, water was
stored in six main reservoirs: Monceau, rue Racine, rue Saint-Victor, Observatoire, Panthéon (Place de l'Estrapade), Vaugirard. Old, sometimes even
decaying, they contained barely enough for a few hours' consumption
(43,816 cubic yards). The extension of the city limits gave Paris the six
reservoirs that the Compagnie Générale des Eaux ran in the suburban communes (where it was the official holder of the concession). Haussmann was
able to get six large modern reservoirs built at high points in the outer
arrondissements, at Passy, Ménilmontant, Belleville, Buttes-Chaumont,
Charonne, and Montsouris, with a total capacity of 320,448 cubic yards. At
the same time he enlarged and modernized the sewage system. Between
1852 and the end of 1869, the municipality laid nearly 523 miles of sewers
in addition to 438 miles already contained within the old city limits; some
of the new pipes had a diameter as great as 3.6 feet.

When Haussmann first took over, water was distributed to private consumers in conditions that a present-day Parisian would find hard to imagine.
In 1854 little more than 1 house in 5 was connected to the mains. Water
under pressure sometimes reached the first or second floor, but most often
there was a tap in the yard from where buckets had to be carried up the
stairs. In July 1860, Haussmann signed a contract with the Compagnie
Générale des Eaux,[7] whereby it became the distributor of water to private
customers all over the capital. The price of a cubic meter (1.308 cubic yards)
was fixed at 60 francs for water from the Ourcq canal and 120 for water from

the Seine—which represented a 20 percent increase over the former price within the old city limits of Paris but a major reduction for users in the former suburban communes. Thanks to the company's energetic activity, the number of consumers connected to the service rose sharply, from 21,921 in 1860 in the Paris of the twenty arrondissements, to 37,889 on December 31, 1872 (out of 63,963 residential blocks).[8] But when the baron left office, "water on every floor" was a feature of scarcely half the blocks in the city, and many Parisians still had to make do with water carriers. It was landlords who decided whether or not a block was connected to the mains, and by no means all of them had yet been persuaded.

Maxime Du Camp saw in the system of sewers due to Haussmann and Belgrand the most important achievement in Paris after the new road systems: "When the time finally came to transform Paris, when the activity of our railways in daily bringing a large number of passengers into the city (passengers whose simple presence meant greater movement of carriages and a huge supply of extra commodities) had necessitated the widening of our streets and the creation of new public highways, the idea naturally occurred of providing the city with all the elements of environmental health that it required and whose inadequate supply had been so painfully remarked during the cholera epidemics of 1832 and 1849." The new system of drains was "the largest in existence," "making Paris, in this respect at least, a city unique in the world."[9]

In 1852 there were just over 66 miles of sewers in the old municipal area of Paris, plus some 25 miles of various types in the suburbs with a smaller diameter. Haussmann's administration renewed and enlarged the small existing sewers and created more than 248 miles of new ones, so that by 1869 the capital had a network of more than 347 miles of tunnels, two-thirds of which were at least 7.5 feet high and 4.26 feet wide. The main sewers, totalling 109 miles in length, were equipped with rails on which boat-sluices operated a clearing system similar to the one that Haussmann had seen as a young subprefect in the Blaye marshes. Another 5 miles carried liquid waste into the Seine, at Asnières and Saint-Denis. Sewage farms producing fertilizer for agriculture were tried out in a pilot experiment at Gennevilliers. But the baron's colleague, the engineer Mille, did not convince him of the benefits of main-drainage. His doubts on this score, as in the case of electric lighting, show the limits of his forward vision.

Investment in water and sewers rose to more than 153 million francs between 1852 and 1870, and the running costs of the water and drainage board accounted for nearly 3.5 million francs in the 1869 budget. The Paris administration deserved well of modernity: "Paris, today's Paris, is the source of that great movement for public health which other nations come to study in order to apply its benefits. The work conducted by M. Belgrand on underground tunnels to introduce drinking water and remove waste water would be enough to illustrate an epoch and a nation. Never has the application of science to public health needs been carried to such a high level."[10]

MOBILITY, OMNIBUSES, AND HIRED CARRIAGES

≋ Firmly believing that Parisians should be able to move around as they wished, Haussmann fought against the narrow winding streets that hindered mobility. He even dictated that café and restaurant terraces should not encroach more than ten feet, and shop fronts more than 3.3 feet, onto the widest boulevards.

Haussmann also attempted to restrict parking. Hackney carriages (or "cabs," as they came to be known) had 158 allotted stands in the capital. As to private and commercial vehicles, the Seine prefect could only leave the task of regulation to the chief of police, although he more than once accused him of insufficient firmness. Louis Véron, a journalist and businessman who served on the municipal council for a while, tells us: "One day I said to the Seine prefect: 'Your widest streets are now too narrow.'—'They seem too narrow,' he replied, 'because we shrink them by letting carriages park in front of every door, every store.'"[11]

In any event, there had been a large rise in the number of carriages moving around Paris. A little more than 25,000 were counted in 1850, but by 1860 the figure was certainly between 30,000 and 35,000.[12] Out of this total, in 1860, Véron reckoned that there were 530 omnibuses and 5,600 hired carriages and cabs, against 20,000 to 25,000 private carriages. Hired vehicles and cabs were used almost as much as private vehicles by Parisians who needed to move around quickly: "In the great city of Paris," Véron notes, "where the most ambitious emulation and the most feverish competition make each person want to get ahead of his neighbors, everyone today understands the price of time."[13]

The task of carrying Parisians and their provincial or foreign guests fell mainly to public transport. Haussmann's compulsory merger of the various concessionaires into a single Compagnie Générale des Omnibus—a move that favored the Pereire brothers—permitted a better organization of the service as well as a degree of control over the quality of materials and the regularity of fares and timetables. Within ten years the mobility of Parisians doubled: in 1855, a total of 347 vehicles carried 36 million passengers (an average of 33 trips per person per year); in 1866, the 664 omnibuses of the Compagnie Générale carried 107 million passengers (an average of 60 trips per person per year).[14]

Those who preferred to use a private vehicle, without having the means or the desire to own one of their own, had recourse to hired carriages and cabs. Coachmen had the reputation of being rough types, and there was a growing number of complaints against them. In 1855 the emperor arranged for the cab monopoly to be awarded to the former prefect Ducoux. But the surrender of older licenses took a long time to complete, and in 1863 the cab drivers declared a strike that brought Paris to a standstill. The regime then changed tack and restored the previous freedom of enterprise; a decree of March 25, 1866, declared that "every individual has the right to operate within Paris hackney carriages and hired carriages intended for the conveyance of persons that are hired out by the hour or by the trip." The city of Paris bought out the monopoly held by Ducoux's Compagnie Générale des Voitures de Paris. The number of licensed carriages rose from 4,487 in 1855 to more than 9,000 in 1870, half of which belonged to the company, half to 1,800 independent operators. Free enterprise did not work too badly, even if Haussmann had trouble solving other problems, especially the persistent lack of courtesy shown by drivers and the development of a reliable meter to end the constant haggling over the price of a journey.

According to Maxime Du Camp, it had become dangerous to cross certain heavily congested roads. What would happen if, "as some overly bold inventors propose, steam power were applied to special carriages on our macadamized roads!"[15] Rail tracks had already appeared in the streets of Paris; a horse-drawn tram operated on the Sèvres-Vincennes route, and other lines were being introduced in the suburbs; soon the light Auteuil-Grenelle tram would be serving the 15th and 16th arrondissements. Steam trains on the circular railroad helped Parisians move between Gare Saint-Lazare and Auteuil. And in 1854 the engineers Brame and Flachat presented Haussmann with a plan for a metropolitan railway beneath the Boulevard de Strasbourg and the Boulevard de Sébastopol, to serve the Halles market. The Seine prefect left it to the Third Republic to create the Paris Metro.

URBAN DÉCOR AND FURNITURE

≈ Beneath the eyes of residents and visitors, the city was developing a strongly homogenized *décor* in accordance with the baron's wishes. Haussmann, who had shown a certain flair for urban settings, concerned himself with everything visible: the façades of residential blocks as well as colors, plants, and the thousand objects that furnish streets and squares. His tastes were certainly well defined: he liked regular façades with a touch of the monumental; he did not care for surface color, as the materials were supposed to be enough by themselves.

It was under the Second Empire that Paris became the City of Light. "Light before all else" was one of Haussmann's mottos. He gave the Compagnie du Gaz, also controlled by the Pereires, every facility to install a mains supply beneath the streets for such large-scale users as cafés, restaurants, hotels, theatres, and stores. The company began to supply daytime gas in September 1856 and already had fifteen hundred customers signed up by February 1860.[16]

With regard to the cityscape, Haussmann's aesthetic was also classically inspired, with a preference for straight lines and symmetry. But he admitted that the art of gardens had developed since the age of Le Nôtre, and he did not oppose curved shapes or undulating terrain so long as they did not give an impression of artifice.

The prefect confessed his love of chestnut trees, which he preferred over any other for the lining of streets. At the same time, the spread of plane trees in Paris owed much to his discovery of their qualities in the Var, although he was not so keen on their irregular, "badly clustered" branches.[17] The prefect would have liked to rehabilitate the elm, which had been rejected by municipal experts because of the scolytid parasite that doomed it to an early death. He was less attached to the lime tree (which "shed its foliage too soon") and the acacia (which gave too little shade). As to maples, sycamores, catalpas, and paulownias, they would be kept within the confines of garden squares.

Haussmann organized a number of nurseries to supply the tens of thousands of trees necessary to his plans, and to cater to the future needs of maintenance and replacement. As early as 1853 he set up the nurseries at Auteuil, and in 1859 he created a new arboretum of eleven acres in the Longchamp plain. That same year the city acquired forty-four acres of land at Petit Pry beyond Vincennes for the growing of street trees, while the College of Arboriculture in the Bois de Vincennes, near the Porte Daumesnil, concentrated on bushes and fruit trees.

Haussmann's long periods in the southwest had left him with a taste for brightly colored flower beds mingled with exotic plants. He and his colleague Barillet-Dechamps also created hot, cold, and temperate glasshouses, first at La Muette in 1855 and ten years later in the Bois de Vincennes, between the Porte de Picpus and the Porte de Charenton.

The body in charge of public walks and planted areas was one of the most powerful within the Paris administration. The prefect had it under his personal control and refused to allow the private sector to have a say in the green-space policy that so closely affected the city's image.

Finally, Haussmann was the first to have an overall policy on urban *furniture*, those various objects with multiple uses such as benches, litter and garbage bins, rain and sun shelters, drinking fountains, urinals and public conveniences, awnings, kiosks, announcement pillars, and, of course, lampposts. The homogeneity of this furniture—one of the most original features of the Haussmannian city—was due to Gabriel Davioud, who had learned his lessons with Deschamps in the survey department before Haussmann gave him his chance by appointing him architect for the Bois de Boulogne in 1853. The street furnishings designed by Davioud or proposed by private firms were mainly functional in character, but they came under careful aesthetic scrutiny as elements in the urban décor. Their style reflected a quest for the picturesque: bulbs, creepers, and festoons expressed Napoléon III's urge to urbanize nature even in such symbolic representations, while garden square kiosks, with their cupolas and little bell-shaped pinnacles, attested to the influence of Turkey and the orientalist fantasy that kept the French dreaming for generations.

Some kinds of urban furniture were provided by private companies; the Morris firm of theatrical printers, for example, secured rights in 1868 over 150 pillars reserved for the announcement of forthcoming shows. The city fixed technical constraints as to location and operation, financial constraints (concessionaires had to pay a charge for the use of public space), and maintenance standards. The Haussmann administration was concerned to ensure that everything belonging to the urban décor be of faultless quality and be kept scrupulously clean.

PUBLIC AND PRIVATE

The management of the public highways was not subject to a uniform legal framework; Haussmann was in this sense an opportunist. Surveys, water supply, and the sewers came under the Seine prefecture, whereas water for private consumption, omnibus traffic, coach and cab hire, and the gas supply were "delegated services" for which entrepreneurs were responsible under the system of public-private partnership or concessionary awards. Whenever possible, Haussmann also preferred to hand the construction of new roads to private contractors instead of carrying it out directly under local authority control.

What mattered most was to control the means enabling the objectives set by the emperor to be fulfilled. So long as the planning was right, authoritarianism and a spirit of centralization went very well together with "getting others to do things" rather than "doing it oneself."

When Napoléon III presented Haussmann in 1854 with his plan for water to be supplied from the Seine under a monopoly concession held by Charles Laffitte, the prefect guessed that this would stop him from carrying through his ideas on the provision of spring water. He therefore torpedoed the proposal—in the name of morality. "I hastened to tell him [the emperor] how grave in every way would be the direct concession of such an undertaking to private industry, without the guarantee of free competition and rival bidding."[18] A few years later, in his report of 1858 on the Paris water supply, he gloried in the implementation of his program under direct local authority control. "The undertaking was conceived at the top, like all those that the public good demands."[19]

For the organization of transport, however, the public authorities limited themselves to a regulatory role. Concessions were awarded for omnibus traffic, and cabs and hired carriages were left to private initiative. Haussmann claimed to derive a law from this: "Whereas monopoly is the most expedient way of assuring the smooth organization of mass transport in a large city, free competition is better suited for the adaptation of individual transport services to the very diverse tastes of the public."[20] In reality, pragmatism was in command—and therefore a wish that the community should remain capable of guidance and decision. Monsieur Morris obtained the right to put up his pillars, but the flowers of Paris would remain municipal.

22

>>>-->>>-->>>-->>>-->>>-->>>-->>>-->>>

Public Buildings

"Not only did the works executed under M. Haussmann's direction give to Paris communications and public health that it had never known before," wrote Maxime Du Camp; "their aim was also to bring Parisians benefits of a higher order. Numerous public schools, medical establishments, a Hôtel-Dieu have been constructed . . . ; great asylums for the mentally ill have been built; and as the moral needs of a nation are as pressing as its material needs, huge churches have been erected where pious souls can find the cherished satisfaction that is their due."[1] Apart from the roads and the water supply, Haussmann's *grands travaux* also concerned buildings of many different kinds: utilitarian structures, administrative buildings, hospitals and asylums, prisons, schools, religious edifices.

PLACES OF WORSHIP

❧ According to statistics quoted by Maxime Du Camp for Paris in the year 1870, a large majority of the resident population of 1,851,792 were Catholics: 1,760,163 declared themselves to be of the Roman persuasion. In addition there were 19,423 Calvinists, 12,634 Lutherans, and 9,615 members of dissident Protestant sects. The non-Catholics also included 23,434 Jews and 1,572 Muslims and Buddhists. Finally, 13,905 people said that they did not practice any religion while 11,041 reported holding beliefs that the census department was unable clearly to define.

Places of worship were the responsibility of the state, and all the religions save Islam and Buddhism had ones of their own. The Haussmann administration built a large number. It is true that the less fortunate Muslims and Buddhists were not very numerous in Paris, but Maxime Du Camp also gives one the impression that the middle classes tended to regard those religions as rather peculiar in a Parisian setting. "The 1,572 Muslims and Buddhists in our midst have no place of prayer, but with the help of a compass the former have no difficulty finding their kiblah, while the latter can easily buy a statue of Cakia-Mouni: there is no shortage of them in our curiosity shops."[2] Yet Maxime Du Camp was a cultivated and seasoned traveler who fervently admired the Arab East and the civilizations of India.

When Haussmann took over at the Seine prefecture, he shepherded through the work on the churches of Sainte-Clotilde and Saint-Vincent-de-Paul that had come to a halt for lack of funds. Next he had no fewer than six churches built within the old city limits: Trinité, Saint-Augustin, Saint-Ambroise, Saint-Joseph, Saint-François-Xavier, and Notre Dame des Champs. The communes later incorporated into the capital were also provided with new churches: Notre Dame de Clignancourt in the former commune of Montmartre, Saint-Bernard at La Chapelle, Saint-Jean-Baptiste at Belleville, Notre Dame de la Croix at Ménilmontant, Saint-Pierre-de-Montrouge at the Alésia crossroads, and Saint-Lambert in the commune of Vaugirard that became part of the 15th arrondissement. The city also bought up some churches built by private individuals: Saint-Eugène, Saint-Martin-des-Champs, and Saint-Éloi in the old area of Paris, Saint-Marcel, Saint-Honoré, and Saint-Michel-des-Batignolles in the newly incorporated communes.

The Church of Saint-Augustin had the peculiarity that, in order to mask the changed angle of Boulevard Malesherbes, it occupied a site too narrow for classical buttresses to balance the thrust of its stone vaults. In 1862, Haussmann's appointed architect Baltard, a convert to the use of metal fresh from work on Les Halles, spontaneously proposed an iron framework to support the vault and dome of the church. Stone remained as a dressing but only as a dressing, so that the faithful would not feel disturbed in an age when metal still seemed suitable only for railway stations, market halls, or exhibition palaces.

The church-building was supplemented with five new presbyteries for the use of priests inside the old city limits, and with restoration, consolidation, and enlargement work on a number of existing churches: Saint-Étienne du Mont, Saint-Leu, Saint-Germain-l'Auxerrois, Saint-Germain-des-Prés, Saint-Laurent, Saint-Ferdinand, L'Annonciation et Notre Dame de Passy, Notre Dame de Bercy, Saint-Jean-Baptiste-de-Grenelle, Sainte-Marie-des-Batignolles, and Saint-Pierre-de-Montmartre.

Religious minorities were not neglected. Haussmann built the Reformed Church of the Holy Spirit in rue Roquépine, which replaced a place of worship demolished during the widening of rue Saint-Lazare. He also put up the consistory of the Temple de l'Oratoire and restored the Protestant churches at rue Quinault in the 15th arrondissement, Boulevard Ornano in the 18th, and Ménilmontant in the 20th. Two synagogues were also built, at rue de la Victoire and rue des Tournelles.

MUNICIPAL BUILDINGS

≈ A large number of public buildings sprang up. Apart from the Hôtel de Ville and its annexes, we should first mention the five new town halls of the 1st, 3rd, 4th, 7th, and 9th arrondissements, and the enlarged or restored ones of the 13th, 14th, 15th, 16th, 18th, and 20th arrondissements. Haussmann also decided that the newly acquired Hôtel Carnavalet should be restored and turned into the Historical Museum of the City of Paris. In relation to the Seine department, he had one subprefecture built at Saint-Denis and another at Sceaux.

In addition to five theatres—the Châtelet and the Théâtre Lyrique on the Place du Châtelet, the Gaîté, the Vaudeville, and Panorama—the city built barracks for the fire brigade and the municipal guard as well as the Halles Centrales, several abattoirs including those at La Villette, the cattle market at La Villette, and a number of neighborhood markets. After building the markets at Porte Saint-Martin (1854) and Gros Caillou (1855) as direct municipal projects, Haussmann turned to the banker Prosper Ferrere in 1863 for the rebuilding of the Marché du Temple. It proved a decisive experiment, and the next year he awarded the reconstruction of the Marché Saint-Honoré to the same concessionaire, then in 1865 the task of creating five new markets in the 8th (Marché de l'Europe), 10th (Saint-Quentin), 11th (Saint-Maur-Popincourt), 13th (Place d'Italie), and 14th (Montrouge) arrondissements. In the closing days of 1865, seven more orders were placed with Ferrere and his Compagnie Générale des Marchés for the building of the Marché Necker (in the 15th), Marché d'Auteuil and Marché Saint-Didier (16th), Marché des Batignolles (17th), Marché Saint-Pierre (18th), Marché de la Villette (19th), and Marché de Belleville (20th). By the time that Haussmann left his prefect's office, the 13th, 15th, 16th, 17th, 18th, and 19th arrondissements had spanking new market halls, both functional and hygienic. In return, Ferrere secured the rights to operate them for a period of fifty years.

Haussmann's achievements were also considerable in the field of education. He acquired the buildings necessary for the expansion of the Sorbonne (a task actually executed by the Third Republic), and began reconstruction of the Faculty of Medicine. The Lycée Condorcet and Lycée Saint-Louis were restored, and work was carried out on the Lycée Charlemagne and Lycée Henri IV. Haussmann rebuilt the Collège Rollin on Avenue Trudaine (Lycée Jacques Decour), the Lycée Chaptal, and Lycée Turgot, and constructed, enlarged, or restored a host of public schools all over Paris, including seventy-one in the newly incorporated suburbs.

Always a supporter of education for all, Haussmann wanted Parisians to retain the option of sending their children to either religious or secular schools. This policy worked to the advantage of religious schools, since secular education had a preponderance in Paris. The churches would now be able to offer free education and hence to compete more effectively with secular schools among poorer sections of the population. Soon after the extension of the city limits, Haussmann, with Napoléon III's agreement, persuaded the municipal council to approve the establishment in each *quartier* of one secular and one religious school for boys, one secular and one religious school for girls, one secular nursery and one run by religious sisters. Our Lutheran prefect made it a point of honor to award generous subsidies at the same time to non-fee-paying Protestant and Jewish schools.

The total cost of the municipal works for the investment budget of the Paris architecture department, which managed the program of works between 1853 and 1869, was nearly 183 million francs, including subsidies paid to the Public Assistance Board.

PUBLIC ASSISTANCE

❧ Public Assistance dated from the early days of Louis-Napoléon's presidency, before Haussmann took over at the Seine prefecture. This public institution, placed under the authority of the Seine prefect and the operational control of a watch committee, had a director appointed by the Ministry of the Interior on the prefect's suggestion. The director had responsibility for home help, hospitals, and old people's homes, and acted as a guardian over foundlings, destitute orphans, and the mentally ill. When Haussmann came to Paris, the director Davenne was close to retirement age and showed little enthusiasm for the dynamic policy required by the new prefect. But Husson, his active and ambitious successor, wholeheartedly embraced Haussmann's views. The watch committee consisted of eighteen members appointed by the emperor, senators, deputies, doctors, and municipal councillors; in 1853 a bookseller by the name of Louis Hachette was sitting on it on behalf of the Chamber of Commerce.

The establishments grouped under the director's authority included eight general hospitals that treated patients of all classes: the Hôtel-Dieu, Saint-Antoine, Beaujon, La Charité, Cochin, La Pitié, Sainte-Marguerite, and Necker. A ninth, Lariboisière, was under construction. The list also included the Municipal Health Center and six special hospitals: the Cliniques, the Sick Children's Hospital, the Childbirth Center, Saint-Louis, the Midi, and Lourcine. Altogether the various hospitals had 6,593 beds available, and the municipal health center a further 150.

The Public Assistance ran five homes: for foundlings and destitute orphans, for incurably sick men (at rue des Récollets), incurably sick women (at rue de Sèvres), elderly men (at Bicêtre), and elderly women (at La Salpêtrière)—a total of 8,844 places. There were also three retirement homes: La Rochefoucauld, Les Ménages (at the site of today's Square Boucicaut, at Sèvres-Babylone), and Sainte-Périne—a total of 1,214 places. Five foundations together offered a further 369. In each of the twelve arrondissements prior to expansion, Public Assistance ran a relief committee. It also owned a number of undertakings such as the bakery on rue Scipion, the central pharmacy on the Quai de la Tournelle, the butcher shop on the Boulevard de l'Hôpital, the central vaults, the central warehouse, and the anatomical amphitheatre on the rue du Fer-à-Moulin.

The Public Assistance budget for 1852 showed expenditures of 13,345,000 francs against income of just under 9.5 million francs; the difference was made up by a municipal subsidy. Its own funds came from housing and farm rents and investments in securities, which brought in approximately 4 million francs, as well as from a million entrance charges for theatre performances, dances, and concerts (Paris liked to have fun), which brought in more than 1.8 million francs in 1869. Haussmann improved the finances by concentrating his efforts on farm-related products, laundering, needlework shops and ladies' work parties, cowsheds and piggeries, and the canteens operated by Public Assistance at public building sites. The income from such activities rose from 1.2 million francs in 1852 to more than 3 million in 1869. But the city subsidy remained indispensable, especially after the incorporation of the suburban communes, rising inexorably to 7 million francs by the end of the 1850s and to more than 10.4 million francs by 1869.

Haussmann took one principal measure to avoid heavy extra investment in hospital beds: he introduced a major home-care program in 1854. Apart from its economic impact, this move had considerable social implications in that it brought screening and treatment closer to poor people in particular. Home management, in this field as in others, had Haussmann's enthusiastic support. Sixty doctors spread through all the *quartiers* of Paris, together with a number of midwives that varied according to needs, offered consultations at each of the relief committees, and paid home visits to patients who reported sick. In its first year the number of patients visited at home was already above the 30,000 mark, and the number of surgery consultations already exceeded 110,000. In 1869, 70,000 patients were treated at home, and there were more than 200,000 consultations.

Less expensive than hospitalization, such home care represented the equivalent of nearly 6,000 hospital beds, or ten hospitals. Haussmann could thus be content that only one new hospital would be built during his tenure, the 560-bed Tenon at Ménilmontant, on which work began in 1868. The creation of convalescent homes with the emperor's financial support at Le Vésinet and Vincennes (accommodating 18,000 patients in 1869) helped to relieve the pressure on Parisian hospitals. Some patients were sent outside the capital to Chatel-Guyon, and two centers for children suffering from scrofula were opened at Forges-les-Eaux and Berck-sur-Mer.

The extension of the municipal area led to the opening of new relief committees in the outer arrondissements. Other investment expenditure had to be allowed to the Public Assistance Board, since although the prefect set a limit on new construction, he could not avoid building work due to the physical relocation of an institution. Apart from the case of the Hôtel-Dieu on the Île de la Cité, Haussmann had to find a new home for Sainte-Périne after the opening of Avenue Kléber: this retirement home reopened at Auteuil in 1862 over an area of almost 20 acres, having cost only 9 francs a square meter (1.196 square yards) to purchase; the construction expenditure, however, came to more than 1.5 million francs. The second operation of this kind, also decided in 1857, was completed in March 1863; the Petits-Ménages home on the rue de la Chaise, and the Fondation Devillas on rue du Regard, were transported to a 15-acre site at Issy, part of which came from a legacy (the rest being purchased at a very favorable average rate of 4.5 francs per square meter); this time, the spending on construction work and the provision of facilities was in the region of 5.5 million francs. In 1864, Haussmann decided to transfer the homes for incurably ill men and women to Ivry; the new institution came into service in 1868 and provided 2,000 places instead of the combined total of 1,200 in the two original homes. It is true that 8.75 million francs went toward all the work, but the city made a good deal on the compensation it received for the land at the home for incurably ill men in rue des Récollets and the added value from the site of the women's home at rue de Sèvres. On July 15, 1866, a new retirement home opened on land belonging to Public Assistance near Sainte-Périne, at Auteuil, but all the expenses were borne by its founders.

JUSTICE

≈ We have already noted the contribution made by the Seine department to spending on the Palais de Justice. The commercial court was also a new departmental building—and there were others. The opening of the rue de Turbigo meant that something had to be done about the old prison of Les Madelonettes. Haussmann had designs on a site called the Enclos de la Santé in the 13th arrondissement, a municipal property that was made over to the department. The *préfecture de police* scheduled the institution to hold six hundred persons of both sexes (convicts and prisoners on remand) in cells rather than communal rooms; the new prison would make it possible to apply modern ideas on penitentiary matters. Haussmann entrusted the project to the architect Vaudremer—a holder of the Grand Prix de Rome, naturally. But as no one thought such an assignment to be very gratifying, Haussmann, "in order to make better use of that artist's talents and pure taste,"[3] gave him the Saint-Pierre-de-Montrouge project, whose simplicity of style recalled that of the early Christian churches. Vaudremer was also given the job of maintaining and repairing the other prisons.

THE MENTALLY ILL

≈ Modernization of the treatment of mental patients was a subject that preoccupied Haussmann from the beginning of his career. As soon as he arrived in Paris, the new Seine prefect undertook to change the practices at Bicêtre and La Salpêtrière; Public Assistance housed old people there but also used the more squalid parts to keep mentally ill men (at Bicêtre) and women (at La Salpêtrière). Although 3,600 patients were thus crammed together in deplorable conditions, the capacity was still insufficient, and the Seine had to find room for a further 1,800 in 20 provincial departments, sometimes a long way from Paris. In thinking of the asylum that he built at Auxerre for people from the Paris region, Haussmann once remarked that patients were certainly better treated there, both materially and morally, than they would have been in Paris. "It is always unfortunate," he added, however, "to keep a patient a long way from his family, especially if he is very poor. He does not receive any visits, and soon the sense of abandonment can make him incurable."[4] Medical statistics confirmed this view: for although the asylums at Bicêtre and La Salpêtrière had their shortcomings, their cure rates were higher than among Parisians sent elsewhere in the country. Haussmann decided to look for new solutions in the Paris area.

In 1860 a specially appointed commission studied the problem on the ground for ten months in considerable depth; Haussmann himself accompanied its members to Auxerre and showed them round "his" asylum. The commission's report to the departmental council concluded that it was necessary to build further establishments in or near the capital, so that patients of either sex could be housed in separate quarters and kept busy working in the open air. For those who could live in their family without presenting any danger, home care should be the preferred option. In 1862 the departmental council accordingly voted to purchase land at Sainte-Anne in Paris, Ville-Évrard at Neuilly-sur-Marne, and Vaucluse at Épinay-sur-Orge (the latter two communes then being within the Seine-et-Oise department). Sainte-Anne came into service on May 1, 1867, Ville-Évrard early in 1868, and Vaucluse at the end of the same year. The therapeutic principles, identical to those practiced at the Saint-Lizier and Auxerre asylums, were among the most advanced in France at that time. The creation of an admissions office at Sainte-Anne was also a novelty, making it possible to follow more closely what happened to the patients while they were there. Sainte-Anne cost 2 million francs to acquire, Ville-Évrard and Vaucluse almost as much again— they were both located in the countryside but were magnificent properties measuring 704 and 272 acres respectively. The construction and furnishing work added another 14 million francs to the total.

MONUMENTAL ARCHITECTURE:
THE "SCHEDULE," METAL, AND ECLECTICISM

≈ In Paris the Second Empire was long on grand gestures but produced few architectural masterpieces to match them.

Two seemingly contradictory requirements—the "schedule" and monumentalism—dominated the conception of public buildings. In that age enamored of science and rationality, the schedule (that is, a coherent functional description of the building and spaces that the architect was supposed to design) held a crucial position. With regard to the public buildings of the

Haussmann administration, sometimes this schedule was laid down by the *préfecture de police* (for example, for Santé prison), sometimes it was developed by the prefect together with various experts (doctors for hospitals and mental asylums), sometimes it was directly provided by the architecture department at the Hôtel de Ville (in the case of primary schools, for example). As a general rule, those who created order knew what they wanted; only rarely would a conflict arise. Once, Haussmann defended common wards against doctors who wished to introduce private rooms everywhere, but he did so in the name of economy, not because he thought his solution was better.

Similarly, Haussmann took full responsibility for the often-criticized theatres on the Place du Châtelet designed by Davioud. The high attic area was said to be unsightly, but technicians had to be given enough space to operate the stage scenery. In his "schedules," the prefect also concerned himself with questions of safety and mobility, ventilation and heating. The summary of his instructions to Davioud for the Place du Châtelet structures contains all these issues: "Make the new theatres worthy of the capital of France; build them solidly and decorate them richly; make the access to them broad and easy; large halls, well lighted and well aired, so that the public can move about easily and spend time there in comfort; finally, profit from the advances of modern industry to make these theatres attractive and comfortable."[5]

Technical constraints made architects ever keener to use iron in their designs. Both they and the general public had been won over by the station halls, the Crystal Palace in London, and its emulations at Paris fairs. Baltard resisted Haussmann's demands for metal sheltering at the central Halles, but six years later it was he who advocated iron for the Church of Saint-Augustin. The technical accomplishments of the Opéra Garnier (as of all the rival plans submitted) had depended upon the use of metal. Labrouste's reading room at the Bibliothèque Nationale in rue de Richelieu was another spectacular example of a bold ironwork structure.

From an aesthetic point of view, the possibility of immense nonbearing surfaces that emerged with metal structures led to a new profusion of glass. The central conservatory, often called the *marquise*, became an almost obligatory feature that was also adopted by hotels, large stores, banks, cafés, and restaurants.

This fondness for metal was not without implications for the architect's trade, since it placed special value on the engineer. The two professions coexisted for a while in the same individuals: men like Hittorff (the redesigned Gare du Nord, 1861–1862), Armand (Gare Saint-Lazare), Duquesney (Gare de l'Est), Labrouste, and a number of other talented architects who had mastered the new techniques. But it was not long before a split opened between architect and engineer.

The tastes of clients naturally played a role. Napoléon III, with his Saint-Simonian faith in progress and the resources of the iron age, favored the bold new trends—as we have seen in the case of the central Halles. Haussmann accepted them as aids to construction and greater comfort, but they did not inspire in him any truly aesthetic feeling. What did move him was the monumental style. Characteristically, his reproach against Baltard's municipal buildings on the Place de l'Hôtel de Ville was that his design should have given more prominence to the façades—for example, by means of strongly projecting pilasters. Haussmann shared the cult of *le monument* so widespread in his time—a term that applied both to historical buildings and to major works of contemporary architecture. It was this concern for the monumental that led him to open up so excessively the cathedral square in front of Notre Dame, to clear the Place du Louvre for Perruault's colonnade, to build a dome above the Tribunal de Commerce, or to flank its façade with a pastiche of the Loggia of the merchants of Brescia (a special wish of Napoléon III). Haussmann got his own copy at the *mairie* of the 1st arrondissement, designed by Hittorff, although he would later realize that it resembled a little too closely the Church of Saint-Germain-l'Auxerrois.

Everyone vied in technical prowess and assorted cultural references; the Napoléon III style was a triumph of eclecticism. According to François Loyer: "The fluency of the triumphalist monument designed by Charles Garnier was better suited to the public opinion of his time than were the intellectual rigor and uncompromising functionalism of Viollet-le-Duc" (the illustrious restorer of historical buildings and an unsuccessful candidate for the design of the new opera house).[6]

23

━━━━━━━━━━━━━━━
≫≫-≫≫-≫≫-≫≫-≫≫-≫≫-≫≫-≫≫
━━━━━━━━━━━━━━━

The Golden Age of
Real Estate

IN THE eighteenth century, the most common Parisian house had a narrow front measuring barely 20 feet on a deep plot that might stretch back over 131 feet. Artisans and tradesmen were in lively competition with each other to have a space on the street, where everything happened; stores faced onto it, and the trades of blacksmith, water-carrier, and greengrocer might be partly or fully practiced there. With its clutter of buildings and trades, the street was a place of activity more than of movement. The house was the center of a restricted horizon, the microcosm of a city whose inhabitants had the principal urban functions more or less at their doorstep.

In the second third of the eighteenth century, the so-called Turgot Plan presented a low city of houses with two or three floors and plenty of internal gardens and courtyards. It was a virtually unchanging model. On the ground floor was the craftsman's workshop-cum-store, and on top of that an *entresol* (that is, a floor with an extra-low ceiling) which served for accommodations and sometimes also as a working area for the artisan and his family. Then came one or two more floors and, finally, beneath the large tiled roof, an attic that had once been used to store grain and later to house a growing population of lower-class newcomers, mostly from the provinces. The first floor was the so-called *étage noble*.

The houses of Paris grew taller under the pressure of the influx. There was nothing very difficult about this from a technical point of view, as they were half-timbered constructions of beams and planks filled either with the unsorted demolition material that was much sought-after, or sometimes with bricks. To raise the height of the building, the usual procedure was to remove the top part of the structure and to build in its place (with the same half-timbering) a kind of cage slightly set back from the lower floors, so that it formed an extra floor that could then be simply covered with the same structure as before. In the central *quartiers*, where the demographic pressure was greatest, such houses often reached five or even six storys; sometimes the *entresol* retained its distinctive features, sometimes it became just one more story like the others. These houses, which were characteristic of the Paris of the Great Revolution, have not completely disappeared from rue Saint-Antoine, rue du Faubourg Saint-Antoine, or rue Saint-Honoré, where almost continuous rows still exist. On rue Saint-Honoré one can still see the house where Robespierre rented an apartment from the joiner Duprat.

Our modern system of co-ownership was unknown. Usually the house remained the property of the tradesman-artisan who had it built in the first place; he would live on the ground floor and the *entresol* and lease the other floors. Those who inherited the property from him kept jealous guard of it. Already under the Ancien Régime, rents helped to enrich a Parisian petty bourgeoisie for whom investment in an apartment block was good business. Since owners were not prepared to sell, it became necessary to find new building land for the *noblesse de robe* and the parliamentary bourgeoisie, rich with their income from public office and from rural properties whose value continued to rise with the general prosperity. Successive kings and grandees of the realm found a way to profit from this mass of unattached money by launching urban development schemes whereby a general plan and façade architecture were imposed upon those who bought up parcels of land for the construction of apartment blocks. This was how Henri IV carried out the plan for the Place Royale (later the Place des Vosges) and the Place Dauphine; Louis XIV did the same with the Place Notre Dame des Victoires and the Place Vendôme, and the Prince of Condé for the Odéon neighborhood; and a businessmen's syndicate divided up the Île Saint-Louis along similar lines in the early seventeenth century, upon the initiative of Marie de' Medici.

Supported by these major royal or princely operations, and by the fame and prestige associated with them, private speculative ventures soon gathered momentum. In his *Tableau de Paris* of 1782, Louis-Sébastien Mercier reported feelings of admiration mingled with unease: "Huge buildings rise from the earth as if by magic, and new *quartiers* are composed of the most magnificent town houses. The construction frenzy is giving the city an air of grandeur and majesty. . . . Speculators have called forth entrepreneurs who, a map in one hand and an estimate in the other, have excited the passions of capitalists."

In the late eighteenth century this speculative fever led the royal authorities to issue regulations for a more disciplined organization of construction ventures, thereby further increasing land values by setting a more acceptable maximum height. These regulations of 1784 were still in force when Haussmann undertook his *grands travaux*. Their justification was security against fire and against people in the street, as well as the greater salubrity permitted by freely circulating air in a context where cities were regularly locked in battle with epidemics of disease. It was in the name of these two principles that the minimum width of streets was set at thirty-three feet—although for the time being this remained no more than a pious wish.

The regulations also expressed the desire for a citywide framework that would correspond to a certain idea of the classical organization of urban architecture. The grandeur and majesty evoked by Mercier would be in danger if the government did not go out of its way to control the construction fever. Paris, capital of the kings of France, should send out to the world the image of order and harmony that they had defined as the justification for their mission on earth.

The ideal model set forth in the regulations of 1784 was the one that may still be seen on the Place des Victoires and Place Vendôme: a ground floor, mezzanine, *étage noble* and middle floor, and at the top an attic with little windows slanting at 45 degrees. The whole took on the aspect of a palace; there were long pilasters (flattened columns with ornamental molding inserted into the façade), cornices, and entablatures inspired by Greek temples. The four levels climaxed at 57.55 feet, at the cornice on top of the last story. Together with the attic, the building rose to a maximum height of 73.52 feet at the level of the roof.

The existing Parisian house benefited from these regulations and continued to gain height within the limits defined by them. For it did not need high ceilings as in the buildings of the Place Vendôme; it could contain a ground floor and four upper storys in the statutory 52.55 feet. Moreover, an astute interpretation of the new regulations could create a fifth story above the ground floor, slightly set back within the attic space. The technique of raising the height of buildings thus continued to operate, although developers realized that it was better to build on a wider base than the traditional 20 feet of the street façade. Beginning in the seventeenth century, new houses in a number of developments tended to be wider than before—a tendency that gathered momentum toward the end of the eighteenth century, when the consolidation of landholdings doubled the width of street façades. The Parisian house thus grew wider at the same time it gained added height and gradually became more like a residential block.

A ROMAN DREAM OF ORDERLY FAÇADES

❦ Parisians in the late eighteenth century nursed a dream of Rome that would inspire the ideologies, institutions, fashions, and vocabulary of both the Revolution and the First Empire. It was an image replete with monuments and palaces, such as the palace for the king of Rome (Napoléon II) that never saw the light of day but whose 1,312-foot façade was planned to dominate the Chaillot hill. There were already a number of Roman-inspired façades by the time of the Revolution: the Louvre colonnade, the palace on the Place de la Concorde, the École Militaire, the Church of Saint-Sulpice, the Palais Bourbon, and to these were added the Pantheon, the Madeleine, and the Bourse in the decades around the turn of the century. Each builder of a residential block wanted to catch for himself a little of the fragrance of ancient Rome. The line of orderly façades gave a shiver of pride to Parisians, who have never liked anything more than the spectacle of festive or military parades passing down boulevards, streets, and avenues as rigorous as a Cartesian discourse. To make them more enjoyable still, developers took the risk of adding balconies. The first continuous balcony was doubtless the one that appeared on the Montholon block, at the Carrefour de Buci, in 1771.

Demographic pressure built toward the end of the 1820s as thousands of people looked in vain for somewhere to live and even prosperous families did not know where to find decent accommodations. Parisians with money to invest found an interest in the construction of residential blocks for leasing to tenants, giving them a palacelike appearance that accorded with the vision of social equality characteristic of the triumphant bourgeoisie. Ceiling height became the same on each story. As to the façade, balconies became a common feature all the way up, while new industrial techniques made it possible to mass-produce luxurious ornamentation within everyone's reach. For this conformist bourgeoisie, the ideal was uniformity and standardization that not only lowered building costs but also promoted the rental market. The bourgeois family, with an owner-occupied house to which it gave a little of its own personality, no longer had any place in these new Parisian centers of construction investment; it moved out to take refuge in Passy and Auteuil, beyond the Monceau plain. The residential block became simply a financial product, banalized in such a way that it could be easily exchanged or sold whenever its owner decided to diversify his portfolio.

Nevertheless, a certain hierarchy between storys persisted in the shape of a subtle balcony code. The mezzanine was now like any other story, but memories of its origin as a store kept it without a balcony. The next floor up, the successor to the *étage noble*, had the right to a continuous balcony, while the ones above it had to make do with a partial balcony. But the continuous balcony reappeared on the fifth floor, which enjoyed clean air and an open view, and the attic windows had the right to a kind of mini-balcony. After 1860 the continuous balcony tended to become established on every story, for in the bourgeois way of life reception rooms were in the brighter and generally more pleasant front of the apartment. Here the balcony enabled people to enjoy the street scene—but also to be seen and admired themselves. How many paintings of the period show a Paris street from a vantage between front room and balcony, with serious gentlemen or pretty ladies seen from behind or from the side looking down on the spectacle of the city.

THE HAUSSMANNIAN BLOCK

❧ This is what we have come to call the Haussmannian apartment block. But in fact it began to take shape in the 1840s under the July Monarchy, at the time when Rambuteau was in charge of the Seine prefecture. What was really new about the Haussmannian block was its external ornamentation. The Rambuteau period was sparing in its use of ashlar, a rare and costly material, and relied largely upon plaster, even if this meant painting and grooving it to create the appearance of building stone. The full-scale balcony of old, now too expensive for the petty bourgeoisie, gave way to windows with shutters and little parapets. But regularity remained an absolute rule: the openings alternated on the façade at the rate of four feet of window, followed by four feet of solid wall, and so on for the length of entire streets. To prevent the façade from blurring into the appearance of a foam-flecked sea, it became customary to add vertical pilasters or columns which, together with the strongly protruding cornices and entablatures, formed a rigorous square design.[1]

During the Second Republic and the early years of the Second Empire, the character of residential blocks did not change. But the scale of construction increased with the *grands travaux*, the incorporation of the suburban communes, the third road system, and the wide straight avenues favorable to quick and easy movement around the city. Powerful new companies took charge of urban complexes stretching over several blocks. Haussmann's policy favored these companies, as he had no interest in the persistence for years of yawning gaps created by his road-building program. Sometimes, at street corners, the prefect's office itself constructed the apartment blocks that defined the direction of the new axes, thereby showing the public that the Seine prefect knew how to build as well as to demolish.

It was thus to Haussmann's advantage to deal in whole blocks with the finance companies, which could be pliant enough in respecting the wishes of the powerful city administration. This satisfied the municipal architects who issued "advice" about construction plans and standardized street façades: the strict regularity of the façades on the Place de l'Opéra, for example, was due not to any formal directive but to "friendly" advice received by the Pereire brothers and their architects; and the extraordinarily consistent lines of Boulevard Voltaire or the Avenue de l'Opéra expressed the key role of the municipal architects who had been working under Deschamps since Haussmann's administrative reorganization of 1859. "The truly Haussmannian apartment block, which came after 1860 and created the image of Paris with which we are familiar," is seen by Loyer as stemming from "an unwritten typology of regulations" and "a more or less authoritarian issuing of architectural advice by people in responsible positions" at the Hôtel de Ville.[2]

Haussmann wished to ban the widespread practice whereby architects on the municipal payroll charged additional fees under the terms of contracts with private clients. It does not seem that the baron succeeded in this aim. Paradoxically, the presence of the same architects on both sides was a peculiar yet effective means of promoting uniformity of views between the administration and private developers. All that finance companies asked was to receive swift permission to build standardized accommodations that met the public demand and could therefore be easily sold or leased. A new regulation, issued in 1859, removed the ambiguities in the regulation of 1784 that had led to the development of attic storys, so that henceforth, in roads with a width of 66 feet or more, it was permitted to raise the cornice above the last story from 57.55 feet to 66 feet. This meant that 5 storys could now be built above the ground floor—but the attic story was integrated with the rest of the façade, in such a way that the apartment block actually seemed to have 6 storys above the ground floor. There was no longer any place for individual imagination: "Each house was no longer anything other than a component of a whole set of apartment blocks."[3] The cut-off corner so distinctive of the Haussmann style, which was made compulsory in order to improve visibility at intersections, marked the limits of the street block with its spectacular circular shape and, whenever feasible, its connected windows.

VIVE L'ARCHITECTURE!

☞ One should not conclude that public opinion was indifferent to architecture. César Daly, director since 1840 of the *Revue générale d'architecture*, believed that the journal should not so much engage in aesthetic reflection as help further the development of the art of construction. A building was "the illustration of a practice facing unprecedented problems that mostly corresponded to new needs."[4]

The *Revue* gave architects the possibility of making their creations better known through visual images. Its impact was so great that rival periodicals soon appeared: the *Moniteur des architectes* in 1847, the *Encyclopédie d'architecture* in 1851, the *Nouvelles Annales de la construction* in 1855. In 1863 the *Encyclopédie d'architecture* merged with the *Gazette du bâtiment* (a listing of legal announcements) to form the *Gazette des architectes et du bâtiment*. All these journals reached a varied readership of businessmen and construction professionals, who found in them ample material for historical and sociological reflection, a plethora of technical information on metal structures or site machinery, and the use of various materials. Their quality earned them an international reputation.

Architects and builders were continually developing construction technology. In this field the Paris administration laid down various safety standards (such as the minimum width of 19.7 inches for the side walls of apartment blocks) and health requirements (such as the size of guttering and precautions against dampness). On the other hand, the facing of internal walls and surface ornamentation (paving, flooring, baseboards, molding, stucco, staircase handrails, iron work, balcony lattice, guttering, window frames, or caryatids) were left to the builder's imagination and to the availability of supply from industries capable of mass-producing such items.

The more rapidly the technology advanced, the longer it took for basic comforts to become more widespread. For these generally depended on the landlord, who weighed up the rate of return on his investment before engaging in any expenditure. Except at the top of the range, rental prices did not tend to increase when apartments included a bathroom or running water in the kitchen.

The supply of gas to apartments also lagged. Gas was used to light the entrance hall and sometimes the dining room, but not the living room (where it was said to fade the paint) or the bedrooms (where one retired at night carrying the traditional oil lamp). It was not yet customary to use gas for heating, and women still preferred wood or coal in the kitchen. Maxime Du Camp thought that within a hundred years "it will be recognized as a cheap means of heating more likely than any other to keep people safe from fires," and that "it will replace the unbearably hot stoves that Paris installs in its narrow kitchens."[5] He was glad to see the rise in the number of households connected to the gas supply. On December 31, 1872, he notes, there were 94,774 in a city with 700,000 dwellings. By 1880 the president of the Compagnie Générale du Gaz put the figure at 135,500, although 74,400 of these were artisans or tradesmen using gas in connection with their work.[6]

Among other household equipment, the old ice chest was still to be seen around Paris, but only very rich people had one of their own at home. Others bought fresh produce daily in accordance with what shopkeepers had to offer, the latter also having no adequate way of keeping it stored. Fish still arrived "with the tide," as carriages brought it daily from the ports closest to Paris: Dieppe and Fécamp. Meat arrived on foot in the capital, and animals were slaughtered at La Villette and other places in the immediate vicinity of the consumers.

REAL ESTATE COMPANIES, BUILDERS, AND BANKERS

❧ The construction industry was one of the traditional branches of the Parisian economy. Surveys conducted by the Paris chamber of commerce in 1847–1848 placed it second only to clothing in number of employees: 12 percent of the working population (41,000 wage earners) in 1847, but 17 percent (71,000 wage earners) in 1860. In revenues, it was in third place behind clothing and food: 140 million francs (or 9 percent of the total for Parisian industry) in 1847, and 315 million francs in 1860. The branch was quite highly concentrated, with 13 workers per enterprise against an average of 4 for the whole of Paris. But the concentration was more marked in the structural trades of masonry and carpentry than among the secondary occupations of joinery, roofing, locksmithing, and housepainting. Construction work used to stop for the winter until 1860, when canvas covers came into general use.[7]

For a long time the fragmentation of real estate meant that construction operated to individual order; Paris in 1841, before Haussmann, had 14,000 landlords per 29,000 houses. Things began to change around 1851–1856, when the reselling of land compulsorily purchased by the city of Paris encouraged the growth of speculative operations. Contractors now built on this land on their own initiative, hoping to sell the resulting blocks with the greatest possible profit. They therefore needed more money than in the past, since they had to pay up front for the initial acquisition of land. The loans they raised from notaries or usurers were underwritten by a mortgage agreement. Thus, in the Seine department alone, mortgage debt totaled approximately 800 million francs around the time in 1852 when Louis-Napoléon was preparing to create Crédit Foncier—and the loans in question attracted a high interest rate of roughly 11 percent. Crédit Foncier, by making extra capital available to contractors at a low interest rate, naturally prompted developers to increase the scale of their speculative operations.

It was now that the Pereire brothers (not themselves building contractors) formed a real estate company with the aim not so much of expanding capital values as of making large rental profits on investments. They set up the company at the request of Napoléon III and Haussmann, both of whom wished to influence the level of rents and to stabilize investment in the rental sector. By 1859 real estate accounted for 74 percent of their investments.[8] After the rue de Rivoli and the rue du Louvre, the Pereires stepped up the scale of their operations. They were present on the Monceau plain and in the *quartier* of the Opéra—in fact, between 1860 and 1862 their company, the Compagnie Immobilière, acquired forty acres of land in various parts of Paris.[9]

The returns were high: real estate on the rue de Rivoli brought in 8.22 percent in 1856, 9 percent in 1857, and 8.69 percent in 1860. Eventually the Pereires aroused the envy of others, and the large banks, which had previously stuck in principle to one-shot operations, now also decided to invest in rental accommodations. Newcomers to the market, such as the insurance companies, followed suit. The growing competition among investors pushed up the price of apartment blocks and lowered the return on real estate capital. Pereire properties on the Boulevard des Capucines brought in 6.02 percent in 1864 and 6.98 percent in 1866, but their rivals generally fared much worse.

In one of those swings of the pendulum common on the capital markets, the major investors suddenly switched from real estate to the railways and industry, then responded to difficulties in industry by returning to real estate but mainly in speculative areas from which they could later execute a speedy withdrawal. They built new dwellings and put them on the market, but these were only enough to cover needs resulting from the destruction of older accommodations and the accompanying rise in population. Napoléon

III and Haussmann were disappointed that the supply was not large enough to bring down rents. Apartments remained expensive: a Compagnie du Gaz engineer, for example, earning the fairly high salary of 1,800 francs a year, would have had to pay a quarter of it (450 francs) on rather ordinary accommodations—and that was the most he could afford without threatening the family budget.

HOW MANY DWELLINGS?

✍ Public opinion accused the authorities, and especially the Seine prefect, of unbalancing the market. Haussmann took this to heart and set about answering "the frequent accusation that the Parisian *grands travaux* had involved thoughtless demolition that reduced the number of dwellings, at a time when the number of inhabitants was rising because of the series of newly developed railway lines that ended in the city."[10] Having kept a careful record of demolition and new construction, he was able to reply that between 1853 and 1870 the balance had never once been negative, "so that the total number of vacant dwellings on offer to the public did not decline but constantly increased, and must obviously have mitigated the rise in rents caused by the declining value of money for which my administration could certainly not be blamed."[11]

From the end of 1852 until the end of 1859, in the twelve arrondissements into which Paris was then divided, there were 4,349 house demolitions—of which 2,236 were the sequel to compulsory purchases, and 2,113 (almost as many) were carried out by landlords hoping to make an additional profit through timely rebuilding. Since, during the same period, 9,617 new houses were delivered for habitation, there was a net gain of 5,268. The number of dwellings did increase as a result of this huge movement of demolition and reconstruction: whereas the vanished blocks had contained 25,562 dwellings, the 9,617 new constructions supplied 58,207 (or 32,645 more). With an average of three persons per household, all the new housing units created during Haussmann's first seven years at the Seine prefecture made it possible to accommodate 175,000 people—a net gain of 98,000 that represents an average additional capacity of 14,000 per year.

In quantitative terms, there was no housing crisis in the Paris of the Second Empire. At the end of 1859 the old city limits contained 32,734 houses, or 451,374 dwellings. Out of this total, 11,000 dwellings were empty. In the 440,000 occupied units, it would have been possible to house 1,320,000 people on the basis of three per household, and the population at the beginning of 1860 was 1,200,000. The expansion of Paris to the limits of the twenty newly defined arrondissements brought the total number of dwellings to 567,917 (through the incorporation of 116,543 units from the old *banlieue*), with a theoretical capacity of 1,680,000 for a now only slightly smaller population of 1,600,000. Between 1860 and 1869 the rhythm of construction grew faster. Demolition, mostly voluntary, eliminated 15,373 houses containing 91,991 dwellings, but at the same time the construction of 34,160 new apartment blocks supplied 215,104 dwellings. Paris therefore gained 18,787 houses and 123,113 dwellings. By January 1, 1870, the city's housing stock had reached 691,030 units, which could accommodate 2,070,000 people. The 1866 census had recorded a population of 1,825,271. By extrapolation, Haussmann calculated that there were a little under 2 million Parisians at the time of his departure from the prefect's office—which would have meant that a surplus capacity existed for 100,000 persons.

What were the consequences of Haussmann's policy for the social composition of Paris? The fiscal wealth of the Seine department obviously increased: taxes on land, personal income, and property rose from less than 15 million francs in 1853 to nearly 25 million francs in 1869. Was this trend due solely to the rise in the amount of property, or also to higher rents? Legislation then in force did not permit the taxation of dwellings occupied by tenants considered to be poor, whatever their level of rent. And the city of Paris also fully exempted from personal or property taxes anyone whose rent was below 250 francs (a figure raised in 1867 to 400 francs).

According to a survey conducted in 1865 by the prefecture, the city's total stock of 637,369 dwellings included 259,604 units not liable to taxation because of poverty. This was a huge proportion—40 percent of the total stock, accommodating some 780,000 individuals. The figure shows without a shadow of doubt that, contrary to an endlessly repeated view, the very poor layers of the population were far from having being swept out of Paris. Furthermore, 109,634 dwellings (with a rent below 250 francs) were in practice exempt from all taxes; it was here that the small shopkeepers and artisans lived, at the mercy of the first crisis to come along, a total of 330,000 persons. The survey also recorded 203,277 dwellings whose level of rent, between 250 francs and 1,500 francs, made them partially exempt from taxation; these were the houses of the middle bourgeoisie. The most expensive dwellings, which attracted a rent above 1,500 francs and therefore the full rate of taxation, numbered only 17,851, theoretically inhabited by 50,000 persons, the elite of society. There were also 17,040 empty housing units and 29,963 premises occupied not for purposes of accommodation but for commercial or industrial activities. The rich had become richer—which explains the marked increase in tax revenue. But the poor, the workers, and the common people were still also present in the capital.

Although the poor had not been driven out, it is true that the *grands travaux* brought about an unprecedented upheaval. "You do not move 117,553 families . . . , you do not dislodge 350,000 people and the industrial or commercial establishments run by many of them, without causing a general upheaval of which the masses (who cannot appreciate its indispensability) rapidly grow tired, especially when it stretches over seventeen long years."[12] Haussmann forgets to mention that this great shake-up, directly affecting an average of 20,000 people a year, was greatest in the central *quartiers* of old Paris, where the workers and, more generally, the least affluent sections of the population traditionally lived.

It is undeniable that rents underwent a sharp increase. Haussmann said as much himself, but he was of the view that it was not as great as the improvement in wages and living standards. The baron writes that some people blamed him for "the rise in the general level of rents in Paris since its transformation—a rise that is unfortunately true." But he commented: "They were careful not to add that this extra cost—largely offset by rising wages and all manner of gains, and due to the same cause in the development of business and public prosperity—would have been incomparably larger without our *travaux*, without the extra houses and dwellings that they gave to Paris. Everyone understands that the worker, who found it quite natural to earn five francs a day instead of three, would have preferred not to have to pay an extra fifty or one hundred francs for a less cramped, better-aired, better-lighted, in short, more salubrious dwelling than the foul, dark, and unhealthy hovel where he used to pack in his family."[13]

HOUSING AND DOMESTIC BUDGETS

❦ The figures given by Haussmann indicate a steady rhythm of construction and a housing stock that kept pace, quantitatively, with the needs of the population. In order to check whether the price of real estate in Haussmann's time allowed the poorer sections to find accommodations, we need to look more closely at a few typical household budgets.

According to Eugène Sue, an unmarried worker spent a total of 1.55 francs a day on subsistence: 20 centimes on lunch, 75 centimes on dinner, 10 centimes on liquor, 20 centimes on tobacco, and 30 centimes (a little more than a fifth) on furnished lodgings. In a four-person family (husband, wife, and two children), the skilled male worker received 2.50 francs a day for a year of 350 days: a total of 875 francs; his wife or older children therefore needed to work to bring this up to the 1,500 francs that allowed them to scrape out a living. Of those 1,500 francs, 1,000 went to food, 250 to clothing, 60 to miscellaneous expenses—and 90 francs to rent. The apprentice or young worker earning 120 francs a year, but fed, lodged and heated, had a more enviable existence.

It was only in the middle bourgeoisie that budgets compatible with the level of rents were to be found. A family of four persons (the parents, one child, and one domestic servant) would have 6,000 francs a year for living expenses, including 2,500 francs for food, 1,000 for clothing, 600 for the servant's remuneration, and 900 for miscellaneous expenses—which left 1,000 francs, or a sixth of the family income, for rent.[14]

There was a gulf between these two types of families. The income ratio between them was 1 to 4 (1,500 francs to 6,000 francs), but the rent ratio was 1 to 11 (90 francs to 1,000 francs). The figures thus point to the burning necessity for new formulas for working-class accommodations. One idea was to subsidize working-class estates, offering housing at prices that ordinary people could afford. In 1849, some time before Haussmann's arrival at the Hôtel de Ville, the Société des Cités Ouvrières launched the first such experiment with social housing at 58, rue de Rochechouart, which the prince president assisted both financially and with advice drawn from his knowledge of England. (Hence the name "Cité Napoléon," or "Napoleon Estates," which was given to the completed project in 1853.) The architect Veugy designed five main buildings of three storys each, with heated and ventilated units of one or two rooms, including a kitchen. Each story had its water points, sinks, and toilets, and provision was made for collective laundries, baths, and children's creches. The rents, fixed between 100 and 150 francs, were considerably below market level.

Napoléon III next bought a plot of land on Boulevard Mazas (today's Boulevard Diderot) in order to build seventeen buildings for workers' housing; 2 million francs were spent on the project, which was part of a longer-term policy. Thus in 1853 the emperor announced that he planned to have at least one working-class estate built in each arrondissement: "The government has decided . . . that new multi-story houses should be built simultaneously in several areas of Paris . . . for unmarried workers as well as family households, in such a way as to combine affordable prices with all the desirable conditions of salubriousness, well-being, and morality."[15]

Property confiscated the previous year from the Orléans family had raised 10 million francs that could help finance the housing program. But it was taking a long time to get underway, and in any event the workers did not wish to be housed in barracks. The Cité Napoléon, already nicknamed "The Barracks," repelled them with its military aspect, its ten o'clock curfew, and its system of police surveillance. The best-intentioned philanthropists were uneasy about the risks of such large concentrations of workers. "It is desirable that the workers should all have healthy, comfortable, and inexpensive housing, but crowds of them should not be gathered together in kinds of large barracks where the bad constantly exert a deplorable influence upon the good," wrote Doctor Villermé, whose work *L'État physique et moral des ouvriers dans les fabriques de coton, de laine et de soie* (1840) made a great impact and led to the first legislation on child labor.[16]

An expert on working-class communities, Armand Audiganne, noted in 1860 that "housing projects have never been popular in France" because they extend an oppressive factory discipline into the intimate space of the home: "When we went home, the workers say, we would find another regulation pinned to our door, affecting nearly all our private activities. We would not be masters in our own home."[17]

The comte de Madre, founder of a "charitable association for the achievement of cheap and improved workers' housing," drew the obvious consequences from the workers' distaste for military-style estates and campaigned for wealthy individuals or well-endowed organizations to take the initiative in providing housing as a business venture. In 1863 he completed work on a set of apartment blocks complete with water and washhouses on rue Saint-Maur, in the 13th arrondissement, built around a large inner yard with workshops in its central area. Rents were 200 francs a year for two rooms and a kitchen; there were no regulation of people's lives and no moral designs; each apartment was snapped up in a few weeks.[18]

Action to improve workers' housing also took place in old blocks left untouched by the demolition program, which, being run-down and insalubrious, could still be afforded by poorer layers of the population. They formed what is known in a present-day euphemism as the *parc social de fait*, the de facto stock of social housing. In order to control such housing, and to try to make it more healthful without changing its place in the provision of accommodations for workers, Haussmann could use a special commission of doctors, philanthropic industrialists, and landlords set up under the terms of the Melun legislation of 1850. Each year this body carried out a large number of inspections: between three thousand and four thousand per year in the period from 1860 to 1869. In a field where subjective assessment plays an important role—exactly what counts as unhealthful?—the commission helped to raised general standards by insisting that there was at least one water point in the inner yard of apartment blocks and that washroom installations were acceptable.[19]

But it seemed that there could be no end to the war on slums. Unhealthful dwellings might be cleaned up in Paris, but others were being hastily constructed of brick and plaster in Belleville or Ménilmontant, and near the fortifications wooden huts were accommodating families newly arrived from the provinces or others driven from pillar to post by successive landlords because their children had been making too much noise. Was Haussmannization not a modern version of Penelope's web?

24

"An Epoch in the History of City Planning"

"WHAT IS KNOWN as Haussmannization—that is, the method of driving new roads and gutting old neighborhoods in a kind of surgical redevelopment—truly marked an epoch in the history of city planning that one hopes may now have passed. After all, the technology of city planning has made some advances in the last hundred years." This view of Haussmann's influence, expressed by Pierre Lavedan in 1954, summed up the debate on the philosophy and significance of the *grands travaux*.[1]

CRITICAL ASSESSMENTS

As a technique for the transformation of existing urban space—in contrast to the creation of new towns—Haussmannization was meant to adapt the city by means of redevelopment. It was thus at the opposite pole from the principles that guided Paul Delouvrier's replanning of the Paris region in the 1960s. Operations on the existing urban fabric inevitably involve considerable destruction, and from this point of view all epochs have vandalized the work of their predecessors. Under the July Monarchy, Victor Hugo had already deplored the modernist enthusiasm with which the disappearance of vestiges of the past was daily greeted. "Vandalism is flourishing and prospering beneath our eyes. Vandalism is celebrated, applauded, encouraged, admired, caressed, protected, consulted, subsidized, bankrolled, and assimilated. . . . Vandalism has its newspapers, its coteries, its schools, its professorships, its public, its arguments. . . . Every day it demolishes some of what little remains from that admirable old Paris." Georges Pillement, who after Hugo took up the struggle against the "destruction of Paris,"[2] placed the original blame on the artists' commission at the end of the eighteenth century: "The artists' plan contained the best and the worst; the artists were mainly architects and engineers who worshiped the straight lines and perspective that Baron Haussmann would later have. For the sake of a fine perspective, they were prepared to demolish everything before them. . . . What the artists did not have time to achieve, Napoléon I or Napoléon III would make their own responsibility."[3]

To see Haussmann's activity in the context of his times is to place the condemnations in perspective. "In the early nineteenth century," Pillement argued, "no value was accorded to the structures of Gothic art or the Renaissance, . . . whereas in later years, even when romanticism brought the Middle Ages into fashion, no distinction was made between the genuine historical article and the pastiche. So long as they were in the presence of Gothic arcades, many prominent artists felt themselves in a sentimental or literary trance. Instead of the ruined archbishop's palace, Balzac hoped that one would be built 'in the Gothic style' which would follow up 'so many subtle harmonies.' "[4] When a Mérimée or a Viollet-le-Duc gave new favor to a testimony of the past, the interest was in historical buildings, not in an old *quartier*. Perhaps only the polemicist Louis Veuillot, in keeping with his Legitimist beliefs, was sensitive to the totality of a city landscape, with its ordinary buildings existing alongside more prestigious structures. "In the new Paris," he wrote, "there will no longer be any residence, any tomb, or even any cemetery. Each house will be only a piece of that enormous inn through which everyone has passed and where nobody remembers having seen anyone else. . . . City without a past, filled with memoryless minds, tearless hearts, loveless souls. City of uprooted crowds, a mobile mass of human dust."

Critics have also focused on Haussmann's aesthetic conceptions. As the pieces fell into place, was the new Paris at least the bearer of a new beauty? On this, intellectuals were of a single mind: the baron's straight lines were deadly boring; no building exhibited any quality whatsoever. But the response to this dual verdict was not complicated: the straight line is at the heart of the French intellectual and aesthetic heritage; "straightness" is a quality, a "swaying" character a personality defect. Only toward the end of the twentieth century would civil engineers begin to ask whether highways should not have an occasional little bend, if only to avoid the sleepiness induced by boredom.

As far as the architecture is concerned, Haussmann's role as prefect for

the Seine meant that his responsibility was not as great as that of the architects themselves. The station halls, marked by the irruption of new construction materials, strike us today as more forceful than the eclecticism of so
many other buildings that went up in the capital during the same period.
But good-quality architecture cannot be decreed, and it would be wrong to
hold such things against Haussmann. His cityscape preserves such a unity
that late-twentieth-century planning projects in Paris (having previously
been a slave to the fashion of towers and huge complexes) are now rediscov-
ering the Haussmannian sites and incorporating some features from the
1930s that produced such happy results in Paris—while molding themselves to the roads and templates of the Second Empire.

More technical accusations have also been leveled at Haussmann. It is
true that the design of the radiating *places* is not the best suited to traffic;
that the cult of perspective regrettably gained the upper hand over function-
ality; and that old blocks and appalling housing conditions often persisted
behind the curtain of new façades. Haussmann counted on the landlords'
self-interest as businessmen to demolish what needed to be demolished—
and many did do this, as we have seen from the statistics on the number of
housing units. In the prefect's defense, it took time for public intervention
in private spaces to become an acceptable practice, and, closer to our own
day, General de Gaulle and Georges Pompidou did not think that the built
structure of Paris could be transformed in any other way than through the
initiative of those who owned the land.

A final set of criticisms concern the vision of redevelopment expressed in
Haussmann's activity. While removing slums within *vieux Paris*, he allowed
new ones to be created in outlying areas. Suburbs beyond the line of the city
fortifications were not integrated into his policy. No doubt this would have
been done within the framework of the "Greater Paris" that was supposed to
coincide with the limits of the Seine department. But as this new enlargement of the capital never happened, Haussmann neglected the development
of areas within what is now defined as the "first ring" of suburbs. These were
industrialized and urbanized in a chaotic manner for which we have not yet
finished paying the price.

In order to ensure the success of his urban policy, Haussmann offered the
most favorable terms to those who were bought out. Compensation was swift
and sizable. The historian Jeanne Gaillard has described the thrill of excitement that spead among Parisian landlords as they realized that compulsory
purchase was synonymous with enrichment. Petitions came thick and fast,
but the main complaint was at not having yet been "expropriated."[5] As the

machinery raced away, Haussmann himself waxed indignant about the scandalously high compensation awards, which benefited professional speculators as much as petty-bourgeois owners of apartments. At least this earned him the support of an influential social group. Tenants, on the other hand, were trampled underfoot—acknowledged only when the rent fell due, dependent upon the landlord's whim for a water or gas supply, subject to arbitrary regulations concerning children or animals. It is the image of the simple man from the country in the vulture's clutches.

The year 1868 saw the publication of *Paris désert. Lamentations d'un Jérémie haussmannisé*. The anonymous author describes a new Babylon where Jeremiah wanders complaining: "I do not see here any houses and cottages; all they build now are palaces. And these palaces belong to Vulture. . . . A man of prey, this Vulture waits in his lair for his victims, and he must have only choice game because he does not stoop to the simplehearted or those with few means." The new Paris is made for people with money. The deportation of the poor has not been organized by Haussmann, but he accepts it as a logical consequence of the transformation that is raising the price of land and apartments.[6] It seems to him natural that the workers should move and find shelter farther out. He lacks any of our modern conceptions of social mixing. The social segregation that began before his arrival keeps developing. Nostalgics can ponder how Cochin, an eminent Parisian notable, celebrated the lost neighborhood communities in which all classes lived together: "Birth, proximity, and trade, use of the same rights on the same day, the closeness that comes of performing the same duties—all this had gradually made of each arrondissement in Paris a little civil and industrial province."[7] And yet the legislative elections that always resulted in a republican victory, then the Commune, showed that at the end of Haussmann's tenure Paris was far from having become the exclusively bourgeois city that is so often painted.

Émile Ollivier did not miss the easy opportunity for wordplay with *Haus* (German for "house") and *Mann* (German for "man"), and with *Hausmann* itself ("houseman" or "porter"), in order to describe the prefect as the "lackey of a great house." That the Second Empire's worship of money did not pass the prefect by, is certainly evident enough. But this is not really adequate as the sole explanation for everything he did. For we would have to suppose a peculiar blindness on the part of all those foreigners who, in Haussmann's own time and for decades after, took Haussmannization in its most favorable sense. César Daly noted even in 1862 in the *Revue générale de l'architecture*: "The *grands travaux* in Paris daily arouse the astonishment and often the admiration of foreigners; they have been less favorably judged by some of the Parisian press." British and German architects, in particular, reported on the baron's work to their respective academies of architecture. The Germans found it a little extravagant and ostentatious, in excess of strictly functional requirements. The British observed that it rested in principle upon rising land values and therefore upon a higher density of construction, and expressed surprise that the prefect was not concerned about the lack of comfort so apparent in the interior design of Paris apartments. All, however, went into raptures over the power and unity of Haussmann's conception.[8]

HAUSSMANNISM IN PROVINCIAL CITIES

≈ Before spreading abroad, the spirit of Haussmannism left its mark in the great transformations that affected other French cities in the Second Empire and the early Third Republic.

In Rouen, the rue de l'Impératrice (today's rue Jeanne d'Arc) was driven in 1861 between the station and the river port. Together with rue Impériale (now rue Thiers), it constituted the main crossing of the Norman metropolis. The creation of these arteries involved the disappearance of five hundred old houses and two churches, Saint-Martin and Saint-André-aux- Febvres.

In Toulouse two similar streets—rue d'Alsace and rue de Metz—were planned in 1864 but built only after 1870; they intersected at right angles and sliced a corner off the Augustinian priory (now the Musée des Augustins).

Avignon was more profoundly transformed. Between 1856 and 1867 the Boulevard de la République ripped through the city from north to south, from the railway station to the city hall and the Papal Palace. The project was much criticized, not because it caused ancient neighborhoods to disappear but because the boulevard created a funnel for the mistral to blow through more intensely.

Even more dramatic was the redevelopment of Marseilles, where the presence of characters already familiar to us from the *travaux* in Paris, Mirès and the Pereire brothers, helps to explain the amazing similarity between the changes in the two great cities. Marseilles had already experienced the major construction project of the Prado, in the reign of Louis-Philippe, and the coming of Napoléon III signaled a new round of city planning. Major growth occurred in the period of exceptional prosperity that followed the conquest of Algeria, shortly before the digging of the Suez Canal (1859 to 1869). The city's population increased by nearly 50 percent in twenty years, from 132,000 in 1831 to 195,000 in 1851. The Vieux Port could no longer cope, and a law of August 5, 1844, ordered the construction of new docks at La Joliette; the project took nine years to complete, but a partial service was operating by 1847. Growth accelerated between 1851 and 1872 as the population soared to 312,000—a further gain of 117,000, or 60 percent. The port continued to expand with installations at Arenc, Le Lazaret, and the Imperial Docks (now the seaport docks).

This posed the urgent problem of linking the new port with the old port and city center. Mirès and the Pereires, who took a close interest in the harbor installations, had every reason to become involved. A hill 98 feet high separated the Vieux Port from the Joliette docks. The Mirès project, submitted in 1858, caused a stir in the city government because of its immoderate scale, and in 1860 the emperor approved a more modest version featuring the straight-lined rue Impériale (today's rue de la République). This operation was entrusted to the Pereires, who destroyed 935 houses and 38 streets as they cut the new street through Marseilles between 1862 and 1864. They had hoped to make of it a second Canebière,[9] but the city's inhabitants did not fall over one another to occupy the new Haussmann-style apartments flanking the street. The outcome, though magnificent in its way, spelled financial disaster for Mirès and the Pereire brothers.[10]

In Lyons the initiative fell to the prefect Vaïsse, who in 1853 had taken the position that Haussmann had turned down before his appointment in Paris. According to Émile Ollivier, Vaïsse—who remained in office until 1864—was as intelligent and efficient as Haussmann, but less brutal in character. "An administrator distinguished by the opposite qualities of moderation, tact, graciousness, and modesty, he obtained the same success."[11] He also had strategic concerns such as the need to avoid a repetition of the major riots of the 1830s. The Maréchal de Castellane, military governor of Lyons, confided to him in connection with the rue Impériale (rue de la République) driven between Place Bellecour and the Place des Terreaux: "This street is even more indispensable strategically than it is from the point of view of salubriousness, embellishment, and public utility."

The rue Impériale connected with the rue de l'Impératrice (now the rue de l'Hôtel de Ville), which ran straight for almost a mile between Bellecour and the Place des Terreaux. The acute angle that the rue de l'Impératrice formed with Place Bellecour meant that it was possible to respect the Church of Saint-Nizier and the former abbey of the Benedictines (Palais Saint-Pierre); the street also gave access to the Place des Jacobins. The rue de la République, on the other hand, did not observe rectilinearity. Running perpendicular to Place Bellecour, it extended one of its sides but was in fact made up of two straight sections that came together at the Place de la République (Place Impériale); it was, in different conditions, equivalent to the schema of the Boulevard Malesherbes in Paris. Starting from Place de la République, the rue Impériale and rue de l'Impératrice ran down in parallel before ending one before, the other behind, the Hôtel de Ville. They were both crossed by rue Grenette, a street lined up with the Pont Lafayette that provided a wider link than the older ones between the city center and the Brotteaux district via the Place des Cordeliers.

"Place Bellecour should be thought of as the Place d'Armes of Lyons," the Maréchal de Castellane said to Vaïsse. "It is from there that the columns will be able to set off. Once rue Impériale has been built, the troops will easily be able to move into the city center." Five hundred houses were destroyed, and height restrictions imposed architectural discipline upon the new blocks that went up. The project was given to the architect Dardel, who, between 1855 and 1860 also rebuilt the Bourse façade on rue Impériale in a rather heavy Renaissance style. Finally, the Tête d'Or park that opened in 1856 beside the Rhone had echoes of the Bois de Boulogne, and embankments built around the same period made the city safe from disastrous floods.

The Haussmannization of Paris did not end with Haussmann's departure or with his death. Under Alphand's leadership, the Third Republic inaugurated the Garnier Opera, finally leveled the Moulins hill, and completed the Avenue de l'Opéra in 1879. After some hesitation, Boulevard Saint-Germain was driven from the rue de Bac/Saint-Germain crossroads to the Place Saint-Germain-des-Prés, achieving the great east-west artery on the left bank that Haussmann had always had in mind. The following century realized more of his plans with Boulevard Raspail in 1907, and the Boulevard Haussmann extension to the Carrefour Richelieu-Drouot in 1925, where it joined the *grands boulevards*.

Another book would be required to separate what has and has not been due to Haussmann's influence in the subsequent history of the French capital. To make the dead speak in order to recover—or to challenge—their legacy is an endless exercise. Did Haussmann deserve the nickname "Pasha" that Parisian children bestowed upon him? No doubt he enjoyed the pomp of imperial Paris. Belonging as he did to a society hungry for easy money, he was often treated as a thief or a corrupt official—and yet he did not leave a large fortune at his death. Sharply aware of his duties as a public servant, he was insensitive to criticism and proved able to carry out Napoléon III's program while rounding it off in various ways. A strong man was certainly needed to turn a still medieval Paris into a great modern city. It is hardly surprising that Haussmann gave the impression of a vandal: he bought out tens of thousands of Parisians and dislodged hundreds of thousands more. Authoritarian, pragmatic, and efficient, he was concerned that there should be order in all things. Few people have done so much to shape the environment and the atmosphere of a city!

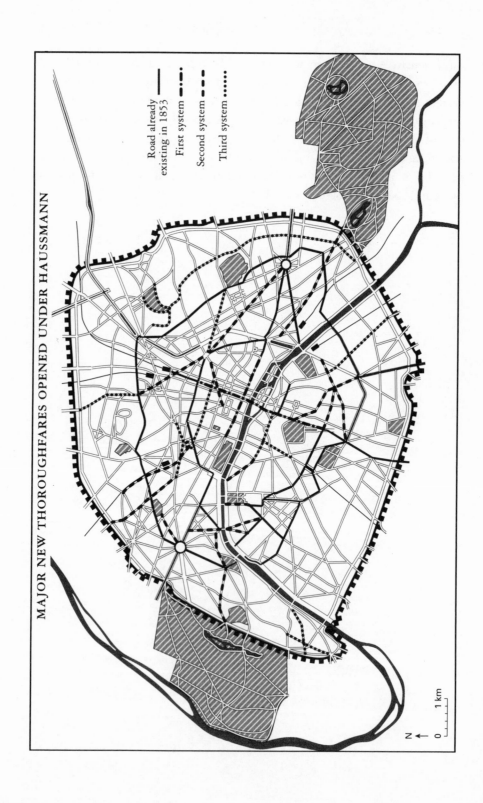

MAJOR NEW THOROUGHFARES OPENED UNDER HAUSSMANN

Road already
existing in 1853 ——

First system •—•—•

Second system •••—•••

Third system •••••••

N ← |——————| 1 km
0

TWO RADIATING SQUARES

Place de l'Étoile

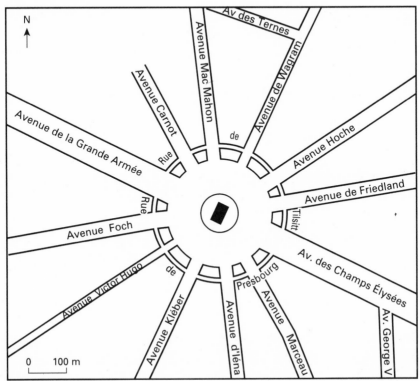

Place de la République

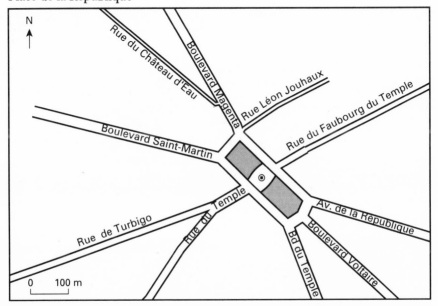

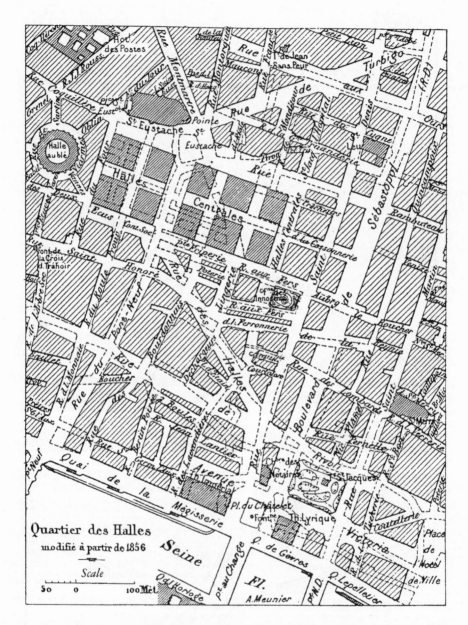

CENTRAL HALLES AREA AS MODIFIED AFTER 1856

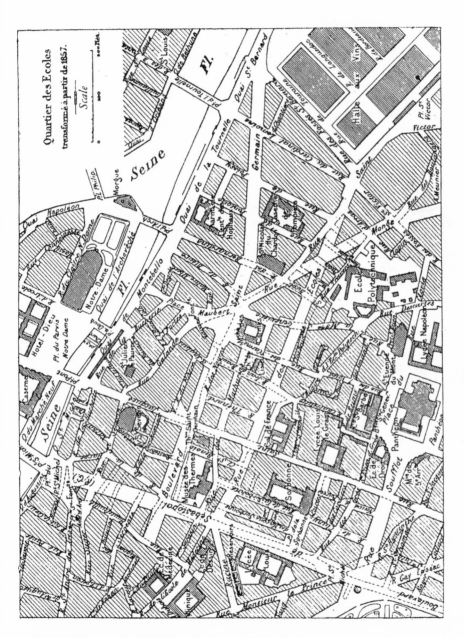

THE ÉCOLES AREA AS MODIFIED AFTER 1857

SUCCESSIVE ENLARGEMENTS OF THE LOUVRE, 1858

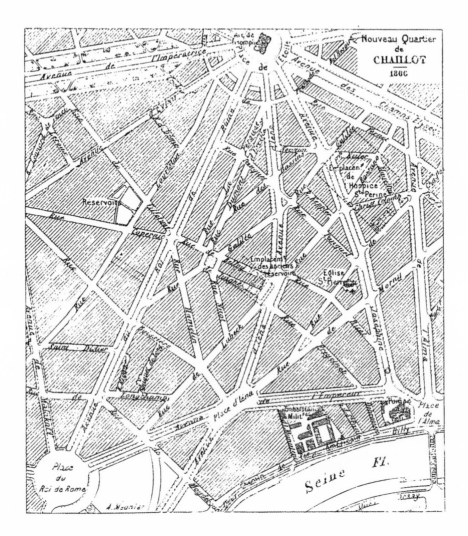

NEW AREA OF CHAILLOT, 1866

Chronology

1806

June 6 — Marriage of Haussmann's parents, Nicolas-Valentin and Ève-Marie-Caroline Dentzel.

1808

April 20 — Birth of Louis-Napoléon Bonaparte, son of Louis of Holland and Hortense de Beauharnais.

1809

March 27 — Birth of Georges-Eugène Haussmann in Paris.
June — General Dentzel appointed governor of Vienna.

1815

June 18 — Battle of Waterloo.

1816

June 12 — Law banishing the regicides. Haussmann's father exiled in Basle.

1821

May 5 — Death of Napoleon I on Saint Helena.

1830

July 27–28–29   The *"Trois Glorieuses"* of the Revolution. Fall of Charles X. Haussmann wounded in fighting on the 29th.

August 9   Louis-Philippe accepts the crown. Beginning of the July Monarchy.

August 21   Popular movement against what are seen as light sentences handed down to Charles X's last ministers.

1831

February 14   Rioting in Paris. Sacking of Saint-Germain-l'Auxerrois and the archbishop's palace.

March 13   Government of Casimir Périer.

March 22   Law establishing the National Guard.

April 15–16   Disturbances in Paris.

May 22   Haussmann appointed secretary general of the Vienne prefecture.

June 15   Disturbances in Paris.

July 14   Rioting on the Place de Grève, Place de la Bastille, and Place de la Concorde.

September 16–19 Disturbances in Paris.

1832

March 22   First day of the cholera epidemic.

April 1–3   Riots.

May 16   Death of Casimir Périer from cholera.

June 5–6   Republican and Bonapartist riots on the occasion of the funeral of General Lamarque.

July 22   Death of the duc de Reichstadt (the "Eaglet") at Schoenbrunn castle.

1833

June 15   Haussmann accepts the position of subprefect for Yssingeaux, in Haute-Loire.

June 22   The comte de Rambuteau, then a parliamentary deputy, is appointed prefect for the Seine department.

July 7   Law concerning procedures for compulsory purchase.

October 9   Haussmann appointed subprefect for Nérac, in Lot-et-Garonne.

December 23   Arrival in Paris of the Luxor obelisk.

1834

February 21–23	Disturbances in Paris.
April 12–13–14	Riots near the Saint-Merry cloister. Massacre at rue Transnonain on the 14th.
April 20	Law on the municipal organization of Paris.
May 31	Law concerning work on embellishment of Champs Élysées and the Place de la Concorde.

1835

June 28	Law on primary education.
August 23	Ordinance concerning street alignment plans.

1836

July 17	Haussmann appointed Knight of the Legion of Honor.
July 29	Unveiling of the Arc de Triomphe at Étoile.
October 25	Erection of the Luxor obelisk.
October 30	Attempted coup d'état by Louis-Napoléon Bonaparte at Strasbourg.
November 21	Louis-Napoléon is placed on a ship bound for New York.

1837

Early August	Louis-Napoléon returns to Europe to be at the bedside of his ailing mother, ex-Queen Hortense, at Arenenberg in Switzerland.
August 26	Opening of the Paris to Saint-Germain-en-Laye railway.
October 5	Death of ex-Queen Hortense.

1838

October 17	Haussmann's marriage to Octavie Laharpe in Bordeaux.

1839

May 12–13	Rioting in Paris (the so-called Seasons Plot).
July	Publication of *Idées napoléoniennes* by Louis-Napoléon Bonaparte.
August 2	Opening of Paris to Versailles railway for passengers (right bank).

1840

January 17	Birth of Haussmann's first daughter, Marie-Henriette.
February 19	Haussmann appointed subprefect for Saint-Girons, in the Ariège.
August 5	Attempted coup d'état by Louis-Napoléon Bonaparte at Boulogne-sur-Mer.
September 1	Beginning of construction work on the Paris fortifications.
September 4	Workers' riots in the Quatre-Vingts *quartier* in Paris.
September 28	Start of trial of Louis-Napoléon and the other Boulogne conspirators before the Chamber of Peers.
October 6	Sentencing of Louis-Napoléon to life imprisonment and his transfer to the Ham fortress.
December 14–15	Return of ashes of Napoleon I to Paris and their deposition in the Invalides.
December 29	First legislation on child labor passed by the Chamber of Deputies.

1841

February 27	Water starts to flow from the artesian well at Grenelle.
May 3	Law on compulsory purchases.
November 23	Haussmann appointed subprefect in Blaye.

1842

May 8	Railway disaster at Meudon-Bellevue.
May 18 / June 11	Legislation concerning the railways.
July 13	Accidental death of duc d'Orléans.

1843

May 2	Opening of Paris to Orleans railway.
May 3	Opening of Paris to Rouen railway.
October 20	Electric lighting trials on Place de la Concorde.

1844

March 14	New legislation on patents.

1846

March 26	Opening of Paris to Tours railway.
April 26	Ordinance permitting creation of the Lariboisière hospital.

May 25	Louis-Napoléon Bonaparte escapes from the Ham fortress.
June 7	Opening of the Sceaux railway.
June 14	Opening of the Northern Railway.
July 24	Death of Louis, ex-king of Holland, father of Louis-Napoléon Bonaparte.
September 30	Disturbances in the *faubourg* Saint-Antoine.

1847

January 13	Wagons carrying wheat are looted at Buzançais, in the Indre.
February 20	Haussmann is promoted to officer of the Legion of Honor.
July 8–17	Teste-Cubière trial at the Chamber of Peers.
August 17	Duchess of Praslin murdered by her husband.
August 24	Duc de Praslin commits suicide in prison.

1848

February 22	Banquet canceled at Chaillot. Beginning of the "February Revolution."
February 24	Fall of Louis-Philippe and appointment of a provisional government.
February 26	Official proclamation of the Second Republic. Creation of National Workshops.
March 5	Garnier-Pagès becomes finance minister.
March 9	Armand Marrast appointed mayor of Paris.
March 16	So-called fur coat demonstration by conservatives in streets of Paris.
March 17	Haussmann removed as subprefect in Blaye and appointed prefectural counselor for the Gironde.
March 19	Start of operations of the Comptoir d'Escompte in Paris.
April 23	Legislative elections.
May 3	Decree providing for *grands travaux* in Paris (completion of Louvre Palace and extension of rue de Rivoli).
June 4	By-elections. Louis-Napoléon elected four times over.
June 18	Louis-Napoléon resigns his seats.
June 21	Decree dissolving the National Workshops.
June 23–26	The "June Days" in Paris.
July 4	Death of Chateaubriand.
July 19	Marrast elected president of the Assembly; resigns as mayor of Paris.
July 21	Neveux appointed prefect for the Gironde.

September 17	Legislative elections. Louis-Napoléon Bonaparte elected.
September 24	Louis-Napoléon arrives at the Gare du Nord in Paris carrying the "color-coded map" for the redevelopment of Paris.
November 4	Adoption of the Constitution.
November 19	Proclamation of the Constitution on the Place des Quinconces in Bordeaux.
November 22	Proclamation of the Constitution on the Place de la Concorde in Paris.
December 10	Louis-Napoléon Bonaparte elected president of the Republic.
December 20	Louis-Napoléon Bonaparte installed as president of the Republic.

1849

January 10	Law reorganizing Public Assistance.
January 24	Haussmann appointed prefect for the Var.
March 3	Outbreak of cholera in Paris.
April 9	City of Paris borrows 25 million francs for ten years from Bechet-Dethomas Company.
April 30	French expeditionary corps of General Oudinot greeted with gunfire by republican insurgents in Rome.
May 8	First stone laid for the Cité Ouvrière housing project on rue Rochechouart.
May 13–14	Legislative elections.
June 13	Disturbances in Paris.
June 14	Disturbances in Draguignan; the prefecture under threat.
July 3	General Oudinot's forces in control of Rome, where the pope is reinstated on the 17th.
July 13	By-elections.
October 4	Law approving agreements between the central government and the city of Paris for clearing of the area between the Tuileries and the Louvre, with a major central subsidy.

1850

February 3	Chief of police Carlier has Trees of Liberty removed as a traffic obstruction.
February 13	Disturbances at the Vidauban carnival in the Var.
March 10–11	By-elections in the Var.
March 15	The Falloux law is passed.
May 11	Haussmann appointed prefect for the Yonne.

May 31	Election law stipulating residence requirements for right to vote.
June	Melun's draft legislation on unhealthful dwellings.
August 12	Louis-Napoléon visits Burgundy.
August 26	Louis-Philippe dies in exile.
October 10	The military review at Satory; shouts of "Vive l'Empereur!"
October 27– November 3	Municipal elections in Sens.
November 2	Changarnier forbids soldiers to shout anything when bearing arms.
November 9	Disturbances at Ligny in the Yonne.
November 23	Disturbances at Avallon.

1851

January 3	Changarnier relieved of his duties by Louis-Napoléon.
March 1	Municipal elections in Auxerre.
April 10	New government. Léon Faucher minister of the interior.
May 25	Municipal elections in Joigny.
May 31–June 1	Official visit to Sens by Louis-Napoléon.
June 5	Work on the Louvre launched by Louis-Napoléon.
July 14	Start of Assembly debate on constitutional amendment requested by the prince president.
July 19	The amendment is not adopted.
August 4	Law authorizing the rue de Rivoli extension to the Place de l'Hôtel de Ville.
October 27	New government. Thorigny appointed interior minister.
November 14–19	Disturbances in the Puisaye cantons in the Yonne.
November 26	Haussmann appointed prefect for the Gironde.
December 1	During the night a decree appoints Morny interior minister; Haussmann's misunderstanding at the Élysée Palace.
December 2	Coup d'état.
December 3	The deputy Baudin killed on a barricade in the Sainte Marguerite *quartier*. In Bordeaux, Haussmann takes control of the city and department.
December 4	Shooting on the boulevards. End of the disturbances.
December 10	Decree authorizing creation of a circular railway inside the fortifications of Paris, linking the Gares de l'Ouest, du Nord, de l'Est, de Lyon, and d'Orléans (Austerlitz).
December 13	Decree on completion of the Louvre.

December 15	Reorganization of the Environmental Health Board at the *prefecture de police*.
December 20–21	Plebiscite endorsing the coup d'état and the constitutional amendment.
December 31	Official declaration of results of the plebiscite.

1852

January 1	The prince president leaves the Élysée and moves into the Tuileries Palace.
January 4	Ball given at the Hôtel de Ville by Seine prefect Berger in honor of the prince president.
January 14	Adoption of the new Constitution.
January 23	Decree authorizing the sale of the Orléans family estate.
February 17	Decree introducing tougher regulation of the press.
February 29–March 1	Legislative elections.
March 1	Victor Hugo's article "War on the wreckers."
March 26	Decree on the streets of Paris and compulsory purchases.
March 27	The state of siege is lifted.
July 17	Opening of the Paris to Strasbourg railway.
July 25	First stone laid for new wings of the Louvre.
August 17	Declaration of public benefit for the circle line between Gare Saint-Lazare and Auteuil.
October 7–10	Presidential trip to Bordeaux; the "Empire means peace" speech.
November 7	Senate calls upon citizens to vote for restoration of the empire.
November 20	Decree establishing the Crédit Mobilier company.
November 20–21	Plebiscite approving restoration of the empire.
December 2	Proclamation of the empire. Louis-Napoléon takes title of Napoléon III.
December 23	Decree of public benefit for enlargement of Place du Louvre and Place Saint-Germain-l'Auxerrois.

1853

January 1	Haussmann elevated to rank of commander of the Legion of Honor.
January 22	Napoléon III announces his marriage to Eugénie de Montijo.
January 29	Civil wedding at the Tuileries Palace.

January 30	Religious wedding at Notre Dame.
February 19	Decree of public benefit for enlargement of Place de l'Hôtel de Ville.
February 20	Haussmann summoned to Paris by Persigny.
March 8	Decree for organization of a world's fair of agricultural and industrial products, to open May 1, 1855, in Paris.
March 11	Ponsard's five-act play *L'Honneur et l'Argent* performed at the Odéon theatre.
March 13	Opening of the Lariboisière hospital.
June 3	Napoléon III visits the new pavillion of the central Halles built by Baltard (the so-called *fort de la Halle*).
June 22	Haussmann appointed prefect for the Seine.
June 29	Haussmann is sworn in.
July 14	Paris municipal committee begins debating the budget.
September 1	Establishment of the Bakery Trade Fund.
December 16	Official opening of the Boulevard de Strasbourg.
December 24	Prince Napoléon-Jérôme appointed chairman of the imperial committee for the World's Fair.

1854

January 26	Ball at the Hôtel de Ville.
March 27	War declared on Russia.
April 2	First issue of *Le Figaro* daily newspaper.
April 8	The emperor and empress open the artificial river in Bois de Boulogne.
April 27	Ball, concert, and drama evening at the Hôtel de Ville.
May 2	The Gare d'Auteuil opens to the public.
May 24	Haussmann lays foundation stone for the Belleville Church.
June 22	Law awarding state lands of former Chaillot walkway to the city of Paris.
June 23	Persigny resigns as interior minister; he is replaced by Billault.
June 29	Decree of public benefit for the clearing of area around Hôtel de Ville between Place de Grève and Place du Châtelet, and for the creation of the square attached to the Tour Saint-Jacques.
August 4	Haussmann's first report to municipal council on the water supply.
August 13	Decree providing for redevelopment of the Place de l'Étoile.

August 15	Festival commemorating Napoleon I.
September 19	Victory on the Alma River in the Crimea.
September 29	Declaration of public benefit for extension of rue de Rivoli from the Hôtel de Ville to rue Saint-Antoine, and for cutting of the "Boulevard du Centre" (Boulevards de Sébastopol, du Palais, and Saint-Michel).
November 14	Morny appointed president of the Legislature.
December 3	An old five-story house collapses on rue de la Tannerie, near the Châtelet.

1855

January 22	Ball at the Hôtel de Ville.
January 25	Death of Gérard de Nerval.
January 30	Funeral of Gérard de Nerval.
February 22	Haussmann orders creation of the Compagnie Générale des Omnibus.
March 2	Death of Tsar Nicholas I.
March 20	*Le Demi-Monde*, by Alexandre Dumas, Jr., performed at the Gymnase theatre.
April 13	Law authorizing the city of Paris to acquire plain of Longchamp and the Parc de Madrid.
April 16	Napoléon III and the empress leave for state visit to Britain. Haussmann in London on official business.
April 16–24	Law authorizing city of Paris to borrow 75 million francs.
April 22	Return of imperial couple to Paris.
April 28	Pianori's attempt on the emperor's life.
May 5	Law on municipal organization. In Paris, members of the municipal council (new name for municipal committee) are still appointed by the emperor.
May 15	Execution of Pianori. Opening of the World's Fair.
June 21–22	Legislative elections. The opposition wins five of ten seats in Paris.
July 5	Offenbach opens the Bouffes Parisiens theatre in the Salle Lacaze, at the Carré Marigny.
August 11	Decree opening Boulevard Saint-Michel between Place Saint-Michel and rue de Médicis. Decree opening Boulevard Saint-Germain between Quai de la Tournelle and rue Hautefeuille.
August 16	Russians repulsed at Traktir Bridge.
August 18	Queen Victoria arrives in Paris.
August 23	Reception for Queen Victoria at the Hôtel de Ville.

August 27	Queen Victoria returns to London.
September 8	Capture of the Malakov Tower.
September 10	French, British, and Sardinian forces enter Sebastopol. Delamarre's attempted assassination of Napoléon III.
November 15	Ceremony closing the World's Fair.
November 22	The king of Sardinia, Victor Emmanuel, and his prime minister Cavour arrive in Paris.
November 24	Official party at Hôtel de Ville in honor of Victor Emmanuel.
December 29	Offenbach's Bouffes Parisiens theatre reopens at Passage Choiseul with *Ba-ta-Clan*. French forces arrive in Paris from Crimea; popular celebrations.

1856

February 25	Opening of the Congress of Paris.
March 16	Birth of the imperial prince.
March 30	The Peace of Paris is signed.
April 3	Offenbach's *Tromb Al-Ca-Zar* a great success at the Bouffes Parisiens.
April 12	Banquet offered by Napoléon III for delegates to Congress of Paris.
April 27	Napoléon III purchases four and a half acres of land on Boulevard Mazas (now Diderot) for cheap workers' housing.
May 6	Ponsard's five-act *La Bourse* opens at the Odéon theatre.
June 14	Imperial prince baptized at Notre Dame. Evening banquet organized by city of Paris at the Hôtel de Ville in honor of the emperor and empress. Haussmann is made Grand Officer of the Legion of Honor.
June 24	Haussmann awards Société d'Encouragement contract for Longchamp racecourse.
October 7	Napoléon III receives in Saint-Cloud a delegation of workers complaining about high rents.
November 7	Napoléon III assigns 100,000 francs to the *préfecture de police* for the opening of "cheap kitchens."
December 6	Verdi's *La Traviata* opens at the Théâtre Italien.
December 28	The Maison Eugénie-Napoléon opens its doors in faubourg Saint-Antoine.

1857

January 24	Monseigneur Morlot becomes archbishop of Paris. Gustave Flaubert tried for offense against public morals with *Madame Bovary*.
January 31	*La Question d'Argent*, a five-act play by Alexandre Dumas, Jr., opens at the Gymnase.
April 8	Charles Lecocq's *Le Docteur Miracle*, joint winner of Offenbach operetta competition, performed at Bouffes Parisiens.
April 9	Georges Bizet's *Le Docteur Miracle*, joint winner of Offenbach operetta competition, performed at Bouffes Parisiens.
April 26	Opening of Longchamp racecourse.
June 9	Haussmann appointed senator.
June 21–22	Legislative elections. Opposition has five of ten Paris deputies.
August 14	Opening of new Louvre buildings.
August 29	Decrees opening the Avenue des Amandiers (today's Avenue de la République) and Boulevard du Prince Eugène (Voltaire).
September 26	Napoléon III travels to Stuttgart and meets Tsar Alexander II.
November 30	Opening of Sainte-Clotilde Church.

1858

January 14	Orsini's assassination attempt.
February 7	General Espinasse replaces Billault as interior minister; Boittelle replaces Pietri at the *préfecture de police*.
February 27	Law on public safety.
March 13	Execution of Orsini.
March 18	The "180-million-franc accord" between the central government and the city of Paris.
April 5	Official opening of the Boulevard de Sébastopol.
April 21	The Palmier fountain is moved to the Place du Châtelet.
May 28	The Legislature amends and approves the 180-million-franc accord and authorizes the city of Paris to borrow 130 million francs.
June 14	Delangle appointed interior minister in place of General Espinasse. Dumas becomes president of the muncipal council.

July 15	Work starts on bell tower located between the Church of Saint-Germain-l'Auxerrois and the *mairie* of the 1st arrondissement.
July 16	Haussmann's second report on the Paris water supply to the municipal council.
July 21	Discussions at Plombières between Napoléon III and Cavour.
August 10	Foundation stone laid for new Church of Saint-Bernard at La Chapelle.
October 21	*Orpheus in the Underworld* at the Bouffes Parisiens (libretto by Hector Crémieux, score by Offenbach).
November 14	The Council of State authorizes the imperial decree (issued on the 19th) establishing the Caisse des Travaux de Paris.
December 10	Secret treaty of alliance with Piedmont.
December 27	Decree concerning compulsory purchases.

1859

January 3	The Caisse des Travaux begins operation.
January 13	The Council of State approves creation of Crédit Industriel et Commerciel.
January 30	Prince Napoléon-Jérôme marries Princess Clotilde.
February 9	Decree for opening of a public enquiry on the incorporation of suburban communes into Paris.
February 14	Party given at Hôtel de Ville by city of Paris in honor of Prince Napoléon-Jérôme and Princess Clotilde.
March 12	Declaration of public benefit for Boulevard Magenta up to the Place du Château d'Eau (today's Place de la République).
March 19	Gounod's *Faust* at the Théâtre Lyrique.
May 3	War declared on Austria.
May 10	Napoléon III travels to Italy to assume command of army.
June 4	Victory of Magenta.
June 16	Law on incorporation of suburban communes is signed.
June 25	Victory of Solferino.
July 11	Preliminaries leading to Peace of Villafranca between Napoléon III and Franz-Joseph of Austria.
July 19	Napoléon III back in Paris.
August 11	Consecration of the new Church of Saint-Jean-Baptiste at Belleville.
August 14	Triumphant entry into Paris by troops returning from Italy.

August 15	Opening of Pont Solferino and of Square Louvois.
August 16	General amnesty decree.
October 10	Decree modifying the division of responsibilities between the *préfecture de police* and the Seine prefecture.

1860

January 1	Incorporation of the suburban communes into the territory of Paris.
January 11	Decree giving Haussmann the right to be present at sessions of the Council of State.
January 22	Franco-British trade agreement.
February 7	Ball at the Hôtel de Ville.
March 27	Marie-Henriette Haussmann, the prefect's elder daughter, marries the attaché Camille Dollfus.
April 22–23	Plebiscites in favor of attachment of Nice and Savoy to France.
June 12	The Court of Cassation reverses its ruling on compensation for tenants of compulsorily purchased properties.
June 24	Death of ex-King Jérôme, Napoléon III's uncle.
July 3	Solemn funeral of Jérôme.
July 9	A production of Rossini's *Semiramide* at the Opera.
July 24	The state makes over the domain of Vincennes to the city of Paris on condition that it develops it into a public park.
August 15	Unveiling of the fountain on Place Saint-Michel. Opening of the new Pont au Change.
September 10	Labiche's four-act farce *Le Voyage de M. Perrichon* opens at the Gymnase.
September 18	Papal forces defeated by the Piedmontese at Castelfidardo.
September 29	Declaration of public benefit for construction of a new opera house.
October 6	The Jardin d'Acclimatation is officially opened by Napoléon III in the Bois de Boulogne.
October 9	The Jardin d'Acclimatation opens to the public.
November 24	Decree increasing the powers of the Legislature (right of address).
November 29	Competition opens for construction of new opera house.
December 16	Haussmann asks the emperor to create a Paris ministry for his benefit.
December 22	Decree giving Haussmann access to the Council of Ministers.

December 24   *Barbouf*, Offenbach's three-act opera-bouffe, opens at the Opéra Comique.

1861

January 8   The Bank of France raises its discount rate to 7 percent.

January 10   *Les Effrontés*, a satirical play in five acts by Émile Augier, opens at the Théâtre Français.

January 28   Death of Henry Murger, author of *Scènes de la vie de bohème* (the source for Puccini's opera).

February 13   The Interior Ministry moves to offices of the Algeria Ministry on Place Beauvau.

February 17   Arrest of Mirès.

March 13   Wagner's *Tannhäuser* is whistled and booed.

March 14   The Bank of France lowers its discount rate to 6 percent.

April 2   The remains of Napoleon I are placed in a special tomb in the presence of the imperial family.

May 10   Haussmann's third report on the Paris water supply to the municipal council.

June 2   Hittorff's committee unanimously chooses Charles Garnier's design in the competition for the new opera house.

June 6   Walewski appoints Garnier architect for the opera house.

July 11   Mirès sentenced to five years' imprisonment.

August 13   Napoléon III officially opens the Boulevard des Malesherbes.

October 6   Wilhelm I of Prussia is received at the Château de Compiègne.

November 9   Death of Artaud, deputy education officer for Paris and Haussmann's brother-in-law.

November 12   Achille Fould is appointed finance minister.

November 21   The Bank of France lowers its discount rate to 5 percent.

1862

March 4   Declaration of public benefit for diversion of waters of the Dhuys.

March 24   Funeral at Père-Lachaise of Ludovic Halévy, who died in Nice on March 21.

April 16   Loans authorized for construction of new opera house.

July 14   Circular freight railway is opened for passenger traffic.

July 21   Minister without portfolio Walewski lays foundation stone for new opera.

July 22	Declaration of public benefit for purchase of land at Buttes-Chaumont.
July 27	Opening of new Church of Sainte-Périne at Auteuil.
August 19	Opening of the Théâtre du Châtelet.
September 3	Opening of the Théâtre de la Gaîté.
October 30	Opening of the Théâtre Lyrique on the Place du Châtelet.
November 22	Unveiling of the statue of Esquirol at Charenton mental asylum.
December 1	Émile Augier's *Le Fils de Giboyer* at the Théâtre Français.
December 7	The emperor officially opens the Boulevard du Prince Eugène.
December 16	Napoléon III visits the Château de Ferrières, owned by James de Rothschild.
December 24	End of restoration work on Notre Dame and its reopening for worship.
December 30	Opening of the new Théâtre des Folies Dramatiques on Boulevard Saint-Martin.

1863

January 15	First ball of the year at the Hôtel de Ville.
May 18	Capture of Puebla in Mexico.
May 31	Legislative elections. Imperial failure in Paris, where the entire opposition list is elected.
June 10	The French expeditionary corps enters Mexico City.
June 22	Decree restoring the freedom of the bakery trade.
June 23	Victor Duruy appointed education minister.
June 27	Renan's *Vie de Jésus* goes on sale.
August 13	Death of Eugène Delacroix.
September 30	Verdi's *Rigoletto* a great success at the Théâtre Lyrique.
November 4	A new statue of Napoleon I is placed on top of the Vendôme Column.

1864

January 20	The Court of Cassation confirms its ruling of June 12, 1860, on compensation for tenants of compulsorily purchased apartments.
March 5	Archduke Maximilan arrives in Paris en route for Mexico.
March 19	Gounod's *Mireille* at the Théâtre Lyrique.
March 28	Races at Vincennes.

June 11	Ernest Renan removed from his chair at the Collège de France.
July 31	Napoléon III writes to Marshal Vaillant, his imperial household and arts minister: "It is very important to me that the monument to pleasure [the opera house] is not built before the refuge from suffering [the Hôtel-Dieu hospital]."
August 31	Death of Prosper Enfantin.
September 28	Creation of the International Workingmen's Association in London.
December 17	*La Belle Hélène*, with words by Meilhac and Halévy and music by Offenbach, enjoys great success at the Variétés theatre.

1865

February 1	Decree scheduling a world's fair to open in Paris on May 1, 1867.
February 15	Speech from the throne in which the emperor emphasizes the need people feel for greater freedoms.
February 18	Émile Pereire condemned over the merger of Marseilles Port Corporation with the Compagnie Immobilière.
February 23	Valentine, Haussmann's younger daughter, marries Maurice-Joseph de Pernetty.
February 25	Napoléon III publishes his book *Julius Caesar*.
March 10	Death of Morny.
March 27	Émile Ollivier's speech supporting government policy causes a sensation.
May 20	The Legislature passes a law on trade union associations.
May 22	Decree authorizing the clearing of the site for the new Hôtel-Dieu, on the Île de la Cité.
June 22	Declaration of public benefit for Montsouris park.
July 12	Law authorizing the city of Paris to borrow 250 million francs for "various works in the public interest."
October 15	Water from the Dhuys reaches Paris.
October 17	The cholera outbreak in Paris, first declared on September 22, causes a record of 213 deaths for one day (4,349 for the whole of October).
October 20	The empress visits cholera patients at the Hôtel-Dieu.
October 23	The empress visits hospitals of Beaujon, Lariboisière, and Saint-Antoine.

November 25   Decree authorizing rue de Médicis to be driven through part of the Luxembourg estate.

1866

February 15   Opening of the Théâtre des Délassements Comiques.
March 15   Victor Hugo's *Travailleurs de la Mer* goes on sale.
June 15   Decree establishing the freedom to operate hackney carriages in Paris.
July 3   Prussian victory over Austria at Sadowa.
October 31   *La Vie parisienne*, with words by Meilhac and Halévy and music by Offenbach, at the Palais Royal.
November 17   Successful opening of Ambroise Thomas's opera *Mignon*.

1867

January 1   The abattoir at La Villette begins service.
January 19   The Legislature formally receives the right to question members of the government.
February 8   Decree regulating relations of the Senate and Legislature with the emperor and Council of State.
March 11   Verdi's *Don Carlos* at the Opera.
April 1   World's Fair opens on the Champ de Mars.
April 12   Offenbach's *Grande-Duchesse de Gérolstein* at the Variétés.
April 27   Gounod's *Romeo and Juliet* at the Théâtre Lyrique.
April 28   Brother of the emperor of Japan received at the Tuileries Palace.
April 29   The king of Greece arrives in Paris.
May 1   The Sainte-Anne asylum comes into service.
May 14   King and queen of Belgium arrive in Paris.
May 23   Dinner at the Hôtel de Ville in honor of the Belgian royal couple.
May 24   The royal prince of Prussia arrives in Paris.
June 1   Tsar Alexander II arrives in Paris.
June 5   Wilhelm I of Prussia arrives in Paris.
June 6   Military review at Longchamp. The Polish refugee Berezowski fires on the tsar.
June 8   Ball at the Hôtel de Ville in honor of sovereigns then visiting Paris.
June 16   Ismail Pasha, viceroy of Egypt, arrives in Paris.
June 30   Abdul Aziz, sultan of Turkey, arrives in Paris.
July 1   Presentation of awards at the World's Fair.

July 2	The emperor orders thirty days of mourning for death of Maximilian in Mexico.
July 15	The Seine assizes sentence Berezowski to hard labor for life.
July 20	King and queen of Portugal arrive in Paris.
August 2	Charles XV, king of Sweden, arrives in Paris.
October 14	Funeral of Achille Fould, former minister of finance.
October 24	Franz-Joseph, emperor of Austria, arrives in Paris.
October 28	Banquet at the Hôtel de Ville in honor of Franz-Joseph.
October 31	Closing of World's Fair.
November 3	Battle of Mentana, near Rome: "The chassepots worked wonders."
November 4	Departure of Franz-Joseph.
December 2	Agreement signed for Crédit Foncier to lend 465 million francs to the city of Paris.
December 5	Rouher, minister without portfolio, tells Legislature that France will *never* allow the Kingdom of Italy to gain possession of Rome. *Le Moniteur* publishes a report by Haussmann on Paris finances.
December 7	Haussmann elected to Academy of Fine Arts.
December 1867 to May 1868	Jules Ferry publishes *Les Comptes fantastiques de Haussmann*.

1868

January 6	A new type of gas lighting is tried out on the Place de l'Hôtel de Ville.
February 22– March 8	Parliamentary debates on "debt assignment."
April 21	*Le Figaro* publishes a letter from Olympe Audouard attacking Haussmann and his violation of people's last resting place.
May 28	Opening of the Église Saint-Augustin.
June 18	*Le Moniteur* publishes a report by Haussmann on the financial situation in Paris.
October 6	Offenbach's *La Périchole* at the Variétés.
November 13	Death of Rossini in Paris.

1869

| February 28 | Death of Lamartine. |
| April 19 | Law approving agreements made between the city of Paris and Crédit Foncier. |

April 23	Opening of the new Vaudeville theatre.
May 23–24	Legislative elections. Opposition candidates sweep the board in Paris.
May 29	Work starts on Montsouris reservoir.
July 12	Message from the emperor to the Legislature.

1870

January 1	Liquidation of Caisse des Travaux de Paris.
January 2	Formation of Émile Ollivier government.
January 5	Haussmann is dismissed and replaced as Seine prefect by Henri Chevreau.
January 10	The journalist Victor Noir is shot and killed by Prince Pierre Bonaparte.
January 12	Funeral of Victor Noir.
February 7	Arrest of Henri Rochefort.
April	Discovery of the Roman amphitheatre of Lutetia during construction work on rue Monge.
June 12	The Grand Prix race at Longchamp; Haussmann is invited to lunch the next day by the emperor.
July 12	The Hohenzollern candidate for the Spanish throne is withdrawn.
July 13	The Ems telegram.
July 15	Debate in the Legislature on efforts to obtain a commitment from the Prussian king never to make any claim to the Spanish throne.
July 19	War is declared on Prussia.
July 25	Defensive preparations in Paris.
July 26	The regency is entrusted to the empress.
July 29	The emperor departs for Metz.
August 9	The Palikao government replaces that of Émile Ollivier.
August 17	General Trochu is appointed military governor of Paris by imperial decree.
September 4	French capitulation at Sedan made public. Fall of imperial regime and proclamation of the republic.

1871

January 28	Armistice.
May 21–28	The *"semaine sanglante"*: bloody crushing of the Paris Commune.
September 3	Haussmann becomes director of Crédit Mobilier.

1873

January 9	Death of Napoléon III.
March	Haussmann travels to Constantinople.
May 23	MacMahon succeeds Thiers as head of state.

1875

March 2	General meeting of Crédit Mobilier shareholders; Haussmann fails to gain control of the company.

1877

May 16	De Broglie dissolves the Assembly; Haussmann is elected deputy for Corsica in autumn by-elections.

1879

June 1	Death of the imperial prince.
August 20	Auctioning of Compagnie Immobilière property near the Opera. Rente Foncière, with Haussmann as chairman, wins the bidding.

1882

May	Jules Simon's article in *Le Gaulois* on the *grands travaux*.

1890

March 5	Death of Marie-Henriette, Haussmann's elder daughter.
December 24	Death of Octavie.

1891

January 11	Death of Haussmann.

Notes

CHAPTER 1. THE PRINCE, PARIS, HAUSSMANN

1. It is now the Victor Hugo Museum, in the historic Place des Vosges at the heart of the Marais district of Paris.
2. Haussmann, *Mémoires,* II, 53.
3. Haussmann, *Mémoires,* II, 58–59.
4. Haussmann, *Mémoires,* II, 59–60.
5. Ibid., p. 60.

CHAPTER 2. HAUSSMANN BEFORE HAUSSMANN

1. Haussmann, *Mémoires,* I, 15.
2. Ibid.
3. Ibid., p. 20.
4. Ibid., p. 10.
5. Ibid., p. 23.
6. Ibid., p. 26.
7. Ibid., p. 27.
8. A reference to the future poet and playwright Alfred Musset.—*Trans. note.*
9. Ibid., p. 33.
10. Ibid., p. 34.
11. Ibid., p. 34.
12. Ibid., p. 5.
13. Ibid., p. 11.
14. Ibid., p. 11.
15. Xavier Marmier, *Journal,* I, 329.
16. Haussmann, *Mémoires,* I, 36.
17. Ibid., p. 37.
18. Ibid., p. 42.
19. Ibid., pp. 46–47.
20. Ibid., pp. 47–48.
21. During Haussmann's time in Poitiers, the prefect ordered a search of the château of the duc d'Escars, or des Cars, a remote ancestor of the Jean des Cars whose enthusiastic biography of Haussmann was published in the 1980s. As it happened, Haussmann did not take part in the police operation.

22. The French departments were divided into a number of arrondissements or districts, each administered by a *sous-préfet* or subprefect.—*Trans. note.*

23. The seventeenth-century persecutions of French Huguenots at the hands of dragoons sent in by Louis XIV.—*Trans. note.*

CHAPTER 3. SUBPREFECT IN THE AGE OF THE BOURGEOIS KING

1. Maxime Du Camp, *Souvenirs d'un demi-siècle,* I, 62–63.
2. Ibid., pp. 60–61.
3. Haussmann, *Mémoires,* I, 89.
4. Ibid., p. 91.
5. Haussmann, *Mémoires,* I, 124.
6. Ibid., p. 126.
7. Ibid., p. 169.
8. Ibid., p. 171.
9. Xavier Marmier, *Journal,* I, 329.
10. Haussmann, *Mémoires,* I, 230.

CHAPTER 4. THE END OF LOUIS-PHILIPPE'S REIGN

1. Maxime Du Camp, *Souvenirs d'un demi-siècle,* I, 75.
2. Du Camp, *Souvenirs de l'année 1848,* pp. 30–31.

CHAPTER 5. FIRST STEPS IN THE SECOND REPUBLIC

1. Maxime Du Camp, *Souvenirs de l'année 1848,* p. 231.
2. Maxime Du Camp, *Souvenirs d'un demi-siècle,* I, 86–89.
3. Maxime Du Camp, *Souvenirs d'un demi-siècle,* I, 89.
4. Maxime Du Camp, *Souvenirs de l'année 1848,* p. 138.
5. Haussmann, *Mémoires,* I, 269.
6. Haussmann, *Mémoires,* I, 268.
7. Haussmann, *Mémoires,* I, 272.
8. Haussmann, *Mémoires,* I, 274.
9. Haussmann, *Mémoires,* I, 277–279.

CHAPTER 6. PREFECT FOR THE VAR

1. Haussmann, *Mémoires,* I, p. 284.
2. In 1860 the transfer of the Comté de Nice to France by the king of Italy, together with the incorporation of the arrondissement of Grasse from the Var, gave rise to the present department of Alpes-Maritimes. This meant that the River Var no longer marked the border between France and Italy, and indeed that it no longer flowed through the department to which it had given its name. For this reason, Haussmann thought that the department would be more appropriately named "the Argens."
3. Haussmann, *Mémoires,* I, 297.
4. Haussmann, *Mémoires,* I, 312.
5. Haussmann, *Mémoires,* I, 314.
6. Ibid., p. 324.
7. Quoted in ibid., pp. 366–367.
8. Ibid., p. 346.
9. Later, as prefect for the Seine, Haussmann remembered Duval and helped get him appointed brigadier.
10. Haussmann, *Mémoires,* I, 381–382.

CHAPTER 7. FROM AUXERRE TO BORDEAUX

1. Haussmann, *Mémoires,* I, 385.
2. Ibid., p. 385.
3. Ibid., pp. 387–389.
4. Ibid., p. 408.
5. Ibid., p. 467.
6. Haussmann, *Mémoires,* I, 423.
7. Ibid., p. 434.
8. Haussmann, *Mémoires,* I, 434.
9. Ibid., p. 436.
10. Ibid., p. 418.
11. Haussmann, *Mémoires,* I, 494.
12. Ibid., p. 494.
13. Ibid., p. 496.
14. Haussmann, *Mémoires,* I, 504.

CHAPTER 8. THE FRENETIC GROWTH OF A CAPITAL

1. Maxime Du Camp, *Paris, ses organes, ses fonctions et sa vie jusqu'en 1870,* pp. 8–9.
2. Ibid., p. 8.
3. Hillairet, *Dictionnaire historique des rues de Paris,* I, Paris: Éditions de Minuit, 1964; Guy Le Hallé, *Les Fortifications de Paris,* Paris: Horvath, 1986.
4. See Jeanne Pronteau, "La commission et le Plan des Artistes," in *L'Urbanisme parisien au siècle des Lumières,* Paris: Délégation à l'Action artistique de la ville de Paris, 1997.
5. Fontaine's *Journal,* quoted in Henri Malet, *Le Baron Haussmann et la rénovation de Paris,* Paris: Éditions municipales. 1973.
6. Las Cases, *Mémorial de Sainte-Hélène,* Paris: Jean de Bonnot, 1969, II, 299.
7. Chateaubriand, *Mémoires d'outre-tombe,* IV, 197.
8. Las Cases, p. 300.
9. Ibid., p. 299.

CHAPTER 9. THE SPLENDOR AND THE SQUALOR

1. *Statistique de l'industrie à Paris,* Part One, p. 17, quoted in Daumard, *La Bourgeoisie parisienne de 1815 à 1848,* Paris: Albin Michel, 1996, p. 443.
2. Buret, *De la misère des classes laborieuses,* II, 215.
3. Quoted in Daumard, op. cit., p. 456.
4. *Journal des Débats,* 30 September 1830.
5. Tocqueville, *De la démocratie en Amérique,* I, 2, p. 259.
6. Archives de la Seine, V*bis,* 78, letter dated November 1830, quoted in Daumard, op. cit.
7. Rambuteau, *Mémoires,* p. 354.
8. Turgan, *Les Grandes Usines,* II, 14ff.
9. Frédéric Barbier, *Finance et politique. La dynastie des Fould XVIIIe-XXe siècle,* Paris: A. Colin, 1991.
10. Say, *Traité d'économie politique,* II, 72.
11. *Journal des Débats,* 28 October 1836.
12. Tocqueville, *De la démocratie en Amérique,* I, 1, p. 216.
13. Say, *Traité d'économie politique,* II, 221.
14. *Journal de la Société française de statistique universelle,* 1843, XIV, 250.
15. Quoted in Daumard, op. cit., p. 8.
16. Ibid., pp. 8–9.
17. Ibid., pp. 15–16.
18. Daumard, op. cit., pp. 185ff.

19. Lanquetin, *Question du déplacement de la population,* 1842.
20. Frégier, *Des classes dangereuses de la population dans les grandes villes et des moyens de les rendre meilleures,* 1840, II. 51.
21. Parent-Duchatelet, *La Prostitution dans la ville de Paris,* 1837, p. 164.
22. Bayard, *Mémoire sur la topographie médicale du IVᵉ arrondissement de Paris,* 1840.
23. *Journal des Débats,* 29 October 1830.
24. *Journal des Débats,* 23 February 1832.

CHAPTER 10. THE TRANSFORMATION OF PARIS: THE CURTAIN RISES

1. Haussmann, *Mémoires,* II, 257.
2 Émile Ollivier, *L'Empire libéral,* Paris, 16 vols., 1895–1918.
3. Ibid., p. xiii.
4. The copy of the original plan given to Wilhelm I was found in 1930 at the Schloss-Bibliothek in Berlin by André Morizet, who published a photographic reproduction in his book *Du Vieux Paris au Paris moderne,* in 1932. The plan of 1873 with Napoléon III's shading is reproduced at the end of Merruau's *Souvenirs.* The historian Pierre Pinon has made a comparative analysis of the two plans in *Paris-Haussmann,* a work jointly edited with Jean des Cars (Paris: Éditions de l'Arsenal, 1991).
5. Maxime Du Camp, op. cit., p. 626: "Before a tenant could take over an apartment in a newly built house, the latter had already returned 5 percent of its value to the city tolls (to be precise, 4,915 francs and 22 centimes for a building valued at 1,000,000 francs)."

CHAPTER 11. PARIS GETS A NEW PREFECT

1. The proceeds of the sale were meant to be allocated as follows: 10 million francs to the friendly societies, 10 million to workers' housing, 10 million to Crédit Foncier (the real estate loan company), 5 million for the pensions of sick priests, and the rest to the Légion d'Honneur.
2 Haussmann, *Mémoires,* I, 514.
3. Ibid., p. 516.
4. Haussmann, *Mémoires,* I, 530–531.
5. Haussmann, *Mémoires,* I, 561.
6. Ibid., p. 527.
7. Ibid.
8. Ibid., p. 529.
9. Ibid., p. 566.
10. Haussmann, *Mémoires,* I, 575.
11. Haussmann, *Mémoires,* I, 580.
12. Haussmann, *Mémoires,* II, 2.
13. Ibid., pp. 11–12.
14. Haussmann, *Mémoires,* II, 9.
15. Haussmann, *Mémoires,* II, 11.
16. Henri Malet, *Le Baron Haussmann et la rénovation de Paris,* Paris: Les Éditions municipales, 1973, p. 107.
17. Haussmann, *Mémoires,* II, 21.
18. Ibid., p. 24.
19. Haussmann, *Mémoires,* II, 34–35.
20. Ibid.
21. Doubtless an allusion to Pierre du Terrail, seigneur de Bayard, whose illustrious military exploits in the early sixteenth century won him the name of "the knight beyond fear and reproach." The word *bayard,* however, could also be an adjective derived from the verb *bayer,* to stand gaping—*Trans. note.*
22. Haussmann, *Mémoires,* II, 51.

CHAPTER 12. HAUSSMANN IN CONTROL

1. The administrative audit [*compte administratif*] is the document that reviews the implementation of the budget forecast for the financial year in question.
2. Haussmann, *Mémoires*, II, 85–87.
3. Fierro, *Histoire et dictionnaire de Paris*, Paris: Robert Laffont, 1996, p. 140.
4. The statue may be found today in the Musée Carnavalet.
5. Haussmann, *Mémoires*, II, 141–142.
6. Ibid., p. 245.
7. Ibid., p. 251.
8. Ibid., p. 252.

CHAPTER 13. FRIENDS AND ENEMIES

1. Haussmann, *Mémoires*, II, 57.
2. Ibid., p. 153.
3. Ibid., p. 154.
4. Ibid., pp. 154–155.
5. The allusion to Ernst Hoffmann's *Fantastic Tales* also involves a play on *comtes* (the French word for tales) and its homonym *comptes* (accounts).—*Trans. note.*
6. Ibid., p. 233.
7. Ibid., p. 311.
8. Ibid., p. 397.
9. Ibid., p. 229.
10. Ibid., p. 61.
11. Ibid., pp. 209–210.
12. Ibid., pp. 58–59.
13. Ibid., p. 59.

CHAPTER 14. THE FIRST NEW SYSTEM

1. Haussmann, *Mémoires*, II, 2.
2. Ibid., p. 3.
3. Ibid., pp. 3–4.
4. Ibid., pp. 2–3.
5. Haussmann, *Mémoires*, III, 15.
6. The reference level for measuring the height of any point in the city was an ideal point 164 feet above the level at which the water of the Canal de l'Ourcq entered the basin of La Villette, which was itself 168.93 feet above the average sea level.
7. Haussmann, *Mémoires*, II, 9.
8. Haussmann, *Mémoires*, II, 26.
9. Émile de Labédollière, *Le Nouveau Paris*, Paris: Gustave Barba, 1860, repr. Paris: SCAELP, 1986, p. 6.
10. Two-thirds of net expenditure for the section of the rue de Rivioli from the Passage Delorme to the rue de la Bibliothèque, and for the operations to open up the Place du Carrousel, the space between the Tuileries and the Louvre, and the area around the Théâtre Français and the Palais Royal; a half of net expenditure for the section running from the rue de la Bibliothèque to the Place Saint-Germain-l'Auxerrois.
11. Haussmann, *Mémoires*, II, 26.
12. That is, approximately 2.5 miles.—*Trans. note.*
13. Claude Perrault (1613–1688): the French architect who originally proposed the idea of the Louvre colonnade.—*Trans. note.*
14. Haussmann, *Mémoires*, III, 501.
15. Ibid., p. 502.

16. In his *Mémoires*, Haussmann wrote by mistake "the Gare de l'Est."
17. Haussmann, *Mémoires,* III, 480.
18. Haussmann, *Mémoires,* III, 527.
19. Haussmann, *Mémoires,* III, 54.
20. Ibid., pp. 54–55.
21. Haussmann, *Mémoires,* III, pp. 490–491.
22. Haussmann, *Mémoires,* III, p. 76.
23. Haussmann, *Mémoires,* III, p. 497.

CHAPTER 15. IMPERIAL FESTIVITIES

1. The reference is to the Palmier fountain.
2. That is, "Slaughter Street."
3. "Old Lantern Street."
4. Alexandre Dumas, quoted in Charles Simond, *Paris de 1800 à 1900,* II, 469–471.
5. Haussmann, *Mémoires,* III, 27–28.
6. *Le Moniteur.*
7. Quoted in Robert Pourvoyeur, *Jacques Offenbach,* Paris: Seuil, 1994, pp. 52–53.
8. Letter quoted in Bertrand Gille, *La Banque en France au XIXe siècle,* Geneva/Paris: Droz, 1970, pp. 132f.
9. Claudin, *Paris,* Paris: Dentu, 1862.
10. See Aurélien Scholl, *Les Dames de Risquenville,* 1865.
11. See Henri de Pène, *Paris intime,* 1859.
12. Alfred Delvau, *Les Dessous de Paris,* 1860.
13. Victor Fournel, *Paris nouveau et Paris futur.*
14. Alfred Delvau, *Les Dessous de Paris,* 1860.
15. Maxime Du Camp, *Paris, ses organes, ses fonctions et sa vie jusqu'en 1870,* reprint, Paris: Rondeau, 1993, p. 74.
16. Jean des Cars, *Haussmann, la gloire du Second Empire,* Paris: Perrin, 1978, p. 249.
17. Haussmann, *Mémoires,* III, 294–295.
18. The ending of the French word *aqueduct* (or *aqueduc,* as Haussmann playfully spells it) rhymes with that of *duc.—Trans. note.*
19. Haussmann, *Mémoires,* III, 534–536.
20. This was at the old Opera on rue Le Peletier, almost on the corner of the *grands boulevards.*

CHAPTER 16. THE 180-MILLION-FRANC AGREEMENT

1. Haussmann, *Mémoires,* II, 307.
2. Haussmann, *Mémoires,* II, 307–308.
3. Henri Malet, *Le Baron Haussmann et la Rénovation de Paris,* Paris: Les Éditions municipales, 1973, p. 201.
4. Surveys begun in 1856 had led to agreement in principle by the Council of State on August 12, 1857, and to a declaration of public benefit on August 29.
5. Haussmann, *Mémoires,* II, 318.
6. Sue, *Les Mystères de Paris,* Paris: Robert Laffont, 1989, p. 1042.
7. Labédollière, op. cit., p. 243.
8. The rue de Lourcine corresponded to what are now rue Broca and rue Léon-Maurice-Nordmann, from the Saint-Médard circus to Santé prison.
9. Haussmann, *Mémoires,* III, 79.
10. Sue, op. cit., pp. 31–32.
11. Haussmann, *Mémoires,* II, 487.
12. Sue, op. cit., p. 33.
13. Quoted from Jacques de Brunhoff, *La Place Dauphine et l'Île de la Cité,* Lyons: La Manufacture / Délégation à l'action artistique de la ville de Paris, 1987, p. 27.

14. Labédollière, op. cit., p. 63. The years have passed, but the descriptions have scarcely changed. The authors of *Vie et histoire du IVe arrondissement*, published in 1988 by Éditions Hervas, do not find to their taste the "mediocre sacristy" (p. 75) that partly replaced the old archbishop's palace.

15. Haussmann, *Mémoires,* III, 521.

16. Haussmann, *Mémoires,* III, 522.

17. Ibid., pp. 524–525.

18. Haussmann, *Mémoires,* II, 326–327.

19. Frédéric Barbier, *Finance et politique. La dynastie des Fould, XVIIIe-XXe siècle,* Paris: A. Colin, 1991, p. 228.

20. Ibid.

21. The decree of January 7, 1859, authorized the first issue up to a limit of 30 million francs, which was later raised to 60 million francs and then to 100 million francs by the law of June 9, 1859. In 1860 and 1861, the laws of July 26, 1860, and June 26, 1861, renewed the approval for a value of 100 million francs in each case. The law of July 2, 1862, raised the total amount to 125 million francs, but this was reduced to 100 million by the law of May 13, 1863, to 80 million by the law of June 8, 1864, and then raised again to 100 million for each of the years 1865, 1866, 1867, and 1868.

CHAPTER 17. INCORPORATION OF THE SUBURBAN COMMUNES AND THE THIRD SYSTEM

1. Haussmann, *Mémoires,* II, 230.

2. Ibid., p. 495.

3. Ibid., p. 230.

4. Ibid., p. 495.

5. Bernard Rouleau, *Villages et faubourgs de l'ancien Paris,* Paris: Seuil, 1985, p. 218.

6. There had originally been fifty-four barriers, but eight were closed between 1818 and 1855, while ten more were opened at various times (one in 1790 and nine between 1820 and 1854).

7. Haussmann, *Mémoires,* II, 47.

8. The population of Paris today is a little more than 2 million. In 1914 it was as high as 2.9 million, and on the eve of World War II and in the 1950–1954 period it was hovering on the brink of 3 million.

9. Labédollière, op. cit., p. 218.

10. Touchard-Lafosse, quoted in Pillement, *Destruction de Paris,* Paris: Grasset, 1941, p. 217.

11. Pillement, p. 218.

12. Haussmann, *Mémoires,* II, 166.

13. Ibid., p. 176.

14. Ibid., p. 178.

15. Ibid., p. 177.

16. Ibid., p. 197.

17. Ibid., p. 200.

18. Ibid., p. 203.

19. Ibid., pp. 211–212.

20. Ibid., p. 213.

21. Ibid.

22. Haussmann, *Mémoires,* II, 238.

23. Marmier, op. cit., p. 330.

24. Ibid.

CHAPTER 18. FINANCIAL DIFFICULTIES

1. Haussmann, *Mémoires,* III, 210–211.

2. Ibid., p. 212.

3. Ibid., p. 237.

4. Ibid., pp. 371–372.

5. Hector Fleischmann, *Napoléon III et les femmes,* Paris: Bibliothèque des curieux, 1913, p. 276.

6. Marmier, op. cit., pp. 244–245.

7. Viel-Castel, *Mémoires,* IV, 263.

8. Haussmann, *Mémoires,* II, 390.

9. Ibid., p. 391.

10. Ibid., p. 389.

11. Haussmann, *Mémoires,* II, 389.

12. Ibid., p. 543.

13. Ibid., p. 547.

14. See *Autour de l'Opéra, naissance de la ville moderne,* Paris: Délégation à l'action artistique de la ville de Paris, 1995.

15. Its main axis, perpendicular to the Seine, measured no less than 1,581 feet, compared with a maximum width of 1,214 feet.

16. Quoted in Haussmann, *Mémoires,* II, 279.

17. See also the mention and note in Chapter 13 above.

18. Jules Ferry, *Les Comptes fantastiques d'Haussmann,* Paris: Guy Durier, p. 2.

19. Ibid.

20. See Haussmann, *Mémoires*, II, 185–186, for an account of this meeting.

CHAPTER 19. THE LION GROWN OLD

1. Joseph-Marie Pietri, younger brother of Pierre-Marie, who had had to leave his post after Orsini's attempt on the emperor's life and died in 1864. Joseph-Marie Pietri had succeeded Boittelle as chief of police in 1866.

2. Jean des Cars, op. cit., pp. 338ff.

3. Haussmann, *Mémoires,* III, 487–488.

4. Ibid., p. 182.

5. Ibid., pp. 154–155.

6. Michel Lescure, *Les Banques, l'État et le marché immobilier,* Paris: EHESS, 1982, p. 285.

CHAPTER 20. THE ENDS AND THE MEANS

1. Maxime Du Camp, *Paris, ses organes, ses fonctions et sa vie jusqu'en 1870,* Paris: Rondeau [reprint], 1993, p. 703.

2. See Délégation à l'action artistique de la ville de Paris, *Autour de l'Opéra. Naissance de la ville moderne,* Paris, 1995.

3. Ibid.

4. Haussmann, *Mémoires,* II, p. 523.

CHAPTER 21. MODEL INFRASTRUCTURES

1. A land occupation coefficient was not used at the time, so it is a question here of what city planning law terms the 'de facto coefficient.'

2. The total road surface was nearly 1290 hectares (12,894,000 square meters) within a municipal area of 7802 hectares. The figures used here are those given by Haussmann in *Mémoires,* II, chapter 20.

3. Haussmann, *Mémoires,* III, p. 142.

4. Ibid., p. 163.

5. Ibid., p. 164.

6. Ibid., p. 261.

7. See Chapter 17 above.

8. Maxime Du Camp, *Paris, ses organes, ses fonctions et sa vie jusqu'en 1870* [reprint], Paris: Rondeau, 1993, p. 581.

9. Ibid., p. 605.

10. Ibid., p. 727.

11. Louis Véron, *Paris en 1860,* Paris, 1860.

12. These figures relate only to the movement of individuals. There were approximately 26,000 vehicles conveying goods, including 1000 water tankers. See Nicholas Papayanis, *Horse-Drawn Cabs and Omnibuses in Paris, Baton Rouge and London,* Louisiana State University Press, 1996, p. 97.

13. Véron, op. cit.

14. Maxime Du Camp, op. cit., p. 74.

15. Ibid., p. 78.

16. These included 64 hotels, 163 restaurants, 233 bakers, and more than a thousand cafés. See Leonard R. Berlanstein, *Big Business and Industrial Conflict in Nineteenth-Century France,* Berkeley: University of California Press, 1991, p. 15.

17. Haussmann, *Mémoires,* III, p. 254.

18. Haussmann, *Mémoires,* III, p. 294.

19. Ibid., p. 373.

20. Haussmann, *Mémoires,* II, p. 322.

CHAPTER 22. PUBLIC BUILDINGS

1. Maxime Du Camp, *Paris, ses organes, ses fonctions et sa vie jusqu'en 1870,* op. cit., p. 706.

2. Ibid., p. 706.

3. Haussmann, *Mémoires,* III, p. 557.

4. Haussmann, *Mémoires,* II, p. 493.

5. Haussmann, *Mémoires,* III, p. 543.

6. François Loyer, *Histoire de l'architecture française. De la Révolution à nos jours,* Paris: Mengès, 1999, p. 149.

CHAPTER 23. THE GOLDEN AGE OF REAL ESTATE

1. Cf. François Loyer, *Paris XIXe siècle. L'immeuble et l'espace urbain,* Paris: APUR, n.d.

2. Ibid, II, p. 139.

3. Ibid., II, p. 140.

4. Marc Saboya, 'La presse architecturale en France (1840-1871)', *Cahiers du CREPIF* No. 18, March 1987, p. 185.

5. Maxime Du Camp, *Paris, ses organes, ses fonctions et sa vie jusqu'en 1870,* op. cit., pp. 596–597.

6. Lenard R. Berlanstein, *Big Business and Industrial Conflict in Nineteenth-Century France,* Berkeley: University of California Press, 1991, p. 17.

7. Michel Lescure, *Les Banques, l'État et le marché immobilier en France à l'époque contemporaine, 1820–1940,* Paris: EHESS, 1982.

8. Michel Lescure, *Les Sociétés immobilières en France au XIXe siècle,* Paris: Publications de la Sorbonne, 1980.

9. The Pereires proceeded in like manner (but on a much larger scale) in Marseilles, where they eventually found themselves in possession of 520,000 square meters of land.

10. Haussmann, *Mémoires,* II, p. 454.

11. Ibid., pp. 454–455.

12. Ibid., p. 458.

13. Ibid., p. 461.

14. Pierre Bleton, *La Vie sociale sous le Second Empire,* Paris: Les Éditions ouvrières, 1963.

15. Quoted from Jean-Paul Flamand, *Loger le peuple,* Paris: La Découverte, 1989, p. 64.

16. Quoted from Flamand, op. cit., pp. 64–65.

17. A. Audiganne, *Les Populations ouvrières et les industries de la France,* Paris, 1860, II, pp.

315–316; quoted from Michelle Perrot, 'Manières d'habiter', in *Histoire de la vie privée*, IV, ed. by Philippe Ariès and Georges Duby, Paris: Seuil, 1987, p. 291.

18. Flamand, op. cit.
19. Ann Louise Shapiro, *Housing the Poor of Paris, 1850–1902*, Madison: University of Wisconsin Press, 1985, p. 31.

CHAPTER 24. "AN EPOCH IN THE HISTORY OF CITY PLANNING"

1. Pierre Lavedan, 'L'influence de Haussmann,' in *L'Oeuvre du baron Haussmann*, Paris: PUF, 1954.
2. Georges Pillement, *La Destruction de Paris*, Paris: Grasset, 1941.
3. Ibid., p. 223.
4. Ibid., p. 225.
5. Jeanne Gaillard, *Paris, la ville (1852–1870)*, thesis, 1976.
6. Maurice Halbwachs, *Les Expropriations et le prix des terrains à bâtir à Paris (1860–1900)*, Paris: Cornely, 1909.
7. Cochin, *Paris, sa population, son industrie*, p. 84.
8. Philippe Gresset, 'L'urbanisme de Georges Haussmann vu d'ailleurs,' in *Paris-Haussmann*, Paris: Éditions du pavillion de l'Arsénal, 1991.
9. Canabière: the ancient thoroughfare leading north from the Vieux Port.—*Trans. note.*
10. See Roger Duchêne and Jean Contrucci, *Marseille*, Paris: Fayard, 1998.
11. Émile Ollivier, *L'Empire libéral*, III, p. 87.

Bibliography

THE FOLLOWING bibliography, which is only a selection from the numerous works and documents that we have consulted, implies no value judgment about those not appearing in the list; it is intended simply to reflect the approach adopted in this book.

Exhaustive bibliographies on Paris may be found in Alfred Fierro, *L'Histoire et diction-naire de Paris* (Paris: Robert Laffont, 1996), and, specifically for the period in question, Louis Girard, *La Deuxième République et le Second Empire, 1848–1870* (Paris: Nouvelle Histoire de Paris, 1981).

Paris-Haussmann, by Jean Des Cars and Pierre Pinon (Paris: Arsenal/Picard, 1991/1998), contains a good listing of works on the baron and his immediate predecessors.

As the archives of the Hôtel de Ville disappeared in the fire of 1871, the main sources are:

—in the Archives de Paris (former archives of the Seine department), series DQ18 (land registry), series DP2 of the Seine finance department, and the disparate but very rich "V *bis*" collection;

—in the Archives Nationales, series VO on street alignments, and C.

We should also mention the interest of contemporary press reports and literary testimony. The names of Balzac, Eugène Sue, and Zola immediately come to mind, but they represent only a small part of what is available to researchers.

Haussmann himself left three of the originally intended four volumes of *Mémoires* (as well as some late poetry, in the Bibliothèque Nationale). In addition, personal papers preserved by his descendants cast an interesting light on his psychology.

HAUSSMANN

Louis Bergeron and Marcel Roncayalo, "D'Haussmann à nos jours," in *Paris, genèse d'un paysage*, Paris: Picard, 1989.

Paul Boiteau, *Les Finances de Paris*, Paris: Guillaumin, 1865.

Anne-Marie Chatelet, "La conception haussmannienne du rôle des ingénieurs et architectes municipaux," in Jean Des Cars and Pierre Pinon, *Paris-Haussmann*, Paris: Arsenal/ Picard, 1991.

Anne-Marie Chatelet, "L'esthétique haussmannienne. D'Haussmann à nos jours," in Georges Duby (dir.), *Histoire de la France urbaine*, vol. 4, *La Ville de l'âge industriel*, Paris: Seuil, 1983.

Jean Des Cars, *Haussmann, la gloire du Second Empire*, Paris: Perrin, 1978.

Jean Des Cars and Pierre Pinon, *Paris-Haussmann*, Paris: Arsenal/Picard, 1991.

Jean-Jacques Dudilleu, "Les Concessions à l'époque d'Haussmann," in Jean Des Cars and Pierre Pinon, *Paris-Haussmann*, Paris: Arsenal/Picard, 1991.

Jules Ferry, *Les Comptes fantastiques d'Haussmann*, n.p., Guy Durier, 1979.

Philippe Gresset, "L'urbanisme de Georges Haussmann vu d'ailleurs," in Jean Des Cars and Pierre Pinon, *Paris-Haussmann*, Paris: Arsenal/Picard, 1991.

Georges-Eugène Haussmann, *Mémoires*, 3 vols., Paris: Victor Havard, 1890–1893.

Gérard Lameyre, *Haussmann "Préfet de Paris,"* Paris: Flammarion, 1958.

Georges Laronze, *Le Baron Haussmann*, Paris: F. Alcan, 1932.

François Loyer, *Paris XIXᵉ siècle. L'immeuble et la rue*, Paris: Hazan, 1987.

Henri Malet, *Le Baron Haussmann et la Rénovation de Paris*, Paris: Éditions municipales, 1973.

André Morizet, *Du vieux Paris au Paris moderne. Haussmann et ses prédécesseurs*, Paris: Hachette, 1932.

Thierry Paquot, "Le baron Haussmann, le mal-aimé?" in Jean Des Cars and Pierre Pinon, *Paris-Haussmann*, Paris: Arsenal/Picard, 1991.

David H. Pinkney, *Napoleon III and the Rebuilding of Paris*, Princeton: Princeton University Press, 1958, 3rd ed. 1972.

Pierre Pinon, "Les conceptions urbaines au milieu du XIXᵉ siècle," in Jean Des Cars and Pierre Pinon, *Paris-Haussmann*, Paris: Arsenal/Picard, 1991.

Pierre Pinon, "Les procédures et les services," in Jean Des Cars and Pierre Pinon, *Paris-Haussmann*, Paris: Arsenal/Picard, 1991.

Louis Réau, Pierre Lavedan, Renée Plouin, Jeanne Hugueney, and Robert Auzelle, *L'Oeuvre du baron Haussmann Préfet de la Seine (1853–1870)*, Paris: Presses Universitaires de France, 1954.

Marcel Roncayolo, "Le modèle haussmannien," in Georges Duby (dir.), *Histoire de la France urbaine*, vol. 4, *La Ville de l'âge industriel*, Paris: Seuil, 1983.

Léon Say, *Observations sur le système financier de M. le préfet de la Seine 1865*, Paris: Guillaumin, 1865.

Guy Surand, "Haussmann, Alphand: des promenades pour Paris," in Jean Des Cars and Pierre Pinon, *Paris-Haussmann*, Paris: Arsenal/Picard, 1991.

Anthony Sutcliffe, *The Autumn of Central Paris: The Defeat of Town Planning, 1850–1970*, London: Edward Arnold, 1971.

P. A. Touttain, *Haussmann: artisan du Second Empire, créateur du Paris moderne*, Paris, 1971.

Louis Ulbach, *Portraits contemporains: Haussmann*, Paris, 1869.

PARIS

Béatrice de Andia, "Les barrières de Ledoux," in *L'Urbanisme parisien au siècle des Lumières*, dir. Michel Le Moel, Paris: Délégation à l'action artistique de la ville de Paris, 1997.

Jean Bastie, *La Croissance de la banlieue parisienne*, Paris: Presses Universitaires de France, 1965.

Jean Bastie, *Paris en l'an 2000*, Paris: SEDIMO, 1979.

Jean Bastie, *Géographie du Grand Paris*, Paris: Masson, 1984.

Dr. Henry Bayard, *Mémoire sur la topographie médicale du IVᵉ arrondissement de la Ville de Paris*, Paris, 1840.

Dr. Henry Bayard, *Mémoire sur la topographie médicale des Xᵉ, XIᵉ et XIIᵉ arrondissements de la Ville de Paris*, Paris, 1840.

Jacqueline Beaujeu-Garnier, *Place, vocation et avenir de Paris et de la région parisienne*, Paris: La Documentation française, 1974.

Walter Benjamin, "Paris—The Capital of the Nineteenth Century," in idem, *Charles Baudelaire: A Lyric Poet in the Era of High Capitalism*, London: New Left Books, 1973.

Louis Bergeron (dir.), *Paris, genèse d'un paysage*, Paris: Picard, 1989.

Lenard R. Berlanstein, *Big Business and Industrial Conflict in Nineteenth-Century France: A Social History of the Parisian Gas Company*, Berkeley: University of California Press, 1991.

Henri Besnard, *L'Industrie du gaz à Paris depuis ses origines*, Paris, 1942.

Ch. Blancot and B. Landau, "La direction des travaux de Paris au XIXe siècle," in *Le Paris des Polytechniciens*, Paris: Délégation à l'action artistique de la ville de Paris, 1994.

Jacques de Brunhoff, *La Place Dauphine et l'île de la Cité*, Lyons: La Manufacture/Paris: Délégation à l'action artistique de la ville de Paris, 1987.

Michel Cabaud, *Paris et les Parisiens sous le Second Empire*, Paris: Belfond, 1982.

Michel Carmona, *Le Grand Paris*, 2 vols., Paris, thesis, 1979.

André Castelot, *Le Grand Siècle de Paris*, Paris: Perrin, 1963, repr. 1999.

Ernest Chabrol-Chameane, *Mémoire sur le déplacement de la population dans Paris et sur les moyens d'y rémédier présenté par les trois arrondissements de la rive gauche de la Seine à la commission établie près le ministère de l'Intérieur*, Paris, 1840.

Guy Chemla, *Les Ventres de Paris. Les Halles, La Villette, Rungis. L'histoire du plus grand marché du monde*, Grenoble: Glénat, 1994.

Auguste Chevalier, *Du déplacement de la population dans Paris, de ses causes et de ses effets, des mesures à prendre pour y mettre un terme*, Paris, 1850.

Louis Chevalier, *La Formation de la population parisienne au XIXe siècle*, Paris: Presses Universitaires de France, 1949.

Louis Chevalier, *Classes laborieuses, classes dangereuses à Paris pendant la première moitié du XIXe siècle*, Paris: Plon, 1958.

Timothy J. Clark, *The Painting of Modern Life: Paris in the Art of Manet and His Followers*, Princeton: Princeton University Press, 1984.

Augustin Cochin, *Paris, sa population, son industrie*, Paris, 1864.

Jean-Louis Cohen and André Lortie, *Des fortifs au périf: les seuils de la ville*, Paris: Pavillon de l'Arsenal, 1991.

Colloque de Créteil, February 9–10, 1990, *Île-de-France: pouvons-nous éviter le scénario catastrophe?*, Paris: Économica, 1990.

Eugène Defrance, *Histoire de l'éclairage des rues de Paris*, Paris, 1904.

Philippe Delahaye, *L'Éclairage dans la ville et dans la maison*, Paris, n.d.

Jean-Michel Derex, *Histoire du bois de Boulogne*, Paris: L'Harmattan, 1997.

Jean-Michel Derex, *Histoire du bois de Vincennes*, Paris: L'Harmattan, 1997.

Lucien Dubech and Pierre D'Espezel, *Histoire de Paris*, Paris: Payot, 1926.

Maxime Du Camp, *Paris, ses organes, ses fonctions et sa vie jusqu'en 1870*, repr., Paris: Rondeau, 1993.

Marc Dupont and Françoise Salaun, *L'Assistance publique-Hôpitaux de Paris*, Paris: Press Universitaires de France, 1999.

Émile Durand, *Guide de l'abonné au gaz d'éclairage*, Paris, 1859.

Jean El Gammal, *Les Hauts Quartiers de l'Est parisien d'un siècle à l'autre*, Paris: Publisud, 1998.

Raymond Escholier, *La Place royale et Victor Hugo*, Paris: Firmin-Didot, 1933.

Alphonse Esquiros, *Paris ou les sciences, les institutions et les moeurs au XIXe siècle*, Paris, 1847.

Alfred Fierro, *Histoire et dictionnaire de Paris*, Paris: Robert Laffont, 1996.

Bruno Fortier and Fernando Garcia Vega, "Le quartier de la Bourse de Paris," *Cahiers du CREPIF* No. 18, March 1987.

Jeanne Gaillard, *Paris, la ville (1852–1870)*, thesis, 1976.

Marc Gaillard, *Du Madeleine-Bastille à Météor. Histoire des transports parisiens*, Amiens: Martelle, 1991.

Louis Girard, *La Deuxième République et le Second Empire, 1848–1870*, Paris: Nouvelle Histoire de Paris, 1981.

Maurice Guerrini, *Napoléon et Paris—Trente ans d'histoire*, Paris: Téqui, 1967.

Maurice Halbwachs, *Les Expropriations et le prix des terrains à Paris (1860–1900)*, Paris: Publications de la Société nouvelle de librairie et d'édition, 1909.

Eugène Hénard, *Études sur les transformations de Paris*, Paris: L'Équerre, 1982.

Renée Héron de Villefosse, *Couronnes de Paris*, Paris: Grasset, 1952.

F.-R. Hervé-Piraux, *Les Folies d'amour au XVIIIᵉ siècle*, Paris: H. Daragon, 1911.

Jacques Hillairet, *Évocation du Vieux Paris: I. Le Paris du Moyen Âge et de la Renaissance. II. Les Faubourgs de Paris. III. Les Villages de Paris*, Paris: Éditions de Minuit, 1954.

Jacques Hillairet, *Les 200 cimetières du vieux Paris*, Paris: Éditions de Minuit, 1958.

Jacques Hillairet, *Dictionnaire historique des rues de Paris*, Paris: Éditions de Minuit, 1964.

Jacques Hillairet, *Connaissance du vieux Paris*, Paris: Éditions Princesse, 1977.

Gustave Hirschfeld, *Le Palais du Luxembourg*, Paris: Henri Laurens, 1931.

Émile de Labédollière, *Le Nouveau Paris. Histoire de ses 20 arrondissements en 1860*, Paris: Gustave Barba, 1860, repr., Paris: SACELP, 1986.

Jacques-Séraphin Lanquetin, *Ville de Paris. Question du déplacement de la population*, Paris, 1842.

Vicomte de Launay, *Lettres parisiennes*, 3 vols., Paris, 1856.

Pierre Lavedan, *La Question du déplacement de Paris et du transfert des Halles au Conseil municipal sous la Monarchie de juillet*, Paris: Impr. Municipale, 1969.

Pierre Lavedan, *Histoire de l'urbanisme à Paris*, Paris: Hachette, 1975.

Félix and Louis Lazare, *Dictionnaire administratif et historique des rues de Paris et de ses monuments*, Paris, 1844.

Leblanc de Ferrière, *Paris et ses environs. Description historique statistique et monumentale*, Paris, 1844.

Guy Le Hallé, *Les Fortifications de Paris*, Paris: Horvath, 1986.

Michel Le Moel (dir.), *L'Urbanisme parisien au siècle des Lumières*, Paris: Délégation à l'action artistique de la ville de Paris, 1997.

Jean-Marc Léri, "Les travaux parisiens sous le préfet Rambuteau," *Cahiers du CREPIF* No. 18, March 1987.

Jean-Jacques Lévêque, *L'Hôtel de Ville de Paris—Une histoire, un musée*, Paris: Horay, 1983.

Giovanni Macchia, *Paris en ruines*, Paris: Flammarion, 1988.

"La maison parisienne au siècle des Lumières," *Cahiers du CREPIF* No. 12, Sepember 1985.

Bernard Marchand, *Paris, histoire d'une ville (XIXᵉ–XXᵉ siècle)*, Paris: Seuil, 1993.

Patrice de Moncan, *Baltard, les Halles de Paris*, Paris: Éditions de l'Observatoire, 1994.

Patrice de Moncan, *Les Grands Boulevards de Paris*, Paris: Éditions du Mécène, 1997.

Daniel Oster and Jean Goulemot, *La Vie parisienne*, Paris: Sand/Conti, 1989.

Nicholas Papayanis, *Horse-Drawn Cabs and Omnibuses in Paris*, Baton Rouge: Louisiana State University Press, 1996.

Annick Pardailhe-Galabrun, "L'habitat parisien: comment on loge dans Paris aux XVIIᵉ et XVIIIᵉ siècles," *Cahiers du CREPIF* No. 12, September 1985.

Alexandre Jean-Baptiste Parent-Duchatelet, *Hygiène publique, ou Mémoires sur les questions les plus importantes de l'hygiène publique*, 2 vols., Paris, 1836.

Alexandre Jean-Baptiste Parent-Duchatelet, *De la prostitution dans la Ville de Paris, considerée sous le rapport de l'hygiène publique, de la morale et de l'administration*, Brussels: Établissement encyclographique/London: Dulau et Cie., 1837.

Aristide-Michel Perrot, *Petit Atlas pittoresque des quarante-huit quartiers de la Ville de Paris*, Paris, 1834, reproduced in facsimile by Michel Fleury and Jeanne Pronteau.

Georges Pillement, *Destruction de Paris*, Paris: Grasset, 1941.

Pierre Pinon (dir.), *Les Traversées de Paris. Deux siècles de révolutions dans la ville*, Paris: Éditions du Moniteur, 1989.

Jean Prasteau, *Paris, ses places, ses jardins*, Paris: SIDES/Éditions de la Tourelle, 1984.

Jean Prasteau, *Voyage insolite dans la banlieue de Paris*, Paris: Perrin, 1985.

Jeanne Pronteau, *Edme Verniquet*, Paris, 1985.

Jeanne Pronteau, "La Commission et le Plan des Artistes," in *L'Urbanisme parisien au siècle des Lumières*, dir. Michel Le Moel, Paris: Délégation à l'action artistique de la ville de Paris, 1997.

Marcel Raval, *Histoire de Paris*, Paris: Presses Universitaires de France, 1941.

Bernard Rouleau, *Le Tracé des rues de Paris*, Paris: Éditions du CNRS, 1975.

Bernard Rouleau, *Villages et faubourgs de l'ancien Paris*, Paris: Seuil, 1985.

Bernard Rouleau, *Histoire d'un espace*, Paris: Seuil, 1997.

Sainte-Marie Gauthier, "Initiative privée et service public: mobilier urbain et espaces publics parisiens au XIXe siècle," *Cahiers du CREPIF* No. 56, September 1996.

Horace Say, *Études sur l'administration de la Ville de Paris et du département de la Seine*, Paris, 1846.

Charles Simond, *La Vie parisienne au XIXe siècle*, vol. 2, Paris: Plon, 1900.

Jean-Jacques Terrin, *Cent Vingt Dessins sur la formation de la ville*, Paris: Hazan, 1989.

Marie de Thézy, *Marville Paris*, Paris: Hazan, 1994.

Marie de Thézy, "Grandeur du mobilier urbain parisien au temps du Second Empire," *Cahiers du CREPIF* No. 56, September 1996.

Jean Tiberi (dir.), *Almanach de Paris, II, De 1789 à nos jours*, Paris: Encyclopaedia Universalis, 1990.

Jean Valmy-Baysse, *La Curieuse Aventure des boulevards (1786–1950)*, Paris: Albin Michel, 1950.

Th. Vincens, *Mémoire sur les moyens d'assainir et d'embellir les quartiers de la rive gauche de Paris*, Paris, 1848.

Voltaire, *Des embellissements de Paris*, Paris, 1749.

GUIDEBOOKS AND PERSONAL VIEWS OF PARIS

Amédée de Cesena, *Le Nouveau Paris*, Paris: Garnier Frères, 1864.

Victor Fournel, *Paris nouveau et Paris futur*, Paris: Jacques Lecoffre, 1865.

Galignani's New Paris Guide, Paris: A. & W. Galignani, 1841.

Girault de Saint-Fargeau, *Les 48 quartiers de Paris*, Paris, 2nd ed., 1846.

Jules Janin, *L'Été à Paris*, Paris, 1843.

Jules Janin, *Un hiver à Paris*, Paris, 1845.

Adolphe Joanne, *Paris illustré. Nouveau guide de l'étranger et du Parisien*, Paris: Hachette, 1870.

Adolphe Joanne, *Paris illustré en 1870*, Paris: Hachette, 1870.

André Kaspi and Antoine Marès (dir.), *Le Paris des étrangers depuis un siècle*, Paris: Imprimerie nationale, 1989.

Henri Lecouturier, *Le Paris des rois et le Paris du peuple*, Paris, 1850.

Lemaistre, *Le Guide pittoresque des voyageurs*, Paris, 1855.

Paris. Guide par les principaux écrivains et artistes de la France, 2 vols., Paris: Librairie internationale, 1867.

Giorgio Perrini, *Paris: deux mille ans pour un joyau*, Paris: J. De Bonot, 1990.

Edmond Renaudin, *Paris-Exposition ou Guide Paris en 1867*, Paris: Delagrave, 1867.

Luc-Vincent Thiéry, *Guide des amateurs et des étrangers voyageurs à Paris*, Paris: Hardouin et Gattey, 1787.

Frances Trollope, *Paris and the Parisians in 1835*, New York: Harper and Brothers, 1836.

Auguste Vitu, *Paris il y a cent ans*, Paris: Bonnot, 1979.

Charles Yriarte, *Paris grotesque. Les célébrités de la rue*, Paris, 1864.

WATER SUPPLY AND SEWERS

Adolphe Alphand, *Note du directeur des travaux de Paris. La situation du service des eaux et égouts. Les mesures à proposer au conseil municipal*, Paris: A. Chaix, 1879.

Maurice Barrois, *Le Paris sous Paris*, Geneva: Hachette, 1964.

Laure Beaumont-Maillet, *L'Eau à Paris*, Paris: Hazan, 1991.

Georges Bechmann, *Salubrité urbaine. Distributions d'eau et assainissement*, 2 vols., Paris: Ch. Béranger, 1899.

Eugène Belgrand, *Recherches statistiques sur les sources du Bassin de la Seine qu'il est possible de conduire à Paris, exécutées en 1854*, Paris: de Vinchon, 1854.

Eugène Belgrand, *Monographie des eaux de sources de la banlieue de Paris*, Paris: Dubuisson, 1855.

Eugène Belgrand, *Les Travaux souterrains de Paris*, 5 vols., Paris: Dunod, 1872–1887.

François Caron et al., *Paris et ses reseaux: naissance d'un mode de vie urbain, XIXᵉ–XXᵉ siècle*, Paris: Bibliothèque historique de la ville de Paris, 1990.

Philippe Cébron de l'Isle, *L'Eau à Paris au XIXᵉ siècle*, thesis, Paris, 1991.

A. Daverton, *Assainissement des villes et égouts de Paris*, Paris: Dunod, 1922.

Alphonse Debauve, *Distribution d'eau. Égouts*, 2 vols., Paris: P. Vicq-Dunod, 1897.

Alfred Des Cilleuls, *Les Anciennes Eaux de Paris, du XIIᵉ au XVIIIᵉ siècle*, Paris: Berger-Levrault, 1910.

Gabriel Dupuy and Georges Knaebel, *Assainir la ville hier et aujourd'hui*, Paris: Dunod, 1982.

Louis Figuier, *Les Eaux de Paris. Leur passé, leur état présent, leur avenir*, Paris: M. Lévy Frères, 1862.

Jean-Pierre Goubert, *La Conquête de l'eau. L'avènement de la santé à l'âge industriel*, Paris: Robert Laffont, 1986.

Félix-Eugène-Edmond Humblot, *Les Égouts de Paris à la fin de 1885*, Paris: Chaix, 1886.

Charles Kunstler, *Paris souterrain*, Paris: Flammarion, 1953.

Simon Lacordaire, *Histoire secrète du Paris souterrain*, Paris: Hachette, 1982.

Simon Lacordaire, *Les Inconnus de la Seine. Paris et les métiers de l'eau du XVIIIᵉ au XIXᵉ siècle*, Paris: Hachette, 1985.

F. Liger, *Les Égouts de Paris*, Paris: Guillaumin, 1883.

Aimé-Jean Linas, *Quelles eaux veut-on faire boire aux Parisiens? Les eaux de Paris étudiées du point de vue de la santé publique*, Paris: E. Dentu, 1862.

Adolphe-Auguste Mille, *Assainissement des villes par l'eau, les égouts, les irrigations*, Paris: Dunod, 1885.

Prefecture du département de la Seine, Direction des eaux et des égouts, *Renseignements généraux sur les eaux et les égouts de la ville de Paris*, Paris: Gauthier-Villars, 1875; *Assainissement de la Seine. Épuration et utilisation des eaux d'égout*, Paris: Gauthier-Villars, 1876.

Donald Reid, *Paris Sewers and Sewermen. Realities and Representations*, Cambridge, Mass.: Harvard University Press, 1991.

Stéphane Robinet, *Eaux de Paris. Lettre à un conseiller d'État pour servir de réponse aux adversaires des projets de la ville de Paris*, Paris: Vve Bouchard-Huzard, 1862.

Francisque Sarcey, *Les Odeurs de Paris. Assainissement de la Seine*, Paris: Gauthier-Villars, 1882.

Catherine de Silguy, *La Saga des ordures du Moyen Âge à nos jours*, Paris: Éditions de l'Instant, 1989.

René Suttel, *Catacombes et carrières de Paris*, Paris: SEHDACS, 1986.

Louis Veuillot, *Les Odeurs de Paris*, Paris: Georges Crès, 1866.

Paul Wery, *Assainissement des villes et égouts de Paris*, Paris: Dunod, 1898.

GENERAL AND POLITICAL HISTORY

Édouard Alletz, *De la démocratie nouvelle ou des moeurs et de la puissance des classes moyennes en France*, 2 vols., Paris, 1837.

Éric Anceau, *Dictionnaire des députés du Second Empire*, Rennes: PUR, 1999.

René Arnaud, *La Deuxième République et le Second Empire*, Paris: Hachette, 1929.

François Bluche, *Le Bonapartisme aux origines de la droite autoritaire (1800–1850)*, Paris: Nouvelles Éditions latines, 1980.

J. P. T. Bury, *Gambetta and the Making of the Third Republic*, Harlow: Longman, 1973.

Victor Considérant, *Principes du socialisme*, Paris, 1843.

Adrien Dansette, *Louis-Napoléon à la conquête du pouvoir*, Paris: Hachette, 1961.

Adrien Dansette, *Du 2 décembre au 4 septembre*, Paris: Hachette, 1972.

Adrien Dansette, *Naissance de la France moderne. Le Second Empire*, Paris: Hachette, 1976.

Jean Dautry, *1848 et la Deuxième République*, Paris: Éditions sociales, 2nd ed., 1957.

Maxime Du Camp, *Souvenirs d'un demi-siècle, I. Au temps de Louis-Philippe et de Napoléon III, 1830–1870*, Paris: Hachette, 1949; *II. La chute du Second Empire et la IIe République, 1870–1882*, Paris: Hachette, 1949.

Maxime Du Camp, *Souvenirs de l'année 1848*, Geneva: Slatkine Reprints, 1979.

Georges Duveau, *Histoire du peuple français, 4. De 1848 à nos jours*, Paris: Nouvelle Librairie de France, Gründ, 1953.

Georges Duveau, *1848*, Paris: Gallimard, 1965.

Jean El Gammal, *Histoire politique de la France de 1814 à 1870*, Paris: Nathan Université, 1999.

Sanford Elwitt, *The Making of the Third Republic. Class and Politics in France, 1868–1884*, Baton Rouge: Louisiana State University Press, 1975.

Louis Girard, *La Politique des travaux publics du Second Empire*, Paris: A. Colin, 1952.

Louis Girard, *Les Élections de 1869*, Paris: Rivière, 1960.

Louis Girard, *La IIe République (1848–1851)*, Paris: Calmann-Lévy, 1968.

André Jardin and André-Jean Tudesq, *La France des notables (1815–1848)*, Paris: Seuil, 1973; translated as *Restoration and Reaction, 1815–1848*, Cambridge: Cambridge University Press, 1983.

Richard Kuisel, *Capitalism and the State in Modern France*, Cambridge: Cambridge University Press, 1981.

Ernest Labrousse, *Aspects de l'évolution économique et sociale de la France et du Royaume-Uni de 1815 à 1880*, Paris, 1954.

Ernest Labrousse, *Aspects de la crise et de la dépression de l'économie française au milieu du XIXe siècle (1846–1851)*, Paris: Bibliothèque de la révolution de 1848, 1956.

Herman Lebovics, *The Alliance of Iron and Wheat in the Third French Republic, 1860–1914: Origins of the New Conservatism*, Baton Rouge: Louisiana State University Press, 1988.

Charles Moraze, *Les Bourgeois conquérants*, Paris: A. Colin, 1957.

Inès Murat, *La IIe République, 1848–1851*, Paris: Fayard, 1987.

Émile Ollivier, *L'Empire libéral*, 16 vols., Paris: 1895–1918.

Hippolyte Passy, *De l'aristocratie considerée dans ses rapports avec les progrès de la civilisation*, Paris: A. Bossange, 1826.

Hippolyte Passy, *Des causes de l'inégalité des richesses*, Paris: Firmin-Didot, 1848.

Hippolyte Passy, *Des formes de gouvernement et des lois qui les régissent*, Paris: Guillaumin, 1870.

Nathalie Petiteau, *Élites et mobilités—La noblesse d'Empire au XIXe siècle*, Paris: La Boutique de l'histoire, 1997.

Harold Pinkney, *Decisive Years in France, 1840–1847*, Princeton: Princeton University Press, 1986.

Alain Plessis, *De la fête impériale au mur des Fédérés*, Paris: Seuil, 1979.

Félix Ponteil, *Les Classes bourgeoises et l'avènement de la démocratie (1815–1914)*, Paris: Albin Michel, 1968.

Pierre-Joseph Proudhon, *Système des contradictions économiques ou philosophie de la misère*, 2 vols., Paris, 1846.

Pierre-Joseph Proudhon, *Idée générale de la révolution au XIXe siècle*, Paris, 1851.

Pierre-Joseph Proudhon, *La Révolution sociale démontrée par le coup d'État du 2 décembre*, Paris, 1852.

Adolphe Robert, Edgar Bourloton, and Gaston Cougny, *Dictionnaire des parlementaires français*, 5 vols., Paris: Bourloton, 1889–1891.

Philippe Sussel, *La France de la bourgeoisie (1815–1850)*, Paris: Denoël, 1970.

Alexis de Tocqueville, *De la démocratie en Amérique*, 2 vols., Paris; *Democracy in America*, New York: Harper and Row, 1966.

Alexis de Tocqueville, *L'Ancien Régime et la Révolution*, Paris; *The Old Regime and the French Revolution*, New York: Doubleday, 1955.

Jean-André Tudesq, *Les Grands Notables en France (1840–1849)*, Paris, 1964.

Jean Tulard (dir.), *Dictionnaire du Second Empire*, Paris: Fayard, 1995.

Vincent Wright, *Le Conseil d'État sous le Second Empire*, Paris: Presses Universitaires de France, 1972.

Benoît Yvert, *Dictionnaire des ministres (1789–1989)*, Paris: Perrin, 1990.

Theodore Zeldin, *The Political System of Napoleon III*, London: Macmillan, 1958.

BIOGRAPHIES

Charles Almeras, *Odilon Barrot, avocat et homme politique: 19 juillet 1791–6 août 1873*, Le Puy: Mappus/Paris: PUF, 1950.

A. Augustin-Thierry, *Le Prince impérial*, Paris: Grasset, 1935.

Jean Autin, *Les Frères Pereire*, Paris: Perrin, 1984.

Robert Christophe, *Le Duc de Morny, «Empereur» des Français sous Napoléon III*, Paris: Hachette, 1951.

Jacques De la Faye, *La Princesse Mathilde, 1820–1904*, Paris: Émile-Paul, 1928.

S. Desternes and H. Chandet, *Napoléon III, homme du XXe siècle*, Paris: Hachette, 1961.

Georges Duveau, *Raspail*, Paris: Presses Universitaires de France, 1948.

Jean-Michel Gaillard, *Jules Ferry*, Paris: Fayard, 1989.

Lothar Gall, *Bismarck Der Weisse Revolutionär*, Frankfurt/Main: Ullstein, 1986; *Bismarck, the White Revolutionary*, London: Allen & Unwin, 1986.

Louis Girard, *Napoléon III*, Paris: Fayard, 1986.

Paul Guériot, *Napoléon III*, 2 vols., revised ed., Paris: Payot, 1980.

Pierre Guiral, *Adolphe Thiers*, Paris: Fayard, 1986.

Thierry Lentz, *Napoléon III*, Paris: Presses Universitaires de France, 1995.

Maurice Paz, *Un révolutionnaire professionel, Auguste Blanqui*, Paris: Fayard, 1984.

Robert Schnerb, *Rouher et le Second Empire*, Paris: A. Colin, 1949.

Philippe Séguin, *Louis-Napoléon le Grand*, Paris: Grasset, 1990.

MEMOIRS

Comtesse Marie d'Agoult, *Mémoires, souvenirs et journaux*, 2 vols., Paris: Mercure de France, 1990.

Baron de Barante, *Souvenirs: 1782–1866*, 8 vols., Paris: 1890–1901.

Madame Baroche, *Le Second Empire, Notes et souvenirs (1855–1871)*, Paris, 1921.

Maréchal de Castellane, *Journal, 1804–1862*, 5 vols., Paris, 1897.

Granier de Cassagnac, *Souvenirs*, 3 vols., Paris: 1884–1885.

Baron de Hübner, *Neuf ans de souvenirs*, Paris, 1904.

Jacques Laffitte, *Mémoires de Laffitte (1767–1844)*, published by Paul Duchon, Paris: Firmin-Didot, 1932.

Xavier Marmier, *Journal (1848–1890)*, vol. 1, Geneva: Droz, 1968.

Charles Merruau, *Souvenirs de l'Hôtel de Ville*, Paris: Plon, 1875.

Persigny, *Souvenirs*, Paris, 1895.

Rambuteau, *Mémoires du comte de Rambuteau*, published by his grandson, Paris: Calmann-Lévy, 1905.

Dr. L. Véron, *Mémoires d'un bourgeois de Paris*, 6 vols., Paris, 1853–1856.

Viel Castel, *Mémoires sur le règne de Napoléon III*, 6 vols., Paris, 1883–1884.

ADMINISTRATION

Maurice Agulhon, et al., *Les Maires en France du Consulat à nos jours*, Paris: Publications de la Sorbonne, 1986.

Alfred des Cilleuls, *Histoire de l'administration parisienne au XIXᵉ siècle*, 2 vols., Paris, 1900.

Édouard Ebel, *Les Préfets et le maintien de l'ordre public, en France, au XIXᵉ siècle*, Paris: La Documentation française, 1999.

Françoise Fichet-Poitrey, *Le Corps des Ponts et Chaussées: du Génie civil à l'aménagement du territoire*, Paris: Ministère de l'urbanisme et du logement, 1982.

Pierre Henry, *Histoire des préfets*, Paris: Nouvelles Éditions latines, 1950.

Jacques Lanquetin, *Édilité parisienne, vues administratives d'ensemble en considération des besoins de l'avenir*, Paris, 1843.

Louis Lazare, *Paris, son administration ancienne et moderne*, Paris, 1856.

Bertrand Le Clère and Vincent Wright, *Les Préfets du Second Empire*, Paris: Colin, 1973.

Jean Meyer, *Le Poids de l'État*, Paris: Presses Universitaires de France, 1983.

ECONOMY, FINANCES

J.-P. Alline, *La Caisse des Dépôts et Consignations: son rôle, ses opérations de 1816 à 1895*, Paris, 1976.

J.-P. Alline, *Le Crédit foncier de France, de l'affaire à l'institution, 1852–1920*, Paris, 1978.

Robert Bigo, *Les Banques françaises au cours du XIXᵉ siècle*, Paris: Receuil Sirey, 1947.

P. Birnbaum, *Les Sommets de l'État. Essai sur l'élite du pouvoir en France*, Paris, 1977.

Jean Bouvier, *Le Crédit lyonnais, les années de formation d'une banque de dépôts (1863–1882)*, 2 vols., Paris: SEVPEN, 1961.

Jean Bouvier, *Les Rothschild*, Paris: Fayard, 1967.

Gaston Cadoux, *Les Finances de la Ville de Paris de 1789 à 1900*, Paris: Berger-Levrault, 1900.

J. H. Calmon, *Le Baron de Soubeyran*, master's diploma, University of Poitiers, 1973.

François Caron, *Histoire des chemins de fer en France, I. 1740–1883*, Paris: Fayard, 1997.

Auguste Chirac, *Les Mystères du crédit: le Crédit foncier de France*, Paris: Amyot, 1876.

Alphonse Courtois, *Manuel des fonds publics et des sociétés par actions*, Paris, 1878.

Herman Daems and Herman Van Der Wee (eds.), *The Rise of Managerial Capitalism*, papers of a conference held at the University of Louvain, Louvain, 1974.

Kimon Doukas, *The French Railroad and the State*, New York: Octagon Books, 1945.

Georges Duchêne, *L'Empire industriel: histoire critique des concessions financières et industrielles du Second Empire*, Paris, 1869.

Charles Freedman, *Joint-Stock Enterprises in France, 1807–1867*, Chapel Hill: University of North Carolina Press, 1979.

Bertrand Gille, *Histoire de la Maison Rothschild*, 2 vols., Geneva: Droz, 1965–1967.

Bertrand Gille, *La Sidérurgie française au XIXᵉ siècle*, Geneva: Droz, 1968.

Bertrand Gille, *La Banque en France au XIXᵉ siècle. Recherches historiques*, Paris: Droz, 1970.

Louis Girard, "Le financement des grands travaux du Second Empire," *Revue économique*, 3/1951.

David Landes, *Bankers and Pashas*, Cambridge, Mass.: Harvard University Press, 1979.

David Landes, *Unbound Prometheus: Technological Change and Industrial Development in Western Europe from 1750 to the Present*, London: Cambridge University Press, 1969.

Jacques Lanquetin, *Situation financière du département de la Seine*, Paris, 1850.

Michel Lescure, *Les Sociétés immobilières en France au XIXᵉ siècle. Contribution à l'histoire de la mise en valeur du sol urbain en économie capitaliste*, Paris: Publications de la Sorbonne, 1980.

Michel Lescure, *Les Banques, l'État et le marché immobilier en France à l'époque contemporaine, 1820–1940*, Paris: Éditions de l'EHESS, 1982.

Maurice Lévy-Leboyer and François Bourguignon, *L'Économie française au XIXᵉ siècle: analyse socio-économique*, Paris: Economica, 1985.

Geneviève Massa-Gille, *Histoire des emprunts de la ville de Paris, 1814–1875*, Paris: Ville de Paris, Commission des travaux historiques, 1973.

Arnaud de Maurepas, *Économie et finances au XIXᵉ siècle: guide du chercheur*, Paris: Comité pour l'histoire économique et financière de la France, 1998.

Frederick Morton, *Les Rothschild*, Paris: Gallimard, 1962.

Henry Peyret, *Histoire des chemins de fer en France et dans le monde*, Paris: SEFI, 1949.

Roger Price, *An Economic History of Modern France, 1730–1914*, London: Macmillan, 1981.

Gaston Ramon, *Histoire de la Banque de France*, Paris: Grasset, 1929.

Julien Turgan, *Les Grandes Usines. Études industrielles en France et à l'étranger*, 10 vols., Paris, 1860–1874.

Charles-Joseph-Auguste Vitu, *Guide financier: répertoire général des valeurs financières et industrielles*, Paris, 1864.

Jacques Wolff, *Les Perier. La Fortune et les Pouvoirs*, Paris: Economica, 1993.

SOCIETY

Maurice Agulhon, *Le Cercle dans la France bourgeoise, 1810–1848. Étude d'une mutation de sociabilité*, Paris: A. Colin, 1977.

Henri d'Alméras, *La Vie parisienne sous Louis-Philippe*, Paris: Albin Michel, n.d.

Henri d'Alméras, *La Vie parisienne sous La République de 1848*, Paris: Albin Michel, n.d.

Henri d'Alméras, *La Vie parisienne sous le Second Empire*, Paris: Albin Michel, 1933.

Philippe Ariès and Georges Duby (dir.), *Histoire de la vie privée*, vol. 4, *De la Révolution à la Grande Guerre*, Paris: Seuil, 1987; *A History of Private Life*, vol. 4, *From the Fires of the Revolution to the Great War*, Cambridge, Mass.: Harvard University Press, 1990.

John Armstrong, *The European Administrative Elite*, Princeton: Princeton University Press, 1973.

Jean-Paul Aron, *Essai sur la sensibilité alimentaire à Paris au XIXe siècle*, Paris: A. Colin, 1967.

Jean-Paul Aron, *Misérable et glorieuse, la femme du XIXe siècle*, Paris: Fayard, 1980.

Armand Audiganne, *Les Ouvriers d'à présent et la nouvelle économie du travail*, Paris: E. Lacroix, 1863.

Armand Audiganne, *Mémoires d'un ouvrier de Paris, 1871–1872*, Paris: Charpentier, 1873.

Paul Bérard, *L'Économie domestique de l'éclairage*, Paris, 1867.

Lenard R. Berlanstein, *The Working People of Paris, 1871–1914*, Baltimore: Johns Hopkins University Press, 1984.

Pierre-Nicolas Berryer, *Derniers voeux d'un vieil électeur de 1789 pour l'avenir de la France et de la civilisation*, Paris, 1840.

Pierre Bleton, *La Vie sociale sous le Second Empire. Un étonnant témoignage de la comtesse de Ségur*, Paris: Éditions ouvrières, 1963.

A. Brunot and R. Coquand, *Le Corps des Ponts et Chaussées*, Paris, 1982.

Eugène Buret, *De la misère des classes laborieuses en Angleterre et en France*, 2 vols., Paris, 1840.

Édouard-Thomas Charton, *Guide pour le choix d'un état, ou dictionnaire des professions*, 2nd ed., Paris, 1851.

Michel Chevalier, *Lettres sur l'Amérique du Nord. De la bourgeoisie en Amérique et en France*, 2 vols., Paris, 1836.

Alain Corbin, *Le Miasme et la Jonquille: l'odorat et l'imaginaire social*, Paris: Aubier Montaigne, 1982.

Fred Cottrell, *Energy and Society: The Relation Between Energy, Social Change, and Economic Development*, New York: McGraw-Hill, 1955.

Adeline Daumard, *La Bourgeoisie parisienne de 1815 à 1848*, Paris: SEVPEN, 1963; Albin Michel, 1996.

Adeline Daumard, *Maisons de Paris et propriétaires parisiens au XIXe siècle—1809–1880*, Paris: Cujas, 1965.

Adeline Daumard, *Les Fortunes françaises au XIXe siècle*, Paris: Mouton, 1973.

Georges Duveau, *La Pensée ouvrière sur l'éducation pendant la Seconde République et le Second Empire*, Paris: Domat-Montchrestien, 1948.

Georges Duveau, *Les Instituteurs*, Paris: Seuil, 1957.

Georges Duveau, *Sociologie de l'utopie et autres essais*, Paris: Presses Universitaires de France, 1961.

Arlette Farge, *Vivre dans la rue au XVIIIe siècle*, Paris: Gallimard-Juillard, 1979.

Suzanne Fiette, *La Noblesse française des Lumières à la Belle Époque*, Paris: Perrin, 1997.

Théodore Fix, *Observations sur l'état des classes ouvrières*, Paris, 1846.

Comte Fleury and Louis Sonolet, *La Société du Second Empire*, 4 vols., Paris: Albin Michel, 1921.

Honoré Antoine Frégier, *Des classes dangereuses de la population dans les grandes villes et des moyens de les rendre meilleures*, 2 vols., Paris, 1840.

Anne-Marie Frugier, *La Vie élégante ou la formation du Tout-Paris, 1815–1848*, Paris: Fayard, 1991.

Gerald L. Geison, *Professions and the French State, 1700–1900*, Philadelphia: University of Pennsylvania Press, 1984.

Louis Girard, *La Garde nationale (1814–1871)*, Paris: Plon, 1964.

Pierre Guiral, *La Société française, 1815–1914, vue par les romanciers*, Paris: A. Colin, 1971.

Pierre Guiral, *La Vie quotidienne des domestiques en France au XIXe siècle*, Paris: Hachette, 1978.

Maurice Halbwachs, *La Classe ouvrière et les niveaux de vie*, Paris: F. Alcan, 1912.

Robert L. Herbert, *Impressionism: Art, Leisure, and Parisian Society*, New Haven: Yale University Press, 1988.

David Higgs, *Nobles, titrés, aristocrates en France après la Révolution, 1830–1870*, Paris: Liana Levi, 1990.

Émile de Labédollière, *Les Industriels, métiers et professions en France*, Paris, 1842.

Lecocq de Montborne, *De la société contemporaine. Religion, noblesse, bourgeoisie*, Paris, 1855.

Maurice Lévy-Leboyer, *Le Patronat de la seconde industrialisation*, Paris: Éditions ouvrières, 1979.

Jean Lhomme, *La Grande bourgeoisie au pouvoir, 1830–1960*, Paris: Presses Universitaires de France, 1960.

Hervé Manéglier, *Paris impérial. La vie quotidienne sous le Second Empire*, Paris: A. Colin, 1990.

Michael Miller, *The Bon Marché: Bourgeois Culture and the Department Store, 1896–1920*, Princeton: Princeton University Press, 1981.

D. Nisard, *Les Classes moyennes en Angleterre et la bourgeoisie en France*, Paris, 1850.

Gérard Noiriel, *Les Ouvriers dans la société française, XIXe–XXe siècle*, Paris: Seuil, 1988.

Philip Nord, *Paris Shopkeepers and the Politics of Resentment*, Princeton: Princeton University Press, 1986.

Annick Pardailhe-Galabrun, *La Naissance de l'intime*, Paris: Presses Universitaires de France, 1988.

Robert Pourvoyeur, *Offenbach*, Paris: Seuil, 1994.

Daniel Roche, *Le Peuple de Paris: essai sur la culture populaire au XVIIIe siècle*, Paris: Aubier-Montaigne, 1981.

Daniel Roche, *Histoire des choses banales. Naissance de la consommation, XVIIe–XIXe siècle*, Paris: Fayard, 1997.

Jacques Rougerie, "Remarques sur l'histoire des salaires à Paris au XIXe siècle," *Le Mouvement social* No. 63, 1968.

Wolfgang Schivelbusch, *Disenchanted Night: The Industrialization of Light in the Nineteenth Century*, Berkeley: University of California Press, 1988.

Haine W. Scott, *The French Café*, Baltimore: Johns Hopkins University Press, 1996.

Terry Shinn, *L'École polytechnique, 1794–1914*, Paris: Presses de la Fondation nationale des sciences politiques, 1980.

Louis Sonolet, *La Vie parisienne sous le Second Empire*, Paris: Payot, 1929.

Ezra Suleiman, *Elites in French Society*, Princeton: Princeton University Press, 1978.

Hippolyte Taine, *Vie et opinions de Monsieur Frédéric Thomas Graindorge*, Paris: Hachette, 1959.

Philippe Vigier, *La Vie quotidienne en province et à Paris pendant les journées de 1848 (1847–1851)*, Paris: Hachette, 1982.

Henri Vincenot, *La Vie quotidienne dans les chemins de fer au XIXe siècle*, Paris: Hachette, 1975.

Rosalind H. Williams, *Dream Worlds: Mass Consumption in Late Nineteenth-Century France*, Berkeley: University of California Press, 1988.

CITY PLANNING

Françoise Choay, *L'Urbanisme. Utopies et réalités. Une anthologie*, Paris: Seuil, 1965.

M. Coste, "Perreymond, un théoricien des quartiers et de la reconstruction," *Annales de la recherche urbaine* No. 22.

Adeline Daumard, *La Bourgeoisie parisienne de 1815 à 1848*, Paris: SEVPEN, 1963; Albin Michel, 1996.

Sophie Descat, "Pierre Patte, théoricien de l'urbanisme," in *L'Urbanisme parisien au siècle des Lumières*, dir. Michel Le Moel, Paris: Délégation à l'action artistique de la ville de Paris, 1997.

Roger Duchêne and Jean Contrucci, *Marseille*, Paris: Fayard, 1998.

Baron d'Ernouf and Adolphe Alphand, *Traité pratique et didactique de l'art des jardins et des promenades. Parcs-Jardins-Promenades*, Paris: J. Rotschild, n.d.

Yankel Fijalkow, *La Construction des îlots insalubres, Paris 1850–1945*, Paris: L'Harmattan, 1998.

Jean-Paul Flamand (dir.), *La Question du logement et le mouvement ouvrier français*, Paris: Les Éditions de la Villette, 1981.

Jean-Paul Flamand, *Loger le peuple*, Paris: La Découverte, 1989.

Michel Fleury, "L'urbanisme éclairé à Paris: Aménagement et Législation de Louis XV à la Révolution," *Cahiers du CREPIF* No. 12, September 1985.

Roger H. Guerrand, *Les Origines du logement social en France*, Paris: Éditions ouvrières, 1967.

David Harvey, *Consciousness and the Urban Experience*, Baltimore: Johns Hopkins University Press, 1985.

Bertrand Lemoine, *Les Passages couverts en France*, Paris: Délégation à l'action artistique de la ville de Paris, 1990.

Pierre Merlin, *Géographie de l'aménagement*, Paris: Presses Universitaires de France, 1988.

Pierre Merlin and Françoise Choay (dir.), *Dictionnaire de l'urbanisme et de l'aménagement*, Paris: Presses Universitaires de France, 1988.

Donald J. Olsen, *The City as a Work of Art: London, Paris, Vienna*, New Haven: Yale University Press, 1986.

Thierry Paquot (dir.), *Le Familistère Godin à Guise. Habiter l'utopie*, Paris: Éditions de la Villette, 1982.

Jean-Luc Pinol, *Le Monde des villes au XIXᵉ siècle*, Paris: Hachette, 1991.

Prince Hermann von Pückler-Muskau, *Aperçus sur l'art du jardin paysager*, assortis d'une *Petite revue du parc anglais*, précédés d'un essai biographique sur l'auteur et d'une étude sur l'esthétique du parc à l'anglaise par E. de Rubercy. Traduction par E. de Rubercy, Paris: Klincksiek, 1998.

Michel Ragon, *Histoire de l'architecture et de l'urbanisme modernes, I. Idéologies et pionniers, 1800–1910*, Paris: Casterman, 1986.

Ann-Louise Shapiro, *Housing the Poor in Paris, 1850–1902*, Madison: University of Wisconsin Press, 1985.

Anthony Sutcliffe, *The Rise of Modern Urban Planning*, London: Mansell, 1980.

ARCHITECTURE

B. Chemetov and B. Marrey, *Architectures: Paris 1848–1914*, Paris: Dunod, 1983.

César Daly, *L'Architecture privée au XIXᵉ siècle. Nouvelles maisons de Paris et de ses environs*, 3 vols., Paris, 1870.

Mark Girouard, *Cities and People: A Social and Architectural History*, New Haven: Yale University Press, 1985.

"Hitorff (1792–1867)," *Cahiers du CREPIF* No. 18, March 1987.

Michel Jantzen, "Place de la Concorde: Étude de restauration des colonnes rostrales," *Cahiers du CREPIF* No. 18, March 1987.

Bertrand Lemoine, *Les Halles de Paris*, Paris: Éditions de l'Équerre, 1980.

Bertrand Lemoine, *L'Architecture de fer, France XIXe siècle*, Paris: Champ Vallon, 1986.

François Loyer, *Histoire de l'architecture française. De la Révolution à nos jours*, Paris: Mengès, 1999.

Michel Ragon, *Histoire de l'architecture et de l'urbanisme modernes, I. Idéologies et pionniers, 1800–1910*, Paris: Casterman, 1986.

Marc Saboya, "La presse architecturale en France (1840–1871)," *Cahiers du CREPIF* No. 18, March 1987.

Anthony Sutcliffe, *Paris: An Architectural History*, New Haven: Yale University Press, 1993.

David Van Zanten, "La polychromie dans l'architecture française de 1830," *Cahiers du CREPIF* No. 18, March 1987.

Index

A NOTE ON THE AUTHOR

Michel Carmona, a graduate of the prestigious École Normale Supérieure, is professor of geography and town and country planning at the Sorbonne in Paris. His specialty is urban geography—especially that of Paris—and urban issues in France and large foreign cities. He has served as adviser to various French cabinet ministers and administrations, and has also written *The Devils of Loudun*, *Richelieu*, and *Marie of the Medicis*.